**Occupation for Health**
**Volume 2**

# A Journey
# From Prescription to Self Health

**Ann A Wilcock**

*With contributions from*
*Vincenza Pols*
*Catherine F. Paterson*
*Irene Ilott*
*Sidney Lock*
*Bruce Crowe and Peggy Jay*
*Beryl Warren*
*Gwilym Roberts*
*Sue Kennedy*
*Annette Leveridge*
*Felicity McElderry*

British Association and College of Occupational Therapists 2002

British Association and College of Occupational Therapists
106-114 Borough High Street
Southwark
London SE1 1LB
UNITED KINGDOM

Website www.cot.org.uk

ISBN number   0-9539375-4-2 (Limp Cover)
0-9539375-2-6 (Cased Cover)

British Library Cataloguing in Publication Data
A catalogue record for this book is available from the British Library


*Editor:* Judy Waters, JJ Editorial Services, Victoria, Australia
*Frontispieces:* Tracey Greenway and D.A.T. Nelson
*Clerical Assistants:* Derek Wilcock, Kathleen Moran, Matthew Ebden and Daniel Pitman

Indexed by Dr Laurence Errington in association with First Edition Translations Ltd, Cambridge.
Printed by The Lavenham Press Limited, Suffolk

This history is dedicated to the memory of Nathalie Barr (née Smythe) MBE
FCOT 1910-1993 whose generous legacy to the College of Occupational
Therapists made it possible.

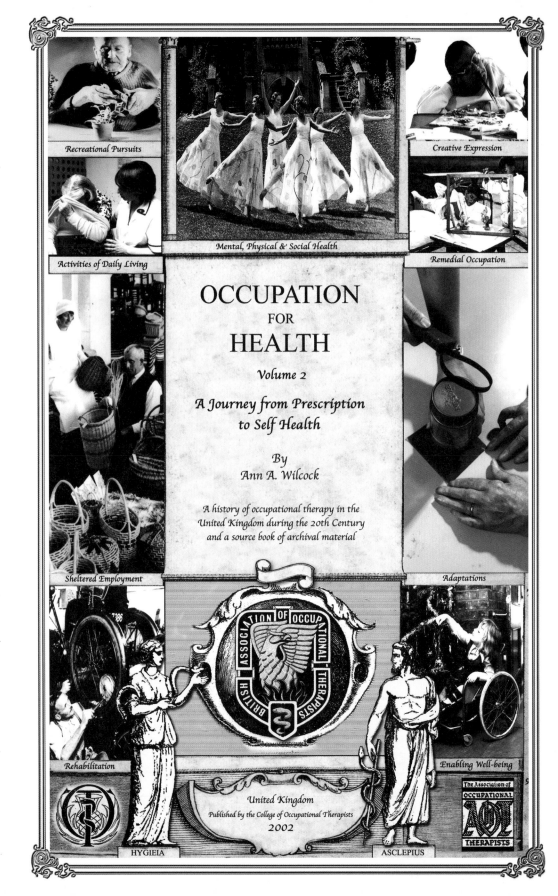

Recreational Pursuits

Creative Expression

Mental, Physical & Social Health

Activities of Daily Living

Remedial Occupation

# OCCUPATION
## FOR
# HEALTH

*Volume 2*

### A Journey from Prescription to Self Health

*By*
*Ann A. Wilcock*

A history of occupational therapy in the
United Kingdom during the 20th Century
and a source book of archival material

Sheltered Employment

Adaptations

Rehabilitation

Enabling Well-being

United Kingdom
Published by the College of Occupational Therapists
2002

HYGIEIA

ASCLEPIUS

The Association of
OCCUPATIONAL
THERAPISTS

Ann Wilcock DipCOT(UK), BappScOT(SAIT), GradDipPublicHealth, PhD(Adel), President of the International Society of Occupational Scientists & Historian to the British Association and College of Occupational Therapists.

Dr Ann Wilcock qualified as an occupational therapist in the UK in 1961. She worked in several hospital settings in the UK before emigrating to Australia in 1964 where she continued in clinical practice until 1976. Her first experiences of lecturing were as a part time lecturer at the University of Newcastle, New South Wales in 1966 and she went on to an academic post at the University of South Australia where she was Head of School from 1987 to 1993. In 2002 she became Professor of Occupational Science and Therapy in the School of Health Sciences at Deakin University in Geelong, Australia where she is establishing a new programme. She is also continuing her role as Visiting Professor at Brunel University in London, England.

Ann has contributed to many articles and books during her career and is respected throughout the world for her work on occupational science. She is the author of the best selling title *An Occupational Perspective of Health* and is Executive Editor of the *Journal of Occupational Science*.

Volume I of *Occupation For Health* was published in September 2001.

# Contents

# Volume two

**Editor**
Judy Waters of JJ Editorial

**Content Editors**
Peggy Jay, Alicia Mendez, Beryl Steeden

**Copyright and Illustrations Editor**
Christopher Ryan

**Frontispieces**
Tracey Greenway, D.A.T. Nelson

**Contributors**
Vee Pols, Catherine F. Paterson, Irene Ilott, Sidney Lock, Bruce Crowe and Peggy Jay, Beryl Warren, Gwilym Roberts, Sue Kennedy, Annette Leveridge, Felicity McElderry
Appendix A: Schools: Christine Craik, Averil Stewart, Catherine Mounter and Graeme Barber, Margaret Foster, Martin Booy, Clare Brewis, Anna Forte, Zielfa B Maslin, Lynn Summerfield-Mann, Catherine Usher.

**Clerical Assistance**
My late husband Derek Wilcock, and the late Kathleen Moran; Matthew Ebden, Daniel Pitman.

**Research Assistance**
Janet Crowe, Anne Kendall, Caroline Marshall, Alison Wicks, Hugh Stewart, Margaret Smith, David O'Halloran.

**Acknowledgements**
My sincerest thanks go to:
- Natalie Barr, for her generous bequest.
- Beryl Steeden, Christopher Ryan, D.A.T. Nelson, Irene Ilott, Gwilym Roberts, Ritchard Ledgerd, colleagues and associates at the College of Occupational Therapists who provided practical assistance, and very necessary support and encouragement.
- The many participants and organisors of the focus groups throughout the UK.
- My family, friends and colleagues in Australia, the UK, and elsewhere in the world, who supported me throughout what proved to be an arduous but a very fascinating project. In addition to those already mentioned thanks go to Cecilie Bearup, Cathy Captainino, Ann Carnduff, Christine Craik, Jennifer Creek, Sally Crofts, Mary and Bill Dobbie, Maeve Groome, Elizabeth Grove, Bruce Heyward, Clare Hocking, Coralie Law, Matthew Molineux, Barry Pitman, Therese Schmid, Josephine Snowdon, Elizabeth Townsend and Gail Whiteford.
- To the friendly and efficient bespoke service provided by the Lavenham Press Limited, Terence Dalton, Elisabeth Whitehair, and Trudy Wilcox.
- The Wellcome Library, the British Library, Imperial War Museum, the Royal Star and Garter Homes, Richmond, The Octavia Hill Birthplace Museum, Wisbech, and the Dorset House School.

# Part1

# The Dawning

# Chapter 1

# The Phoenix, Staff and Serpent

## Contents

In this book, the second of two volumes devoted to the history of occupational therapy, the story of the British Association of Occupational Therapists is told. British occupational therapy had its dawning and development early in the twentieth century when it became a separate and acknowledged profession. Although the use of occupation for health has a history that is as old as human existence, a specific group of people committed to learning more about the relationship, namely, occupational therapists, did not emerge until the second decade of the twentieth century. Initially, they applied that knowledge to assist people with psychological and physical illness and handicap.

## Foundations

Occupational therapy came into being because of a basic need and an underlying belief that there is a connection between what people do and their health. To explore those premises the first volume of the history traced the fluctuations of occupational regimes for health in the Western World from earliest times up to the end of the nineteenth century. It should have wide appeal to occupational therapists throughout the world, as well as to medical and social historians, and policy makers of all kinds.

For the benefit of readers who do not have access to the story that was told in the first volume it is useful to begin by recapping briefly the journey of 'occupation for health' throughout the history of humankind.

From the beginning of human life, occupation was the means of providing the necessities of life and, so, was a major mechanism for the maintenance of health and the prevention of illness as well as survival. The occupations of day to day living also kept the organism as a whole working well by exercising physical and mental capacities. Life depended, to a large extent, on people working co-operatively within communities which met their social health needs. Gradually, they found remedies and adapted their lifestyles to best effect in times of illness and injury and so developed the concept of 'medicine.' As time went on, humans began to explain many health problems according to spiritual beliefs and activities associated with them, so, for thousands of years, health interventions were often the province of priests.

That was the case in the earliest times of what is now regarded as the classical period. Then, because of territorial and warrior tendencies, physical health, strength, fitness, youth and beauty were venerated and deemed the essence of health. As the physical occupations of daily life became the province of conquered peoples and slaves, it was necessary to replace the health benefits of those activities of daily life with another form of occupation. That was achieved through the development of multi-purpose gymnasia where physical exercise existed alongside that of the mind, which was provided by philosophers like Socrates, Plato and Aristotle. It is said that the beginnings of modern medicine started in ancient Greece, and it was there that a humoural theory of physiology led to the establishment of six rules to maintain health and to prevent illness.

Those rules were promulgated, widely, during medieval times, when they became known as the *Regimen Sanitatis.* They remained in vogue until the nineteenth century. Through the *Regimen*, occupation was linked with mainstream medicine in both preventive and curative prescriptions. Two of the rules were of particular interest in that regard, that about 'action', 'motion' or 'exercise' and rest, and another which concerned emotional states. Alongside those rules, monastic medicine reigned supreme and so a spiritual view of health once more gained supremacy. The belief that the ultimate health and salvation of the soul was more important than the body led to the occupations of prayer, pilgrimages, charitable works and 'labour' being deemed of prime medical importance.

With the reformation, the dissolution of the monasteries meant that health care for the masses was no longer available. In the hiatus that resulted, one interesting development was the establishment of Bridewell Hospital for the occupationally deprived and occupationally depraved, which used occupation as the principle method of remediation. It was one of only five Royal Hospitals in London. Responsibility for the sick, poor and homeless was, eventually, taken up by the state in Elizabethan times with the Poor Law Act of 1601. Parishes, administered by Justices of the Peace answerable to the Privy Council, became the communities of care and for about a century and a half the system worked well with occupation being provided for those under care. That occupation was regarded as important is clear, because the 1601 Act required of parishes 'a convenient stock of flax, hemp, wool, thread, iron, and other stuff to set the poor to work.'

Philanthropic activity began to take over as the system started to fail with the beginnings of the industrial revolution, which was to result in the genesis of huge occupational change for the whole population. Social reformers at philosophical and action level sought to change the injustices which led to massive physical, mental and social ill-health. They gradually effected changes in industrial conditions, employment practices, housing, education and environment, further developing the bases of public, occupational, ecological and social health practices. Asylums for the mentally ill were established and within them occupation, benevolence and justice became the major form of remediation as part of what was known as moral treatment. Gradually that focus declined as asylums became overcrowded and occupation began to be used for economic as well as for therapeutic purposes, and as doctors sought other forms of treatment more in line with their 'internal medicine' backgrounds. Sir David Henderson, who might be regarded as a prime instigator of occupational therapy in the United Kingdom reported, in 1923, that:

> ...it is surprising that more progress has not been made in the occupation of mental patients, but the good work of those early years instead of being continued seems to have been gradually allowed to fade. The development of occupational work is nowadays looked upon as a new means of treatment, whereas it is a method which was perhaps more thoroughly utilised in the middle and early part of the last century than it has been in the course of the last forty or fifty years. The fact anyway remains that mental hospitals in the British Isles have not utilised occupational work as much as possible.[1]

By the end of the nineteenth century institutions for the physically disabled and handicapped were being established, and occupation was being used within them as well as being prescribed for the treatment of tuberculosis.

In this second volume, which picks up the story in the twentieth century, the genesis, development and growth of the occupational therapy profession in Britain and its association with other parts of the world are explored, along with stories of many of the people, ideas and practices which contributed significantly to its progress. Many themes flow over from Volume 1. For example, it was very exciting to find, for the first volume, evidence of practices which have resurfaced or been reinvented in the twentieth century. Earlier, but relatively unknown, antecedents included practical issues like the invention of something almost identical to 'the Nelson knife' for the one-handed, the need for rails on steps and stairs being referred to as early as the late Renaissance, and the discovery that long before 'sensory integration', 'rocking' was considered a useful treatment technique for a multitude of disorders.

Throughout the earliest centuries, underlying interest, goodness of fit, as well as basic need were apparent in occupation being utilised for health purposes. What was needed to spur on the evolution of the profession was some sort of catalyst. There were probably two major ones in the first decade of the twentieth century. They built upon those earlier philosophies about labour, industry, exercise and health, the use of occupation in asylums and in the treatment of tuberculosis, as well as the establishment of institutions for the physically disabled. The first catalyst was the impact of women's suffrage and their forays into education and the professions in the earliest decades of the century. The second was the impact of World War I, which led to a huge population of injured young men who were needed back at the front. That resulted in some members of the medical profession establishing occupational workshops to 'reconstruct' battered minds and bodies, drawing upon lessons learnt in the care of crippled children. Those catalytic stories provide the core of the story told in the next two chapters.

As in the first volume the approach taken to gather and examine the material is that used by the historian of ideas. As well as cataloguing stories of the past this includes an analytic process to gain insight into the what, why and how of particular phenomena, in this case, of occupational therapy in twentieth century Britain. Arthur Lovejoy, who first used the term 'history of ideas' in the 1920s, proposed that a researcher could take substantially the same material as others and subject it to analysis from a different perspective so that new insights emerged. It is an excellent method to examine the idea of occupation for health from an occupational therapy perspective rather than a medical one.

In seeking to clarify the history of the idea behind the profession of occupational therapy it is important to bear in mind that, in post-industrialised societies, the ideas and practices in health care are dominated by medical science. Although occupational therapy practice has altered with the passage of time in line with concomitant changing medico-socio-cultural-contexts, it was grounded in medical science concepts early in the twentieth century. It grew according to the acceptance of its value, and through the patronage of medical men and women, and was initially used as a prescribed adjunct to medicine. Only recently have some therapists suggested that occupational therapy can be much more, and that occupation is a health determinant in its own right, which does not require medical interpretation.

Providing a look at the profession's history in a critical and analytical way will be helpful in determining what the future may hold. Catherine F Paterson, a few years ago, wrote in a similar vein. She said:

> History is interesting for its own sake, but also facilitates understanding of contemporary roles and relationships. Just as our sense of personal identity demands roots in the past from family history, our professional identity and understanding of the contexts in which we work are enhanced by knowledge of their development. [2]

She added, by way of example, the sort of misconceptions that could damage current therapists faith in the foundation ideas of their calling, as well as the proper pride felt by earlier occupational therapists who pioneered services in conditions very different to the present:

> There is also the myth that past occupational-therapy practice lacked rational theoretical underpinning and was essentially diversional. What the history of occupational therapy in work practice services demonstrates is that the humanistic concern for the well-being of workers incapacitated through disease or injury has always been accompanied by genuine efforts to understand biomechanical, physiological and psychological processes. [3]

Delving into primary literature sources in relation to occupational therapy has been the process of choice. To that end information has been gathered from reports, minutes, documents and written material from the College Archives housed in the Wellcome Trust Medical Library. Also, substantial use has been made of the *British Journal of Occupational Therapy*, and its antecedents *Occupational Therapy* and *The Scottish Journal of Occupational Therapy* as well as other texts and papers written by British Occupational Therapists. As in the first volume use will be made of substantial extracts so that readers can appreciate the approaches better in terms of the values of the time when they were written. Photographs or documentary evidence of the profession's past have been collected or viewed and in some cases illustrate the text.

Additionally, to ensure that this is a 'people's history,' stories have been sought from individual occupational therapists and from groups within the many professional regions of the United Kingdom. Early in the data gathering process each region in Britain was contacted and invited to hold a focus group at which participants could discuss their ideas of what should be included in the history. Focus groups were held in all regions which responded affirmatively. Figure 2.1.1 features some members of the profession who attended the focus group held in London at the College Headquarters, and Figure 2.1.2 some who attended the group in Aberdeen. In addition to those focus groups, five retired members were convened separately in Scotland by Margaret Smith. An analysis of the ideas and suggestions that emerged at the groups is provided later in this chapter; as far as was possible they were followed up.

**Figure 2.1.1:** **Some members of the profession who attended the focus group held in London at the College Headquarters. From the right Betty Collins, Alicia Mendez, Peggy Jay, Elizabeth Grove and Eileen Bumphrey**

**Figure 2.1.2:**
**Some members of the profession who attended the focus group held in Aberdeen. From the right Catherine F. Paterson, Margaret Rothney, Isobel Aitkenhead, Margaret Johnston and Agnes Cook**

Also within the text there will be some original contributions by other authors. They draw upon particular expertise within the community of occupational therapists, such as Catherine F Paterson's extensive knowledge of Scottish occupational therapy history, Sidney Lock's of rehabilitation equipment, and Irene Ilott's of research. Additionally, the stories of some schools of training were provided by academics within them, and specialist groups within the British Association tell of their own history. The story, which emerges from this process, enmeshes those 'authors' interpretation of the past', so that 'new avenues of investigation, criticism and reflection' are opened up.[4]

In terms of access to and quantity of resource material, it is an easier process to reconstruct the story of occupational therapy in Britain in the twentieth century than over the vast periods of time covered in the first volume. Here, it is important to record the considerable pride I experienced as I read of the profession's rich and varied contributions, of the indomitable spirit and enterprise of the pioneers, and of today's practitioners. I wanted to tell every story, to include all the material into a source book that few people could find the time to read in their busy daily schedules. Of course that was not sensible or feasible. Material, on the whole, though, was so plentiful that, at a point of overload, arbitrary decisions about what or what not to include have had to be made. Those decisions will never satisfy all readers, but provide a place for more histories to be undertaken, and more insights to be experienced. Other material which could have added to the history, no doubt, still lies dormant in libraries, studies, cellars, sheds, spare rooms and attics, and no apologies are made for not seeking further. The time line, although generous, has been tight for so much material, and that has limited what has been possible. But no one history ever tells the whole story, and no end of histories will still fail in that respect. All will only tell according to a historian's interest bounded by the time constraints of external circumstances.

Indeed, the selection of material that makes up any history, as well as the direction of the analysis, depends upon the historian's point of view however rigorously that is held in mind and guarded against. An acknowledged aspect of any qualitative research it is deemed a requirement within such methods to acknowledge that no research can be totally unbiased, and that any researcher needs to consider and acknowledge particular interests and direction. As was acknowledged in the first volume, this history is likely to reflect my long-term engagement in occupational therapy in both physical and psychological fields of practice and academia. It will also be influenced by a current fascination in the relationship between occupation and health, and the need for occupational justice to ensure health and well-being for all people and not only those with recognised disability.

As in the first volume, immersion in the data was an important step in understanding and interpreting how the profession was changing and developing as the decades passed. Early in the process some trends were apparent, in part, as a result of my own reading of the changes I had experienced as an occupational therapist. The very obvious one was the change from hospital based remedial activity, often of a creative nature to activities of daily living working within the community. I started to analyse in themes rather than times. Later in the process I made the change to 'flexible' decades because some of the themes were apparent for much of the century and it became clear that more subtle directions within them should be connected more closely with contextual changes of different times.

The division into decades is 'flexible' because in some cases it made sense to carry particular themes over a few years or to report on earlier aspects of what happened during a period. This has resulted in, for example, the first decade covering from 1900 to World War I, and the second decade covering, mainly, that event from 1914 to 1918, and its immediate repercussions. A similar adjustment is made at the time of World War II for the same reason.

Apart from therapeutic processes, several important themes emerge in the history. Many relate to the status of occupational therapy, to its largely feminine membership, to its relationship to medicine, and to how occupational therapists responded when the ideas and philosophies on which the profession is based were challenged as socio-technical development created rapid cultural change. The challenges led to modifications, and this volume will be testament to the way remedial objectives gave way to adaptation and independence; therapist/patient communication altered from expert prescription towards partnerships with clients; an emphasis on craft activity was replaced by activities of daily living; practice in institutions was extended into the community; therapy informed largely by word of mouth reports of successful practice was gradually replaced by research-informed intervention; and interest in wellness as well as illness is emerging at the present time.

The twentieth century was a time of unprecedented change, which accelerated as the years rolled by. It was a period when what is described as the industrial age merged into the post-industrial, the service, the technological, and the information age. As with all change on a large scale these developments brought with them enormous alterations in how people spent their time in both obligatory and chosen occupations and which of them they valued, along with 'to be expected according to this story', concomitant changes in health status. Throughout the history it becomes apparent that as the social, physical and medical environment changes so do the types of clients and their problems as well as theory and practice. Some of the more obvious manifestations of this are the effects of war, technological development, economic depression, recession, and periods of affluence. Other harbingers of change include the authority and influence of older or younger populations in society itself; medical research, priorities and technology; belief systems; political will; and, increasingly, multicultural societies and care of the environment. Occupational therapy has also been influenced by its relationship with other professions, with health authorities, and with politicians. As it has been influenced by others so too has the profession's sphere of influence fluctuated. The effect of such influences has led to changes in education, in the professional association, and in who choose to become occupational therapists.

In considering the contextual nature of the profession's evolving story, it is important to uncover what occupational therapists did, in what context, and how this developed. Setting the story down took on an order of its own as the century unfolded, and as occupational therapy developed as a formal profession. The context of a decade emerged as the place to start, followed by the major changes within the professional body and some of its associations with occupational therapy in other parts of the world. What happened in education and in practice seemed the obvious next steps, and as research became more and more important it too demanded a section of its own finishing up the chapters in the second half of the volume. Choosing the stories used as examples could have been cramped by my own experience and interests however hard I tried to be objective. To prevent that I engaged research assistants to help in the selection, all but one of whom had trained and worked in the UK for some time over the last forty years. They helped to establish important aspects to include because of their experiences in the field, at different times. The other, also an occupational therapist, I found valuable as an entirely independent voice in choosing articles from the journals which appeared to illustrate particular trends of the times, but who was not constrained by prior knowledge of who or what it would be politically correct to include.

Inquiry regarding the indoctrination of those who chose to take up this work is also necessary. To that end the history will attempt to illustrate what was it like to be a student, a therapist, an educator, or a scholar 'then,' and what was read and written about. Such material will draw attention to the qualities sought in leaders of the field, in future education, and in professional organisations, as well as appreciating what therapists did and do. Topics such as these were addressed in discussions with occupational therapists throughout the research phase of history gathering and inform the ideas and stories which make up this volume.

## Focus groups: Remembering the past
### By Vincenza Pols[5]

A number of focus groups were conducted throughout the United Kingdom between 1998 and 1999. All regions were approached and groups were held in those that responded positively. The occupational therapists who attended the focus groups agreed to discuss their ideas about what they believed important to include in a history of British occupational therapy, and there was a remarkable degree of consistency. The group discussions were audio-taped and five were chosen randomly to be subjected to content analysis. The process used is described below.

There were three stages to the process of analysis. First, as I listened to the focus group conversations on audio tape, I précised them into a journal. At times, the participants' conversations became involved and enthusiastic and were difficult to follow despite many checks. As a result it is possible that some of the stories and experiences described by them may have been misinterpreted. Next, I read the journal notes to discover the range of topics that had been discussed in the groups. In general, the participants reminisced about their experiences in their work settings and during their training. Many considered it was important to name people who they considered were significant role models and had made important contributions to the development of occupational therapy practice especially from World War II to the present. Others reflected on changes in occupational therapy practice that they believed were a response to shifts in medical practice and the delivery of health services. They thought these changes were consistent with cultural shifts that have occurred in Great Britain over the past decades. The participants also reflected on their experience of workplace systems and their relationships with peers, associates, educators and students. Those experiences were described within the context of occupational therapy practice in psychiatry and in physical medicine, either as graduates or undergraduates. In addition, some participants reflected on their views about the particular character of the profession and how this may be important as occupational therapy practice continues to develop. The third and final stage of analysis was a review of the range of topics, which clearly showed that all the participants were reflecting on their own histories as occupational therapy practitioners. This emerged as the primary theme of the focus groups, and was typified by reminiscences about student days.

## Significant people

Often the participants began to describe their own history as an occupational therapist by remembering people who were significant in their lives. Several distinct groups emerged as they told their stories about people who challenged them to review their occupational therapy practice, encouraged them to learn, and enabled them to adapt to shifts in medical practice, health service delivery and other cultural changes such as workplace relations and dress code.

The first group was family members and careers advisers. Some participants thought that these people influenced them to make the decision to 'do occupational therapy'. One person said that her father's experience of working with occupational therapists, during his recovery from injuries sustained during World War II, encouraged her to take up occupational therapy studies. Another said her decision to do occupational therapy came from her mother and grandmother's attitude that 'a job was more important than family'. Yet another said her mother 'thought it would be nice (for her daughter) to be a special craft teacher' at a time when there was a 'big emphasis on craft' in occupational therapy practice. Several others said they chose occupational therapy because 'the job was creative', they liked 'making things and being with people' and they had 'an interest in medicine'.

The next group was educators, more particularly heads of schools (Principals) like Miss Macdonald who was mentioned by many throughout the focus groups. In their view she 'had a big influence' because she wrote a textbook which, for many years, was used by undergraduate students. One participant who trained at Dorset House with Miss Macdonald remembered that:

*...she lived at the school in a bed sitting room. There were Nissan huts. She had a little wooden toy; if it faced the wall you knew you were in trouble. She had this sense of humour without saying anything.*

Another participant said that educators 'had a big influence on the (professional) formation of students' and, in her view, undergraduate education was 'a mixture of occupational therapy practice and finishing school.' Indeed it was the experience of some participants that students tended to come from 'nice middle class backgrounds' and one participant said that when:

> *...posh mothers and fathers brought their daughters to Dorset House and saw the Nissan huts, they were surprised that their daughters wanted to stay.*

**Figure 2.1.3:   Nissan huts, Dorset House**
*(Reproduced courtesy of Dorset House Archives, Oxford Brookes University)*

Some of Miss Macdonald's other pioneering activities were remembered; in particular that she took a team of occupational therapists out to Argentina: 'That's how occupational therapy started in the Argentine. She is still remembered there today. Miss Mac is part of their tradition.'

Indeed, many memories of undergraduate days were shared and one person said that 'students held educators in fearful respect' Students would exchange ideas with one another regarding strategies to deal with routine three-monthly interviews with their Principal because 'this was the way then.' Another said 'I went in for my interview and sat down and the Principal said "Who told you to sit down?"' In one focus group a participant remembered her interview prior to commencing occupational therapy training:

> *'I went into the interview wearing a hat and gloves. Miss Fitchett asked about the dress I was wearing, I said I made it myself, she was very impressed.'*

Another participant remembered Iris Fitchett, who started the Derby school, as a fellow student, explaining that: 'she was in the same group as me; (as) mature students we completed a short course during the war.' Whilst she was Principal, Miss Fitchett married and participants, who were undergraduates at that time, remembered that 'she wore blue' and 'we all went to the wedding.' Participants remembered that her successor was Miss Burdon who 'came from Australia' where she had 'started the school in Perth.'

It was a general view that educators, in the very early days of undergraduate study, clearly outlined their expectations of students. For example, one principal was reported to have said: 'Don't wear lots of perfume or make-up as this can be offensive. Occupational therapists need to be pleasant to work with, not overnice.'

Several other educators were mentioned by participants who considered that their contribution to the development of occupational therapy was worthy of inclusion in the history of occupational therapy in Great Britain. Amongst these were Betty Collins who one participant remembered as a 'marvellous person (who) did a lot to advance the profession', and Mavis Wallace 'who was very innovative with training.' 'It was her idea to go to a four year course', and she set up set up the first in-service pre-registration programme for OT helpers. They also named Diana Grey, who set up the Salisbury Technical School, and Doris Sym who started the Glasgow School, and Rita Goble from the Exeter school.

In one focus group the participants thought it was important to record a brief history of Dorset House because, 'Dr Casson started the first school of occupational therapy in a private psychiatric hospital in Bristol which was called Dorset House.' They then went on to explain that in later years the school, which retained the name, moved to Oxford and also that particular occupational therapists are invited to deliver the prestigious Casson Memorial Lecture' to recognise and acknowledge the very significant contribution made by that pioneer.

The third group of people identified by the participants was educators in clinical settings, some of whom became role models for participants when they were either undergraduates or new graduates. One participant said she was a student of Miss MacCaul, a fieldwork educator at 'Kings', who was 'very good.' Others named different people for particular reasons, such as Joy Blakely who was remembered as 'a visionary in paediatric practice' who also 'set up a leisure library.' One person remembered that 'Betty Hollins was seconded to the Argentine for six months to set up rehabilitation following a terrible outbreak of polio.' Another named Jean Herrington, and said she was 'inspirational'. She set up St Jude's laundry and Riding for the Disabled in paediatrics in the 1950s and 1960s. Yet another named Peg Fulton and said she was:

> ...always very kind. She spent time talking to each patient and included students very well. [On their] first day of training [she told students they] need to be very strong academically and physically because the job requires a great deal from you. Her unit was highly respected nationally and internationally and she had a lot of overseas visitors.

Of the numerous other pioneering clinicians who were named in the focus groups, some of apparently outstanding worth were: Natalie (Smythe) Barr, who went to Hong Kong and later to Taiwan; Mary Smith-Rose; Sidney Lock who originally trained as a nurse; and Mary Jones who 'used adapted machinery to rehabilitate limbs and designed many dynamic splints.'

In some of the focus groups the participants discussed the issue of men joining the profession. One person remembered that an ex-Sergeant Major was the first male student in 1945. He was on staff as a technical instructor. Another thought that in earlier years 'male students made an impact; even though they were a rarity, they went straight to the top—it was an hierarchical thing.' Someone else said they 'came because they couldn't be a doctor—some came from nursing.' Yet another said that they often 'went off and did other things' (such as become a prison governor) because salaries for occupational therapists were low and men looked for work that was better paid to support their families. They reflected that there are now many more opportunities for employment, and that in addition salary conditions have improved so many more men are joining the profession.

Some participants spoke about technicians and other support staff who made a significant contribution to the development of occupational therapy practice. As one said, 'We worked with technicians—we had the ideas but they had the skills' (and the tools to make adapted equipment for clients). Another thought that occupational therapists:

*...value the support worker [and] this is different than other professions, occupational therapists enabled them to grow—it is a tradition [that] occupational therapists work more with them.*

The relationship between occupational therapists and support workers was highlighted in another focus group, when one participant expressed the opinion that: 'support workers helped young new graduates enormously, they provided stability'. Someone else summarised the discussion by saying that many clinicians (both professional and support staff) '...were trailblazers, they may not have worried about systems [but] they shaped the world' of occupational therapy practice.

## About uniforms!

Often participants reflected on the impact of social change on their professional behaviour. For example, in more than one focus group, the subject of dress code elicited lively discussion. One person remembered that: 'We did not go to anatomy lectures without our uniform on,' and 'We were praised if we wore a long dress to balls,' rather than the 'fashionable short-length dresses'. Another said that: 'In the 1960s the journals contained many letters about uniform styles' and it was considered that 'dark colours were practical in light workshop areas of work'. As someone else said: 'At work I always wore a skirt. The wearing of trousers was an issue. Some patients found trousers offensive but this has changed.'

## Adapting to shifts in medical practice

Several participants described their experience of changes in medical practice and health systems since World War II. For example, the medical treatment for tuberculosis shortened from 18 months or longer to just a few weeks. It was the view of one participant that: 'Historically occupational therapists have responded very quickly to new demands; they see a gap and move into it—other professions have done this too.' Another participant said the response to shifts in medical practice was that: 'We were desperate to get rid of the "basket weaver" image to promote the remedial image, but that got rid of a range of occupations.' Yet another said: 'Occupational therapy managers were faced with priorities, therefore craft and diversional activities were handed over to volunteers.'

Listening to the discussions, it became obvious that some participants held particular memories of their work in psychiatric settings. One said:

*When major tranquillisers came into use and were taking effect, this caused a big change. All admission patients were referred to occupational therapy as a matter of routine. The occupational therapy departments were the last outpost of British craft. Patients coped with great difficulty. Some couldn't reach the high level that was expected. Some items were presented at shows. The patients took a pride in their work.*

Another participant remembered that: 'Occupational therapists were given considerable autonomy to plan and implement treatments.' That experience was shared, with one person recalling that '…the medical superintendent gave occupational therapists tremendous power—the system was a benevolent autocracy; we could do what we wanted.' As the memories continued, another explained that occupational therapists were integral to:

*…therapeutic community type experiments. [There was] much bridging between disciplines—the lines were indistinct. Occupational therapists took on the role of advocating for nurses with doctors. Occupational therapists could bridge the space between them.*

Many participants thought there was a common emphasis in both psychiatric and physical settings to 'resettle patients into the community' and this included helping them return to work. However, resources were very limited so in psychiatric settings occupational therapists established hospital workshops, which provided opportunities for people to learn work skills so they could be 'set-up in employment'. The workshops had 'contracts for light manufacture'; they employed:

*Institutionalised patients who didn't want to go back to the community. Many were unemployable. Hospitals used patients to perform hospital jobs [which] caused some collision with the Unions.*

In physical settings, patients were involved in activity-based rehabilitation. Occupational therapists and technicians adapted industrial machinery and craft equipment to encourage specific limb and joint movements. Adapted equipment, such as one handed knitting machines, and adapted games, such as shuffleboard and chair hockey, were developed by occupational therapists. To enable patients to engage in everyday occupations, a range of adapted equipment, like the bath-board and teapot-tipper, were developed. In one setting:

*…a 'mock-up' mine, which was paid for by the National Union of miners, was set up purely as an assessment tool. It was clean. Patients had to load and unload a train. They were usually ready to go back to work by this time.*

One participant expressed the view that changes in medical practice and health care systems had a significant impact on the practice of occupational therapy. In a very few years occupational therapy practice made a transition from 'craft in groups' to 'individual involvement' with people to look at conditions in the home or work environment. Others talked about the development of private practice and the new and different opportunities it posed.

## Anxieties about the future

Even though it was the experience of participants across the focus groups that new areas are opening up for occupational therapy practice, several expressed their anxieties about the future. One person said that multidisciplinary teams have had a negative effect on occupational therapy practice and 'occupational therapists need to be strong to promote their role.' This idea was taken up by another participant who said a 'common attitude' can be found in health care systems that, 'anyone can do the job' of an occupational therapist. Many others agreed with those concerns and with the idea that 'lots of people don't understand what we are trying to do.' One added that promoting the role of occupational therapy is made more difficult because the profession suffers from a lack of numbers when compared with physiotherapists. The discussion continued as one person shared her strong view that 'other professions keep pinching occupational therapy ideas', some 'making decisions only an occupational therapist should make.' Many participants shared such concerns.

## The core ethos has not changed

From time to time throughout the focus groups, participants would challenge one another 'to think what we are really on about.' These discussions became very animated. Some thought that the role of occupational therapy is still not well understood by many in Great Britain, and is often confused with physiotherapy. One person said it was different in other countries, and excitedly told a story about encountering a young lift attendant in Canada who understood the distinction because he said:

> Physiotherapy is about range of movement and muscles and things, occupational therapy is about interaction with the environment.

Someone else thought, '...historically, occupational therapists are do-ers' and in her view this has not changed. However, as another said, occupational therapists are now expected to:

> ...justify our doing. We now have to prove and record it. It is good for therapists to do this. We need standardised assessments, we need research (and) we need to be reactive whilst at the same time retain spontaneity. The modern world forces us not to do this but there is value in going with the moment. Anything can come up, as long as it comes from the patient and addresses their aims and objectives.

To support this point of view another person said:

> ...the occupational therapist is often the only person who can enable the patient to 'go home and be with the cat;' the alternative being life in a 'nursing home.

In another focus group, one participant, who is an educator, thought that today's undergraduate students recognise that occupational therapy is more than assessing how well patients can wash and dress themselves. In her experience students 'want to explore what is the essence of what people are about.' However, another participant added that there were, 'limited opportunities to look at other aspects of a person's life apart from personal care issues.' In this focus group several people shared the view that occupational therapy practice needs to become 'more creative' in spite of 'limited resources'. They accepted, though, that it is important to consider 'how far we can go before the quality of the service suffers.'

Many of the participants in the focus groups were experienced and senior occupational therapists and they related their stories about past work experiences with considerable nostalgia. One participant said that, regretfully, occupational therapists have: 'modified practice to respond to the emergence of a litigious culture.' They have had to address issues of accountability for resources. Yet another shared her experience that:

*...the fear of litigation has knocked the health service on the head. (Professionals) are afraid to step out of line in case they find themselves in court. In one instance the whole team was taken to court by one patient.*

Some shared that they had learnt different ways of working and, as one person said, more occupational therapists:

*Are now working collaboratively with other professionals, for example in pain management. Occupational therapy practice is getting better, rather than different, and we are looking to [further] explore changes in practice.*

Another participant in a different focus group, who said that occupational therapists are now working in non-traditional areas, shared that view. She noted areas such as in Ear Nose and Throat at Queen's Hospital, private practice, and work with early redundancy workers—in a general practice offering primary health care. Another said, 'We are servants of the people we serve.'

Throughout the focus groups as the participants told the history of their own practice as occupational therapists they appeared to enjoy remembering people who had made an impact on their development as health service practitioners. Some of those people had challenged them to adapt their practice as shifts in medical knowledge and the delivery of health care services occurred. Their experience spanned forty-five years and it was frequently acknowledged that huge changes in the practice of occupational therapy had taken place in that time. They also acknowledged that change would continue to occur as health and social care services are further examined and rationalised. In spite of such change, participants were generally hopeful that the practice of occupational therapy would remain important in health service delivery. They remain committed to promoting occupation in the lives of the recipients of occupational therapy to enhance their health and well being.

The most senior occupational therapist to attend one of the focus groups was Olive Jeff. She was the first occupational therapist to practice in the North East and started the first occupational therapy course in the area. Blind by that time, at the focus group she made contact with Jennifer Creek, another participant, and a fellow embroiderer. Unable to use her collection of fabric scraps, Olive passed them on to Jennifer for use with a student group making a patchwork quilt as part of their course, but, unfortunately, died before completion of the quilt.[6]

Because of the importance given by the focus groups contributors to their own history and student days, it was felt important to chronicle, if only briefly, the stories of all the British schools of occupational therapy. These are grouped in Appendix A. Making an informed decision about which stories of particular people to tell was much more difficult. There are so many outstanding occupational therapists. So an arbitrary choice had to be made; the people who have been honoured by the Association with a Fellowship are singled out. Their stories will be told, briefly, in Appendix B to the rear of the history, but most will be referred to at other times in the text. Before the advent of the Associations there were some people of particular note who were not occupational therapists and whose stories are also told. Apart from those, many others will be mentioned once or many times, and even though that is the case it will be inevitable that some who should have mention in this history will not appear. To them or those who believe the stories of others should have been told, I apologise, and claim the tyranny of time as an excuse. I also appeal to others to collect and tell those stories for there cannot be too many tales of inspirational people, their ideas, and their work.

In this volume, as well as the first, chapter frontispieces provide a conceptual map of the material presented. The maps are encased in pictorial material illustrative of the social context of the decade. The main frontispiece of this volume is based, like the first, on Robert Burton's 17th century sepia frontispiece of *Anatomy of Melancholy*. The collage within it, for this volume, is a collection of photographs representing different aspects of occupational therapy's history, linked with the classical gods Aesculapius, the god of medicine, and Hygiea, the goddess of health. Shown, too, are the current British Association badge, and the early badges of English and Scottish Occupational Therapy Associations, which suggests that we should know more about the choice of emblems and the myths that surround them.

## The Phoenix, Staff and Serpent

The badge of the British Association is one of great beauty and mythical significance. Pictured in Figure 2.1.4 the central image is of the phoenix rising from the flames, with the 'Staff and Serpent of Aesculapius' underneath. That combination represents the coming together of AOT and SAOT. The Scottish Association's original badge was the 'Staff and Serpent of Aesculapius' set against a thistle which is depicted to the bottom left of the volume's frontispiece. The first badge of AOT, which simply depicted those letters calligraphically, is displayed to the bottom right. AOT adopted the phoenix rising from the flames for its badge in the 1950s.

**Figure 2.1.4:** **The Association badge (2002) with the phoenix rising from the flames and the snake coiled around the staff introduced 1974**

It is of interest in this introduction to consider the myths that surround the symbol of the snake around the staff, and the image of the phoenix rising from the ashes, which were chosen early in the British Professional Association's histories to represent their focus.

The symbolism of the 'staff and serpent of Aesculapius' has a long history. According to Cornutus in the 1st Century AD it represented help and support given to the sick[7], and to Eusebius Caesariensis (c. 260-340 AD) the staff was seen as a symbol of support whilst the serpent represented preservation of body and soul[8].

The serpent was regarded by the ancients as 'the life of the earth'. The earth was not only the realm of the dead. It renewed itself year in and year out, and was thought capable of providing all the instruction necessary for salvation. As 'serpent oracles and earth oracles are fundamentally the same' so the snake was deemed capable of providing all necessary instruction and prescription for the sick. In that way it was representative of the healer rather than the art and science of healing.[9]

Aesculapius' serpent, which curled around the staff, is best known as the symbol of medicine. Its home, with Aesculapius, was in the depth of the underworld, in the realm of the dead, where the mystery of life and recovery could best be revealed. Macrobius (c. 400 AD) explained that the snake's capacity to revive as it sloughed off its skin symbolised the ill throwing off disease and regaining former strength. He told how the serpent represented the daily rebirth of the sun, which also linked him to Aesculapius whose healing force emanated from the sun.[10]

It is thought by some that Aesculapius' staff was originally a long travelling staff, signifying the arduous life of a travelling physician, and that it was later, as he was deified, that the staff became the symbol of the support he offered to the sick.[11] However it too had religious significance. Often portrayed as a branch, sometimes with a leaf or two still attached, it also symbolised the life-giving secrets of the earth, embodying both death and awakening. The similar symbolic meanings of the serpent and the staff were emphasised by their union.[12]

The image of the phoenix rising from the flames has, possibly, an even longer history. The phoenix was a mythical bird, sacred to the sun. It was a very large, male bird, often with magnificent, brightly coloured plumage and a lovely voice. Only one phoenix existed at a time and it was reputed to live for hundreds of years. Its story is part of the mythology of many countries such as Egypt, Arabia, Greece, China, and the Americas.[13]

The 'Phoenix Fire Story' made its earliest known appearance in the ancient Egyptian Pyramid Texts of the third millennium BC. Those versions which survive are placed in 'the golden age' which is said to have existed before history began, and which scholars suppose to be a mythical time before anger, strife or tumult came into being.[14] The story is linked with that of the Nun and the Primeval Mound, and of the Bennu bird and the Benben stone. It goes like this:

Before history began, Atum, 'the god before all other gods', it is said, lay alone, naked and motionless in 'the infinity, the nothingness, the nowhere and the dark'[15] which the ancient Egyptians called 'the Nun' The god, however, maintained full control over his own will, intellect, and wisdom, and was filled with magic and energy to create, transform and 'author his own forms.'[16] At a preordained moment he surged up through the waters of the Nun, creating something out of nothing which is expressed in ancient Egyptian scriptures as three parallel and interlinked symbols—the Primeval Mound (the first land), the sacred Benben stone, and the Bennu bird. The three symbols were grouped together in the City of the Sun—Heliopolis, within the 'Temple of the Benben', which was also sometimes referred to as the 'Mansion of the Phoenix.'[17]

The Bennu, which appeared at the moment of creation, in the form of a grey heron, was the model for the Greek phoenix.[18] It epitomised the breath of life, the victory of light over darkness and spirit over death[19]. In ancient Egypt the phoenix 'was born before death existed'[20] and 'symbolised the eternal return of all things and the triumph of spirit over matter,'[21], and just as the new sun rises to replace the old one each day so the Bennu or phoenix was reborn from the ashes of his predecessor:

> As its end approached the phoenix fashioned a nest of aromatic boughs and spices, set it on fire, and was consumed in the flames. From the pyre sprang a new phoenix, which after embalming its father's ashes in an egg of myrrh, flew with the ashes to Heliopolis where it deposited them on the altar in the temple of the sun god Ra.[22]

The phoenix was frequently reputed to have come from Arabia and it is possible that the stories of the large mythical bird known there as the roc or rukh which was associated with strength, purity and life, is the basis for that idea. Greek mythology which links the phoenix with the sun god, Apollo, and tells much the same story as that of Egypt, also placed the origin of the phoenix in Arabia. In North America the stories of the thunderbird resonate with similar ideas, and the theme of the phoenix rising again from its own funeral pyre are also part of pre-Colombian Central American mythology.[23]

The Association of Occupational Therapists (AOT) had run a 'badge competition' in the thirties for adoption as the Association's crest, which could be worn as a badge by members.[24] It would also be used on the Association's notepaper and diplomas. An exhibition of the design entries was held at a meeting on March 11th 1939, and, apparently voting was keen. It was won by Molly Cawley from the Dorset House School, with runners up, Mr P. Jennings from Runwell Hospital, Essex, and Miss M. Dawson, a student at the Maudsley School.[25] Unfortunately when the design was 'reduced in size and carried out practically' it did not look 'nearly so well', so further designs were called for.[26,27] Eventually the calligraphical AOT was chosen.

It was in the 1950s that the phoenix made its debut. The badge was designed by Francis Cooper, an eminent silversmith and a Freeman of the Goldsmiths' Company. The Phoenix was silver against a blue enamelled background, with the pyre flames in red and the border in a deep green with silver lettering. This is how he described the significance of the design, which is shown in Figure 2.1.5:

*...It is therefore the symbol of self-regeneration and as such seems to me as appropriate a legend as we are likely to find, in that your methods make people heal themselves, through their own efforts as against the doctor's medicine and the surgeon's knife.*

*In the design I have shown the Phoenix rising by its own efforts to renewed strength and youth through the Association of Occupational Therapists. It will be noted that the head and wing tips extend on to the outer border, suggesting that it is leaving the members of your Association behind it to proceed to its new life.*[28]

## Figure 2.1.5: Badge designed for AOT by Francis Cooper

It is fascinating that both Associations chose symbols of re-awakening, of re-growth after disaster, and new life replacing the thought of death, or perhaps, of living death, as representative of occupational therapy. The stories support the notion of occupational therapists being involved in enabling people who have experienced physical, mental or social disease or disorder of whatever degree to overcome the difficulties that surround them in their daily lives and create a new life through what they do. The ancient myths of rebirth and reawakening pre-empt modern ideas about occupational discontinuity, as a result of personal or community disorder, being overcome through intervention based on meeting needs and enabling the development of untapped capacities.

During the final stages of the amalgamation of the Associations in the 1970s one difficult problem was the question of a badge for the British Association of Occupational Therapists. Both former Associations wanted to retain the symbols they had chosen in earlier days—the staff and serpent and the phoenix rising from the flames. Many different designs were submitted to the Councils of both Associations, none of which was suitable. Nathalie Barr knew a promising young local designer who was asked to help and it was his design that became the official badge as illustrated in figure 2.1.4. Despite its appeal, the Phoenix lost some of Cooper's beautiful self-health symbolism.

**In summary,** this chapter has introduced the second volume of the history of occupational therapy, which tells the story of the profession's development in the United Kingdom during the twentieth century and its links to practice in other parts of the world. A short précis of the pre-history was given to set the scene and the historical method was explained, along with an analysis of the focus groups that were attended by occupational therapists throughout the United Kingdom in 1998 and 1999. The colourful myths of the symbols that make up the badge of the British Association and their significance to past and future were discussed. What follows is an outline of important dates which are derived from the stories told in the following pages.

# Significant dates in the twentieth century tale

The Association has noted in reports the major steps forward in the profession's progress throughout the seventy-five years from the appointment of Margaret Fulton, the first trained occupational therapist in the UK. The dates it picked out as seminal are recorded below together with others from the beginning of the century, which have emerged as significant during the research into the profession's history. These provide a chronological outline of issues that are discussed in more detail throughout the text.

| | |
|---|---|
| 1900– | Occupation programmes are a central part of treatment in many psychiatric hospitals throughout the UK such as at Crichton Royal, Denbigh, Edinburgh, the Retreat, and Wakefield. |
| 1902– | Schools open for the physically and mentally handicapped. |
| 1908 | Dr David Henderson goes to USA to work with Adolf Meyer at the New York Psychiatric Institute and Johns Hopkins University Medical School where the latter instigated occupational therapy. |
| 1910 | 19th century occupation as treatment in tuberculosis, pioneered by Sir Robert Philip, is expanded to include a farm colony. Other substantial occupational initiatives follow for those with TB. |
| 1914–1918 | Work study experts, Jules Amar, and Frank and Lillian Gilbreth engage in making the environment easier for 'cripples', using 'activity analysis', and 'the discovery, invention or adaptation of devices that will make it possible for the cripple to "fit back" into all the ordinary activities of life.' |
| | Use of occupation in the trenches, and in Red Cross hospitals, convalescent, and 'residential' facilities. |
| | The establishment of long-term training and psychological and social support for the disabled at the Lord Roberts workshops. |
| | Use of occupation as treatment in Curative Workshops established by Sir Robert Jones. 'The intimate relationship' between 'treatment and curative |

training' is described as 'one of the most prominent discoveries of the orthopaedic centres in the War.'

North American occupational therapy 'reconstruction aides' teach 'various forms of simple handicraft to patients in military hospitals' in Europe, especially to patients in orthopaedic wards or those 'suffering from nervous and mental diseases.'

1917   The (American) 'National Society for the Promotion of Occupational Therapy' is founded. Profession is named 'occupational therapy.'

1919   Occupational Therapy, by that name, is established in Britain by Dr Henderson at Gartnavel Hospital with the co-operation of the Matron, Miss Darney.

The Ministry of Health takes over the functions of the National Health Insurance Commission and the Local Government Boards.

The Ministry of Labour takes over Government Instructional Factories for disabled ex-servicemen, which are renamed Government Training Centres.

The 'Central Council for the Care of Cripples' is established and in 1962 becomes the 'Central Council for the Disabled'.

1922   Dr Henderson appoints Dorothea Robertson as an occupational 'therapist',within Gartnavel Hospital's occupational therapy department.

1925   The first trained occupational therapist, Margaret Barr Fulton, is employed in the UK, at the Royal Mental Hospital, Aberdeen.

1920s  Dr Elizabeth Casson pioneers psychiatric occupational therapy at Dorset House, her private clinic in Bristol.

1930   The first occupational therapy school in the UK, Dorset House, opens in Bristol.

1932   The Scottish Association of Occupational Therapists (SAOT) is founded.

1936   The Association of Occupational Therapists (AOT) is founded for England, Wales and Northern Ireland.

Scotland's first purpose built occupational therapy department for the treatment of physical illness and disability opens at the Astley Aislie Institute in Edinburgh.

1937   The Astley Ainsley Institute establishes Scotland's first Occupational Therapy School.

| 1938 | AOT offers the first final diploma examinations for occupational therapy in England. |
|------|------|
| | The AOT journal *Occupational Therapy* is inaugurated. |
| | The first department of occupational therapy in London is established at the Royal Free Hospital. |
| 1939 | The Astley Ainslie Institute awards the first Scottish Occupational Therapy diplomas. |
| 1943 | AOT adopts its first code of professional practice. |
| 1945 | England and Scotland run short courses to train Auxiliaries as assistants to occupational therapists in order to meet wartime needs. |
| | AOT sets up its first office in London, a single rented room on Brompton Road, South Kensington. |
| 1948 | The NHS is established. AOT and SAOT appoint representatives to the Whitney Council to negotiate national salary scales and conditions of service for NHS employees. (Social Service employees still have nonational salary scale.) |
| 1950 | SAOT starts publishing a quarterly journal, *Scottish Journal of Occupational Therapy*. |
| 1952 | The World Federation of Occupational Therapists (WFOT) is formed. |
| | The Joint Council of Occupational Therapy Associations in the United Kingdom is established to provide SAOT and AOT representation in WFOT. |
| 1954 | The First International Congress, which launched WFOT, is held in Edinburgh. |
| | SAOT establishes its first office in Edinburgh, on George Street. |
| 1956 | AOT Board of Studies is reconstituted with responsibility for all educational and examination functions and awarding the Diploma. |
| 1957 | A monthly journal replaces the quarterly AOT publication. |
| | Statutory Registration of Professions Allied to Medicine introduced. |
| 1960 | The Professions Supplementary to Medicine Act includes occupational therapy as one of the professions accountable to the Privy Council. |

| | |
|------|-----------------------------------------------------------------------------------------------------------------------------|
| 1964 | The first occupational therapy school in Wales is established. |
| 1966 | The 4th International Congress of the World Federation of Occupational Therapists is held in London. |
| 1969 | A referendum shows the membership of SAOT and AOT in favour of a merger. |
| 1971 | Salford College of Higher Education becomes the first college of higher education to run an approved occupational therapy course. |
| 1972 | The first occupational therapy school in Northern Ireland established at the Ulster Polytechnic. |
| 1974 | The British Association of Occupational Therapists (BAOT) is formed from a merger of AOT and SAOT. Peggy Jay is the first Chairman. |
| | The AOT and SAOT journals merge into the *British Journal of Occupational Therapy*. |
| | The first BAOT conference takes place in Newcastle. |
| 1976 | Elizabeth Grove becomes the first occupational therapy officer at the Department of Health and Social Security. |
| 1977 | BAOT hosts the first European Congress in Edinburgh. |
| 1978 | BAOT forms the College of Occupational Therapists (COT), a registered charity primarily involved in the professional and educational aspects of occupational therapy. BAOT becomes the nationally recognised trade union for negotiating pay and conditions of service for occupational therapy staff in the NHS. |
| 1979 | *Occupational Therapy News* makes its debut as an insert in the *British Journal of Occupational Therapy*. |
| 1980 | The first BAOT annual conference in Wales is held. |
| 1982 | The first BAOT annual conference in Scotland is held. |
| 1985 | BAOT hosts the second European conference in London. |
| 1986 | HRH The Princess Royal becomes the patron of the College of Occupational Therapists. |
| | Committee of Occupational Therapists for the European Communities (COTEC) is established. |

| | |
|---|---|
| | BAOT moves to 6–8 Marshalsea Road, Southwark, London SE1 |
| 1989 | HRH The Princess Royal officially opens the BAOT new headquarters building, on Marshalsea Road in Southwark. |
| | The Blom-Cooper Independent Commission of Inquiry highlights the need to increase the occupational therapy workforce, continue educational development towards degree status, adapt a community focus and raise the public profile of the profession. |
| 1992 | Occupational therapists across the United Kingdom celebrate the profession's diamond jubilee. |
| | Averil Stewart is awarded the first chair of occupational therapy in the UK, at Queen Margaret College in Edinburgh. |
| 1993 | BAOT members agree to contract with Unison for Trade Union Services. |
| | *Occupational Therapy News* (OTN), the BAOT house magazine, becomes an idependent publication. |
| 1994 | BAOT hosts the 11th WFOT Congress in London. |
| 1998 | HRH The Princess Royal officially opens the BAOT new Borough High Street headquarters, in Southwark, London. |
| | The first BAOT annual conference in Northern Ireland is held. |
| | The COT unveils its first national advertising campaign *Able to Make You Able*. |
| 1999 | Devolution in Scotland, Wales and Northern Ireland leads to the launch of Country Boards for the three countries. |
| | The BAOT celebrates its silver jubilee. |

[1]Henderson DK. Report of the Physician Superintendent for the year 1923. In: *The One Hundreth and Ninth Annual Report of the Glasgow Royal Asylum for the Year 1923*. Glasgow: James Hedderwick & Sons Ltd., 1924: 23.
[2]Paterson CF. An historical perspective of work practice services. In Pratt J, Jacobs K, eds. *Work Practices: International Perspectives*. Oxford: Butterworth-Heinemann, 1997: 25–38.
[3]Paterson CF. An historical perspective of work practice services....25–38.
[4]Hamilton DB. The idea of the history and the history of ideas. *Image: Journal of Nursing Scholarship*. 1993; 25 (1): 45–48.

[5]Vincenza Pols is an Australian occupational therapist with experience in analysis of qualitative research data. She has provided the above analysis independent of preconceived ideas about relevance because of no previous contact with the profession in Britain.

[6]Creek J, James J. An Occupational Therapy Quilt. *Mental Health OT* 2001; 6(1): 7–8.

[7] Lang C, ed. Cornutus. Theologiae Graecae Compedium. op. 33. Liepzig: Teubner, 1881. In: Schouten J. *Serpent of Asklepius: Symbol of Medicine.* Amsterdam, London, New York: Elsevier Publishing Company, 1967; 35.

[8]Gifford EH, ed. Eusebius Caeariensis. Praeparatio Evangelica, III, II, 26. In: Schouten J. *Serpent of Asklepius....;* 35.

[9]Schouten J. *Serpent of Asklepius....;* 36.

[10]Macrobius. Saturnalia, 1, 20, 1–4. In: Eijssenhardt F, ed. Opera. Leipzig: Teubner. 1893. In: Schouten J. *Serpent of Asklepius....;* 40.

[11]Edelstein EJ, Edelstein L. Asclepius, II. Baltimore, 1945; 229. In: Schouten J. *Serpent of Asklepius....;* 40.

[12]Schouten J. *Serpent of Asklepius....;* 41.

[13]*The Encyclopaedia Britannica.* 14th ed. London and New York: The Encyclopaedia Britannica Company Limited, 1929; vol 17: 772.

[14] Faulkner RO, ed. *The Ancient Egyptian Pyramid Texts.* Oxford: Oxford University Press, 1969; 225.

[15]Rundle Clark RT. *Myth and Symbol in Ancient Egypt.* London: Thames & Hudson, 1991; 54–55. In: Hancock G, Faiia S. *Heaven's Mirror: Quest for the Lost Civilisation.* Michael Joseph Ltd, 1998; 105.

[16] Ellis N. *Awakening Osiris: The Egyptian Book of the Dead.* Phanes Press, 1988; 102.

[17] Nauval R, Gilbert A. The Orion Mystery. London: Heinemann, 1994; 16,17. In: Hancock G. & Faiia S. *Heaven's Mirror...;* 106.

[18] Habachi L. *The Obelisks of Egypt.* Cairo: The American University Press, 1988; 4–5.

[19] Rundle Clark. *Myth and Symbol in Ancient Egypt....;* 245–6.

[20] Faulkner. *The Ancient Egyptian Pyramid Texts....;* 225–7.

[21]Hancock G. & Faiia S. *Heaven's Mirror...;* 321.

[22] Hancock G. & FaiiaS. *Heaven's Mirror...;* 243.

[23]Hancock G. & Faiia S. *Heaven's Mirror...*

[24]Notices: Badge Competition. *Occupational Therapy* 1939; Winter: 7.

[25]Notices: Results of Badge Competition. *Occupational Therapy* 1939; Spring: 8.

[26]Notices: Badge Competition. *Occupational Therapy* 1939; Summer: 10.

[27]Association of Occupational Therapists. *Annual Report.* 1939–1940.

[28]Cooper FJC. In: Occupational Therapy 1954; 17(2):44.

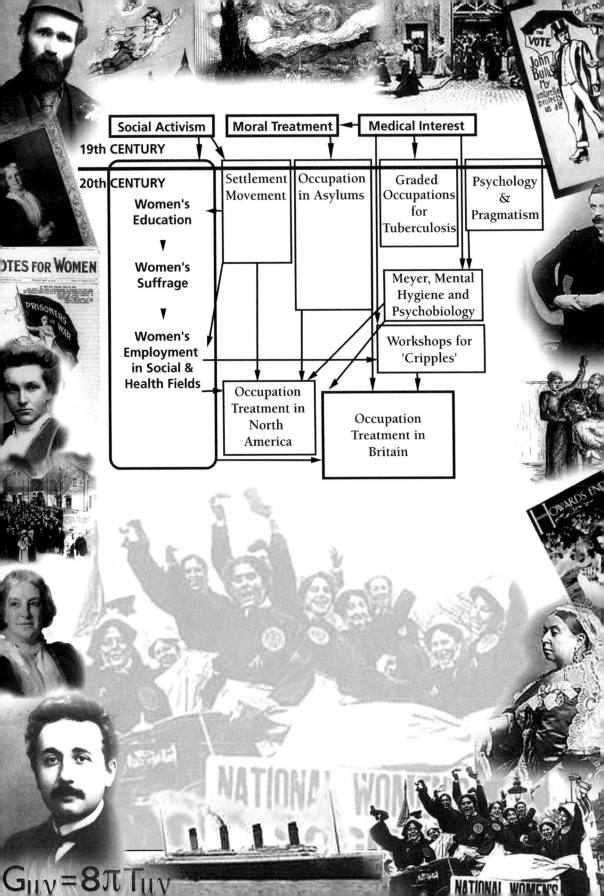

**Social Activism** | **Moral Treatment** | **Medical Interest**

**19th CENTURY**

**20th CENTURY**

Women's Education ▼ Women's Suffrage ▼ Women's Employment in Social & Health Fields

Settlement Movement

Occupation in Asylums

Graded Occupations for Tuberculosis

Psychology & Pragmatism

Meyer, Mental Hygiene and Psychobiology

Workshops for 'Cripples'

Occupation Treatment in North America

Occupation Treatment in Britain

$G_{\mu\nu} = 8\pi T_{\mu\nu}$

# Chapter 2

# The Dawning Decade:
# New Roles for Medicine, and for Women

## Contents

Women's suffrage
Intellectual and physical disability: Awakening of occupational consciousness
    In Britain
    In America
Psychological approaches within mental health
    In Britain
    In Europe and America
Adolf Meyer and his influence in Britain

T he history of the use of occupation for health during the twentieth century has to start with an exploration of what occurred during the first decade—the focus of this chapter. The context of the decade reflects an awakening social conscience at the start of the twentieth century, a movement towards increased productivity using time and motion studies, and a growth of psychological approaches within the domain of mental health. Although, in reality, there was a carry over of ideas and practices from the latter half of the 1800s, the turn of the century was viewed as a fresh start. In some ways, the combination of ideas that evolved during the nineteenth century and the fresh start fostered the rapid development of increasingly sophisticated medical knowledge and possibilities. It also resulted in the evolution of new allied health services. In this chapter, the beginnings of one such evolution is told. Occupational therapy, a profession concerned specifically with the relationship between occupation and health and its therapeutic application, was close to its dawning

The idea behind occupational therapy was definitely not new. It had been part of health practices since the dawn of humankind; but no one group had recognised it as a factor that could form the basis of a profession in its own right. Some had come close to that possibility in the nineteenth century when there was extensive use of occupations for curative purposes in lunatic asylums. Other initiatives which had a goodness of fit with occupational therapy were the sociopolitical, health, and welfare changes of the previous century resulting from social activism on an unprecedented scale, coupled with scientific management, and public and occupational health and safety developments. Those changes were largely in response to the gross inequities, and health and social problems that arose as a result of the industrial revolution.

# Women's suffrage

Alongside those factors, and a probable catalyst to the emergence of the profession, was the move towards women's suffrage. Parliamentary bills for women's suffrage were repeatedly introduced between 1886 and 1911, but were always defeated. A militant campaign of organised violence was launched in 1906, which prompted a reporter at the *Daily Mail* to coin the term *suffragettes*. Women took action, such as heckling at public meetings, chaining themselves to railings, and refusing to pay taxes, to advertise their plight and demand their rights. They went so far as to bomb the home of the Chancellor of the Exchequer, Lloyd George. Many were imprisoned and whilst on hunger strike force fed. These activities stopped with the outbreak of World War 1 in 1914, and ceased for its duration. Women activists busied themselves in war work, which resulted in a softening of attitude towards them. Limited suffrage was granted in 1918 and, finally, to all women in 1928.[1,2] Cecile Dorward, who was to become an occupational therapist, records in *Anything but Ordinary: The Nine Lives of Cecile* the jubilation felt at that time. At only 16 years of age, she worked as a home decorator in a women's firm whose workers chose to wear 'breeches with gaiters and lots of buttons' as their uniform because other forms of trousers were socially unacceptable. She describes her fellow workers as 'well-connected feminists making a point about equality of employment opportunities across genders.' One, for example, was Dorothy Bruce, Lady Balfour of Burleigh, who had been secretary of the National Union of Societies for Equal Citizenship. During the war she worked for the French Red Cross collecting the seriously wounded from railway carriages and preparing them for surgery. It is hardly surprising that, with such companions, Cecile recalls the 'atmosphere of excitement wherever we went' following the victory of women's suffrage after 'forty years of activism.'[3]

Suffrage was viewed as the pinnacle of justice at the time. The movement grew out of years of frustrated and deprived lifestyles, and as a result of increasing opportunities for women to engage in education and to use this in following careers that had not previously been available. Women, able to take advantage of those opportunities, often pioneered the service industries, taking their caring, and previously family oriented, talents to the ministration of others in the extended community. As such they led the way in social reform, recognising, with reference to the mores of their times, issues of social justice that were often of an occupational nature. They were, for example, involved in both the improvement and the phasing out of earlier occupational paradigms of care, such as the workhouse. As social and economic conditions throughout the country began to improve, and workhouse populations declined to manageable numbers, there was a gradual alleviation of discipline and conditions. Workhouses started to provide more for the relief for the sick and destitute, and the old and infirm, through the 'medium of restricted outdoor relief', workhouse infirmary, or 'if necessary, in an external hospital.'[4]

Four women of particular note fought battles, many of which preceded the suffragette movement. Dorothea Lynde Dix fought and won battles on both sides of the Atlantic to improve conditions for the mentally ill. Elizabeth Fry took up the cause of prisoners in jail. Jane Addams established the Chicago Settlement House, to assist migrants to adjust to a different way of life. And Octavia Hill pioneered improved environments, particularly for the urban poor. Others, who will be introduced in this chapter, are Mary Denby, Agnes Hunt, and Mrs Kimmins who brought the needs of 'mentally defective' and 'crippled' children and adolescents to the attention of a wider community by the establishment of excellent services to meet their needs.

The sort of initiatives developed by these women led to a more humanitarian approach to social and health problems which, in many ways, were entwined. The entwining encompassed notions of the health and well-being of people being associated with their opportunities to engage in occupations. Most of their stories were included in the previous volume, but some of them cross the pragmatic and purely artificial boundary between the volumes, and will be revisited in this chapter.

# Intellectual and physical disability: Awakening of occupational consciousness

The transition of women toward the public sector, and toward suffrage was, in part, responsible for a shift in social consciousness regarding others less fortunate than themselves. As they stepped, one imagines somewhat fearfully but determinedly, into the worlds of education, social need and health care, women took with them views which differed from their male contemporaries. One such woman was Octavia Hill, whose incredible tale was told in the first volume.

Octavia Hill can be considered something of a 'grandmother' to modern occupational therapy. She is the, once unknown, link between the development of occupational therapy in the United Kingdom and the nineteenth century educational, health and social activists. Hill can be seen as a direct descendant of activists such as her mother, Pestalozzian teacher, Carolyn Southwood Smith; her grandfather, occupational health reformer, Dr Thomas Southwood Smith; and the social reformers, Robert Owen and John Ruskin. She was also a link to the dawning of the profession in America, through the Settlement movement, and Jane Addams and Hull House in Chicago, where education for embryonic occupational therapists occurred from 1908. In their own ways, all those visionaries aimed toward the social well-being of individuals and communities, closely aligned with recognition of everyone's need to find satisfaction through participation in meaningful occupation. It is clear, though, that these aims were not necessarily spelt out in the same way that occupational therapists of the twentieth century might do. This interest was evident in Hill's work with the Ragged School children, and the play grounds, halls and green environments she established to encourage wide ranging occupations for her tenants and others. She began her work assisting disadvantaged children to develop their potential through what they did in a toy-making workshop and throughout her long career she continued to become more and more aware of the power of doing to help personal growth. For example, in her annual report to her workers in 1911, she affirmed that:

*...the usefulness of the employment given to poor and not over skilful tenants...impresses me more every year as I watch the feeble and helpless man growing.* [5]

Elizabeth Casson, who started the first British school for occupational therapists, and whose story will feature in a later chapter, was trained by Hill as a housing estate manager. She obviously absorbed much from her employer, and in her own right was skillful in promoting the many kinds of recreational, theatrical and educational occupations which took place in Red Cross Hall, of which she had charge.[6] Hill, in a letter to *The Times*, had explained how the Hall and garden which were part of the complex in Southwark known as Red Cross Cottages, which she built in the 1880s, would be used in summer for 'music, flower shows, reading room, and library, and it will be available in winter for our various concerts, entertainments, musical drill, lectures, and parties!'[7] She acknowledged the 'impetus' given by 'our spirited young secretary' (Casson) to 'performances by the people themselves' as 'most satisfactory (and) long desired'.[8] In 1910 Hill reported that the Hall had 'gone remarkably well', and that 'Miss Casson (had) still further developed her plan of bringing in local clubs and other institutions (which) develops power in local workers and creates local interest.'[9] Surely, those words foreshadow both the community development ideals and the enabling and empowering messages of the profession during the late twentieth century.

In America, too, by the end of the nineteenth century educational opportunities had begun to open up for women. Jane Addams was one of those who benefited, gaining the foundation of the strength and confidence she would need for the future from one of numerous women's colleges in the American North-East. Her story was told in the first volume, but a quick reference must be made here to the classes for attendants and nurses of the insane, which were instigated at Hull House, the settlement house she established in Chicago, to learn about 'invalid occupations'. It was in 1908 that the first Special Course in Curative Occupations and Recreation was organised there, by Julia Lathrop, Rabbi Hirsch and Dr Graham Taylor. Eleanor Clarke Slagle, who was to become a founder of the American Society of Occupational Therapists, completed the fourth class,in 1911, following her enrolment in the Chicago School of Civics and Philanthropy as a social work student.[10]

Barton, another of occupational therapy's American founders, and himself physically disabled, wrote on this topic that:

*...for too long our civilization has merely pitied the cripple, has considered him as being in a class by himself. The cripple is, indeed, in a class by himself, but is by no means to be considered merely as an object of pity. The time has come when society must not only admit its duties, its obligations to the members of this class in itself, but also must allow those members — coerce them if necessary — to fulfill the obligations involved in their being members of this class by itself—the obligations of self-respect, of self-support, and the obligation of proving that, though maimed, they are at least not crippled in their wills.*

*The sudden and tremendous need of assistance for cripples has produced numberless applicants for the position of helpers for them; but because of its non-development and obscurity there is but little definite information regarding the subject of how the sick or crippled can best be helped.*[11]

Although the word cripple is legislatively proscribed in the present day, when most forms of discrimination have become a focus of human rights, it was used generally in the early twentieth century. It had originated when those who were unable to walk normally were forced, by the nature of their disability, to creep about, so becoming known as 'creeples'.

## In Britain

During the early decades of the century there was increased recognition of people with special needs. Specialised homes, hostels, hospitals, schools and workshops began to be established during this period. These included institutions for people with learning disabilities or difficulties, who were described at the time as 'mentally defective' or 'feeble minded'. Schools for them and for children with epilepsy were established by local authorities, according to the 1899 Elementary Education Act.[12] An example is provided by a facility situated in Lancashire, which became a blueprint for the management of other similar institutions in the early years of the twentieth century.[13]

Helped by local and national support, the Sandlebridge Boarding Schools or Colony, opened in 1902. Known later as the Mary Denby Hospital, after its founder, the institution catered for both children and adults. Denby, a member of the Manchester School Board, had carried out an extensive investigation of 40,000 Manchester School children, in 1898, before formulating a plan to provide institutional care for high grade 'mental defectives'. Boys and girls were housed in different schools and by 1909 the residents numbered 204.

Occupation was deemed an important element of the Institution's life from the start, based on the 'ideological and practical centrality of productive work' within society in general. 'Apportioned employment according to contemporary gender constructions of work' the boys engaged, mainly, in farm and garden work whilst the girls were provided with domestic and needle work.' The 1905 Report of the Lancashire and Cheshire Society for the Permanent Care of the Feeble-Minded put forward the idea that if:
> *we can show that they are able through the farm to contribute considerably towards their maintenance, we shall have done a great deal to solve the sad problem of their lives.*[14]

The ideology mirrored that of other institutions in which occupation was used as a 'fundamental feature of social control in prisons and workhouses'. Denby used, as publicity for the colony, the idea that work within the institution would act to partially reclaim 'defectives' from potential unemployment, criminal activity, promiscuity and alcoholism. However, at Sandlebridge, occupation was used, not only to manage and control, but distinctly and effectively for therapeutic ends, but, although:
> *...like modern occupational therapists...[Denby] attempted to provide a scientific, and explicitly medical, rationale for her management strategies and expertise, it was her recognition and integration of complex social and individual needs within a specific geographical environment and political framework that ensured her initial success.*[15]

Similar, in many respects to the nineteenth century moral treatment, Denby's view of occupation was based on neither 'capitalist exploitation' nor 'naive therapeutic optimism'. For her it was useful in several ways: 'it produced capital; it promoted the mental and physical health of inmates; it encouraged socialisation; it facilitated education and promoted discipline and religious commitment; and it encouraged and rewarded creativity.'[16] In 1911 she wrote:

> Occupation is the keynote of success in dealing with the mentally defective:— occupation, incessant, pleasant to the child, easily within its capacity, and useful in itself. From the time the boy or girl rises in the morning until it goes to bed at night he or she should be occupied. The day should be one succession of mealtimes, work and play. It is well to remember that, for the feebleminded, all work may be made as delightful as play, and our object is not attained until our children look forward to their daily business with as much interest as to their games or their dinners.[17]

Also in the early decades there was increased recognition of the special needs of the physically handicapped. In 1902 the Liverpool 'Workshop and Home for Cripples' was set up, and a year later the Belfast 'Cripples Institute Workshops'. In 1906 there was the 'Lord Mayor Treloar's Cripples Hospital' at Alton, Hampshire; in 1912 hostels for invalid and crippled girls, opened in London; and in 1914, the Liverpool 'Open-Air Hospital' was opened.[18] Schools for them were opened and local authorities were advised by the Government Health Board and the Board of Education to set up school clinics to provide medical services to 'cripples, blind children, deaf-mutes, and those with ear, nose, throat and dental problems.'[19] However, because of World War I, it was not until 1926 that the provision of special schools for physically handicapped children became compulsory. By that time:

> …the total number of children ascertained to be physically defective throughout England and Wales was 150,779. Including the blind, deaf and mentally defective, the total was 200,149, of whom 120,277 were attending ordinary elementary schools.[20]

Agnes Hunt, pictured in Figure 2.2.1, was an influential force in the development of such facilities. In *Reminiscences* she writes that:

> In 1900, England had no realisation of the magnitude of her crippled population, nor yet of its crying need. Some of the towns had cripples' guilds, and in London there was an Invalid Children's Aid Association. These societies gave treats to the crippled children, and paid for convalescent treatment. Much money was also expended on splints. Unfortunately, as there was no one to supervise the application of these appliances, they were seldom worn, although much admired and greatly prized by the parents…No proper treatment, no after-care, and no hope for the future, except the gloomy portals of the workhouse—a burden to their loved ones, wretched and utterly helpless, alternatively spoilt and smacked by their people, and systematically cold-shouldered by a world which had no room and little sympathy for the physically disabled.[21]

**Figure 2.2.1:** **Agnes Hunt**

*(By courtesy of Robert Jones
and Agnes Hunt
Orthopaedic Hospital,
Oswestry)*

Disabled herself, Hunt reflected on the difference between her own opportunities, because of a sheltered childhood and financially comfortable circumstances, and those of crippled children from the slums. She had been able to undertake nursing training and so achieve independence, meaning and purpose:

> *It was, however, not until I was myself a patient of Robert Jones' in 1903 that a real and certain hope was born that something might and could be done to help the dreary lot of the cripple.*[22]

Hunt started Baschurch Home, Oswestry, in 1900 originally for convalescence of patients from the Salop Infirmary. There she had sheds built and adapted to house crippled children, and herself, because the house itself 'was in no ways suited' to their needs. Despite its unsuitability, Baschurch 'exerted a magnetic attraction' for the physically handicapped, and by 1904, the year she persuaded Robert Jones to join the staff, she needed more sheds because of demand. To raise money for them she had a:

> *...brilliant idea, we could produce a play in the open air, acted by the cripples, and charge five shillings a seat...The first play we acted was 'The Court of Oberon' and Wells made some little trolleys to fit the frames on which many of the cripples lay. The children who were either on crutches or calipers were dressed as bats, with wings made out of old umbrellas, and were harnessed to the trolleys which carried the small patients dressed as goblins. They all pranced around the stage, singing songs set to music by my cousin, Eva Hunt...After this we acted plays every year.*[23]

As one reads that story, the spirit embodied in the modern profession of occupational therapy is evident, as the fun, the trolleys and the opportunity to express hidden abilities conjure up similar visions from paediatric practice.

Over a period of thirty-four years Baschurch Home turned into a 320-bed orthopaedic hospital, later to be named after Robert Jones and Agnes Hunt. It boasted clinics extending through eight counties, a staff of after-care nurses, and a training college for the physically handicapped, plus 'the nucleus of a village settlement'. The success of the work done at the Baschurch Home is testament to Hunt's courage, perseverance, and adaptability. With always limited funds, but great ingenuity, she turned sheds into wards, workshops, and more, according to the need at the time. Despite official awareness that the physical conditions at the Home were poor, they were overlooked because 'the work done in it was a shining example to the whole of the hospitals in the kingdom.'[24] Similar training schools opened at Heswell, Ruislip, Pinner and Chailey.[25]

The Chailey Heritage Craft School, which started in 1903, was, in fact, the first residential school in England for physically handicapped children which combined hospital treatment with education and training. Based in the country, and utilising a refurbished workhouse and industrial school, Chailey initially provided a home for boys drawn from the *Guild of Brave Poor Things*, started by a Mrs Kimmins in the South-East quarter of London. Later it housed, treated and trained both boys and girls, the latter in many domestic tasks such as laundry and housewifery. Educationally, the institution was often at the forefront of new ideas due to the influence of Mrs Kimmins' husband, who was the chief inspector of London's County Council Schools. Its uniqueness was the provision of 'normal and healthy training for useful work and a happy social life' to combat a disabled child's previous treatment as a 'sad and sorry helpless creature.' The aim was to prove that he or she could 'be mentally freed from the old legends of deformity.' One armless boy carved a sign above the door with his feet. It read: *Men Made Here*.[26]

Robert Jones said of Chailey and its 'healthy looking children':
*They are hard at work or hard at play, irrepressible in spirit, and yet fully disciplined...he is filled with emulation and a desire to excel. If he has lost an arm, or leg, he still has one or other so trained as to minimise disability. It is a perfect joy to see a one legged boy run a race, and the pride of a one-armed boy, when he shows you what the remaining one has accomplished. Every boy and girl realise that they are to be of service in the world. There are no drones at Chailey! See them at work in the carpenter's shop or in other industrial developments, and you will realise the happiness of it...They are taught the joy and morality of work!*[27]

**Figure 2.2.2:** **Toymaking by the handicapped children of Chailey**[28]
*(Chailey Heritage School)*

Such pioneer work established a long held tradition in England of special schools for the physically handicapped attached to hospitals, rather than special classes in ordinary schools as was the case in other countries such as America. Under the English system, handicapped children were provided with the opportunity to regain or acquire confidence during recovery or treatment, but could lose touch with ordinary life in which they may, sooner or later, have to take their place. Different approaches were used elsewhere. In Prague at the Jedlicka Institute, for example, Dr A. Bartos treated handicapped children and adults within a 'collective' community by 'throwing' them on their own resources and learning, for instance, how, with suitable appliances, to dress themselves. Managed by their own committee which aimed at self-support, there the handicapped encountered 'the outer world by excursions' rather than through personal contacts.[29]

The establishment of training schools for the physically handicapped, whatever their fundamental strategies, reflected a growing perception of the part occupation could play within the lives of people with long term physical disorders. There seems to have been at least the beginnings of an understanding that occupation could be instrumental in improving physical health as well as providing a starting point for later economic independence. There was, however, at that time, no official scheme in England for either the rehabilitation or training of the physically handicapped generally. Watson described how, when the voluntary county scheme went in search of 'cripples', 'the houses of the poor in slums and country cottages revealed pitiful secrets of grown or partially grown men and women, usually quite unlettered, quite useless, quite hopeless and often uncurable.' There were, in addition, 'children who required training and the uninsured accident cases.'[30]

Watson argued that, until crippling diseases were prevented or cured, the lack of an official scheme posed three principal concerns. The first was for the handicapped child, who was not able to contemplate every type of work and would, probably, be untrained for any. The second was for the adult who, following an accident, was unable to return to his former job and required rehabilitation and retraining. And the third was for the adult who was only able to work in particular fields and required medical supervision or less arduous duties than the norm.[31]

Because of lack of funds it was only possible to open workshops in association with some major hospitals and to offer training and education to as many of the disabled as the funding would allow. One training scheme took place in a special ward opened by Dr Rollier, for men unable to leave their beds. Another was started by the orthopaedic surgeon, G. R. Girdlestone, at Wingfield. Participants, usually starting at 16–19 years of age, learnt cobbling, surgical bootmaking, and woodwork during an 8 hour day, and over a period of three years. Included within this programme was an hour and a half of daily education.[32] Apart from training schemes like that, Watson believed that the best prospect, for those only able to work at home or in a workshop, or under direct medical supervision, was offered 'by such work as splint-making, etc., in connection with orthopaedic centres or rural industries and handiwork.' The latter was being promoted by the National Council of Social Service in view of a 'small but not over-developed market'.[33] By 1929, such was the interest in this subject, there was even an *International Exhibition of Cripple's Work*. Whilst such schemes did not adequately meet the needs of any of the three areas of concern he had identified, Watson said that within such 'small beginnings' he believed that 'crafts as handiwork' offered the 'germ of progress'.[34] This statement may provide an indication of how occupational therapy became so closely linked with handicrafts in its formative period.

Another group who benefited from the growing perception of the part occupation could play in the remediation of long term physical disorders were people with tuberculosis. Workshops for them were expanded or developed, and sanatoria included rest and activity programmes. In Chapter 10 of the first volume, the story was told of Sir Robert Philip, who pioneered occupation as therapy in the field of tuberculosis in Scotland. It was in the last decade of the 19th century that he developed a graduated programme based on rest, movement, and progressively demanding occupations for the patients at both the Royal Victoria Dispensary and Royal Victoria Hospital, in Edinburgh.[35]

The programme of regulated work and recreation was expanded in 1910, when a farm colony was opened. Philip, in delivering the Introductory Address to the Edinburgh Sanitary Society in that year, reminded his audience that, 'for us all health is largely governed by the harmonious alternation of activity and rest.' This truth was extended into the treatment of patients with tuberculosis, with the proviso that 'the amount of activity allowed must in every case be determined with exactness.' Indeed 'there must be a careful estimation of the dosage' the adjustment of which 'must be guided by the needs of the individual patient.' Because of this, Philip, in ways similar to how occupational therapists carefully controlled 'the dosage' of occupation for tuberculosis sufferers some decades later, advised that:

> The possible occurrence of...untoward effects implies the need for most careful supervision of persons undergoing treatment by movement for some little time at least. It is only the watchful observer in frequent relationship with the patient who can quickly discriminate the effects of excessive dosage and who can wisely determine the decrease or increase of dose in a given case.
>
> On this account such treatment can be more efficiently initiated in a hospital or farm colony, where the patients are more or less constantly under the eye of a trained observer, and where increase of dosage is sanctioned only when no contra-indication is present. Under such conditions the degree of tolerance on the part of the patient can be studied with great exactness. The regulation of dosage becomes a scientific procedure.
>
> ...Where no...contra-indication occurs, it is found possible to increase the activity undertaken until its amount is as great as, or indeed, until it is much greater than, the activity previously undertaken by the individual in health.
>
> After sufficient trial at this high level, the patient may commonly be allowed to guide himself as to the discharge of energy which is sufficient to keep him in condition and is not excessive.[36]

With regard to the farm colony, he explained that:

> For the majority of patients under treatment this regimen, as carried out within the hospital, is found to be complete. In the case of some 25 per cent. of the patients, however, there is need for something more. It has been found that, after the disease seems to have been arrested and the muscles have recovered size and tone, these persons remain unduly liable to relapse. An immediate return to their ordinary vocations, more especially in the

*case of indoor workers, means frequently recurrence of trouble...It is for this class of persons that the farm colony was conceived. The colony is a kind of post-graduate school suited to the requirements of a certain number of individuals who need more prolonged surveillance and direction than is convenient in hospital.*[37]

W. Leslie Lyall wrote that the farm colony development was 'the last link in the chain...which makes the Edinburgh system practically complete in its bearings towards tuberculosis in all its stages.' The Chain, he said:

*...was forged by the purchase of an estate at Polton, where a farm colony is in process of development...Here patients are employed (both male and female) who have already been inmates of the hospital, but who still require a lengthened period of supervision before returning to ordinary life. To each of these work is assigned in accordance with his condition and abilities.*[38]

That programme demonstrates very clearly the notion of occupation as cure. It was used prescriptively, in the same way as pharmaceutical therapy, and was aimed at the elimination of symptoms. The results demonstrated a greater effect than could be expected from rest or drug therapy alone.

It is hardly surprising that Sir Robert Philip, who pioneered the use of occupation with his tuberculous patients, later became a member of the Board of Governors of the Occupational Therapy Department and Training School, established at the Astley Ainslie Institution, Edinburgh. In England, too, a pioneer of the use of craft occupation in the treatment of tuberculosis, Dr Jane Walker of Nayland, a Sanatorium in East Anglia, was to become an early force in establishing the discipline as a founding vice-president of the English Association.

In the early twentieth century the concept of social services, provided by the government as a type of justice which could rank with the legal variety, began to gain ground. Replacing the 'charitable good works' of the previous century, the beginnings of state responsibility were obvious in the Old Age Pensions Act of 1908, and the establishment of employment exchanges in 1910.[39] At the beginning of the second decade Local Government Boards were instigated to set up various treatment facilities, including sanatoria, in the community. At about the same time, inspired by Bismarck's social legislation in Germany, and paid for by employers, employees, and Government, the National Insurance Act (1911) proposed by Lloyd George, was activated to cover the costs of sickness and unemployment benefits.[40] The majority of medical practitioners joined the scheme, probably glad to have an assured income, in which the state guaranteed and paid an annual fee to them to provide medical treatment to contributing working men.[41]

## In America

In America, Herbert J. Hall, a doctor, began in 1904 to prescribe as medicine what he called 'work cure' to enable his patients to direct their interests and to regulate their lives. Two years later, with a grant of $1000 from Harvard University to forward the study of 'progressive and graded manual occupation' in the treatment of neurasthenia, Hall set up a workshop in Massachusetts to capitalise on the normalizing effect of specially chosen manual work. There, he used hand weaving, pottery, woodcarving, and metalwork as treatment because of their 'universal appeal'. In the Journal of the American Medical Association, he wrote that: 'Suitable occupation of hand and mind is a very potent factor in the maintenance of the physical, mental and moral health in the individual and the community.'[42]

About 1908, Hall established a training programme in the use of occupation as treatment for young women nurses and social service workers. Later he published *The Work of Our Hands—A Study of Occupations for Invalids* in which occupation was described as either diversional or remedial according to whether it was for patients with incurable disease or had therapeutic and economic value.[43]

Also in Massachusetts, in 1905 a nurse, Susan E. Tracy, observed during her training how occupation appeared to make bedrest more tolerable for orthopaedic patients. It relieved tension and she came to believe that happiness and contentment were essential attributes for rest and therefore recovery. After establishing training courses for psychiatric nurses, six years later she was conducting a training course in occupation for nurses at the Massachusetts General Hospital, and in 1914 became director of an 'Experiment Station for the Study of Invalid Occupations'. That provided instruction to 'invalids', nurses in training, and trained nurses who might become teachers.[44] In the flier for the course the need to consider the body, mind and spirit of each patient was highlighted, whilst aiming towards:
1. The patient's physical improvement
2. His educational advancement
3. His financial betterment
through:
1. The realization of resources
2. The ability to initiate activities
3. The participation in such activities of both sick and well subjects. [45]

# Psychological approaches within mental health

The twentieth century was, without doubt, a time when psychology came into its own, and assumed an important part of assisting the mentally disturbed to carry on meaningful lives. Like occupational therapy, its antecedents can be observed in the work of philosophers such as John Locke, and in 'Moral Treatment', the term 'moral' often being referred to as meaning the same as 'psychological'.

## In Britain

Remnants of occupational aspects of moral treatment, perhaps the earliest form of large scale psychological intervention, were still in evidence in many psychiatric hospitals throughout Britain. In the North Wales hospital at Denbigh, for example:

*Recreation and entertainments were revitalised in 1902 with the appointment of Dr Frank Jones who joined Dr Herbert as Assistant Medical Officer. He was a talented*

*musician and sportsman, and organised a variety of musical events and many sporting*
*activities such as athletics, football and tennis Along with Dr Herbert who provided Magic*
*Lantern shows and organised dramas and musicals, they ensured that patients were well*
*provided with recreation.*[46]

In many hospitals though, the economic rather than the curative ideas behind the use of occupation appeared to be most valued. Some occupational therapists today hold the opinion that earlier forms of the use of occupation with inmates of mental hospitals cannot be described as occupational therapy. Yet, the association of moral treatment with occupational therapy was recognised by early pioneers in the profession, as it is by some scholars of the profession today. For example:

> *...Louis Haas, who wrote one of the first textbooks on occupational therapy, pointed out*
> *that its first impetus came from the Quakers in the 18th Century, when the Retreat at York*
> *began its work of treating mental patients to aid their recovery and return to normal life*
> *by awakening their interest in occupations carefully designed for them. This successful*
> *treatment spread through England and America.*[47]

It is, perhaps, not surprising that occupation was still in use at the home of moral treatment, The Retreat in York. In the written instruction booklet given to members of the nursing staff in 1902, for example, nurses were advised that they should endeavour to 'rouse the interest' of patients and encourage them 'to occupy themselves usefully.' Nurses were further instructed to 'assist' patients in 'their amusements and pursuits', and it was noted that these instructions applied to all patients not only the more intelligent.[48]

Occupation continued to be utilised in other asylums throughout the United Kingdom and the subject continued to be of interest to the medical fraternity. For example, in reference to an article that had appeared in *The Lancet* of 28 October, 1900 about the economic benefits of employment of the insane in American asylums, one critic pointed out that:

> *Old established asylums such as Wakefield and Utica are veritable hives of industry;*
> *it is years since machinery was introduced in the shoemaking department at the former,*
> *and the old men were encouraged to make and repair stockings; while the useful trades at*
> *Utica are representative of the greatest possible variety , and would be still more efficient*
> *but for the interference of trade unions. Of course every asylum ought to have a farm*
> *proportionate to its size. It is late in the day to advocate that primitive measure.*[49]

Some enlightened administrations sought to improve what they offered in this treatment mode. A case in point was the Royal Edinburgh Mental Hospital, where in 1900 'a lady possessing the South Kensington certificate was engaged to teach fancy needlework to the lady patients.' Also, Dr Easterbrook, the Medical Superintendent of the Crichton Royal Hospital, visited twenty-four mental hospitals in the USA and Canada, which were considered to be 'state of the art', with the major objective of gathering ideas for a proposed Recreational and Therapeutical building.[50]

At Crichton Royal Hospital the tradition of occupation started by W.A.F. Browne in the previous century continued. The farm remained substantial, gaining many honours at agricultural shows, which linked patients and hospital with the community. It was extended in 1901 to give private as well as pauper patients the opportunity of working on the land. The policy of such employment remained therapeutic and not economic in the belief that:

> Insanity is a disease which demands a stimulus, and there is no stimulant equal to fresh air and exercise...In short the patients are not in the Asylum for the farm, but the farm has been provided for the patients.[51]

Recreational occupations also continued to thrive at Crichton Royal, with a nine hole golf course, and a splendid new cricket pitch both established in 1901. Matches against Morningside Asylum as well as others were regular features. The results were published in the in-house *New Moon Magazine*. For winter sport, by the end of the decade a three rink curling pond and a skating rink were in place to extend the already available pursuits of skiing and tobogganing.[52]

That occupation had, indeed, made the transition from the nineteenth to the twentieth century as an important component of treatment in asylums for the mentally ill, is evidenced by the sixth edition of a *Handbook for Attendants on the Insane*, published in 1911. Within it, Campbell Clark and colleagues state that: 'Occupation is the most important means in the treatment of our Patients.'[53] When stressing the importance of regular occupation, they recognised that integral to that were: 'regular hours for rising, taking food, work, exercise, amusement, and retiring to bed.' Such temporal factors were, and still are, 'beneficial not only to the bodily health, but also to the mental state,' as well as educating patients in 'good habits'. They added:

> It is not the amount and value of the work done that is here considered—it is that suitable occupation, however simple in itself, by exercising alike the bodily and the mental powers, has a most salutary effect on both the body and the mind. It diverts the Patient from his morbid fancies, and leads his thoughts into a healthy channel. Hence whenever the bodily strength allows of it, we should try to get the Patient to occupy his time usefully and engage in some work that is suitable and congenial to him. Such occupation is found in housework, in the garden or workshops, on the farm, in needlework, in the laundry, in drawing, writing, or any other work that the Patient is able for. It is not enough for the attendant to take the Patient out with the working party, and then let him lounge about idly. He ought rather to make diligent efforts to get every Patient to engage in some steady work, however simple that may be. The willing must not be over-tasked; and the idle are to be induced to work.[54]

In stressing the 'importance of the routine of work' they recognised similar benefits in 'all the other arrangements of the asylum, which are intended to secure the safety or promote the comfort of the Patients.' They advocated that the instructions provided by the hospital for 'supervision when at work or taking walking exercise' needed to be followed carefully.

When discussing the 'treatment of the different mental states' and individual cases, the authors sounded a personal note. They said:

> ...we try to lead the mind into a more healthy groove of action, to repress morbid acts or habits. We endeavour to cheer the depressed by kind sympathetic conversation and conduct towards them, and divert their thoughts from the distressing fancies by getting

*them to take an interest in the things around them, and by inducing them to engage in*
*active work and amusement when their bodily health permits it...When the excitement is*
*severe and long-continued, we try to provide a healthy outlet for it in active muscular*
*work or active open air exercise.*[55]

By way of suitable 'amusements' which as many as possible should be encouraged to
join, they recommended that 'dancing and games were of value' because they introduced
'variety and interest into the life of the Patients'.[56]

## In Europe and America

Gutersloh, in Germany, and Santpoort, in Holland, stand out as the mental hospitals
on mainland Europe where occupational (excluding recreational) treatment was carried
out during the early part of the century. Dr Simon was renowned for his re-organisation
of the Gutersloh Mental Hospital with the introduction of 'occupational treatment' in
about 1905. The hospital, which provided villa accommodation for 1,240 patients, was
situated within a 447 acre estate of which 125 acres were forest. It appears that the aim
was for occupation to be used for 100 per cent of the patients. His treatment programme
was based on the following factors:

*(i) The means of occupation are in the main provided by the ordinary work necessary to*
*the institution very little in the way of fancy crafts is undertaken.*
*(ii) No special occupation therapy officers are employed.*
*(iii) Apart from the workshops there are no special occupation therapy rooms; the work*
*treatment is carried on in the wards which themselves largely serve as work-rooms.*
*(iv) The proportion of staff to patients is large where it is required, but in the quiet or*
*chronic wards it is probably less than in England and Wales.*[57]

Apparently the keystone of Dr Simon's principles was the elimination of disturbing
behaviour from the patient's environment. To this end he isolated patients who became
disturbed and allowed them to return to their occupation when they became calm. Later, Dr
Thum, instigated similar work at the Constanz Mental Hospital with good results, so that
the practice eventually spread to other parts of Germany and to neighbouring countries.[58]

At the Santpoort Mental Hospital, near Amsterdam, occupational treatment was
originally carried out almost entirely by the nursing staff trained in occupational work by
'lectures, demonstrations and handicraft training' after Dr Van der Scheer, the Medical
Director, sent 60 of his nurses to Dr Simon for training in 1926. Probationers, too, were
taught the principles and practice of what was called active therapy. Gradually it became
necessary to introduce technicians in the central workshops who had not previously
undergone training as nurses. Arrangements were then made for the nurses to receive
assistance in training from the technicians.[59]

In Malta since the mid nineteenth century occupation as treatment had been used in
psychiatric hospitals: in Franconi Hospital, for example, at that time, it was introduced
by Dr Chetcuti and included cotton spinning, the rearing of animals, social and
recreational activities like fetes and dancing, and the use of gymnastic machines to
prevent physical deterioration. At Attard Asylum, which was a replica of Wakefield
discussed in Volume 1, priority had been given to the occupations of patients such as the
cultivation of lands and the rearing of animals. Well before 1900 the Asylum was self

sufficient, with the main instigator of the industrial occupation of patients being Dr Xuereb. One set back, in 1909 when the criminal ward opened, was from patients under sentence who often incited working patients from engaging in occupation by tempting them with cigarettes. During the First World War, the patients work helped the general population with the provision of agricultural products which had risen to exhorbitant prices in the market place as a result of the conflict. They were praised for 'not only providing therapeutic advantages to themselves, but ... also benefitting the hospital and the Public Treasury'. It was not, however, until 1926 that treatment by occupation was referred to as 'Occupational Therapy' by Dr Ralph Toledo.[60]

In America, Susan Tracy, mentioned earlier in the chapter, became director of nurses training at a Boston Asylum in 1906. An advocate of wholesome interests, self help, and interpersonal relationships between teacher/nurse and patient, Tracy began to prepare instructors to teach occupations to patients with mental illness. That was the first time in the USA that nurses, or 'kindergarteners' with the addition of a nurse's training (rather than crafts people) were picked out as best fitted for the work. This was because of their ability to recognize signs of fatigue, eyestrain or the limitations caused by illness. In 1910, Tracy's lectures, including an illustrated guide of occupations to be used with patients, were published in a book titled *Studies in Invalid Occupations: A Manual for Nurses and Attendants*. While it was primarily a craft book, it provided instructional methods and rationales for the use of specific activities according to diagnosis and ward, bed, workshop, or home environment.[61]

Tracy's concept of occupation was adopted from the work of educational philosophist, John Dewey, whose ideas were also influential at Jane Addams' Hull House. It is an important concept:

> By occupation is not meant any kind of 'busy work' or exercise that may be given to a child to keep him out of mischief or idleness when seated at his desk. By occupation I mean a mode of activity on the part of the child which reproduces or runs parallel to some form of work carried on in the social life...The fundamental point of the psychology of an occupation is that it maintains a balance between the intellectual and the practical phases of experience.[62]

Tracy, who conducted numerous training courses on the use of occupation as treatment, similarly believed that well chosen occupation could assist the retention of social connections and the preservation of self-respect and ambition.[63]

William Rush Dunton Jr is sometimes called the 'father of the profession' in America, because of his 'endeavors on behalf of occupational therapy, as a practitioner, as a theoretician, as a philosopher, and as an officer of the national group.'[64] As early as 1895, as staff psychiatrist of an asylum in Baltimore, he was involved in the establishment of a metalworking shop for the treatment of patients. Other craft occupations were added later to the extent that an arts and crafts teacher was engaged in 1908. Dunton noted that patients benefited by direction and the careful choice of occupation, and followed Tracy's lead, after reading her book, by conducting a series of classes for nurses on occupations and recreation which became ongoing. The following year, in 1912, he was charged with responsibility for the hospital's occupation programme.[65] His first textbook on the subject *Occupational Therapy—A Manual for Nurses* was published in 1915 and outlined the basic tenets of occupation therapy as he saw them and described simple occupations for therapeutic use. Reflecting the long-held medical belief described in the first volume he, too, claimed that occupation's primary purpose was to 'control' and 'divert' attention into more 'healthy channels'. A further purpose was to facilitate rest, act as a 'safety valve', train and re-educate mental processes, hands, eyes, muscles, and so forth, and to provide a 'new vocation.'[66] The American Association was, later, to grant him life membership and the right to describe himself as an occupational therapist. His personal creed, which reflects the earlier claims of people such as Cheyne, in the eighteenth century, was:

*That occupation is as necessary to life as food and drink*
*That every human being should have both physical and mental occupations*
*That all should have occupations which they enjoy or hobbies—at least two, one outdoor and one indoor*
*That sick minds, sick bodies and sick souls may be healed through occupation.*[67]

In terms of psychology and occupational therapy in America, William James is of considerable importance. The 'functional' and 'utilitarian' philosophy of pragmatism[68] that he espoused was central to Slagle's work. She quoted his words in her syllabus:

*The moment one tries to define what habit is, one is led to the fundamental properties*
*of matter...habit diminishes the conscious attention with which our acts are performed.*[69]

James was closely associated with the University of Chicago, where fellow pragmatists John Dewey and George Herbert Mead worked and the study of pragmatism flourished. The themes of pragmatism were tried on the community through the offices of Hull House and through that association pragmatism influenced occupational therapy. The psychiatrist, Adolph Meyer, also accepted the philosophy precepts and, in his practice, recognised that 'personality is fundamentally determined by performance,' and so stressed the integration of mind and body, activity and habit, time and environment, in real life.[70,71]

The first two decades of the twentieth century, though, are probably best known as the years when the theories and ideas of neurologist, Sigmund Freud (1865–1939), first emerged. Arguably the most well-known figure in the treatment of mental disturbance, despite perhaps also being one of the most controversial, he brought into vogue the idea of looking for deeper meanings of human behaviour than appear on the surface, with his theory and practice of psychoanalysis. In the early 1900s a group of psychoanalysts which included the noted Alfred Adler and Carl Gustav Jung gathered around Freud, although they were later to disperse as their ideas took different directions. Alfred Adler went on to write *The Practice and Theory of Individual Psychology and Social Interest* and, amongst other issues, postulated 'the importance of achieving self-realization through the use of abilities, interests and skills, and adaptation to the environment.'[72] Eventually the dominance of psychoanalytic approaches was to have significant and detrimental effects on the use of occupation as psychological therapy. This was not yet the case, and occupation was to be re-invented, within a dynamic new approach to mental health at the start of the twentieth century which was known as 'mental hygiene'.

Mental hygiene encompassed the notion that many mental illnesses were preventable. It held that there was a need to 'study the causation and prevention of mental disturbances, including the influences of environment, heredity, alcohol, lead, [and] syphilis.' A further aim was 'to improve the conditions of treatment of mental disorders, particularly in the early stages.'[73]

Mental hygiene organisations started as a result of the experiences of Clifford W. Beers as a patient in several mental hospitals in the United States. Following his recovery, he wrote *A Mind that Found Itself* as a way to promote improvement in future treatment.[74] Through his efforts, first the Connecticut Society for Mental Hygiene, then the National Committee for Mental Hygiene, were set up in 1908 and 1909 respectively.[75] These bodies comprised men and women of influence who were interested in medical philanthropy and social work, and held the objectives:

1. To work for the conservation of mental health.
2. To promote the study of mental disorders and mental defects in all their forms and relations.
3. To obtain, and disseminate, reliable data concerning them.
4. To help in raising the standard of care and treatment.[76]

Gradually the movement spread world wide; societies for the promotion of mental hygiene were started in Australia, Belgium, Brazil, Canada, France, and South Africa, as well as in the United Kingdom, where the British National Council for Mental Hygiene was established.

Probably the most influential psychiatrist within the mental hygiene movement was Adolf Meyer. It was he who encouraged Beers to write about his experiences and it was he who suggested the name, mental hygiene.[77] Meyer was such an inspirational force within the genesis of modern occupational therapy in the United Kingdom, as well as in the United States, that his story is included here from the former perspective.

# Adolf Meyer and his influence in Britain

Adolf Meyer has long been known as a significant figure in the evolution of modern occupational therapy in the United States, where he lived and worked from the 1890s. He is credited with the major philosophical paper, which the profession embraces, presented in 1921, in which he suggested that 'psychiatry has been among the first to recognise the need for adaptation and the value of work as a sovereign help in problems of adaptation.' He argued that in the remediation of mental illness 'we must provide opportunities rather than prescriptions.[78] Parts of that paper are still quoted frequently and world wide in occupational therapy theoretical and historical papers.

**Figure 2.2.3:** **Adolf Meyer**
*(Sketch made from a photograph in the Archives of the American Psychiatric Association)*

Meyer was born in Neiderwenigen in Switzerland in 1866 and studied medicine at the University of Zurich, qualifying in 1890. He won a travel scholarship and spent four months in Paris and six in Britain. In Edinburgh, he studied the organisation of mental health services,[79] and in London he was fortunate to observe the work of several notable medical men including the renowned neurologist, Hughlings Jackson. Indeed, in his 'Maudsley Lecture' some years later, Meyer referred to the influence of Hughlings Jackson on his thinking, as well as to Scottish teachers he encountered such as John Wyllie, Alexander Bruce, Byron Bramwell, and Sir Thomas Grainger. He expressed a 'real personal indebtedness to British medicine and British psychiatry.'[80]

When he returned to Switzerland, Meyer's interest in specialising in neurology was furthered by neuropathological research on the forebrain of reptiles. In 1892, having completed his thesis on the topic, he decided that his future lay in America. On the way there he again visited Britain where he attended the International Congress of Psychology in Edinburgh and heard William James the American pragmatist philosopher and pioneer psychologist speak.

Soon after his arrival in Chicago, Meyer presented his first ever medical paper to the Chicago Pathological Society in December 1892. In it he described how:

*I asked my new neighbors and colleagues for suggestions as to the tastes and best lines of occupation of American patients. The proper use of time in some helpful and gratifying activity appeared to me a fundamental issue in the treatment of any neuro-psychiatric patient.*[81]

In 1921, Slagle who, among her 'valuable possessions' had 'an autographed extract of some length' of this paper, referred to it as one of the early 'seeds' of occupational therapy.[82]

Meyer appears to have been less successful than he had hoped in furthering his aspirations within the neurological field. So, in 1893 he accepted a post as a pathologist in the Illinois Eastern Asylum at Kankakee a small town some 60 miles south of Chicago. From this time on Meyer set about establishing improvements in pathological and clinical services in psychiatric practice. Innovations included the training of medical and nursing staff, organising preventive programmes, and increasing 'understanding (of) the personal, social and environmental situations which had a bearing on the particular problem.'[83] Although at Kankakee he found 'some ward work and shop work, and later, under the inspiration of Isabel Davenport, some gardening for the women in the convalescent cottages' he was not, on the whole, impressed by the clinical practice he observed. In an 1894 report to the Governor of Illinois on the treatment of the insane, which detailed his ideas, he suggested the establishment of 'divisions of occupational and recreational therapy as an integral part of treatment facilities.'[84] In terms reminiscent of the Retreat, he suggested:

> The ideal asylum or hospital for the insane should furnish the patients most of the advantages of home…the attendants should be nurses not supervisors, they should live like patients…and share the recreations and amusements with the patients with as little bossing as possible. Everything that suggests detention in prison must be strictly avoided.[85]

Following his time at Kankakee, between 1895 and 1902 Meyer worked at the Worcester Lunatic Asylum, as pathologist, clinician, and teacher of psychiatry. It was from there, in 1901, that he represented Clark University at the 450th birthday celebrations of Glasgow University, which enabled him to strengthen what was to become a strong link with Scottish psychiatrists and physicians.

By that time, Meyer described himself as a mental hygienist, and helped to establish the (American) National Committee. Eventually this, and sister societies for the promotion of mental hygiene in other parts of the world, sustained preventive as well as curative interests. The focus was on 'working for the conservation of mental health' and 'promoting the study of mental disorders, as well as 'raising the standard of care and treatment.'[86]

Meyer's growing reputation led to several prestigious appointments in New York State from 1908. Recently graduated David Henderson, a young Scottish physician, went to work with Meyer, remaining at the New York Psychiatric Institute for three years before returning to Glasgow to take up a junior physician post at Gartnavel Hospital. However, before he could take up that post, Meyer invited him to return to the United States become senior resident of the new Phipps Psychiatric Clinic at Johns Hopkins University Medical School after he was made Director. Henderson accepted the challenge, and described the 1913 opening of this facility as both 'significant and joyous.' It was the time when 'Meyer saw all his cherished hopes and wishes being realised' having 'planned every part of it' with 'tremendous thought and care.' Henderson described it as 'an historic occasion when, for the first time, a psychiatric clinic was integrated within a general hospital in an English speaking country.'[87] Henderson's admiration for Meyer and his wife grew when he lived with them for the first six months of his stay, and as he became 'steeped in Meyer's ideas and practices' working with him pioneering the new clinical service.[88] Meyer was to remain at Phipps Clinic until his retirement at age 74.[89]

Above heredity, Meyer maintained as part of his psychobiological approach the importance of environment, background and learning 'considered in relation to the life of the individual.' He was interested in the social nature of illness, prevention, and the care of patients after they left hospital, and this 'comprehensive viewpoint…constituted (a) great departure from the formal descriptive methods which had preceded it.' Henderson told how Meyer used to ask why 'surrender to neurology the wholesome pluralism of practical life?' He maintained 'that it was infinitely more satisfying to use the broad concepts of instincts, habits, interests and specific experiences and capacities than the concepts of structural analysis at the present stage of our biological knowledge.'[90]

That belief also led him to be a great advocate for the use of occupation with his patients, ably supported by his wife, who Henderson described as a pioneer of social psychiatry and occupational therapy.[91] Programmes offered at the clinic included organised games, exercises, dancing and music as well as arts and crafts.[92] But this approach, as were his others, was based on factual results rather than on 'hypothetical formulations'. 'He never allowed us to go beyond the actual facts revealed, and he constantly utilised his anatomical, physiological, and neuropathological knowledge as a check or brake.'[93]

Meyer 'borrowed' Eleanor Clark Slagle after her 'occupational training' at Hull House to work for a couple of years at the Phipps Clinic. It was here that he insisted upon workers in the field, such as occupational therapists, incorporating both guidance and re-education of habits to help patients to deal better with individual life stressors.[94] Obviously, Henderson was of like mind. Indeed Slagle mentions his contribution to the establishment of occupational therapy in America along with his mentor, and Lathrop and Addams.[95] Henderson mentions her as a 'valuable therapeutic asset' who gave 'imaginative guidance to the occupational therapy department.'[96]

Henderson described Meyer as being in 'the tradition of Pinel, Tuke, Rush, Connolly, Charlesworth, Gardiner and Hill, and all the other great reformers.' He took many of his mentor's approaches with him when he returned to Gartnavel in 1915,[97] including the need to develop occupational therapy. His story, in relation to occupational therapy's development in Britain, will be told in a later chapter.

It is appropriate to note, at this time, that there were other influential British physicians who went to the United States to work with Meyer in Baltimore. They included: MacNiven, who became physician superintendent at Gartnavel after Henderson and who described Meyer as 'a great and lovable man';[98] and Gillespie, who collaborated with Henderson on a *Textbook of Psychiatry*, which was dedicated to Meyer, embodied many of his ideas, and became from 1927 a standard text in Britain for more than fifty years. Gillespie later became physician for psychological medicine at Guys Hospital, thus extending a direct Meyer influence to the south of England. Sir Aubrey Lewis also spent time with Meyer and brought many of his ideas back to Britain, incorporating them into practice and teaching. Lewis was to become Clinical Director of the Maudsley Hospital from 1936 in which was developed one of the earliest, if short-lived, schools of occupational therapy.

**In summary,** the foundation for the dawning of occupational therapy was well laid in the first decade of the twentieth century. Pockets of practice utilising occupation as a therapeutic medium and for therapeutic purposes existed throughout the western world as governments began to take on more responsibility for social services. Women played a significant role in its emergence, and their entry into the social and health arena was a major stepping stone. But it must be appreciated that without the patronage of some very special medical men the profession would not have had the impetus which propelled it forward. That was to continue in the next decade, when World War 1 shook the foundations of the century.

[1]Norton A-L, ed. *The Hutchinson Dictionary of Ideas.* Oxford: Helicon Publishing Ltd., 1994. Revised paper back ed, 1995; 493.

[2]Girling DA, ed. *New Age Encyclopaedia.* Sydney: Bay Books; vol 30:168.

[3]Dorward C, Davidson R. *Anything but Ordinary: The Nine Lives of Cecile.* Fremantle: Fremantle Arts Centre Press, 2000; 38–43.

[4] O'Connor J. *The Workhouses of Ireland; The Fate of Ireland's Poor.* Dublin: Anvil Books, 1995; 196.

[5]Hill O. Annual Report to her Workers. 1911; 8

[6]Hill O. Public hall and garden for Southwark. Letter to the Editor. *Times,* 14th March, 1887; 7.

[7]Hill O. *Times...;* 7.

[8]Hill O. 1909; 10

[9]Hill O. 1910; 5.

[10]Wilcock AA. An Occupational Perspective of Health. Thorofare, NJ: Slack Inc., 1998.

[11]Barton GE. *Teaching the Sick: A Manual of Occupational Therapy and Re-Education.* Philadelphia: W.B. Saunders Company, 1919; 15.

[12]An Act to make Better Provision for Elementary Education of Defective and Epileptic Children in England and Wales. 62 & 63 Vict. c.32, 1899; An Act to amend the Elementary Education (Defective and Epileptic Children) 1899, 3 Edw. 7 c.13, 1903.

[13]Jackson M. From Work to Therapy: The Changing Politics of Occupation in the Twentieth Century. British Journal of Occupational Therapy 1993; 56(10): 360–64.

[14]Jackson M. From Work to Therapy: The Changing Politics of Occupation in the Twentieth Century. British Journal of Occupational Therapy 1993; 56(10): 360–64.

[15]Jackson M. From Work to Therapy: The Changing Politics of Occupation in the Twentieth Century. British Journal of Occupational Therapy 1993; 56(10): 360–64.

[16]Jackson M. From Work to Therapy: The Changing Politics of Occupation in the Twentieth Century. British Journal of Occupational Therapy 1993; 56(10): 360–64.

[17]Denby M. On the Training and Management of Feeble Minded Children. In: Lapage CP. Feeblemindedness in Children of School-age. Manchester University Press, 1911: 275.

[18] Central Council for the Disabled. *A Record of 50 Years Service to the Disabled from 191— 1965.* London: 1969; Intro.

[19]Macdonald EM. *World-Wide Conquests of Disabilities: The History, Development and Present Functions of the Remedial Services.* London: Bailliere Tindall, 1981.

[20]Hill AH. Special Schools in Britain. *The Cripple,* October, 1928.

[21]Hunt A. *Reminiscences.* Shrewsbury: Printed for the Derwen Crippled Training College by Wilding & Son Ltd., 1935; 118–119.

[22]Hunt A. *Reminiscences....*; 119.

[23]Hunt A. *Reminiscences....*; 120–121.

[24]Hunt A. *Reminiscences....*; 5, 107.

[25]Macdonald EM. *World-Wide Conquests of Disabilities....*; 131-133.

[26]Burt Sir C. Preface. In: Kimmins (Mrs). *Heritage Craft Schools and Hospitals, Chailey 190–1948: Being an Account of the Pioneer Work for Crippled Children.* Chailey: 1948; 7–8.

[27]Jones Sir R. Cited in: Kimmins. *Heritage Craft Schools....*; 68.

[28]Kimmins. *Heritage Craft Schools....*; 71.

[29]Watson F. *Civilization and the Cripple.* London: John Bale, Sons & Danielsson, Ltd., 1930; 33

[30]Watson F. *Civilization and the Cripple....*; 36.

[31]Watson F. *Civilization and the Cripple....*; 35.

[32]Reported in The Cripple. January 1929; 166. Cited in: Watson F. *Civilization and the Cripple....*; 36–37.

[33]Reported in The Cripple. October, 1928. Cited in: Watson F. *Civilization and the Cripple....*; 88–89.

[34]Watson F. *Civilization and the Cripple....*; 89.

[35]Philip R. Rest and Movement in Tuberculosis. *British Medical Journal*, 24th December, 1910.

[36]Philip R. *Collected Papers on Tuberculosis.* London: Humphrey Milford: Oxford University Press, 1937; 138–140. Originally published as: Rest and Movement in Tuberculosis. *British Medical Journal*, 24th December, 1910.

[37]Philip R. *Collected Papers on Tuberculosis...*; 141.

[38]Lyall WL. In: Sutherland H., ed. *The Control and Eradication of Tuberculosis.* Edinburgh: Wm. Green and Sons, 1911.

[39]Randle APH. Rehabilitation and Society. *Occupational Therapy.* January 1974; 15–17.

[40]Macdonald EM. *World-Wide Conquests of Disabilities.....*

[41]Porter R. *Disease, Medicine and Society in England, 1550–1860.* Basingstoke: Macmillan Education, 1987.

[42]Hall HJ. Work Cure, a report of five years' experience at an institution devoted to the therapeutic application of manual work. *Journal of the American Medical Association* 1910; 54: 12.

[43]Hall HJ, Buck MMC. *The Work of Our Hands—A Study of Occupations for Invalids.* New York: Moffat, Yard and Co., 1915.

[44]Tracey SE. *Studies in Invalid Occupations—A Manual for Nurses and Attendants.* Boston: Whitcomb and Barrows, 1910.

[45]Tracey SE. *Flier on Occupational Course.* Experimental Station for the Study of Invalid Occupations. Jamaica Plains MA, 1914. In: Hopkins HL, Smith HD, eds. *Willard and Spackman's Occupational Therapy.* 7th ed. Philadelphia: J.B. Lippincott Co., 1988; 19–20.

[46]Wynne C. *The North Wales Hospital, Denbigh, 1842–1955.* Denbigh: Gee & Son, 1995; 23.

[47]Casson E. Occupational Therapy in Great Britain. *Journal of the American Medical Women's Association* 1947; 2 (6): 303–305

[48]*The Retreat, York: Instructions to Members of Nursing Staff.* Committee of the Retreat York: City Press, 1902; 4.

[49]No author given. The Employment of the insane. *Journal of Mental Science,* Vol CLVI: 1900; 13.

[50]Groundes-Peace ZC. An outline of the development of occupational therapy in Scotland. *The Scottish Journal of Occupational Therapy* 1957; (30): 16–39.

[51]Williams M. *History of Crichton Royal Hospital 1839–1989.* Dumfries and Galloway Health Board, 1989; 37, 57.

[52]Williams M. *History of Crichton Royal Hospital 1839–1989.* Dumfries and Galloway

Health Board, 1989; 37, 57.

[53]Campbell Clark A, M'Ivor Campbell C, Turnbull AR, Urquhart AR. *Handbook for Attendants on the Insane.* 6th ed. Bailliere, Tindall and Cox, 1911; 50.

[54]Campbell Clark, et al. *Handbook for Attendants on the Insane....*; 50.

[55]Campbell Clark, et al. *Handbook for Attendants on the Insane....*; 48.

[56]Campbell Clark, et al. *Handbook for Attendants on the Insane....*; 50–51.

[57]Board of Control. *Memorandum on Occupation Therapy for Mental Patients.* His Majesty's Stationery Office, London, 1933; 8–9.

[58]Board of Control. *Memorandum on Occupation Therapy for Mental Patients.* His Majesty's Stationery Office, London, 1933; 8–9.

[59]Board of Control. *Memorandum on Occupation Therapy....*; 9.

[60]Busuttil J. Occupational Therapy: Origins and Development in Malta and Gozo. Prosan, 1986.

[61]Tracey SE. *Studies in Invalid Occupations—A Manual for Nurses and Attendants.* Boston: Whitcomb and Barrows, 1910. In: Hopkins HL, Smith HD, eds. *Willard and Spackman's Occupational Therapy.* 7th ed. Philadelphia: J.B. Lippincott Co., 1988; 19–20.

[62]In: Barton WE. Training Programs for Occupational Therapists in the US Army. *Occupational Therapy in Rehabilitation* 1944; 23: 282.

[63]Hopkins & Smith. *Willard and Spackman's Occupational Therapy....*; 19–20.

[64]Hopkins & Smith. *Willard and Spackman's Occupational Therapy....*; 21.

[65]Bing R. William Rush Dunton, Jr. American Psychiatrist: A Study in Self. University of Maryland: PhD Dissertation, 1961. In: Hopkins & Smith. *Willard and Spackman's Occupational Therapy....*; 21.

[66]Dunton WR, Jr. *Occupational Therapy: A Manual for Nurses.* Philadelphia: WB Saunders, 1915.

[67]Reed KL, Sanderson RS. *Concepts of Occupational Therapy.* Baltimore: Williams & Wilkins, 1980; 203–204.

[68]James W. *Pragmatism, and Four Essays from the Meaning of Truth.* Cleveland: Meridian Books, The World Publishing Co., 1970. (*Pragmatism* was first published in 1907, and *The Meaning of Truth* in 1909).

[69]Slagle EC, Robeson HA. *Syllabus for Training of Nurses in Occupational Therapy.* Habit training is adopted from pragmatism through the Meyer influence, but is also central in Arts and Crafts movement. See: Mayhew KC, Edwards AC. *The Dewey School: The Lab School of the University of Chicago, 1896–1903.* New York: Appleton-Century, 1936; 206.

[70]Breines E. Pragmatism as a foundation for occupational therapy curricula. *American Journal of Occupational Therapy* 1987; 41(8): 522–525.

[71]Breines E. *Origins and Adaptations; A Philosophy of Practice.* New Jersey: Geri-Rehab, Inc, 1986; 67.

[72]Macdonald EM. *World-Wide Conquests of Disabilities....*; 106.

[73]Henderson DK. Aims of British National Council for Mental Hygiene. In: Mental Hygiene. *Glasgow Medical Journal* June 1923; 2.

[74]Beers CW. *A Mind that Found Itself: An Autobiography.* New York: Longmans, Green, 1917.

[75]Macdonald EM. *World-Wide Conquests of Disabilities....*; 108–9.

[76]Henderson DK. *Mental Hygiene.* Glasgow Medical Journal June, 1923.

[77]Henderson DK. Introduction. In: Winters EE, ed. *The Collected Papers of Adolf Meyer, Volume II: Psychiatry.* Baltimore: The Johns Hopkins Press, 1951; xix.

[78]Meyer A. The philosophy of occupational therapy. (Read at Fifth Annual Meeting of the National Society for the Promotion of Occupational Therapy) *Archives of Occupational Therapy* 1922; (1) 1: 1–10.

[79]Meyer A. Die Irrenpilege in Schottland. Correspondenz-Blatt fur Scheizer Arzte. 23. Reprinted in *Collected Papers*. 1893; 445.

[80]Meyer A. British influences in psychiatry and mental hygiene. *Journal of Mental Science* 1933; 79: 435–463.

[81]Meyer A. The philosophy of occupational therapy. (Read at Fifth Annual Meeting of the National Society for the Promotion of Occupational Therapy) *Archives of Occupational Therapy* 1922; (1) 1: 1–10.

[82]Slagle EC. Training aides for mental patients. Read at Fifth Annual Meeting of the National Society for the Promotion of Occupational Therapy) *Archives of Occupational Therapy* 1922; (1) 1: 11–18.

[83]Henderson. Introduction. In: Winters. *The Collected Papers of Adolf Meyer....*; xviii.

[84]Henderson. Introduction. In: Winters. *The Collected Papers of Adolf Meyer....*; xviii.

[85]Meyer A. 1895; 45. In: Gelder M. Adolf Meyer and his influence on British psychiatry. In: Berrios GE, Freeman H., ed. *150 Years of British Psychiatry, 1841-1991*. London: Gaskell, 1991; 422.

[86]Henderson DK. Mental Hygiene. *Glasgow Medical Journal* June 1923; 1.

[87]Henderson. Introduction. In: Winters. *The Collected Papers of Adolf Meyer....*; xvi-xvii.

[88]Gelder M. Adolf Meyer and his influence on British psychiatry. In: Berrios GE, Freeman H, eds. *150 Years of British Psychiatry, 1841–1991*. London: Gaskell, 1991; 430.

[89]Gelder. Adolf Meyer and his influence on British psychiatry....; 430.

[90]Henderson. Introduction. In: Winters. *The Collected Papers of Adolf Meyer....*; xiii.

[91]Henderson DK. *The Evolution of Psychiatry* in Scotland. Edinburgh: E & S Livingstone Ltd, 1964; 161.

[92]Henderson. *The Evolution of Psychiatry* in Scotland....; 161..

[93]Henderson. Introduction. In: Winters. *The Collected Papers of Adolf Meyer....*; x.

[94]Gelder. Adolf Meyer and his influence on British psychiatry.

[95]Slagle EC. Training aides for mental patients. Read at Fifth Annual Meeting of the National Society for the Promotion of Occupational Therapy) *Archives of Occupational Therapy* 1922; (1) 1: 11–18.

[96]Henderson. *The Evolution of Psychiatry in Scotland....*; 191.

[97]Gelder. Adolf Meyer and his influence on British psychiatry....; 430.

[98]MacNiven A. The first commissioners: Reform in Scotland in the mid-nineteenth century. *Journal of Mental Science* 1960, 106 (443): 451–471.

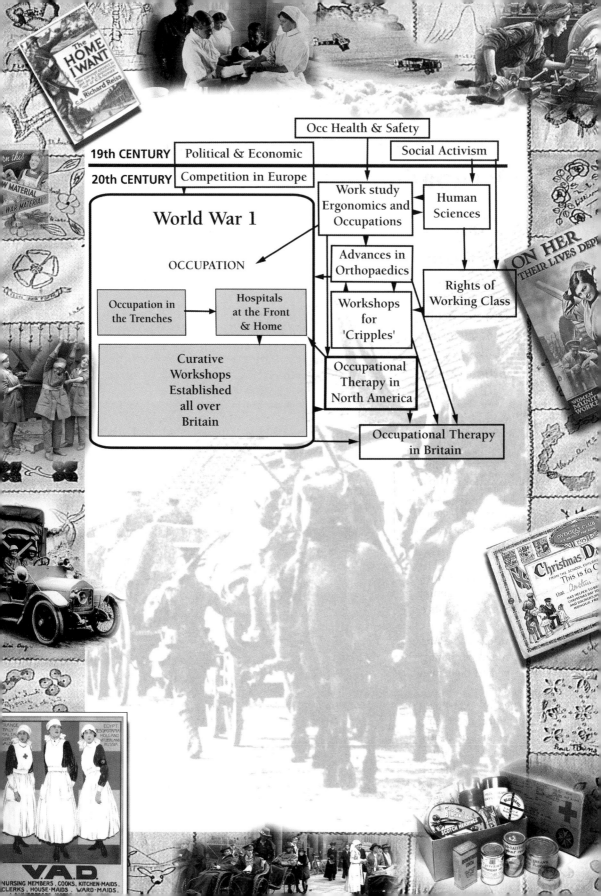

Occ Health & Safety

**19th CENTURY** Political & Economic

**20th CENTURY** Competition in Europe

Social Activism

World War 1

OCCUPATION

Occupation in the Trenches → Hospitals at the Front & Home

Curative Workshops Established all over Britain

Work study Ergonomics and Occupations

Human Sciences

Advances in Orthopaedics

Workshops for 'Cripples'

Rights of Working Class

Occupational Therapy in North America

Occupational Therapy in Britain

# Chapter 3

# The War To End All Wars: Occupation for Reconstruction

## Contents

The events relating to the use of 'occupation for reconstruction' during World War I form the focus of this chapter. As social and health services workers united to help solve problems that appeared as a result of the conflict, 'scientific management' emerged as a discipline. This was an early name for 'work study' and was to lay groundwork for occupational therapy later. Additionally, initiatives of the first decade relating to occupation for the 'crippled' were employed during the war years. To some, the emergence of a concept of 'rehabilitation' was the most important outcome of one of the most destructive periods of human history. The use of occupation within curative workshops in Europe and Britain was central to rehabilitation, but the value of workshops for civilian 'reconstruction' was disregarded after the war as economic and political expedients once more gained dominance over the humanitarian. The period of the War saw the naming and framing of occupational therapy in the USA and was a powerful catalyst to its establishment in Britain.

Regarded as the War to end all Wars by contemporaries, the conflict was endured as 'an experience without parallel, eclipsing all previous wars'. Indeed, all the great powers of Europe and the United States were involved, and the hostilities extended to Asia and Africa, the South Atlantic, and the Pacific. This was despite the fact that once it had begun 'the ostensible reasons for war were lost sight of...'.[1] The social order everywhere was shaken, four great empires were destroyed, and worst of all, the combatants, the wounded and the dead were more numerous that ever before. The British Empire lost a million troops; France, one and a half million; Germany, one and three-quarter million; and Russia, more that all those put together. It seems incredible that:

> *Though soldiers hated the trenches and civilians grumbled against harsh conditions, public opinion in every country applauded the warmakers and condemned those who sought a way out.* [2]

Indeed, the outbreak of the war had been 'greeted by cheering crowds in every belligerent capital. The popular mood in every country was one of nationalistic self-righteousness, and everywhere the war was expected to be short, glorious, and victorious.'[3]

In turning to the question of 'occupation for reconstruction,' which emerged as an entity during the conflict years to meet the needs of the many casualties of war who were injured and shell shocked, it is necessary to consider first the part played by exponents of scientific management.

# Scientific management

In the late nineteenth century, the best known of the pioneer 'time and motion study' experts was American engineer Frederick W. Taylor (1856–1915). He began to investigate industrial processes in a Philadelphia steelworks in the early 1880s, with an aim to increase productivity. In his classic work of 1911 *The Principles of Scientific Management* Taylor described how work processes around machines could be analysed according to movements and the timing of component parts of a whole task; any which appeared unnecessary could be reduced or eliminated, and so increase efficiency.[4] No longer in vogue, that approach, which revolutionised industry, is now criticised. It is believed that it takes the meaning out of work, making tasks personally unrewarding and potentially alienating, as well as increasing the risk of repetitive strain injury as a result of static muscle work and postures.[5]

But that criticism anticipates the future, and it is fair to say that in its early years time and motion study was to prove a useful tool to explore aspects of occupation in a new way. Its value was recognised by governments during the 1914–18 war, and principles of scientific management were used to help the disabled return to employment.

# Scientific management: occupation for therapy in World War I

Occupation was recognised across Europe, by both sides involved in the 1914–18 conflict, as essential to the curative process, to the economic future of disabled servicemen, and to their feelings of well-being. The French government, early in the War, also recognised the place of occupation in the social fabric of the community and in their nation's health, especially with regard to the manpower shortage in both the armed services and civilian life. They appointed Professor Jules Amar, a French physiologist, who was influenced by Taylor, to study scientific management and its application to the training and re-employment of wounded soldiers.[6]

In his book *The Physiology of Industrial Organisation and the Re-employment of the Disabled*, which was published after the war, Amar described:

*The object of professional orientation is to react against social prejudices by placing the wounded soldier in the position for which he is fitted, in order to realise his full economic output.[7]*

The most common form of rehabilitation was the re-education of amputees. This reflects both the numerous incidences of amputation in the trenches and the limit of medical intervention at that time. Amar outlined three stages of rehabilitation for the amputee which can be summarised as follows:

1. Functional re-education: analysis of the patient's movements to determine his functional condition; restoration towards the patient's previous work capacity; evaluation of the patient's capacity for prolonged exertion

2. Fitting the prosthetic appliance 'not to replace the lost limb or segment of a limb, but to supplement or replace a lost or badly impaired function'

3. Professional re-education in special workshops, for which, following successful completion they received a certificate.[8]

**Figure 2.3.1:** **An artificial hand, designed by Amar[9]**
*(By permission of The British Library 08248 bb 49)*

AN ARTIFICIAL HAND DESIGNED BY THE GREAT GENIUS, PROF. JULES AMAR, DIRECTEUR, CONSERVATOIRE DES ARTS ET METIERS, PARIS

We recommend to the attention of all workers for the handicapped the study of the wonderful works of Prof. Amar, especially *Le Moteur Humain* (*The Human Motor*), English Translation by Elsie Butterworth Daniels (Routledge) ; and *Organization Physiologique du Travail*, English Translation by Bernard Miall (The Library Press).

Amar developed a prosthesis known as a 'worker's arm' which, in common with more modern upper limb prostheses, had both a 'functional' (universal holder or pliers) and 'dress' hand (parade hand). His particular focus of re-education was suited to the agricultural pursuits followed extensively in France and to men who required strength and simple but foolproof methods of holding or steadying. He provided an example of the rehabilitation of a farmer using the occupations in which he would typically engage:

*When he first enters the school the farmer invariably informs me, if he has lost an arm, that he can no longer perform any agricultural operation, unless to give food to the live-stock. But when he has been re-educated, when he is equipped with the worker's arm, with the universal holder and ring, he accustoms himself, first of all, to the use of the dynamographic shovel: then he employs, turn by turn, the ordinary spade and shovel, leaning on them and pressing them into the soil as they should be pressed; then he strikes and pulls with the mattock, or presses and pulls the hoe and rake. In a few days after his return to the country the farmer writes to tell me that he is performing all his agricultural tasks without assistance from anyone.[10]*

He also made comment on road workers' ability to return to their job:

> *Even in a navvy's work, road-making etc., there is room for one armed men...It appears that this sort of work suits the one armed man far better than it does the one legged man, although the reverse is true of the removal of soil. Two wheeled barrows. which are easy to guide, are obviously indicated for work of this kind.*[11]

Amar's use of special equipment such as the 'dynamographic shovel' is an indication of the adaptive equipment phase that re-occurred in occupational therapy's later history. Amar 's adaptation led him to the conclusion that:

> *An examination of agricultural implements, with a view to adaptation to the use of war cripples, has become a necessary undertaking, but has not sufficiently attracted the attention of the State.*[12]

So, it is not only present day authorities who overlook the perceived needs of a minority. At that earlier time, even in spite of manpower shortage, Amar, like occupational therapists at present, had to have economy firmly in mind as he recommended occupations suitable to those he helped to 're-educate'. For example, he suggested that during re-education consideration should be given to the making of wooden toys. Not only was it a craft in which a peasant's ingenuity and 'habit of making something out of everything with his own hands would find useful scope', but also appropriate wood (beech) was available, as well as 'the most skilful labour' and 'little in the matter of outlay.'[13]

Amar recommended that during re-education the wounded should work within their home communities at cottage industries or with willing employers, with appropriate opportunities for consultation and input at a central 'school' and 'workshop' both available and provided.

> *The technical department of the school will be consulted by the pupils for all sorts of reasons: some wishing to undergo a course of physiological training, which seems full of promise; others seeking some improvement of the prosthetic appliances, or to their more careful adjustment, or simply—and I have had thousands of such before me—a circumstantial examination of their capacities, in order that they may obtain their certificate of qualification; this they will send to manufacturers inclined to employ them, or they will profit by it directly by setting up on their own account. For my part I hope to see this effort to revive the life of the complete workman, the homemaker, encouraged. In this there would be nothing inconsistent with the tendency toward industrial centralisation, as the large workshops would, without loss to themselves, become accustomed to leave the smaller crafts and petty commissions to this class of worker, a class capable of great ingenuity and inventive power. The state also would benefit by this condition of affairs, provided the home-workers did not fail to turn out good apprentices. As for the workshops which are established for purposes of their re-education, their object is perfectly well defined: to perfect the technique of the handicrafts, and to adapt the wounded soldier to selected professional exercises, accordingly as he is obliged to change his calling or to specialise in that one of the departments of his craft which is best calculated to husband his energies without diminishing their output.*
>
> *The time required for this re-education varies. Although as far as manual labour is concerned a year constitutes a sufficient average, it must be remembered that the theoretical education will require a longer time; and it will be of a compleat nature, so that it may form a working class elite which will itself be qualified to teach.*

*The principle of the school will be that of a boarding-school, the men receiving board and lodging, while their wages will be reckoned according to a scale which may vary according to locality, remembering the loss of output in the majority of cases of amputation of the lower leg or thigh is practically nil.*

*Under exceptional circumstances it may be useful to adapt the system of the day-school in the case of married cripples, so that they may return to their own homes every evening. Thus the schools established for the purpose of re-education distribute the benefits of instruction in pursuance of a definite aim; they develop the minds of the workers and complete their technical training. They determine, being familiar with the facts of the case, the industrial or commercial destination of the wounded soldier, preparing him securely to find employment and to take his place in the ranks of society.*

*...For everything must converge upon the real object, which is to find employment for the wounded soldier.[14]*

Despite his obvious interest in amputees, Amar recognised the power of occupation in adaptation to other changes of bodily function. He argued that:

*Reeducation is not confined to the motor organs; it is being extended increasingly to all the agents of human activity; to those which dispense energy (the heart and lungs) and those which maintain our relations with the outer world (the senses). It is indeed possible, as we have seen, to re-adapt the sense of touch, a sense very highly developed in the blind, and a sense upon which the prosthesis of the upper limbs is very largely dependent. The sense of hearing, diminished as the result of accidents to the outer ear, appears also to be capable of substantial improvement; but of this I have no personal experience. And everybody knows that the sense of sight is susceptible, after appropriate treatment, of remarkable ameliorations.*

*What I can assert in this connection is, that most of the senses are blunted as a result of nervous disorders or shock, and also as a result of traumatisms of the skull. When the patient has recovered we find the senses recovering their acuteness, under the influence of constant and intelligently supervised exercise.[15]*

Amar obviously believed in rigorous assessment based on scientific management techniques to understand the physiology of work applied to the re-education of the injured. He used specially devised equipment, such as an 'ergometric cycle', for measuring and recording muscular activity, respiration, energy expenditure, and fatigue.[16] However, because of their complexity, Amar's assessments were not used extensively, despite medically supervised curative workshops being set up throughout France, Britain, Canada and the United States.

Time and motion study was a product of the period, and in many ways was a process similar to activity analysis which became one of occupational therapist's primary tools, particularly in the 'curative' and 'remedial' eras. There is a link. Occupational therapy, within the United States, and probably in Britain too, was influenced directly by the other giants of scientific management—husband and wife team, Frank and Lillian Gilbreth, who, at the very least participated in conferences held by early American occupational therapists. The more senior amongst readers may recall the film about the Gilbreths, *Cheaper by the Dozen*, starring Clifton Webb.

Frank B. Gilbreth (1868–1924) was a disciple of Taylor, and Lillian (1879–1972) was an industrial psychologist and teacher who took a particular interest in making the environment easier for 'cripples'. When, during 1914 and 1915, Frank Gilbreth visited hospitals in Europe he became aware of Amar's research, but took a different approach to the re-education of crippled servicemen. Instead of adapting the man to the work as Amar did, Gilbreth, whose focus was on the manufacturing industry rather than on agriculture, adapted the work to the man. When concentrating on workers with physical disabilities this meant:

> ...rearranging the surroundings, equipment and tools. It may consist of slight modifications of machinery. It may consist of changing the method by which the work is done, that is, of allowing some other member of the worker's body to perform the motions that formerly were made by the member that is now maimed or missing. In any case the need is for invention.[17]

They used cinematography, a specially devised clock, and 'Simultaneous Motion Cycle Charts' to assist them with analysis.[18]

While, according to the nature of the industrial environment of the day, they advocated for greater and greater division of labour, interestingly they still recognised that there was less monotony where the greatest skill was used. Anticipating the future role of occupational therapists, the Gilbreths recommended arousing interest in the:

> ...discovery, invention or adaptation of devices that will make it possible for the cripple not only to have a productive and paying occupation but also to "fit back" into all the ordinary activities of life.[19]

Those adaptations could be attached to a maimed limb, or be simple devices like a magnetized hammer to make nailing with one arm possible; but in either case the adaptation must be mastered easily so that a feeling of capability was experienced. Some of their devices are remarkably similar to many used at some time by occupational therapists over the years. Some were created by the users such as the dressing aids shown in figure 2.3.2. This man had:

> ...complete stiffening of many of his joints since 23 years of age...he has very little use of his legs and very little motion in his back and neck. He has, however, invented and made for his own use special devices such as peculiar shaped crutches, long handled hooks for pulling on his shoes, and tongs for pulling on his trousers.[20]

**Figure 2.3.2:**   **Special appliances made by user. One of the crutches, when reversed, is used to push off his boots.[21]**

*(By permission of The British Library 08248 bb 49)*

Touching further on the psychological aspects of the need to feel capable in the occupations of daily life, the Gilbreths opposed the suggestion that countries were obliged to support crippled servicemen in idleness, for life. That view, they said, was contrary to the one held by the majority of injured soldiers who were horrified by the idea of becoming non-productive members of the community, and that 'the last thing in the world the sufferer wants' was 'enforced or continuous idleness'. Additionally, disabled servicemen may be 'shocked' and have 'horrible recollections' which required diverting. It was, therefore, important for them to be occupied with other 'attractive, inspiring and stimulating' interests.[22] They argued that 'the health and happiness of the cripple' demand that he be 'kept busy from the earliest stage in his recovery', as well as that he 'be re-educated at the earliest possible moment.'[23] This was in order to overcome what was reported as the greatest problem—persuading an injured man that life was worth living despite disability, and that he was still needed. That being the case, it was seen as a duty to furnish real work that could be done efficiently and profitably, whilst providing satisfaction, self-respect, and happiness.

Because the Gilbreths held broad views encompassing an economic, educational and 'waste-eliminating' perspective of re-educating the 'crippled soldier', their work was invaluable to enable their return to the front or to become a part of the industrial effort which supported the war. Like Amar, they saw that in many countries the economic balance was changed negatively by the sudden withdrawal of men to fight in the war; even if they returned many of the men would have changed capabilities. This, they thought, was 'especially true of those (people) who have only a manual education, since when they are physically disabled they find themselves unable to adapt to new occupations without considerable assistance.'[24]

To tackle such issues the Gilbreths 'insisted upon' the need for trained personnel, and teachers, being sent to base hospitals, so that re-education could commence as soon as possible under military regulations, as was the case in France. They recognised that handicapped workers often preferred their previous type of employment, and that this should be facilitated whilst bearing in mind 'the greatest prosperity to both worker and employer'. Apart from that they suggested three kinds of opportunities:

1. Of so adapting cripples to jobs already existing, or so adapting such jobs to cripples, that cripples may become competitors with the whole worker.

2. Of finding occupations that do not exist, but which should exist for public prosperity, and assigning these to crippled workers.

3. Of reserving certain jobs for cripples, and putting them in these jobs on a non-competitive basis so far as uncrippled workers are concerned.[25]

Research was needed to progress such ideas, they said, including the collection of data about how: individuals with disability succeeded in becoming 'useful, efficient and happy'; machinery could be changed to make its use by disabled workers both possible and profitable; and unnecessary fatigue could be eliminated, avoided or relieved. They stated that any results should be immediately disseminated to all establishments and workers in the field.[26]

The Gilbreths' approach contributed, in more ways than one, to the burgeoning profession of occupational therapy. Dunton, one of the founders of American occupational therapy introduced in the previous chapter, compared the Gilbreths' and Amar's methods and believed that the former followed 'the better principle'.[27] Indeed, concentration on adapting 'the environment' to the needs of patients or clients has long been a particular concern of occupational therapists; however occupational therapists have also employed Amar's principles in their approaches to prosthetics, and, sometimes, in the development and use of complex physiological assessments.

Compatible with the industrial nature of his previous work, Gilbreth was, of course interested in resolving the manpower shortage created by the War. However although he upheld his view that 'the world needs the work of every person existing and able to be a producer' he also recognised that 'most important of all is the cripple's own need for constructive activity', as well as, in line with commonly held views and rhetoric of the times, that 'he is still able to do "a man's job" in the world.'[28]

Thomas Kidner, another of the founders of North American occupational therapy, was interested in 're-education' of cripples, and in scientific management. Born in London, he left England for Canada at the age of 34 to establish a technical education program in New Brunswick and Nova Scotia. As a result of the War, services for disabled soldiers began to be developed in Canada and Kidner accepted an appointment as Vocational Secretary of the Military Hospitals Commission in 1915.[29] In that post he developed a system of vocational rehabilitation for disabled veterans which included 'teachers giving instruction in various crafts, stenography and type-writing, drawing, shop arithmetic, and in fact, anything which will aid the patient to fit himself to earn a living.'[30]

# Other occupational initiatives

Some of the most significant occupational initiatives during the war were taken by the troops themselves. In the trenches, or at sea, servicemen tried to keep their spirits up and forget the horrors of war by engaging in any number of occupations. They wrote, not only letters home, but also stories and poetry; they drew and painted pictures, often in miniature because of shortage of supplies and sometimes used unusual materials, such as soot, for the same reason. They carved bone and mortar shells, made models out of dead matches, and jewellery for their loved ones. A collection of such artifacts, known as trench art, is displayed in the Imperial War Museum in London. They are testament to the importance of occupation for survival and mental health.

Also sometimes called trench art is the work done by injured servicemen when in hospital, having been stretchered back to Britain. The collection held in the Imperial War Museum are examples of such work. There is, for example, a beaded necklace made by Private Walter Cressey at the Queen Alexandra Military Hospital, after he had lost four fingers and been blinded by a gas attack.

**Figure 2.3.3:** **Soldier fashioning Trench Art in World War I**
*(Imperial War Museum Q2960)*

**Figure 2.3.4:** **Bullet crucifix**
*(Copyright NJ Saunders)*

Turning to other occupational initiatives which took place in World War I, Watson observed in his 1930 book *Civilization and the Cripple*:

> *...one of the most prominent discoveries of the orthopaedic centres in the War was in the intimate relationship between treatment and curative training. The wounded soldier, confined for weeks and even months to a hospital ward, found time lay heavy on his hands, idleness deepened his sense of tedium and anxiety, his exercises were performed without concentration and his moral fibre deteriorated along with his physical health. To meet this problem and accelerate interest and good heart, the famous curative workshops were instituted to facilitate restoration and with a view to employment.*[31]

That comment is true of both world wars, which had a marked effect on the establishment of the concept of modern rehabilitation, and on the formation of specific disciplines to deal with separate aspects of care resulting from the inevitable traumas of such conflict.

In World War I every fighting man was considered essential, as casualties were enormous and return to the front was paramount. The account of his convalescence (which did not have a particular curative work orientation) given by Harris of the New

Zealand Rifle Brigade, found in the Archives of the British War Museum, provides an indication of earlier procedures:

*24th. All of us who are fit enough are sent to Codford Convalescent camp so as to make room for more wounded coming in. Codford is a convalescent camp and as the men become fit enough for it are given light training. The Command depot is made up of 4 camps...patients are classified each Monday by the Dr and when they get to B camp they go off to Training camp and back to France.*

*At the foot of our camp is the YMCA and institute which is always very popular amongst the men and in a place like this makes life bearable for the men. There are billiard tables (4d for half hour) a refreshment buffet which supplies tea, coffee and eatables...Entertainments of various kinds are arranged sometimes as often as 4 nights a week...the idea is to provide the men with some form of entertainment of an evening and through the day as a counter attraction to places that would be less profitable to the mens welfare.*[32]

Hospital staff and others used a variety of means to entertain injured servicemen. Figure 2.3.5 shows a 1916 concert which patients and their visitors enjoyed.

**Figure 2.3.5:** **Hospital staff, visitors and patients enjoying a concert, the singer stands on a table. Lithograph after L. Ibels, 1916**
*(The Wellcome Library, London)*

The British Red Cross took a lead in establishing programs of occupation and entertainment for injured servicemen. That organisation owed its existence to the initiative of a Swiss Banker, Henri Dunant, who, moved by the sufferings of those wounded at the Battle of Solferino in 1859, had set about establishing an international voluntary aid society to succour such victims at a time of war. The British Red Cross, which was first active in 1870, was granted a royal charter in 1908, and held as primary objectives the furnishing of aid to the sick and wounded in wartime. During the 1914–18 conflict they formed a joint committee with the Order of St John to co-ordinate their endeavours.[33] Red Cross Hospitals were established across many parts of the country at, for example Cheltenham, Birkenhead, Southampton, Bristol, and Middlesex.[34] The East Lancashire Branch provides an example of their contribution during the first year of the War. At Woodlawn hospital, in West Didsbury, apart from numerous entertainments, the large grounds provided opportunities for many types of recreations in the open air. The orchards became not only a source of interest and profit, but 'to the patients so inclined a means of indulging in a favourite occupation.'[35] Similar programs were offered at Fairhope Red Cross Hospital, Manchester, where patients included 81 with bullet wounds to the head, trunk, upper or lower limbs, 30 with shrapnel wounds, 37 with frostbite, and eight with rheumatism; and at Catterick Hall, Didsbury, which also placed social club premises at the disposal of patients affording them additional opportunities for indoor amusements and outdoor games. In contrast, at the Heaton Chapel Division they organised a splint padding class,[36] and at the British Red Cross Hospital in Netley they took a more craft-oriented tack:

> *Embroidery and needlework was commenced in this Hospital early in 1915, and has been an increasing industry ever since. Large numbers of patients pass away the weary hours of hospital life in doing pieces of work, and a very high degree of skill has now been attained and most artistic results have been achieved by those who, up to the time of admission, had never threaded a needle.*[37]

The Roses of Picardy embroidery, shown in Figure 2.3.6, done in Netley Hospital, which was an 'early landing place' near Southampton where the injured were held when very sick and prior to going on to reconstruction workshops.

| | |
|---|---|
| **Figure 2.3.6:** | **Roses of Picardy - embroidered at Netley Hospital** <br> (*Archives of the Imperial War Museum* <br> *Photograph A Wilcock*) |

In one hospital in North London, a plate, now housed in the Imperial War Museum, was decorated with candle smoke using fingers, matchsticks and rags to create the detail, and lacquered with a mixture of cordite from rifle bullets dissolved in whiskey. The artist was a South African soldier who lost both legs in France, and used his decorated plates as currency for cigarettes.[38]

One of the best known of the Red Cross establishments was the Royal Star and Garter Home at Richmond, started in 1916. The disabled servicemen who went to live there were engaged in a variety of occupations that could provide them with some income. In the Minutes of the House Committee, dated 24 July 1917, it is recorded that:

> *A statement was read from Lady Sloggett relating to the money received from the sale of the patients work. The committee agreed that the patients should have the money realised at the sale for their work, after the cost of mounting has been deducted.*[39]

It appears that Lady Slogett was very involved in several aspects of the Home during its formative years, including the organisation of activities and exhibitions of work. As well as direct involvement in the patients' occupations she was concerned with their lifestyles generally, for example, she provided cakes for the first Christmas of 1916, just as others contributed a variety of items to make the occasion festive. Lord Farqhar, another of the supporters, gave individual presents for residents, and the singer, George Robie, sent a number of gramophone records. It appears Lady Slogett worked so strenuously in her charitable tasks that she felt unable to continue her 'work amongst the patients' as recorded in the minutes of 1 June 1918.[40] The people engaged in the provision and instruction of occupations apparently varied, with many offering their services voluntarily. Whilst some of the work, no doubt, provided the chance for ladies with time and inclination, such as Lady Sloggett, to help the war effort, some tradesmen and teachers were also engaged.

**Figure 2.3.7:** **Nurse, man in bed, man in wheelchair, doing tapestry/embroidery**
*(Star and Garter, Richmond-upon-Thames)*

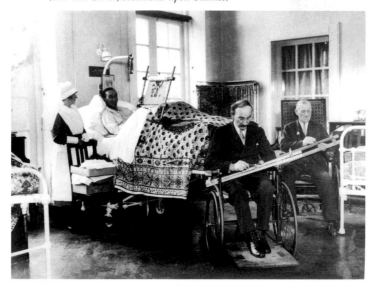

It seems that 1918 was a very creative year with regard to extending the occupational opportunities of residents. In June:

> *The House Committee approved of providing a workshop and instruction classes for the patients...also that an enquiry be made as to the equipment required for a business training class, and the cost of the same, and that opinion of a competent musician be obtained as to the forming of an orchestra by the patients.*[41]

Those initiatives were, on the whole, successful, for in October it was recorded that:

> *...music classes for the patients have been begun, and the House Committee hope after Christmas to give an Entertainment by the Star and Garter Orchestra. Bootmaking classes will be started as soon as possible. The proposed Carpentry Class has been abandoned for the present as it was found that the number of men physically fit for the work was not enough to justify the expense which would have been incurred. The work of adapting the old Conservatory for use as a workshop has now been completed.*[42]

And in the following month:

> *The shoemaking classes were commenced on 25th November. The commercial classes are attended by a large number of patients, and the Orchestra formed under the tuition of Dr Jolley is proving a source of great interest to the men.*[43]

By the following year the Home was applying for a cinema licence.

**Figure 2.3.8: Shoemakers' Shop**
*(Star and Garter, Richmond-upon-Thames)*

Apart from the Red Cross contribution, existing facilities within the broader community were also utilised for the war wounded. A prime example was Chailey, which accepted over 500 wounded soldiers during the war as well nearly 600 raid-shock children. The former worked alongside the usual residents and were sometimes supervised by them:

> *One could see a tall and well-built guardsman who had lost a limb being trained and supervised by a tiny youngster who was even more gravely crippled. In this way the mutilated soldier came at once to realise that his sad condition could be accepted without destroying all hope of a healthy future; and the moral cure was as marvellous as the physical.*[44]

The boys even built what were known as the *Kitchener Huts* to free their own building for the use of the wounded soldiers. After the Armistice, Chailey's 'special surgical military hospital' was used for wounded pensioners. (During World War II both soldiers and 'blitz children' were again accepted at Chailey.)[45]

Other facilities that were utilised, but which concentrated on the employment aspects of occupation, were St Dunstan's for the Blind, and what became known as the Lord Roberts Memorial Workshops. The latter had come about as a result of the after effects of the South African (Boer) War (1880–81). At its close the Soldiers' and Sailors' Help Society had found it extremely difficult to find employment for those who were disabled as a result of the campaign. It was decided to establish self-supporting workshops where those capable of some work could be taught a trade. These had operated for the 10 years preceding World War I, but had been small scale. It soon became obvious that it would be necessary to greatly extend the original Workshop Scheme. Whilst their expansion was being considered Field Marshal Lord Roberts, who had always taken the greatest interest and active participation in the Scheme, died and as a memorial to him the workshops came to bear his name.

The 'Lord Roberts Memorial Fund For Workshops For Disabled Soldiers And Sailors', was approved and arrangements were made to establish substantial manufacturing businesses in London, Edinburgh, Belfast, and Brighton, in which to provide employment for all disabled men who wished to work there. The types of industry included the making of brushes, wooden household goods, wooden toys and children's games, and the appeal for funds explained that:

> ...we provide not for the present only, but for the whole future life of these brave men. We take them as they come, lame and halt, from the battlefield, and make of them efficient, capable workmen; not receivers of charity, but valuable units of a huge industrial and economic scheme.[46]

Dr H.J. Hall, at the First Annual Meeting of the National Society for the Promotion of Occupational Therapy in America, discussed the Memorial Workshops which had been established all over England. He described how, with the very latest machinery, they were hoping to supplant Germany in the field of toy making and were already 'turning out a great product.' However, he went on to say that 'one of the industries which has been taken on by the crippled soldiers is cigarette making.' Although that 'should profitably employ a great many workers whose hand and arm motions have become limited', he had a cautionary aside to relate:

> A friend who has just returned from the other side, brought me a box of these new hand made cigarettes. The cover bore a silhouette of Lord Roberts on horseback and an appeal to patriotism in the use of this product. But alas, the tobacco was bad and it was packed too tightly. There have been other defects which should have been apparent to an expert. My devotion to the Allies runs high and I am a cigarette smoker but I had to throw away half the box. I could not even palm them off on my friends.[47]

The other establishment mentioned earlier, St. Dunstan's for Blind Soldiers and Sailors, provided hostel accommodation and work training. In the workshops instruction was provided mainly by people who were blind, backed up by sighted foremen. The blind instructors were recruited from the ranks of the more 'intelligent and apt soldiers' who were trained to be pupil teachers. The men could learn one or more of several occupations such as massage, shorthand-writing, telephone operating, boot-repairing, mat-making, basket-making, joinery, poultry farming, and market gardening. Most of them also learnt 'netting', Braille, and type-writing. As hand writing almost inevitably deteriorates following blindness, typing was taught as a means to keep in touch with family and friends and, when the blinded soldiers had passed the test given at the end of the typing course, each was given a typewriter to own. On leaving St. Dunstan's the men were also supplied with Braille literature.[48]

The war also heralded major areas of growth within the medical profession in dealing with psychological trauma resulting from shell shock. The 'hormic' and social psychologist, W. McDougall, whose work focussed on purpose and conation (from the Latin—to strive),[49,50] was involved in the treatment of people following shell shock during the war. Rhodes scholar Rupert Reynell, after studying medicine at St Bartholomew's, was a pioneer in the field of neurology and was another of the few people who understood what needed to be done for patients with shell shock. It was through him that renowned Australian artist Margaret Preston became involved in trying 'to help mend soldiers' at the Seale-Hayne Neurological Memorial Military Hospital in Devonshire using pottery and other crafts. There 'improvisation' was the key word due to wartime shortages—an aspect that must have appealed to Margaret's delight in self-sufficiency. Shortages of cane for the basket-weaving were compensated for by young rose shoots, raffia and Paddy's lucerne, 'with the result that baskets sold in the town sometimes flowered in spring'.[51]

Development also occurred in orthopaedic surgery, and Sir Robert Jones is, perhaps, the best known of the orthopaedic specialists. Occupation was to be used as an integral part of the treatment of both shell shock and orthopaedics, and 'proto occupational therapists' from the New World played a role within that.

In March 1918 four women, Mrs Clyde Myers, Laura LaForce, Corrine Dezellor, and Amy Drenenstred, sailed to France from America and were assigned to Base Hospital 117, near La Frauche, which specialised in shell shock. Without rank, uniforms and no specific duties, they were designated civilian aides and assigned the central portion of a barracks 20 feet by 100 feet long between a Red Cross Supervisor of gardens and the hospital carpenter. In home made smocks, using supplies they took with them, old beds from dumps which they made into work benches, and tin cans from the kitchen with which they lined the kiln, they set about assisting the soldiers to regain confidence and concentration. Within a few weeks, as a result of their work, a thousand such aides were requested.[52]

As, in the beginning, little training was available, potential aides were sought with expertise in social work, library, arts and craft teaching, or commercial skills, but not necessarily with any medical background. Intensive six to twelve week courses were run in twenty-six different locations, and some of these programmes were expanded and continued after the war, although most closed permanently at its conclusion.[53,54] Those who went over next to work in European military hospitals were called 'reconstruction aides'. Both 'physiotherapists' and 'occupational therapists'—were recruited.[55] Approximately 1685 reconstruction aides were eventually in service, of whom about 460 served abroad, and of which about 116 were occupational therapy aides. Others worked in army hospitals in America. Their duty was:

> ...to teach various forms of simple handicraft to patients in military hospitals and other sanitary formations of the Army, especially to those patients in the orthopaedic wards as well as to the patients suffering from nervous and mental diseases.[56]

Gutman, in the 90s, argued that the relationship between 'reconstruction aides' and orthopaedists influenced the development of the profession establishing a willing acceptance of the medical model by occupational therapists.[57] In that argument it was noted that occupational therapy aides practised in settings controlled by strict supervision of physicians:

> To maintain a connection with medicine and the curative aspects of activity, the aides relied on physicians to direct the selection of activity. The physicians accepted and supported the aides as technical assistants. The female aides were nurturers who provided diversional activity that, while very important to successful convalescence was not to be

*considered on a par with vocational training that was handled by men.*[58]

Paterson, with a similar view, suggested that some considerable time would pass 'before there was a body of professional, qualified occupational therapists who could challenge this situation.'[59]

Although the profession did not start in a formal way in Britain at that time, what happened then was influential in terms of much of twentieth century practice. Two British pioneer occupational therapists, Elizabeth Casson and Mary Macdonald, made comment on this special time in the profession's history. Casson, when explaining the development of occupational therapy in Britain to an American medical audience, told how:

> *...Louis Haas, who wrote one of the first textbooks on occupational therapy, pointed out that...it was the 1914–18 War that began its application to (physical) illness and injury. It is generally recognised that the first organised war occupational therapy was provided by the Canadian Army. It was quickly followed by that of the United States of America, while at the same time Sir Robert Jones organised, at the request of the British War Office, a magnificent orthopedic service which was grouped around his large curative workshop at Shepherds Bush in London, where as many as 600 men were under occupational treatment in a hospital of 800 beds.*

She added that, 'At that time, and ever since, occupational therapists have kept in touch with each other across the Atlantic.'[60]

Macdonald acknowledged how 'early in the First World War' the impact of:

> *...the large numbers of casualties in the German and Allied armies, combined with the shortage of civilian manpower, forced the European governments to develop services for vocational rehabilitation, particularly for amputees. In Britain, the two most significant people in this vocational rehabilitation of the war wounded, through the establishment of curative workshops, were Sir Robert Jones (1857–1933), founder of orthopaedic surgery, and King Manuel (1889–1932), the deposed King of Portugal, who lived in exile in England.*[61]

# King Manuel, Robert Jones, occupation and curative workshops

King Manuel and Robert Jones, did indeed, play particularly important roles in establishing rehabilitation as a necessary adjunct to orthopaedic after-care. As part of that process, they recognised the potential of programmes of occupation within rehabilitation and the links to psychological well-being and return to community life. They endeavoured to make the links closer by melding hospital to community through work.

Manuel II of Portugal was born the second son of Carlos I. He succeeded to the throne at just 19 years of age following the assassination of his father and older brother, the Crown Prince, in 1908. His reign lasted only two years before the outbreak of the revolution which established Portugal as a Republic. He chose Twickenham, in England, as his new home. In 1914, he established a private hospital for officers in Brighton developing a major interest in rehabilitation as he became immersed in the plight of those who were disabled.[62] The following year, with the support of the Joint War Committee of the Red Cross and Order of St John, he visited European hospitals. At the Anglo-Belgian Hospital at Rouen he saw the war wounded engaged in a variety of occupations in workshops established as part of the facility. This, along with work being carried out at the Canadian Hospital at Ramsgate, impressed him so much that he became a champion for the establishment of curative workshops to aid in the rehabilitation of wounded servicemen.[63] His social status, no doubt, assisted in the amassing of funds, which made the establishment of workshops in British hospitals a viable possibility:

> *The scheme which I had in mind for a long time was only put into practice owing to the generosity and foresight of the Joint War Committee of the British Red Cross Society and Order of St. John of Jerusalem, and also owing to the splendid financial support I received from the public in the different places where the centres have been established.*[64]

Robert Jones (1857–1933) came from a background with demonstrated interest in the treatment of skeletal disorders. His uncle, Hugh Owen Thomas, invented the Thomas Splint. Jones qualified, in 1878, from the Liverpool School of Medicine, later becoming a Fellow of The Royal College of Surgeons. He pioneered orthopaedics, working and teaching in Liverpool. His status was recognised internationally as he became an Honorary Fellow of medical and surgical societies in Ireland, France, Sweden, Italy and Germany; and in 1909 he was elected the President of the Orthopaedic Division of the 'International Congress of Medicine'.[65]

**Figure 2.3.9:**     **Sir Robert Jones 1857-1933**
*(The Wellcome Library, London)*

In 1903 Jones demonstrated his interest in the after care of his patients when he became involved with Agnes Hunt in the Baschurch Home for Cripples. Later he insisted that the after care be extended to include 'a regular training centre to teach the badly-crippled adolescents to earn their living.'[66] With similar intent, at the beginning of the 1914–18 war, he established a service at the Alder Hey Hospital near Liverpool, with an emphasis on continuity of care and the restoration of physical function, to 'eliminate military wastage'.[67] Being aware that occupations, such as joinery, were offered as part of treatment for the wounded at a Canadian hospital in France, Jones advised the adoption of occupations in Britain. He recognised 'the psychological contribution to recovery through this form of treatment in which he either had the patients introduced to the former occupation in which they were interested, or to a more suitable new one.'[68] Helped in his persuasion of the War Office by Manuel, who as his ally had prevailed upon the Joint War Committee of the Red Cross and St. John to provide the first £1000, Jones established a curative workshop at the Military Orthopaedic Hospital, Shepherd's Bush, in 1916.[69]

In Jones's 1916 work *Notes on Military Orthopaedics*, dedicated to Manuel, he writes of combining exercise with meaningful occupation, in a way remarkably similar to physical rehabilitation methods later in the century, such as those described by Mary S. Jones in *An Approach to Occupational Therapy*. He used 'direct' exercise in which:

> *...a screwdriver may be employed to supinate the arm, a saw to exercise the elbow, painting to move the shoulder—but with an ingenious instructor, special ways are constantly devised in order to directly affect the joint involved.*

and, what he described as, the indirect method of attack:

> *For example, when a man with a stiff ankle is set to plane or saw wood, he unconsciously uses the ankle as he gets interested in the work which his hand is doing.*[70]

He found that voluntary movements were more effective than passive, and made more so with interest and purpose, particularly as many of the soldiers spent eighteen months or more in the hospitals.[71]

> *Men with stiff ankles are set to drive a treadle, lathe or fretsaw. If put on a treadle-exercising machine the monotony soon wearies the mind, but if the mind is engaged not on the monotony of the footwork but on the interest of the work turned out, neither mind nor body becomes tired. Men with defective elbows and shoulders find exercise and mental diversion in the carpenter's and blacksmith's shops. If their hands and fingers are stiff, working with a big swab to clean windows or with a paint brush is a more interesting occupation than gripping spring dumb-bells.*[72]

**Figure 2.3.10: Shepherd's Bush Orthopaedic Hospital: Curative treatment for the left foot**
(*Unable to trace copyright*)

There was an economic benefit too. At Shepherd's Bush, patients carried out the hospital's maintenance work, including the installation of the wiring and plumbing for electro- and hydro-therapeutics. Patients also manufactured splints, surgical boots, artificial limbs, and orthopaedic appliances required for the war wounded and pensioners in the London District utilizing metal workers, leather-workers, smiths, fitters, and oxy-acetalene welders.[73,74] This may be one of the origins of the manufacture of splints and appliances within modern occupational therapy. Such work 'gives the patients the feeling that they are doing something which is of great benefit to their fellow comrades in hospital'.[75] Apart from those occupations, patients engaged in basketry, book-binding, boot and shoe-making, cane seating, carpentry, cigarette making, fretwork, leather-work, machine-drawing, motor repairs, netting, painting and sign-writing, papier-mache work, photography, printing, raffia-work, rug-making, surgical knife grinding, tailoring, telegraphy, upholstery, weaving, and wood-carving. They were also involved in outdoor occupations such as gardening, farming, forestry and poultry keeping; commercial occupations like shorthand, typing, book-keeping and commercial correspondence; as well as more social occupations such as playing in an orchestra.[76]

Recognising the psychological benefits of occupation, Jones maintained that:
*Those of us who have any imagination cannot fail to realize the difference in atmosphere and moral in hospitals where the patients have nothing to do but smoke, play cards, or be entertained, from that found in those where for part of every day they have regular, useful and productive work.*[77]

A chapter about curative workshops, written by Manuel, was included in Jones's 1921, *Orthopaedic Surgery, Vol. II*. Extracts from that work are provided below because of the importance of workshops at the time, and also to illustrate the similarity which can be observed between what was implemented then and later occupational therapy rehabilitation practices. One of the most important requirements of the workshops was:
*...to create an atmosphere of contentment amongst the men who had in a large number of cases been many months in hospital. I had always thought that the best method of creating this atmosphere was to occupy and give work to...wounded men (who) thought they would never again be able to work, or that they would never again be able to earn their living when they were discharged from the army.*[78]

*There is no doubt that the hospitals where curative workshops have been established have assumed an industrious aspect as well as an atmosphere of contentment.*[79]

Manuel described the four major objectives of the workshops as:
1. To give occupation to the men
2. To find work which would be useful for their respective injuries
3. To find occupations which would have a beneficial psychological effect
4. To consider occupations which would, later on, be of benefit to the men when they were discharged from hospital either to the army or into civil life.
Whilst the last three of those objectives are probably self explanatory, the first of them is particularly interesting. To me it implies an intrinsic value given to occupation. This concept was implicit in the early professional literature and is being rediscovered today, but was largely overlooked and, in some ways condemned, in the years between. As occupational therapists have sought a medical explanation of their contribution they have, perhaps unconsciously, overlooked the unique but central place occupation plays in everyone's life, and what happens to people when they are without it. More in terms of the medical thrust of occupational therapy during much of the twentieth century, Manuel explained: 'Training and work may be extremely useful and give good results

under medical and surgical supervision, but without that supervision it may do more harm than good especially at the beginning.'[80]

> *This form of treatment is ordered by the surgeon directly, and can therefore be considered as theoretically compulsory...practically it is still voluntary, as the men receive for their treatment encouragement and especially rewards and privileges which stimulate their desire to get better and to work...we must bear in mind that it is of great importance for the man to be able to realize for himself that while he is undergoing his treatment he is doing useful and productive work.*[81]

In terms of specific curative occupation, Manuel provided some case histories such as:

> *Pte. A. (Liverpool). Gunshot wound of thigh—stiff knee-joint. Began work on treadle lathe in March 1917. In June he had easy flexion up to 40o, and dispensed with crutches after three weeks' treatment.*

> *Pte. C. (Oxford). Wounded 11.4.18 by bullet through neck to right of cervical spine. There was no use at all in left arm, which was flail-like. Slight movements returned in fingers and shoulder under treatment by massage and electricity on 1.6.18. Work in carpenters' shop then commenced, and in three weeks half normal power with complete co-ordination was established. Other treatment nil.*[82]

Jones was appointed Military Director of Orthopaedics in March 1916, and was Knighted in 1917. By the end of the war, he had extended his concept of curative workshops to twenty special military hospitals, with approximately 20 000 beds, in many parts of Britain which were run on lines similar to Shepherd's Bush. The Scottish centres were in the Edinburgh War Hospital at Bangour, Glasgow and Aberdeen. At the former were competent trade instructors, up-to-date machinery and tools and a wide range of study provided by the Education Department.[83]

> *Work as a rehabilitative measure was first introduced to Bangour hospital during the first world war when curative workshops were established for the rehabilitation of wounded servicemen. Under the direction of a Royal Engineers Captain, the workshops were equipped and each trade was taught by a qualified craftsman. In the aftermath of the war, mentally ill patients returned to the Village Hospital and benefited from the opportunities provided by constructive activity and, together with other mental illness hospitals, continued the work under the direction of tradesmen...*[84]

**Figure 2.3.11: Oldmill Curative Workshop, Aberdeen**
*(By permission of Aberdeen Medico-Chirurgical Society)*

Manuel finished his account with a summary of the work done and a plea for it to continue after the war:

> The social question connected with the problem of the disabled is for the nation of a capital importance. We have been living in times when brains, strength, imagination, and knowledge have been used for the purposes of destruction. They must now also be used for reconstruction—reconstruction of those who have offered their lives to their country and who have been disabled in her cause. One must not forget the needs of the country not only now but in the future, when useful and skilled workers will be required in all branches of industry. A more complete co-ordination and organization should exist to obtain the results which can still be easily obtained. We have started an organization, we have obtained results, we have done good to the men, we have restored their injured limbs by the direct treatment in our workshops, we have improved their general physical and mental condition by the psychological treatment, we have produced useful work, we have created amongst our patients an atmosphere of satisfaction and industry, we have prepared men for the Army more rapidly than was done previously, we have re-educated those who were to be discharged from the Army—all this has been done and is still being done, I will not say without difficulties, and we have obtained most wonderful results. My wish is that further organization should create a real link between the authorities and societies which are dealing with the training and professional re-education of the disabled men. We are the first stage of the problem, and I am proud to say that we have established our work on a solid basis.[85]

# The use of occupation treatment in Germany

In Germany, too, occupation was recognised as essential to the rehabilitation of the war wounded, as was the need for diversion from the destructive occupations of war to maintain the well-being of the fighting men.

> The furnishing of recreation and amusement for the soldiers both in the trenches and the hospitals is regarded as an important feature of welfare work. 'The soldiers in the field want games,' was the information that came back from the trenches soon after the outbreak of the war. To forget the fearful realities of his life, the soldier needs diversion in his hours of rest and relaxation. At times he is too exhausted to read and simple games fill a great want. Games in the hospitals have a much greater usefulness than is generally realized.[86]

The furnishing of that need was provided, in part, by organisations such as the Red Cross and Care of Cripple societies, and the ranks of newly 'working' women. The Woman's League, for example:

> ...made a systematic course in wholesome, interesting games as part of the army nurse's training course. Printed outlines have been prepared of the games suitable for the various kinds of welfare work carried on by the society. In this are listed games suitable for hospital patients, for the trenches, for blinded soldiers, for the children in municipal playgrounds; games for adolescents and entertainments of all kinds for the disabled and convalescents.[87]

Simple, fun occupations were provided for soldiers to take into the trenches such as checkers, chess, dominoes and other well-known board games played with dice and figures:

*These are made as small as possible so as not to overburden the soldier's knapsack. The boards are made of stiff oilcloth or leather and can be folded up; the figures are kept in small linen bags. Puzzles, card games of all kinds, including the educational series are also very popular. Booklets containing riddles, puzzles and amusing tricks of all sorts are furnished.[88]*

Similar enjoyable but simple occupations were used in the early stages of hospitalisation:

*...for patients who are not bed-ridden, games involving active motion are planned and many long-forgotten simple games have been revived; light gymnastics with music are also found to be valuable. For the blind many books, magazines and games are provided. Through entertaining games the blind are most apt to regain their cheerfulness and self-confidence. After their interest in life has been thus reawakened it becomes easy to train them in useful remunerative occupations.[89]*

Following treatment in regular military hospitals, patients, for whom it was deemed necessary, were transferred to orthopaedic hospitals for further 'orthopedic, medico-mechanical and occupational treatment.'[90] The 'occupational' treatment within the orthopaedic-neurologic military hospitals was organised from a special department within the hospitals as part of the extended therapeutic plan:

*'Occupation' therapy begins as soon as possible. Practical participation in the school serves not only to increase the flexibility of joints and tissues, the usefulness of which has been reduced by ankylosis or paralysis, but is also of inestimable value in overcoming the numerous psychic neuroses developed in modern war.*

*The actual medical treatment of those who are confined to bed takes only a few hours during the day. There is danger that the enforced inactivity will impair the spirits of the otherwise healthy men and paralyze their energy and desire to work.*

*Here some suitable occupation is a beneficial and very necessary antidote. The school offers the possibility of work of such kind not only as a diverting occupation but in a manner which, at the same time, offers each one some immediate economic advantage. The men can fill the gaps in their previous general or special vocational education and satisfy their desire of adding to their knowledge and mechanical training. The theoretical instruction in the elementary branches in the industrial and commercial fields especially contributes to this end. As a consequence a man who is disabled for the practical work of his calling may, with his increased technical knowledge acquired in the school, be enabled to return to his former trade and place of employment in a higher and better-paid capacity.[91]*

From the start of the war, existing hospitals, specialising in orthopaedics, had begun to provide instruction of school type subjects, to assist disabled service men with future employment. To determine the nature of the courses a questionnaire was circulated among the injured and, as a consequence of that, writing, arithmetic, shorthand, typewriting, English and French were offered. Patients were also engaged in handwork such as 'basket weaving, carving handles, lattice and fence building.' The military-hospital schools, which were known as Lazaretteschule, aimed to restore the wounded to usefulness. That idea was not entirely new. In Germany, like other countries, institutions already existed which specialised in the care and education of cripples, such as schools specially equipped for the 'one-armed'. But the idea was extended to all servicemen who experienced mental or physical dysfunction as a result of war service.[92]

As the war progressed the need for more extensive schemes became apparent, not only for 'orthopaedic treatment and restoration to usefulness', but also for a follow-up system of reconstruction and care. A collaboration of military and civil authorities, the Welfare Commission for the War Disabled was established, which brought together industrial and trade organisations, polytechnic and commercial schools. The Commission sought, as part of its brief, to 'enlighten the public through the press and by literature and lectures, and lastly to give direct aid in special cases.' Probably as part of that process, by the end of 1916 statistics appeared 'to warrant the claim that nearly 95 per cent of the disabled would be made self-supporting' with their employment status improved in some respects.[93]

It was after the acute treatment phase that an injured serviceman's future employment became the primary issue of consideration. Those who were discharged as unfit for military service by the military authorities were assigned to specialised military hospital-schools for extended training or retraining with the future in mind. These were situated in former seminaries, schoolhouses, Catholic institutions and such, with ample grounds about them, and which were large enough to provide accommodation for up to 1000 patients. One such institution was established for a group of hospitals of 8–10,000 beds. An orthopaedic specialist directed a staff of physicians and nurses alongside workshop instructors. 'The orthopedists and instructors must be men not only of ingenuity but of limitless patience in order to succeed in this work.' Special departments for the treatment of 'nerve injuries and neurologic pathologies' were developed which worked 'hand in hand' with the orthopaedic hospitals.[94]

As far as was possible people were trained to continue their previous employment despite their disabilities. In many cases a major factor was overcoming lack of will-power, energy or ambition to prevail over handicap. Patients were helped to use contrivances, special tools or 'their accessory muscles and other limbs'. In cases in which a change of vocation could not be avoided, retraining in hospital workshops was found to be more effective than competition with younger or 'normal' workmen in outside training facilities:

*If for instance, a one-legged man in a large factory, surrounded by the physically competent, were to become tired it would be rather discouraging to him to give up even temporarily and to see others around him able to continue their work. On the other hand, in the special hospital workshops he can tell his troubles to the doctor who sympathises with and is familiar with his physical limitations and working ability and who will understand and encourage him. In this way and through the stimulation of the instructors and the nurses, who in the orthopedic hospitals are very carefully selected he gradually becomes used to harder work until a sound foundation is laid in his vocational training.[95]*

Several different organizations were developed and subsidised, at local and national levels, for disabled servicemen to learn new ways of making a living, for example, in the building, clothing, furniture, metal and food trades, or as mechanics, surgical appliance makers, electricians, watchmakers, sail or ropemakers. Special attention was given to disabled farmers and farm labourers because it was deemed important that they return to the land. Later they could attend special hospital-schools established at Graudenz or West Russia, where they learnt not only theoretical but practical farming in the extensive grounds or nearby farms where they participated in 'even the heaviest farm work, such as mowing, ploughing etc., using the artificial limbs and 'working arms' made specially for this purpose'. Adaptive devices, working splints and functional fittings for prostheses were also developed and used, such as Thilo's Glove to aid either finger flexion or extension, and a 'work-arm' which did not replace a prothesis but was a tool for tradesmen.[96] (See Figures 2.3.12 and 2.3.13)

**Figure 2.3.12:  Thilo's glove to aid finger flexion or extension[97]**

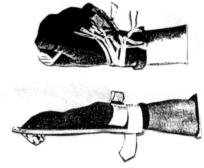

**Figure 2.3.13:  Work-arm attachments as tradesman's tools[98]**

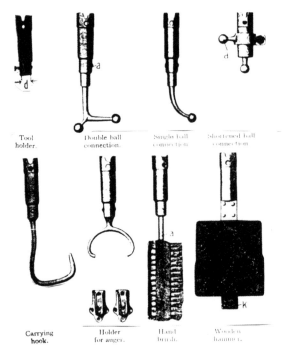

Like many of the remedial workshops in Britain some German centres, like the Coblenz Orthopaedic Hospital School, specialised in:

a) the wholesale manufacture of artificial limbs and supports,

b) training in 'all kinds of bodily exercises in the large gymnasium' before 'inducting the men into their chosen occupation.'[99]

Reconstruction and re-education were also available for officers 'forced to enter civilian professions on account of their injuries'. Physical defects or age were 'not to be considered as impediments except where absolutely necessary for the good of the service'. Large industrial concerns took, without remuneration, hundreds of the war disabled into their workplaces to train them according to their 'adaptability'.[100]

# After the war

At the 1919 Allied Conference on the After care of Disabled Men, in Washington D.C. the English novelist, John Galsworthy, made a statement about the process of restoration He said:

*Restoration is at least as much a matter of spirit as of body, and must have as its central truth: Body and spirit are inextricably conjoined. To heal the one without the other is impossible. If a man's mind, courage and interest be enlisted in the cause of his own salvation, healing goes on apace, the sufferer is remade; if not, no mere surgical wonders, no careful nursing, will avail to make a man of him again. Therefore I would say: From the moment he enters the hospital, look after his mind and his will; give him food; nourish him in subtle ways; increase the nourishment as his strength increases. Give him interest in his future. Light a star for him to fix his eyes on, so that, when he steps out of the hospital, you shall not have to begin to train one who for months, perhaps years, has been living, mindless and will-less, the life of a half dead creature.*

*That this is a hard task none who knows hospital life can doubt. That it needs special qualities and special effort, quite other than the average range of hospital devotion, is obvious. But it saves time in the end, and without it success is more than doubtful. The crucial period is the time spent in hospital. Use that time to recreate not only the body, but mind and will power, and all shall come out right; neglect to use it thus and the heart of many a sufferer and of many a would be healer will break from sheer discouragement. A niche of usefulness and self-respect exists for every man however handicapped; but that niche must be found for him. To carry the process of restoration to a point short of this is to leave the cathedral without a spire. To restore him, and with him the future of our countries, that is the sacred work.*[101]

Despite that impassioned and powerful message, the willingness of the British War Office to set up curative workshops had been, perhaps, more to do with their economic benefit than acceptance of the remedial effects of occupation. This attitude may also account for the closure of the workshops when they served no immediate or substantial economic purpose. Casson wrote:

*Unfortunately, the English War Office closed down the curative workshop at the end of the war, against the advice of Sir Robert Jones and despite the efforts of all the experts who deplored the shortsightedness of those who would not see that the great lessons learned in the war could now be applied to all in civil life who were injured or diseased. Sir Robert then threw all his energies into his work for cripples, but many of his valuable lessons were lost.*[102]

Macdonald held a similar view. The War Office, she wrote:

*…took little interest in this experiment and, while after the 1918 Armistice Canada and*

*the U.S.A. forged ahead, Occupational Therapy was viewed in England as a luxury, and for all but the most seriously and permanently wounded service pensioners, it was dropped.*[103]

Even in North America, and despite the impetus given by the conflict, the development of occupational therapy, post-war, was slow. Hopkins, for example, reported that programs and personnel in all US army hospitals were reduced until only three occupational therapists were employed.[104]

Orthopaedic specialists, other than Jones, bemoaned their virtual demise following the armistice. It was recommended that such services be reinstated, so that people with disability could make use of 'the one and only plank which could carry him from the life of a derelict to that of useful work and self-respect.'[105] As the founders of the Central Committee for the Care of Cripples explained:

> *The experience of the war gave a great impetus to the work of caring for cripples and to orthopaedic surgery in general. The treatment and education of the crippled soldier was such an important matter that it obtained wide publicity and great experience was gained both in surgical and educational methods and in organisation. It was, perhaps, too little recognised that much of the work then done for the soldier was based upon the experience of a small group of people who had for years been doing their best towards alleviating the sufferings and assisting in the education of civilian cripples, more particularly of crippled children. Treatment had been lacking owing to the rarity of special hospitals the impossibility of providing effective treatment for cripples in general hospitals with their town sites and bed pressure, and the absence of any system of after-care. The only attempt at a complete scheme of treatment or after-supervision for cripple children had been that of Miss Hunt. This scheme which has constituted Miss Hunt's life work, served as a general basis upon which most of the ideas of organisation of the Central Committee for the Care of Cripples are based.*[106]

In the United States the system of orthopaedic surgery, restoration of function and vocational rehabilitation developed by Jones and Manuel was adopted by two orthopaedists, Joel Goldthwait and Elliott Brackett. They were responsible for creating the Division of Orthopedic Surgery within the Medical Department of the Army and for organizing a reconstruction programme for soldiers who had been disabled.[107] A letter written early in 1918 from Dr Herbert Hall, to one of the committees starting a school of occupational therapy, outlined the process of rehabilitation to be followed in the United States:

> *The government plan divides the rehabilitation of the crippled soldiers into three parts, which may merge into each other. First, the bedside occupations such as weaving, woodworking, etc. The effect of these is purely medical and not commercial. The next step is the curative workshop where the patient has opportunities to use tools in the machine shop. This stage is intended to restore the functions of the nerves and muscles. The patient can make splints and orthopedic apparatus. This stage is not intended to be vocation, the aim being still medical. The third stage is reached when the workshop has accomplished its purpose. The soldier then comes under the Bureau of Vocational Education where the individual is studied with the view of giving him training in technical schools, from this the man is placed in a trade or professions.*[108]

In Britain, in 1919, the Ministry of Health was set up, taking over the functions of the National Health Insurance Commission and the Local Government Boards. The Ministry of Labour took over the Government Instructional Factories for disabled ex-servicemen from the Ministry of Pensions. The Factories which were renamed Government Training Centres, and using the King's National Roll Scheme, the Government directed businesses to offer employment to disabled ex-servicemen.[109] Also in 1919, the League of Nations was formed to establish peace and security and promote international co-operation. Formed in the same year, and connected with it was the International Labour Organisation, which was responsible for advising governments on issues of social justice such as employment. The following year a permanent Health Committee was set up as part of the League, and members were expected to be concerned with, and co-operate in the prevention and treatment of illness.[110]

Other closely related initiatives were the foundation, in Britain, of the National Institute of Industrial Psychology and the Industrial Fatigue Research Board, which collaborated on the scientific study of human performance in industry.[111] However, the worldwide economic depression of the 1930s led to lack of interest in such research, in large part, because of high levels of unemployment and the resultant cheapness of labour.[112]

Apart from the war, another event of note for this history, which occurred during the period was the establishment of a society of occupational therapists in the United States.

# Occupational Therapy in North America

When Gilbreth returned from Europe to the United States in 1915 he and his wife presented papers about the re-education of crippled soldiers to different professional groups. One was given at the first conference of the National Society for the Promotion of Occupational Therapy, during which he and Amar were elected as honorary members.[113]

The National Society for the Promotion of Occupational Therapy was founded on March 15 1917 at a meeting between George Edward Barton, William Rush Dunton, Susan Johnson, Thomas Kidner, Isabel Newton, and Eleanor Clarke Slagle. Susan Tracey was unable to attend because, at the time of the founders meeting, she was involved in another new course at the Presbyterian Hospital in Chicago.[114] Because vocational teachers, who had sometimes been employed to engage patients in occupation, had little knowledge of how to link activity to patient's problems a change of tactic was needed. In earlier years, doctors with an interest in moral treatment had taken on the role of occupational therapist themselves, but they often had little knowledge of occupations. In some places, attendants and nurses had been involved but they too required more training in occupations, so it had been decided, in some mental hospital in America, to include 'occupational and diversional subjects' within nurses training.[115] Apart from those already mentioned, courses were established in Baltimore, Boston, Milwaukee, New York, Philadelphia and St Louis, often associated with universities.[116]

Eleanor Clarke Slagle (1876–1942), a social work student from an affluent and politically active family, completed the course in 'Curative Occupations and Recreations' at Hull House in 1911. She taught there before going to the Phipps Clinic with Adolph Meyer, and returned in 1918 to become Director of the Henry B. Favill School of Occupations, which was a part of the Illinois Society of Mental Hygiene. One of the founders, Slagle served the American Occupational Therapy Association in all its offices. The First Lady, Mrs Franklin D. Roosevelt, and Adolf Meyer attended her farewell banquet on retirement from the American Association in 1937. A few extracts from her work demonstrate a way of thinking which echoes ideas discussed in the first volume as well as remarkably modern concepts of the relationship between social problems, health and occupation. Her association with Hull House, no doubt, provided her with a knowledge of Ruskin and Morris's 'Arts and Crafts Movement', and demonstrates that the suggested associations between those British social activists and occupational therapy have some justification. Slagle proposed that it was important for a student of occupational therapy to have 'learned to have respect for the utilitarian and acknowledge(s) what Ruskin calls the 'stout craftsmanship' that is easily applicable to this work.' Additionally, in a way reminiscent of Octavia Hill's concern with children's play, in 1922 Slagle talked about '...the necessity of creating or recreating the play spirit' particularly for those from big cities who have had little opportunity for 'spontaneous play'. She added:

> How many present have lived in a congested part of the city and watched children day after day in their vain pursuit for continuity in their play...and we get what Jane Addams so clearly described as 'the fatal passivity that leads to social deviations, all too many of which lead to state institutions of one kind or another.' Therefore, we include games, folk dancing because it is founded on the play spirit, gymnastics, playground activities, competitive games, etc.[117]

In terms of modern concepts of the profession, she recognised that training of occupational therapists needed to include social rehabilitation and preventive work:

> ...placing the emphasis all through the training upon the relation of directed activity to mental adjustment and social rehabilitation. By social rehabilitation, I mean three distinct groups—one group that will in all likelihood remain in the hospital the balance of their days, the second group that may be returned to community life and activity and a third group who may profit by work directed with understanding in a pre-hospital work clinic with an idea and hope of preventing hospital experience.[118]

Another of the American founders who had a connection with the British Arts and Craft movement was George Edward Barton, born in Brookline, Massachusetts, in 1871. He became an architect and early in his career visited London where he met and was influenced by William Morris.[119] On his return to the United States, Barton incorporated the Boston Society of Arts and Crafts, and became its first secretary. Later, it was he who called the meeting at Consolation House, his centre for vocational re-education in Clifton Springs, at which the American Society for the Promotion of Occupational Therapy was founded. It was at this meeting, too, that Barton persuaded the others to accept 'occupational therapy' as the name for the new profession, about which he had decided ideas.

> The term Occupational Therapy, which was first used by the author (Barton) at a conference of hospital workers called by the Massachusetts State Board of Insanity at

*Boston, December 28, 1914, has run like a contagion all over the country, with the result that the very meaning of the words used in many cases has been entirely overlooked. That the reader may have some idea to what an extent this is true and dangerous, the Surgeon-General of the United States at the beginning of the war announced broadcast over the country that Occupational Therapy was to be developed and utilized, and that a large number of teachers would be required. Yet, in the call for Reconstruction Aides issued August 8, 1918, there is no word either definite or implied which makes any knowledge of the sick, or of teaching the sick, or of therapeutics (in any sense) necessary.*[120]

Barton's criticism was based on his own case and preparation for the job. His interest in such work grew from his own experiences following tuberculosis, the amputation of his left foot following gangrene, and an hysterical paralysis of his left side. He prepared himself for the job by 'studying anatomy, surgery, nervous diseases and drug treatment...attending lectures for nursing students at the Clifton Springs Sanitarium Training School', and corresponding with others such as Dunton who used occupation as treatment.[121] Pre-empting a complaint of many modern therapists, he obviously disapproved of 'untrained' people describing what they did as occupational therapy:

*The craft teacher, who a year ago considered herself a teacher of basketry or weaving now, merely because her pupil is sick continues to teach the same subject in the same way as before and calls herself an 'occupational therapeutist'. This not only is an absurdity, but will inevitably cause much unnecessary waste and pain in the future...For a doctor or an occupational director to allow or to prescribe the use of a hammer is every bit as inadequate, childish, unprofessional and absurd as it would be for a doctor to tell an ignorant woman to give her baby a little stimulant, leaving it to the mother whether that stimulant shall be malted milk or strychnine—and she to determine the dosage...the teaching of the sick man is a fundamentally different subject from the teaching of the well man. Indeed, past experience in trade teaching is almost a hindrance rather than a help, because so many of the pedagogic axioms when applied to the sick man not only are not self-evident truths, but are not truths at all.*[122]

Barton wrote three books on occupational therapy between 1916 and 1919. Gilbreth recommended the second *Re-education: An Analysis of the Institutional System in the United States* as a resource addressing the need for psychotherapy for crippled soldiers.[123,124] In the third *Teaching the Sick: A Manual of Occupational Therapy and Re-education* Barton discussed the differences and similarities between occupational therapy and vocational training, which has featured markedly in this chapter. He did so in relation to the re-education of crippled servicemen because 'the popular interest in the subject at the present moment is that devoted to the actual needs of the moment; that is, the needs occasioned by the war.'[125] He prefaced this by commenting that:

*...there appears to exist in the minds of many people a total misconception of what vocational re-education is, as applied to disabled soldiers and sailors. The Federal Board for Vocational Education, which is charged with the duty of re-educating the injured men, is constantly receiving communications from people who have this, or that or the other supposed 'art' or 'craft' which is offered as being 'just the thing to teach the poor dear wounded soldiers.'*

*The difficulty appears to be that many of these well-intentioned advocates of gilded peanut hulls and gim-crack nick-nack making are mentally confused, and do not know either what 'occupational therapeutics' and vocational education are, or the part they play. The former is given to divert the patient's mind, to exercise some particular set of muscles or a limb, or perhaps merely to relieve the tedium of convalescence. Occasionally these activities have little if any practical value beyond the immediate purpose they serve, nor are they intended to have any other value. But even in occupational therapy the idea now is to give that sort which will be preliminary to, and dovetail in with, the real vocational education which is to begin as soon as the patient is able to go further along.*

*The business of re-education is, first of all, common sense and practical. The idea is to turn out thoroughly trained men. It is necessary to realize first that the great fundamental upon which re-education rests is not the making of an object, but the making of a man. To this end, any occupation, however trivial or seemingly absurd, which will assist in the re-birth of the desire to do—the Will—and which will at the same time involve such exercises and such efforts as will assist the body to resume its normal functioning, is no more wasted than is the multiplication table.*[126]

Thomas Kidner (1866–1932) was the second architect in the founder's group. Kidner's position led to him being invited by Barton to the meeting at Clifton Springs. Later, in 1918, Kidner crossed the border from Canada to work in the United States as Special Advisor on Rehabilitation to the United States Federal Board of Vocational Education.[127] Early in the same year, Winifred Brainerd, who was in charge of occupations at the sanatorium adjacent to Barton's Consolation House, crossed the border in the opposite direction, going to Toronto to help plan and participate in the first course for 'instructors in bed-side occupation'. Those courses, required for the emergency of war, were discontinued in the summer of 1919, by which time over 350 young women were trained and posted to military hospitals throughout Canada.[128] Demobilized Canadian occupational therapy reconstruction aides were involved in the formation of curative workshops in Toronto and Winnipeg in 1920 and 1922 respectively. The Canadian Association of Occupational Therapists was established in 1926 the same year that the University of Toronto was persuaded by the Ontario Society to introduce a two-year diploma course.[129] The Profession had established itself on the world stage.

**In summary** the years of World War I were memorable: on the downside, for the degree of horror experienced by so many, and for the number of casualties; and on the up side, for the effort that was expended in providing better curative services to the injured than ever before. Indeed, 78 per cent of soldiers treated returned to active service. It appears incredible that such success was not recognised by governments as worth utilising for the civilian sick or disabled. The events relating to the use of 'occupation for re-education and cure' during the War formed the focus of the chapter. Several organisations and professional groups played important roles in what can truly be conceived as global recognition of occupation as an essential and curative factor in the treatment of a wide range of physical disorders. It had already been recognised for mental disorders. Individuals in the trenches also used it for essential purposes to assist their own survival and well-being. The discipline of 'scientific management' or 'work study' laid substantial groundwork for occupational therapy at government and health care levels. The Red Cross pioneered approaches using occupations in hospitals and homes across Europe, and curative workshops were, possibly, the outstanding factor in returning people to some sort of normality. The war years saw the final breakthrough in terms of establishing a profession which was founded on:

> ...the advancement of occupation as a therapeutic measure;
> the study of the effect of occupation upon the human being;
> and the scientific dispensation of this knowledge.[130]

[1]Taylor AJP. Introduction. In: Shermer D. *World War 1*. London: Octopus Books, 1973; 7–13.
[2]Taylor AJP. Introduction. In: Shermer D. *World War 1*. London: Octopus Books, 1973; 7–13.
[3]Shermer D. *World War 1*. London: Octopus Books, 1973; 31.
[4]Merkle JA. *Management and Ideology: The Legacy of the International Scientific Management Movement*. California: University of California Press, 1980.
[5]Pheasant S. *Ergonomics, Work and Health*. Macmillan, 1991.
[6]Creighton, C. The origin and evolution of activity analysis. *The American Journal of Occupational Therapy* 1992; 1: 45–48.
[7]Amar J. *The Physiology of Industrial Organisation and the Re-employment of the Disabled*. Translated by Bernard Miall, edited with notes and an introduction by Professor AF Stanley Kent. London: The Library Press Ltd., 1918; 347.
[8]Amar. *The Physiology of Industrial Organisation....*; 257.
[9]Amar. *The Physiology of Industrial Organisation and the Re-employment of the Disabled*. In Gilbreth FB, Gilbreth LM. *Motion Study for the Handicapped*. London: George Routledge & Sons Ltd. 1920; facing page 44..
[10]Amar. *The Physiology of Industrial Organisation and the Re-employment of the Disabled*. Translated by Bernard Miall, edited with notes and an introduction by Professor AF Stanley Kent. London: The Library Press Ltd., 1918; 257, 343.
[11]Amar. *The Physiology of Industrial Organisation....*; 343.
[12]Amar. *The Physiology of Industrial Organisation....*; 343.
[13]Amar. *The Physiology of Industrial Organisation....*; 343.
[14]Amar. *The Physiology of Industrial Organisation....*; 347-348.
[15]Amar. *The Physiology of Industrial Organisation....*; 350.
[16]Amar. *The Physiology of Industrial Organisation....*
[17]Gilbreth FB. Motion study for crippled soldiers. Richard D. Irwin, Inc., 1915. In: Spriegel WR, Myers CE. eds. *The Writings of the Gilbreths*. 1953...; 282.
[18]Gilbreth. Motion study for crippled soldiers...
[19]Gilbreth. Motion study for crippled soldiers....; 24
[20]Gilbreth FB, Gilbreth LM. *Motion Study for the Handicapped*. London: George Routledge & Sons Ltd. 1920; Caption under plate facing p. 27.
[21]Gilbreth & Gilbreth. *Motion Study for the Handicapped....*Facing frontispiece.
[22]Gilbreth. Motion study for crippled soldiers....; 26–27.
[23]Gilbreth. Motion study for crippled soldiers....; 41–42.
[24]Gilbreth & Gilbreth. *Motion Study for the Handicapped....*; 19.
[25]Gilbreth. Motion study for crippled soldiers....; 23–24.
[26]Gilbreth. Motion study for crippled soldiers....; 37.
[27]Dunton WR. *Reconstruction Therapy*. Philadelphia: W. B. Saunders Company, 1919; 107–8.
[28]Gilbreth, F. B. (1917). The re-education of the crippled solider. Reprinted in: Spriegel WR., Myers CE., eds *The Writings of the Gilbreths* (1953) Richard D. Irwin, Inc.: 278
[29]Reed KL. Sanderson RS. *Concepts of Occupational Therapy*. Baltimore. Williams & Wilkins, 1980..
[30]Dunton. *Reconstruction Therapy....*; 108.

[31]Watson F. *Civilization and the Cripple*. London: John Bale, Sons & Danielsson, Ltd., 1930; 30.

[32]IWM HARRIS RE 86/66/1 P58-61. Archives: London: British War Museum.

[33]Girling DA, ed. *New Age Encyclopedia*. Sydney. Bay Books, 1983; vol 24: 145–146.

[34]Imperial War Museum. Section VI. Red Cross and General Hospitals. In: *Exhibition for Encouraging Work done by Wounded and Discharged Soldiers and Sailors June 20th to June 27th, 1917*. London: Imperial War Museum, 1917; 52.

[35]Sherratt J, ed. *East Lancashire Branch of the British Red Cross Society: An illustrated Account of the Work of the Branch During the First Year of the War*. Manchester: Sherratt & Hughes, 1916; 85.

[36]Sherratt. *East Lancashire Branch of the British Red Cross Society....*; 81, 191,195-196.

[37]Imperial War Museum. Section VI. Red Cross and General Hospitals. In: *Exhibition for Encouraging Work....*; 52

[38]Trench Art Archives. Imperial War Museum.

[39]Star and Garter Home. *Minutes of the House Committee, May 1917–Jan. 1919*, Richmond: Star and Garter Archives, 24th July, 1918; 41.

[40]Star and Garter Home. *Minutes of the House Committee, May 1917–Jan. 1919...*; 175.

[41]Star and Garter Home. *Minutes of the House Committee, May 1917–Jan. 1919...*; 183.

[42]Star and Garter Home. *The Star and Garter Monthly Report*. October 1918.

[43]Star and Garter Home. *The Star and Garter Monthly Report*. November 1918.

[44]Burt Sir C. Preface in: Kimmins (Mrs). *Heritage Craft schools and Hospitals, Chailey 1903–1948: Being an Account of the Pioneer Work for Crippled Children*. Chailey: 1948; 8.

[45]Kimmins. *Heritage Craft schools and Hospitals....*; 30.

[46]Imperial War Museum. Section IV. The Past, Present and Future of the Lord Roberts Memorial Workshops. In: *Exhibition for Encouraging Work...*; 36, 39-40.

[47]Hall HJ. Arts and crafts in medicine. *Proceedings of the First Annual Meeting of the National Society for the Promotion of Occupational Therapy*, New York, 1918, p.1

[48]Imperial War Museum. Section II: St. Dunstan's Hostel for the blind soldiers and sailors. In: *Exhibition for Encouraging Work...*; 20.

[49]Knight R, Knight M. *A Modern Introduction to Psychology*. 5th ed. London: University Tutorial Press Ltd., 1957; 56–57.

[50]McDougall W. *Introduction to Social Psychology*. 23rd revised edn Methuen, 1936.

[51]Preston M. Pottery as a profession. In: Botel E. *Margaret Preston: The Art of Constant Rearrangement*. NSW: Penguin Books in association with the Art Gallery of NSW, 1985; 17–20.

[52]Reed & Sanderson. *Concepts of Occupational Therapy....*; 214.

[53]Hopkins HL. An historical perspective on occupational therapy. In: Hopkins HL, Smith H, eds. *Willard and Spackman's Occupational Therapy*. 7th ed. Philadelphia: J.B. Lippincott Co., 1988.

[54]Low JF. The reconstruction aides. *American Journal of Occupational Therapy* 1992; 1, 38–43.

[55]Gutman SA. Influence of the US military and occupational therapy reconstruction aides in World War I on the development of occupational therapy. *American Journal of Occupational Therapy* 1995; 3: 256–262.

[56]Low. The reconstruction aides....; 38–43.

[57]Gutman. Influence of the US military....; 256–262.

[58]Low. The reconstruction aides....; 38–43.

[59]Paterson CF. An historical perspective of work practice services. In Pratt J, Jacobs K, eds. *Workπpractices: International Perspectives*. Oxford: Butterworth-Heinemann, 1997; 25–38.

[60]Casson E. Occupational Therapy in Great Britain. *Journal of the American Medical Women's Association* 1947; 2 (6): 303–305.

[61]Macdonald EM. *World-Wide Conquests of Disabilities: The History, Development and*

*Present Functions of the Remedial Services*. London: Bailliere Tindall, 1981; 131–133.

[62]Cooter R. *Surgery and Society in Peace and War. Orthopaedics and the Organization of Modern Medicine, 1880–1948*. The Macmillan Press Ltd, 1993.

[63]H.M. King Manuel. The scheme of curative workshops in the orthopaedic centres of the United Kingdom. *American Journal of Orthopaedic Surgery* 1918; 3: 149–156.

[64]H.M. King Manuel. Scheme and organization of curative workshops. In: Jones R. *Orthopaedic Surgery, Volume II*. 1922; 632.

[65]Macdonald. *World-Wide Conquests of Disabilities....*

[66]Hunt A. *Reminiscences*. Shrewsbury: Printed for the Derwen Crippled Training College, by Wilding & Son Ltd., 1935; 132.

[67]Cooter. *Surgery and Society in Peace and War....*

[68]Macdonald. *World-Wide Conquests of Disabilities....*; 140–141.

[69]Cooter. *Surgery and Society in Peace and War....*

[70]Jones R. Notes on Military Orthopaedics. London: Cassell & Co Ltd. for British Red Cross Society, 1917. In: Jones R, ed. *Orthopaedic Surgery of Injuries*. Henry Frowde & Hodder & Stoughton, 1921; x.

[71]H.M. King Manuel. The scheme of curative workshops in the orthopaedic centres of the United Kingdom. *American Journal of Orthopaedic Surgery* 1918; 3: 149156.

[72]Jones R. *Notes on Military Orthopaedics*. London: Cassell & Co Ltd. for British Red Cross Society, 1917.

[73]Cooter. *Surgery and Society in Peace and War....*; 118

[74]Manuel. Scheme and Organization of curative workshops....; 636.

[75]Manuel. Scheme and Organization of curative workshops....; 640.

[76]Manuel. Scheme and Organization of curative workshops....; 636.

[77]Jones. Notes on Military Orthopaedics. In: *Orthopaedic Surgery of Injuries....*; iii.

[78]Manuel. Scheme and Organization of curative workshops....; 636.

[79]Manuel. Scheme and Organization of curative workshops....; 638.

[80]Manuel. Scheme and Organization of curative workshops....; 642.

[81]Manuel. Scheme and Organization of curative workshops....; 636.

[82]Manuel. Scheme and Organization of curative workshops....; 634.

[83]Edinburgh War Hospital, Bangour 1915–1920. Printed Brochure: Curative workshops of the hospital. Cited in: Groundes-Peace ZC. An outline of the development of occupational therapy in Scotland. *Scottish Journal of Occupational Therapy* 1957; (30): 16–39.

[84]Hendrie WF, Macleod DAD. *The Bangour Story—A History of Bangour Village and General Hospitals*. AUP, 1991; 184.

[85]Manuel. Scheme and Organization of curative workshops....; 642–3.

[86]McDill JR. *Lessons from the Enemy. How Germany Cares for Her War Disabled*. Philadelphia: Lea and Febiger, 1918; 153.

[87]McDill. Lessons from the Enemy....; 153.

[88]McDill. Lessons from the Enemy....; 153–154.

[89]McDill. Lessons from the Enemy....; 153–154.

[90]McDill. Lessons from the Enemy....; 176.

[91]McDill. Lessons from the Enemy....; 185–6.

[92]McDill. Lessons from the Enemy....; 192, 167.

[93]McDill. Lessons from the Enemy....; 156–157, 174.

[94]McDill. Lessons from the Enemy....; 183.

[95]McDill. Lessons from the Enemy....; 225.

[96]McDill. Lessons from the Enemy....; 167, 221.

[97]McDill. Lessons from the Enemy....; 183.

[98]McDill. Lessons from the Enemy....; 225.

[99]McDill. Lessons from the Enemy....; 186.

[100]McDill. Lessons from the Enemy....; 165–168.

[101]Galsworthy J. Statement on Rehabilitation, 1919. In: *Occupational Therapy*. Summer 1946; 5–6.

[102]Casson E. Occupational Therapy in Great Britain. *Journal of the American Medical Women's Association* 1947; 2 (6): 303–305.

[103]Macdonald. *World-Wide Conquests of Disabilities....*; 140–141.

[104]Hopkins. An historical perspective on occupational therapy. In: *Willard and Spackman's Occupational Therapy*...

[105]Watson. *Civilization and the Cripple....*; 30–31.

[106]Central Council for the Disabled. *A Record of 50 Years Service to the Disabled from 191–1965*. London, 1969; 4.

[107]Gutman. Influence of the US military....; 256–262.

[108]Spackman S. A history of the practice of occupational therapy for restoration of physical function: 1917-1967. *American Journal of Occupational Therapy* 1968; 2: 67–71.

[109]Macdonald. *World-Wide Conquests of Disabilities....*; 146.

[110]Macdonald. *World-Wide Conquests of Disabilities....*; 145.

[111]Murrel KFH. *Ergonomics: Man in his Working Environment*. London. Chapman & Hall, 1965.

[112]Paterson. An historical perspective of work practice services...

[113]Creighton C. The origin and evolution of activity analysis. *American Journal of Occupational Therapy* 1992; 1: 45–48.

[114]Reed & Sanderson. *Concepts of occupational therapy....*

[115]Macdonald. *World-Wide Conquests of Disabilities.....*

[116]Macdonald. *World-Wide Conquests of Disabilities.....*

[117]Slagle EC. Training aides for mental patients. (Read at Fifth Annual Meeting of the National Society for the Promotion of Occupational Therapy) *Archives of Occupational Therapy* 1922; (1) 1: 11–18.

[118]Slagle EC. Training aides for mental patients. (Read at Fifth Annual Meeting of the National Society for the Promotion of Occupational Therapy ) *Archives of Occupational Therapy*, 1922; (1) 1: 11–18.

[119]William Morris's story is told in the first volume of this history.

[120]Barton GE. Re-education: *An Analysis of the Institutional System in the United States* New York. Houghton Mifflin, 1917.

[121]Reed & Sanderson. *Concepts of occupational therapy....*; 194–5.

[122]Barton. *Re-education: An Analysis of the Institutional System....*

[123]Barton GE. *Teaching the Sick: A Manual of Occupational Therapy and Re-education*. Philadelphia. W.B. Saunders 1919.

[124]Gilbreth FB. First steps on the solution of the problem of crippled soliders. Richard D. Irwin, Inc., 1918. Reprinted in: Spriegel WR, Myers CE, eds. *The Writings of the Gilbreths*. 1953.

[125]Barton. *Teaching the sick....*; 23.

[126]Barton. *Teaching the sick....*; 59–61.

[127]Reed & Sanderson. *Concepts of Occupational Therapy....*

[128]Robinson IM. Muriel Driver Memorial Lecture: The mists of time. *Canadian Journal of Occupational Therapy* 1981; 4: 145–152.

[129]Driver MF. A philosophical view of the history of occupational therapy in Canada. *Canadian Journal of Occupational Therapy* 1968;2: 53–60.

[130]Certificate of Incorporation of the National Society for the Promotion of Occupational Therapy, Inc. (1917). *Then and Now: 1917–1976*. American Occupational Therapy Association, 1967; 4–5.

# Part 2

# The Founding Years

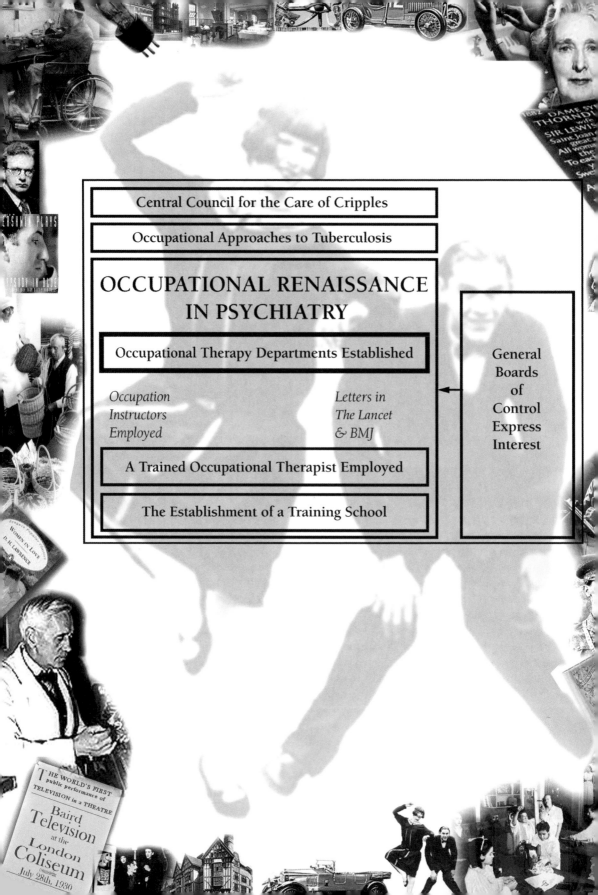

Central Council for the Care of Cripples

Occupational Approaches to Tuberculosis

# OCCUPATIONAL RENAISSANCE IN PSYCHIATRY

Occupational Therapy Departments Established

*Occupation Instructors Employed*

*Letters in The Lancet & BMJ*

General Boards of Control Express Interest

A Trained Occupational Therapist Employed

The Establishment of a Training School

# Chapter 4

# And so it Began...

## Contents

This chapter is about the recognition, in Britain, of occupational therapy as a separate entity within the health field. The 1920s was a significant period, which saw acceptance of the specific use of occupation as a treatment modality being called 'occupational therapy'. The first occupational therapy departments were established and named as such; the first debates about occupational therapy occurred in *The Lancet*; the first trained occupational therapist was appointed; and, by the end of the decade, the first training school was established. It was the time when the earliest exponents of the profession in Britain began to teach others about its importance. Its message, at that time, was essentially curative.

The chapter tells three very important stories about special people in the history. The subjects are: David Henderson, who has to be considered the first of the major twentieth century medical practitioners to give support and patronage of the highest order to the burgeoning profession; Margaret Barr (Peg) Fulton, the first trained British occupational therapist to work in the United Kingdom, and whose story is told, appropriately, by a fellow Scot, occupational therapy historian, Catherine F. Paterson; and, psychiatrist, Elizabeth Casson, a pioneer of the profession in the 1920s who founded the first school in 1930. I have chosen to place Casson's story in this chapter of 'firsts' as the idea and the organisation started during the 1920s, and because the school can be considered the culmination of a remarkable period. Other accounts which surround those three stories are told, to a large extent, using the words of the people who experienced them.

# Context of the times

**B**efore progressing to the tales of those three legendary figures, it is useful to set the scene, by looking first at the context of the times starting with what was happening with occupational therapy in some other parts of the world. In Canada, following the successful efforts of the specially trained aids during the War, the Ontario Society of Occupational Therapy was established in 1920, under the guidance of Dr Goldwin Howland. He also facilitated the establishment, in 1925, of the two-year course at Toronto University. The Canadian Association of Occupational Therapists was founded in 1926, and a quarterly journal began. In Germany, occupational treatment also developed post-war and, from beginnings in mental hospitals, was gradually spreading to some hospitals for the disabled. The Cripples' Hospital at Volksdorf, Hamburg, was to house one of the most up-to-date therapeutic workshops of its kind and, in the Humanitas Hospital for crippled children in Saxony, workshops with central playrooms were provided on each floor. In 1926 Holland introduced the teaching of occupations into wards and workshops of mental hospitals, where advanced handicrafts were organised under the supervision of technicians. In Switzerland, the curative value of occupations was recognised as a supplement to other methods of treatment and introduced into the Burgholzli Mental Hospital at Zurich in 1930 and a number of other institutions. Occupational treatment was prominent in sanatoria and, in the Leysin International Sun Hospital, Dr Rollier originated the simultaneous use of occupation and heliotherapy in which occupations, mostly of the mechanical type, were carried out during graduated exposure to the sun. Success of work treatment at Leysin led to its use in other general hospitals throughout the country.[1]

Apart from what was happening in occupational therapy, it is important to understand the background against which such exciting developments occurred. In some ways they appear all the more remarkable when that background is explained.

Except in Russia where the Bolsheviks had assumed power, the prevailing post-war supposition in most of Europe and North America was that there would be a resumption of pre-1914 values and a continuance of nineteenth century liberalism, national imperialism on a world wide scale, and faith in progress. Instead, an age of anxiety emerged, in which there was both a clinging to the orthodoxies of the church, and a frantic searching after the new in terms of society and the arts. This activity masked a general sense of bewilderment which culminated in the great economic depression that set in late in the twenties. The feelings were summed up well by the French poet and critic Paul Valery who wrote:

> *The storm has died away, still we are restless, uneasy, as if the storm were about to break. Almost all the affairs of men remain in terrible uncertainty…One can say that all the fundamentals of our world have been affected by the war, or more exactly by the circumstances of the war; something deeper has been worn away than the renewable parts of a machine…Among all the injured things is the Mind. The Mind has been cruelly wounded; its complaint is heard in the hearts of intellectual men; it passes a mournful judgement on itself. It doubts itself profoundly..[2]*

Perhaps, the development of occupational therapy then, is not so strange. Perhaps, indeed, it was a manifestation of society, or of some members of society, recognising that they needed to 'do something' about needs which needed to be met.

The burgeoning of occupational therapy in the United Kingdom appears to be associated with its adoption by members of the medical profession. It occurred as local authorities began to assume responsibility for hospitals previously administered by the poor law Boards of Guardians, and the care of people with disability and handicap.[3] But the dawning of twentieth century medical interest in occupational therapy was of earlier origins as traced in Chapters 2 and 3. It was evident in the work of medical experts such as Adolph Meyer, Sir Robert Philip, and Sir Robert Jones. The next section briefly reviews the progress of the Central Council for the Care of Cripples with which Jones was intimately concerned, and which occupational therapists were to be associated with in the future. It goes on to relate the remarkable growth of 'occupational' approaches in the treatment of tuberculosis where so many early therapists began their careers. These accounts suggest how closely occupational therapy allied itself with medicine, and with the patronage of some prominent members of that profession who were visionary in attempting to meet the holistic health needs of their patients. In hindsight, that was a strategic move. Alliance with medicine, fast developing a strong voice in many matters that would concern occupational therapists, could only be of benefit to the fledgling profession which consisted, in the main, of women. Whether that has proved to be of benefit in the longer term is a matter of debate that has exercised the mind of not a few occupational therapists in recent years. It will be one issue that can be addressed more clearly at the end of the history in Chapter 12.

# Central Council for the Care of Cripples

In 1919, Sir Robert Jones, with orthopaedic specialist, G. R. Girdlestone, published a proposal for a National Scheme for Cripples and in the same year the Central Council for the Care of Cripples (CCCC) was set up in conjunction with the Central Council for Infant and Child Welfare (CCICW).[4] In 1962 together they became the Central Council for the Disabled.[5]

Some members of the Council determined, early in 1920, that diminution of war work rendered the time favourable to organise the care of civilian cripples on a national scale. Two years earlier, when the Education Act of 1918 was under consideration by the House of Commons, the Joint Parliamentary Advisory Council had brought forward a report on the need for increased facilities for the education of physically handicapped children. The CCCC and CCICW merged forming a Council of people concerned with different aspects of care but a central belief that 'rehabilitation involved the whole person and every aspect of life'. Although the organisation started its work addressing the needs of children, it was always intended that its activities of 'general enquiry, propaganda and organisation' would extend to adults. It had few financial resources, but was rich with exceptionally able members who saw it as the vehicle to initiate and co-ordinate local action. Over the years the CCCC evolved and extended with a network of orthopaedic hospitals, after-care clinics, and local associations for the disabled.[6]

In 1924 *The Cripples' Journal* (later *The Cripple*) was founded, actively encouraged by Robert Jones and Agnes Hunt, and edited by Frederick Watson, another orthopaedic specialist. It had been intended originally as a local Shropshire publication but such was its influence and readership that within a couple of years it became the official Journal of the Organisation.

A major problem facing the CCCC was how to reduce the difficulties for disabled people in finding suitable employment. In consultation with the Ministry of Labour in 1925, a special committee was proposed for each 'orthopaedic' area. It would contain hospital representatives aware of 'the capacity and limitations of the cripple from the surgical point of view together with representatives from the Juvenile Employment Exchanges, Employers and Trade Unions who would know the local trade conditions and openings.' This was tried out at the Wingfield Orthopaedic Hospital in Oxford, and in Hertfordshire, Essex and Shropshire, and local associations for the disabled were urged to establish committees in every town and country district. A general shortage of vocational training was evident, and the CCCC prepared a scheme to provide a training centre to serve the London area. Eventually, a property near Leatherhead was acquired and the Queen Elizabeth Training College for the Disabled was established. Other training colleges were also established about the same time and some local associations developed sheltered and training workshops for the severely handicapped.[7]

In the mid 1930s the Central Council was transformed by generous donations from Lord Nuffield 'whose sympathy for the cause of the disabled had been largely due to his admiration for the work of Mr. Girdlestone one of the Council's founders.' The Lord Nuffield Fund for Cripples was set up in 1936, and during the next few years organisers were recruited, trained and established in Derbyshire, Durham, East Anglia, Essex, Gloucestershire, Kent, Leicestershire, Middlesex, Lincolnshire, Scotland and South Wales. They promoted clinics and after-care schemes, and county associations with the assistance of disabled individuals.[8]

An increase in the demand for sheltered employment for those only able to work under such conditions was partly met by a workshop opened at Yateley in 1936 and another, the Searchlight Cripples' Workshops, opened at Newhaven in 1937. And, in a field very closely related to the burgeoning occupational therapy, the CCCC also supported 'home work' by launching International Exhibitions of Cripples' Work in Exeter in 1929, Nottingham in 1931, Bristol in 1934, and in Edinburgh in 1937. Additionally, in an effort to improve the design and quality of the products, handcraft teachers were appointed to spend time instructing disabled people in various parts of the country.[9]

# Occupation in holistic approaches to tuberculosis

In 1917, some years after Philip's innovative approach to tuberculosis, Sir Pendrill Varrier-Jones (1883–1941) with the support of Sir German Sims Woodhead, professor of pathology at Cambridge University, went even further in using occupation as the foundation of treatment for people with tuberculosis. Believing that the disease was incurable, and that 'we work to live,'[10] he founded the Papworth Village Settlement. It was planned as a 'Garden City', with hospital, sanatorium, and industries in which patients, after the acute phase of their treatment, could work at union rates, while living in specially designed cottages with their families, or alternatively, in hostels if they were single.

Papworth was built according to Varrier-Jones' holistic approach to medicine aimed at 'treating the whole man or woman, and not merely the diseased portion.'[11] He explained that the basis of the Village-Settlement scheme implied consideration of the social and psychological environment, as well as the physical manifestations of the disease. Further, he took a person-centred approach, arguing that:

> ...we are dealing with persons, not cases, and with this firmly fixed in our minds we shall be more likely to find a solution. In reality these considerations should often have the first place in our minds and the medical picture the second.[12]

His revolutionary approach, which resulted in the segregation of families where tuberculosis was present, was controversial and commercially challenging. Papworth, however, was not designed primarily as a colony that sought, in principle, to remove infectious people from the general community, although that was a suggestion by some authorities at the time. Nor was it only to provide a favourable environment to prevent the recurrence of the disease after it had been arrested. It was, as well, a resurgence of a Utopian dream (the establishment of Utopian communities featured in Volume 1). This time it was a settlement based on work therapy firmly 'rooted in the cult of domesticity' and family 'privacy', within a 'green' environment combining the advantages of urban and rural life.[13]

The occupations available at Papworth were wide-ranging, but work was largely of a manual trades nature from joinery to cabinet making, printing to sign writing, tailoring to boot-making, and leather bag to jewellery making, as well as outdoor jobs such as horticulture and poultry-keeping. The Settlement also provided many sporting and social opportunities, so that residents could engage in swimming, tennis, golf, cricket, or amateur dramatics, or those provided by the Womens' Institute, church or chapel, Boy Scouts, or Horticultural Society, or attend the cinema, or pub.[14 15] Surprisingly, Papworth proved a commercial success, which was what Varrier-Jones had hoped for mainly to better the psychological well-being of his patients but also for obvious economic reasons.[16] Watson suggested that 'as a voluntary training scheme it presents a practical basis far in advance of hospital workshops.'[17]

Other occupation-based facilities were opened for similar purposes. Preston Hall, in Kent, opened in 1919 for 300 tubercular ex-servicemen, offering outdoor work, such as gardening, poultry keeping, green keeping, agriculture, small holding work and boat-building on 98 acres of gardens and 287 acres of woodland. Some of the patients were involved in laying golf courses and bowling greens, which were later available as social amenities. The social program extended to evening entertainment such as organised lectures, billiards, whist drives, theatre and music. Advertisements for staff also had an occupational flavour; that for the Assistant Medical Officer required the playing of association football as a qualification, and ex-RAMC orderlies who had also been bandsmen were employed to provide additional musical options for staff and patients. Its first years do not appear to have been an unqualified success. Critics reported Preston Hall as a deplorable waste of money and time, and questioned the need, for example, for the 25 gardeners who obviously objected to patients working with them. The British Legion took over Preston Hall in 1925 and called upon Varrier-Jones to reorganise it in a way similar to Papworth.[18]

Of other treatment and training colonies, one, at Wrenbury Hall in Cheshire, for ex-servicemen who were 'intellectually and temperamentally capable of learning a new mode of living,' admitted them early after diagnosis of tuberculosis.[19] At first agricultural work was the focus, but this later changed to woodwork.[20]

Many sanatoria, too, adopted the 'work for therapy' principle:

> In 1920, Newman outlined the 'true sanatorium principle', in which he believed exercise, suitably alternating with rest, played an important part. In his opinion, games were an inappropriate form of exercise as they could cause strenuous exertion and competition leading to undue stress. Walking exercise alone was apt to be either too monotonous or incapable of sufficient gradation under the close supervision of the resident officer, and tended to the formation of 'loafing' habits. He believed that the provision of training at every sanatorium was essential, for without occupation of the mind and body there would be physical and moral deterioration.[21]

For women this usually meant graduated domestic work and, in this vein, at the North Wales Sanatorium for Women, and later at the Cheshire Joint Sanatorium, a widely commended scheme was established. Cottages antipathetic for those with tuberculosis were set up with the women patients living in them being given a weekly sum of money to learn to make the necessary changes and to keep house in a way which would ameliorate the disease.

Sometimes, rather than an optimal balance of activity and rest, the work aspect appears to have been taken too far, such as in the West Wales Sanatorium for women and children. There, apart from heavy physical house keeping chores, patients carted manure and sawed trees—on occasion, it was reported, 'on their knees in the snow'. An investigation followed one death which it was claimed resulted from the hard physical labour. Following this, and in explanation of the treatment regimes in sanatoria, it was reported in the *Western Mail* that:

> The life of a patient in a sanatorium is controlled as to diet and movements…the object of the discipline is to benefit his health and aid his recovery…It is now agreed that a system of graduated walking and some form of manual work has proved of great benefit to tuberculous patients who are free from fever…Manual work in the snow, which would naturally raise the heat of the body, can be very pleasant.[22]

Work therapy which encapsulated the notions of rest and activity continued well into the late 1930s and, as occupational therapy began to be established as a separate profession, those medical officers who developed such regimes regarded their programs as fitting within its boundaries. McDougall, who administered Preston Hall, after it was taken over:

> ...equated the knowledge required by physicians practising occupational therapy with that required for surgical operations: Occupational therapy is a form of treatment, it is not a business...What is required...is a thorough grasp of the principles underlying occupational therapy, and in this respect occupational therapy differs in no way from any other form of treatment for tuberculosis or any other disease.[23]

However, despite acceptance that what was offered as work therapy with tuberculosis patients was in the spirit and philosophy of occupational therapy, 'instructors were (usually chosen) from among patients or ex-patients.' This was because experts such as Varrier-Jones,[24] along with the Ministry of Health,[25] took the stance that 'being a patient or an ex-patient was deemed to be the best qualification for the job.' In that period, though, there were too few occupational therapists, and 'occupational therapy as a separate paramedical profession (which was being instituted in the inter-war period) had not yet made an impression on sanatoria.'[26]

Some doctors, based principally in America, challenged the rationale behind work therapy for tuberculosis. They remained firmly convinced of the efficacy of rest rather than activity alternating with rest. This view gained ground in the United Kingdom during the 1930s and 1940s as surgery became a treatment of choice for some specialists. Bryder argues that the change from occupational treatment, based on an holistic approach to medicine, to surgical intervention 'can be seen as an attempt to bring tuberculosis treatment more into line with the orthodox medical treatment of the twentieth century.'[27] This 'had more to do with professional interests and economic and social pressures than with any inherent superiority of surgery over conservative treatment.'[28] Work therapy was disadvantaged; it was so different from other more obviously medical interventions that it did not enhance the status of doctors involved in it. Similarly, in the present day occupational therapists are disadvantaged by the same sort of perceptions within medical ranks and the general public. To overcome such misconceptions and disadvantage McDougall, the Medical Administrator of Preston Hall after it was taken over by the British Legion, asserted that:

> ...it seems clear that any successful village settlement must always insist that medical principles shall take precedence over every other factor in the life of the community. I should prefer to go even further and say that the work which is taking place from day to day in any of the departments of a village settlement is a specialised form of treatment.[29]

It will be clear to readers of this history that a situation similar to that experienced by the medical superintendents of lunatic asylums who practised moral treatment was being re-enacted with medical superintendents of tuberculosis institutions such as McDougall. 'If cures could be effected by non-medical means, then the administrators were reduced to mere custodians of the patients and their status and very existence were threatened.'[30]

Despite such negative influences, occupation continued to be used in many tuberculosis institutions as an essential background to other forms of treatment, and as an important component of post-sanatorium advice. There was general agreement that return to a way of life which had allowed the disease to flourish would be counter productive. Advice ranged from complete change by, for example, emigration to Australia or New Zealand where a more outdoor lifestyle in a warmer clime was possible, to re-housing schemes and special workshops. The latter allowed ongoing contact and supervision that was reinforced by domiciliary and after-care schemes.

# Occupational renaissance in mental health

It was in the field of psychiatry that the first doctor in the United Kingdom adopted, whole-heartedly, the modern concept of occupational therapy as a separate discipline. Dr David Henderson established 'Occupational Therapy,' by that name, at Gartnavel Hospital, Glasgow, in 1919. It was noted in an earlier chapter how he had worked in the United States with Adolf Meyer, who he recognised as the instigator of occupational therapy in America. Henderson described occupational therapy as 'the most enduring of our remedial aids.'[31] His story must now be told.

## Sir David Henderson

David Henderson was born in 1885, attended Dumfries Academy, and was a medical graduate of Edinburgh University in 1913. He travelled widely following his graduation seeking the most eminent psychiatrists as his post-graduate teachers. He spent several months in Munich working with Emil Kraeplin who is renowned for his classification of the psychoses, and also had contact with the work of Alois Alzheimer. Referring to his time in America with Meyer, in an address at the 25th anniversary of the Scottish Association of Occupational Therapists, he described his introduction to the field:

> My first experience of occupational therapy as a remedial help on a properly organised basis takes me back to 1908 at the Manhattan State Hospital, Ward's Island, New York. A small part of that hospital constituted the New York Psychiatric Clinic of which Adolf Meyer was director. Dr Meyer was tremendously interested in 'the creation of an orderly rhythm in the hospital atmosphere' and constantly stressed the importance of creating balance between work and play, rest and sleep. With the assistance of Mrs Meyer he strove to establish a blending of work with pleasure so as to instill a spirit of achievement. This form of treatment caught on, and it was not long before every mental hospital organisation began to develop its own occupational department. In this instance I would mention particularly the pioneer work of Dr W R Dunton Jr, at the Shepherd and Enoch Pratt Hospital, Baltimore.[32]

He went on to tell his audience how:

> Miss Beau a nurse on the staff of the St Lawrence State Hospital, Ogdensburg, N.Y., was deputed to attend a course of instructions for Nurses and Attendants in hospitals for the insane which was organised by the Chicago School of Civics and Philanthropy. That, I believe, was the first attempt to develop an organised occupational therapy course as a means of promoting cure in the treatment of mental illness. Miss Julia Lathrop—assisted

*by Miss Helen Berling and Professor Graham Taylor—was the moving spirit. The value of handicrafts, folk dances, competitive games, and rhythmic exercises was demonstrated: the importance and comprehensive nature of the course was made evident by lectures on: 'Value of Occupations in improving the Minds of the Insane', by Professor James Angell, University of Chicago; 'The Value of Occupations from Physician's Standpoint' by Dr Frank Billings, President Illinois State Board of Charities; 'Occupations as a Means of Directing Energy' by Edwin F. Worst, Head of Industrial Arts, Chicago Normal School. These are only a few examples of the topics discussed. Miss Beau was also greatly impressed by a visit to a mental hospital at Anne, Illinois, where she saw 'a class of calisthenics consisting of 360 men who, with few exceptions went through the exercises with spirit...an effort was made in the male department to employ as many patients as possible...each patient was given a task adapted to his intelligence and taste'. The New York State Hospital medical superintendents received Miss Beau's report with acclamation and in 1910 Dr Mabon of the Manhattan State Hospital, Ward's Island, arranged that Miss Wright, one of the senior nurses should also attend the Chicago course; on her return a Department of Occupational Therapy was established at the Manhattan State Hospital.*[33]

Henderson was, apparently, a highly visible force during the early days of occupational therapy in America. Slagle named him as one amongst a small group of notable others who 'sowed the seeds'. She said at the fifth Annual Meeting of the National Society for the Promotion of Occupational Therapy in the US that:

*Thirty years ago the seed of occupational therapy for mental patients was sown by a group that became known throughout the length and breadth of the land as one of the greatest humanitarian forces at work on the social, charitable, custodial, correctional and dependent problems of the time. They scarcely need to be named to this audience: Dr Adolf Meyer, Julia Lathrop, Jane Addams and Dr Henderson. To their vision and knowledge of the need we may trace the first training class in occupations for mental patients given at the Chicago School of Civics and Philanthropy, under state funds, with an idea of interesting nurses and attendants in something more than custodial care and routine duties.*[34]

That Henderson was considerably influenced by Meyer's interest in occupational therapy is evident. He was also inspired by his psychobiological model which stressed that each individual should be treated as a 'whole' which is similar, in many respects, to today's biopsychosocial model. At Johns Hopkins Hospital Henderson had 'particularly interested himself in the establishment of workshops and the occupational training of patients.'[35] In Britain he became a major exponent of its development, even before his appointment as Physician-Superintendent of Gartnavel Psychiatric Hospital in 1921. This followed a few years of secondment as an army psychiatrist in World War 1, and an important series of papers on 'Psychological Disorders of War.'[36]

In 1919, he had introduced occupational therapy into patient treatment at Gartnavel Hospital. With the co-operation of the Matron, Miss Darney, basketry, raffia work, rug-making and leatherwork were introduced to the 'more intelligent patients' and 'those who were convalescing.' Henderson explained the limitation as being because it wasn't possible 'to have more than one class per day.'[37]

**Figure 2.4.1    Professor Sir David Henderson**[38]
*(Unable to trace copyright)*

At Gartnavel, 'one of (his) first and most enduring developments was the creation of the occupational therapy department with the appointment in 1922 of the Occupational Therapist, Miss Dorothea Robertson.'[39] Henderson, in the Report of the Physician Superintendent for the year 1922, described this event:

> I am glad to report that during the year the Directors agreed to the appointment of an Instructor in Occupational Therapy. This is the first time, so far as I know, that such a teacher has been appointed to a similar position in a hospital of this kind in Scotland. For many years occupational work has been recognised as a great asset in the treatment of mental patients, but it has lacked organisation. It has been a question largely of mechanical outdoor work for the men and needlework of various kinds for the women. These things are of great importance, and much good has accrued from them, but a great deal more is needed, and it should not simply be a question of providing work for those who are willing to do it, but those others who are dull, uninterested, and apathetic should be stimulated to take up definite interests. Nothing, we are told succeeds like success, and although what is accomplished may not be of material importance, yet good habits will be substituted for bad ones, the tone of the institution will be improved, and the results obtained will be reflected in the mental outlook of the patients, and in the atmosphere of the institution.[40]

In his report of the following year, Henderson reminded his readers of the successful and wide ranging occupational regimes in Asylums in the previous century, which had been allowed to diminish and in many cases to disappear so that occupational therapy was regarded as a new form of treatment. In the same report, Henderson went on to discuss the problems of patient populations largely drawn from professional and business classes, and the different occupational programs required for those rather than for people within 'rate-aided institutions.' He said 'they are not adapted for strenuous outdoor work,' and that called for occupations that were 'not only useful, but of a more or less aesthetic kind.' He continued:

> ...it is more a question of realising that it is not work as work which is important, but the fact that the work is of such a nature as to be thoroughly engrossing and satisfying,

*and only difficult enough to meet an individual's requirements. By the time patients come to a mental hospital they are usually in such an enfeebled condition of mind and body that in one way or another they feel that they have failed, that they have not been able...to stay the course, and in consequence it is necessary to restore their self-confidence and self-esteem. This cannot be done by prescribing a bottle, or even by therapeutic talks, unless such are backed up by getting the patient to prove for himself that he is still capable of doing something...This, then, is what is meant by occupational therapy. It is really a practical way of promoting the patient to a better mental attitude and to the idea that life even yet may have something in store. In a way, I suppose, I may say it is not so much occupational therapy that one instills, but rather a philosophy of occupation.*[41]

In 1924 he lectured on occupational therapy to the Royal Medico-Psychological Association in Glasgow. This, one of many lectures he gave on the subject to different audiences, was particularly important because Dr Elizabeth Casson, who went on to establish the first occupational therapy school in Britain, was in the audience.[42] The following year a new occupational therapy pavilion was built at Gartnavel, shown in Figure 2.4.2. 'This innovation was to prove a rapid success, lauded by both patients and Directors, the service being gradually expanded over the ensuing years.'[43]

**Figure 2.4.2:** **The exterior of the new occupational therapy pavilion built at Gartnavel in 1925**

*(From the Gartnavel Hospital Annual Report, 1928. Unable to trace copyright source.)*

Ahead of his time, Henderson advocated the development of psychiatric clinics in general hospitals such as there were in America and Germany. 'Such a department' he said, should 'be equipped with laboratories, and with all remedial facilities in the way of occupation department, hydrotherapeutic department, gymnasium.'[44] In addition to those ideas in his annual reports he anticipated modern ideas of practice with regard to the 'future possibilities' of 'community services' and 'home treatment'. Not surprisingly, the beliefs he held about occupational therapy are enjoying a resurgence at the present time. They embraced notions such as:

- **Occupational balance.** He said, 'the lives of people...should not be too lop-sided. There should be work and play, rest and sleep, and proper employment of leisure depending on personal likes and dislikes';
- **Meaningful occupation.** He advocated that it was, 'essential to create a sense of success and worthwhileness';
- **People are occupational beings even in sickness.** He believed that, 'interest, and activities of a vocational, recreational, and educational nature' not only effect recovery but 'add something to life itself';
- **Development of potential.** Therapeutic occupation, he reasoned, 'should lead to a resumption of family and community life at a more stable and understanding level, so that the future will not be drudgery, but an opportunity to make life, through work, more efficient and happier than previously';
- **Holism.** He recognised that, 'there can be no division of body and mind...the one reacts on the other';
- **Health promotion and illness prevention.** Occupation, he argued, 'will lead to the preservation of health but will also prevent illness. Life and work are indivisible just as mind and body are.'[45]

With Henderson's adoption of the term 'Occupational Therapy' for the occupation programs he developed, and his wide dissemination of its value, occupational therapy became a topic worthy of discussion in the *Lancet* and other prestigious medical journals. The letters that ensued as a result of such reports provide an indication of the type of interest at the time. One *Lancet* report gave rise to the following correspondence which is to be found in the Gartnavel archives.[46] (Where a question mark is inserted in brackets it indicates the handwritten text was impossible to decipher.)

*Dear Sir,*

*I am writing to you for a little information which, if you will be kind enough to give me will be appreciated.*

*I should say, however, that I am a physician from America doing some research work at Oxford University along the lines of Occupational therapy in certain forms of insanity. I notice in the last issue of the Lancet, that you have introduced this form of therapy in your institution and I thought that perhaps you can give me the information I crave. What I desire to know is, whether this form of treatment is used in this Country, and if so, just where I may go or write, to find out something about it in more detail than a general news item affords.*

*I may say that we use it very extensively in America and that I have had occasion to apply it freely, but before closing my paper on the subject I should like to know just what is being done over here on the subject.*

*I thank you kindly for any information it may be your pleasure to give me.*

*Very truly yours,*

*Chas. E. McPeek BSc. MD*

Henderson replied to McPeek's letter thus:

*July 18th, 1923*

*Dear Sir,*

*I beg to acknowledge receipt of your letter, and was very interested to know that you were doing research work at Oxford University, along the lines of Occupational therapy. I did not know that Oxford University offered any work along these lines, and I am interested to hear about it. I also did not know that the 'Lancet' had taken any notice of the introduction of occupational therapy into this hospital. So far as I know, this is the only hospital in the British Isles where any attempt has been made to introduce occupational therapy in an organised way, and certainly this is the first hospital in which, or to which, a teacher of occupational work has been appointed. Although this is so, it is only right to point out that the value of occupation has been recognised, but at the same time, the work prescribed has been in the nature of gardening or other manual labour, without any particular attempt being made to interest the patients in any other form of activity. In this hospital we have approximately five hundred patients, all of the private class, and in consequence we have constantly been faced with the position that a great many of our patients would not do outside work of any kind, and therefore it became necessary to attempt to organise some form of indoor work. At the present time we have a lady in charge of the department, and helping her there is one male instructor. In addition we attempt to give our nurses a certain amount of training, and later, when our occupational building is completed, we will be able to develop things more. At the present time, however, and since the beginning of this work less than a year ago, we have already over one hundred patients occupied in this form of work, and I have no hesitation whatsoever in saying that in many cases it is of very great benefit. Some time ago, Dr Dunton, who you personally know, asked me to contribute something to the Archives of Occupational Therapy on this topic of occupational work, but, so far, I have not had time to do so.*

*If there is any further information which I can give you, I will be glad to do so.*

*I am,*

*Yours faithfully,*

*(sgd) D.K.Henderson.*

*P.S.*

*The occupational work being done consists of basket work, raffia work, the caneing of chairs, the weaving of rugs, by hand with a needle, and by means of looms. We have also done various other things, such as china painting, metal work, art needlework, and so on. We have four different classes, and a special attempt is being made to re-educate and employ those who have never done anything, but have been idle in the wards.*

McPeek replied:

*My Dear Dr Henderson,*

*I thank you kindly for your prompt and detailed reply to my inquiry of a few days since, and I assure you that I am in full sympathy with your starting occupational work in your institution.*

*To answer your question; I would respectfully advise that Oxford University does not give any course in this (?). I am doing research work for my D.Sc. and I chose this subject ('Early Application of Occupational Therapy in Dementia Praecox') (...?) I have been engaged for nearly two years.*

    *I have had some four years experience in this subject in America, where we have it in full working system in some twenty five States—in the several hospitals for the insane in that many states and in a great many private institutions. (After having prescribed this work for these four years in my State Hospital work, I have gathered together a mass of evidence, material, cases to substantiate all that is claimed for the new science. In America it has been placed on a scientific, therapeutic basis, and the States (...?) is at this time spending more on statistics to establish the efficacy and practical application of this comparatively new treatment.*

    *I should be glad to run up to Glasgow and tell you and your staff anything I know about it, that you might care to know.*

    *I say this assuming that, like in my own country, not a great deal of material is to be had, and there is practically no literature on the subject, as it has too recently been argued? (I hope to visit a number of institutions in England, for ar...? I have introductions from M...? Dickinson, of the Board of Control in Lunacy.)*

    *I am very glad, indeed, to have had this enlightenment from you.*

*Faithfully yours. etc.*

Henderson's response was welcoming.

A report in *The Lancet*, dated March 22, 1924, read:

    *In recent years, the revival of occupational therapy as an aid to the treatment of early mental disorder has attracted a good deal of attention; and a considerable part of Dr Henderson's report is devoted to this aspect of institutional life. In such a hospital as the Glasgow Royal Mental Hospital the majority of patients are drawn from the professional and business classes. From both a physical and psychical point of view routine work is unsuitable for these patients. What is required is a task, suitably interesting and aesthetic for people of culture, and, moreover, planned that it is capable of fulfilment by the particular patient. The confidence engendered and restored by a course of such occupational therapy is often of striking service in enabling the patient to make the mental readjustment necessary for his cure. Bearing this in mind, the Glasgow Royal Mental Hospital is to be congratulated on being 'the first mental hospital in the British Isles to appoint a full-time occupational teacher, and to provide a separate occupational pavilion for the development of this type of therapy.' Dr Henderson concludes by making an appeal for a 'well-educated, intelligent, refined type of girl' to take up mental nursing, which, as he points out, is a far more specialised calling than is generally supposed.*[47]

The fact that no training facilities in occupational therapy per se were yet available in Britain is the reason Henderson supposed that entry into this type of work would be through 'Mental Nursing'. What is interesting is that there was also a supposition that occupational therapy would be, essentially, 'women's work' which called for a good education, intelligence and refinement. One wonders if this was influenced by Eleanor Clarke Slagle and others he had worked with in America, and why it was the women rather than the men he had met that made him believe they were most suited to it.

That *Lancet* report engendered the following response that queried Henderson's claim of being first, and suggests that similar action was taking place elsewhere:

*Telephone No. 15.*
*Kent County Mental Hospital*
*Maidstone April 1st 1924.*
*Dear Sir,*

    *Would you be good enough to let me have a copy of the annual report of your*
*hospital. I was much interested in the account of the Lancet (22/3/24) especially in the*
*report on Occupational Therapy—from this report I note that yours is the first hospital*
*in the British Isles to appoint a full time occupational teacher—we were under the*
*impression here that (we were the first when I?) took up my duties here as Occupational*
*Officer in October (date?) last year. Then I appointed some (assistant?) after three years*
*similar work under the Minister of Pensions at their (Name?) Hospital at Epsom (?) —*
*I am naturally very interested in this branch of mental work and therefore like to hear*
*what other Mental Hospitals are doing with regard to occupation. Do you have any*
*system of reward?*

*Yours very Truly*
*Charles F. de Salis Lt Colonel*

Henderson replied immediately in a manner that tells of justifiable pride in getting
occupational therapy off the ground in Britain:

*3rd April 1924.*
*Dear Sir,*

    *I am in receipt of your letter, which has interested me very much. I shall send a copy*
*of my Annual Report as soon as I receive it from the printers. This should be in the*
*course of a week or two. Before I made the statement that this was the first hospital in*
*the British Isles to appoint a full-time occupational teacher, I had made a fairly*
*comprehensive inquiry, and was unable to find any other mental hospital which had an*
*occupational teacher at all. Miss Robertson was appointed to this hospital in December*
*1922, so that I think we can still claim the credit of being first in the field. I should be*
*interested in knowing from you whether in addition to your own hospital there is any*
*other hospital in England with an organised occupational department. In the annual*
*report which will shortly be published, Miss Robertson has also made a report of the*
*types of work we are employing. I, of course, believe that this type of therapy can be*
*utilised to a very much greater extent than heretofore, and perhaps at a later date those*
*of us who are specially interested in this matter might get together and have a*
*discussion.*

    *I have never instituted any system of reward. I, of course, know that there has*
*always been a great deal of discussion in regard to whether inducements should be held*
*out, but I, personally, have always been opposed to it, owing to the fact that I have felt*
*that such a system did not appeal in the correct way.*

    *I shall be glad to hear further from you, and will give you any details which you*
*might like to ask about.*

*Yours faithfully,*
*(sigd). D.K. Henderson.*

Whether Lt Colonel de Salis replied to Henderson's response is not known, but he was
involved some years later in the establishment of the Association of Occupational
Therapists (AOT). His potential contribution was recognised when he was elected as a

member of the original Council of AOT. Unfortunately, he died shortly after it was formed.

Henderson's 1924 report on occupational therapy was also highlighted in the *British Medical Journal* in a piece titled 'Occupational Therapy in Mental Disorder,' which referred to earlier reports on the topic by his whole team:

> *In his annual report for 1924 Dr. D.K. Henderson, the physician-superintendent of the Glasgow Royal Asylum…draws attention, as in previous years, to the importance of the development of organized occupational therapeutic work. The Glasgow Royal Asylum now has two pavilions under skilled instructors, whose sole interest it is to occupy groups of patients. It is found that the value of this work is reflected in the general atmosphere of the hospital—the wards have been quieter and the patients better conducted. A series of papers by Dr Henderson, Dr A. G. W. Thomson, senior assistant physician of the hospital, Miss Brodie, lady superintendent, and Miss D. Robertson, instructress in the occupational department respectively, dealing with various aspects of this important work was published in the Journal of Mental Science last January. There can be no doubt that occupational therapy is one of the most important means of interesting the chronic patients in external affairs and in preventing them from sinking into regressive fantasies and general dilapidation. The ultimate aim of occupational therapy is not merely to interest the patients in modes of activity which are of no real value; it is to start them on work in the schoolroom, as it were, with the idea that they may in time gain a pleasure in useful work and become serviceable social units in the asylum community. In many cases, of course, to arouse interest in work is the first stimulus towards recovery.*[48]

In his 1927 *Textbook of Psychiatry*, co-authored with R.D. Gillespie, Henderson devoted a chapter to occupational therapy. In it he detailed the therapeutic gains to be achieved and provided examples of patients at Gartnavel. In again recognising that occupation, as such, had been an aspect of asylum life since its inception, he quoted a passage from the 1820 Annual Report of the Glasgow Asylum to this effect, emphasising both continuity and change at Gartnavel, but went on to state:

> *All this was excellent, but did not go far enough. Indirectly no doubt it led to betterment or recovery, but the tendency was to consider such work from the institutional and economic viewpoint rather than from the individual and curative…Such work was often 'mere drudgery' and 'sometimes must have antagonised rather than helped the patient.*[49]

In 1932 Henderson initiated the establishment of the Scottish Association of Occupational Therapy, inviting the small numbers of people working in the field to attend a meeting at Gartnavel to explore the possibilities. Margaret Fulton recalls that he 'saw to it that we had the machinery to establish, support and develop this advancing profession.'[50] In that year he also took up the appointment of Professor of Psychiatry at Edinburgh University and Medical-Superintendent of the Royal Edinburgh Mental Hospital where he worked for close to quarter of a century until 1954. There, too, Henderson established occupational therapy and out-patient services.[51] After World War II, during which Henderson served on the Government Committee on Nervous and Mental Disorders, he assisted the Scottish occupational therapists to reconstitute their Association, taking over as Inaugural President when Sir John Fraser, principle of Edinburgh University, died unexpectedly.[52]

It is important to consider not only Henderson's role in the development of occupational therapy, but also what occurred at the 'coal face.' To that end, correspondence and reports are now included which tell the story of the early instructors (therapists) and therapy at Gartnavel. It must be remembered that therapy 'instructors' did not have formal 'therapy' qualifications, just as many of the American pioneers did not, because no training was yet available in the country.

## 'Occupational instructors' of the 1920s

The first person to be given a full time post as occupational instructor at Glasgow Royal Mental Hospital was Dorothea Robertson. She applied for the position in 1922 when she was 30 years old, having been educated at Elgin Academy where, as well as being Dux of the School, she attained both the Leaving Certificate and the teacher's training required by the Scottish Education Department. At Newnham College, Cambridge, she sat the Modern Languages Tripos, and was found to be 'practical', 'resourceful', 'enthusiastic', 'level-headed' and a 'harmonious member of the community'. Her employment application told of a deep interest in 'mental work' which she was convinced was her 'real vocation.' In accepting the position she planned to undertake additional training to assist with handcraft skills. She sought advice from a teacher of 'Educational Handwork' at the Provincial Training College, presumably in Glasgow, who was said to have taught a 'great many of the disabled soldiers.'[53]

In 1923, Robertson wrote her first report, which is given below in full:

GENTLEMEN,

The Occupational Department was opened on March 1st, 1923, with one instructor. Mr Murray was appointed as Assistant in May 1923.

The work of the Department is done under the immediate supervision of the Medical Staff; a notice being sent, of each patient, with the Medical Officer's recommendation as to the work most suitable.

The average daily attendance for the first three months was 35. This number has steadily increased, until at the present time the average attendance is 98.

Each class is about 1 1/2 hours' duration, but a good many 'parole' patients attend regularly both morning and afternoon. These latter are encouraged as far as possible to help the others.

The Department is still experimenting with the most suitable forms of work, and at present the following are being taught: – Simple woodwork, basketry, cane chair making, raffia and pine needle work, china painting, metal work, rugmaking, embroidery, and decorative colour craft work.

The main crafts amongst men are woodwork, cane chair making, and rugmaking. A fret-machine has been recently added to the equipment, to provide facilities for toymaking, as it is hoped this craft, though extremely simple in itself, will provide greater scope for interest and originality. Rugmaking has been found to be very successful with a certain type of patient, and some very beautiful rugs have been produced. Several wireless crystal sets have also been made.

The women are occupied with raffia and pine needle work, embroidery, and glass and china painting. The latter craft has been specially successful, and has been found to appeal to many patients, both men and women, who could not be persuaded to take an *interest in anything else. One lady remarked, 'The week I learned china painting has been the happiest I've spent since I have been in hospital.'*

*The hand loom has now been set up, the cloth being woven being a piece of striped shirting, which will be utilised by the Institution.*

*At the beginning the work was handicapped by the lack of space in the old class-rooms, but since the new class-rooms were opened in December, all objections on this score have been removed. The improved accommodation and brighter surroundings have been highly appreciated by the patients, who have shown a keener desire to participate in the work of the class.*

*On the invitation of the Glasgow Council of Social Organisations, an exhibition of handicrafts was given at a Conference held at Row in October 1923. A letter was received later from the Secretary of the Conference Committee expressing their pleasure at the varied and artistic nature of the exhibit.*

*A sale of the work produced by the Department was held on December 1st, 1923, at which the patients displayed great interest, several of the ladies acting as Saleswomen.*

*Yours Faithfully,*
DOROTHEA ROBERTSON[54]

A year later Robertson, in her report, concerned about the saleability of work, explained:

*While the therapeutic value of the work is much more important than the commercial value, and is, in fact, the chief end and aim of an occupational department, I feel that such a department ought to be sufficiently self-supporting to defray the cost of raw materials. For that reason it is necessary to consider the taste of our buying public, and it is better, other things, of course, being equal, to make articles which will sell readily, and which may be required by the hospital, rather than those for which there is little demand.[55]*

In that 1924 report Robertson refers briefly to the meeting of the Medico-Psychological Association at which papers about occupational therapy were read by Robertson and the Matron, as well as by medical staff. It can be supposed that it was at this meeting that Casson first heard Henderson speak. Other practical issues mentioned in the report included the pleasures and advantages of holding classes outside during the summer and the building of a second occupational pavilion so that, after that time, males and females were segregated. Finally Robertson alluded to her lack of experience, and noted somewhat wistfully that:

*...it is not possible to gauge its [interest in particular occupations] depth or extent. It would be interesting and helpful in dealing with new patients to know why a certain kind of work appeals to a particular patient, but one would need to have a much larger experience, spread over a much longer time, to be able to arrive at any such conclusions.[56]*

That was Robertson's last report as she resigned in September 1925, her place being taken by Annie Melrose who answered a newspaper advertisement for 'a lady to teach art and craft and to organise an occupational department' at Gartnavel. She, too, was 30 years of age when she applied for the post. Melrose had experienced, what she described as a 'thorough scholastic education,' and had attended the Edinburgh College of Art and Crafts as a full-time day and evening student for six years between 1914 and 1921. Along with that course she took other training in relation to individual and class instruction including

'Health and Hygiene' and 'Psychology'. She had, since that training, had full charge of the Art and Needlework department in two evening schools and was a secretary for an organisation responsible for entertainments for wounded soldiers. She took up her appointment on 26 October 1925 at an annual salary of £200, resident. This meant that she was expected to live at the Asylum during the week, but could, if she wished, spend 'every week-end at home.' She was told that 'the work can be arranged to suit yourself for the most part, but the regular hours will be from 9.30 a.m. until 4.30 or five o'clock.'[57] Henderson, who later was to describe her as 'the founding mother of occupational therapy' at Gartnavel, obviously found her and her work to be of great value. [58]

In her first report Melrose explained how the central hall of the pavilion was no longer used solely for the display of finished work, but in great part as an art and craft studio. She described a 'normal atmosphere...where the working conditions are almost those of any ordinary workshop or studio.' She noted that this change had enabled patients, who had been previously unable to settle to occupations in smaller classrooms, to work quietly and with concentration.[59]

Melrose's next report was extensive when compared with the brief reports of the previous three years. Some sections demonstrate considerable depth of critical analyis of the therapeutic process and a sense of joy, which must have been infectious in promoting a happy and productive environment. She described a 'gradually developed scheme' in which patients were classified according to 'mental condition and prescribed occupation,' and which enabled direct observation and encouragement where necessary and a freer, more stimulating environment for others. Some of the report is particularly worth recording. There is, for example, the relatively modern notion that shared participation can be more therapeutic than an approach based on the therapist as an authoritarian expert:

*...our nurses and attendants learn the different crafts, working as fellow-workers beside the patients. This contributes to an atmosphere less suggestive of the supervision of hospital life, and by supplying common interests, helps to promote a more friendly feeling between patients and staff.[60]*

Melrose described a process whereby the interests and potentialities of patients drove the therapy:

*It is interesting to note the particular crafts that appeal to certain patients, and how much their choice may be influenced by former associations, delusions and ambitions...A schoolmaster, who, using his pen, prints our calendars and posters, while a clergyman, determined to improve our minds, resorts to texts printed in bold lettering. A farmer made a rug—the wool appealed to him. Delusions affect the work of a University graduate, who, firmly convinced that he is an architect of great repute, and that he has various and involved connections with the peerage, does a type of illuminated architectural designs and coats of arms, all of the heraldic order...they have supplied a definite object for his daily walks in the grounds which hitherto have been meaningless. He has become quite sociable, and sings and plays to us, and can make himself quite charming.[61]*

Despite the apparent freedom of choice, it is obvious that Melrose also considered the therapeutic effect of the occupations on patients:

*The crafts have, in many cases, to be simplified and adapted to suit each case, else the results could not be gratifying or encouraging for the patients whose ambitions often exceed their capabilities.*

*One must watch carefully with rug-making, as this occupation, even when worked from an intricate chart tends to become mechanical...we had a young boy patient, dreamy and introspective... The occupation did not help him much because his mind was free to indulge in and to create morbid thoughts and fancies.*[62]

Similarly, 'a girl patient of the same age' when engaged in embroidery and raffia work 'continued to be moody and asocial, and so intensely depressed that even her colour schemes were affected, and were all of the sombre black, purple, brown and grey tones.' When introduced to batik work she became ' brighter, less asocial and quite talkative, helping with other patients and often working all day with us until her discharge.'[63]

Quite obviously Melrose was a thoughtful and erudite ambassador for the emerging profession; she was chosen, or volunteered, to write about occupational therapy as part of a trade leaflet for Dryad Handicrafts who were to play such a large role in the formative years. In that leaflet *Craft Work—A Medicine* Melrose briefly explained the purpose and value of occupational therapy for physical and mental invalids. Extracts provide an outline of her ideas:

*The necessity may arise by the home fireside, in the sickroom, or the nursing home, and the timely introduction of occupational treatment may do much to contribute to the peace and beauty of the home, give pleasure to the worker and may even ward off a complete nervous breakdown. For the mind that would remain in good health, occupation is essential and craftwork is one of the most easily accessible, enjoyable, satisfying and mentally stimulating hobbies...*

*Unless given an outlet and means of being turned into normal fatigue, unused energy soon corrodes, thereby causing mental and physical friction...*

*For those wavering between unreality and reason, whenever possible keep to the primitive crafts, weaving, basketry, pottery and metal work, by which man has supplied his needs and beautified his abode throughout the ages; these crafts can be adapted to suit special mental and physical handicaps.*[64]

Melrose went on to work as an occupational therapist at the Hartwood Mental Hospital in Lanarkshire. While there she published a description of her work in a 1929 edition of *Hospital Social Service*. She described her part of an extensive occupational therapy program within the hospital. The latter she saw as so outstanding and extensive that no one paper could:

*...do justice to the wonderful scheme that is the order of the work and play in this institution, with its extensive interests, its social life, made up of concerts, series of ward parties, musical 'at homes,' picnics, games, sports, its links and interests with the outside world, societies and dramatic clubs, its after care, social and clinic work...*

*Horticulture and agriculture proved of such therapeutic value, physically and mentally, that, solely to give farther scope for the development of these occupations— additional lands were acquired and Hartwood has over one acre to offer each patient.*[65]

Those occupations were used in preparation for discharge and, for some, as a means of future livelihood.

Patients chose their own occupations, subject to the medical officer's approval, and even when they were of a domestic or service nature 'the staff receives every encouragement, and reasonable means, to give each patient his or her own niche, and a real interest in life.' On the downside of what she described so warmly:

> ...with a population of nearly thirteen hundred patients made up of ex-service men, professional, business and working men and women, girls and youths, it is, alas, inevitable, that even this great sea of wholesome work and interest cannot sweep all before it. For very many diverse reasons, there are patients left—sometimes for months and years—quite unmoved by its tide.
>
> For such patients the Occupational Therapy department was inaugurated.[66]
>
> Another type of patient makes up the nucleus of steady workers...These patients were social failures in the outside world... Their energy having been misdirected, many of them bring records of having caused ward disturbances, of having been 'difficult', destructive, or homicidal.[67]

It seems that those who were considered 'too hard' for the rest of the program were assigned to occupational therapy. Melrose, undaunted, described how:

> Many patients have been passive for years, they are deteriorated, dis-orientated, often mute, or again they may be noisy, excited, destructive, homicidal, and resistive, but these patients have first claim to our best energies and resources.
>
> ...And, after all, what is occupational therapy? It is merely a means of mental contact whereby the patient is gradually brought back to reality and all existent energy is held and increased, or non-existent energy is generated. An occupation—simple or complicated— is not therapeutic unless it holds all available power and reason and tends to increase it, to restore self confidence by giving the feeling that accomplishment alone can give.[68]

In 1919, the year that Henderson formally introduced 'occupational therapy' into Gartnavel, similar moves were afoot elsewhere. A head attendant was appointed as Supervisor of Men's Recreations at the Crichton Royal:

> This is the first appointment of the kind in a Scottish Mental Hospital. He accompanies the physicians and matrons on their morning ward visits at 9 a.m., supervises the carrying out of the occupational and recreational treatment prescribed for individual male patients, acts as an intermediary between the wards and the working parties, and sees that the equipment required for outdoor and indoor games and pastimes is properly provided.[69]

And in 1928, the same hospital appointed Miss J. Crawford, DA, an art teacher, as instructress and therapist at a salary of £200 per annum, plus dinner. At the Ayr District Asylum, by 1923, eighty per cent of the patients were reported to be employed. Without doubt, though, the most exciting advance was the appointment of Miss M. B. Fulton as 'occupational therapist' to the Royal Mental Hospital, Aberdeen, in 1925.

# Margaret Barr Fulton[70]
# By Catherine F. Paterson

**M**argaret Barr (Peg) Fulton, MBE (1900-1989) has a special place in the history of occupational therapy, since she was the first qualified occupational therapist in the UK. Peg, as she was known throughout her life, was employed by the Aberdeen Royal Cornhill Hospital from 1925, shortly after she qualified, until her retirement in 1963. During that time, she gained an international reputation for her department and for her part in the development of both the Scottish Association and the World Federation of Occupational Therapists.

Peg was born in Manchester on 14 February 1900, the youngest of the five children of Elizabeth Barr and Dr Andrew Boyd Fulton, both of whom were Scottish. Her father, a graduate of Glasgow University Medical School, first practised in Ayrshire before taking up a large practice in Salford. Peg recalled that with the changes wrought by World War I, even the girls of the family turned their thoughts to careers.[71] Many of the pioneer occupational therapists came from similar professional backgrounds in which the girls were educated, but only the boys were expected to follow their fathers into medicine.

After her father died in 1919, Peg accompanied her mother to the United States, and it was there that she first heard about occupational therapy and was put in contact with the Philadelphia School of Occupational Therapy.[72] The course comprised an academic year followed by six months of hospital training. Apart from a wide range of craft activities, subjects included the history and theory of occupational therapy and art, social aspects of occupational therapy, hospital organisation, psychology, anatomy, kinesiology, orthopaedics, paediatrics, psychiatry, and medical conditions such as tuberculosis.[73] She recalled that the staff were excellent and the practical work was always related to its therapeutic use.[74] Memories of the exciting blocks of practical experience in a children's hospital, a general hospital and a psychiatric hospital, remained vivid throughout her life.[75]

After working in downtown New York, Fulton returned to Great Britain, with a sheaf of testimonials including one from Thomas Kidner, then President of the American Association of Occupational Therapists. Another was a letter from her principal, Miss Florence Fulton, who lived long enough to see her young protegée become President of the World Federation of Occupational Therapists. She wrote:
> *I am very sorry to have you go...you have given of your best to the work. I shall miss you but I shall always be glad that you have been one of my girls and I know, wherever you go, that you will make good.*[76]

As occupational therapy, by that name, was unknown in the UK, Fulton spent seven months looking for a post before being put in contact with Henderson at the Glasgow Royal Asylum. Unable to employ her himself, Henderson contacted a colleague, Dr Dods Brown, medical superintendent of the Aberdeen Royal Asylum, who sent her an urgent message to accept no other post while he set out to persuade the Board to employ her.[77]

Aberdeen, one of the seven Scottish Royal Asylums, was founded in 1800. By 1925, it had about 800 beds and accepted both private and rate-aided (public) patients. As in the other asylums, occupation, particularly physical activity in the open air, was considered therapeutic. However, there seems to have been a long-standing difficulty with the occupation of the female paying patients, so Dods Brown's recommendation to appoint Fulton was adopted by the Board on the salary suggested by her (£120 a year, living out, a modest salary even by 1925 standards.)[78] On commencing employment, her impact was immediate and the Annual Report of the Aberdeen Royal Asylum for 1925 recorded that:

> Occupational Therapy was commenced here in August under Miss Fulton, who was selected as Instructress...This special occupation is of therapeutic value not only in convalescent cases, but in those whose progress towards recovery has become stationary, and in irrecoverable cases...They acquire a new outlook and gain self-confidence, and these, in many cases, are the beginning of a larger usefulness to the general community...My thanks are due to Miss Fulton, who had the responsibility of commencing the department, for the very able, painstaking, and tactful manner in which she has managed it.[79]

From the start Dods Brown was highly appreciative of his therapist, and Fulton considered herself very fortunate in her patron. Nearly thirty years later she recorded that no pioneer had ever had more ideal conditions for starting an occupational therapy department than she had found in Aberdeen, as with 'a Superintendent endowed with vision, wisdom, unflagging enthusiasm and a sense of humour, all things become possible.'[80] It is difficult to imagine the challenge and skill required to engage patients in activities, while they were in deep depression or in acute psychotic states, when there were no other effective means of controlling symptoms. In 1929, Dods Brown published an article entitled *Some Observations on the Treatment of Mental Diseases* in which he discussed, mainly, the use of malaria[81] and occupational therapy in the treatment of general paralysis, in his view the two most effective treatments available.[82] As part of his paper, Dods Brown included the following case study:

> A woman who had been in a depressed, and somewhat agitated condition, and who had maintained almost complete silence for about two years, and who, on account of delusions of unworthiness, had refused her food, and had been tube-fed for several months, was put to the occupational therapy department. From that time she began to converse, and to take an interest in things outside herself. She improved steadily and rapidly, and was discharged recovered.[83]

In May 1937, Alfred Adler, the famous Viennese psychologist, visited Aberdeen and during a tour of the hospital talked with Fulton. *The Aberdeen Press and Journal* of 28 May 1937 reported Dr Adler as saying:

> At the Royal Mental Hospital, which I visited yesterday, everything is arranged in the best possible way. I was particularly struck with the Occupational Therapy department and with the high degree of interest which is shown in psychological problems.[84]

Fulton certainly did have a very real interest in psychological problems and the personal life histories of all her patients. Unfortunately she never published or even wrote much on her guiding philosophy of occupational therapy. It is known that she set very high standards in craft work, which she considered to be a medium of treatment through which patients could be relieved of their symptoms, develop new skills and increase their self-confidence and self-esteem. Above all, however, she believed that the relationship which developed between the therapist and the patient was central to the therapeutic process. She wrote:

> *I always considered the practical work as an important medium establishing, as it does, good interpersonal relationships with the patient and, may I even suggest, more helpful in some cases than the more technically rigid approach of the doctors, good as they are.*[85]

However, she underestimated the importance of her relationships with the patients as is evident from this moving tribute from an unknown former student, who was recalling her introduction to the hospital during the Annual Sport's Day:

> *...we followed Miss Fulton as she walked up the long rows of spectator patients. It was then that the remarkable happened. As she paused to speak, first to one and then to another, these apathetic masks were transformed. Smiles appeared; further up the line one woman nudged her neighbour. The nudging spread like an incoming wave and people leaned forward, beaming as Miss Fulton approached—quite unconscious of the effect she was creating...more than once as we followed her, we saw a hand reach out—not mischievously or compulsively—but very gently, to touch her coat as she turned away. It was both moving and unforgettable.*[86]

At the start of World War II, 330 patients and their staff from Kingseat Hospital, which had been commandeered as a naval hospital, were transferred to Cornhill. Fulton recalled that: 'Bereft of our workshops, life was very strenuous trying to keep the patients employed all over the wards.' And at night, indifferent to her own safety, she would cycle to different wards and play the piano, trying to keep the patients calm during the frequent air raids on Aberdeen, one of which, in 1943, resulted in the death of three employees and one patient.[87]

Despite the war, however, the building of a new occupational therapy department continued and was completed in 1942. The Hospital Board was justly proud of this specially designed and equipped facility. The 1943 *Annual* Report recorded that:

> *The new Occupational Therapy Department is situated on the first floor above the recreation hall, and its main workshop windows look out on a pleasant vista of tree tops. Beautiful Oregon pine has been used almost exclusively for panelling, doors and cupboards.*
>
> *The men's department consists of a main work-room, long and spacious, with one continuous bench in front of the windows and a room for heavy woodwork separated by a sound deadening door. There is also a paint room. The women's department has work tables, looms and a paint room. There are ample tubs, cupboards, and there is a store room as well as a Show Room.*[88]

It was at this point that Dods Brown retired and Dr Andrew Wyllie, formerly deputy physician superintendent of the Crichton Royal Institution, Dumfries, was appointed physician superintendent. An early disagreement arose because Wyllie appointed a nurse to organise a department of social and recreational therapy and annexed part of the new occupational therapy department. Fulton had always considered social and recreational activities as part of the occupational therapy role and this schism had a long-lasting detrimental influence on inter-staff relationships at the hospital.[89]

Fulton's relationship with Wyllie and the Board was not helped by her tendency to speak out on what she considered deficiencies of the service, although she did not court publicity. In 1957, her address to the 25th Anniversary Congress of the Scottish Association of Occupational Therapists resulted in a headline in *The Scotsman* 'How Juggernaut of "Red Tape" has hit the hospitals'.[90] Fulton was complaining of the large volume of paperwork which had accompanied the introduction of the National Health Service: 'These new schemes—carried out in glorious triplicate and at fabulous expense—have already encroached to an alarming extent on the time essential for adequate patient treatment'.[91]

**Figure 2.4.3:** **Miss Margaret (Peg) Barr Fulton**
*(Courtesy of Catherine F. Paterson)*

On another occasion, Fulton was lamenting to a Rotary Club the dearth of aftercare facilities for ex-psychiatric patients. Unbeknown to her, an MP was in the audience, and subsequently he raised a question in the House of Commons. But Miss Fulton did not just speak about deficiencies—she was prepared to do something about them. In 1950, Fulton and Dr Mary Esslemont, a prominent general practitioner, started the Amity Club for isolated female ex-patients, where they could carry on their craft work while developing social contacts. Fulton trained other Soroptomists as support workers for what was a pioneer after-care facility.[92]

Following the appointment of Robertson at Glasgow in 1923 and Fulton at Aberdeen in 1925, other Scottish mental hospitals were encouraged by the Commissioners of the General Board of Control for Scotland to appoint instructresses in the arts and crafts. By

1932, there were eleven such ladies, most of whom had formal art and teaching qualifications, who formed themselves, with the encouragement of Dr Henderson, into the Scottish Association of Occupational Therapy (SAOT).[93] The first meeting was held in Glasgow on 27 May 1932. Margaret Menzies, who was the occupational therapy instructress at the Glasgow Royal at that time, was elected President. Fulton was elected secretary/treasurer and remained on the committee until the meetings were suspended in 1939 because of World War II. Contact was maintained with the fledgling Association of Occupational Therapists south of the border and with the Canadian occupational therapists who were setting up a department and course at the Astley Ainslie Institution during the 1930s.[94] However, Fulton's main achievement during these pre-war years of the association was the support she gave the unqualified members.[95]

The Scottish Association of Occupational Therapists[96] was reconstituted in Edinburgh on 27 July 1946. Miss Fulton was elected Chairman, a position she held until 1949, and she remained actively involved in the Council almost continuously until 1971.[97]

In 1952, representatives of six countries, including Miss Fulton, met in Liverpool to discuss the setting up of an international organisation for occupational therapists. In the official history of the World Federation of Occupational Therapists (WFOT) it is recorded that:

> It was an enormous achievement that during the four days of the Commission the Constitution and Standing Orders were completed and the machinery organised to set up the necessary committees to deal with Membership, Legislation, Finance, International Relations, Education and Congresses. How much we stand indebted to the members of that Commission who ensured that the initiative that had been engendered became a reality.[98]

It was at this inaugural meeting that Miss Fulton was elected President, a position she held for the formative first eight years of the WFOT. One of the earliest decisions of the young organisation was to hold an international congress in Edinburgh, 16–21 August 1954. It was attended by almost 400 delegates from 21 countries, and by all accounts was an extremely successful event. Alicia Mendez, President of WFOT 1974–8, considered that:

> The organising committee of the first Congress set a very high standard and a pattern for the Scientific programme and Social Events that was to be followed for many subsequent Congresses. Their courage in accepting the challenge to be responsible for the first Congress must be recognised, for much weighed on its success. Had Edinburgh failed the World Federation may have failed with it.[99]

Following the success of the Congress Fulton was awarded the MBE in 1954, but with her usual modesty, she maintained that the award belonged to the young Edinburgh-based occupational therapists who were members of the conference organising committee.[100] She was elected an Honorary Fellow of the WFOT in 1960.[101]

Fulton retired in September 1963 to live in Edinburgh. She remained a member of the Council of the Scottish Association until 1971, and up to her death in 1989 continued to take an active interest in the development of the profession, including the Grampian School of Occupational Therapy, founded in Aberdeen in 1976. The Council for the National Academic Awards selected her for an honorary degree to be awarded in 1990, but not in time for her to be told. However in 1995, the Grampian Healthcare NHS Trust decided to name a new day care centre in her honour.[102] HRH the Princess Royal, Patron of the College of Occupational Therapists, officially opened the Fulton Clinic and Memorial Garden in the grounds of Royal Cornhill Hospital on 12 May 1995. It is a fitting tribute to one who gave so unstintingly of her time and talents to the residents of the hospital for more than 38 years, and who pioneered the continued care of patients in the community.[103]

# Involvement of Boards of Control in occupational treatment

In the 1920s English and Scottish General Boards' of Control, showed interest in occupation as therapy and made recommendations to many hospitals that they should open occupational therapy departments.[104] They regularly recorded in annual reports details of what members of the Boards observed regarding occupational therapy when they made visits of inspection to hospitals. The General Board of Control for Scotland, for example, in its 1924 Report noted that, at the Dundee Royal Asylum:

*...(the patients') general health appeared to be good and their appearance indicated that all who were physically fitted were suitably exercised or engaged in useful and health-giving occupations in the beautiful and well kept grounds of the institution.*[105]

In the same year the Board, which inspected the Glasgow Royal Asylum four times, also noted:

*The energy and activity shown in the care of the patients was apparent in the results of the occupational therapy which has been a feature of the institution for some time...*

*Part of the special building erected for occupational therapy has been found to be so useful that the whole building as originally planned is now in process of completion.*[106]

Returning to the Glasgow facility in 1925, they found that:

*The occupational therapy referred to in previous reports continues to enlarge its scope and usefulness. The original building contemplated for this work is now almost completed, and the work done by the patients was seen in operation. It is most creditable to the instructors and the patients.*[107]

There, on 10 August 1926, they found:

*128 patients were attending the class of Occupational Therapy, which continues its excellent curative work. Many of the other patients are employed at varied work in the wards and in the garden or grounds with manifest advantage to their bodily and mental health.*[108]

At the Royal Edinburgh Asylum in that year:

*The class in Occupational Therapy at Craig House was visited. The patients were markedly interested in the work which will doubtless undergo steady development in an institution in which every suggested method of treatment that may lead to a beneficial result is promptly and fully explored.*[109]

In the Fourteenth Annual Report in 1927 it was reported that:

*...many patients are benefited by work especially in the open air and the advantages of having male nurses experienced in the varying forms of mental disorder cannot be over-estimated.*

*During the past year Occupational Therapy has been further extended and it is now in general operation. The benefits to the patients have been frequently commented on and it only required the Exhibition of work from all the institutions throughout Scotland which took place at Bangour in July to demonstrate into what varied and useful channels it is possible to direct the energies of patients who before the introduction of Occupational Therapy were unable or thought to be unable to do anything of a useful nature and whose habits were destructive, degraded and costly from the point of view of nursing.[110]*

In the 1929 Report of the Board it was recommended that all members of asylum staffs should attend courses of instruction given to mental nurses. The object was not only that they could then teach a trade, but also that they should have a better understanding of their patients.[111] The following year the Board commented on the Brabazon Scheme at Woodilee:

*Reference is made to the death of Miss Aikman. It was she who, on 14th January 1898, introduced the Brabazon Employment Scheme for the first time into an Asylum, and weekly since that time, even during the war, visited the institution and taught and worked with the patients in all those varieties of work which are now seen and used in Occupational Therapy. It was as a result of the inspection of the Brabazon work in this country that the idea of Occupational Therapy arose in America.*

*Occupational Therapy is now much used in this country and largely employed with great success in many of our Mental Hospitals as a means of care and treatment. It differs from the original Brabazon employment in this respect, that instead of voluntary there are paid instructors. It would do honour to Miss Aikman's memory and to the work which she has done for this institution if Occupational Therapy were now started.[112]*

Readers may recall that the Brabazon scheme started in the late nineteenth century and was mentioned in Volume 1 of this history.

There was similar interest in occupational therapy south of the border. A circular, No 639, dated 8th August 1924, sent to the Chairman of the Visiting Committee of each County and Borough Mental Hospital in England and Wales, reads as follows:

*The Board of Control have recently had under their consideration the question whether something more should not be done to provide manual, physical and recreational training for certain of the juvenile and young patients who have for the time being to be retained in mental hospitals.*

*The proportion of patients who could benefit from such training no doubt varies considerably in different institutions but the Board are satisfied that in some instances the numbers are sufficient to justify training being provided. They have ascertained that the Central Association for Mental Welfare would be willing to send an experienced trainer for a few weeks to any hospital for the purpose of starting the work. After a few weeks some of the nurses would be able to continue it. The expense of employing a trainer would be quite small (about 25 pound for 1 month) and I am to enquire whether your committee and the Medical Superintendent would care to make an experiment on the lines indicated.*

*From the limited amount of experience already available there is ground for thinking that such training is of value in promoting the welfare and happiness of the patients.[113]*

In response to that circular J. Iveson Russell sent the following report:

*The Board of Control Circular letter No. 369 dated 8th August 1924 refers to manual, physical, and recreational training for juvenile and young patients, but gives no indication of the nature of the occupations recommended, and a letter of enquiry addressed to the Central Association for Mental Welfare merely elicited the fact that the Secretary was on holiday. It may be presumed however that the training recommended is similar to that which is carried out in Institutions for the care of young mental defectives, and as a result of correspondence I am satisfied that the methods practised in these Institutions do not differ widely...*

*It is interesting to note the comparatively small numbers in the early age groups. Approximately 5% of the patients are under 25 years of age and 83% are over 35. Moreover a large proportion of the younger patients are already engaged in useful and necessary employment. Therefore if consideration be confined to the class referred to in the Circular letter, the number available would not be sufficient to justify training being provided.*

*But there is a reason to believe that the interests of many older patients might be enlisted and that the introduction of such industries as Mat-making, Basket making, Envelope and Paper Bag Making would prove in time to be profitable and beneficial...*

*To commence work on a small scale the initial cost would be trivial and most of the apparatus required could be made by our own workmen.*

*The training of Instructors could be arranged without any difficulty and without expense.*

*Success, however, would depend essentially upon the enthusiasm of both Nurses and Patients and while the former may be confidently hoped for, the latter may demand considerable stimulation. In the older class of psychotic patient the spirit of play and competition is less active than in the younger mental defective and an ounce of tobacco is a stronger lever of encouragement than is a word of praise. Therefore although somewhat beyond the scope of this report, I would request that sanction be granted to open a Canteen within the Hospital grounds, where patients and their visitors might have tea or refreshment on payment and that a system be instituted whereby patients might be rewarded for work done, with cheques bearing a small purchasing value at the Canteen.*

*(Signed) J. Iveson Russell*

*Medical Superintendent*

Iveson Russell was to prove a very interested advocate for occupation as treatment, and wrote the first full length, twentieth century, British textbook on the topic which will be discussed at length in the next chapter.

In 1928 the Royal-Medico-Psychological Association visited Dutch mental hospitals at Santpoort, Maasoord, Apeldoorn, Brinkgreven, Den Dolder and Bloemendaal, and a number of mental clinics, where they observed occupation used as treatment based on Dr Simon's ideas. Readers will recall from chapter 2 that Simon was renowned for the introduction of 'occupational treatment' at the Gutersloh Mental Hospital early in the century. Dr A.E. Evans reported that they saw a thorough application of therapeutic principles, an atmosphere of quiet industry, and a noteworthy absence of noisy brawling or introspective idleness. The obvious success of occupational treatment impressed the members of the Tour, many of whom immediately introduced it into their respective hospitals, notably at the Devon County Mental Hospital, the North Riding Hospital, Cardiff City Mental Hospital, Severalls, Chester, and Barming Heath, as well as at several others. Some of those became training centres where other mental hospitals sent nurses for instruction.[114]

Instruction of nurses and others to undertake occupational therapy is a topic which has been central within the chapter. To complete this chapter the story of the next step in training people to do the work is told. It is the story of Elizabeth Casson. She, too, became fascinated by the concept and the need for occupational programs with psychiatric patients during the twenties. She started to investigate what was happening in that respect in other places and instigated programs herself. That was to lead to the establishment of the first school of training for occupational therapists in Britain, which opened its doors to students in 1930.

# Elizabeth Casson

Elizabeth Casson was born in 1881 into a talented family of dramatic and musical ability. Her father, Thomas Casson of Denbigh, was an expert in organ-building, her brother, (Sir) Lewis Casson, was to become a well-known actor who married Dame Sybil Thorndike. Casson, herself, loved to sing and act, and enjoyed listening to organ music, although she resisted pressures to play an instrument herself. Awakened to nature's beauty as she grew up in the Welsh countryside,[115] she was also a gifted sketcher and painter. On the more practical side she loved tools, and enjoyed mechanics, 'mending locks or motor-car gadgets,' in preference to playing with dolls. As a child she was neither strong nor robust and her sister revealed that although she was a talented writer she was never 'regarded as particularly clever till in her teens at St. Mary's College, Paddington, when she was fortunate in her teachers and very happy.'[116]

After a period of secretarial work with her father, Casson trained as a housing estate manager in South London as a member of the staff of Octavia Hill, whose story is told in the first volume of the history, and mentioned again in chapter 2 of this volume. Hill (1838–1912), who is known as a leader of the open space movement which culminated in the formation of the National Trust,[117] also sought to improve conditions and provide positive experiences for those less fortunate than herself. A case in point is the annual open day Hill held for her poor tenants at a house in Hammersmith (which later became William Morris's London home, Kelmscott). At these open days the poor and 'intellectual and artistic do-gooders' shared in many activities including play acting, games and country dancing.[118] The 'intellectual and artistic do-gooders' sharing these experiences were social activist friends and colleagues such as Samuel Barnett who founded Toynbee Hall and the Settlement Movement, and leaders of the Arts and Crafts Movement, William Morris and John Ruskin. That this group of social activists shared experiences with those they tried to help was perhaps influential in Casson's participatory approach to occupational therapy, which could well serve as a model for the twenty-first century.

**Figure 2.4.4:    Red Cross Hall and Cottages**
*(Courtesy of Octavia Hill Birthplace Museum)*

Casson appeared well fitted to her work as secretary at Red Cross Hall, which was attached to a group of quaint cottages and a communal, specially designed, occupational garden. Her office was a large room at the back of the Hall that was a centre for many kinds of recreational and educational activities for Hill's tenants. In the Society of Housing Managers Newsletter, Casson was recalled by one of her four fellow workers who started at about the same time, in1909, as 'slight, rather short, with an untidy crop of hair, and with a very intelligent and vivid expression...alive and keen'.[119]

> *Miss Hill, I suppose knowing of Miss Casson's brother and sister-in-law's connection with theatrical work, passed over largely to her the running of the activities of Red Cross Hall. The Sunday concerts were very popular at that time...and Miss Casson was largely responsible for their success.*[120]

Casson's experiences convinced her that 'appalling ignorance and neglect of physical weakness and disease accounted for much of the misery and poverty she found,'[121] and that the people themselves required first aid as much as their tenements.[122] So, at about the age of thirty, and whilst working for Hill, she surprised family and friends by deciding to take matriculation so that she could study medicine. This led, ultimately, to her becoming the first woman to be awarded the degree of Doctor of Medicine of the University of Bristol in 1929. Her picture in academic dress, is shown in Figure 2.4.5. Vyrnwy Biscoe, the reporter of an article in a Bristol newspaper at the time, claimed for Casson that she was 'one of the first to realise the power of creative handiwork'. Occupational therapy, she wrote, was a 'new healing method which is working such miracles with the mentally disordered and the victims of long and tedious convalescence.'[123]

**Figure 2.4.5:** **Dr Elizabeth Casson in academic dress**
*(Reproduced courtesy of Dorset House Archives, Oxford Brookes University)*

Whilst an undergraduate Casson revelled in the carefree life of being a student. She enjoyed the delightful surroundings of Clifton Hill House, the Hall where she lived, the formalities of University life and academic pageantry, and made a pleasure of the extra duties called for as a result of World War I. With others, she pulled 'the great roller over the lawn,' 'milked Jane the goat,' 'made quilts for French refugees, and knitted socks of unusual shapes'.[124]

Interested in specialising in psychiatry, the newly qualified Dr Casson 'went to one of the best mental hospitals as a clinical assistant' where she 'found it very difficult to get used to the atmosphere of bored idleness in the day rooms.'[125] As a moment of great significance, she remembers how:

*...one Monday morning, when I arrived at the women's wards, I found the atmosphere had completely changed and realised that preparations for Christmas decorations had begun. The ward sisters had produced coloured tissue paper and bare branches, and all the patients were working happily in groups making flowers and leaves and using all their artistic talents with real interest and pleasure. I knew from that moment that such occupation was an integral part of treatment and must be provided.[126]*

A few weeks after this determination Dr Casson accepted an appointment at the Royal Holloway Sanatorium, Virginia Water, where she took her diploma in psychological medicine. At that institution a tradition of occupations such as games, entertainments, competitions, annual sports days and craft exhibitions remained from earlier days. As well, the nursing staff encouraged those 'who were well enough to organise their own needlework and embroidery', but 'no work was regularly prescribed by the medical officers.' Casson, at this point, attributed her 'real introduction' to occupational therapy to a description by Henderson of his work at Gartnavel Hospital in Glasgow.[127]

Casson's growing interest in and commitment to occupational therapy was not surprising when one considers her own diverse talents and social activist experience, coupled with stories of ancestors, of whom she was very proud. Apparently her great-grandmother, in answer to problems that arose during 'the blockade' in Napoleonic times, organized community meals and slate-quarrying for the villagers of Festiniog. And, back in the eighteenth century, another ancestor, a curate at Seathwaite-in-Dudden, kept school on week-days as well as finding pleasure in walking, spinning, and teaching his own family how to weave.[128] Additionally there was a growing interest, generally, in rehabilitation and Casson recalls the American 'Kessler Film' on rehabilitation being shown in England.[129]

Dr Casson describes the first occupational therapy department she saw when on a holiday in the mid-1920s at Bloomingdale Hospital, New York:

*It had a beautiful Craft House, built in hospital grounds, with large rooms for printing, book-binding, metal work, weaving, pottery and a variety of other forms of employment. There was a large gymnasium nearby with a team of games instructors. The patients left their wards at stated times for work.[130]*

A few days later Casson visited the Boston School of Occupational Therapy, and the idea of an English School was implanted in her mind. On her return to England Casson sought out all the occupation programs she could find, such as those at Lady Chichester Hospital, Brighton, Miller's Home at Harrow, and the East Anglican Sanatorium at Nayland. At the latter Dr Jane Walker, one of the first women to qualify in medicine, and a founder of the Medical Women's Federation, was a leader in the open air treatment of tuberculosis along with the use of occupation which she pioneered. She later became one of the founding vice-presidents of the Association of Occupational Therapists.[131]

Not surprisingly, Casson soon began to organize occupational therapy at Virginia Water employing people with particular skills and expertise as there were no specifically trained occupational therapists at that time:

*Miss K. Phillips who had retired from the post of Chief Inspector of L.C.C. (London County Council) Infant Schools came first, to hold regular classes in embroidery...Miss Allen, who had worked with mental defective patients, started full-time work with a few looms, and very soon needed more help, so Miss Tebbit was added to her staff for a few months.[132]*

Constance Tebbit (whose married name was Owens) explains how, in 1925, 'it was a most exciting experience for a nineteen year old to meet her (Casson) at that time and to be caught up in, and infected by, her enthusiasm to start occupational therapy.' However, before being employed, Tebbit was subjected to Casson's test of suitability for the work through assessment of her relationship with patients at a social evening and being left to her own devices in an acute ward. Tebbit later went off to train at the Philadelphia School and returned to become the first principal of the Dorset House School.

Having served her apprenticeship to the idea and application of occupational therapy, Casson returned to Bristol in 1929. She borrowed money to set up her own residential clinic for women psychiatric patients and to establish a school of training for occupational therapists. Her sister describes how 'with characteristic courage she began with very little money, in a very large house, which she soon filled with patients, staff and her first batch of students.'[133] The very large house was known as Dorset House on Clifton Down, and it was here that Casson determined to develop all the ideas about treatment that had been growing in her mind, married to her strong religious beliefs. These included a full-time, planned day for all patients[134] which served their needs and offered them wholeness in living.[135] She established:

*...a treatment centre where each patient's daily life would be so planned that it fitted the individual's need like a well-tailored garment. She planned that each member of her household, whether patient or staff, should feel an integrated part of the whole and that each would contribute, according to capacity, to the welfare of the whole. There would be no sharp social or professional distinctions between members of staff and every patient would be made to eradicate any unnecessary dividing line between the patients and the staff. In this community everyone would be essential and therefore would feel valued and valuable. Recreations would be shared by all, recovering patients could undertake duties such as gardening or housework, and occupational therapy would be available to all.*[136]

**Figure 2.4.6:    Dorset House, Clifton, Bristol - view from the promenade**
*(Reproduced courtesy of Dorset House Archives, Oxford Brookes University)*

In early lectures to students, Casson told them that it was particularly important for them to understand that:

*...all stimuli that reached the brain resulted in instinctive or in voluntary action. This may occur immediately, but if thwarted the mental energy is stored and the urge to action becomes involved and combined in sentiments that later become **the motives of organized activities.***

She recognised this in herself: 'There were plenty of these motives stored up in me, and it has taken all my activities since 1929 till now to express them.'[137]

Constance Owens remembered 'incredibly busy days' as both School and Clinic grew according to Casson's dream and what now might be called her 'occupational perspective' on life, because in addition to the more expected duties:

*...we sandpapered and painted doors and furniture, colour washed walls, stained*

*floors, wove cushion covers, made stools and trays, curtains, traycloths, rugs and waste paper baskets. We danced and sang and, with Owen Reed's help, produced plays, gave parties and played cards with the patients. In the main sitting room a Jig Saw Puzzle (often of immense proportions) was always on the go. This was a great gathering point, especially before lunch and dinner and Dr. Casson was frequently one of the party. Occupational Therapy went on in the evening as well as by day.*

*...In the Mendips we had a cottage to which parties of patients and staff went for day trips or week-ends and where they cooked and kept house. There was never a dull moment and, though there was little money, there was unlimited enthusiasm.*[138]

Casson's student friend, Irving, describes an 'atmosphere of serenity and helpfulness' that made visits to Dorset House a time of 'refreshment and content.' This despite the fact that:

*...her visitors were expected to take part in activities of the patients. We had to join in folk-dancing on the lawn, to give fictitious help in the solution of these difficult crossword puzzles which seemed to be child's play to some of her patients, or to find missing pieces in the current jig-saw puzzle.*[139]

By the beginning of the 1939 war, Dorset House had spread to four large houses in Clifton and a household of well over a hundred. Indeed between 1929 and 1941, (when the Clinic and School were forced to moved because of bombing), about 800 patients had been residents. Her sister believed that 'the collapse of all this when bombing attacks grew too frequent and fierce must have been an almost unendurable shock and grief to her, but she uttered no word of complaint.'[140] Casson moved with the Nursing Home to Clevedon. The Ministry of Health borrowed the Occupational Therapy School building for the duration of the war, relocating the students and staff to Barnsley Hall, Bromsgrove.

Dr Casson continued to be intimately involved with the School after the move and its ultimate establishment in Oxford. She held the position of Medical Director, and motored between Bristol and Oxford to meetings. Indeed, she financed the School from her personal funds until 1948. Then she turned it into a non-profit-making Limited Company, before creating the Casson Trust a year later to which she handed over her financial interests in the School. Her family continued to be involved with the School for many years. Sir Hugh Casson was Chairman of the Board of Governors, for example. In his Diary he provided a little story and picture of his aunt which he shared at a Dorset House lunch:

*Saturday 7th: Oxford*

*Jubilee lunch at Dorset House School of Occupational Therapy, Oxford. For 20 years I was chairman of the governors of this school founded and run by my formidable doctor aunt Elsie. She was a beautiful, compassionate, strong-minded and public-spirited woman with the most individual dress sense. (I remember at the age of nine being conducted, rebellious and humiliated, across Paris, together with my equally embarrassed sister, by Aunt Elsie wearing a full length black evening dress and a straw hat and carrying an alpen-stock.) Lots of old pupils and staff at the lunch and my speech received indulgently.*[141]

**Figure 2.4.7:    Elizabeth Casson crossing Paris: A sketch from Hugh Casson's diary**[142]

*(Reproduced by permission of Sir Hugh Casson Ltd)*

Elizabeth Casson died on 17 December 1954, and is buried in the village churchyard at Backwell in sight of the sea and the Welsh mountains she loved as a child.[143]

Like any good story there are many more embedded within it and some will be explored later, but a final comment in this chapter addresses the lived experience model clinic that Casson established as an integral part of the first British Occupational Therapy School.

The communal nature of Casson's Dorset House was, indeed, intriguing. It seemed to draw upon and epitomise the communal Utopias that were conceptualized in nineteenth century philosophy and social activism, and those like Thomas More's from even earlier times. It seemed to have much in common with the ideology and action associated with the Settlement movement, in both England and the USA, which found a central place for people of different persuasions, social standing and capacities to share resources and grow, helping each other in many ways. The holistic, communal and participatory model also seems to anticipate the newer ways of thinking about occupational therapy practice—that it needs to be client centred and aimed at enabling occupation which has meaning, as well as, or despite, a curative focus. It points the way for occupational therapists to embrace, once more, a participatory model of learning and to work towards overcoming the constraints and difficulties of the consultative model of practice which is in vogue. This latter model is imposed largely by managerial, economic rationalist philosophies of life, and the current approach of medical science.

**In summary,** Chapter 4 described how the profession began in Britain, and gives credit to three very special people, two doctors of psychiatry, David Henderson and Elizabeth Casson, and the first trained occupational therapist in the country, Margaret Barr (Peg) Fulton. Against a background of growing interest, which they had a share in creating, in a very few years they established a strong foundation for a new and very different profession. And, so it began.

[1] O'Sullivan ENM. Textbook of Occupational therapy: With Chief Reference to Psychologcal Medicine. London: H.K. Lewis, 1955.

[2] Valery P. In: Kohn H, ed. The Modern World: 1848 to the Present. New York: Macmillan, 1963;179–180.

[3] Randle APH. Rehabilitation and Society. Occupational Therapy 1974; January: 15–17.

[4] Macdonald EM. World-Wide Conquests of Disabilities: The History, Development and Present Functions of the Remedial Services. London: Bailliere Tindall, 1981.

[5] Central Council for the Disabled. A Record of 50 Years Service to the Disabled from 191--1965. London: 1969; intro.

[6] Central Council for the Disabled....; 4, 7.

[7] Central Council for the Disabled....; 14–16.

[8] Central Council for the Disabled....; 25

[9] Central Council for the Disabled....; 27

[10] Watson F. Civilization and the Cripple. London: John Bale, Sons & Danielsson, Ltd., 1930; 38.

[11] Varrier-Jones PJ. Tubercle 1936; 17: 529.

[12] Varrier-Jones PJ. Lancet 1941; 1: 368.

[13] Bryder L. Below the Magic Mountain: a Short History of Tuberculosis in Twentieth-Century Britain. Oxford: Clarendon Press, 1988.

[14] Papworth Annual Report, 1923; 14,16,24.

[15] Papworth Annual Report, 1935; 19.

[16] Bryder. Below the Magic Mountain....

[17] Watson. Civilization and the Cripple....; 39.

[18] Bryder. Below the Magic Mountain....

[19] Provisional Report of Cheshire Branch of British Red Cross Society, Proposed Training Colony. 21 May 1919; 3.

[20] Bryder. Below the Magic Mountain....

[21] 2nd CMOH Annual Report 1920, 96. In :Bryder. Below the Magic Mountain....; 166.

[22] Western Mail 1 May, 1924.

[23] McDougall JB. British Journal of Tuberculosis 1927; 86,87. In: Bryder. Below the Magic Mountain....; 169.

[24] Varrier-Jones PJ. British Journal of Tuberculosis 1926; 20: 16.

[25] PRO MH55/132, Ministry of Health. Training Sections for Ex-Servicemen at Sanatoria, Jan 1920; 3–5.

[26] Bryder L. Occupational Therapy and Tuberculosis Sanatoria. SSHM Bulletin 40 1987; 64–6.

[27] Bryder. Below the Magic Mountain....; 173.

[28]Bryder. Below the Magic Mountain....; 157.

[29]McDougall JB. British Journal of Tuberculosis 31/3/1937; 203–4.

[30]Bryder. Below the Magic Mountain....; 170.

[31]Henderson DK. Introduction. In: Winters EE., ed. The Collected Papers of Adolf Meyer, Volume II: Psychiatry. Baltimore: The Johns Hopkins Press, 1951; xix.

[32]HendersonDK. Life and work. Scottish Journal of Occupational Therapy 1957; 7–10.

[33]Henderson DK. The Evolution of Psychiatry in Scotland. Edinburgh: E & S Livingstone Ltd, 1964; 161–162.

[34]Slagle EC. Training aides for mental patients. (Read at Fifth Annual Meeting of the National Society for the Promotion of Occupational Therapy) Archives of Occupational Therapy 1922; (1)1: 11–18.

[35]Obituary Notices: Sir David Henderson M.D., S.Sc., F.R.F.P.S. (GLAS.), F.R.C.P. British Medical Journal 1st May 1965.

[36]Andrews J, Smith I, eds. Let There Be Light Again: A History of the Gartnavel Royal Hospital From its Beginnings to the Present Day. Glasgow: Gartnavel Royal Hospital, 1993; 73.

[37]Henderson DK. Occupational Therapy. Journal of Mental Science. 1925; 71.

[38]In: Creek J, ed. Occupational Therapy and Mental Health. Second ed. Edinburgh: Churchill Livingstone, 1997; 8.

[39]Andrews & Smith. Let There Be Light Again....; 75.

[40]Henderson DK. Report of the Physician Superintendent for the year 1922. In: The One Hundreth and Ninth Annual Report of the Glasgow Royal Asylum for the Year 1922. Glasgow: James Hedderwick & Sons Ltd., 1922.

[41]Henderson DK. Report of the Physician Superintendent for the year 1923. In: The One Hundreth and Tenth Annual Report of the Glasgow Royal Asylum for the Year 1923. Glasgow: James Hedderwick & Sons Ltd., 1924; 23.

[42]Fulton MB. Obituary: Sir David Henderson, M.D., S.Sc., F.R.F.P.S. (GLAS.), F.R.C.P. Journal of Occupational Therapy 1964; 3.

[43]Andrews & Smith. Let There Be Light Again....;75.

[44]Henderson DK. Mental Hygiene. Glasgow Medical Journal June 1923; 1.

[45]Henderson. Life and work. SJOT...

[46]Henderson DA. Correspondence. Glasgow Royal Mental Hospital Archives, 1923–1924.

[47]From our own Correspondents. Scotland: Occupational therapy in early mental disorder. The Lancet March 22, 1924; ccvi: 621.

[48]Occupational therapy in mental disorder. The British Medical Journal. June 20, 1925.

[49]Andrews & Smith. Let There Be Light Again....; 75.

[50]Fulton. Obituary: Sir David Henderson....

[51]Andrews & Smith. Let There Be Light Again....; 76.

[52]Fulton. Obituary: Sir David Henderson....

[53]Robertson D. Correspondence. Glasgow Royal Mental Hospital Archives, 1922.

[54]Robertson D. Occupational department. In: The One Hundreth and Tenth Annual Report of the Glasgow Royal Asylum for the Year 1923. Glasgow: James Hedderwick & Sons Ltd., 1924.

[55]Robertson D. Occupational department. In: The One Hundreth and Eleventh Annual Report of the Glasgow Royal Asylum for the Year 1924. Glasgow: James Hedderwick & Sons Ltd., 1925.

[56]Robertson D. Occupational department. In: The One Hundreth and Eleventh Annual Report of the Glasgow Royal Asylum for the Year 1924. Glasgow: James Hedderwick & Sons Ltd., 1925.

[57]Melrose A. Correspondence. Glasgow Royal Mental Hospital Archives, 1925.

[58]In: Andrews & Smith. Let There Be Light Again....; 75.

[59]Melrose A. Occupational department. In: The One Hundreth and Twelfth Annual Report of the Glasgow Royal Asylum for the Year 1925. Glasgow: James Hedderwick & Sons Ltd., 1926.

[60]Melrose A. Occupational department. In: The One Hundreth and Thirteenth Annual Report of the Glasgow Royal Asylum for the Year 1926. Glasgow: James Hedderwick & Sons Ltd., 1927; 31.

[61]Melrose. Occupational department. In: The One Hundreth and Thirteenth Annual....; 32–33.

[62]Melrose. Occupational department. In: The One Hundreth and Thirteenth Annual....; 34.

[63]Melrose. Occupational department. In: The One Hundreth and Thirteenth Annual....; 35.

[64]Melrose A. Craft Work—A Medicine. Dryad Handicrafts Leaflet No 70. Leicester: The Dryad Press, 1928; 3–5.

[65]Melrose AH. Occupational therapy at Hartwood. Hospital Social Service 1929; XIX (55): 55–64.

[66]Melrose. Occupational therapy at Hartwood....; 57.

[67]Melrose AH. Occupational Therapy Department. Report of Lanark District Asylum 1927; 45.

[68]Melrose AH. Occupational Therapy Department. Report of Lanark District Asylum 1927; 45.

[69]Easterbrook CC. The Chronicle of the Crichton Royal. Dumfries: Courier Press, 1940.

[70]Adapted from Paterson CF. Margaret Barr Fulton, MBE (1900–1989): Pioneer occupational therapist. In: Adam A, Smith D, Watson F, eds. To the Greit Support and Advancement of Helth. Aberdeen: Aberdeen History of Medicine Publications, 1996.

[71] Fulton MB. The Memoirs of Miss Margaret Barr Fulton, MBE, 1900–1980. Unpublished Typescript. 1989 (SAOT Archive 5.2)

[72]Fulton. The Memoirs…1989.
The National Society for the Promotion of Occupational Therapy, later the American Occupational Therapy Association (AOTA) had only been founded in 1917, so occupational therapy was still a very new profession.

[73]Prospectus of the Philadelphia School of Occupational Therapy 1925–26, Greater Glasgow Health Board Archive 3/11/7.

[74]Fulton. The Memoirs....; 1989; 10.

[75]Fulton. The Memoirs....; 1989; 11–12.

[76]Fulton F. Letter to Margaret Fulton, 17 July 1924; SAOT Box 5.1.

[77]Fulton. The Memoirs....; 1989; 23.

[78]Minute of the Aberdeen Royal Asylum Board of Directors 15 July 1925; Northern Health Services Archive Grampian Regional Health Board (hereafter NHSA GRHB0 2/1/19).

[79]Annual Report for 1925, op. cit.

[80] Fulton MB. Review of 25 years. Scottish Journal of Occupational Therapy 1957; 30: 44–48.

[81]'The use of malarial spirochaetes to induce a pyrexia which would kill the bacteria responsible for syphilis, thus delaying the effects of the tertiary phase, general paralysis of the insane'. In: Hume CA. 1930s: Ourselves as others see us. British Journal of Occupational Therapy 1992; 55 (7): 260–262.

[82]Dods Brown R. Some observations on the treatment of mental diseases. Edinburgh

Medical Journal 1929; 36: 657–686.

Other medical treatments in vogue at the Aberdeen Royal Hospital between the wars included prolonged narcosis, electric stimulation therapy, insulin shock therapy, and pre-frontal leucotomy. Sedatives were used, particularly paraldehyde, but there were no effective drugs until the 1950s. Stelazine was introduced and evaluated in Aberdeen in 1958.

[83]Dods Brown. Some observations on the treatment of mental diseases....

[84]Welfare work in Aberdeen Professor Adler pays tribute. Aberdeen Press and Journal 28 May 1937.

Dr Adler died suddenly in Aberdeen on 28 May 1937 before the end of his visit.

[85] Fulton. The Memoirs...1989.

[86]Alpha, Miss Margaret Barr Fulton, MBE, MSAOT, OTR., Scottish Journal of Occupational Therapy; 55: 18–19.

[87]Fulton. The Memoirs.... 1989; 33.

[88]Annual Report of the Aberdeen Royal Mental Hospital. 1943, NHSA GRHB 2/8/15.

[89]Fulton. The Memoirs.... 1989.

[90]How Juggernaut of 'Red Tape' has hit the hospitals. The Scotsman. 2 November 1957.

[91]Fulton MB. Address delivered to Opening Meeting of Scottish Association of Occupational Therapists 25th Anniversary Congress. Scottish Journal of Occupational Therapy 1958; 32: 8–12.

[92]Fisher H. Amity has a new home. Aberdeen Press and Journal c. 1950. SAOT Box 5.5.

[93]Groundes Peace Z. An outline of the development of occupational therapy in Scotland. Scottish Journal of Occupational Therapy 1957; 30: 16–44.

[94]Minutes of the Scottish Association of Occupational Therapists 1932–1939. SAOT Box 1.4.

[95]Paterson CF. Interview with Bunty Elliott (nee Isabella Veitch). Edinburgh, 6 April 1999.

[96]Since there was by that time a body of qualified occupational therapists, the name of the association was appropriately changed from Scottish Association of Occupational Therapy.

[97]Minutes of the Scottish Association of Occupational Therapists 1946–1971. SAOT Box 1.5 & 1.6, Box 2.1, Box 3.1.

[98]Mendez MA. A Chronicle of the World Federation of Occupational Therapists: The First Thirty Years: 1952–1982. Jerusalem: WFOT. 1986; 2.

[99]Mendez. A Chronicle of the World Federation of Occupational Therapists...

[100]Fulton, MB. Personal notes, (unpublished). SAOT Archive Box 5. 1985.

[101]Mendez. A Chronicle of the World Federation of Occupational Therapists...

[102]The Grampian Healthcare NHS Trust was set up in 1993 to manage the community and mental health services throughout Grampian including the Royal Cornhill Hospital.

[103]I am grateful for the assistance given by David Smith and Fiona Watson in the preparation of Margaret Barr Fulton's story, and for the support of the Wellcome Trust. I am also indebted to the family of Margaret Fulton, who have generously shared with me personal papers and memorabilia of her life and career.

[104]Twelfth Annual Report of the General Board of Control for Scotland For the Year 1925. Edinburgh: His Majesty's Stationery Office, 1926

[105]Eleventh Annual Report of the General Board of Control for Scotland For the Year 1924. Edinburgh: His Majesty's Stationery Office, 1925; xviii.

[106]Eleventh Annual Report of the General Board of Control for Scotland For the Year 1924. Edinburgh: His Majesty's Stationery Office, 1925; xix.

[107]Twelfth Annual Report of the General Board of Control for Scotland For the Year 1925. Edinburgh: His Majesty's Stationery Office, 1926; xxiii.

[108]Thirteenth Annual Report of the General Board of Control for Scotland For the Year 1926. Edinburgh: His Majesty's Stationery Office, 1927; xxi.

[109]Thirteenth Annual Report of the General Board of Control for Scotland For the Year 1926....; xxi.

[110]Fourteenth Annual Report of the General Board of Control for Scotland For the Year 1927. Edinburgh: His Majesty's Stationery Office, 1928.

[111]Groundes-Peace ZC. An outline of the development of occupational therapy in Scotland. The Scottish Journal of Occupational Therapy 1957; (30): 16–39.

[112]Sixteenth Annual Report of the General Board of Control For the Year 1929. Edinburgh: His Majesty's Stationery Office, 1930.

[113]Fairley W. Circular No 639. London: Board of Control, 1924.

[114]O'Sullivan ENM. Textbook of Occupational therapy: With Chief Reference to Psychologcal Medicine. London: H.K. Lewis, 1955.

[115]Irving NS. University Days and After: by a fellow student. Occupational Therapy 1955; 18 (3): 90–91.

[116]Reed E. Dr Casson's Early Life. Occupational Therapy 1955; 18 (3): 87–89.

[117]The Macmillan Encyclopedia. Aylesbury: Market House Books, 1990; 574.

[118]MacCarthy F. William Morris: A Life for Our Time. London: Faber and Faber, 1994; 392.

[119]M.C.G. Dr E Casson. Society of Housing Managers News Letter No 2, 1955.

[120]M.C.G. Dr E Casson. Society of Housing Managers News Letter No 2, 1955.

[121]Reed E. Dr Casson's Early Life. Occupational Therapy 1955; 18 (3): 87–89.

[122]AWR. Profile: Elizabeth Casson, M.D., D.P.M. Occupational Therapy 1955; 18 (3): 85–86.

[123]Biscoe V. Bristol Women. Cutting in Dorset House Archives. Unknown Newspaper Source. c.1929.

[124]Irving. University Days and After....

[125]Casson E. Dr Casson tells how the Dorset House School of Occupational Therapy came into being. Occupational Therapy 1955; 18 (3): 92–94.

[126]Casson. Dr Casson tells....

[127]Casson. Dr Casson tells....

[128]AWR. Profile: Elizabeth Casson...

[129]Casson E. 1947. Occupational Therapy in Great Britain. Journal of the American Medical Women's Assocation 2 (6), 303–305.

[130]Casson. Dr Casson tells....

[131]Obituary Jane Walker, C.H., M.D., LL.D. Occupational Therapy Winter 1939; 12.

[132]Casson. Dr Casson tells....

[133]Reed. Dr Casson's Early Life....

[134]Casson. Dr Casson tells....

[135]Glyn Owens C. Recollections 1925–1933. Occupational Therapy 1955; 18 (3): 95–97.

[136]Glyn Owens. Recollections....

[137]Casson. Dr Casson tells....

[138]Glyn Owens. Recollections....

[139]Irving. University Days and After....

[140]Reed. Dr Casson's Early Life....

[141]Casson H. Hugh Casson Diary. London: Macmillan. 1981; 66.

[142]Casson H. Hugh Casson Diary....

[143]Irving. University Days and After....

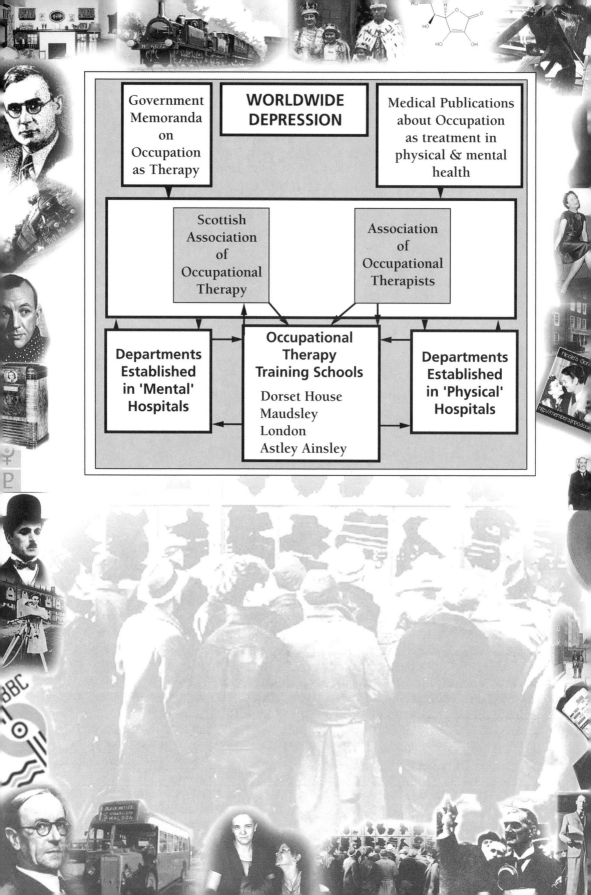

**WORLDWIDE DEPRESSION**

Government Memoranda on Occupation as Therapy

Medical Publications about Occupation as treatment in physical & mental health

Scottish Association of Occupational Therapy

Association of Occupational Therapists

**Departments Established in 'Mental' Hospitals**

**Occupational Therapy Training Schools**

Dorset House
Maudsley
London
Astley Ainsley

**Departments Established in 'Physical' Hospitals**

# Chapter 5

# Living and Learning Curative Occupational Therapy

## Contents

Context of the time
Early Schools of training
   Dorset House
   Maudsley Hospital
   London Training Centre
   Astley Ainslie Training Centre
Memorandum on Occupation Therapy for Mental Patients
Publications
   Dr W.H.F. Wilson
   Dr R. Eager
   Dr J. Iveson Russell
Associations of Occupational Therapists
   The Scottish Association of Occupational Therapy
   The Association of Occupational Therapy
   The Journal
Developing occupational therapy practice around the country
   For the treatment of physical conditions
   For the treatment of mental conditions

In this chapter the story of the early years of occupational therapy, between 1930 and 1939, continues with the genesis of several schools. It was also the time of another very significant Board of Control Memorandum on Occupation Therapy; the first major publications about occupation for health in the twentieth century; and the formation of professional associations. One was formed in Scotland, and another in England, serving Wales and Northern Ireland as well. It was a time of intense activity, unbounded enthusiasm, commitment, excitement and creativity. People such as Mary Macdonald, Angela Rivett, Muriel Tarrant, and others played a major role in establishing the profession and setting its future directions. Many pioneers 'lived' occupational therapy, and as they grew they learned, and set up both services and opportunities for others to learn, despite the worldwide economic crisis that characterised much of the period. The chapter uses the words of the people who pioneered the world of occupational therapy in order to capture the spirit of the time and to recreate their experience in some small way. The length of stories varies according to the availability of records. For example Mary Macdonald's collection, housed at the Oxford School, provides a veritable and varied treasure trove of information, but for the short-lived occupational therapy training course at the Maudsley Hospital material was hard to find.

Following a brief look at the nature of the 1930s up to the advent of World War II, the stories of the establishment of training schools during this period are told in addition to the school histories told in appendix A. These early training schools were closely allied with developing practices around the country, so the practices too need to be considered in the final section of the chapter. That follows a look at related medical publications and government initiatives at the time. The written material from the period is presented at some length because of its importance in terms of the development, future directions and philosophies of the profession.

# Context of the times

During the period between the two world wars, unemployment was to become a major concern throughout much of the world. In the United Kingdom it was caused by a combination of factors such as a surplus of labour and of manufactured goods, under-consumption, and a disorganised labour market aggravated by tariff and free trade policies. By 1921, the number of unemployed in Britain had risen to over two million, and, by 1932, to almost three million—about 22 per cent of the insured population. The 1929 general election, which resulted in a Labour victory, had been fought on the issue of unemployment, but that failed to stop the economic depression that followed two years later. The problem did not diminish, in a real way, until the outbreak of war towards the end of the decade, despite government policies aimed at developing new industries in areas where unemployment was greatest.[1] Along with lack of employment, and apart from the monetary concerns, were the emotional problems that result from the lack of meaning and purpose which are part and parcel of engagement with the world through work.

So, the 'depression' was not just economic! Issues relating to unemployment would have been in the minds of almost everyone in the country and may have been instrumental in the political and general recognition that engagement in occupation is absolutely necessary for well-being. So, the lack of potential employment in the everyday work force would have influenced the pioneer occupational therapists' views about the role of the profession in work. It can be speculated that the social illness issues of the time were so overwhelming that it would have been beyond their scope even to consider it as an area of concern. Indeed, it would have been almost impossible to determine how to assist their patients' return to a normal life, including paid employment, within the context of the decade. That idea developed during and after the war, in response to the demand for manpower.

But the idea of occupational therapy, or the need for occupation within the broader health environment, was catching on. For example, in 1934, public awareness was generated by an exhibition about occupational therapy in London, and in 1938, there were reports from as far afield as the Lebanon, and in publications as disparate as *The Lancet* and the *Christian Christmas Annual*. In the first of those we read of a one year diploma course for teachers and trainers of mental defectives being set up;[2] in the latter, about establishment of occupational therapy in the Holy Land at Lebanon Hospital for the treatment of patients with mental health problems. There 'a large new house—the Irish House—has been opened, housing forty eight quiet patients, and the Hall of Occupational Therapy, given in memory of Lady Scott-Moncrieff.'[3] In the *Bristol Evening Post* of the same year, a report tells of the establishment of occupational therapy utilising 'nature study and weather recording' at the Winsley Sanatorium.[4] And a 'Women's Feature' in Southampton's *Southern Daily Echo* explained that 'the idea is that when a patient is absorbed in useful or beautiful hand work, the mind, which has become out of touch with reality and is usually entirely self-absorbed, gradually finds the way back to normal.' They recommended that people taking it up should have 'deft fingers...ability to teach, initiative and keenness, patience and sympathy.'[5]

**Figure 2.5.1:    Exhibition of Occupational Therapy: London, 1934**
*(Reproduced courtesy of Dorset House Archives, Oxford Brookes University)*

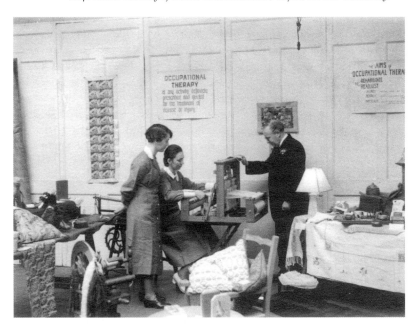

Pioneer occupational therapists appear to have been remarkably generous with their time in terms of disseminating information through talking to interested groups as well as to news media. Casson and Fulton were particular cases in point. However the paper given by Mrs Nesta Clarke, the occupational therapist at Chester County Hospital, to the North Wirral Soroptomist Club holds particular historical appeal. There was, she said:

*...little authentic history of occupational therapy until comparatively modern times. Our belief in its ambiguity was not in historical documents so much as vague references in ancient writings...With the opening of the nineteenth century came a new era; occupation began to be used in many hospitals both in England and America.*

*It was important to understand from the beginning that occupational therapy was not a form of treatment confined to craft rooms and workshops. It consisted in the ordering of the patient's whole day, so that work, leisure, recreation, eating and sleeping formed a balanced whole, varied and directed in accordance with his individual needs.[6]*

# Early schools of training

Occupational therapists tend to think of the existing training schools and their histories as telling much of the early story of establishing the profession. That is, in large case, true. However there were other opportunities for training which are less well known and which typified the interest of the early years. For example, when a reader asked, in 1938, 'Could I study occupational therapy without giving up my present post as a non-resident sister in charge of a mental ward?', the Nursing Mirror replied that they knew of 'no evening classes' but that there were two methods of training: 'the best of which was to take a full diploma course' at Dorset House, the Maudsley, or London's Occupational Therapy Centre.[7] (There was also a full time course available at the Astley Ainslie Training School in Edinburgh which was mentioned in an article in the *Nottingham Evening Post* ).[8] Alternatively:

*...to take one of the shorter courses offered by many mental hospitals to nurses, but this is also a full time occupation, and could not be arranged by evening classes. An important part of all training in occupational therapy is the practical work with patients, and this must, naturally, be done during the day.[9]*

In the *Nursing Mirror and Midwives Journal* that information was extended to advise that such training was often free at a nurse's own hospital under a trained officer. In addition to a mental nurse's course there was a further 6–9 months' training. The article advised that yet another Diploma course was available at the Central Association for Mental Welfare, in London. This offered a three-term course for training supervisors of occupation centres and home teachers of mental defectives.[10]

The story of the establishment of Dorset House has already been told, but how it developed in the 1930s will be told here, along with the stories of the genesis of the other three full time courses offered in the decade. The rest of their stories will be continued in Appendix A with those of the others. The early history of Dorset House as a School of Occupational Therapy is inseparable from its history as a Nursing Home for the treatment of female patients with neurotic and psychotic disorders, which Dr Casson started in 1929.[11] In 1930, students were accepted to work with those patients and from this grew the Dorset House School which opened, in the Nursing Home, on New Year's Day, 1930. Miss Constance Tebbit, who had trained in Philadelphia, was its first principal.

**Figure 2.5.2:** **Example of the work of Rosemary K. Hogg, an early Dorset House student**
*(Reproduced courtesy of Rosemary K. Baker (née Hogg))*

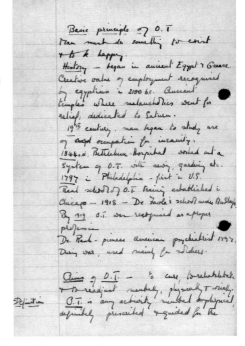

Dr Casson considered that the aim of Dorset House was:

*...to form a community where every individual was encouraged to feel that she had a real object; for a patient the object was to get well and to go out to a worth-while life; for a member of the staff it was to serve others with all the talents she possessed; for a student, to develop all her capacities for her life as an Occupational Therapist and to find the individual job that only she could do.*[12]

The School's premises continued to expand until it filled three adjacent houses, Dorset, Alva and Litfield. Eventually it was in Litfield that the 'occupation rooms' and 'playroom' were housed. One contained the looms, and, in another, other types of craftwork were practised. The playroom, shown in Figure 2.5.3, had very little furniture and was used for dancing, games, Margaret Morris Movement, and parties. Margaret Morris Movement, which became part of the curriculum and treatment at Dorset House in 1932,[13] was also carried out in the garden as pictured in Figure 2.5.4.

**Figure 2.5.3:** **The playroom at Dorset House**
*(Reproduced courtesy of Dorset House Archives, Oxford Brookes University)*

**Figure 2.5.4:** **Margaret Morris Movement in the gardens**
*(Reproduced courtesy of Dorset House Archives, Oxford Brookes University)*

During its first three years, the bulk of the clinical experience was psychological, for two reasons; the demand for trained occupational therapists was for those equipped for mental hospital work; and at the same time it was far easier to provide facilities for this type of experience. The physical aspects of occupational therapy were never forgotten, though, and during 1939 an embryonic occupational therapy department to demonstrate the use of this treatment for physical cases was opened at the Bristol General Hospital. The work was confined to ward work and the patients treated were mostly heart cases. Some students helped to run the extension Guide Companies at Frenchay Sanatorium and Winfield Orthopaedic Hospital. Peggy Reed recalled:

> We were very sorry when Dorset House gave up guide work at the Winfield Orthopaedic Hospital. Miss Tebbit and Miss Goscombe started the company, and Peg and Bates had it for nearly a year, but when they went up to Chester there was no one to carry it on. Those Friday afternoons were memorable, especially for the shouts of the children...Once in the summer we had a picnic, to which the stretcher cases came in the car.[14]

Mary Macdonald became the Principal in 1938. She told how, at that time Casson had 'enthusiastic ideas for expansion' into the treatment of patients with physical disorders. 'So what was termed "an adventure in rehabilitation" was started at Allendale Curative Workshop' opened in 1939 for outpatients suffering from varying forms of physical disease or disability.[15] This acted as a demonstration treatment unit and provided clinical practice opportunities for students.

**Figure 2.5.5:** **Mary Macdonald**
*(Reproduced courtesy of Dorset House Archives, Oxford Brookes University)*

**Figure 2.5.6: Dorset House School of Occupational Therapy Plan of Training**

*(Reproduced courtesy of Dorset House Archives, Oxford Brookes University)*

One of the early Dorset House students was Margaret Inman, who had been a trained nurse. Dr Casson recommended her to the New Zealand Government when they wrote seeking a qualified occupational therapist to employ in psychiatric work at the Auckland Psychiatric Hospital. Inman, somewhat nervously because of the war, sailed to New Zealand in 1940, on the SS *Remura* via the Panama Canal. In that year, she established a service at the hospital with the support of Dr Buchanan, and inaugurated the first School in New Zealand. That offered a six-month training to mature students with previous work experience. She held the position of Principal for ten years. This is a romantic story with a happy ending. Inman married Dr Buchanan. It was he who had advised the Government about occupational therapy following a visit to England.[16]

Whilst Dorset House is, arguably, the best known of the English Schools because of its longevity, another, which is probably the least well known nowadays, started only two years later, replacing earlier, less formal 'occupation training' for nurses. This was situated at the Maudsley Hospital, and it, too, went hand in glove with psychiatric practice in the first instance.

In an earlier chapter it was noted that Sir Aubrey Lewis, of the Maudsley Hospital, spent time in America with Adolph Meyer and brought many of his ideas back to Britain; one of which, it must be presumed, was the need for occupational therapy. This seems to have been implemented at the Maudsley with some speed as it was well established before he became Clinical Director in 1936.

The previous Medical Superintendent, in his report of 1932–35, commented upon particular difficulties in the provision of occupational therapy because of 'the large number of patients...necessarily confined to bed,' in comparison with other hospitals of like kind. 'Much attention,' he said 'has to be concentrated upon forms of occupation which are suitable for wards' as well as for the much faster turnover of patients attending a central department, than would generally be the case in most mental or orthopaedic hospitals. As a result, he stressed the necessity for occupational therapy 'to concentrate upon the benefit to the patient rather than upon striking products,' and that the crafts taught must be interesting, satisfying and achievable with the patients quickly reaching 'a degree of proficiency.' He went on to discuss economic concerns associated with the need for the department to be self-supporting 'apart from the salary of the officer in charge.' In the main that was to do with the provision of materials for the occupations used as treatment, but he concluded that 'in practice an attempt to run the department on a self-supporting basis proved hopelessly cramping to its proper functions.'[17]

Another difficulty reported was 'the absence of any suitable quarters for a central department.' As in many other places it seems that occupational therapy at the Maudsley started life, in 1931, in a basement which was 'equipped as far as its limited size would allow.' In this case the basement was regarded as 'makeshift,' and somewhat proudly, the Medical Superintendent boasted that:

> ...the premises provided for occupational treatment in the first extension of the hospital, and opened in the autumn of 1935, compare favourably with any in this country. The room is perhaps large enough not only to take all in-patients fit to go there but also to provide space for a limited number of out-patients. [18]

The male patients were apparently able to use the hospital maintenance workshops, and it was planned that a second extension to the hospital would include the provision of a new workshop. The original one was to be adapted to provide 'satisfactory facilities for carpentry and upholstery' as part of the occupational therapy programme. The appointment of a male officer was anticipated to take charge of those occupations, which were particularly 'adapted to men, but also of the physical training and drill of male patients.' The report also considered the possibility of special facilities being provided for 'either out-patients or former in-patients' at a 'training centre in arts and crafts under control of the Council and in the neighbourhood of the patient's home.' This, the Medical Superintendent believed, would be particularly useful for 'patients with unhappy home circumstances or unoccupied lives.'[19]

The report went on to discuss the training of occupational therapists. This started in a way similar to the early years in the United States, with training being available to hospital staff and, possibly, interested others:

> ...training has been given almost since the opening of the hospital to those desiring to take up as a career, supervision of occupational treatment in cases of mental disorder. Up to 1932 this was of very informal kind and derived almost wholly from practical work done in conjunction with the occupation officer here.[20]

Presumably that type of training had applicability only to the treatment of those with mental illness. In 1932, 1933, and 1935, a six-month course was offered under the charge of Dr Tennent who was to be another significant figure in the development of the profession. The Medical Superintendent's report describes the course thus:

> The first regular course was held from October, 1932, to March, 1933. In this the

*College of Nursing and Goldsmith's College participated and it was limited to six candidates. It was agreed that priority should be given to registered nurses, although in the absence of sufficient number of applications from such candidates it was arranged that others might be accepted.*

*Dr. Tennent, who has throughout been responsible for the organisation of the occupational treatment here, gave to those attending the course a series of lectures upon such aspects of psychiatry as were relevant.*

*A similar course was held from October, 1933, to March, 1934. Owing to alterations in the building which rendered the old premises unavailable, while the new were not yet ready, no students were enrolled in October, 1934, but in January, 1935, three students started a six months' course.[21]*

Each week students were required to work six and a half days, three and a half learning handicrafts at the Goldsmith College, and three days at graduated practical work with patients at the Maudsley. Apart from that students received, from a doctor, twenty-four lectures followed by clinical demonstrations of cases.[22]

In the autumn of 1935 a course lasting a full year was implemented:

*The Camberwell School of Arts and Crafts has agreed to provide the technical training in weaving, rug-making, basketry, bookbinding, cardboard construction, leather work, sewing, embroidery, and design. The general management of the course is being transferred from the College of Nursing to the Maudsley itself. While it is hoped and believed that support from the College will be forthcoming, this change will make it possible to try and attract students who are not nurses. In fact, it is specially hoped that the course may be taken by those who already have a considerable knowledge of handicrafts and require particularly to learn how to apply their knowledge for the benefit of those suffering from mental disorder.*

*Indeed, unless those with some such previous training can be induced to take up occupational therapy for patients of this class, it is hard to see how the best standards sometimes reached in America can ever be approached in this country.*

*The students here help, of course, as part of their practical training to instruct patients and supervise their work. [23]*

A special nine-month course for nurses was also run in 1935 which was so popular that it was over-subscribed:

*Two classes have been organised, each of fifteen, working in each week for one session in the mornings and for another session in the afternoons, under the same instructor. This was intended to make it possible that all nurses who wished to avail themselves of the opportunity should do so, but the number of applicants was double those who could be accommodated.*

*...It is hoped that similar courses will be held for the remaining applicants next year and there-after that these classes in occupational treatment shall become a recognised part of the training of every nurse here.*

*The possession of such a training by a nurse would not only be a very useful supplement to any possible provision for the instruction of patients by more highly skilled occupational therapists, but it would be a particularly valuable possession for any nurse who may afterwards take up private work.*[24]

Miss English, a state registered nurse trained at the London Hospital who, during the Great War, served in Salonica and while there became interested in spinning and weaving, trained as an occupational therapist at the Maudsley. She became the founding sub-editor of *Occupational Therapy*.[25] So, too, did Angela Rivett, a founder of the London School. However, because it was such an early school, there are now few occupational therapists who were Maudsley Diplomates left. Fortunately the whereabouts of one, Joyce Keam, an Australian, was known, and she agreed to provide her reminiscences.[26]

Joyce Keam grew up on a dairy farm on the banks of the Yarra River at Heidelberg in Victoria. She first heard about occupational therapy from a Canadian physiotherapist visiting Melbourne who thought that she would be 'good at it' because she could do all manner of crafts, games and sport. Keam wrote to America and England to enquire about courses, and recalls receiving masses of information from America and almost nothing from the two English Schools—'just a small scrap of paper really.' She had heard that there was a school in Scotland as well but didn't know more about it.

She journeyed to England to undertake a one-year training course at the Maudsley in 1937. She can't recall the names of any of the lecturers or how many people were in the course, but described her training as learning lots of craft and lots of psychiatry and not much else. She does remember a strong emphasis on fieldwork, with a typical day involving seeing patients followed by lectures. In the main, doctors delivered the lectures; and although some anatomy and physiology was taught it was very basic, and most of the lectures dealt with psychiatry. The psychiatry lectures were shared with the student social workers and nurses.

According to Keam, the female director of the Maudsley course was trained at Dorset House, and gave the impression that occupational therapy was solely about doing craftwork with patients. Despite that, Keam maintained her own strong view that all activity came within the domain of occupational therapy, from mending the roof to digging a ditch—so long as it had a therapeutic purpose. David O'Halloran, who interviewed Keam for this history, reports that during their discussions, she mainly used examples from the vocational domain. Apparently another girl doing the course with her shared her views, as did a therapist from Dorset House whom she met at a conference. That person suggested that Keam should visit the Bristol School before returning to Australia.

It is probable that Keam followed up that idea because at the completion of her training someone at the Maudsley arranged for her to go to Dorset House for a month of additional work. Keam thought that one important distinction between Dorset House and the Maudsley was that you 'couldn't tell who were patients and who were staff at Dorset House.' This probably relates to the strong community ideal that was discussed in the last chapter. Indeed, Keam reports that there was a 'community' feel, but gave the impression of being a visitor rather than ever feeling part of the community. She added that she had to do lots of study while she was there which kept her apart.

Macdonald organised a tour of occupational therapy departments in America for Keam on her way back to Australia, similar to one she had made a few years earlier. Keam's departure was noted in *Occupational Therapy*,[27] and she had to provide a record of her tour for publication in the American Journal. The tour included a tuberculosis clinic in Milwaukee, a paediatric service in Boston, a psychiatric service, possibly, in New York, and a physical rehabilitation service in Philadephia, which Keam had never seen before. She recalls seeing a poster there about 'What is Occupational Therapy?', which struck her as unusual having never seen this kind of thing in Britain.[28]

**Figure 2.5.7:** **Major Joyce Keam**
*(Courtesy of Joyce Keam)*

In 1939, on her return to Australia, Keam followed a lengthy, varied and important career. In 1941 she established an occupational therapy department in a 2000 bed military hospital, and two years later, as Major, was promoted to the position of Chief Occupational Therapist at Army Headquarters in Melbourne, and Advisor of Occupational Therapy to the Director General of Medical Services. In the beginning, she was one of three pioneer occupational therapists in the country, along side Ethel Francis who trained at the Philadelphia School, and Sylvia Docker, who trained at the London School.[29]

The Occupational Therapy Centre and Training School, which was to become the London School of Occupational Therapy, was established in 1935. It was founded in Tottenham Court Road by Muriel Tarrant (Figure 2.5.8) and her friend Angela Rivett (Figure 2.5.9), who were to become affectionately known as the 'Aunts' to successive groups of student occupational therapists. Like the other early Schools, the one in Tottenham Court Road started life as an occupational treatment centre, and provided at least some of the staffing for that service with students in training. The initial course was of six months' duration.[30] The motto adopted for the London School of Occupational Therapy, 'Without vision we perish,' encapsulated her attitude in many fields of activity.

**Figure 2.5.8:    Muriel Tarrant**

**Figure 2.5.9:    Angela Rivett, one of the founding principals of the London School, in 1993**

*She is pictured with the 1993 staff. Front row from left: Frances Reynolds, Anne Loch, Jenny King, Lynn Summerfield-Mann, Anne Murdoch (former head of school visiting with Miss Rivett), Angel Rivett, Bernadette Waters (then head of school), and Sally Curson; back row: Paul Roden, Gwilym Roberts, Linda Gnanasekeran, Rosemarie Dravnieks, Gaynor Sadler, Sydney Klugman and Deborah Kemp. (By permission of Brunel University)*

Many well known occupational therapists trained there. Included in that group was Sylvia Docker, an Australian who worked as a physiotherapist in World War 1 and in 1935 travelled to England to train as an occupational therapist at the London School. Returning to Australia in 1938, she pioneered the profession in Melbourne with the Victorian Crippled Children's Society and at the Austin Hospital. Later she became Director of Occupational Therapy Training which was started in Sydney early in World War II, to fill a need recognised 'as being of national importance.' (That phrase echoed how occupational therapy's contribution was described in Britain at the start of World War II[31]). She is commemorated by the Sylvia Docker lecture given at the bi-annual conference of *OT Australia*.[32]

The first Scottish occupational therapy department specifically for patients with physical disorders was at the Astley Ainslie Institution in Edinburgh, and in 1937 the first training school was established there.[33] The visionary behind these initiatives was Lt Colonel John Cunningham, the first Medical Superintendent of the Astley Ainslie

Institution. He wrote in 1931 of 'the importance of graded occupation and recreation, both mental and physical as a factor in bringing about an ultimate return to health.' To introduce graded activity, Cunningham enlisted the help of the Canadian Association of Occupational Therapists, who provided a series of therapists during the 1930s and 1940s to promote both the practice and education of occupational therapists.

The training school offered a two and a half year diploma course based on the one in Toronto with the Canadian, Gloria Langmaid, in charge. The intake was small with only nine students over the first two groups, and they were, in the main, 'daughters of prominent medical and other men connected with the hospital.' Cunningham's daughter, Mary, was one of them.[34] Another who started in the earliest group was Jean Blades. She qualified in 1938, and during the war pioneered the development of occupational therapy at the military hospital at Strathcathro in Angus, before moving on to the Princess Margaret Rose Hospital in Edinburgh in 1944.[35] Another was Dorothy Bramwell who was stranded at the outbreak of World War II in Egypt. In the next chapter the story of how she spent the war years setting up Occupational Therapy departments in the Middle East is told. On her return in 1944 she was awarded the MBE and became the first Scottish trained director of the school. Meanwhile back in Edinburgh, wartime circumstances led to the course being halted temporarily after the first diplomas were awarded in 1939.

## Memorandum on Occupation Therapy for Mental Patients

The Board of Control *Memorandum on Occupation Therapy for Mental Patients* issued in 1933, noted the courses offered by both the Maudsley and Dorset House Schools, and made recommendations about what training they perceived occupational therapists required:

*...an occupation therapist should undergo a course of training extending over something like two years to include :*

*(a) Nine months to one year devoted to the learning of crafts in an approved training school.*

*(b) A series of lectures on basic subjects, with clinical demonstrations of cases suffering from physical and mental illness.*

*(c) A period of training in a mental hospital where occupational work is being done- possibly six months would be sufficient.*

*(d) A short course in a large colony for defectives. This will be valuable as an introduction to the methods of training of low grade defectives which, with the necessary modifications, can be applied to deteriorated patients in mental hospitals, until training in the application of the treatment to such patients can be obtained in the mental hospitals of this country.*

*(e) Three months training in recreational activities, including indoor and outdoor games, dancing, drill, music, dramatics, etc.* [36]

The *Memorandum* is of such importance that it is essential to consider the paper in depth. Within it Occupation Therapy was defined as:

*...the treatment, under medical direction, of physical or mental disorders by the*

*application of occupation and recreation with the object of promoting recovery, of creating new habits, and of preventing deterioration.*[37]

Its purpose was also outlined:

*Rest may be essential in acute states, but, if unduly prolonged, it is attended with no less undesirable results in cases of mental disorder than in physical disorders. At the earliest possible moment, therefore, the use of the mind should be promoted by the mildest measures of occupation or by encouraging the patient to take interest in things external to himself.*[38]

It is also valuable to reproduce, in full, the advantages of the profession as they were pronounced some 70 years ago:

**(i) The patient's mental attitude is favourably influenced.**

*Occupation therapy provides at least a means whereby he may escape from the boredom of inactivity, and from depression. It offers new outlets, with the chances of an increase of interest, a lessening of concentration on immediate mental troubles and a reduction of emotional disturbance. Moreover, it induces a hopeful attitude not only towards the benefits to be derived from occupation therapy itself, but to other forms of therapy which may at the same time be applied for the amelioration or cure of the illness.*

**(ii) Good habits are induced and maintained.**

*The treatment can be regarded as a medium for the establishment of controlled behaviour; it promotes regulation of habits to the advantage of the work of mass nursing. It maintains not only the habit of occupation, but the equally important capacity for co-operation, in patients who may otherwise sink into mental isolation, and it helps also to maintain a sense of responsibility. All this may be curative, but where cure is not possible, deterioration and degradation are retarded.*

**(iii) Physical health is promoted.**

*The result directly of exercise and change of posture and indirectly of increased interest will be improved physical health.*

**iv) The whole atmosphere of the hospital is improved.**

*Monotony is the bane of institutional life! Occupation is a form of treatment especially calculated to counteract it. Occupation therapy breaks up the routine institutional life of the hospital and relieves monotony, and induces a busy activity with resulting cheerfulness and hope of recovery. It allows social contact between mental patients in circumstances of common interest to those under treatment.*

*The economic value of occupation need not be stressed. But if the result of the treatment is to raise the general level of social behaviour, it follows that misuse and destruction of clothing and property will be a less prominent feature of the activities of those undergoing treatment and their capacity for useful work will be greater.*

*We consider, too, that the stabilisation of conduct resulting from the treatment will, in many cases, enable patients to be boarded out with their friends and relatives. Occupational treatment, continued into the convalescent phase of the illness, will often make the re-adjustment to a working world a more agreeable task, and must inevitably lessen the anxiety and dread with which the recovered patient takes up again the burden of life.*

*In conclusion, we think that the value of the proper application of the treatment as a socialising factor can hardly be over-estimated, not only from the point of view of the patient, who will more readily come for early treatment, but also from the effect created upon the public mind.*

*We believe, indeed, that the introduction of a well organised system of occupation therapy will mean a considerable step forward towards the time when mental hospitals will cease to be regarded as closed units within our social system.*[39]

The memorandum noted that:

*Many doctors who have applied the system to the most diverse types of patients say that occupational treatment, more than any other single factor, is instrumental in preventing much of the deterioration of mind and habit occurring in dementia.*[40]

The Memorandum offered ideas about the classification and scope of 'occupation therapy' as it was envisaged in the 1930s as 'employment', handicrafts, occupations like gardening and poultry-keeping, recreational occupations encompassing mental and physical education and 'amusements', and social opportunities. From the figures available within existing mental hospitals, the Memorandum recognised that more than 80 per cent of the patients should come within the scope of occupation therapy:

(a) Bed occupations for patients who are not prescribed absolute rest.

(b) Habit training in the wards with deteriorated and disturbed patients…

(c) In the wards for patients who, though disturbed and active, are able to respond to the appeal of craft work…

(d) Handicrafts and industries in Occupation Centres…

(e) Industries forming part of the normal services of the hospital…

(f) Recreational and social activities throughout the hospital…[41]

It is worth noting the opinions expressed in the section entitled *Occupation Therapy in Relation to the Utility Services of the Hospital*, which reads as follows:

*The object of occupation is primarily therapeutic, and it is of the utmost importance that it should be regarded as such and not as a means of providing commodities for use in the hospital at a low cost compared with that of ordinary supplies from commercial sources. A sharp distinction between therapy and mere occupation, of whatever kind, should be maintained, though it is recognised that any form of occupation may have a therapeutic value if applied under the direction of the physician and in the hands of staff who are specially trained in this branch of medical therapy.*

*The utility services, the kitchen, laundry and sewing room, with the household departments in which women work, and the various shops with the farm and garden for men, are centres where occupation has been provided over almost the whole period during which mental hospitals have existed. In these places are employed only the more stable and industrious inmates.*

*Again, other work, for the purpose of providing some of the articles and garments used or worn in the hospital, is often not done within the hospital because it is believed to be more economical to buy in the open market. We suggest, however, that the therapeutic value of the occupation which would be provided for patients needing just this kind of work by the making of these same articles in the hospital may be such as to outweigh the small monetary gain obtained by purchasing them from outside sources.*

*The primary factor is the therapeutic value to the patient, so that too much stress should not be laid on output and finish. But if the work in the utility shops and departments is to be used as a means of treatment, the medical officer must have the same freedom to move patients from and to them, and to change the occupations of patients working in them, as he will have in the case of those occupied in the handicraft centres.*

*We do not dispute that the utility shops and departments of the hospital may often fittingly be regarded as the proper sphere of occupation for patients who have undergone treatment to secure stabilisation, but whose cure is found to be no longer likely. They may quite well maintain the standard of skill and output, and thus themselves, by making the shop a useful centre to the hospital, facilitate the treatment of other curable patients who may come there for continued therapeutic treatment, but the need of the individual patient must be the determining factor in every case. It may be, especially on the male side, that these shops and departments may provide the finishing treatment of convalescent patients who are soon to resume their social activities in the outside world. If these departments of the hospital are to serve as treatment centres as well as providing material service, it may be necessary to make some modification in the present method of using them.[42]*

It was noted that in the USA a distinction was drawn between occupational therapy and service departments. Patients who were not well enough to be employed in less protected surroundings worked with occupational therapists under medical prescription. Only when they were considered fit to work in the community were they transferred to service departments, discharged, or sent out on parole.[43]

The Memorandum, whilst accepting the idea of occupation therapy and being committed to working out how best to implement it, looked overseas for ideas about how it might best be done:

*The Americans apparently hold that the addition to the ordinary hospital staff of a number of what are known as occupation therapists, who have had two years' training in various crafts and the therapeutic application of them, is necessary, while the Dutch and Germans take the view that this form of treatment can best be carried on by the ordinary staff of the hospital. It appears, however, that the Dutch have recently found it necessary to include in their personnel technicians in special crafts, who are not nurses, and the Americans use them in their industrial shops, farm, garden and laundry which are regarded as being outside the domain of the occupation therapist.[44]*

In Italy, occupation was not introduced into the major mental hospital in Rome until 1931, although 'Clinics of Work' had been established after the 1914–18 war to deal with the acute problem of the rehabilitation of the wounded and disabled soldiers. In Denmark, occupation treatment was a feature of many mental hospitals and sanatoria where it was developed on vocational as well as therapeutic lines. In France also, occupation treatment was practised in many mental hospitals and sanatoria as well as in hospitals for crippled children, but had not been extended into general or convalescent hospitals.[45]

In the 1933 Memorandum three ways in which occupation therapy could be carried on under medical control were recognised:

- First, existing nurses and staff could be trained and utilised. That was regarded as 'the most important link in the whole chain' and unless it was properly carried out 'the entire scheme will fail';
- Second, technicians, without mental health training, could augment existing staff; or
- Third, someone else (occupation therapists, perhaps) could be employed, in addition to nurses and technicians.

The last option appeared to be favoured, as doctors, matrons, chief male nurses, or even tutor sisters, it was surmised, had too large and too different a work load to take on an additional organisation role. However, in order for occupation to be used 'throughout the hospital as a socialising factor or as a method of cure' it had to be organised with that object in view by 'the Medical Superintendent himself.' As well, a doctor, they insisted, 'without whose help occupational treatment must fail in its main purpose', should bear the burden of directing work, prescribing the treatment, generally supervising its application and keeping in touch with the work his patients were doing. Technicians would provide high level skills, but by utilising the staff of existing service departments of the hospital only a very small additional number of technician-instructors would be required. Nurses would call upon a working knowledge of the simpler arts and crafts; and an occupational therapist (or 'somebody' else) would be employed who knew how to do handicrafts, 'how to teach them to mental patients, and how to instruct the nurses in the application to the patient of all the wide training, including habit training, which occupation therapy comprises.' The Memorandum recommended:

> ...the introduction of the occupation therapist as a new grade of staff in the mental hospital, who, working with but independently of the matron or chief male nurse, will carry on therapeutic treatment by occupation under the doctors. We are also of opinion that technicians, who have not undergone training as nurses, will be necessary in certain of the special crafts and in the industrial shops.[46]

The authors envisaged one occupation therapist would be required on each side of a hospital of 1000 beds, that it might be well for them to be non-resident, and suggested that their pay scale be £200–300 per annum. They briefly outlined the position of an occupational therapist:

> Here is a new class of officer who has to be fitted into an organisation designed in the first place without any thought of the intrusion; we assume that a woman will occupy this post on the female side and on the male side a man.
>
> The occupation therapists will, under the medical officer of the section, be responsible for initiating and giving general direction to the therapeutic work.
>
> Their knowledge of many handicrafts will enable them to train the nurses in this field, and, during the progress of the work, to deal with difficulties in technique and therapeutic application. Though their work at first may be confined to the training of the nurses in the occupation centres, as soon as a few of the latter have been trained, the sphere of the therapists will be enlarged to include the whole of their respective sides of the hospital. We suggest, also, that in order to ensure that recreational activities will assume their proper place in the scheme, it may be well to make the occupation therapists responsible for all recreational as well as occupational treatment. For such a responsible post, we must have somebody who has considerable knowledge of the theory and practice of occupation therapy, and who has the education and mentality to interpret the doctors' instructions in the widest therapeutic sense.[47]

Also recommended was employment of a small group of occupational therapy assistants called 'craft workers.' Severalls Hospital used such a system, which had been found to work well. It was recommended that they may be certificated nurses with considerable experience and some craft training, or persons 'from outside' who had received training in crafts, with a view to qualifying as occupation therapists. Two or three would be required on each side of 1000 bed hospitals. It was envisaged that officers in charge of service industries in the hospital 'must serve two masters—the matron, the clerk and steward or the chief attendant on the one hand, and the occupation therapist on the other.'[48]

Not stated, but implicit within the terms of duties associated with the application of occupation across all patients within a hospital, was the controversial notion that nursing staff too would, in effect, be answerable to two masters. All nurses were to be trained to value 'occupational and recreational treatment as an important part of their daily work' because the patients' occupational regime needed to be continued during the hours of rest and recreation. Indeed, especially in the case of deteriorated patients, 'recreational training including physical drill, etc., should be combined with the occupational treatment, not only during the hours of leisure, but also as part of the general scheme.' Some nurses, who formerly 'devoted their energies to the control and supervision of their charges' on the wards, would have the 'alternate and much more agreeable task' of attending and working in the occupation centre with their patients. Such a system would not impose on the nurse added duties so much as a change of work, and no additional numbers were envisaged.[49]

Russell, in similar vein, asked at a special general meeting of the Association: 'Would the future of the profession be better...if we adopted the policy (a) that occupation therapy is a special subject outside the sphere of mental nursing, or (b) that actually it is mental nursing?' He was in favour of the second option, and went so far as to suggest that 'occupational therapists should aim to become the matron of the hospital, with a staff of nurses under her control, some of whom would be trained and some would be training in occupational therapy.' Whilst that would mean that occupational therapists would need to be trained nurses, it would mean that they and nurses would each be 'approaching the same goal, but from different angles...'[50]

An interesting letter, which drew upon the Board of Control's use of the term *occupation therapist*, was published in the Spring 1939 issue of the Journal. It reads:
> Dear Editors,
>
> Are we Occupation Therapists practising Occupation Therapy or Occupational Therapists practising Occupational Therapy? May we be either, or must we be both?
>
> It would be interesting to know from whence originated this particularly ugly, awkward and unnecessary adjective, occupational, as applied to Therapy. We cannot, I am afraid, plead lack of direction, for as far back as 1933, the Board of Control set us an example when they issued their memorandum on Occupation Therapy and discussed therein the training and duties of the Occupation Therapist.
>
> Dr. J. Iveson Russell in his writings on this subject favours 'Occupation Therapist' and 'Occupational Therapy.' Dr. Elizabeth Casson in her paper, 'The Prescription of Occupational Therapy' in the Winter number of the 'Journal,' while acknowledging perhaps unconsciously, the general trend, appears to pull herself up with an isolated **Occupation** Therapy in paragraph 5.
>
> These are only a few examples to illustrate my point. There are many others. Is it yet too late to drop this horrible AL and return with consistency to the more dignified noun? This letter expresses my own view. What do other **Occupation** Therapists think?
>
> Yours very truly, Dorothy McLuskie.

# Publications

M edical interest in occupational therapy was becoming evident in various spheres. There were papers given by them to occupational therapists and published in the Association's Journal, as well as letters such as the one from JR Rees, the Medical Director of Tavistock Clinic in London. He wrote: 'Of all the ancillary medical services, I doubt if any one is more important than occupational therapy.'[51] Occasionally there were articles about occupational therapy in medical journals, such as one by Lt Col. Cunningham in the *Edinburgh Medical Journal* that discussed occupational therapy in 'Recovery and Rehabilitation'. In the paper he maintained it was 'essential that the treatment should be carried out by Occupational Therapists who have been specially trained for this type of work.'[52]

## Dr W.H.F. Wilson

Illustrating how a young medical officer viewed the emerging profession at that time, William Hamilton Fraser Wilson, resident medical officer at Astley Ainslie, wrote *Recent Developments in Occupational Therapy*, towards the degree of MD of Edinburgh University in 1936. He began his thesis by referring to the conjoint nature of body and spirit, and the impossibility of healing one without the other. Bearing this in mind, along with the knowledge that hospital admissions tended to be much lengthier and riskier than in the present day, it can be understood from his thesis that Wilson appreciated the holistic need to nourish and motivate a patient by providing an interest in the future to prevent 'living mindless and will-less, the life of a half dead creature.' Remarkably, Wilson recognised that to motivate patients who are ill 'is a hard task' and that 'it needs special qualities and special effort quite other than the average range of hospital devotion.'[53] Recognition of the difficulty of the job is not an issue that has received much attention, though it is long overdue. It could be blamed for some of the attrition that has occurred within the ranks of occupational therapy, for changes of direction, and for lack of appreciation of the value and complexity of the job by more specifically focussed members of treatment teams.

Occupational therapy, Wilson explained, at that time had been known as ergotherapy, psychotherapy, work cure, diversional therapy, as well as by other names which provide modern readers with some notion of its breadth and concentration early in its twentieth century history. But, he said, its establishment had not been taken up with as much enthusiasm in Britain as in Canada and the USA partly, he suspected because of the relatively little publicity it had received in medical journals. One wonders what he might have said of the almost absent coverage of the profession in medical journals of today.

Its value in the 'mental field' he saw as 'developing sustained effort and attention', 'awakening interest', 'inducing regular habits', 'replacing morbid ideas with healthy ones', and 'establishing mental and motor control and co-ordination.' In the physical field he saw occupational therapy exercising, restoring and retraining 'function of specific muscles and joints', and 'stimulating circulation' leading to improved 'digestion, sleep and physical health.' He also described its purpose in the social field as 'improvement in individual and group morale', and 'opportunities for social adaptation in work and recreation.'[54]

The occupational therapist's 'tools' of the times he described as 'crafts, physical education and recreation'. He also posed the question that must be central to any history of occupational therapy, although it is one which tends to be avoided or ignored, as if it had never been the case. The question he asked was, 'Why are handicrafts so generally used in occupational therapy treatment?' The answers, as he saw it, were:

1. Scientific—because of the reaction triggered in 'the motor centres of the brain to work stimuli; and the resultant improvement of higher centres of the brain.'

2. 'Crafts are a primitive means of expression; an instinctive healthy outlet of individuality.'

3. They have an instinctive appeal at times of sickness.

4. They '...can be easily graded and selected to meet the mental capacity; the interests of a day labourer or a genius.'

5. They 'can supply all the physical movements required in restoration' of impaired function. Additionally there is 'psychological value of that peculiar pleasure derived from work accomplished with one's own hands.'[55]

Not content with generalising, Wilson concluded his thesis with fifteen pages of description of actual 'therapeutic' occupations, their detailed remedial use and adaptations, and finished with several case histories to illustrate his views.

## Dr R. Eager

In a small booklet *Aids to Mental Health* published in Exeter in 1936, Dr Richard Eager spelt out the benefits of occupation, recreation and amusement. Eager had been the Medical Superintendent of the Devon Mental Hospital, Exminster, and his text was a composite of addresses given to The Mental Hospitals Association in 1934 and the Public Health Congress in 1936. The fact that there was sufficient interest in the topic by attendees for such papers to be given at all, signifies the place occupational therapy was beginning to assume. Eager began by discussing the importance of meaningful and balanced occupation for all people if they were to lead happy and healthy lives. However, he made a distinction between occupation and recreation:

*I would first state that 'work,' although disliked by so many, is the salvation of civilized man and that unemployment is a curse to any community and brings in its train many ills which must eventually lead to physical and mental deterioration if allowed to continue.*

*The happiest individual is he, or she, who has work which compensates for his feelings of inferiority and brings into being a 'superiority complex.'...Those who are constantly changing are those who are not only dissatisfied with their job but with work generally. They are the individuals who think that happiness consists only in leisure and relaxation.*

*They consider that there should be no difficulties to overcome and, like a horse, shy at the first fence, never to face it again and eventually become social parasites.*

*But even though our work may be all that could be desired, times of relaxation and leisure must be suitably spent. Therefore everyone in his youth should develop activities which will carry on this function into old age. The wise man has a variety of hobbies and is constantly fortifying himself with new ideas and new contacts. If we are to live healthy lives this requires some thought and will be considered under the heading of Recreation and Amusement as distinct from Occupation.*

*The high pressure business man however, is usually so engrossed in his work that he disregards the need for amusement and recreation as well as the danger signals in respect to his own health and the crash comes when least expected. Lack of occupation also affects both mind and body as so many during the unemployment troubles of the past few years know only too well.*

*Occupation therefore with reasonable periods of relaxation is necessary to every one of us if we want to remain healthy both mentally and physically.'* [56]

After that general admonishment of great importance, Eager went on to discuss the case in mental hospitals. With very few trained occupational therapists available to employ, he argued that nurses must, of necessity, be concerned with eliminating idleness. Numbers of patients sitting about doing nothing was depressing in itself but in order to turn their thoughts into useful channels and eliminate unhealthy retrospection a system of organised occupations was necessary. According to the title of his booklet and introductory words it appeared that Eager, did not hold an integrated concept of occupation, so it comes as no surprise that he divided therapeutic occupations into sections, describing them as useful work in the sewing room, farm, gardens, ward and kitchens, for example, and separate from recreation and amusement. Even so, and somewhat confusingly, Eager also appeared to accept occupational therapy, conceptually, as inclusive of the others by the following definition and subdivisions:

*Whereas **Occupational Therapy** may be defined as the organisation of suitable employment for the purpose of combating idleness, this can be further sub-divided into **Physical Therapy**, or the organisation of recreations during relaxation from such occupation and **Social Therapy**, or the organisation of amusements...*[57]

His booklet was historically significant as Eager was, perhaps, the first to pose apparently simple but very important questions about defining occupation. He must have pondered long over the perennial problems of dividing 'doing' or 'occupation' into work, labour, recreation and amusement. His writing briefly reflected some of these difficulties which are the subject of renewed debate today. In discussing the 'recreation/work' divide in occupation, he used the example of 'young children about the house during school holidays' arguing that their cry 'What can I do'? signified a want of *occupation* without the slightest resemblance to *work*. The word *work*, he said, implies *'labour*, by which we earn our living, in contrast to the term *occupation* which seems to imply more the idea of 'passing away the time!' He recognised then, as in modern debate, that 'one person's work may be another person's recreation; but the man who earns his living as a fisherman would surely be the last to select this form of occupation *as a recreation.'* Eager was obviously struggling with the concepts, finally admitting that 'I always avoid calling *Occupational Therapy* WORK, because this word seems so repugnant to the modern mind, whereas it is really very difficult to define the difference.'[58]

In a brief historical overview he, along with others such as Rees-Thomas, ascribed to Dr Simon, of the Gutersloh Mental Hospital in Germany, earlier in the century, the first 'proper', systematic and supervised grouping and classes to induce idle patients to 'do something.'[59] Simon had been so successful that his methods were introduced and being used in the 1930s in Dutch Mental Hospitals. Patients in British Mental Hospitals had long been encouraged to work, he said, but only about 35 per cent of the inmates were so engaged. He argued that:

> Where such a system has been introduced on intensive lines, the change in the general atmosphere has been most noticeable, and the hospital which had formerly been a refuge for idlers, becomes a hive of industry.[60]

Indeed, Eager said, 'the Mental Hospital which practises occupational therapy creates a spirit of hopefulness and happiness which is absent in one which does not do so.' He advised that such results were possible only with the co-operation of the staff as a whole, and could 'never be achieved by one or two enthusiasts alone.'

Eager assigned roles to all groups of staff because 'the main purpose of the hospital is the treatment of the patient's mental state, and if occupation in a certain department is considered the correct treatment, the hospital staff must co-operate towards that end.' The medical staff must not only allot patients to suitable classes, but prescribe the occupations:

> Indeed, one might venture to suggest that the prescribing of suitable occupations for patients is as important as the prescribing of drugs; one might even go further, and suggest that the latter might be largely dispensed with, if more attention were given to the former.[61]

All members of staff, including the Matron, the head Male Nurse, 'nurse, probationers, laundrymaid, housemaid, kitchenmaid, or a member of the artisan staff' should be involved, along with all heads of departments, such as the clerk, steward, clerk of works, and engineer. They must 'encourage the occupation of as many patients as possible in their several departments' even if 'various officials have to devote a certain amount of time to helping and supervising the patients.' Additionally, staff in charge of the programs needed to know each patient's peculiarities and habits.[62]

Eager considered that it was essential to class patients according to their individual capabilities, with their progress carefully graded as interest or proficiency increased or decreased. Emphasising that occupational therapy was not a 'means of reducing the staff or a form of cheap labour' he specified that 'the occupational hours' which often lasted less than two hours morning and afternoon, were definitely for *treatment*. [63] Some of the occupations he prescribed for particular diagnostic groups were as follows:   .

- For 'mental defectives'—picking threads out of rags for upholstery or waste (which was preferable to them tearing their clothes into rags) and, with help and competent guidance, coir mat making or rubber tyre mat-making, wire-netting, weaving, boot-making, knitting socks and sweaters and jumpers on machines under competent supervision;
- For various types of dementia—rag picking, paper bag making, weaving face cloths, floor cloths, and dish cloths on frames, making curb stones or tiles from concrete often for later use in a large hospital;
- For various types of delusional psychoses including cases of dementia praecox (schizophrenia)—fancy ties on frames, plaited straw baskets, envelopes, cardboard boxes, socks, etc. (hand knitted), wool rugs, French polishing, basket and brush making;
- For epileptics—all kinds of net making, and the making of fire lighters;

- For early admissions—fancy ties on frames, floor cloths, dish cloths, and face cloths, slipper making, fancy knitting, stuffed toy making, raffia work;
- For those who show some special aptitude—under the supervision of a member of the staff, cabinet making and carpentry, tinsmith, painting, plumbing, bookbinding, bootmaking, upholstering, tailoring, engineering, and printing;
- For the restless and noisy patient—pulling or pushing a heavy roller, lawn mower, hand cart, or wheelbarrow, levelling ground, re-laying football and cricket pitches, making excavations for new buildings, carrying baskets to the laundry, and classes of physical drill.[64]

In progressing to the notion of recreation Eager prescribed that it must be free from monotony, a complete change from work, and must 'rope in' those patients who sat about doing nothing in non-occupation therapy hours. As well as dances, cricket, football, hockey, bowls, and tennis, which had long been popular in mental hospitals, his recommendations included walks round the hospital estate, or neighbouring country lanes, and 'Swedish Physical Drill' which the patients themselves welcomed with enthusiasm, saying 'this is the best hour of the day.'[65]

Regarding amusements or 'Social Therapy,' Eager recommended the use of the hospital's recreation hall for theatrical productions. After occupational therapy hours, he recommended that cards, dominoes, draughts and chess be encouraged, along with inter-ward parties and competitions, table tennis and billiard tournaments, dancing, glee singing, the wireless, cinema and the Staff Concert. Eager concluded that 'the prescribing of occupation is often of greater importance than the prescribing of drugs.'[66]

## Dr J. Iveson Russell

Indicative also of growing interest, the first full length textbook on occupational therapy in Britain *The Occupational Treatment of Mental Illness* by John Iveson Russell was published in 1938. In the Foreword, William Rees-Thomas recognised its original status remarking that it was appropriate that 'it should come out of Yorkshire', the county in which the Tukes and Ellis historic experiments with occupation as treatment for the mentally ill were carried out. Whilst acknowledging that 'occupation therapy can be applied to patients suffering from any form of bodily or mental disease' Rees-Thomas disclaimed it as a method of cure, but endorsed it as a solution to 'many problems which arise in the nursing and management of patients suffering from mental illness.'[67]

In order to apply an occupational philosophy to the treatment of illness Russell, like Eager, considered the occupational nature of people generally, in the first instance:

> ...the problem is one of human nature...We have all seen men deteriorate when they have left an active occupation and retired to a life of ease with nothing to do. We are all familiar with the sad state of mind of the young man who has never had a job, and the good-humoured self-assurance that he displays when at last he gets one. Undoubtedly idleness has an evil influence, and worthy occupation a beneficial influence, on the human mind, and the explanation is not far to seek. By education and social experience man acquires an 'idea of an ideal self,' in other words, a personal opinion regarding his particular status, obligations, and duties, in the society of mankind, and a sense of

*propriety for his own conduct and for the courtesies which he deserves from others.*

*The happiness of his whole life depends upon the welfare of this ideal. Any thought, act, or circumstance which frustrates it produces a feeling of unhappiness, and any thought, act, or circumstance which expands or enhances it produces happiness. Thus failure, insult, and criticism cause unhappiness; success and approbation cause happiness. In brief, a person is made happy by circumstances that cause him to think well of himself, and only by acts worthy of approval can he avoid the humiliating feeling of failure and the frustration of the ideal self.[68]*

The book was prepared mainly for mental hospital nurses although it might prove helpful to occupation therapists as it was written for 'the student of the art of mind healing' who used crafts as the 'instruments'.[69] He defined occupational treatment as a:

*...deliberately planned means of attaching a patient's interests to material objects and their common relationships, in a manner that will persistently emphasise his own value and importance, and so prevent the troubled mind from seeking refuge in morbid introspection in which it can find but a nightmare of unworthiness and despair.[70]*

In his judgement, no particular occupation was especially suitable for a particular type of illness, that being dependent on the individual patient. Despite that, Russell deemed it essential that the treatment was prescribed, directed and supervised by a physician. To ensure that the 'occupational officer' had all the information required, along with the case records, he applied a simple 'formulary', This questioned the choice of indoor or outdoor work, whether the occupation should be stimulating or sedatory, requiring high or low levels of concentration, was of a skilled, simple, repetitive, or habitual nature, was active or sendentary, whether dangerous tools were permitted or to be avoided, and whether the patient needed to be observed whilst engaged, or not.[71]

Russell reflected that ordinarily, 'during illness and convalescence, nothing occurs in the daily life of the invalid to make him feel proud of himself...but the mental hospital patient endures the most humiliating illness of all.' In part, to overcome that difficulty, 'occupation treatment aimed to give each patient a worthy place in the active life of his restricted environment, to assist him to fill that place creditably, and thereby to make him think well of himself.'[72] 'We believe,' wrote Russell, 'that idleness is a positive evil, and that it is the cause rather than the effect of the social, moral, and intellectual deterioration of patients suffering from mental illness of long duration.' Therapeutic occupations, on the other hand, offered the easiest and best return path to the realities of community life and social relationships. Without prevarication, he added that:

*...suitable occupation, carefully chosen and skillfully presented, will improve the mental and social condition of every patient in a mental hospital, but this is easier to preach than to put into practice. Therapeutic occupations must be conducted under medical supervision, and in some cases specifically prescribed; but the main secret of success lies in the method and the manner in which the occupation is presented. [73]*

In order to be used more effectively in response to individual differences and needs, therapeutic occupations themselves were classified according to types such as: artistic, executive, physical, inventive, intellectual, competitive, altruistic, submissive, and dominative. Practical assessment to effect those classifications, which was used as a tool to aid preliminary choice of occupations, took place not only in the occupation centres but throughout the hospital whilst observing whether the patient was:

- Designing or copying, and more interested in the aesthetic effect than the workmanship.
- Happy to spend hours in fine stitchery, or fitting an intricate mechanism.
- Preferring laundry or domestic work, or land work.
- Studying and inventing new methods and modifications.
- Anxious to learn, but without desire to apply the knowledge acquired.
- Ready and willing to take part in competitions.
- Delighting in altruism.
- Anxious to receive orders, and pleased to obey without question.
- Delighted to be 'in charge' of something and responsible for its care.[74]

However, that assessment was but a guide, for specific occupation could not be prescribed by this method alone, as illustrated by the following case:

> A.B., aged 67, had retired two years previously from the sub-editorship of a well-known newspaper. Hallucinatory voices taunted him with the remark, 'You never were sub-editor of the Blankshire Post,' and, believing that his neighbours were saying this, he was constantly trying to prove that he had, in fact, held that position. His conversation, although muttered and hardly audible, was high-brow and scornful, and as far as he could be credited with any interests at all, they were concerned with history, literature, finance, European politics, and self. He was placed in the intellectual category, and every means available was tried to woo his lofty and elusive interests, but always with complete failure, until without any theoretical reason he was introduced to the joiners' shop, where the craft of wood-turning immediately fascinated him and incidentally silenced his hallucinations.
>
> The case illustrates the danger of placing a too confident reliance upon obvious signs. The whole truth is rarely obvious. This patient had been apprenticed in his youth to the printing trade, and his subsequent 'success' and promotion had placed him at the age of fifty in a position of responsibility in which he lived for fifteen years at the limit of his ability, and although passably efficient he was constantly apprehensive of impending failure, and suffered from the stress of concealing his difficulties. When he retired from business he collapsed mentally. Hallucinatory images told him first that he had not been worthy of a sub-editorship and later that he never had been sub-editor. Defensively he was obliged to pose as a scholar and at the same time evade every intellectual test, but in the joiners' shop his superior education was taken for granted without question, and the turning lathe was to him like a raft to a drowning man.[75]

The final section of Russell's text that will be visited here is the section on habit training. Eleanor Clarke Slagle in the USA had centred on this when she worked with Meyer and, as Henderson was so influenced by their work, it appears particularly relevant to consider it as a concern on both sides of the Atlantic. Russell went so far as to suggest that 'the general principle of any system of occupational treatment might be described as habit training.' He discussed it particularly with regards to 'training in the manners of common decency' which was applicable to patients exhibiting 'a very low standard of behaviour.'[76] The following schedule was provided as a guide for male patients. A similar one was used for women patients:

*Schedule A.—Men*

7 a.m.  Rise. Dress in trousers and slippers. Turn down bedclothes. Fold pyjamas or nightshirt. Walk in group to lavatory, carrying shoes. Brush shoes, with pol ishing brush only. Wash, being stripped to the waist. Brush teeth. Return to dormitory and complete dressing. Brush hair. Dress inspection

8 a.m.  Walk in group to breakfast, which is to be served and consumed with decorum. (Other patients may have had breakfast earlier.)

8.30 a.m.  Lavatory. Wash hands.

9 a.m.  Don overalls. Walk smartly to place of occupation, which may be a distance of half a mile.

10 a.m.  Urinal. Remove overalls and jackets and parade for P.T.

10.30 a.m.  Cup of tea out of doors.

10.40 a.m.  Don overalls and resume work.

11.30 a.m.  Deposit implements, carts, etc., in proper place and in orderly arrangement, and walk smartly to ward. Remove overalls, and hang them in proper places. Wash hands and face and brush hair. Dress inspection.

12 noon.  Dinner, to be served with careful attention. Spoons should not be used when knives and forks are indicated; two separate courses should not be served together; and bread should not be tossed to the patient from the opposite side of the table.

12.30 p.m.  Wash hands and rest till 2 p.m.

2 p.m.  Dress inspection. Don overalls and walk to work.

3 p.m.  Cup of tea. Return to ward as at 11.30 a.m.

3.30 p.m.  Parade at bath-room. Clean and polish shoes; be shaved if necessary. Bathe and, if necessary, change underclothes. Dress. Brush hair. Brush clothes. Dress inspection.

5 p.m.  Tea, with the same care as at dinner.

6 p.m.  Attend indoor entertainment or outdoor recreation.

7.30 p.m.  Lavatory. Brush teeth. Bed. [77]

# Associations of Occupational Therapists

Two associations of occupational therapists were established in Britain in the 1930s. They were the Association of Occupational Therapists, and the Scottish Association of Occupational Therapy. These were antecedent to the British Association formed in the 1970s.

## The Scottish Association of Occupational Therapy

A group of eleven Scottish 'occupational therapists', with the encouragement of Dr Henderson, established the *Scottish Association of Occupational Therapy* (SAOT) in 1932.[78] Most were not trained in occupational therapy, but held art college diplomas and worked in mental hospitals as instructresses in the arts and crafts. Stories of the pioneer work of two such instructresses were included in the previous chapter. Peg Fulton was the exception.

The first meeting was held in Glasgow on 27 May 1932. Miss Margaret Menzies, who was the occupational therapy instructress at the Glasgow Royal Hospital at that time, was elected President. Miss Fulton was elected secretary/treasurer and remained on the committee until the meetings were suspended in 1939 because of World War II.

From its inception to 1939, when the war started, there were thirty members of the SAOT. The Scottish Association maintained contact with the fledgling Association of Occupational Therapists south of the border, and with the Canadian occupational therapists who were setting up a department and a training course at the Astley Ainslie Institution during the 1930s.[79] No meetings were held during the war years.

Although that description is brief it is not because of any preconceived notions about importance. It is partly because of availability of resources and time constraints, and also that the fuller story of the early days of the Scottish Association will be told by Catherine F Paterson in the history of Scottish occupational therapy which she is currently completing.

## The Association of Occupational Therapists

Mary Macdonald was the instigator and first secretary of an informal committee of people who were interested in forming an association of English, Northern Irish and Welsh occupational therapists. She was also the Convenor of the first General Meeting at which the Association came into being. Because of those roles she was asked to write an account of the Association's history to commemorate its twenty-first birthday year. This she did in a series of articles published between March and July 1957, in the Association's official journal *Occupational Therapy*.[80] Her account, which has the authenticity and, of course, the personal bias, of being written by one intimately involved in its unfolding, is used as the basis for this section of the chapter.

The editorial of the first Journal told how the Association was founded at the insistence of a number of students who saw the need for some such organisation.[81] Macdonald was one of those students, and she began her history by explaining her part in instigating the initial meeting, which got the founding of the Association under way:

> *Those who knew the Dorset House of early Bristol days will remember the week-end cottage in the Mendip Hills. It was when walking on these hills that a question was put to Dr. Casson...by two of the Occupational Therapy students:–*
> *'Could a professional association be set up for Occupational Therapists?'*
> *Dr. Casson's reply was characteristically brief and to the point:–*
> *'It's up to you!'*
> *This was a challenge in itself.* [82]

The challenge was taken up, and a meeting 'of those interested in forming an Association of Occupational Therapists' was called on 7 August 1935. Macdonald chose to tell the tale of that meeting, which was held at Dorset House, using 'the actual words of the first records, which, though kept in a stiff-covered exercise book, were properly formal.'

> *Present: Dr. Casson, Mrs. O. Reed, Miss Jackson, Miss Dahl, Miss Dennett. (Students) Miss Plater, Miss Brown, Miss Hick, Miss Hogg, Miss Parsons, Miss Macdonald.*

*Dr. Casson opened the discussion by saying that the present students at Dorset House had talked of the possibility of forming an Association of Occupational Therapists, and this gathering was to consider and plan how this could be done.*

*Careful consideration should be given to what was to be the standard of eligibility to the proposed Association.*

*It was suggested that all Medical Superintendents of Mental and other likely hospitals be written to and asked to inform practising Occupational Therapists in their hospitals of the idea of forming an Association, and of fixing a meeting in London.*

*It was agreed that there was an opening for an Association and the meeting then discussed who to approach first.*

*It was suggested that a Committee be formed of leading and qualified occupational therapists, to make proposals and arrangements. It was felt that the unqualified students, though interested, were hardly in a position to make a general appeal.*

*An Association of Occupational Therapists could deal with matters of standards of qualification, syllabuses, uniforms, and be of use in discovering openings and recommending trainees to posts, etc. etc.*

*It was felt that those present at the meeting should approach the suggested Committee and leave further arrangements in their hands.*

Macdonald, in a slightly humorous aside, then added:

*In less time than it seems to take nowadays, a second meeting was called. This was attended by trained Occupational Therapists and the following are extracts from the recorded account of it.* [83]

That, apparently brief but significant meeting, as well as establishing the procedure for the formation of an Association also raised central issues with which the body would concern itself for many years. These were issues of professional education such as 'standards of qualification' and 'syllabuses', and professional practice such as 'discovering openings and recommending trainees to posts' and, surprisingly, what turned out to be a long-running issue about 'uniforms'. It took until 1939 for the Association to undertake the provision of the excellent and helpful service it has long provided between employers and potential employees, that of notification of vacant posts.

The next meeting was held less than three weeks later at 2.00 p.m. on 24 August, also at Dorset House. Present on that occasion were Miss Baily from the Maudsley Hospital, Mrs Clarke from the Chester Mental Hospital, Miss Crousaz from Fishponds Hospital, Bristol, Miss Jackson from Dorset House, Mrs Reed (Non practising), and Miss Macdonald. In a letter Mrs Owens, who was not present, suggested:

*...a London Meeting in the New Year. Those present voted for a date in The New Year, 15th February being suggested. Members of this meeting could undertake to circularize hospitals in their respective areas. It was felt that Miss Darwin would be an excellent chairman, and that Mrs. Owens should be asked to speak on 'The Definition of Occupational Therapy.' It was felt that the Orthopaedic side should be represented and the meeting decided to invite Mr. Seddon of the National Orthopaedic Hospital, Stanmore, Middlesex, to speak. A third speaker was to be chosen representing the Psychological field.*

*It was felt that Miss Fulton from Scotland should be invited to the London Meeting,* [84]

Macdonald again added a personal aside, which possibly reflected some of her own feeling about how matters were proceeding. She recorded that: 'with considerable satisfaction, and in high hope the group dispersed.' Of significance, the three subjects deemed to be representative of the central focus of the proposed association, were defining occupational therapy, orthopaedics, and psychology. Also of significance is the choice of at least one medical expert, presumably to 'tell' the occupational therapists what would be expected of them.

The next meeting on 9 November was held at 71 Bedford Street South, Liverpool, at Mrs Owens' invitation. There were four others present: Miss Baily, Mrs Clarke, Miss Jackson, and Miss Macdonald. The minutes of the meeting suggest that a rumour was circulating that an Association had already been formed. To dispel it, and to arouse interest, a letter was sent to the *Mental Welfare Journal*. Despite some obvious disappointment in the 'apathy' and 'distrust' expressed in letters from the two hospitals which replied to the circular sent earlier, such was the spirit of the instigators, that they deemed there was sufficient interest to warrant going ahead with a General Meeting to establish an Association. This was held on 14 March 1936.

In the following extracts the agenda and report of the General Meeting, provided by Macdonald, have been combined and comments added:

*Chairman's Speech.*

*MISS DARWIN explained the formation of the temporary Committee, and named them, asking them to stand up in turn. The question the meeting was to decide was 'Should an Occupational Therapists' Association be started?' In the last five years there had been great developments in occupational therapy, not only in the work done but in interest gained.*

*In America and on the Continent occupational therapy was carried on, although in different ways. Perhaps, while not necessarily taking either as they stood, a system could be evolved adapting the best of both methods. In Holland and Germany occupational therapy was done under the direction of the Medical Superintendent through the nursing staffs. In America trained occupational therapists worked quite apart from the nursing staff, except for the necessary co-operation. The Royal Medico-Psychological Association had an occupational therapy course for nurses; the Maudsley Hospital and Dorset House trained students other than nurses. In planning the formation of an Association there seemed an opportunity to arrange an improved standard of training.*

*H. J. SEDDON, ESQ., C.M.G., M.A., D.M. OXON., F.R.C.S. ENG., M.B. B.S. LOND., M.R.C.S. EDIN., L.R.C.P. LOND. (Occupational Therapy in relation to Orthopaedics).*

*Mr Seddon said he was not very well qualified to talk as he had no Orthopaedic occupational centre in his hospital, but it was hoped to open up a new part of the hospital for rehabilitation of patients. He had, however, taken a survey of his patients with a view to considering where and how Occupational Therapy could be beneficially used. His findings were as follows:—*

*•Surgical T.B. 150 of his 310 patients might have occupational therapy. He considered occupational therapy of value only as occupation and entertainment, as good for general treatment but of no local value.*

•*For Fractures. Occupational therapy was of very great value, locally and generally.*
•*In General Orthopaedics. i.e. Infantile Paralysis, Spastic Paralysis, Rickets, etc.– 6 out of 110 would benefit directly, i.e. 5%. The exercise in a swimming pool was best and most efficacious treatment, but Occupational Therapy was good for morale.*

*Summary 90% do not benefit directly. Occupational therapy was helpful in maintaining morale in all cases. Treatment of fractures in this country was unsatisfactory, but this was being considered by the Royal Medical Council, and Insurance Companies were becoming interested. Rehabilitation and re-adjustment were prime needs, i.e. a boy at Oswestry suffering from Hemiplegia, was trained for house-painting There was definite scope for occupational therapy on these lines.*

*DR A. W. PETRIE (C.B.E., M.D D.P.M., F.R.C.P., F.R.C.S.) spoke on occupational therapy in relation to mental treatment, a vast subject on which he could only give general points.*
•*In cases of Traumatic Neuroses—occupational therapy was of value.*
•*In Mental Deficiency where co-ordination of mind and limb were needed occupational therapy was not something new; it was a revival. England had once been recognised as a pioneer country, but she seemed to have slipped back. Occupational therapy should cover all activities and all kinds and stages of illness. The importance of occupational therapy was not so much on the work produced as on the effect of this work on the patient.*
•*Chronic patients may help with work in hospitals but should be given the added interests of needlework, gardening, carpentry, etc.*

*Occupational therapy centres should be formed as a training ground for ability and 'work habit'. A question which needed to be looked into was the advisability of deciding if men and women should work together or in separate centres. According to some methods, doctors prescribed occupational therapy and nurses applied treatment, but craft experts were needed and nurses could not be expert in everything. An organiser was needed too. Which method would meet the requirements?*

*MRS. OWENS said she was amazed to see so many present. She said she felt that they came from many spheres but most had probably had mental hospital training and experience. She then said:*
*'I propose that we form an Association and select a Committee.'*

*MISS RIVETT had great pleasure in seconding the motion. She felt that the great need for such an Association was recognised. New ideas were often regarded with the eye of suspicion, but occupational therapy had passed this stage. Through an Association there would be the opportunity for the exchange of ideas not only among ourselves, but with other countries as well.*

GENERAL DISCUSSION
*COLONEL DE SALIS (Maidstone) having had 16 years experience, thought the idea of an Association was good, but it must be very wide. The time had come when occupational therapy should be recognised. In a mental hospital every nurse should have some knowledge of crafts. Occupational Therapy did not stop in the occupational therapy centre. Occupational therapists should have wider experience and knowledge, i.e. mental, craft and general. It should always be remembered that the patient must come first.*[85]

*MISS JACKSON (Dorset House, Bristol) felt she might tell something of American Occupational Therapists' Association, which was formed in 1917. There were 3 categories into which its members fell.*

*(a) Graduates from training colleges having one year's experience.*

*(b) Anyone having successful experience for 4 years.*

*(c) Anyone having special training in occupational therapy.*

*The Association now governs standards of training.*

*MR. ROWE (Great Yarmouth). Occupational Therapists had much to learn. Occupational Therapy should be efficient in its training and organisation. Medical Officers should select suitable patients. Patients should, if possible, be taken from the ward to other surroundings for occupational therapy. Medical Officers should select nurses as assistants. A balanced attitude to production was important.*

*MISS NEUKIRK (visitor from America). Americans were interested in our new venture and sent good wishes!*

*DR. CASSON would be delighted to see an Occupational Therapists' Association formed. Medical Officers, Nursing Staff and Occupational Therapists should make an ideal team in an institution, for the successful and smooth running of occupational therapy.*

*MISS HICK (Bath Orthopaedic Hospital) gave account of successful work and co-operation of nurses.*

*Mrs. Owens proposal was put to the vote and carried unanimously.*

*After votes of thanks to Chairman and Speakers, there was an adjournment for tea.*

*Nominations for a Council were than accepted and the names of those elected were:– Miss Baily, Mrs. Clarke, Miss Crousaz, Mr. Lawrence, Miss Macdonald (new qualified), Mrs. Oliver, Mrs. Owens, Mr. O. Reed, Miss Rivett, Miss Ross, Mrs. Rowe, Colonel de Salis.* [86]

At the second informal committee meeting it had been decided that any and all the expenses incurred would be shared by the committee members. Macdonald added after the General Meeting that it was perhaps relevant and amusing to note the first accounts, which when divided amongst the eight original committee members came to nineteen shillings and eleven and a half pence each.[87] All too soon, the members of the Council began to experience problems of time and expense, which they needed to give their new commitment. Apart from the many hours they devoted to planning for the new Association, 'many had to travel long distances, and their fares, which came out of their own pockets, were—and are—a heavy burden on purses which in most cases are not too well filled.'[88]

A meeting of the new Council followed shortly after on 13 June 1936, and Mrs Glyn Owens was elected as chairman and Lt Col. De Salis as secretary/treasurer, however, the latter's death just six weeks later was an unexpected blow. He was mourned, despite most of the members' brief acquaintance with him, as apparently 'all felt (he) would be a splendid help by his clearness of thought, his executive abilities, and his experience of 16 years as occupation officer in the West Kent Mental Hospital.' Joyce Baily took over the duties of secretary/treasurer.[89]

Before the first General Meeting of the newly-formed Association could be held:

*A sub-committee was formed to draw up the provisional constitution. As it was felt that the assistance of members of the medical profession and of those experienced in hospital management was, for many reasons, desirable, a number of well-known men and women were invited to act as an Advisory Board. Helped by some of these, another sub-committee began to inquire into the subjects of training, qualifications and examinations. The work of these sub-committees was reviewed by the Council and the enrolment of members and associate members was undertaken.*[90]

Miss Briscoe, Dr. Elizabeth Casson, Professor Mapother, Dr. Minski, Dr. Iveson Russell and Mr. H. J. Seddon and Miss Yates agreed to become members of the Advisory Board, with Sir Hubert Bond of the Board of Control as President, and Ruth Darwin, Jane Walker and Arnold Rowntree as Vice-Presidents. Mr. de Guingand agreed to act as the Honorary Solicitor, and Mr. Glyn Owens as Honorary Auditor, the latter offering 'his London business address to be used as the 'Registered' office of the Association.[91]

Council also set about what has proved to be an ongoing and onerous task, the defining of an Occupational Therapist. The first 'official' definition of the Association was as follows:

*An Occupational Therapist is any person who is appointed as responsible for the treatment of patients by occupation and who is qualified by training and experience to administer the prescription of a Physician or Surgeon in the treatment of any patient by occupation.*[92]

It was also decided that, at least initially, but with a closing date for this form of Membership fixed for 1 March 1939, the first members to be recognised as such:

*...might be either those who had qualified at recognised Schools and who had held whole-time appointments as occupational therapists for not less than a year, or those who had had a minimum of four years' practical experience in occupational therapy... Associate Members, i.e. persons not covered by the two former qualifications, but who were interested in the work of the Association, and anxious to unite with it, were also to be welcomed.*[93]

The Dorset House and Maudsley Hospital training courses were recognised, at least until the development of an official educational policy. Thirty-seven applications for membership were approved, along with twenty-one associate memberships. Members paid an annual fee of £1/1/0, and Associates 10/6.

A Board of Registration of Medical Auxiliaries was set up in 1936, and Macdonald records that 'the remedial professions which were becoming more established were glad to be accepted by it.' The Board's aim was to keep a register of those qualified in the new remedial professions. It was represented at the Ministry of Health and co-operated with it in regard to training, practice, salary and employment conditions.[94]

In October 1937, the Ministry of Labour formally requested information from the Association for publication in a 'careers' pamphlet, which in some ways marked its National recognition as a distinct profession.[95] However, the main work of Council, during that year, was the production of an examination syllabus. In 1938 twelve candidates sat for the first Association preliminary examinations, which encompassed papers on Anatomy and Physiology, Psychology, and First Aid. Of those, eight students were from Dorset House and four were from the London school. Figure 2.5.10 is the official Association record of the 1938 examination results. (The names of those who failed have been covered.) The first Association final examinations were held in September of the same year. In July of 1938 the Association's practice of inspection of schools and approval of curricula began with a statement to the effect that:

*...only such schools as have submitted their syllabus for approval by Council; have been officially visited by two Members or the Council, and entered candidates for the Association's Examinations, shall be recommended by Council.*

**Figure 2.5.10:   The official Association record of the 1938 examination results**

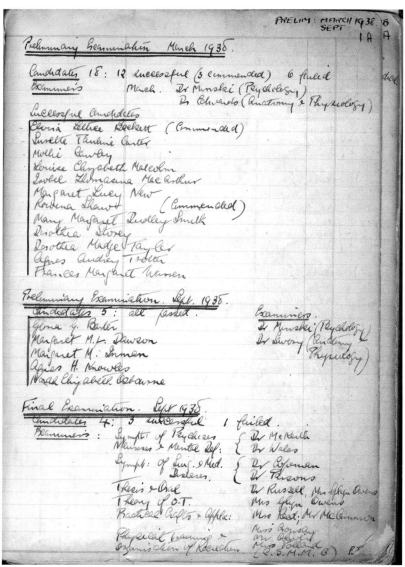

Discussion about Incorporation also commenced in 1938, although this was to take until the 8 January 1945 to achieve, after the statutory period of integration of a new association.[96] During the following year, 1939, the Association became a Constituent Body of the British Federation of Social Workers creating its first link with another professional body with similar aims. The Federation promoted 'consultation and co-operation among its members', provided 'opportunities for the interchange of knowledge', discussed 'matters affecting social legislation', improved 'conditions of work', and facilitated research.

## The Journal

The second half of 1938 saw the advent of the first issue of the Association's journal *Occupational Therapy*. Nancy Ross took on the job of editor, assisted by Miss A. M. English, as sub-editor; both were members of Council. The founding Editorial, not surprisingly, provided a brief history of the early struggles of the Association which have already been referred to, and then went on to list the aims of the publication. These are provided in full because of their importance at that time, and because they are, largely, carried forward today, which makes the British Journal different from, and richer than, many other professional occupational therapy journals of current times. Ross began her editorial with brief mention of the process of establishing the Journal. She recorded that the sub-committee deputed to the task was appointed in the Summer of 1937 and began by investigating the cost of production, Their work had been delayed by the lack of an editor. 'All members of the sub-committee and, according to their own statements, of the Council, had a knowledge of the technique of journalism which is best described in the words of Lewis Carroll as a "perfect and absolute blank."' Ross went on to say about herself and her colleague:

*...and the present editress is one to whom the above dictum applied with the utmost intensity. However, nothing venture, nothing win. It was obvious that we could not have a Journal without an Editor, and experience however dearly bought, is the best teacher. Members will realise with what trepidation we—for in this matter Editress and Sub-Editress stand together—take this plunge into the troubled waters of publicity. With this appeal for your mercy, we lay before you what we believe should be the policy of our Journal.*

What followed was a list of four objectives for the *Journal* which are, refreshingly, open, aimed more at assisting people from a range of disciplines to learn from each other, than simply providing an outlet for scholarly publications.

*Obviously, the first object of the official organ of such an Association as ours must be to make contacts and keep in touch with the members. With this end in view, we are inciting both full members and associate members to send us such personal notes as they think will be of interest, in order that we may feel that we know each other. These notes will be added to the list of members which we intend to publish, and will, we are sure, be a great help in breaking down the isolation of which some complain. As new members join us, we shall add these to the list and incite them to contribute notes about themselves.*

*Our second aim is that the Journal should be a medium for the expression of views on controversial subjects and for the airing of criticisms and suggestions for improvement.*

*Thirdly we hope that by getting into touch with allied professions or kindred subjects, new points for discussions may be raised. It may be that we shall find these in recent research in Psychology or Medical Science; in study within our own profession, in teaching or in nursing; or in the development of occupational therapy in this or other countries. We invite all readers to co-operate in this, and shall always be glad to consider contributions, either in the form of letters or of articles on subjects in which they are interested or in which they have done special work.*

*Lastly, we will endeavour so far as lies in our power to act as an information bureau from which members may obtain information when their questions are neither so difficult nor so lengthy as to warrant the employment of the scheme for the provision of expert advisers.*[97]

Members had received their initial copy free, and Ross ended the historical editorial with two appeals to readers. The first was to request they buy 'at least one extra copy to put in the hands of some person who might become a new member or whose interest it might be helpful to obtain' to offset the excessive costs of producing the Journal for so few members. The second appeal was a general admonition for unity and commitment:

*Do not wait to see what you can get out of the Association, but with all your heart put what you can into it. We can use your energies, your brains, your abilities and your money. We can use your criticisms and suggestion.*[98]

Macdonald noted that much of the stability of the Association depended on the Journal, particularly in the war years, despite its occasional rather than regular publication, and paid tribute to those who produced it. For example, Ross, she said, 'most gallantly carried on her job as "Editress"' until ill-health and pressure of work caused her to resign.[99] Congratulatory letters on the birth of the Journal were received from the President of the Association, Sir Hubert Bond, who wrote that 'the Association's decision to found a Journal is a wise one', and from vice president, Ruth Darwin, who recognised the Journal's potential value because 'workers in the wide field of occupational treatment are often isolated and unaware of the methods in use elsewhere and of the many experiments that are now being tried.'[100]

# Developing occupational therapy practice around the country

Adoption by the medical profession shaped the boundaries of occupational therapy during the early years. Doctors' definitions of this new therapy limited it to obvious remedial or curative work according to prescriptive practice and an eventually reductionist paradigm, although that must have appeared to be the opposite case to the early pioneers. With regards to prescription, Casson, probably representative of many others, had a decided opinion. It involved the triple interchange of doctor, patient and occupational therapist. She considered it the 'crux of treatment' and vital, particularly when cases were not clear cut which, in her opinion, they seldom were. She called to the Association to ensure both the 'high standard of filling prescriptions' and the 'guidance of those doctors who have to learn to prescribe well.' Prescriptions must provide:

> ...not only the diagnosis; but the nature of mental effect the treatment is intended to produce. Even if nothing more explicit is said, 'stimulating', 'sedative', 'encouragement of self expression', or of 'self respect,' gives some idea of what to aim at. It does not matter—in fact it is almost better—for some of the instructions to be verbal and that there should be a periodic consultation over each patient.[101]

## For the treatment of physical conditions

Casson explained in 1935, at a London conference on the welfare of cripples and invalid children:

> You all know how much afraid we are of moving a limb after any injury. It is a necessary provision of Nature to desire to rest a painful joint. In the ordinary course of events our work begins again and we forget the injury because our attention is fixed on something else and constant messages reach the brain that cause the joint to move unconsciously. Careful treatment however often fixes our attention on an injury and fear prevents movement after it is quite safe. We all saw soldiers during the War who came up to hospital for massage and their mental attitude prevented their recovery—'If my leg still needs daily massage it just shows that the doctor knows it is not well' is what he believed consciously or unconsciously. In such cases as this occupation completed the cure much quicker than any other treatment—often a ward dance, a game of football, or, if it was available, a treadle fretsaw was all that was needed. [102]

She went on to outline a few principles of occupational therapy, which sound remarkably simple, yet are too often forgotten in the desire for the complexities of modern medicine. First, 'that every action depends on a stimulus.' She discussed how, in the case of children, when the stimulus provided by a toy, for example, reached the brain, 'the little fingers move in ordered rhythm.' As the child improved so muscular effort could be increased and measured 'to a nicety to suit the amount of movement that the doctor has ordered.' Second, 'to arouse specific emotions that result in the desire to use muscles and thereby to return to health.' Casson recommended making use of 'one of the most powerful motives we have'—curiosity. She provided a story of occupational therapy in physical practice:

> Not long ago Miss Forrester Brown invited one of my Occupational Therapy staff to work under her at the Bath Orthopaedic Hospital, and prescribed occupations for a man with an injured spine. Lying near him were two boys who had lately come to the Hospital from remote farms. They had had infantile paralysis when quite young. Their families had settled down to the fact that they were cripples. They had been washed and fed quite kindly, and that was all. During the long years they had become completely apathetic and seemingly feeble-minded. They lay in bed in Hospital and watched the man in the next bed. Gradually curiosity was stimulated by what they saw and heard and they began to want to do something too. One boy asked for a pencil, and when he saw his drawing and felt his muscles producing his drawing, a whole new life came to him. Both boys are now working well, and quickly showed that their intelligence is excellent. [103]

With regard to another type of 'physical' practice, Dr Walker's occupational work at Nayland East Anglia Sanatorium mentioned in earlier chapters, continued. She was ill by the time of a social meeting of occupational therapists at Friends House early in 1938 where she was scheduled to talk about her program at Nayland.[104,105] Instead Dr Soltau, a colleague, gave a paper. Soltau spoke first of Walker's interest even before the name of 'occupational therapy' was invented, and of how 'the treatment of the body with and through the mind had been one of the leading characteristics of her work for persons suffering from pulmonary tuberculosis.'

Quoting Dr Walker at the 1935 meeting when the Occupational Therapy Association was inaugurated, Soltau reminded the audience of Walker's view that there are three types of occupational therapy:
- diversional therapy, when the patient is not fit for more than simple games and amusements to divert the mind
- ...the occupational type of work, consisting of making useful and artistic things, not only for the purpose of occupying the mind but for the restoration of impaired or weakened functions
- ...vocational work, in the attempt to place the patient in a better position to earn his living when restored to health.

She went on to discuss how, when dealing with tuberculosis, people must be provided with some outlet for their energy, 'or they will give way to irritation, or quarrelsomeness or go off to the local public house.' Gardening was one occupation put to therapeutic use at Nayland, and was, presumably, for women and men. Men, Soltau said, 'are more difficult to cater for than women,' which accounted for the use made of the carpenter's and painter's shop at Nayland in which patients made and painted furniture. She finished with a quote: '"The soul's joy lies in doing," said the poet Shelley, and this is true for all.'[106]

Nancy Ross, in a paper *Gardening as a Remedial Occupation* picked up on Soltau's lecture about its use in tuberculosis. Ross suggested that the benefits were employment in the open air but that, probably, only 'the lighter processes' of gardening would be suitable for the majority of patients. The emphasis needed to be put on 'the inspiring task of promoting growth, and not the depressing work of removing decay.'[107] Gertrude Noyes, who used it experimentally in the tuberculosis wards of a County General Hospital first gained approval for 'the experiment' from the Hospital Committee. The outcomes of the experiment were reported as positive in the following respects:
- Atmosphere in the ward was 'happier';
- Confidence, measured by interest in the work, increased;
- A decrease in worrying behaviour was exhibited.

Additionally some pointers about the nature of the treatment approach were given. Occupational therapy was seen to be more motivating when:
- Work was seen by the patients as 'part of a scheme';
- Work was for their own enjoyment and included choice;
- Work was advised by the doctor but was voluntary and unpressured.

Following that careful preliminary approach, which remains impressive today, it is not surprising that the scheme became a stable part of the treatment in the tuberculosis wards of the hospital.[108]

Arguably, one of the earliest 'occupational therapy departments' for the treatment of physical disabilities was that established at the Astley Ainslie Institution in Edinburgh. The first unit of the hospital had been opened in 1923, when Lt Col. John Cunningham became the first medical superintendent. Cunningham reported that in those early years gardening 'exercise' was prescribed for some cases, that outdoor games were used as a method of treatment from 1930, and a Hospital School for child patients was opened a year later, on an experimental basis. By 1933 the school, which Cunningham argued provided the juvenile patients with occupational therapy, was an accepted part of the program with very few of the patients unable to take part, and an average attendance of 11 weeks. About half to one-third of those who attended did so from their beds, while the number taught in a year was 50–60. Because the children tired easily the best form of instruction was provided through stories and projects, using instructional games, craftwork, and a percussion band, for example.

*Instruction aimed to:—*

*1. Provide children with suitable occupation which would help physical recovery and shorten the long hospital day.*

*2. Make it easier for children to return to the normal world of home and school on leaving the hospital.*[109]

Smith in *Between the Streamlet and the Town: A Brief History of the Astley Ainslie Hospital* described how, in the early 1930s, Cunningham, had 'become increasingly concerned that the hospital should do more to help in the rehabilitation of its adult patients.' Whilst attending an international medical conference, and talking with Dr Goldwyn Howland, Cunningham expressed that concern. Howland, who was the President of the Canadian Association of Occupational Therapists, responded with the words: 'You need occupational therapy!' He then 'outlined the benefits of this then comparatively unknown auxiliary branch of medicine'. Cunningham reported to the Hospital Board on the advisability of introducing occupational therapy and, wisely, having kept in touch with Dr Howland consulted him about possible appointments of Canadian occupational therapists to the Astley Ainslie.[110] Indeed, Members of the Canadian Medical Association visited the hospital. As a result Howland recommended that a Canadian occupational therapist, Amy de Brisay, who was in charge of Toronto General Hospital's occupational therapy department, should come to Scotland and start the Department.[111]

It was in September 1932, that de Brisay, who had undertaken the 1919 Toronto emergency course,[112] arrived in Edinburgh to establish an occupational therapy department at the Astley Ainslie Hospital. 'Initially she was on loan to the hospital for three months but so valuable did her work become that she remained another six months.'[113] Another Canadian occupational therapist, Mrs Macrae took over from her.

In 1936, the same year that the Occupational Therapy Training Centre was opened at Astley Ainsley, a new and specially designed Department was too. It had 'noisy' and 'quiet' workshops and was fully equipped with saws, lathes, and so forth, as the earlier war workshops had been. The Scottish Health Services Committee of 1935 had been very impressed by the Hospital's report on the benefits of various occupations which were provided and the individual supervision which was provided by therapists. It is noteworthy that Sir Robert Philip who had pioneered the use of occupation in tuberculosis was a member of the Board of Governors of both the Occupational Therapy Department and Training Centre. The Board appreciated that the Hospital could not continue indefinitely to depend upon Canadians to staff their facilities and it was for that reason that the training was established.[114]

London, too, was to open its first occupational therapy department, so named, during the decade. In 1938 one was opened at the Royal Free Hospital in Grays Inn Road. Miss Tarrant, of the London School, was 'permitted' to set up the department if she also agreed to superintend the dietetic kitchen and instruct patients in the Bircher-Benner diet. She agreed. Early pioneers obviously thought no price was too high for the chance of advancing the profession. Both enterprises flourished![115]

Allendale Curative Workshop deserves a mention in this section of the chapter. It was established in Bristol in 1939 in the part of Dorset House that had been the premises of a former hotel with nearly an acre of garden. Here again the work was experimental, and each case was a special study. It was staffed by students on clinical practice, under the guidance of Miss Macdonald, Miss K. Barber, Dr Eugen Weissenberg a student from Germany, and Mr R. C. Cole a teacher of joinery. In a report of *Forty Cases Treated at the Allendale Curative Workshop* published in the Lancet we learn that patients came, principally, from fracture clinics and were chosen:

> ...by their surgeons because of some complication calling for special attention—joints fixed by adhesions, or bad habits of posture. No patient was taken without prescription and full instructions from his doctor; in the case of patients from the fracture clinic, the occupational therapists in charge attended regularly at the clinic when the orthopaedic surgeon was re-examining the patient and heard his fresh instructions. [116]

The injuries and disabilities treated included upper limb fractures, arthritic conditions associated with fractures, muscle and tendon lacerations and strains, paresis of median, ulna, circumflex, and musculospinal nerves, polyneuritis, and cerebral palsy. Experience taught some rules:

> 1. The craft chosen must provide the exact muscle movement needed at each stage. It must be changed as the patient changes.
> 2. The occupational therapist must superintend the movements continually; she must, therefore, have a complete training in anatomy and physiology, such as is required for massage.
> 3.The patient's mind must be concentrated on the accomplishment of the work in which he is engaged. Therefore it must be something he enjoys doing and knows to be useful.
> 4. The degree of strenuousness must be carefully regulated.[117]

Figure 2.5.11 shows Grisel MacCaul, an occupational therapist trained at Dorset House, working at the Allendale Curative Workshop.

**Figure 2.5.11: Grisel MacCaul at Allendale**
*(Reproduced courtesy of Dorset House Archives, Oxford Brookes University)*

In a 1939 article in the Journal, some ideas for conditions and requirements within a curative workshop were provided. A thought that appears to have spanned the decades was that the workshop should be in close proximity to the physiotherapy department, and that the two should work co-operatively. Along with that was mooted the need to arrange for patients to return to the workshops, daily, after discharge from hospital until their return to work.[118]

## For the treatment of mental conditions

Although occupation had been used in some asylums since the nineteenth century it was during the 1930s that a growing appreciation of its value began to resurface. This was stimulated, no doubt, by the energy and enthusiasm generated by some of the people and events whose stories have been told in this and earlier chapters. The idea was beginning to spread amongst physicians concerned with mental health. Throughout the decade it began to make its mark in mental hospitals as wide apart as Aberdeen, Barming Heath, Berkshire, Brighton County, Cambridge, Cardiff, Chester, Clifton, Coventry, Derby, Dumfries, Edinburgh, Essex, Exeter, Gloucester, Lancaster, Macclesfield, Montrose, Severalls, Sussex, Shrewsbury, Swansea, Taunton, Worcester, and the North Riding of Yorkshire.

In Scotland, the Nineteenth Annual Report of the Board of Control included a two and a half page section detailing the perceived value of occupational therapy in the treatment of the insane. They deemed of 'primary importance' that it should be 'recognised as part of the treatment and not as a means of securing from the patient's labour a measure of return for the cost of his maintenance though that may be an indirect result.' Suitable and congenial occupation, they said, was 'both health giving and sedative', with 'good results both in contentedness of mind and the consequent improved bodily condition of the patients.' To further outdoor occupations which they favoured, the Board had been given 'statutory powers to authorise Local Asylum Authorities to acquire land.'[119]

'The object,' they said 'of Asylum treatment is to restore the patients to a condition of mind which will enable them to resume their place in the general community and, if possible, to return to the social and occupational position which they held before their breakdown in health.' The limited availability of employment in the early 1930s concerned them in that it affected the occupational opportunities available to patients which they described as 'so essential' to the maintenance of mental health following discharge from hospital. The Board reported that, to provide meaningful occupation in such a case, one District Asylum had instigated a scheme in which discharged patients kept in contact with the Institution visiting residents or assisting them in sports and amusements. For those patients who were unlikely to return to ordinary community life, but no longer required ongoing treatment, they saw that previous experience in gardening, farming or domestic work could fit a patient to live in the community with private guardians. This was a method of care that the Board was being encouraged to promote. Because all occupation was voluntary there was some concern that the recent provision of workshops in which arts and crafts were taught may prove more attractive than outdoor and domestic work to many patients. To prevent that, the Board suggested that the workshops should be used primarily for the patients unfitted to other forms of occupation. The number of patients who were variously employed during that year in Scottish Asylums was close to 10,000, with 3724 men and women patients assisting attendants in wards. Apart from those, 2469 men patients assisted in farms or gardens, while 829 females engaged in needlework, 585 assisted in laundries and 513 in kitchens. In contrast to this, 225 men and 290 women were involved in arts and crafts.[120]

The Board of Control praised the Department at Aberdeen as being one of the most active centres of Occupational Therapy in Scotland. It had a staff of two and was attended by 88 patients. In contrast to that, 28 patients attended the Department at Bangour, which had a staff of four. In the mid-1930s, a department was built at Montrose, and Agnes Nugent, who held the certificate of the RMPA, was appointed to take charge of this.[121]

At the Crichton Royal Hospital, in 1938, Easterbrook Hall, a large central 'therapeutical and recreational building' containing an Occupational Therapy Department, was opened. In the *Edinburgh Evening Dispatch* of 27 March 1939 a report of remarks made by Dr McCowan, the Superintendent, provides a hint of a gnawing issue regarding the division of occupation into fragments. The problem was that occupation was associated with either creative work or of a social or recreational nature, and different people were assigned to be in charge of those programs. In speaking about their recently organised Occupational Therapy Department which, he said, worked in close co-operation with the Recreation Department, McCowan reported, with no apparent concern that there could be an issue: 'Individual attention to each patient is all important if full benefit is to be obtained from these forms of treatment.' He added:

> The Crichton is now unrivalled in this respect. A very careful programme has now been drawn up, covering the whole day of the patient, in which due regard is given to variety of occupation, to recreational and social activities, with necessary rest periods for each individual patient. This has been made possible by the appointment of highly trained experts to be in charge of these activities, a position not unusual in other hospitals in the case of occupational therapy but probably unique in this country in the sphere of Recreational Therapy.[122]

Recreation therapy was the topic of five papers read at the Royal Medico-Psychological Association (RMPA) in May 1938. Dr McCowan was one of the speakers. The others were: Dr J. M. Speer, who advocated folk dancing; Dr T. P. Rees from Warlingham Park Hospital, Surrey, which employed a dual trained ex-army physical trainer and mental nurse and valued rhythmic movement to music; Dr J. R. Curran, who told of scouts, guides and concert parties used with mental defective male adults in Stirlingshire; and Dr N. H. M. Burke, who spoke of the use of team games and athletics for similar patients, at Cell Barnes, St Albans.[123]

South of the border, in many psychiatric institutions, occupation was not valued as extensively as it had been in the middle of the nineteenth century, but it remained a feature at some like the Retreat in York and at Bethlem Royal which were early employers of occupational therapists. Indeed, the Retreat, similar to the Maudsley, was to offer training in occupational therapy combined with nursing, and Bethlem opened an occupational therapy department in July 1932 with the appointment of Miss N. A. Pollard as occupational therapy officer. The Physician Superintendent's report for that year gave statistics on the number of attendances and the range of craftwork offered at Bethlem. He finished his report by saying:

> In the opening of this department a long felt need has been filled and I am glad the recommendations which were made by me so long ago have been adopted. From the results that have been achieved there is no doubt in my mind that both from attractive and effective treatment and monetary points of view this inauguration has been more than justfied. [124]

In Denbigh, the use of occupation appeared to be on the increase at the North Wales Hospital. Clwyd Wynne reports that:

> Patients were now being provided with an ever increasing variety of entertainment and recreation...The wards were being given regular supplies of books, magazines and records and indoor games such as billiards, bagatelle, chess and draughts were played. Whist Drives, along with the weekly dances and cinema shows were held in the hall.[125]

In that hospital, as in many others, previous activities were subsumed under the new title *occupational therapy*, and appointments were made. Wynne tells how:

> This period before the Second World War also saw the beginning of Occupational Therapy. This came about following a visit by Dr J. H. O. Roberts to Holland in 1934 to see it used. It was supervised initially by nursing staff who had been sent to Chester and Cardiff for training, but in 1937 the first qualified Occupational Therapist, Mrs Howe Thomas, was appointed for two mornings a week. It developed into a thriving department on the male and female sides, and patients won prizes at the 1939 National Eisteddfird in Denbigh for their handicraft work. They also contributed to the war effort by making ARP (Air Raid Precaution) lampshades, sandbags and camouflage nets.[126]

Psychiatric care during the 1930 was before the advent of antipsychotic medication. It is difficult for current day therapists to appreciate what that meant in terms of the behaviours exhibited daily by large numbers of the patients. They were variously 'restless, turbulent, quiet, deteriorated and demented.' Authorities saw the introduction of organised occupation as producing 'a lessening of concentration on immediate mental troubles and a reduction of emotional disturbance.'[127] The Association, in 1939, invited Dr Stephen MacKeith from the Coventry and North Warwickshire Hospital to address its Annual General Meeting. In his paper he talked about some modern methods of treatment used in mental hospitals to counter such behaviours, with a few pointers for occupational therapists with regard to them. He said of 'Continuous Narcosis':

In this treatment, by the repeated administration of a narcotic drug, the patient is kept asleep more or less continuously for about a fortnight. He is then allowed to come round.

> *...The occupational therapist has, of course, no contact with the patient during the actual period of narcosis. She meets him again when the treament is over. It is important for her to remember that from the patient's point of view a period of narcosis is not a completely passive and easy time. Often there have been continual terrifying dreams. Physically too, the patient is usually rather exhausted at the end of the treatment, and has lost some weight.*[128]

Of 'Convulsant Therapy' he told how:

> *This method of treatment, introduced by Meduna in 1934, consists of intravenous injections twice a week of a drug which causes the patient to have a major epileptic fit... The method is used especially for stuporose schizophrenia. The increase in 'accessibility' which often occurs gives the Occupational Therapist an excellent opening, but she should remember that on each actual day of treatment the patient may have a considerable degree of malaise.*[129]

The last method he described was 'Insulin Shock Treatment':

> *This is a method of treating schizophrenia introduced in Vienna by Sakel in 1933. ...It is important that the Occupational Therapist should not regard cases receiving insulin treatment as being outside her sphere; for her methods afford an excellent means of stabilising and developing the increasing affective response of cases who are recovering under the treatment. It is surprising to what extent a sort of 'club spirit' may develop among patients responding to insulin treatment who previously were asocial and apathetic.*[130]

That paper was followed up in the same edition of *Occupational Therapy* by one written by English discussing the treatment of schizophrenia. She suggested that this group of patients 'presents the most difficult problem of all' to the occupational therapist trying to provide interesting and therapeutic occupation. Occupational therapy, she said, was 'considered of great importance and one of the best means of preventing degeneration and keeping the patient in touch with reality.' She added:

> *...It is true that the usual crafts are of great value in drawing out and helping patients to keep in touch with reality, as are the activities which increase their physical well-being and provide realities to take the place of fantasies, such as team work in social habits and re-education in a more communal way of life. In these activities the sustained effort of thought required helps to co-ordinate the disordered state of their minds. The great necessity is to fit the appropriate occupation to the level of regression at which the patient has adjusted himself and in this all the skill and intuition of the occupational therapist is called into plays to understand the situation.*[131]

In Ireland, occupation treatment was a feature of a number of mental institutions as well as of mental deficiency institutions, orphanages, blind asylums and sanatoria.

Weaving, basketry, brushcraft, mat-making, upholstery, and suchlike were in use, even prior to the 1914–18 War, but were supervised by paid tradesmen and based more on the economic requirements of the hospitals than on therapeutic reasons. In 1934, an occupational therapy department was established at the Killarney Mental Hospital, and in a number of others throughout the country. Occupation centres, re-education therapy classes and recreational treatment centres were established on both the male and female sides of the hospital. Treatment was based on American-Canadian practice and the Simon system from Germany, and was run by the more skilled members of the nursing staffs. In Killarney daily participation ranged from 85–90 per cent, with special efforts being made to include restless and excited patients.[132]

**In summary,** the story of occupational therapy's development during the years of the depression up to the time of World War II has been told. It was a period of intense activity and excitement with a small group of dedicated people giving their energy and time without appearing to count the economic or personal cost. Several schools were started, medical and political interest and energy was stimulated which resulted in the publication of texts, important Governmental Memoranda, and the setting up of departments in physical and mental hospitals. Possibly the most significant events of the time were the forming of professional associations, one in Scotland, and another in England which served Wales and Northern Ireland as well.

[1]Girling DA, ed. *New Age Encyclopaedia*. Sydney: Bay Books; vol 29: 75–76.
[2]Course for Teachers of Mental Defectives. *Lancet* 1938; 15th October.
[3]*Relief of Mental Trouble: The Lebanon Hospital*. Christian Christmas Annual 1938; 1st December.
[4]Light Occupation as 'Medicine': Successful Experiment at Winsley. *Bristol Evening Post* 1938; 25th October.
[5]Women's Feature: Occupational Therapy. : Southampton's *Southern Daily Echo* 1938; 14th September.
[6]Clarke NIR. Work as a stimulant: Value of Occupational Therapy. *Birkenhead News* 1938; 27th August. Also reported in *Birkenhead Advertiser* 1938; 27th August.
[7]Training: Occupational Therapy. *Nursing Mirror* 1938; 1st October.
[8]Coventry C. Earning a Living: Occupational Therapy. *Nottingham Evening Post* 1938; 24th September.
[9]Training: Occupational Therapy. *Nursing Mirror....*
[10]Mental Welfare Work. *Nursing Mirror and Midwives Journal* 1938; 17th December: 394.
[11]Story provided by Dorset House, adapted from: Collins B. *The Story of the Dorset House School of Occupational Therapy*: 1930–1986. Oxford: Dorset House, 1987.
[12]Casson E. Dr Casson tells how the Dorset House School of Occupational Therapy came into being. Occupational Therapy 1955, 18 (3): 92–94
[13]Morris was primarily an artist and dancer, but trained as a masseuse at St Thomas' Hospital (CSMMG) after noticing the therapeutic effects of colour, design, music and exercise in her school. Indeed her studio attracted backward or ill-formed children. Margaret Morris Movement began to be used specifically as remedial work for orthopaedic, maternity and mentally ill cases. See Welsh JR. The Remedial application of Margaret Morris Movement. *Occupational Therapy* 1939; Summer: 17–20.
[14]Reed P. Guides. In: *External Activities*. Dorset House Archives.

[15]Macdonald EM. 1934–1954 Recollections 2. *Occupational Therapy* 1955; 18 (3): 100.

[16]Buchanan M. The Beginning. *New Zealand Journal of Occupational Therapy: Commemorative Issue. 1940–1990* 1990; 41(1): 7.

[17]Maudsley Hospital. *Medical Superintendent's Report*, 1st January 1932 to 31st December 1935; 40–41.

[18]Maudsley Hospital. *Medical Superintendent's Report*, 1st January 1932 to 31st December 1935; 40–41.

[19]Maudsley Hospital. *Medical Superintendent's Report*, 1st January 1932 to 31st December 1935; 40–41.

[20]Maudsley Hospital. *Medical Superintendent's Report*, 1st January 1932 to 31st December 1935; 40–41.

[21]Maudsley Hospital. *Medical Superintendent's Report*, 1st January 1932 to 31st December 1935; 40–41.

[22]Board of Control. *Memorandum on Occupation Therapy for Mental Patients*. His Majesty's Stationery Office, London, 1933; 25.

[23]Maudsley Hospital. *Medical Superintendent's Report*, 1st January 1932–31st December 1935; 40

[24]Maudsley Hospital. *Medical Superintendent's Report*, 1st January 1932–31st December 1935; 40

[25]Editorial. *Occupational Therapy* 1939; Spring: 5.

[26]David O'Halloran a current occupational therapist known to Keam agreed to talk with her about her time at the Maudsley, and recorded her reminiscences.

[27]Notice. *Occupational Therapy* 1939.Winter: 8.

[28]Keam J. Reflections on the Maudsley: Personal communication Given, with permission to publish, to D O'Halloran, Hobart, 1999.

[29]Anderson B, Bell J. *Occupational Therapy: Its place in Australia's History*. Sydney: NSW Association of Occupational Therapists, 1988.

[30]Obituary: Miss Muriel Tarrant. *The Times*. Wednesday December 2, 1987.

[31]Macdonald EM. The history of the Association of Occupational Therapists: Chapter 2, 1936–39. *Occupational Therapy* 1957; April: 14–16.

[32]Anderson B, Bell J. *Occupational Therapy: Its Place in Australia's History*. Sydney: NSW Association of Occupational Therapists, 1988.

[33] This story of the Astley Ainslie and occupational therapy education in Edinburgh was written by Professor Averil M Stewart.

[34]Smith. Smith C. *Between the Streamlet and the Town: A Brief History of the Astley Ainslie Hospital*. Typeset Pindar (Scotland) Ltd, Printed and bound by Polton House Press, 1988; 39.

[35]Smith M. Notes: *Focus Group, Retired Members*. Edinburgh: July 1999.

[36]Board of Control. *Memorandum on Occupation Therapy for Mental Patients*. His Majesty's Stationery Office, London, 1933; 26.

[37]Board of Control. *Memorandum on Occupation Therapy....*; 2.

[38]Board of Control. *Memorandum on Occupation Therapy....*; 2.

[39]Board of Control. *Memorandum on Occupation Therapy....*; 3.

[40]Board of Control. *Memorandum on Occupation Therapy....*; 6.

[41]Board of Control. *Memorandum on Occupation Therapy....*; 4–6.

[42]Board of Control. *Memorandum on Occupation Therapy....*; 7–8.

[43] Board of Control. *Memorandum on Occupation Therapy....*;12.

[44]Board of Control. *Memorandum on Occupation Therapy....*; 13.

[45]O'Sullivan ENM. *Textbook of Occupational therapy: With Chief Reference to Psychologcal Medicine*. London: H.K. Lewis, 1955.

[46]Board of Control. *Memorandum on Occupation Therapy....*; 14–15, 26.

[47]Board of Control. *Memorandum on Occupation Therapy....*; 16, 23.

[48]Board of Control. *Memorandum on Occupation Therapy....*; 17–18.

[49]Board of Control. *Memorandum on Occupation Therapy....*; 16–18, 23.

[50]Russell JI. Occupational Therapy and Mental Nursing. *Occupational Therapy* 1938; May: 17–19.

[51]Rees JR. Letter to the Editor. *Occupational Therapy* 1938; Summer: 7–8.

[52]Cunninham Lt Col J. Recovery and Rehabilitation. *Edinburgh Medical Journal* 1938.

[53]Wilson WHF. *Recent Developments in Occupational Therapy.* Edinburgh University: Doctor of Medicine Thesis, 1936.

[54]Wilson. *Recent Developments in Occupational Therapy....*; 58–59.

[55]Wilson. *Recent Developments in Occupational Therapy....*; 59–60.

[56]Eager R. *Aids to Mental Health: The Benefits of Occupation, Recreation and Amusement.* Exeter: W.V.Cole and Sons, 1936; 4–5.

[57]Eager. *Aids to Mental Health...*; 13.

[58]Eager. *Aids to Mental Health...*; 13.

[59]Rees TW. Foreword. In: Russell JI. *The Occupational Treatment of Mental Illness.* London: Bailliere, Tindall & Cox, 1938; viii.

[60]Eager. *Aids to Mental Health...*; 5–6.

[61]Eager. *Aids to Mental Health...*; 6.

[62]Eager. *Aids to Mental Health...*; 6–7.

[63]Eager. *Aids to Mental Health...*; 7–8.

[64]Eager. *Aids to Mental Health...*; 10–11.

[65]Eager. *Aids to Mental Health...*; 14–22.

[66]Eager. *Aids to Mental Health...*; 22–28.

[67] Rees. Foreword. In: Russell JI. *The Occupational Treatment of Mental Illness....*; vii–viii

[68]Russell. *The Occupational Treatment of Mental Illness...*; 2.

[69] Russell. *The Occupational Treatment of Mental Illness...*; Preface, ix.

[70]Russell. *The Occupational Treatment of Mental Illness...*; 8.

[71]Russell. *The Occupational Treatment of Mental Illness...*; 31–32, 34.

[72]Russell. *The Occupational Treatment of Mental Illness...*;4–5.

[73]Russell. *The Occupational Treatment of Mental Illness...*; 5–7.

[74]Russell. *The Occupational Treatment of Mental Illness...*;14–15.

[75]Russell. *The Occupational Treatment of Mental Illness...*;15.

[76]Russell. *The Occupational Treatment of Mental Illness...*; 51–52, 55.

[77]Russell. *The Occupational Treatment of Mental Illness...*; 53–54.

[78]Groundes Peace Z. An outline of the development of occupational therapy in Scotland. *Scottish Journal of Occupational Therapy* 1957; 30: 16–44.

[79]*Minutes of the Scottish Association of Occupational Therapists* 1932–1939. SAOT Box 1.4.

[80]Macdonald EM. The history of the Association of Occupational Therapists. *Occupational Therapy* 1957; Chapter I, March: 13–16; Chapter II, April: 14–16, Chapter III, May: 15–17, Chapter IV, June: 30–33, Chapter V, July: 20–22.

[81]Ross N. Editorial. *Occupational Therapy* 1938; Autumn: 3.

[82]Macdonald EM. The history of the Association of Occupational Therapists: Chapter I. *Occupational Therapy* 1957; March: 13–16.

[83]Macdonald. The history...: Chapter I

[84]Macdonald. The history...: Chapter I

[85]Note: It was a letter from Colonel de Salis from Kent County Mental Hospital, dated 1924, to Dr Henderson that was reported in the last chapter. The 16 years experience mentioned above suggests that de Salis started to work as an occupational therapist in

1920, which is earlier than was originally presumed.

[86]Macdonald. The history...: Chapter I.

[87]Macdonald. The history...: Chapter I.

[88]Ross N. Editorial. *Occupational Therapy* 1938; Autumn: 3.

[89]Ross N. Editorial. *Occupational Therapy* 1938; Autumn: 3.

[90]Macdonald. The history...: Chapter 2.

[91]Macdonald. The history...: Chapter 2.

[92]Macdonald. The history...: Chapter 2.

[93]Macdonald. The history...: Chapter 2.

[94]Macdonald. *World–Wide Conquests of Disabilities....*; 191.

[95]Ross N. Editorial. *Occupational Therapy* 1938; Autumn: 4.

[96]Macdonald. The history...: Chapter 2.

[97]Ross N. Editorial. *Occupational Therapy* 1938; Autumn: 5–6.

[98]Ross N. Editorial. *Occupational Therapy* 1938; Autumn: 6.

[99]Macdonald. The history...: Chapter 2.

[100]Bond Sir H. From the President, and Darwin R. Letters. In: *Occupational Therapy* 1938; Autumn: 7.

[101]Casson E. The Prescription of Occupational Therapy. *Occupational Therapy* 1939; Winter: 22–24.

[102]Casson E. Occupational Therapy. (Reprinted from a report of conference on 'Welfare of cripples and invalid children' held at the Drapers' Hall, London, on November 7th and 8th, 1935.) *Occupational Therapy* 1955; 18 (3): 98–100.

[103]Casson. Occupational Therapy...

[104]Ross N. Editorial. *Occupational Therapy* 1938; Autumn: 4.

[105]Dr Jane Walker did not survive her illness and died on November 17th in her eightieth year. Recognised as one of the pioneers of occupational therapy, like many others, she is a link between occupational therapy's origins in the United Kingdom and enlightened medicine, and with the work of women pioneering the professions. She had been one of 'the first women to qualify in medicine; a leader in the open air treatment of tuberculosis and first President of the Medical Women's Federation.' She was described as 'energetic', 'blunt', and 'unconventional', 'yet lovable, entertaining and full of quick sympathy.' With a great deal of enthusiasm for the causes she espoused, as a magistrate, as well, she 'was deeply interested...in economic reforms concerning the well-being of women and children.' (Ross N. Dr. Jane Walker, Obituary Notice. *Occupational Therapy* 1939; Winter: 12.)

[106]Soltau, Dr. Address to Social Meeting Occupational Therapists' Association November 5th 1938. Occupational Therapy and Pulmonary Tuberculosis. *Occupational Therapy* 1939; Winter: 10.

[107]Ross N. Gardening as a Remedial Occupation. *Occupational Therapy* 1939; Summer: 25–31.

[108]Noyes G. Experimental Occupational Therapy in Tuberculosis Wards. *Occupational Therapy* 1939; Summer: 7–10.

[109]Groundes-Peace ZC. An outline of the development of occupational therapy in Scotland. *Scottish Journal of Occupational Therapy* 1957; (30): 16–39.

[110]Smith C. *Between the Streamlet and the Town....*; 39.

[111]Groundes-Peace . An outline of the development of occupational therapy in Scotland...

[112]Driver MF. A philosophical view of the history of occupational therapy in Canada. *Canadian Journal of Occupational Therapy* 1968; 2: 53–60.

[113]Smith. *Between the Streamlet and the Town...*; 39.

[114]Smith. *Between the Streamlet and the Town...*; 39–40.

[115]Author not given. The Royal Free Hospital, Gray's Inn Road, London. *Occupational Therapy* 1957; March: 17–20.

[116]Casson E. Forty Cases Treated at the Allendale Curative Workshop. *Lancet* 1941; Nov, 1: 516.

[117]Casson. Forty Cases...

[118]Goodman HB. A Curative Workshop. *Occupational Therapy* 1939; Winter: 10–15.

[119]*Nineteenth Annual Report of the General Board of Control For the Year 1932* Edinburgh: His Majesty's Stationery Office, 1933; xvii–xix.

[120]*Nineteenth Annual Report of the General Board of Control For the Year1932 ...*; xvii–xix.

[121]Groundes–Peace . An outline of the development of occupational therapy in Scotland...

[122]*Edinburgh Evening Dispatch.* March 27th, 1939.

[123]Royal Medico–Psychological Association. *Lancet* 1938; 3rd June: 1267–1268.

[124]*Physician Superintendent's Report.* Bethlem Hospital, 1932; 12.

[125]Wynne C. *The North Wales Hospital, Denbigh, 1842–1955.* Denbigh: Gee & Son, 1995; 24–25.

[126]Wynne. *The North Wales Hospital...*; 26.

[127]Board of Control. *Memorandum on Occupation Therapy...*

[128]MacKeith S. Some modern methods of treatment used in mental hospitals. *Occupational Therapy* 1939; Spring: 12–15.

[129]MacKeith. Some modern methods...

[130]MacKeith. Some modern methods...

[131]English AM. Occupational therapy applied to the early and incipient schizophrenic group. *Occupational Therapy* 1939; Spring: 20-26.

[132]O'Sullivan ENM. *Textbook of Occupational therapy: With Chief Reference to Psychological Medicine.* London: H.K. Lewis, 1955.

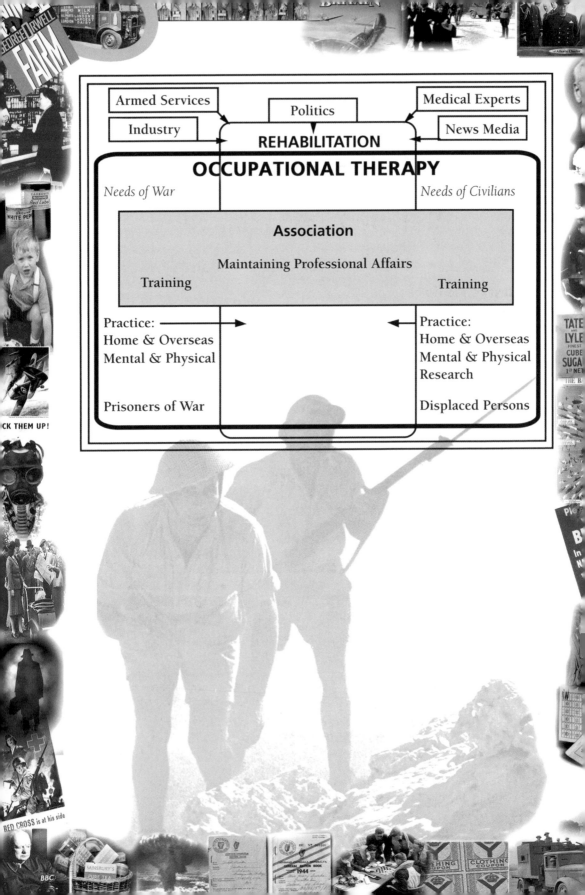

**Armed Services**

**Industry**

**Politics**

**Medical Experts**

**News Media**

**REHABILITATION**

# OCCUPATIONAL THERAPY

*Needs of War*

*Needs of Civilians*

## Association

### Maintaining Professional Affairs

Training

Training

Practice: —
Home & Overseas
Mental & Physical

Practice:
Home & Overseas
Mental & Physical
Research

Prisoners of War

Displaced Persons

# Chapter 6

# Another World War: Occupational Therapy–of Essential National Importance

## Contents

The process of establishing the new profession was interrupted by World War II, which lasted from 1939 until 1945. This chapter is devoted to the history of occupational therapy during that period and the couple of years that followed the conflict. The start of Macdonald's historical account of the time written for the Journal cannot be surpassed. She wrote:

> *1939 was again a full—and troubled—year. War clouds were gathering, and the position of Occupational Therapists in an emergency was discussed. The Secretary was instructed to write to the Director of Medical Services to register the readiness of Members to be called upon. The reply, indicating that the present work of Occupational Therapists was considered '...of essential national importance' was a very real encouragement to those who had worked so hard to prove its value.* [1]

To say this phase of the profession's history was important to its development is almost to understate the matter. It was a time that enabled the newly committed groups of individuals to make their identity known to the world at large, and to prove their claim about how the relationship between occupation and health could be used in a therapeutic way. The Association of Occupational Therapists (AOT) tried to meet the wartime needs as they arose, and to maintain the procedures and the standards they had set in the previous few years. This chapter provides material about both those issues. The Scottish Association chose not to hold meetings during the war years, but its members underwent similar difficulties and growth to those in the rest of the country. The story of how they were assisted by Canadian occupational therapists is told by Catherine F Paterson, and is an example of how occupational therapists from Commonwealth countries, or allies, worked, often alongside British occupational therapists, in various parts of the world as part of the war effort.

# Context of the times

World War II was unique because it was the first to be fought in Europe, Asia, and Africa simultaneously. While many regard it as the 'second round' of a European Civil war which began in 1914, it arose from three separate conflicts: between Germany and Poland in 1939; the Russo-Finnish War in the same year; and the 1937-45 Sino-Japanese War. The bombing of Pearl Harbour in December 1941 brought the United States into the conflict, resulting in global war. Millions fought and millions died, the casualties not restricted to those in the services, but extending to thousands of civilians through systematic genocide, and through the new horrors of mass bombing attacks and atomic warfare.[2]

As in World War I, interest in the study of work performance once more came to the fore, but this time ergonomists were mainly involved in consideration of the man-machine interface, rather than rehabilitation of the war wounded. Military equipment was becoming extremely complex and fast calling for rapid operating responses. That often resulted in failure to get the best out of the equipment or in the breakdown of operatives.[3][4] Interest in work performance as part of rehabilitation of the injured was revived by others, mainly as part of hospital care. The British Medical Association in 1935 had already decreed that rehabilitation should be governed by certain principles: first, segregation of patients to special treatment centres; second, control throughout treatment by the same surgical team; and third, careful after-care.[5] As medical interest in the specialty grew with the needs actuated by the war, occupational therapy was recognised as one of rehabilitation's components, as it had been in World War I.

In an Official British Medical History of World War II it was recorded that:

*After 1918 the orthopaedic centres were dismantled and occupational therapy again reverted, for the most part, to the mental hospital service. On the outbreak of the Second World War, however, the need for providing the best means of rehabilitation after injury assumed a new significance, for not only were there the Service personnel to be considered but also the large numbers of members of the civilian community who were in danger of being incapacitated by air raids. It was accordingly decided that at all the special centres provided under the Emergency Medical Services for the reception and treatment of disabling injuries – orthopaedic centres, long-term fracture hospitals, spinal and head injury centres, neurosis centres, etc. occupational therapy departments should be built and equipped as an integral part of the scheme...* [6]

Because of the acute shortage of trained occupational therapists, such departments were staffed chiefly by male handicap instructors and members of the Educational Corps. As part of the work, though, a few trained occupational therapists who had joined the Women's Auxiliary Services were also engaged in developing rehabilitative occupational therapy. Like almost everyone else during the War they had to do so in an environment short of accommodation and materials.

Occupational therapists were restricted in their choice of therapeutic occupations, as Government authorities deliberately limited their intervention to craftwork and did not permit them into the domain of trade. Many would have preferred to use more realistic occupations. Even the craftwork, which in some cases was considered by the occupational therapists to be too light and more suited to diversion than remedial work, was limited by government control because of availability of materials obtained through special priority systems. [7]

**Figure 2.6.1:    Servicemen making toys**

Not all medical authorities approved of the rehabilitation model that was adopted. Some plastic surgeons, for example, believed that 'real war work' was more appropriate, so between courses of surgical treatment the men were placed in 'war' factories where rehabilitation workshops were set up. The rehabilitees worked at producing war materials using modified machinery to assist the re-education of injured limbs. Their surgeon remained involved. The value of the 'work therapy' was apparent. It was expanded to include ward patients so that they too were able to engage in remunerative and useful work early after injury, which was effective in reducing the duration of handicap. [8]

Women took over unaccustomed worker roles when the men went to fight. They were employed in factories and, by 1943, 80 000 were engaged in many kinds of agriculture in the Women's Land Army and the Scottish Women's Land Army. The Women's Voluntary Service was formed in June 1938 before the outbreak of war at the request of the Home Secretary. Its work was extended from its original brief in Air Raid Precaution Services to include welfare. Many women enlisted in the armed services, and became skilled in trades carried out in the Women's Auxiliary Air Force, Royal Army Corps, and Women's Royal Naval Service. Many served overseas.

The Army Medical Service appointed women doctors. The British Army Medical Corps co-ordinated nursing and paramedical services at home and in treatment centres overseas. To meet the Navy's medical needs, hospital ships and land centres were established. Royal Air Force medical centres were linked with those of both the army and navy. Their Orthopaedic and Rehabilitation Service, developed by Sir Reginald Watson-Jones and Sir Henry Osmond-Clarke, included five rehabilitation centres. Interestingly, a small number of doctors, Eagger, Maskell, Mason, O'Malley, Sommerville, and Zinovieff, who were wartime supervisors of those rehabilitation services, were instrumental to their continuance in peacetime, and in the further development of occupational therapy.[9]

Rheumatologists also turned to rehabilitation of the wounded and injured. When Frank Howitt, the King's heliotherapist, was promoted Brigadier in charge of Physical Medicine in the army 'he chose six physician/rheumatologists to head the team. Basil Kiernander and later Kit Wynn Parry were appointed to supervise physical medicine in the RAF and Frank Cooksey in the Civil Emergency Medical Services.'[10] Both Wynn Parry and Cooksey were later to work closely with occupational therapists, the first with Natalie Smythe in the treatment of hand injuries, and the second with Grisel MacCaul at Kings College Hospital.

Multidisciplinary physical medicine was in its infancy during the war. In 1940, Dr George Kersley, for example, was made responsible for physical medicine in Southern Command and given the brief to open the first so called 'tough' school of occupational therapy at the Army Convalescent Depot in Taunton, as well as reorganising the Army School of Physiotherapy at Netley. Two years later he was promoted to Advisor in Physical Medicine to the Middle East Forces, where he commenced the huge job of turning Convalescent Depots from 'concentration camps' into 'rehabilitation centres and saved five thousand potential fighters from being invalided home by the psychiatrist.' He also reported that he was, 'in close touch with the British Red Cross Society in connection with their occupational therapy role.'[11] In 1942 Kersley's own occupational therapy role made news in a variety of newspapers. The *Birmingham Post* claimed 'the Southern Command has given a lead to the British Army in occupational therapy.'[12] The *Western Morning News* told the story of a patient regaining full use of his hands at the occupational centre, after the tops of his fingers had been blown off.[13] Cardiff's *Western Mail* described 'one of Major Kersley's inventions as an ingenious loom worked by the patient lying flat in bed.[14] And the *Scottish Daily Express* told how Kersley explained that 'an ordinary game of darts and a supervised set of table tennis will do an immense amount of good.'[15]

**Figure 2.6.2:  Col. George Kersley, 1942**[16]
*(Royal Society of Medicine Library)*

That occupational therapy was attracting considerable and appropriate attention at the time is indicated by a notice in the 'Medical Officer,' on 10 August 1940:

> *Sir E. Graham-Little asked the Minister of Health what steps are being taken, and by what Government Departments, to make provision in military and civil hospitals for Occupational Therapy to hasten the resumption of service by wounded men; and what steps are being taken, and by what Government departments, to develop a national system of rehabilitation so that by means of specialised training and the establishment of specially organised workshops, service men who are unfit for further military service may be returned to civilian life with minimal disability?*
>
> *Mr. M. Macdonald (Minister of Health): As to the first part of the question Occupational Therapy is provided for wounded men at the special orthopaedic centres forming part of the emergency hospital scheme administered by the Secretary of State for Scotland and myself, as well as at Ministry of Pensions hospitals and the fracture or orthopaedic departments of a number of general hospitals in the scheme. As to the second part, arrangements are being considered in concert between the Ministries of Health and of Pensions and the Department of Health for Scotland, with the appropriate professional experts. Our aim is to secure a co-ordinated system of rehabilitation designed to produce the maximum restoration of working capacity.*[17]

# The Association of Occupational Therapists (AOT)

Macdonald's account of the time told how:

> *...the elected Council of the Association, together with its Advisory Board, faced the situation with a calmness and realism which spoke much for the quality of the foundations that had been laid. In reading through the records, it is impressive to note that no rushed decisions were made, and that action taken was always consistent with long-term policy and with the maintenance of high standards of treatment and service. This was not achieved easily. Pressure came from many sides to abandon courses and examinations for full qualification – so recently, so successfully attained and so necessary for the future and stability of the profession. Wholehearted in their war effort, although often weary and dismayed, the Council and Members held firmly to the view that there was a definite future*

*for Occupational Therapy, but much – almost too much for a very new profession – would depend on the uncertain present. And they were not proved wrong*[18]

At a meeting of the Council in Liverpool, on September 30th, 1939, a proposal was carried:

> *That an executive committee consisting of six members of Council be formed for the duration of the war, with power vested in the Chairman and Secretary to act on behalf of the Council in the event of the said committee being unable to meet.*[19]

That Committee comprised the Chairman, Mrs Glyn Owens, the ex-officio secretary, Mrs Clarke, and the journal representative, Miss Ross or Miss English, plus Mr McCammon, Miss Crousaz and Miss Worthington.[20] It was dissolved in March 1942, because the Council as a whole appeared able to meet and deal with the necessary business.[21] However, the work of those officials was formally recognised as outstanding by the President of the AOT in the Annual Report of 1941–42.[22]

## Maintaining professional affairs

In addition to work connected with the war, the routine business of the AOT continued. So much did the work increase that it became necessary to appoint an Assistant Honorary Secretary and an Examination Secretary. During the war both critical and mundane matters were dealt with. These included: representation on, or affiliation with, various other official bodies; applying for exemption for occupational therapist trainees or practitioners from being directed into other occupations; and such issues as incorporation, budgets, membership, or obtaining coupons to purchase uniforms. (There was such a shortage of all types of goods that almost every purchase required coupons, which were rationed per head of population.) Preliminary and final examinations were arranged. General meetings and those of Council were held with remarkable consistency, the latter, as need indicated, around the country, and as far apart as London, Liverpool, Bristol, and Cambridge.[23] In the annual report of 1940–41, for example, it was reported that 'in spite of difficulties of transport' Council met 11 times in various places. Journeys may have taken the councilors many hours and were often under trying conditions, with expenses met by the individuals themselves. Later in the war, because members may have been unable to travel to General Meetings, a postal ballot was instituted to maintain a democratic voting process for Council representation.

Annual General Meetings still retained informative and varied programmes. The one in 1940, for example, held in Bristol, programmed: a surgeon to give a paper on occupational therapy in the treatment of neurosis; visits to the occupation rooms of the Allendale Curative Workshop; and, in the evening, 'a display of rhythmic exercises given by students at the Dorset House School of Occupational Therapy under the direction of Miss MacCaul, followed by dancing and games.'[24]

With regard to membership of the AOT, by the 1939–1940 Annual Report the decision had been made that admission was by examination following two and a half years' training, plus 1 year's full time employment. Membership was steadily increasing. In the 1938—39 annual report, 60 members, and 58 associates were recorded, and by the 1942–43 report there were 106 members and 122 associates.[25] Some of the calls upon time were to consider applications for membership from people without qualification who were working in hospitals. In the 1939–40 Annual Report it was recorded that people practising as occupational therapists who had not completed formal training would be able to take an examination devised especially for them. This was to be incorporated as a section of the War Emergency Diploma. However, in the Annual Report of 1942–43 it was stated that:

> For the year 1942 only, the Council decided, subject to certain conditions and at their discretion, to admit such practising occupational therapists who were not aware of the Association's existence or for other reasons failed to apply for membership prior to March 1939 when entrance could be gained other than by qualifying examination. Under this concession 7 applications have been received.[26]

Macdonald records that it was proposed, and later implemented, that 'the certain conditions' were the completion of a written paper and personal interview. In 1943 the decision was taken that members of the Association should be allowed to put the letters MAOT after their names.[27]

The Council decided that the outbreak of war made it expedient to draw up conditions of work and a salary scale. The first were compiled by the British Federation of Social Workers and the second was undertaken by Owens. The suggested salaries were approved and incorporated, and the following scale recommended per annum:

| | |
|---|---|
| *Area organiser and member of A.O.T.* | *£450–550* |
| *Head of Hospital Dept. and MAOT* | *£275–375* |
| *HoHD plus training of students* | *+ £5 per student/6 mths* |
| *Assistant to HoHD and MAOT* | *£200–300* |
| *Junior – qualified by exam: no experience* | *£150–200* |
| *Head of Training School and MAOT* | *£450–550* |
| *Assistant to HoTS and MAOT* | *£250–350* |
| *Auxiliary OT* | *£100–130* |

In 1943 conditions of service and salaries again came under discussion, and better scales, graded according to qualification, were recommended.[28]

During the latter half of the war the AOT found time to seriously consider fundamental issues such as the aims, objectives and future policies of the Association. Historically important regulations for practice were drawn up and passed at the General Meeting of 11 September 1943. They ruled that:

> Occupational Therapists are required and shall agree to give treatment only under medical direction, except in certain specialised fields of work recognised by the Association of Occupational Therapists.
>
> Occupational Therapists will open or conduct the Occupational Therapy department as a separate but collaborating unit among other treatment services in the hospital, clinic or centre.
>
> Occupational Therapists with other qualifications may work in a dual supervisory capacity after having organised and practised Occupational Therapy for the minimum of

*three years (or the part-time equivalent) of which one year must be full-time Occupational Therapy.*

*Occupational Therapists shall not be responsible for the training of students other than for hospital practice except in conformity with the requirements for teaching as laid down by the Association of Occupational Therapists.*[29]

With slight variation, those remained in force for many years.

Also in 1943 a Sub-Committee was elected to investigate the possibility for incorporation of the AOT with the ultimate view of gaining a Charter. Members of the Advisory Board, with the help of a solicitor, drew up the Articles of Association, and on 17 February 1945, the first meeting of the Council of the newly incorporated Association took place. The *Certificate of Incorporation* and a copy of *The Memorandum and Articles* of the new Association were presented to the Council, the assets of the old Association were taken over, and the Seal was 'adopted as the Common Seal of the Association.' It had 'become an incorporated limited liability company, with Board of Trade permission to dispense with the word "limited".'[30]

There were numerous articles in papers and magazines promoting the profession. An example is provided by the report of a 'Broadcast Talk' on the BBC's *Health Magazine* in the Winter of 1941. Occupation was described as far more than recreation. The example was given of a soldier with a facial wound blowing a wind instrument or blowing bubbles for exercise. The interviewer thought that out of keeping with 'the dignity of a Regimental Major', and asked, later in the interview:

*Is there scope here for individual taste?*

*Answer. – Most certainly. The well-trained therapist will consider each patient as an individual and try to find out and develop that patient's innate interests and talents and make him feel an individual person and not just a case...*

*Question. – That sounds like what the papers call 'rehabilitation' or indeed, it goes further – it suggests that the man might be finding his right work that he had not found before he was ill.*

*Answer. – Well, occupational therapy is of basic importance in rehabilitation, which after all, is briefly the treatment, by other than actual medical or surgical means, of sick or injured persons so as to enable them to get back to their old occupation and livelihood, or indeed to change to a more suitable occupation, because a good occupational therapist ...taps... hidden or undiscovered talent or interest in one of his patients...*

*Question. – Well, this sounds as though it is an important post-war work as well as war work.*

*Answer. – It is as important a part of planning for the future as anything else. We have to recreate a new world, and will have to re-create some of the minds that are to live in it.*[31]

Throughout the period and beyond, finances were an anxiety. Secretarial and similar expenses had to be met even though the officers of the AOT were all honorary. Donations from a number of good friends assisted in keeping the AOT afloat, such as the £150 received as a result of an appeal by the Chairman on a visit to the USA, although that was specifically for use towards the establishment of occupational therapy for war casualties. To a struggling Association, it provided great encouragement. The Emergency War Fund on behalf of which the appeal was made was to be devoted primarily to the opening of a 'demonstration' occupational therapy department in a civilian hospital where children were treated, and the extension of training facilities to meet the demands of the war.[32] In 1943 membership subscriptions were increased to two guineas to counter the rising costs.[33]

In the case of representation on, or affiliation with, other organisations, various initiatives were underway. Early in the war, the AOT was invited to join the Board of Medical Auxiliaries, but after investigation it was found to be too small to have full representation, so Council decided against it.[34] Also in those early war years the Chartered Society of Masseurs invited representatives from the AOT to discuss possibilities of joint training in massage and occupational therapy with particular reference to orthopaedics. Discussions did take place, but Macdonald recalls that little came of them, 'as both professions were, of necessity, busy with the extensions in their own work and the claims on them from the Services and the Emergency Medical Service of the Ministry of Health.'[35] In 1943, another link with Masseurs and with the Ling Association (An association of medical gymnasts: The story of Ling is told in Volume 1) was forged.[36] An Advisory Committee on Rehabilitation was formed, but despite much useful discussion, no definite action followed.[37] By the 1941–42 Annual Report, the AOT had become affiliated with the British Federation of Business and Professional Women, and the Central Council for the Care of Cripples. It had also established close connections with the British Federation of Social Workers.[38]

The Journal continued publication during the war years, being produced quarterly even when the editor was ill. There were some variations of dates and format, contributions were 'scattered far and wide', and an 'impending paper shortage' added to the difficulties. In the first year of the war an increase in circulation was urgently needed, and subscribers were asked to induce their hospitals to subscribe.[39] The next year the Journal was said to be a heavy draw on the financial resources of the AOT, which was reported to be the case for some years to come.[40] Later, the Journal was to become a major source of income.

In the Winter of 1939 the Editorial in *Occupational Therapy* addressed the opportunity provided by the war for recognition of the profession's potential contribution to health care:

> *It has often been said in the past that Occupational Therapy received its greatest stimulus in the last war. This being so it is not beyond reason that the present war should give a vast opportunity for service, and though, as yet we are not called upon to do much, the time may come, and we believe will come, when the authorities and the general public will awaken to the fact that a valuable form of treatment is being neglected...Whatever we may be doing now, whether it is one of the various forms of 'war work', or the more prosaic, but still useful 'usual job', let us keep in mind that some day – any day now – a call may come for trained Occupational Therapists, and then we will have to make up our minds, not only as to where we ought to be, but also as to how we can do our work best in the new circumstances that may arise.[41]*

When victory was proclaimed at the end of hostilities in Europe (VE Day), it was described in the Editorial as 'a short breathing space in the war effort – an opportunity to gather our powers together for another journey forward.' A breathing space was very necessary. The AOT hierachy and its Council, sub-committees, Advisory Board, and examiners, had been forced to work at an incredible pace, controlling, encouraging, developing and implementing, assisted by the strength of the first two presidents, Sir Hubert Bond and Dr. Janet Aitken. The Editor concluded that editorial with the reminder that 'the hardest work must come after the battle is over.'[42]

## Training

Throughout the period, training and examination processes remained a priority, for on those processes depended the future of the profession, and in terms of the War, a rapid increase in the numbers of practising occupational therapists was imperative. The special procedures undertaken to meet that imperative are discussed a little later, but here, it is important to recognise the gains made in terms of the number of ordinary qualifiers. In 1939, fourteen students passed the Preliminary Examination, five from the Occupational Therapy Training Centre, London, one from the Maudsley, and eight from Dorset House, and three students passed the Final examinations. Their certificates were presented at a social occasion at Friends Meeting House.[43] Twelve sat for the Preliminary Examination in June 1940. In November sixteen took the Final Examination. It is of interest to note that one of the Preliminary candidates is listed as training at the County Mental Hospital, Runwell. In the previous chapter the Board of Control's *Memorandum on Occupation Therapy for Mental Patients* indicated that mental hospitals should implement occupational therapy training along with that of mental nursing.[44] It is unknown how many hospitals took up that challenge but, in 1939 a *Certificate in Occupational Therapy for Mental Nurses* was instituted by the Royal Medico-Psychological Association (RMPA) for state registered mental nurses and those with the Certificate in medical nursing of the RMPA. It was a two-year course taken in a training school of a hospital recognised by the RMPA.[45] At the Retreat, York, there was a combined occupational therapy/mental nursing course run between 1942 and 1948. It was of four years' duration and met the requirements of the General Nursing Council Examinations in Mental Nursing, and the Occupational Therapy Association Examinations.[46]

Macdonald noted that:
> ...the main professional training and examinations continued as a core of stability throughout the war, and it was both encouraging and satisfactory that there was a steady number who recognised the need for, and importance of, the full training.[47]

The stoicism required to maintain the processes is illustrated by a change of venue for rather than a postponement of the 1940–41 examinations. Intense enemy activity meant that it was impossible for the Association to hold them in London and so they were held in Bristol, instead.

A resolution taken in 1938, that all medical examiners should become members of the Advisory Board throughout their term of office, meant that some eminent authorities became part of the organisation. This included tuberculosis authority, McDougall, and the surgeon, Girdlestone. The latter, in 1943, when he was President of the British Orthopaedic Association, was quoted in the *British Medical Journal* as saying:

*I think we all feel that rehabilitation should begin very soon after the accident or wound and be carried on throughout the patient's period in Hospital in the form of occupational therapy and gymnastic or remedial exercises.*[48]

According to Balme, at the outbreak of war there were not more than 100 occupational therapists on the register of the AOT in England.[49] After the shut down of courses at the start of the war, a steady expansion in training facilities resumed. In 1942 the London School was re-opened, and in the same year the programme at The Retreat started. The Physician Superintendent, Arthur Poole, wrote in his Annual Report: 'During the year the hospital was approved as a Training School for Occupational Therapy by the Occupational Therapy Association and our first student passed the preliminary examination of the Association.'[50] In May 1943, another School was opened at St Andrew's, Northampton, and in April 1945, the St Loyes School in Exeter opened its doors. A memorandum on training sent by the Association to the Ministry of Labour, noted the latter two but did not mention The Retreat.[51] Despite official recognition it appears that the AOT was not wholly in favour of courses offering the combination of mental health nursing and occupational therapy, although it allowed candidates to sit its examinations.

## Special arrangements for the war

The Navy, Air Force, and Ministry of Pensions depended on all the occupational therapy schools, drawing staff from them. Dr Elizabeth Casson told how, when war broke out, organisers of the Emergency Medical Service (EMS) of the Ministry of Health visited Dorset House. They decided 'to entrust to the Dorset House School the training of occupational therapists needed in large numbers to implement their wartime rehabilitation programme.' So, apart from students taking regular courses, 200 others took special war examinations, which were instituted by the Association.[52]

Recognition was given by the AOT to the course established by the War Office at Taunton where the British Army trained its own occupational therapists. Its students were some of their own masseuses, most of whom were sent after training to Army Hospitals abroad.[53] The War Office School was under the direction of Kersley, assisted by Canadian occupational therapists, details of whom are provided later in the chapter by Catherine F Paterson. A Joint Examination Board was set up by the AOT and Military Authorities to deal with the qualifications of candidates trained at the War Office School. Later, successful candidates received the War Emergency Diploma.

It was at the first meeting of the War Executive Committee that, in order to meet the need for additional occupational therapists, it was decided:

*...to draw up a syllabus for candidates wishing to take an emergency course, and to establish an examination, for the duration of the war.*

*As a result of this, a syllabus for O.T. Auxiliaries was drawn up, covering simple first aid, some anatomy, physiology and psychology, elementary symptomatology of medical, surgical and psychiatric illness, including precautions, the aims and principles of occupational therapy, including recreational and social organisation, and various activities. The examination and course were planned to encourage 'up-grading' to full qualification when certain credits would be given. This was a far-sighted policy and one which was followed in arranging later emergency courses. It proved most satisfactory, and an encouragement to some who are now among the best practising occupational therapists of to-day, and who came to the profession through these war-time trainings.*[54]

In June 1940, the first Auxiliary Examinations were held and all six candidates were successful. However the Council decided that 'this examination did not meet the needs of the occasion.' So in November, of the same year, they resolved that:

*...an Emergency Examination be instituted to replace the Auxiliary Examination, this examination to be open only to candidates who have previous qualifications in one of the following professions: – Massage and Medical Gymnastics, Mental or General Nursing, Craft or other teaching.*[55]

So it was that the War Emergency Diploma came into being, for which students were prepared by the existing schools. Designed for the then current state of emergency, examinations were based on the framework of the usual syllabus with some modification. A report in the Lancet explained that for masseuses it was free of charge with free board and lodging for 6 months if they undertook to return to work at EMS centres. Although occupational therapy was a separate profession the report explained that it combined well with Massage because the trained masseuse already had 'a background in anatomy, experience in handling patients, and supple and controlled hands.' The course at Barnsley Hall was 'real war work', it said, in that it was a strenuous and concentrated course.[56] The initiative did not, however, replace the Auxiliary examination but augmented it. In the 1944–45 Annual Report it is recorded that as well as 76 students passing their preliminary examinations, 34 candidates being successful in their finals, and 10 candidates in the War Emergency Diploma, a further 33 passed the Auxiliary Examination.

Despite those initiatives, by 1943, the shortage was still acute, and an extract from the *Yorkshire Post* explained that the Government was 'preparing a scheme for the free training of instructors and auxiliary instructors.'[57] Commencing at Dorset House on 19 July 1943, the scheme was, appropriately, called the '1943 Certificate.' It was instituted at the request of the Minister of Health to meet the demand for the additional supply of trained and semi-trained workers. It was designed for and available to applicants who had some kind of pre-requisite qualification not covered by the War Emergency Diploma. To meet that category applications were subject to approval by the Council. In the 1944–45 report we learn that 36 such candidates passed the examination.[58] The courses were planned with credits to allow for upgrading to a full qualification. Of approximately 250 'special' wartime trainees about 80–100 later joined the profession through upgrading.[59]

There were, therefore, four Association awards possible at the time, and yet another variation, which had been available since the start. The 'Full Diploma' could be either a single qualification in either physical or psychological work or dual with qualification in both.[60] These plus the other possible means of training are pictured on Figure 2.6.3.

Figure 2.6.3: Ways of training in occupational therapy during the war years

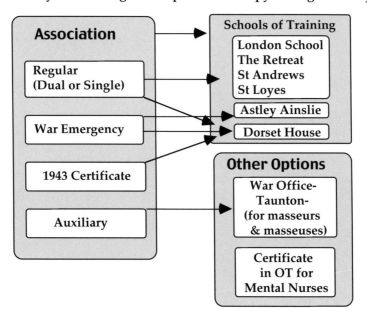

# Rehabilitation becomes newsworthy

In the *Medical Press and Circular* of 17 March 1943 the Editorial proclaimed:

> *There are fashions in medicine just as there are in fashions in Art or Philosophy…and today if there is one fashion which dominates medical thought almost to the exclusion of any rivals it is rehabilitation. But to say so much is by no means to disparage the conception; it is merely to indicate that it is novel, and fashions that are well founded lose their novelty and cease to attract attention in the world of medicine just as soon as they become embodied in standard practice…*
>
> *Rehabilitation, therefore, must include the restoration of function to all those parts of the body and mind thrown out of gear by the original injury…*[61]

The extracts from the BBC interview reproduced previously provide some indication that the common use of the word 'rehabilitation' was relatively new. Miss English reported that it was only in 1939 that the *Report of the Inter-Departmental Committee on the Rehabilitation of Persons Injured by Accidents*, known as the Delevingne Report, was published and used the term formally. Though it was in frequent use by then it still had an unfamiliar ring and was sometimes imperfectly understood even by the speaker. She added that reading the report again after two years of war made her realise how many advances had been made in those years. She saw rehabilitation, occupational therapy and pre-vocational training as a constructive trilogy with an aim to enable patients to regain their confidence and independence, and to help develop latent talent and potential ability, 'which are nearly always to be found.'[62]

Following the Delevingne Report, an Interim Scheme for the Teaching and Resettlement of the Disabled was planned by the Ministry of Labour and the Health Department in 1941. Plans and advice were provided by the Tomlinson Report. Published in 1942 by the Inter-department Committee on the Rehabilitation and Resettlement of the Disabled chaired by George Tomlinson, the Report advocated for specialised and vocational treatment which encouraged the patients. It also called for the registration of disabled persons, and for 3 per cent of them to be (compulsorily) employed by large companies.

In a July 1942 *British Medical Journal* article Sir Robert Stanton Woods, Consultant Advisor in Physical Medicine to the Ministry of Health, quoted from the *Oxford Dictionary* a definition of rehabilitation as 'restoration to privileges.' In the Medical sense, he added, 'this would signify restoration to the privileges of health, so far as this is possible.' Taking a holistic perspective, he recognised, meant not only taking into account 'the whole therapeutic procedure but also the mental and material environment.' In the more restricted sense in which he was addressing the issue he wrote 'efforts to rehabilitate can be considered under the heads of passive physical therapy or the application of physical agents, active (volitional) exercise, and productive occupation.' He added that voluntary effort ought to form a part of rehabilitation at as early a stage as it is safe to do so.[63]

He explained that in the EMS there were extensive facilities for rehabilitation activities:

*Because in the time of war the great preponderance of disability in the Services is due to injury, while in totalitarian war a large proportion of civilian disability is also due to enemy action, the earliest hospitals in the E.M.S. to be fully equipped in this respect were the so-called orthopaedic centres. At each of these there have for some time existed departments of physiotherapy, of local and general remedial gymnastics, and of occupational therapy...*

*Occupational therapy is a standard part of treatment at all orthopaedic centres and at every hospital with a 'Group A' fracture department, and trained personnel for this 'work' are increasing in numbers, the Ministry having instituted an intensive course of training at one of the orthopaedic centres. The remedial aspect of productive occupation is partly physical and partly psychological...'[64,65]*

In November of the same year he wrote about not only dealing with an injured body, but 'with an injured person—body, mind, spirit.' To that effect:

*...Of far greater therapeutic value are purposeful and productive movements of groups of muscles such as those required in the performance of games and handicrafts, or the resumption of Army training, where creative and competitive instincts can be brought into action and the patient's attention is no longer focused on his disability but rather on his returning skill in achievement.[66]*

Malkin and Parker, surgeons working at Harlow Wood Orthopaedic Hospital, Nottingham, explained that:

*The establishment of orthopaedic centres in the Emergency Medical Service stimulated those working in them to tackle the problem of rehabilitation already carefully investigated in the Delevingne Committee. With few exceptions it had been the custom in civilian practice to discharge a patient when fit for light work and still maintain some supervision of his further recovery as an out-patient.*[677]

That was not considered appropriate or wise in the case of Service men who, it was seen, required rehabilitation immediately following the postoperative treatment. They found occupational therapy to be of considerable value.

Not everyone agreed. Watson-Jones, Consultant Orthopaedic Surgeon to the Royal Air Force, expressed a non-committal interest when he commented 'work-shops, occupational-therapy benches, and massage cubicles are like medicine-balls, climbing ropes, and skittles, items of equipment which are sometimes useful but never indispensable.' He favoured non-specialised centres that provided 'the same exercises, the same recreations, the same atmosphere' with the only variation being the duration of treatment.[68]

Impressed by the need to reduce wastage caused by prolonged invalidism, a survey of rehabilitation in civilian hospitals by the Ministry of Health followed the Tomlinson Interdepartmental Committee on Rehabilitation.[69,70] In 1942, the *Birmingham Post* and *The Times* both ran similar stories about industrial injuries and referred back to the interim scheme for rehabilitation introduced in October 1941.[71] Tomlinson, then Joint Parliamentary Secretary to the Minister of Labour, explained the scheme, which was aimed at the training and resettlement of disabled persons, had been extended to all types of industrial accidents. One of the difficulties of rehabilitation in wartime was that shortage of manpower meant that people could get employment whether fit or not, and real difficulties would not be apparent until after the war.[72]

*The Machinery Market* of the 8 January 1943, advised employers, trades unions, and personnel management of rehabilitation facilities available for injured industrial workers which were provided by the EMS and the Department of Health for Scotland. The article described how 21 Orthopaedic Centres included 'complete occupational therapy' and offered 'games, workshop occupation and handicrafts.' Rehabilitation was a part of approximately sixty 'Fracture Departments A' but, which, although providing 'occupational therapy of the handicraft type' did not, usually, include full workshop occupation. 'Fracture Departments B', and 'Fracture Clinics C' were said not to have such facilities.[73] The same information was taken up by the *Walsall Observer*. It reported that the provision of work or suitable training previously available to people injured as a direct result of the war had been extended to include all 'manual workers in war industries' including agriculture and fishing.[74]

On a slightly different but related tack, the prevention of disability within industry was also a topic of concern. The Factories Act of 1937 encouraged the Ministry of Labour to provide advice and for its inspectors to give attention to issues such as safety rates, weight lifting, protective units for machinery, positioning of workers and machinery, eye protection, avoidance of lead poisoning, and work diseases. The Ministry of Labour was asked to provide similar inspection of apparatus and machinery within rehabilitation units of EMS hospitals, and to give advice and training to supervisors.[75]

Within occupational therapy the concept and popularity of rehabilitation was welcomed. On Owens's retirement from her position as Chairman of the AOT in 1942 it was the subject chosen by Irene Hilton, the incoming Chairman, to introduce herself to members. Hilton, who was not an occupational therapist, did so by means of an open letter in the Journal. She wrote:

> *Rehabilitation is on everyone's lips; the doctor, the industrialist, the physio-therapist and the social worker define it differently. Definitions are, at best, misleading, and sometimes dangerous. I would like to think that for the occupational therapist nothing less than rehabilitation in its widest and least specialised sense was the ultimate goal.*
>
> *You have a unique opportunity for service in that you can adapt your materials and your technique to meet the individual need. To you the hospital patient is not primarily a 'fracture,' a 'chest case' or a 'neurosis;' but a human being who must be helped back to normality, given confidence, new interests, and a new job if necessary. More than any other hospital workers, you have it in your power to open windows through which people can look at life with fresh hope and fresh vision.[76]*

A report in the *Birmingham Weekly Post* linking rehabilitation and occupational therapy explained: 'A department will be set up to provide remedial exercises and occupational therapy. And when the injured person is completely rehabilitated there will be available for him (or her) the assistance of an industrial liaison officer...to secure the rehabilitated suitable employment.'[77] The Birmingham Accident Hospital and Rehabilitation Centre, where that department was established, had been reconstituted from the Queens Hospital in 1941. Its rehabilitation service was reported to be a 'novel and most interesting feature of the Centre.' William Gissane, surgeon in Chief and Clinical Director of the Hospital made 'rehabilitation' the topic of his Annual Address to the AOT at its General Meeting in 1942. Rehabilitation, he said, was 'to restore to proper condition', and in order to achieve that the patient had to 'work hard in the interests of his own recovery'. In the past, he added, 'the tendency has been to stress the purely surgical part of the treatment of the injured part.' That created misplaced confidence, and resulted in the majority keeping the whole body at rest as well as the injured part. Occupational therapy, he said, must guide patients through that stage. On the Association's examination team, Gissane had been very impressed by one student's answer to an exam question in which she had drawn a loom with an adaptation worked by an injured lower limb. To him it was 'an outstanding example' of how occupational therapist's 'specialised knowledge' could 'meet the problems of rehabilitation in the early stages of recovery.' But his expectation of the professions' potential service was not only in acute care. He believed that, in the future, occupational therapists would have a role in medical services within big factories.[78] That example points to the major development in occupational therapy, during the war years—that of physical rehabilitation.

# Occupational therapy and physical rehabilitation

Despite the success of the World War I Curative Workshops, occupational therapy for physical disorders had not been greatly developed before 1939, except in isolated pockets of endeavour.

> One of the first considerations of the Council was to prepare to meet the need for a realistic form of Occupational Therapy in the physical field. The demonstration workshop opened by Dr. Elizabeth Casson at Bristol – 'The Allendale Curative Workshop' gave an impetus to this. [79]

Macdonald recalled that at the Curative Workshop:

> ...special adaptations were made on tools and apparatus used in joinery, woodcarving, metalwork, basketry, bookbinding, weaving and rugmaking, gardening, and splintmaking. Provision was also made for the games of billiards and darts, and for gardening, and the patients showed encouraging recoveries.

**Figure 2.6.4:** **Handles fitted to beater of standard loom, adapted by G. MacCaul**
*(Reproduced courtesy of Dorset House Archives, Oxford Brookes University)*

It provided treatment for civilian accident and disability cases from local hospitals and was to become 'the model for occupational therapy departments in the Emergency Medical Service hospitals throughout England.'[80] Macdonald later suggested that the occupational therapy departments run in conjunction with the EMS, at the time when the war effort of the AOT was in top gear, were the prototypes of those opened later as part of the National Health Service. She recalled some of the best of their kind during the war were:

- 'Ashridge Hospital, under Miss Elizabeth Osborn', who was later to become the first Principal of the Melbourne School of Occupational Therapy in Australia.
- Bromsgrove Emergency Hospital which was linked with the Dorset House School after its evacuation there, 'under Miss G. MacCaul' who was to become the Head Occupational Therapist at King's College Hospital, London.
- 'Nill End Hospital, St Albans under Miss Beckett.'

• 'Horton Emergency Hospital, Epsom, under Mrs K.Vidler' a War Emergency Diplomate, who resumed her previous profession to become the Principal of the Physiotherapy School at St Thomas' Hospital.

• 'Upton Emergency Hospital under Mrs Glyn Owens,' who was to become the Principal of the Liverpool School of Occupational Therapy, and who started student training at the Upton Hospital.[81]

Some of the lesser known centres were also excellent and of those Macdonald named:

• The Walsall General Hospital
• The West Bromwich Hospital
• The Grimsby and District General Hospital
• The Miners' Rehabilitation Centres at Tolygarn, S. Wales and Nuneaton, Warwick
• The Royal Naval Hospitals at Barrow Gurney, Bristol, and Sherborne and Malpas, Cheshire
• The Royal Air Force centre at Matlock, and
• The Banstead Military Hospital and Army centres at St Hugh's, Oxford, and Taunton.[82]

**Figure 2.6.5:** **Patients engaged in curative occupational therapy**
*(Imperial War Museum (A11525))*

The accepted closeness of the relationship between occupational therapists and masseuses, at least in terms of the latter being able to obtain a dual qualification quite quickly as a result of the War Emergency Diploma, did appear to lead to some very specific remedial treatments being developed. An article in *Occupational Therapy* by Janet Bunyard, a member of the Chartered Society of Masseurs on the correlation of the massage department with occupational therapy addressed the treatment of the hand as a shared concern. She described how the masseuse 'as she leads the patient one step forward on the way to recovery' had a new helper—the occupational therapist, who 'practise(s) him, by specially chosen work at each stage.' Surely a potential pioneer of hand therapy, a specialty shared by both occupational and physiotherapists, Bunyard wrote, quite lyrically, in 1940, about the re-education of the hand, as a servant of the mind as well as a useful part of the body:

*It first feeds the mind with experience (a baby learns all about an object by handling it, and a scientist learns his great truths by means of manual experiments), and then translates the result of that experience as arrived at by the intellect...On a humbler scale, the hand enables a man to earn his living, that is earn his right to go through life with self-respect and satisfaction and to have anything that he can pay for...The hand then is man's best friend, and to be deprived even temporarily of this wonderful teacher and servant is to lose independence, to be cut off from our share of usefulness.*[83]

One of the newer areas of practice to emerge during the war years was that of the specialised spinal injury centre. Mary Dudley Smith wrote of a unit, which she did not identify by name, established towards the end of the war which, at the time of her writing, housed 62 men and 3 women, the majority suffering from complete lesion of the spinal cord. In the early days many had severe pressure sores and urinary infection but more recently most were admitted soon after injury and sometimes it was only a few months before the patient was able to get around in a self-propelled chair. The Unit, she said, was impregnated with the enthusiasm of the specialist in charge typified by his determination that such patients could become useful citizens in the community, enjoying work and play. The co-operation between staff was 'good' and the atmosphere of the unit was noticeably gay with the regular provision of entertainment in the ward and encouragement of patient activities. Occupational therapy started a fortnight after admission with graded craftwork given to divert the patient's mind from pain and future worries. During that initial treatment the occupational therapist got to know the individual, their education, training, work, hobbies, service experience, marital status, and abilities. Several men learnt the art of fly tying (which used light apparatus, a small range of movement, and was varied). Training fine finger movement was seen as potentially valuable pre-training for lucrative jobs such as fine instrument making. As soon as expedient, the question of vocational training was considered. The Medical Superintendent arranged with the manager of a local radio factory to let patients who could be transported by ambulance work at jobs of national importance for several hours a day amongst the usual workforce. One patient was a shorthand typist with the Metropolitan Police, and as he hoped to continue with the same type of work he worked to increase his shorthand and typewriting speed whilst still in bed. In addition to such initiatives, Ministry of Labour officials and Educational Authorities were consulted, and employees of different local firms adopted various wards and visited them in the evenings and at weekends.[84]

In the field of tuberculosis, 'men from the forces' who contracted the disease were treated at the Preston Hall Settlement, near Maidstone, run by the British Legion with McDougall as Medical Director. A report in the *Portsmouth Evening News* explained that there the British Legion had 'set about the science of occupational therapy.'[85] *The Evening Standard* reported the patients' occupations as the manufacture of fancy goods and soap (for export), printing, carpentry, building and rabbit breeding. Since 1925 more than 6000 ex-servicemen had received treatment.[86] By 1943 *The Times* was reporting that 'so successful has been the work of rehabilitation and occupational therapy among tuberculous ex-service men at the British Legion village of Preston Hall...that a new centre providing similar treatment for ex-service women has been acquired by the Legion at Nayland Hall, near Colchester.[87] That could only have been the sanatorium in which Jane Walker established occupational therapy so many years earlier.

In another Sanatorium at Ham Green, an occupational therapy workshop was completed in May 1938. Richardson, the occupational therapist, began by explaining the meaning of occupational therapy to patients and utilising more orthodox crafts, grading them according to the needs of each. 'Then came a lessening of interest.' A suggestion box was put in the workshop and ideas for new occupations were solicited. Suggestions included: a meteorological station; a shoe repairing depot; a short-wave radio set; a photographic studio; a model aeroplane club; a dark room for developing films; a hospital magazine; and an entertainment committee. All were followed up, with Richardson assuming a facilitatory or 'enabling' approach as his account demonstrates:

*Meteorological Station. First of all we collected money for a rain gauge and with great pride watched the gardener put it in the ground. The patient who made the suggestion was appointed meteorologist to the station and this official may be seen each morning at 10 o'clock hopping out of bed in his dressing gown to measure the rainfall. A few months later the Health Committee was persuaded to purchase for us a Stevenson screen, soon known as 'the bee-hive'. The thermometers, four in number, i.e., a maximum, minimum, and wet and dry bulb, were paid for by the patients and friends. We were then given a cloud atlas which, with its coloured charts, has proved indispensable in the classification of clouds and the state of the sky. Our latest acquisition is a Fortin Mercury Barometer which hangs in the meteorologist's chalet. The Meteorological Office of the Air Ministry have now recognised our work and for the past twelve months our daily readings and other necessary records have been forwarded to them periodically*

*Shoe-Repairing Shop. To further this suggestion I paid a visit to the Shoe Factory in Bristol and the initial requirements for shoe-repairing were bought as advised by the salesman. At first, however, the patients repaired the shoes in a very amateurish way and this made us all rather dissatisfied with our efforts. Finally, I got in touch with a masterman in the trade and the Health Committee sanctioned a dozen lessons in the art of repairing shoes. The expert arrived and advised the necessary apparatus for doing the work adequately and this we were able to procure. Then work started in real earnest. The patients looked most business-like dressed in white aprons with leather bibs over them and they had the satisfaction of learning to do a job really well.*

*Short Wave Set. This was provided by the Health Committee and is a source of great interest to some patients.*

*Photographic Studio. It was possible in the workshop to spare a room, for conversion into a photographic studio – which was named 'The Chelsea Studio'.*

*Model Aeroplane Club. This suggestion met with immediate response and we soon had twenty or so members. Weekly meetings are held and by means of a subscription of 1d. per week per member and profits on the teas provided at meetings, which are organised by the patients themselves, the club is partly self-supporting. The occupation is an ideal one for the indoor work is light and as each plane is finished there comes the thrill of taking it out into the garden for its test flight. All the 'oldest inhabitants' in the Sanatorium turn out to watch the flights.*

*Dark Room. This created a problem from the point of view of adequate ventilation but this difficulty was satisfactorily overcome. No patient is to spend more than fifteen minutes in the dark room.*

*A Hospital Magazine. The two patients who put forward this suggestion were appointed Editor and Sub-Editor. The magazine is published about four times a year – six issues have already made their appearance – and by charging 3d. per copy to cover the cost of paper, ink, etc., this venture has become self-supporting. The magazine has received very good reviews in the local Press. The Public Health Department supplied us with a Bantam Duplicator, and when that ceased to meet our needs, the Editor advertised for a second-hand Rotary Duplicating Machine, with the result that Messrs. Ellams of Bristol presented us, free of charge, with an Automatic Feeding Rotary Duplicator. The Public Health Department also gave us a very good re-conditioned typewriter.*

*Entertainment Committee. A joint Entertainment Committee was formed of men and women and entertainments were for some time given every Thursday afternoon. Then, thanks to the initiative and hard work of one patient we acquired a cinematograph machine for the use of the patients and staff. This is a first-rate Paillard machine, valued at 50 guineas, towards which the Health Committee gave a grant and the remainder of the cost was raised by the patients and staff. We hope eventually to have a talkie machine.*

The more orthodox crafts remained popular with many but Richardson tried to make the 'scope as wide as possible and incorporate every new idea and suggestion that is put forward by the patients.'[88]

**Figure 2.6.6:     Patients with lung tuberculosis at East Fortune Hospital, Lothian, in the 1940s engaged in occupational therapy**

At Croydon Borough Sanatorium, Gladys Goodman, the occupational therapist, organised a team of 40 men and 30 women patients to make hospital supplies and other essential items from materials that were easy to get. They made wooden splints, bandage rolling machines, gloves for men on the minesweepers out of women's old felt hats, scraps of leather and pieces of thick woollen material, and those on bed rest unravelled old knitted garments and reknitted them into useful ones for people on active service.[89]

McDougall, the tuberculosis 'guru', commented that the war had brought 'the need for utilising human economy to the utmost in the interests of the nation.' The 'peacetime methods of Village Settlements have been enlarged and expanded to dimensions which only war could make possible,' he said. At Preston Hall there was an EMS hospital on the same site as the Sanatorium where all who required vocational training and rehabilitation received it through a variety of occupational therapy. EMS hospital patients were involved in land reclamation and planting vegetable crops. McDougall argued that 'there are soldiers, sailors, and airmen out there waiting for articles of one kind or other which can well be made by patients undergoing treatment...'[90]

# Overseas

Some of the occupational therapists trained in the War Office courses, and a few others, went to war centres in Southern Europe and the Middle East. One of the most noted was Dorothy Bramwell (1922–2000) who was one of the first four occupational therapists to be trained at the Astley Ainslie Hospital, and the first Scottish director of the course. When her own course of training was suspended at the outbreak of the war she had completed two academic years, but still needed to complete six months hospital practice before graduating. She was to do that and more in the Middle East. On a visit to Malta to attend her sister's wedding, Bramwell was prevented from returning home because of Italy's entry into the war. She was evacuated to Egypt, and there established occupational therapy services to assist the war injured to recover physically or mentally from their battle scars.[91]

**Figure 2.6.7:** **Dorothy Bramwell**
*(Courtesy of Catherine F. Paterson)*

Extracts from Bramwell's own account of her work tell the story:[92]

*...In the Middle East, a very small percentage of remedial Occupational Therapy was concerned with physical injuries.*

*..As far as I know there was no Occupational Therapy – at least under that name – in any of the Military Hospitals in the Middle East, before the year 1940. On September 13th of that year I started work in a very small way with the psychoneurotic patients in No. 64 General Hospital. At first there was no money on which to run the Department, and very little equipment, and we worked in one end of the ward, as a room could not be spared. To begin with, only six or eight patients were given treatment and of the staff, only those working with the mental patients took any interest in the Department. For the first few weeks all our material was given to us by friends, from whom we also received one or two donations of money. This unsatisfactory method of running the Department could not continue, so I eventually applied to the British Red Cross Society for assistance. Had it not*

been for the kindness and interest shown by this organisation, Occupational Therapy in the Middle East would not have developed as it has done.

...The Department began to grow...very soon the surgeons began to realize the value of the remedial side of the work. Several cases of burns, as well as hand and arm injuries, were treated on the wards and I was invited to attend a weekly fracture clinic held by the senior surgeon. As the work increased it was necessary to have more staff in the Department and also a separate workroom to which the general cases were able to come. A civilian voluntary worker offered her services, and a side ward was given to us for a workroom...it was not until I had given a lecture to the whole unit that the nursing staff showed any desire to helpfully co-operate.

In July 1941, I was posted to No. 1 Psychiatric Centre attached to No. 19 General Hospital...an N.C.O. was detailed to help in the workroom. He took charge of the woodwork – tinsmiths and sign writing, etc...About this time an order was published, that every Military Hospital of 600 beds or over was to open an Occupational Therapy Centre. Still no trained Occupational Therapists had been sent from the United Kingdom and we had to do the best we could without them. Each hospital was allowed on its establishment, one N.C.O. to work in the Centre, and an Occupational Therapy Officer was appointed...Early in 1942 Lt. Col. G Kersley became Adviser in Physical Medicine in the Middle East and took over the organisation of Occupational Therapy in the Middle East.

In June 1943...I was posted to No. 63 General Hospital...This centre had been run for over a year by a sergeant on the hospital staff who, after a few months, was joined by a corporal with six months Occupational Therapy training, and when I arrived there was a flourishing Department...There was an orthopaedic centre attached...which gave us some scope for remedial work...This was now more possible as five masseuses with six months Occupational Therapy training arrived in the Middle East. It was not easy to post these masseuses...They were eventually sent to Nos. 41 and 18 neuropathic hospitals and to Nos. 23, 12 and 27 general hospitals, which were orthopaedic centres, to concentrate on remedial work. It was now found necessary to have someone to whom all centres could apply for help or advice, so, in the end of October, I was given the title of Chief Occupational Therapist in the Middle East.

...The outlook of many of the desert hospitals was rather depressing and various means were used to brighten the surroundings. A great many gardens sprang up and the psychotic compound in No. 1 Psychiatric Centre produced a novel idea. Regimental crests and other designs were outlined in the sand in pebbles wrapped in silver paper. Those patients also built a ping pong table in the sand. The cement top of the table was on a level with the ground while the surroundings were dug out to the correct depth.

Livestock was very popular among the patients, particularly those in the neuropathic hospitals. No. 41 General Hospital kept hens and guinea pigs and budgerigars, while No. 78 General Hospital had an aviary.

During 1941, 1942 and 1943 I visited Nos. 27, 6, 16, 64, and 8 General Hospitals and Nos. 2, 3, and 5 Convalescent Depots and No. 2 New Zealand General Hospital and No. 5 S. African General Hospital. All those hospitals and convalescent depots had departments of varying sizes, and the standard of work in all was high

In 1942 the British Red Cross Society started an occupational therapy store in Cairo:

Each military hospital in the Middle East received from the British Red Cross Society, equipment and materials from the Occupational Therapy store, up to the value of 1/6 per bed *per year...A substore, working in conjunction with the main store, was opened by the British Red Cross Society in Jerusalem for the hospitals in Palestine and Syria. This was the work of Mrs Saunders, who had started several Occupational Centres in Palestine, supervised all hospital centres there and for some time had distributed materials from Jerusalem.*

*...The Occupational Therapy store in Cairo sent large quantities of equipment and materials to hospitals in Italy, Malta, N. Africa and P.A.I. (Persia and Iraq) Force.*

*...In addition to this, every hospital had its own sources of supply...In two or three hospitals, the carpenter's shop made use of bomb boxes for making many things such as chairs, waste paper bins, dirty linen bins, small lockers, and one hospital made one into a baby's cradle...One or two hospitals obtained U/S motor car engines from the salvage depot. These were taken to pieces and used for various types of equipment or kept intact so that those interested could learn by them.*

Throughout her time in the Middle East, Bramwell taught others. These included nursing sisters, orderlies, Red Cross Workers, and VAD.s. As well, she recognised and paid tribute to other workers in the field. She noted:

*Very valuable work was being done by Mrs Lewthwaite who, from a centre in Cairo, distributed to many hospitals patterns of Regimental badges and materials and threads with which to embroider them. Since this work was started, it has proved to be one of the most popular crafts among the men. *[93]

Margaret Lewthwaite was a resident of Haifa, who some time previously had done occupational therapy training (her account did not provide details of where or when). In early 1940 she found herself handing out cigarettes to the wounded on stretchers as they were brought from the Western Desert. Next day, she drove to Jerusalem to suggest that an occupational therapy department should be included when hospitals were set up. Instead she was invited to set up her own department in the 15th (Scottish) Hospital in Cairo and was provided with a small office and two storerooms. She persuaded various organisations and individuals to provide her with cotton material, wood, needles and wool or thick cotton thread at no cost, and volunteer staff to help her. She organised prisoners of war to make up embroidery frames and, an artist herself, she created special designs, sometimes to individual requests, for patients to embroider. She called this 'frame therapy.'

By the end of the first year, 500 hand-made framed embroidery 'kits' were handed out each week to No. 9, No. 63, and No. 15 Scottish Hospitals. In 1941, she was made a member of the latter unit, provided with a car and driver and awarded the MBE for her work. Her work continued until the end of the war in the desert in 1944; by that time she had become Head of Occupational Therapy in the Middle East British Hospitals, and she was assisting other New Zealand, American, Indian and South African hospital units at their request. It is assumed that she must have taken over the head position from Bramwell.

One particular story of Lewthwaite is heart warming. She regularly visited a very young and violent patient in a padded cell. She took crayons with her, and drew. He joined her and filled a page with crosses in a cemetery and planes diving out of the sky. By chance she saw a photograph of him playing a violin and, having told his story, was given money to buy a violin for him. The first day he just looked at it, the second he held it carefully, and the third he played it beautifully. Eventually he recovered.[94]

**Figure 2.6.8:** Sketches after pictures from *Nursing Times* March 21st 1942 and August 1st 1942 at home (Astley Ainslie Institution) and abroad (Middle East)

In the *Nursing Times* of August 1st 1942, a report pictured soldiers in the Middle East in a New Zealand Hospital engaged in treatment. The pictures illustrate the bed bound engaged in sewing, weaving for exercise of upper limbs, 'quoits on the sand' to exercise wrists and elbows and increase muscular co-ordination, tin-foil work for strengthening wrists, a stationary bicycle and treadle sewing machine for lower limb exercise, and a range of other occupations such as making clocks, practising draughtsmanship, and woodwork in the workshop. The report emphasised that:

> ...the men work at their own pace, gradually doing more and more as their mental and physical health improves. So good have been the results of occupational therapy in the treatment of all kinds of injuries – strains, fractures, broken limbs, head injuries, and all other disabilities of war, that the War Office has in hand a steady extension of this form of treatment.[95]

Many other stories could and should be told, but mention will only be made of two occupational therapists sailing to South Africa to start an occupational therapy school at the University of Witwatersrand, Johannesburg. They reached there, via the Cape, having been torpedoed on the way. One of them was Isobel Macarthur of Exeter, and the other was Muriel Crousaz, a pioneer in the establishment of the AOT. Apparently Crousaz lost all her possessions except a fur coat and the notes which she took with her on how to run an Occupational Therapy Training School!

# Canadian Occupational Therapists in World War II
## By Catherine F. Paterson

Occupational therapy within physical rehabilitation during World War II, particularly in Scotland, owes much to Canadian occupational therapists who volunteered for war work. This section of the chapter recounts the contribution to the war effort in Scotland and England, of eleven trained Canadian occupational therapists, whose leadership was vital in both increasing the numbers of trained therapists and assistants and in developing departments in the Emergency Medical

Service (EMS) hospitals. One Canadian occupational therapist was posted to Middleton Park Hospital, Oxford, two to Taunton, three to the Astley Ainsley Hospital (AAH), Edinburgh, and five to Scottish EMS hospitals. These occupational therapy departments, set up and financed by the government within the EMS hospitals, provided the base for the post-war development of the profession in the NHS physical hospitals.

In Scotland from 1939 to 1941 there was a hiatus in the development of occupational therapy. With the outbreak of war in 1939, the occupational therapy department at the AAH was closed and the course was suspended, leaving the training of nine occupational therapy students (four from the first intake and five from the second intake) incomplete.[96] The closure of the department and school was part of emergency procedures to make room for anticipated casualties, when the AAH was requisitioned as part of the EMS. In planning for the expected large numbers of civilian and military casualties, there was early recognition of the need for specialised units, particularly for orthopaedics and rehabilitation, as there had been during World War I. To staff these rehabilitation services, masseurs and rehabilitation orderlies, who were trained in the army, were recruited, but emergency measures to increase the number of occupational therapists were not immediately put into force.[97]

Mary Wilson (1918–1988) was the last of the succession of Canadian occupational therapists, who had worked at the Astley Ainslie Hospital and occupational therapy school before the war. Only 20 when she arrived in Edinburgh, in 1938, she had graduated the previous year from the University of Toronto. Unable to obtain a paid position after completing her internship, due to the recession in Canada, Amy de Brisay, encouraged her to apply to work in Edinburgh.[98] When the department was closed in 1939, Wilson remained at the AAH as a nursing auxiliary, but in July 1940 she was recruited by the Red Cross to establish an occupational therapy department at the Middleton Park Hospital, Bicester, Oxford. This was a military convalescent and rehabilitation hospital, which Goldwin Howland, the President of the Canadian Association of Occupational Therapists referred to as the 'show place for all other hospitals'.[99] and it certainly attracted much publicity.[100] Apart from developing the department, Wilson also provided the final stages of the training of two of the Scottish students Isobel Johnstone and Mary Cunningham. Wilson worked at Middleton Park until 1944, when she was finally allowed to join the Canadian Army Medical Corps (CAMC), becoming the first Canadian occupational therapist in the Corps to serve in the UK.[101] By January 1945, a total of 36 Corps members were staffing 12 Canadian Military Hospitals throughout the UK, and on average 3856 patients were being treated every month.[102]

By 1941, when the need for additional occupational therapists became urgent, the Government agreed to finance an emergency six months' training for suitably qualified personnel as occupational therapy assistants at the AAH in Edinburgh as well as at Bromsgrove and Taunton.[103]

The courses at the Army School of Occupational Therapy, Taunton, were run by Josephine Forbes and Dorothy Grant, Canadian occupational therapists, who had responded to a request by the British War Office. They found, to their initial dismay, that their chief function was to conduct emergency training in occupational therapy for Royal Army Medical Corps masseurs, as well as treat casualties. Forbes and Grant spent some time with Macdonald, at Bromsgrove before starting their first course in December 1941. This was for 28 masseurs, who were either privates, trained in a four-month massage course given by the Army, or NCOs who had the full qualification of the Chartered Society of Masseurs (and masseuses) and Medical Gymnasts. Forbes and Grant ran at least two courses, the first all male and the second mainly female. After some reluctance on the part of the Association, the students sat the examinations of the AOT War Emergency Diploma.[104]

North of the border, the Department of Health for Scotland had requested the Governors of the AAH not only to restart the complete training for the Diploma, but also to run the six-month intensive course for occupational therapy assistants.[105] The courses started on 1 October 1941, and in the Annual Report, the medical superintendent gave an account of the emergency course. The instruction given in the short intensive course was designed to give the students knowledge of the subject sufficient to enable them to understand and carry out the instructions of the trained occupational therapists with whom they would be associated as assistants. The syllabus thus included elementary courses in anatomy, psychology, medicine and surgery, the theory and practice of occupational therapy and craftwork, with as much practical instruction as could be given in the time.[106]

The courses in Edinburgh were organised by another Canadian, Jean Hampson (1895–1968), who at 46 was a very experienced therapist. Originally a teacher, she had trained as an aide in 1919, and had worked in military hospitals in Canada, after the Great War and then in a children's hospital.[107] Unlike Forbes and Grant, Hampson at least had had some experience of occupational therapy education when she arrived in Edinburgh. She had 'not only influenced the nature of occupational therapy in paediatric settings in Toronto but through her participation in the teaching of the students from the sole occupational therapy school, influenced the development of the programmes emerging in Montreal, and other cities in Canada'.[108]

Twelve students were enrolled for the six-month Emergency Course in Edinburgh.[109] One was Isabella Veitch (later Elliott), who had been an occupational therapy assistant and member of the embryonic Scottish Association of Occupational Therapy (SAOT) before the war. According to Elliott, the course was very concentrated and the students took it extremely seriously, especially as the Department of Health was paying the tuition fees and they were each receiving an allowance of £2/10/- per week.[110] At least seven later qualified as occupational therapists in Scotland, adding significantly to the ranks of qualified therapists after the war.[111]

In Edinburgh, in conjunction with the six-month emergency course, the full two-and-a half year course was re-established, also under the direction of Jean Hampson. The initial intakes were small, since the AAH was limited by its charter to producing occupational therapists for its own department. However, due to the demand for occupational therapists, the restriction on numbers accepted on the course was relaxed and each year the intake increased from seven in 1941 to twelve in 1945. One of the first students to complete the course was Miss Rhoda Elizabeth Begg, who expressed the students' appreciation of their mentor:

> It was new work, its traditions still to be formed, and it was rather an anxious time in which to be a student or to teach. But in Jean Hampson, we had a leader whose idealism and belief in hard work were allied to an irresistible sense of fun and our student days were lively and very interesting. We look back on her good counsel with affection and respect.[112]

As well as running the courses, Hampson also supervised the occupational therapy department of the AAH, which was staffed by Canadians, Margaret Langley and Barbara Hope. Patients were principally men from the 'other ranks', who had a mixture of medical conditions, such as tuberculosis, and injuries such as nerve damage and amputations, which had been sustained during service. In 1944, they were able to join the Canadian Royal Army Corps and were transferred to Canadian hospitals in England.[113]

Meanwhile, in response to the request by the Department of Health for Scotland in 1939, in addition to the three occupational therapists at the AAH, five Canadian trained occupational therapists volunteered to set up departments in hospitals, which were part of the EMS. Amy de Brisay, Mary Clark, and Gertrude Ellis, arrived in March 1941[114] and they were joined a year later by sisters Ruth and Deborah Craig.[115] Collectively they set up departments at Killearn, Bangour, and Stracathro, and later at Gleneagles hospitals.

The largest of the EMS hospitals in Scotland was Bangour, which in peacetime was the Bangour Village Hospital, built at the beginning of the twentieth century for the treatment and care of 'the pauper lunatics' of the city of Edinburgh.[116] Bangour became noted for its two specialised units, which were also of particular relevance to occupational therapy. The Neurology and Neurosurgery Unit was pioneered by Norman McOmish Dott (1887–1973)[117] and the Burns and Plastic Surgery Unit was headed by Alexander B. Wallace (1906–1975). Both achieved international recognition.

On the outbreak of war in 1939, Dott set up his Brain Injury Unit at Bangour, where he formed a truly multidisciplinary team, and became a staunch allay of occupational therapy. Speaking in 1967, he recalled that:

> When I was in active practice, during the war, the nurse, physiotherapists and I found that many of our endeavours fell short of what was needful. Often the patients we had worked hardest for just failed to make the grade – drifted into chronic invalidism. Then we called in the OTs. They had their dual approach – the psychological stimulus to do pleasing things within the patients' capacity; and the physical 'know how' of duly advancing gradations. And then we achieved full rehabilitation with the patient the focus and this therapeutic team gathered round him, harmoniously co-operating to achieve his full potential.[118]

The occupational therapy was headed by Amy de Brisay. Three of the five students from the second intake at the AAH, whose training had been suspended, worked at Bangour, for a year under de Brisay's supervision, while studying for their examinations. de Brisay's contribution was well recognised. Dott, when summarising the developments at his Brain Injury Unit, considered that:

> *Among the war-time advances in rehabilitation measures which we were able to secure, the greatest was the return of Miss de Brisay to Scotland and the generous and untiring work with our patients and for the cause of rehabilitation in general and occupational therapy in particular. What we owe to her noble and courageous personality and her capable organisation cannot be overestimated.*[119]

de Brisay made a similar impact in the Burns and Plastic Surgery Unit, which was the second specialised department at Bangour.[120] Alexander Wallace[121], who developed the Unit was not unusual at that time in considering that therapeutic occupations should be prescribed and supervised by the surgeon or physician, however he was even more specific than most other physicians, and published in the next decade, the aims and prescriptions for an illustrative range of patients, who had been treated at Bangour.[122] (More details are provided in Chapter 7.)

After the war the occupational therapy department continued to play an integral part in patient care[123], and both Dott and Wallace took an active interest in the activities of the reconstituted Scottish Association of Occupational Therapists.[124]

One further project that involved de Brisay was the development of occupational therapy for the rehabilitation of miners at the Gleneagles Fitness Centre. One of the most publicised innovations in rehabilitation during World War II was the opening of the Fitness Centre for miners, at Gleneagles, which in peacetime was, and still is, a luxury hotel, famous for its golf.[125] Although there had been some pre-war provision for the rehabilitation of miners to build on (a clinic in Lanarkshire,[126] and a residential rehabilitation centre in the Midlands[127]) Gleneagles was the first residential centre of its kind in Scotland. Dunn concluded that, 'Much of its work was frankly experimental and much was learned.'[128] The centre admitted its first miners in January 1943.[129]

The Medical Superintendent of the Fitness Centre was Dr Peter J. Macleod, and the rehabilitation staff comprised three male physical training instructors, two physiotherapists, two fully trained occupational therapists, and one assistant who had completed the emergency six-month course at the AAH. There was no nursing staff, since the patients were all well enough to look after themselves.[130] After it was initially organised by de Brisay, the occupational therapy department was then delegated to Deborah Craig, who had been working with her at Bangour for a year, and who had had experience at the Toronto Rehabilitation Centre run by the Workmen's Compensation Board.[131]

Craig, writing at the time of Macleod's untimely death in 1951, considered that:

> *In planning the programme of rehabilitation for the Fitness Centre, occupational therapy was one of Dr. Macleod's main interests. He had always believed in the power of work to restore confidence and prove to the patient his ability to recover. In occupational therapy he saw great possibilities for developing this theory, from early ward work to the later stages of rehabilitation at the Fitness Centre. He held that the task set should be just within reach at any particular stage of recovery, and stressed the importance of progression in any scheme of occupational therapy.*[132]

> *Most of the patients were miners and the occupational therapy programme contained*

*all the usual remedial activities, treadle lathes, bicycle saws and foot powered looms, but resistance tended to be greater, and garage and outdoor activities were used as the patients recovered. The heavier activities included digging, the use of two-handed saws to cut logs into boards, and the casting of concrete to make kerbs for the County Council.*[133]

At the end of the war, Gleneagles resumed its normal function and the Fitness Centre was transferred to Bridge of Earn Hospital, where it continued to be a dynamic unit for the treatment and rehabilitation of orthopaedic patients. Eventually, the demise of heavy industry, particularly of the Fife coal mines, and advances in orthopaedic surgery reduced the importance of the service.

Mary Clark had also trained as an occupational therapist at the University of Toronto and worked at the Workmen's Compensation Workshop in Toronto. In response to the request by the Department of Health for Scotland, she set sail with the four other occupational therapists on the SS Georgic from New York in February 1941. Her account of the voyage across the Atlantic in a converted cruise ship, unescorted and in winter gales, is testament to the real meaning of volunteering for overseas service during a war.[134] Clark spent her first three months in Scotland at Bangour Hospital with Amy de Brisay, until Killearn Hospital, which was being built 14 miles north of Glasgow, was ready to receive patients. This emergency hutted hospital eventually had 600 beds and provided specialist treatment in orthopaedics, neurosurgery and peripheral nerve lesions. Killearn took the 'long operation cases' from Glasgow hospitals, who were sent to the country for safety. Some of the patients had been severely injured during the air raids on the Clyde.[135] Clark left Scotland in March 1945, while the war was still on.[136] However, the foundations of the service had been laid and the occupational therapy department continued until the neurosurgery unit was transferred to the Southern General Hospital, Glasgow, and Killearn was replaced by the newly constructed Gartnavel General Hospital in the 1970s. Both hospitals continued to have well-developed and successful occupational therapy departments.

Gertrude Ellis, who travelled to Scotland with de Brisay and Clark,[137] was posted to Stracathro Hospital, one of the seven new hospitals built for the EMS in Scotland at the start of the war. The work at Stracathro was demanding—some of the patients had dramatic injuries, including seamen brought straight from the North Sea with hypothermia and dreadful burns caused by the burning oil from their sunken ships. Jean Waterston, whose training had been suspended at the start of the war, was sent to Stracathro to work under the direction of Ellis. However, Waterston was there for only two weeks when Ellis took leave to be married.[138] She was replaced in 1942 by a Scottish trained therapist, Isobel Johnstone.[139]

Eleven therapists are not very many, but at a time of great demand, these eleven volunteer occupational therapists made a significant contribution to the war effort. Nearly all of the first class of the Taunton course were sent to base hospitals abroad,[140] including six who were posted to the Middle East to work in the service developed by Dorothy Bramwell, one of the first intake of students trained in Edinburgh. They were sent to separate neuropathic and orthopaedic units to concentrate on remedial work.[141]

The Canadians and the newly qualified Scottish therapists and their assistants made a significant contribution to the rehabilitation services, particularly where they were supported by prominent consultants, who took a personal and holistic approach to their patients. As a direct result of Canadian leadership and training, nine of the 34 EMS physical hospitals developed occupational therapy departments – the Astley Ainslie Hospital, the six orthopaedic hospitals: Stracathro, Princess Margaret Rose, Peel, Larbert, Killearn, and Hairmyres and important departments were established at the specialist units of Bangour General and Gleneagles Fitness Centre. These occupational therapy departments, set up and financed by the government within the EMS hospitals, provided the base for the post-war development of the profession in relation to physical medicine.

After the war, the Scottish Association maintained its close links with Canada, with an exchange scheme being organised between therapists.

## Occupational therapy in mental hospitals

At the outset of the war there were fears that the incidence of mental breakdown would increase. Indeed, in 1938 a group of London psychiatrists estimated that, within six months of the outbreak of the war, three to four million people would need their services. Those estimates proved wrong; people's morale raised rather than plummeted with the bombing. Unfortunately for those in hospitals, shortages of staff led to a tightening of the locked door policies that had eased during the 1930s.[142] (Early asylums and mental hospitals had maintained a policy of confining patients behind locked doors. Movement and time outside their wards were controlled and escorted strictly.)

The Army Psychiatric Service provided in- and out-patient clinics for soldiers, casualty clearing stations, and 'base hospital' clearing stations for expeditionary forces. Under military conditions occupational therapy had a place in the first of those, grouping patients in either a neurosis or psychosis stream. Major H. A. Palmer, a senior assistant physician at Woodside Hospital, had worked alongside an occupational therapist since the outset of the war, and he described the usual process. In the mornings patients were either assigned to a special occupational therapy class housed in a different building to the ward, or ward work, or work connected with the well-being of the hospital. A range of occupations was employed, with one of them being a miniature theatre which entailed an excellent combination of individual and group activity. In the afternoons some form of recreation was used such as physical drill, football, a route march, or a visit to the city. Additionally a dance, a movie, a whist drive or chess tournament was organised once a week.[143]

During the war years, departments in many mental hospitals were taken over to provide emergency beds for physically disabled civilian and service cases. So, whilst in the physical field the profession was growing and developing, in mental hospitals it was becoming curtailed. Materials were difficult to get as the demands of physical centres took precedence. Indeed in an extract from *The Lancet* the question of shortage of occupational therapy supplies in mental hospitals was noted:

*Mr. F. MESSNER asked the Minister of Health if he was aware that the present rationing of materials is hindering the work of occupational therapy in mental hospitals; and if he could take steps to secure a relaxation of the rationing regulations in these special cases. – Mr BROWN. replied: I am in communication with the President of the Board of Trade in this matter.*[144]

Whether that query produced any lightening of the problem is unknown; however, occupational therapists working within mental health 'struggled on bravely, showing great ingenuity and devotion', maintaining services with sufficient vigour so that, by the end of the war, they were quickly able to return to normal and then expand.[145] It is interesting to note the trend of occupations at this time. In the physical field the choice was controlled largely by the materials made available through the special government priority system, and by government restrictions on the type of occupations used in treatment. That was not the case in the psychological field, but without the materials required for much of the usual craftwork, occupational therapists had to direct their patients' interests to other 'more realistic occupations'.[146] Macdonald saw that as a progressive step which later extended into physical treatment as well.[147] A *Sunday Express* report 'War Jobs Aid Recovery of Mental Cases' explained that mental patients were given urgent war work to do as a 'rehabilitation experiment' by the Mental After Care Society. Men at a convalescent home were provided with semi-skilled work in conjunction with a local war factory. It was claimed to have 'astonishing results', their work being surprisingly fast and accurate, and their mental health improving at the same time.[148] The report failed to say whether occupational therapists were involved, however, Dorothy Lawrence Paul's report of the occupational therapy at Gartnavel in 1939 told a similar story:

*For several weeks at the beginning of the year many of the patients helped in the hospital A.R.P. (Air Raid Precautions) preparations by sewing sandbags...*

*At the outbreak of war the patients and staff used the pavilion to make A.R.P. blinds and electric light shades for the Hospital. After several weeks we decided to turn our efforts to Red Cross sewing, and the knitting of comforts for the Army and Navy. We have succeeded in winning the co-operation of the patients and the nursing staff, both in the Department and in the Wards, and a number of the male patients have joined in the effort, and are very proud of the socks which they have knitted, after encountering many difficulties. The patients are glad to feel that they, too, are doing their bit, and are creating some article of real use, and they take great pride in doing so.* [149]

By the following year Paul provided an update. The team of male and female patients, and the Nursing Staff:

*...have managed to knit 792 comforts to date...The wool is supplied by the Central Fund Depot...In several of the Wards patients are cleaning and picking Sphagnum Moss ready to be made into dressings which are so urgently needed at the First Aid posts in the bombed areas. The Red Cross Depot supplies the moss and is most grateful for our assistance.*[150]

Another example of realistic work, in a totally different vein, was provided in *Hospital and Nursing Home Management*. This recommended poultry-keeping as 'work' within occupational therapy for the reduction of 'unmanageableness and violence' and the 'acceleration of recovery.' Edward Richmond, the author, obviously found the best laying hen to be a cross between a Rhode Island Red male bird and a light Sussex hen which, he wrote, should be bought at 'point of lay'. The patients apparently fed the birds on scraps from the hospital kitchen—an important economic consideration in a time of shortage.[151]

Joyce Hombersley, who was to become the Director of Training at St Andrews Hospital, Northampton, alludes to the difficulties experienced in mental hospitals during the war years. In a letter to the Journal dated 22 November 1944, she wrote:

*Coming back to occupational therapy in this country after an absence of five years I have been appalled by the difficult conditions due to shortage of Staff and Supplies under which my colleagues have been working. During, a recent tour of Hospitals I was amazed and delighted by the strides made on the Orthopaedic side but at the same time rather saddened by what I felt was a loss of ground in mental work. Mental hospitals have obviously been very hard-hit but I am wondering whether we have been making the wisest and fullest use of what is left to us...Given such limited supplies of material and the admitted shortage of staff should we not have been better employed in research?* [152]

Despite the downturn of practical opportunities for work in mental hospitals there continued to be great interest in the specialty and some articles of note in a number of issues of *Occupational Therapy* are worthy of comment, and current day research. In the Spring issue of 1941, for example, a paper by Dr J. R. Whitwell, the honorary librarian to the Royal Medico-Psychological Society Libary, questioned the procedure for the selection and use of books as therapy.[153] In the same issue Dr Astley Cooper challenged occupational therapists to become more scientific by subjecting occupation used as therapy to experimental study. Whilst recognising that the work involved was significant, he said:

*There is obviously a great lack of data...and I therefore suggest the first essential is the keeping of records of cases, diagnosis, crafts used, grade of work, with details and results. I want to emphasize the importance of diagnosis, not only as a means of sorting cases, but also as a control of our present ideas on classification.*

His rationale was that the 'essence of therapy is the application of treatment to cases.' Any kind of remedial agent 'claims to treat each case specifically, and should be able to lay down general indications for the use or disuse of his remedies.' He queried whether as much could be said of occupational therapy.[154]

An article towards the end of the war by Ruth Darwin attempted to start picking up 'the threads of progress broken in 1939' by beginning to discuss postwar needs in the mental health services.[155] She believed the place of occupational therapy within in-patient treatment of mental and nervous disease to be well recognised, however she cautioned that practice in many places lagged behind recognition, and in others shortage of staff and other wartime difficulties had impeded progress. Not all hospitals employed occupational therapists to do the work. Some hospitals, she said:

*...depend upon almost superhuman achievements of individual medical superintendents, matrons and head male nurses, whose enthusiasm and energy have enabled them to acquire and impart technical knowledge which in the case of more ordinary mortals would be outside their province...*

Whatever the reason, she averred, occupational therapists had to remain militant until 'the sight of unoccupied and apathetic or destructive patients sitting brooding in the wards or wandering aimlessly in the gardens, is less familiar.'[156]

Darwin went on to discuss 'new possibilities outside the realm of the hospital itself' in which the developing awareness of the need for occupation during convalescence and the training and re-instatement in industry of recovering or recovered patients was better understood. With allusion to the suggestions made in the Tomlinson Report she suggested the establishment of facilities:

> ...for occupational treatment in centres attached to clinics; for the training of patients who have recovered sufficiently to enable them to follow a professional or technical course either in their old trade or in a new one; and for industrial shops for mentally disabled persons who are permanently unfit for employment except in sheltered conditions. [157]

Indeed, the war and the years that followed were to mark a new era in mental hospitals. In the North Wales Hospital, for example, that was precipitated by the appointment of Dr J. H. O. Roberts in 1940. He started with the re-classification of wards on both sides, attempting to place similar types of patients, by diagnosis and behaviour, into the same wards, and then, at the war's closure, introduced a holistic approach. That included measures to improve the general health of patients, to re-educate and advise, and the provision of rehabilitation and home assessments.[158]

However two of the most significant changes in terms of future trends were, first, the opening of the first British Day Hospital in 1946. It became the Marlborough Day Hospital, but at that time was called the 'Social Psychotherapy Centre.' Second, a wartime innovation of Maxwell Jones, the use of community and group methods of treatment, was to prove an on-going feature of therapeutic programmes for the remainder of the century.[159]

# Prisoners of war

In 1941 a proposal was made that occupational therapy could help Prisoners of War. Mrs Owens and Miss English were asked to investigate the possibility.[160] Their idea was reported in the Annual Report of 1941–42 as follows:

> A scheme has been thought out whereby some form of occupation could be provided for prisoners of war which would help to alleviate boredom in their captivity. The scheme was presented to the Joint War Organisation of the British Red Cross and St John of Jerusalem by Miss English and Mrs Owens and is still under consideration. Meanwhile, through the Invalids Comforts Section of this Organisation an attempt has been made by Miss English (who was invited by Mrs Bromley-Davenport in October) to prepare parcels of work suitable for some of the hospitals in Germany. A special concession has been permitted and prepared samples of work with the necessary printed instructions are sent.[161]

The parcels were sent by Air Mail and could weigh only 31/2 lb. Dangerous tools, leather, or materials in tubes were forbidden, but a special concession regarding 'sending prepared samples of work, and the necessary printed or typewritten directions and designs' was permitted. The type of work which was despatched is listed below:

| | |
|---|---|
| Small hand looms | Cut out soft slippers with underlay felt for soles. |
| Tablet weaving | Needlework on hessian for big bags to hold work etc |
| Tapestry and embroidery | Netting materials to make bags and hammocks |
| Gloves in felt and rexine | Felt applique pictures |
| Quilting | Small bundles of wood for small models, boats, etc. |
| Material for silhouette cutting | Tobacco pipes in the rough |
| Book-binding apparatus | French knitting frames |
| Norwegian Braid weaving | Raffia work |
| Rugs | Macrame work, string belts, etc |
| Patch-work | Wool and Spindles for spinning |
| Needleweaving belts | Knitting and crotchet |
| Paints and wood for heraldry, crests, etc. | |

The success of this scheme was spectacular. From one camp where prisoners awaited repatriation, a request came for work for 500 men who asked, particularly, for slippers, embroidery, tapestry, and bookbinding materials as their books are getting dilapidated. One RAMC Officer wrote to say how thrilled he was to receive a parcel. He added that as he could quite easily do all the work in a week, he was rationing himself to a little each day. Another request was for something small and difficult, which took a long time to do.

The following year it was reported that the 'work grew to such proportions that it became impossible to continue' in the same way. That resulted, in October 1942, in a subsection of the Red Cross Invalids Comforts Section being opened to carry on the work. Mrs Bromley-Davenport, who took on that responsibility, invited the originator of the idea, the 'tireless' Miss English, to continue to act in an advisory capacity. By the end of 1942 sufficient work had been sent for over 2,000 men. Parcels, by then, could weigh up to 10 lb., and study courses and instruction books were provided through the Educational Book Section of the British Red Cross. A large exhibition of the work was on display at the War Office and at the United Nations Exhibition in Dorland Hall, London. Her Majesty, the Queen visited the Invalids Comforts Section and appeared extremely interested in the work, particularly that which had been prepared by 'Service' patients. Miss English was introduced to her.[162,163] In a short piece in *The Times*, Miss English explained:

> *Physical and mental deterioration, caused from monotony and lack of occupation, is one of the greatest problems for prisoners of war...But generally speaking, prisoners of war need more than just to pass the time. Many are maimed; others are too disturbed and frustrated by their captivity to concentrate on purely theoretical study; and quite a number are only suited for manual work. These men need to be prepared for a definite career after repatriation. To many of them some type of constructive craft-work would provide the solution – work which ensures a creative outlet and a solid promise for the future. Educationalists, doctors, and others who are already engaged in rehabilitation work should*

*be given facilities to construct an organized plan for the prisoners' future, thereby replacing the present lack of vision by adequate and effective action.*[164]

A further scheme was devised to extend the programme. Groups were developed in each county under the auspices of the Red Cross, and 'large quantities of material and samples ready for censorship and dispatch' were received and prepared. The East Lancashire group, for example, headed by Mrs H. McGill, as an initial step issued an appeal for tools and materials. Letters of appreciation were received not only from the prison camps, but also from Major General Sir Richard Howard Vyse who asked members of the Association for their expert help in connection with the new Groups.[165]

Apart from that Scheme, individuals or groups of people chose to engage in a variety of occupations whilst they were prisoners of war. Items deposited in the Imperial War Museum point to the importance given to the occupations, which surely adds credence to the notion of occupation as a form of self-health as discussed in Volume 1. Examples from World War II prisoners of war include:

• Three notebooks put together by Private Geoffrey A. Monument of the RASC, a prisoner of war in Changi, Singapore, and Haito and Sendai in Japan, who recorded details of food, personal weight, diet, Red Cross parcels, books read, notes on fellow prisoners, poems and one which was a recipe book which he called:

> 'Epicurean delights'
> The Grub stake.
> Manager GA MONUMENT
> Eat drink and be merry for tomorrow you may die.
> 'New Rhapsodies compiled by the hungary'

The books were made of oddments of brown paper bags, photo envelopes and so on, tied or sewn together with string or thread.[166]

• 'Floreat medic', an operetta (in one tremendous act) produced in Malang Prisoner of War Camp, Java, 1942. Written and produced by the medical orderlies.

The words were set to music taken from a number of well known operas and shows, such as the 'Mikado', 'John Brown's body', 'Jingle bells', and 'I dreamt I dwelled in Marble Halls'.[167]

• Illustrations of Changi Women's Internment Camp including those of Dr H. I. Worth, a medical doctor in the camp, and Miss A. L. Robertson, a physiotherapist, who collected the illustrations.[168] One by C. Jackson of the Sime Road Women's Camp is shown as Figure 2.6.9.

• Hand made illustrated magazines by Private R.R. Bull, of the Royal West Kent Regiment who was captured in France in 1940. They were compiled in Stalag 1401 POW Camp Germany, May 1942–November 1943, and contained social and sports news and some literary material. Included in the items are mementos of a one-act play, a series of poems compiled in camp, and hand drawn camp theatre programmes.[169]

**Figure 2.6.9:**   **Sime Road Women's Camp, Changi: By C. Jackson**
*(Unable to trace copyright)*

# Textbooks

D
uring the war years, textbooks by occupational therapists for occupational therapists began to appear. Macdonald, in collaboration with Nora Haworth, a medical colleague, published the *Theory of Occupational Therapy* for students and nurses studying the uses and methods of application of occupational therapy.[170] A sign of the times, the book covered occupational therapy in mental nursing, as well as occupational therapy in the treatment of mental disorders, orthopaedic and surgical cases, cardiac cases, and tuberculosis. Chapters on equipment, apparatus, materials and suppliers, records and prescriptions, finance, and training were included.

In cases of mental disorder, occupational therapists' 'means for the re-education of those functions of the mind which are either not functioning or are functioning abnormally' included essential crafts, and 'classes in country dancing, community singing and simple physical exercises.'[171] In a general hospital occupational therapy could be 'general' to prevent depression and to keep up morale. Alternatively it might be 'special' in which case treatment was 'carefully selected and prescribed with some remedial purpose in view' such as re-education of muscles. General medical and surgical, orthopaedic or neurological cases were those for whom occupational therapy was likely to be prescribed.

Another important text, one of a series on rehabilitation according to different specialties, *The Rehabilitation of the Injured: Occupational Therapy*, was published by John Colson for prescribing physicians or surgeons and for occupational therapists who would carry out the prescriptions. Colson worked at Pinderfields Emergency Hospital, the Accident Service at the Royal Sheffield Infirmary, and Berry Hill Hall. The latter was 'a fine old mansion' run by the Mutual Colliery Owners' Mutual Indemnity Co. Ltd where disabled miners were treated with exercises, games and handicraft.

He divided his chapters on occupations according to 'remedial use', 'craft technique', and 'constructional work'. The occupations were graded as 'light', 'intermediate' and 'heavy' and included vigorous pursuits such as gardening, scything and timber work, as well as the more common handcrafts.[172]

Colson discussed the aims of remedial occupational therapy as using occupations to effect the conservation of muscular or joint function, and strengthening weak muscles by localised or general movement using work that produces rhythmic contraction followed by relaxation, a full range of movement, and is progressive in strength and time. He also aimed occupational treatment at mobilising stiff joints, re-educating neuromuscular co-ordination, teaching normal function, and encouraging the patient. He saw the advantages of occupational therapy over other forms of remedial treatment as the variation possible, the creative interest, unconscious movement, the normal use of a part, and that it was of particular use for conditions of hand and fingers. He saw the purposes of diversional occupational therapy as preventing negative psychological effects and ensuring prescribed rest of specific body parts between periods of active therapy of others.

Both the Haworth and Macdonald and the Colson texts included sections on resettlement in industry, and advocated the grading of occupations, so emphasising the need for occupational therapists to be experts in activity analysis.

Colson's book, although acclaimed for being the first of its kind in the physical practice field, did not win universal applause. Seemingly, his biggest critic was Phyllis Lyttleton another dual-trained therapist, who at that time was in charge of the department at Pinderfields EMS Hospital. Extracts from her letter, published in the October 1944 Journal, read as follows:

> *Mr. Colson is to be congratulated on having published what should prove to be a most useful book to those interested in Occupational Therapy. To the students of the profession it will be a great boon to have the craft analysis and constructional work of so many crafts collected for them under one cover. The grading of the crafts under their various effects upon joints and nerves is also very valuable to the student as it will provide her with a safe basis upon which to build, though it should be pointed out that the list is by no means final, and there should be emphasis on certain crafts as being far superior to others for certain purposes.*

More critically, Lyttleton queried:

> *Why does he place woodwork separate from the other crafts because it requires tools? It is just another craft, and much damage may be done to the patient by its being looked*

upon by the authorities as a separate department from occupational therapy and not under the jurisdiction of the occupational therapist, which is the case in many Ministry of Pensions hospitals.

And:

> Occupational Therapy cannot be run in the same quiet and soothing atmosphere of a Physio-Therapy department, where the main topic of conversation is the patient's disability, though this latter is not the fault of the masseuse who usually tries hard to change the topic for her own sake as well as the patient's. Here lies my main quarrel with Mr. Colson. His theory regarding specific treatment is excellent but he has lost sight of the tremendous value a patient gains from joy and pride in construction, from variety of work, from pleasant atmosphere, from good companionship and friendly rivalry. None of these things are incompatible with the undoubted value of the points that Mr. Colson makes, but they are equally essential if the patient is to gain full value from the treatment and to the student these things may not be apparent after reading Mr. Colson's book. [173]

She went on to criticise some of the treatment he recommended for upper limb amputees, to which Colson responded in a return letter:

> I stated (a) that carpentry was of value in the treatment of these cases; and (b) that the aim of occupational re-education was to harden the stump and encourage the patient to use the injured arm as normally as possible. Miss Lyttleton, however, declares: (a) that carpentry is the least valuable craft in the early stages of rehabilitation of the amputee; (b) that efforts should be made to shrink the stump, and not to harden it; and (c) that all re-education is to re-educate the other (sound) arm.
>
> Miss Lyttleton's remarks are altogether too sweeping, for I have been informed by a distinguished medical authority on this subject that carpentry is the **most valuable craft** in the early stages of rehabilitation of the amputee, and that **the patient should be encouraged to use the stump, so as to prepare both the brain and the stump for the use of the artificial limb.** This is extremely important, for during the period that the patient is waiting for the artificial limb to be fitted, he tends to rely entirely on the remaining hand, which is detrimental to the subsequent use of the artificial limb. As for the word 'harden'—which I used in place of 'shrink'—perhaps it is open to misinterpretation, although the accepted definition is 'to make firm'.

The healthy debate continued with further correspondence. Lyttleton had some claim to expertise in the treatment of amputees, having 'had to deal with limbless cases in large numbers', her department having 'received every type of amputee, patients who had lost one arm, one leg, both hands, both legs, and all possible combinations of these disabilities.' Indeed, she published a small book *Occupational Therapy For The Limbless* to inform prescribing medical practitioners as well as occupational therapists.[174] The review of Lyttleton's book suggested it was of wider applicability that its title suggested. It put the case for occupational therapy with clarity and conviction, and was applicable to many types of ill or injured people other than the limbless.[175]

# The aftermath

At the end of the War the United Nations Organisation replaced the League of Nations, and in June 1946, at an International Health Conference held in New York, the World Health Organisation came into being.

In the spirit of international health and well-being which that organisation represents, health and welfare workers, including occupational therapists, responded to the apparent need of former foes:

> *Germany and the Germans have been struggling to exist under conditions which cannot be fully understood until seen...The whole country is as someone who has suffered a long and serious illness drained of initiative and power to help herself towards a healthy life.* [176]

Griselda Thornely explained how teams of welfare workers under the auspices of the British Red Cross had engaged in relief work since hostilities ceased. As part of that a small team started to use physiotherapy at Bad Pyrmont Hospital where 1500 wounded men were still receiving treatment.

In January 1947 Thornely was asked to establish an occupational therapy department as part of a new rehabilitation scheme. She was given three months' leave of absence from her hospital. When she arrived she found that the scope for occupational therapy in the whole hospital was enormous, but knowing her time was limited placed her priorities on getting together equipment, materials, and students who, with training, could carry on the programme. Five students were found. They received tuition each afternoon and treated patients in the mornings despite having few material resources. Thornely's place was taken by Miss Coast who carried forward the training.[177]

On the home front, in Scotland, the Astley Ainslie Institution Occupational Therapists' Club, which was established in 1944, was wound up. It had met the need for a professional society while the original Association was in abeyance, and had held three meetings each year. The Scottish Association was reconstituted in Edinburgh on 27 July 1946, being renamed the Scottish Association of 'Occupational Therapists' in preference to 'Occupational Therapy' which had formerly been the case. Margaret Fulton was elected Chairman, a position she held until 1949. Eight of the original members, under a special clause, became full members, of whom there were 30. Regular meetings were held in different parts of Scotland.

The first meeting of the Association after reconstitution was a luncheon at the North British Station Hotel on 10 May the following year, by which time there were 24 occupational therapy departments in Scotland. It was well attended by its Advisory Panel, which had been formed on the advice of Sir John Fraser, Principal of the Edinburgh University, and Cunningham from the Astley Ainslie. Those two became President and Vice President respectively. Following Fraser's untimely death, Sir David Henderson took over as President until 1951 when Professor Norman Dott assumed the Presidency.[178]

South of the border, a paper titled *The Future of Occupational Therapy* looked back at the almost unbelievable ten years since occupational therapists formed themselves into a corporate body in England:

> The training schools have been crowded, their students earmarked for in-patient hospitals long before the final examinations have taken place. In-experienced and young occupational therapists have had to start new departments with little direction from the over-burdened surgeons, and to cope with large numbers of patients, either singlehanded or with assistants even less trained and experienced than themselves.[179]

The rapid expansion of numbers of trained occupational therapists, in comparison with the few there had been before the war, and the establishment of places for them to work in a range of services, had precipitated the profession into adulthood almost too suddenly. It had little time to catch breath before the advent of social health care changed the environment and demands yet again. However, it was assisted by the equally rapid growth of 'rehabilitation', and the ongoing provision of services for people with disability, even though that was not as extensive as might have been hoped.

One of the downsides of the rapid development of services to meet the needs of war was the lack of time to begin basing what occupational therapy provided on a sound research footing. Instead it tended to develop a pragmatic common sense approach because its benefits appeared so obvious at the time. A few forward thinking members of the profession sought to flag the dangers of taking only that approach.

# Laying the foundations for research in the 1940s
## By Irene Ilott

The need for research was noted by Hombersley in 1944 who considered that the UK was 'a long way behind our American colleagues both in original research and publication of results' and that the Association could initiate 'a scheme of research.' Hombersley's letter suggested:

...What seems to be needed is a certain amount of work on something like the following lines:—

*(a) A group of patients receiving physical treatment together with strenuous*
*Occupational Therapy*
*(b) Control group receiving physical treatment but no Occupational Therapy.*
*(c) Group receiving Occupational Therapy but no physical treatment.*
*(d) Control group receiving no treatment of either kind.*
*The patients in each group should be as nearly approximated as possible and the results tabulated after a period of say six months or a year. Detailed records of work periods, occupation given, patients' reactions to various types of work, etc., would be essential and naturally very close co-operation from the Medical Officers in charge of the physical treatment would be necessary...*

> *What we need, I feel, is a more scientific and critical attitude towards our work if we are not to*
> *slip back twenty years and find ourselves damned once more with the 'Arty-Crafty" label.* [180]

Phyllis Lyttleton endorsed Hombersley's plea for some properly organised research, and well collated results in treatment for physical conditions. However she foresaw a two-fold difficulty:

> *Only in a large hospital with many specialised Units is there the best material for*
> *research, and in these hospitals the shortage of staff is the most acute. Also in these days*
> *of labour shortage, and urgent re-settlement while the going is good it seems wrong that*
> *any group of patients, and the number would need to be considerable, should be debarred*
> *from all the forms of treatment from which they are likely to benefit.* [181]

In 1946, a report of a Social Meeting contained the proposal made on behalf of Council by Mrs Glyn Owens, Miss MacCaul and Miss Tarrant to establish Industrial Research Fellowships. The aim was 'widening the horizon of occupational therapy' from crafts to industrial processes and heavy occupations. The report described how Mrs Mary S. Jones 'gave an account of the need for research into the possibilities of the use of industrial processes'. She reviewed the first ten years since Occupational Therapists formed themselves into a corporate body, using the metaphor of their position as 'an infant prodigy among the ancillary medical services'. She noted the 'urgent necessity for research into industrial processes "preventative rehabilitation" and the ability to restore the patient's confidence in his ability to return to full production in the competitive world.' She advised that 'industrial processes need careful observation and study with a view to their adaptation and adoption for remedial work.' This, one of the first references to research, also by implication refers to development in the statement about using the findings in remedial work. [182]

As a result, a total of £69 was raised in the social meeting for the Fellowship Fund. Council of the Association of Occupational Therapists formed a sub-committee to investigate this problem, which was chaired by Jones. The sub-committee recommended that two fellowships be given for six months to 'allow experienced Occupational Therapists to give their individual attention to the subject' and that the study include the problems in the treatment of patients with either physical disabilities or psychological disturbances. 'It is essential that research should be carried out from both angles, and close collaboration will be expected between the holders of the fellowships'. There was recognition of the short time scale 'for research of this sort to show results' but that 'if the research shows promise it is hoped that a successful appeal for funds may be made to outside bodies interested in Industrial Rehabilitation.' The time lag between research and its application was also acknowledged. 'The research will obviously take time, and even when it shows that certain industrial processes are both suitable for out-work in hospitals and have definite remedial value, there will be a further time lag to be spent training Occupational Therapists in their application.' All members of the Association were asked to help by fund raising and collecting information to assist the research, save time, and assist the spread over 'a wider field, yielding therefore better results.' [183]

In January 1947 it was reported that Priscilla Schwerdt had been awarded the Industrial Fellowship for Research in the Scope and Applications of Industrial work as part of the treatment by occupational therapists of patients with physical disabilities. [184]

For the next eighteen months, progress on this first Association-funded research was reported in Occupational Therapy, particularly the problems with funding. The editorial in July 1947 noted that the fund raising impetus 'seems to have died away.' Members were exhorted to support the fund in every possible way 'even if we, ourselves, are not going to work on these lines, it should be remembered that this is probably a major trend of the future.'[185] In October it was reported that there had been insufficient funding for the Industrial Fellowship Fund for 'psychological fields' and members were again urged to make possible 'the completion of a work which we are all agreed should be of great value to the profession.'[186] Finally, in July 1984 the report of the Annual General Meeting held on 13 March received a report of the Industrial Fellowship Sub-committee. This noted that Miss Schwerdt's report was being circulated amongst committee members and hoped to publish shortly, however it was 'a lengthy document, and in consequence it was taking a considerable time in circulation.'[187]

An extensive conference report entitled 'The Use of Clubs in Social Therapy' was published in the October 1947 issue of the Journal of Occupational Therapy. This was a report on ten years of therapeutic social club work at Runwell Hospital given to the *International Conference on Mental Hygiene*. A subheading 'suggested lines for research' contained points about better record keeping for follow-up studies to help answer questions such as, 'How can one judge when to discharge a member? What is the proportion of success, partial success and failure? How far is improvement in the club accompanied or followed by improvement outside? What types are most helped by social clubs and upon what types is effort wasted? Why did certain members cease to attend and what happened to them?' Such questions about the process and outcomes of interventions are still relevant.[188]

The second decade of the AOT's existence therefore set the foundation by placing research on the agenda of the Council. This was achieved by raising funds to establish a Fellowship to give a practitioner time to investigate a developing area of practice. Unfortunately, this seems to have been bedevilled by the common problem of funding. A second foundation, or emergent theme, was the focus upon outcomes; meaning that research could help answer clinically important questions about the effectiveness of treatments, such as social clubs for adolescents with mental health problems.

**In summary** the chapter told the story of how World War II escalated the growth of occupational therapy between 1939 and the advent of social health care in 1948. The challenges posed by wartime needs were met as they arose, and led to more than maintenance of procedures and standards. The value of the profession's contribution to the emerging model of rehabilitation was well recognised at government level, and acceptance was based on common sense as well as its apparent novelty appeal to the media. Increased opportunities for training arose and, although some were of a short-term nature lasting only for the duration of the war, resulted in long term benefits. Not only was there an increase in critical mass, but also the establishment of particular remedial approaches brought to the profession by those from other fields. Some tales of particular contributions have been told, along with parts of the contribution of Commonwealth members, or allies, who worked alongside British occupational therapists, in various parts of the world as part of the war effort. Many more remain in wait for future historians.

[1]Macdonald EM. The history of the Association of Occupational Therapists: Chapter 2, 1936–39. Occupational Therapy 1957; April: 14–16.

[2]Mayer SL. Introduction. In: Heiferman R. World War II. London: Octopus Books, 1973.

[3]Murrel KFH. Ergonomics: Man in His Working Environment. London: Chapman and Hall, 1965.

[4]Paterson CF. An historical perspective of work practice services. In Pratt J, Jacobs K, eds. Work Practices: International Perspectives. Oxford: Butterworth-Heinemann, 1997; 25–38.

[5]British Medical Association. Report of Committee on Fractures. 1935. Cited in: Wallace AB. The Rehabilitation of the Burned. Occupational Therapy 1955; (18) 1: 20–26.

[6]Balme H. Organisation of Occupational Therapy. In: Cope Z, ed. Surgery. London: HMSO, 1953; 730–31.

[7]Macdonald EM. The history of the Association of Occupational Therapists: Chapter 4 . Occupational Therapy 1957; June: 30–33.

[8]Cope Z. Organisation and work of plastics units. In: Cope Z, ed. Surgery. London: HMSO, 1953; 334 .

[9]Macdonald EM. World-Wide Conquests of Disabilities: The History, Development and Present Functions of the Remedial Services. London: Bailliere Tindall, 1981, p.142.

[10]Kersley GD, Glyn J. A Concise International History of Rheumatology and Rehabilitation. London: Royal Society of Medical Services, 1991; 45.

[11]Kersley & Glyn. A Concise International History of Rheumatology...; 47.

[12]Injured Led to Forget Disabilities: Occupational Therapy in the Army. Birmingham Post 1942; 21st July.

[13]Army Gives Lead: Therapy Makes Injured Soldiers Useful. Western Morning News 1942; 21st July.

[14] Marvels of Therapy in the Army. Western Mail Cardiff. 1942; 21st July.

[15]Darts, Table Tennis Help in Cure of Injured Soldiers. Scottish Daily Express 1942; 21st July.

[16]Kersley & Glyn. A Concise International History of Rheumatology...; 46.

[17]Notices. Medical Officer, August 10th, 1940. Reprinted in: Occupational Therapy 1940; Summer: 14.

[18]Macdonald. The history of A.O.T....; Chapter 2.

[19]A.O.T. Minutes of Council Meeting. Liverpool: September 30th, 1939.

[20] A.O.T. Annual Report. 1939-1940.

[21]Macdonald. The history of A.O.T....; Chapter 2.

[22]A.O.T. Annual Report. 1941–1942.

[23]Macdonald. The history of A.O.T....; Chapter 2.

[24]A.O.T. Annual Report. 1940–41: 2.

[25]A.O.T. Annual Report. 1938–39, 1939–40, 1940–41, 1941–42.

[26]A.O.T. Annual Report. 1942–43: 5.

[27]Macdonald. The history of A.O.T: Chapter 2 and Chapter 3. Occupational Therapy 1957; May: 15–17, and June: 30–33.

[28]Macdonald. The history of A.O.T....; Chapter 2 and Chapter 3.

[29]Macdonald. The history of A.O.T....; Chapter 3.

[30]Macdonald. The history of A.O.T....; Chapter 3.

[31]Broadcast Talk. Reported in: Occupational Therapy 1941: Winter: 16–21.

[32]War Emergency Fund. Occupational Therapy 1941: Spring: 6–7.

[33]Macdonald. The history of A.O.T....; Chapter 2 and Chapter 3.

[34]Macdonald. The history of A.O.T....; Chapter 2.

[35]Macdonald. The history of A.O.T....; Chapter 3.

[36]Ling was a Swedish medical gymnast whose story was told in Volume 1.

[37]Macdonald. The history of A.O.T....; Chapter 2.

[38]A.O.T. Annual Report. 1939–40, 1941–42.

[39]A.O.T. Annual Report. 1939–40: 4.

[40]A.O.T. Annual Report. 1940-41: 2.

[41]Ross N. Editorial. Occupational Therapy 1939; Winter: 5.

[42]Macdonald. The history of A.O.T....; Chapter 3.

[43]A.O.T. Annual Report. 1938–39.

[44]Board of Control. Memorandum on Occupation Therapy for Mental Patients. London: His Majesty's Stationery Office, 1933.

[45]Haworth NA, Macdonald EM. Theory of Occupational Therapy. London: Bailliere, Tindall & Cox, 1940, 1944; 135.

[46]Nursing Records. Retreat Archives. Borthwick Institute. York. 1945.

[47]Macdonald. The history of A.O.T....; Chapter 3.

[48]Cited in: O'Sullivan ENM. Textbook of Occupational therapy: With Chief Reference to Psychological Medicine. London: H.K. Lewis, 1955; 15.

[49]Balme H. Organisation of occupational therapy. In: Cope Z. ed. Surgery. London: HMSO, 1953: 731.

[50]Poole A. Annual Report of the Physician Superintendent. The Retreat, York, 1942; 8.

[51]A.O.T. Annual Report. 1944–45; 3.

[52]Casson E. Occupational Therapy in Great Britain. Journal of the American Medical Women's Association 1947; 2 (6): 303–305.

[53]Casson E. Occupational Therapy in Great Britain...

[54]Macdonald. The history of the A.O.T....; Chapter 2.

[55]A.O.T. Annual Report. 1940–41; 5.

[56]Masseuse in Occupational Therapy. Lancet 1941; 21st July.

[57]To Train Wounded. Yorkshire Post 1943; 8th July.

[58]A.O.T. Annual Report. 1944–45.

[59]Macdonald. The history of the A.O.T....; Chapter 3.

[60]Graeme Barber MSc BA(Hons) DipLib ALA Head of Academic Services, Catherine Mounter BEd(hons) DipCOT SROT Assistant Principal.

[61]Editorial. The Medical Press and Circular 1943; CCIX (11).

[62]English AM. Rehabilitation. Occupational Therapy 1941; Winter: 21–23.

[63]Stanton Woods Sir R. Rehabilitation in the EMS British Medical Journal 1942; 25th July: 4255–6.

[64]Stanton Woods. Rehabilitation in the EMS....

[65]This information was given in a Ministry of Health circular (No 2395) which was sent to local and hospital authorities.

[66]Stanton Woods Sir R. Activity in Rehabilitation. British Medical Journal 1942; 21st November: 610.

[67]Malkin SAS, Parker G. Rehabilitation in an EMS Orthopaedic Unit. British Medical Journal 1943; 13th March: 316.

[68]Watson-Jones R. Rehabilitation in the Royal Air Force. (An address to the Council for

the Development of Orthopaedics in Northern Ireland. Queens University, 1941) British Medical Journal 1942; 28th March; 4238.

[69]Rehabilitation in Civilian Hospitals: Survey by the Ministry of Health. British Medical Journal 1943; 10th April.

[70]Tomlinson G, Chairman. Report of the Inter-department Committee on the Rehabilitation and Resettlement of the Disabled. London: HMSO, 1942.

[71]Injured Workers Rehabilitated: Encouraging Results of Interim Scheme. Birmingham Post 1942; 23rd October.

[72]Industrial Injuries. The Times 1942; (date unknown) October.

[73]Emergency Hospital Scheme for Industrial Workers: Scope of New Services. The Machinery Market 1943; 8th January: 19.

[74]Specialist Treatment: Service extended to injured workers. Walsall Observer 1943; 29th January.

[75]Macdonald. World-Wide Conquests of Disabilities....

[76]Hilton I. An Open Letter to Members of the A.O.T. Occupational Therapy 1942; Spring: 3–4.

[77]Accident Hospital: Policy of Birmingham's New Centre: Refitting Workers for Industry. Birmingham Weekly Post 1941; 26th April; and Birmingham Mail 1941; 21st July.

[78]Gissane W. Rehabilitation. Occupational Therapy 1942; Spring: 9–12.

[79]Macdonald. The history of the A.O.T....; Chapter 2.

[80]Peto G. Dr Elizabeth Casson, OBE, MD, DPM. A tribute to her work. Occupational Therapy 1955; 3: 107–109.

[81]Macdonald. The history of the A.O.T.... Chapter 3.

[82]Macdonald. The history of the A.O.T....; Chapter 3.

[83]Bunyard J. The Correlation of the Massage Department with Occupational Therapy. Occupational Therapy 1940; Winter:10.

[84]Dudley Smith M. Occupational Therapy in a Spinal Injury Centre. Occupational Therapy 1945; Spring (22): 13–16.

[85]Portsmouth Evening News 1941; 21st April.

[86]'Work-Cure' for Invalids: Men from forces may go the Village Settlement. Evening Standard 1941; 22nd August.

[87]Rehabilitation of Ex-Service Men: Work as an Aid the Recovery. The Times 1943; 25th May.

[88]Richardson IE. Some Aspects of Occupational Therapy at Ham Green Sanatorium. Occupational Therapy 1940; Summer : 6.

[89]Notices. Occupational Therapy 1940? Details of date unknown.

[90]McDougall JB. War Time in a Santorium. Occupational Therapy 1942; Summer: 13–16.

[91]Paterson CF. Dorothy Bramwell. Scotsman 9th August 2000.

[92]Bramwell MDB. Occupational Therapy in M.E. Force, 1944. This account was submitted by Bramwell to the Public Record Office. It 'outlined the development of an occupational therapy service or organization in the Middle East Force in the early part of 1941. Miss Bramwell was employed as a civilian as she was in Alexandria staying with her uncle (Admiral Sir Andrew Wingham, the Naval C. in C., Mediterranean) at the time war was declared and she had a diploma in the subject.' Public Record Office WO 222/173.

[93]Bramwell MDB. Occupational Therapy in M.E. Force....

[94]The Work of Margaret Lewthwaite, MBE: In Egypt in World War II. London: Archives of the Imperial War Museum.

[95]Occupational Therapy in the Middle East 'For Idle Hands to Do'. Nursing Times 1942;

1st August: 502–503.

[96]Annual reports of the Astley Ainslie Hospital, 1933–1939.

[97]Dunn CL, ed. The Emergency Medical Services Vol. II. London: HMSO, 1953.

[98]Life memberships–Amy de Brisay. Canadian Journal of Occupational Therapy 1965; 32(4): 147–152. Videotaped interview of Mary Wilson in 1976 by Sharon Brintnell and Helen Madill, copy presented to CFP.

[99]Middleton Park Hospital was developed in one of Lord Jersey's country estates and provided an annex for the Head Injuries Unit of St Hugh's, Oxford. Interview with Mary Cunningham by CFP in Bristol, 9 April 1999. Howland G. Presidential address. Canadian Journal of Occupational Therapy1941; 9(1): 3–6.

[100]Miall AM. Healing from Handwork. Women's Magazine, July 1942. Country House Nursing. Vogue, July 1942.

[101]Dunlop WJ. News. Canadian Journal of Occupational Therapy 1941; 8(1): 23. The Canadian Association of Occupational Therapists had been pressing the Canadian Department of Defence for occupational therapists to staff Canadian Hospitals in the UK from 1940. Wilson transferred to the 13th Canadian General Hospital, where she remained until June 1946. Wilson returned to Canada, where she had a long and successful career, which was recognised by the Canadian Association of Occupational Therapists, when she was awarded Life Membership in June 1965. See: In honour of Miss Mary Wilson. Canadian Journal of Occupational Therapy 1965; 42(3).

[102]Irvine ME. Report on occupational therapy in the Royal Canadian Army Medical Corps hospitals overseas. Canadian Journal of Occupational Therapy 1945; 12(12): 35–40.

[103]Balme H. Organisation of occupational Therapy. In: Cope Z. ed. Surgery. London HNSO 1953: 731.

[104]Forbes J. Army Occupational Therapy Centre. Canadian Journal of Occupational Therapy 1942; 9(2): 54–57.

[105]Minutes of the House and Works Committee of the AAI. Lothian Health Board Archive (hereafter LHB) 35/1/6a, 14 March 1941.

[106]Annual report of the AAH. 1941.

[107]Women's War Work: Popular Toronto teacher goes to Scots hospital, Title and date of newspaper unknown. National Archives of Canada. MG 28 I495.

[108]Driver M. A philosophic view of the history of occupational therapy in Canada. Canadian Journal of Occupational Therapy 1968; 35(2): 53–60.

[109]Annual report of the AAH. 1941.

[110]Interview of Bunty Elliott (née Isabella Veitch) by CFP in Edinburgh, 6 April 1999.

[111]SAOT Register of Membership: 1946–1974. SAOT Box 72.

[112]Begg RE. Obituary: Miss Jean Hampson. Scottish Journal of Occupational Therapy 1969; 77: 48.

[113]Interview of Margaret Lewis (née Langley) by CFP in Toronto, 17 August 1996.

[114]de Brisay, Clark, and Ellis sailed with Josephine Forbes and Dorathy Grant. Dunlop WJ. News. CJOT 1941.

[115]Howland G. Presidential address. Canadian Journal of Occupational Therapy 1942; 9(1): 3–6. The Craig sisters were half-Scottish, and the girls spent part of their lives in Toronto with their Canadian mother and grandmother, who knew the de Brisays. Interview of Mary Cunningham by CFP in Bristol, on 8 April 1999. Amy de Brisay had encouraged the sisters to train as occupational therapists in Toronto. Interview of Miss de Brisay's niece, Mary Campbell, by CFP in Toronto, 17 August, 1996.

[116]McKechnie AA. Forward. In: Hendrie WF, Macleod DAD. The Bangour Story. Edinburgh: Mercat Press, 1991: vi.

[117]Dott was was born in Edinburgh and graduated from the University of Edinburgh MB ChB in 1919, awarded the Syme Fellowship in 1921, and obtained FRCS Ed in 1923. A Rockefeller surgical fellowship later that year led him to Boston, where he worked under Harvey Cushing, the celebrated pioneer of neurosurgery, an experience which shaped his future. Norman McOmish Dott, CBE, MD, FRCS Ed, FRCS Canada, FRSE. Obituary. British Medical Journal 1973; 2: 787.

[118]Dott N. Chairman's opening remarks. Scottish Journal of Occupational Therapy 1967; 69: 4–6.

[119]Dott N. Chairman's opening remarks....

[120]Hendrie & Macleod. The Bangour Story....

[121]Wallace graduated MB ChB in 1929 from the University of Edinburgh, gained his FRCS Ed in 1932 and MSc from McGill University in 1936. After studying in Canada, he became interested in the tissue culture of skin and before the war worked at the Strangeways Laboratory in Cambridge. A. B. Wallace, CBE, PhD MD FRCS Ed FDSRCS Ed FRSE, Obituary. British Medical Journal 1975; 1: 158.

[122]Wallace AB. The rehabilitation of the burned. Scottish Journal of Occupational Therapy 1955; 20: 19–21 (reprinted from Rehabilitation).

[123]Hendrie & Macleod. The Bangour Story...: 184-186.

[124]Both Dott and Wallace joined the Advisory Board of the Scottish Association of Occupational Therapists in 1946 and Professor Dott succeeded Sir David Henderson as President of the Scottish Association of Occupational Therapists in 1951, a position he held until 1972.

[125]Dunn. The Emergency Medical Services...: 25. Making miners fit. Scotsman 1943; 16 January.

[126]Scotland: Orthopaedic clinic for Lanarkshire. British Medical Journal 1935; 1: 1046. For a fuller account see: Miller A. Late rehabilitation of the injured. British Medical Journal 1942; 2: 209–211.

[127]Berry Hill Hall was the first residential rehabilitation centre for miners in the UK. It was set up on an experimental basis in 1939 with 15 beds within a convalescent hospital run by the Miners' Welfare Commission. Nicoll EA. Rehabilitation of the injured. British Medical Journal 1941; 1: 501–6.

[128]Dunn. The Emergency Medical Services....: 76.

[129]Fitness Centre for Miners, The Times 1943; 8th May.

[130]Craig D. Rehabilitation for Scottish miners at Gleneagles Industrial Fitness Centre, Canadian Journal of Occupational Therapy 1944; 11(1): 11–13.

[131]Howland G. Presidential Address. Canadian Journal of Occupational Therapy 1942; 9(1): 53–6.

[132]Craig DMHC. Dr P. J. Macleod, OBE MB ChB. Obituary. Scottish Journal of Occupational Therapy 1952; 9: 4.

[133]Craig D. Rehabilitation for Scottish miners.... The type of programme carried out at Gleneagles and later at Bridge of Earn Hospital was well described in Colson JHC. The Rehabilitation of the Injured. London: Cassell, 1944.

[134]The SS Georgic was a former luxury cruise liner, which had been fitted with armaments as defence from the frequent German attacks. The ship had 2,000 passengers including Australian and Canadian Airforce and was loaded with supplies—ambulances, planes and ammunition. The voyage took 12 days, rather than the normal six days, zigzagging across the Atlantic in fierce gales, avoiding U-boats, mines, and a German bomber. The SS Georgic became the first ship to cross the Atlantic safely unescorted. Unpublished account by Mary Ray (née Clark).

[135]The most serious air raids in Scotland were those on Clydeside during two nights in

March and two in May 1941. The raids were amongst the heaviest experienced in Great Britain. In Clydebank itself, with a war-time population of 55,000, no less than 53,000 were made homeless. Dunn. The Emergency Medical Services....: 112.

[136]In May 1943 in Glasgow, Mary Clark married Donald Ray, a Pilot-Officer of the Canadian Air Force. He became an instructor and was sent home to Canada in December 1944, and Mary followed him in a convoy. Interview of Donald Ray by CFP in Toronto, 16 August 1996.

[137]Little is known of Ellis, except that she graduated from the University of Toronto in 1930 and had been Director of the Occupational Therapy Department of the Children's Memorial Hospital, Montreal, before she volunteered to work in Scotland. Appointments. Canadian Journal of Occupational Therapy 1941; 8 (1): 23.

[138]Interview of Jean Blades (née Waterston) by CFP at Fala Village, 9 April 1996.

[139]Interview of Isobel Walker (née Johnstone) by CFP in Edinburgh, 26 September 1999. Johnstone worked at Stracathro until 1944, when she replaced Wilson at Middleton Park Hospital, where she worked until the hospital was closed at the end of the war.

[140]Forbes J. Army Occupational Therapy Centre....: 55.

[141]Bramwell DB. Occupational therapy in the Middle East, 1944. Public Record Office WO 222/173.

[142]Hume C., Pullen I. Rehabilitation in Psychiatry. An Introductory Handbook. Edinburgh: Churchill Livingstone, 1986.

[143]Palmer HA. Occupational Therapy in relation to the Military Hospital. Occupational Therapy 1941; Winter: 7–11

[144]Occupational Therapy in Mental Hospitals. Lancet 1941; 10th July.

[145]Macdonald. The history of the A.O.T....; Chapter 3.

[146]Macdonald. The history of the A.O.T....; Chapter 3.

[147]Macdonald. The history of the A.O.T....; Chapter 3.

[148]War Jobs Aid Recovery of Mental Cases. Sunday Express 1943; 16th May.

[149]Paul DL. Occupational Therapy Department. In: The One Hundreth and Twenty-Sixth Annual Report of the Glasgow Royal Asylum for the Year 1939. Glasgow, 1939; 24–25.

[150]Paul DL. Occupational Therapy Department. In: The One Hundreth and Twenty-Seventh Annual Report of the Glasgow Royal Asylum for the Year 1940. Glasgow, 1940; 28.

[151]Richmond E. Occupational Therapy and Poultry Keeping: A Topical Exercise for Mental Hospitals. Hospital and Nursing Home Management 1942; September: 6.

[152]Hombersley J. Correspondence. Occupational Therapy 1944-45; Winter (21): 9–10.

[153]Whitwell JR. Bibliotherapy. Occupational Therapy 1941; Spring: 13.

[154]Astley Cooper H. Some reflections on occupational therapy. Occupational Therapy 1941; Spring: 9–12.

[155]Darwin R. Some Aspects of Occupational Therapy in Psychological Work. Occupational Therapy 1945; Spring (22): 13–14.

[156]Darwin. Some Aspects of Occupational Therapy in Psychological Work....

[157]Darwin. Some Aspects of Occupational Therapy in Psychological Work....

[158]Wynne C. The North Wales Hospital, Denbigh, 1842–1955. Denbigh: Gee & Son, 1995; 27–28.

[159]Hume & Pullen. Rehabilitation in Psychiatry....

[160]Macdonald. The history of the A.O.T....; Chapter 2.

[161]A.O.T. Annual Report. 1941–42; 7.

[162]A.O.T. Annual Report. 1942–43; 5–6.

[163]Macdonald. The history of the A.O.T....; Chapter 2.

[164]English AM. Training War Prisoners. The Times 1943; August.

[165]A.O.T. Annual Report. 1942–43; 5–6.

[166]British War Museum. IWM MISC 159 Item 2453.

[167]British War Museum. IWM MISC 188 1tem 2824.

[168]British War Museum. IWM MISC 148 Item 2323.

[169]British War Museum. IWM Bull RR 88/59/1.

[170]Haworth & Macdonald. Theory of Occupational Therapy....

[171]Haworth & Macdonald. Theory of Occupational Therapy....; 10–11.

[172]Colson JHC. The Rehabilitation of the Injured : Occupational Therapy. London: Cassell; 1945.

[173]Lyttleton P. Correspondence. Occupational Therapy 1944 ; October (20):

[174]Lyttleton P. Occupational Therapy For The Limbless. London: H. K. Lewis; 1946.

[175]Book Review. Occupational Therapy 1946; no 24

[176]Thornely G. The Rehabilitation of German Wounded Ex-Servicemen. A British Red-Cross Scheme. Occupational Therapy 1948; July: 21–26.

[177]Thornely. The Rehabilitation of German Wounded Ex-Servicemen....

[178]The Scottish Association of Occupational Therapists. Scottish Journal of Occupational Therapy 1957; 30: 39–43.

[179]The Future of Occupational Therapy. Occupational Therapy 1946; Spring?: 10.

[180]Hombersley J. Correspondence. Occupational Therapy 1944–45; Winter (21): 9–11.

[181]Lyttleton P. Correspondence. Occupational Therapy 1945; Spring (22): 17

[182]Social meeting. Occupational Therapy 1946; 26: 9–11.

183Social meeting. Occupational Therapy 1946; 26: 9–11.

[184] Occupational Therapy 1947; 27: 4.

[185]Editorial. Occupational Therapy 1947; 29: 4–5.

[186]Occupational Therapy 1947; 30: 20.

[187]Report of the Annual General Meeting. Occupational Therapy 1984; 33: 9–10.

[188]The Use of Clubs in Social Therapy. Occupational Therapy 1947; 34: 11–23.

# Part 3

# Rehabilitation and Expansion into the Community

**Chapter 7**
**A National Health Service: Getting Back to Work**

**Chapter 8**
**Activities of Daily Living: Towards Independence**

**Chapter 9**
**New Look Social Services: Into the Community**

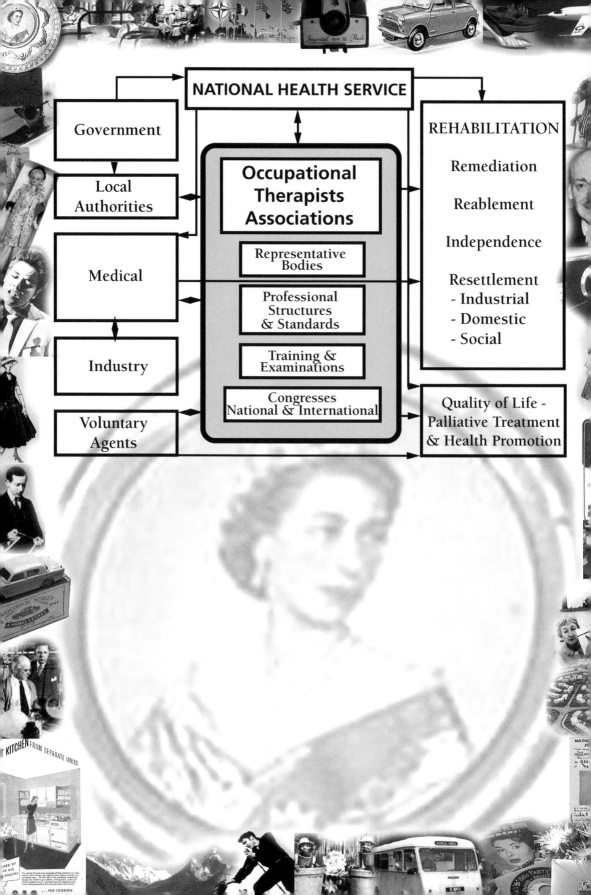

**NATIONAL HEALTH SERVICE**

Government

Local Authorities

Medical

Industry

Voluntary Agents

**Occupational Therapists Associations**

Representative Bodies

Professional Structures & Standards

Training & Examinations

Congresses National & International

**REHABILITATION**

Remediation

Reablement

Independence

Resettlement
- Industrial
- Domestic
- Social

Quality of Life - Palliative Treatment & Health Promotion

Chapter 7

# A National Health Service: Getting Back To Work

## Contents

In this chapter, the story of the emerging profession is picked up in 1948 and covers the post-war reconstructive period of the 1950s. In many ways, reconstruction shares similarities with rehabilitation and, unlike in the years following World War I, the government of the day attempted to maintain the progress made during the war in terms of programmes available for people after injury or with disability. The main thrust of these programmes was 'getting back to work.' In providing a picture of what happened during the late 1940s and 1950s, once again the work of the Associations is considered within the context of the times, before details of training and practice are discussed. It was also the period when the international professional camaraderie of the war years was cemented through the establishment of the World Federation of Occupational Therapists.

# Context of the times

In general, the pioneer period of the profession had come to an end. It was followed by ventures that explored uncharted directions to assist patients with a diversity of health problems. The establishment of a National Health Service (NHS) assisted the development of more extensive programmes within occupational therapy. The written material of the time suggests the beginnings of 'professionalism' along with acceptance of being part of the rehabilitation team, but tends to demonstrate less excitement and entrepreneurial activity, and less 'making do' to prove the value of the concept. Something of the kind must have appeared to be the case to Dorothy Bramwell who, in 1953, was moved to write:

> There is certainly something wrong when we become satisfied with things as they are and no longer strive for something new. Can any one of us be sure that this does not apply to her?
>
> It is not long since there was only a handful of occupational therapists in Great Britain, struggling to prove that they possessed something which was of value to the patient. Now the profession has been established and is fast spreading into new spheres— undreamed of until recently. In order to keep pace with new developments, the therapist must remain eager to learn. She is of no value to the medical profession if her ideas are not up to date or if she is not willing to learn.[1]

In similar vein there appears to have been less excitement about and involvement in occupational therapy by the medical profession, except for a committed few. O'Sullivan in *Textbook of Occupational Therapy* recognised that its universal adoption in the general hospitals had 'yet to await the conviction of the medical and other authorities. In the absence of a practical experience, there may be a tendency to regard it as a "hospital frill" and an unjustifiable expenditure.' O'Sullivan argued that it was not sufficient for psychiatrists, physicians or surgeons associated with occupational therapy to give only nominal supervision. 'The medical director must be conversant with the theory and, to some extent, the practice of the treatment.'[2] That appears to have been a lot to ask of another professional group, especially in a time of monumental change such as the postwar period when many were jockeying for position in the new National Health Service.

In setting the context for this period in the life of occupational therapy the establishment of the NHS is probably the most important issue to be discussed.

# The National Health Service

The NHS had taken some years to come to fruition. The work began during the war years with an investigation of hospitals by the Ministry of Health in 1941. In the following year the Beveridge Report[3] highlighted the need for child allowances, and social welfare and financial assistance for the unemployed, the sick and disabled. Some of Beveridge's proposals for health and hospital services were included in the draft of the National Health Service Bill. However, it was during the period 1945–1951 when Aneurin Bevan was the Minister of Health that major changes came about, as he was directly responsible for the nationalisation programmes being set up under the Labour Government. The programme included the National Health Service Act of 1946, and the National Health Act (Scotland) of 1947.

The Acts, and concomitant changes that ensued from the medical establishment as well as government initiatives, all had an impact on occupational therapy as on other health services. In fact, they supported and encouraged the growth and development of health professions such as occupational therapy, despite limited funds in post war Britain. Prior to the Acts many health and hospital services were provided by local authorities and voluntary organisations but, from July 1948, almost all voluntary and private hospitals were nationalised and re-organised, and new developments were put in place. Mental, general, and isolation hospitals within Regional Hospital Boards were each run by Hospital Management Committees, and Teaching Hospitals were supervised by Boards of Governors with direct links to the Ministry of Health. The health functions of Local Authorities became linked with the NHS.[4]

In terms of rehabilitation and resettlement of people with disability, the Disabled Persons Employment Acts of 1944 and 1958 provided for registers to be kept of employable disabled persons, the reservation of certain jobs for them, specification of a quota of disabled workers according to the number of employees, the provision of sheltered employment and, when necessary, rehabilitation and vocational training. As well, a Committee of Enquiry on the Rehabilitation of Disabled Persons was set up in 1953 by the Ministries of Labour and of Health and the Scottish Secretary of State, with Lord Piercy as chairman. The Piercy Report, published in November 1956, suggested the services which the Welfare State might provide for people with disability, such as rehabilitation centres, hostels, and sheltered work, along with proposals to set up industrial treatment centres which embraced medical care. Interest in the subject was demonstrated by the representative gathering of political, industrial, medical and ancillary professionals at a three-day course held in Newcastle on the rehabilitation of the disabled worker in heavy industry in 1953.[5] The Sheffield Regional Hospital Board set up an ad hoc committee to consider the Piercy Report which visited European and British rehabilitation centres as part of their deliberations. However, it was not until 1962 that they advised on the setting up of comprehensive medical and industrial centres, with hostel accommodation, and paramedical services.

A 1946 Report of the Standing Committee on Disabled Persons issued by the Ministry of Labour had stated that there were occupational therapy departments in 204 out of the

520 General and Special Hospitals in England and Wales selected by the Ministry for rehabilitation, as well as in many other hospitals. The reablement of psychiatric as well as physical cases was authorised, but mental hospitals were still experiencing a shortage of occupational therapists as a result of war priorities. There were a considerable number of schemes for vocational training of disabled people but the Report emphasised that it was impossible to draw a demarcation line between medical and industrial rehabilitation. In the process of enabling a hospital patient to become an active worker mainly recuperative medical treatment coupled with occupational therapy was needed, and that was considered a vital part of the comprehensive Health Service being developed. Occupational therapists were also required to work in permanent sheltered workshops for those whose disability left them unable to work in open employment, or with the home bound. The British Red Cross Society was active in a voluntary capacity with the home bound, under the direction of Doctor Harold Balme. His booklet Making the Unfit Fit described the official organization of the Ministry of Health's rehabilitation schemes and was appreciative of the benefits of employing occupational therapists to develop services.[6,7] Despite the recuperative, medical treatment focus of the 1946 Disabled Persons Report, occupational therapy was not a feature in 'Industrial Rehabilitation Units' (IRUs). A rehabilitation officer was in charge and other staff usually included a doctor, an occupational psychologist, a social worker, a disablement resettlement officer, a technical adviser, and expert craftsmen who ran the workshops and offices. In some there were nurses and remedial gymnasts. In IRUs workers learned to use appropriate tools and machines, and could proceed to Government Training Centres for vocational training. A non profit-making company, Remploy Ltd, was established for those needing sheltered employment.

In 1947 the Minister of Health had required assurance of adequate standards of professionals employed in the NHS. The Chairman of the Medical Auxiliary Board, surgeon, Mr Zachary Cope, with Dr G. A. Clark from the Ministry of Health, and Mr A. B. Taylor from the Department of Health for Scotland, was asked to conduct eight committees, one for each of the professions of: Almoner, Chiropodist, Dietitian, Medical Laboratory Technician, Occupational Therapist, Physiotherapist together with Remedial Gymnast, Radiographer, and Speech Therapist. The committees' terms of reference were to consider and make recommendations about the supply and demand of training and qualifications of those professions. Members from each organisation were invited to attend by the Minister of Health, and the Secretary of State for Scotland, who later presented the Reports of the Committees on Medical Auxiliaries (the Cope Report) to Parliament in April 1951.[8] A further Working Party, with combined professional representatives, was set up in 1953, which led to the 'Professions Supplementary to Medicine Act', which was passed in 1960.[9]

In the late 1940s the government set up the Whitley Council of Health Service Employers and Employees to deal with conditions of service such as hours, work standards, and remuneration. The Council accepted representatives from the Ministry of Health, the Welsh Board of Health, the Scottish Health Office, Regional Hospital Boards, Hospital Management Committees, and Local Authorities. Occupational therapy was one of the remedial professions represented on the Whitley Professional and Technical Council 'A'. Both the AOT and SAOT appointed representatives to the Whitley Council to negotiate national awards and conditions. [10]

The establishment of the NHS divided the country into Regions. As a result of this the structure of the AOT changed and Regional Groups were established with constitutional approval by Council. This later lead to Regional as well as Nationally elected Council members.

# The Associations

T he two British Associations maintained close contact. For example, during July–September 1951, representatives of the Scottish Association attended various meetings in London to discuss both the implications of the Cope Report, and issues of reciprocity.[11] Then there was need to establish a Joint Council because, under the Constitution and standing orders of the World Federation of Occupational Therapists (WFOT) in 1952, each member had to be a country with ambassadorial status. As the two British Associations of Occupational Therapists were already established, the Joint Council was set up to meet the WFOT requirement. It was a supranational body composed of the Chairmen and three other members from each Association. That formal merging forged closer links between the two Associations and, in time, the Joint Council took a leading role on issues like negotiations for State Registration, the preparation of a code of ethics,[12] and the Department of Health regulations for qualifications of medical auxiliaries. [13]

## National and International Conferences and Congresses

Both Associations established impressive programmes of educational events. The Scottish Association's first Congress was put on as early as 1949. In August of 1951 it held a two-day summer school at which the practical sessions and range of papers was extensive. Those by doctors, for example, included information about architecture of the foot, the physiology of muscle, behaviour problems in children, while occupational therapists described their work with tubercular patients, with borstal detainees, and with children suffering from chorea. In 1953, Doris Sym proposed that during the winter months there should be a series of lectures in various parts of the country, followed by discussion and information exchange at postgraduate standard. The lectures were given by medical experts, the first was on *Arthrodesis and Arthroplasty in Disease and Injury of the Joints* , the second on Geriatrics, and a third and final offering was on *The Historical Development of Modern Psychiatric Practice*. With such activities, the secretarial work increased steadily and the need for an official office became paramount. In 1953, they were granted a room in the BMA buildings in Drumsheugh Gardens to which all letters could be sent, and in 1954 office accommodation was rented at 77 George Street, Edinburgh, and a part time Secretary employed.

In England, the Association's first conference was held in London, 15–16 June 1951, with the Minister of Health providing the opening address. The format for the first afternoon of papers typified the period and the relationship between occupational therapy and medicine. First there was a presentation given by a medical man followed by another given about the same subject by an occupational therapist. Lord Amulree, Dr Bach, Dr Guttman, Professor Heaf, Dr Parsons, and Dr Rees Thomas, respectively, discussed geriatric care, rheumatism, paraplegia, tuberculosis, the needs of hospitalised children and, lastly, mentally defective children. Their occupational therapist counterparts, Cynthia Miles, Elizabeth Bright, Daphne Lidiard, Jean Fletcher, Miss Dallas, and Miss Knox, provided an insight into methods of occupational therapy treatment, independence skills, difficulties patients experienced at home, balanced plans to increase confidence in the resumption of normal life and work habits, and productive and creative planning for enforced leisure hours. The next day a range of papers followed much the same format, with topics covering occupational therapy in a general hospital, in child guidance, in orthopaedics, with 'neurotic patients', and as a pre-vocational guide to the physically and mentally handicapped. Visits were made to Belmont Hospital in Sutton, the Cerebral Palsy Unit at Queen Mary's Hospital for Children, and Farnham Park, the rehabilitation service of the Slough Industrial Health Service.

At the conference Miss Fynes-Clinton, from Northern Ireland, reported that whilst hospital authorities were sympathetic to occupational therapy, at that time there were only five occupational therapists working in two hospitals in Belfast. Fynes-Clinton explained that there were diversional services carried out by Red Cross workers, and post-tuberculosis patients could undergo a short training in handicrafts, presumably, to work within sanatoriums or village settlements. There was likelihood, she felt, that occupational therapy would expand, and doctors often asked whether, if they advertised for them, trained people would work there.

Jean Waterston attended from Scotland, and gave a brief overview of recent developments north of the border, like the introduction, by prison officers, of occupational therapy for physically and mentally handicapped boys in a borstal. On a different tack, Waterston offered a cautionary comment worthy of noting. She said of occupational therapy, generally:

> Organization and supplies were being stereotyped, and it was only by each individual member of the profession realizing the great need for her enthusiasm and human understanding that progress and research would not be stifled. [14]

In 1951, a number of senior occupational therapists attended a conference of the International Society for the Welfare of Cripples in Sweden. Alicia Mendez tells how the group 'decided that the increasing growth and strength of the profession warranted and indeed made imperative the establishment of an international body.' The following year, a meeting was held in Liverpool with representatives from Canada, Denmark, South Africa, the United Kingdom and the United States of America, with letters of support received from Australia, New Zealand, India, and Israel.[15] The World Federation of Occupational Therapists was constituted, and Peg Fulton was elected as the first president, with Constance Owens as the first secretary.

The First International Congress, which launched the Federation, was held in Edinburgh, 16–21 August 1954, at the start of the Edinburgh International Festival. The venue was the beautiful George Heriot's School, which was fitting as the School was originally founded as a hospital in 1623 by James VI's jeweller, Heriot, who 'desired to benefit the handicapped and moreover, to do so by means of education with a vocational bias.'[16] A formal government reception was held in Edinburgh Castle.

**Figure 2.7.1: WFOT Council in Edinburgh 1954**

Over 400 delegates from 21 countries attended the Congress. Whilst most were female occupational therapists there were, at least, a few male occupational therapists from Britain and America, some of whom had military titles. Additionally there were representatives of medical and educational interests from 11 countries other than those of the founding members. Of them, eight were later to become either associate or full members of the Federation. Fulton, as President, welcomed the delegates and spoke about some of the problems facing the profession, such as a shortage of occupational therapists, training schools, educational standards, and government and medical support. Despite the latter shortage, it was Professor Norman Dott and five other eminent doctors who chaired the major sessions and gave most of the papers. The themes reflected the major areas of occupational therapy of the period: cerebral palsy, poliomyelitis, psychiatry, rehabilitation and resettlement, and tuberculosis.[17] As the theme titles suggest, the proceedings were medically oriented, with only six occupational therapists giving papers, the others being delivered by 16 physicians, psychiatrists and surgeons.[18]

Early in the chapter a comment was made about the few medical personnel who remained committed exponents of occupational therapy throughout their careers. One of those was Professor Dott, Chairman of the first WFOT Congress, who believed it to be his responsibility that patients should be properly rehabilitated as part of medicine. As a member of the Scottish Association's Advisory Panel, President, and Chairman of the Board of Studies, he was instrumental in making the Congress a resounding success. In his Valedictory Address, he closed the Congress by saying:

*What a magnificent future lies before you. You have unlimited scope for the development of your techniques…What opportunities are yours for adding to the sum of medical knowledge, whereby the patients of the future will be better understood and better treated, for occupational therapy is a potent tool of research as well as an immediate benefit to the sufferer and his circle and community.*[19]

Fittingly, he was the first Advisory Fellow appointed by the World Federation of Occupational Therapists.

At that time engaging medical personnel in the giving of learned papers was one ploy to maintain their interest in the profession. Another was having papers about occupational therapy published in medical journals. Although the concept was no longer novel, occupational therapy was more successful then in that regard, than at present.[20] The nature of the information contained in one paper in a 1951 Lancet suggests that it was an official attempt by the Association to advertise its services, to inform the medical profession as well as to attract prospective students. That makes it a useful document to look at how the official body viewed the profession during the decade. Occupational therapy, the paper proclaimed:

*…is primarily a psychological treatment, whether it is practised upon physical or psychiatric cases, its therapeutic value essentially depends upon the transference of the patient's focus of attention from a subjective to an objective centre. In all cases the patient's interest must be diverted from preoccupation with his disability and inadequacy to purposeful activity and achievement.* [21]

A 'big issue', which still has the capacity to concern or anger occupational therapists, appears to have been critical at that time. It had been addressed as an issue a few years earlier, when it was decided that prescriptions aimed at diverting patients from psychological disturbance should be described as 'general' rather than 'diversional'. In the *Lancet* paper it was pointed out that the growing tendency to distinguish between 'diversional therapy' intended to raise morale and relieve boredom and 'occupational therapy' as treatment directed to a more specific purpose, was 'largely due to a misunderstanding of the fundamental basis of all Occupational Therapy.' It was explained:

*…In all treatment, success will be limited unless body and mind are regarded as an organic whole. An individual can be studied properly only in relation to his environment, and it therefore follows that the economic pressure of security or insecurity has a strong influence on the recovery of the patient.*

*If these principles are borne in mind, Occupational Therapy can contribute greatly to the rehabilitation of all types of patients and the success of this, as of that of any treatment, can only be measured in terms of benefit to the individual. Even when the patient has been brought to the convalescent stage he will need to be encouraged in some activity which will lead more directly to his re-installment in his everyday work.* [22]

The paper went on to describe very briefly the history of the profession, the Association, how, where and in what subjects occupational therapists were trained. It explained that the emergency qualifications established during the war had been discontinued but that those holding them could advance towards the full Diploma. Meanwhile, as well as regularly trained occupational therapists, those with emergency qualifications had recommended salary scales. For holders of the 1943 Certificate it was £330 per annum rising to £350, and for holders of the Auxiliary Certificate it was £270 rising to £290.

## The Journals

*Occupational Therapy*, published by the AOT, continued as a quarterly journal. Connie Henson took over as editor from Nancy Ross in 1949, remaining in that honorary position until July 1952. Between 1950 and 1974 the *Scottish Journal of Occupational Therapy (SJOT)* was published, also as a quarterly. It replaced a Newsletter of articles which, for three years before the publication of the Journal, had been edited by Zara Groundes-Peace, duplicated and sent to members four times a year.[23] Groundes-Peace was, appropriately, appointed the first editor of SJOT.

The contents of several issues of the journals *Occupational Therapy* and SJOT during the 1950s provide a snapshot of the issues addressed at that time. Cerebral palsy was becoming of interest in practice with three articles addressing the topic, including two from the Bobaths.[24,25,26] The Bobaths' physiotherapy approach to problems of motor control through reflex inhibition was to become dominant in the treatment of both children and adults with neurological deficits for decades. Additionally, there was a review of the book *Cerebral Palsy in Childhood*,[27] which was one of two publications on the topic acquired for the AOT Library in 1961. Other publications reviewed in May and June 1958, or acquired later for the library, covered schizophrenia, hand surgery, how to live with disabilities, overcoming arthritis, and the human setting of medicine.

Other new or possible directions in practice were addressed in a report of refresher courses at the Medical Rehabilitation Centre, Camden Road, and the Marlborough Day Hospital, which will be revisited later in the chapter, and in Henderson's *Reflections on Criminal Conduct and its Treatment.* [28] Mental health initiatives reported included 'beauty culture',[29] and the purpose and methods of teaching psychology to students.[30] New initiatives in occupational therapy were also the topic of Dr G. M. Carstairs' address to the Ordinary General Meeting of the Association in May 1958.[31] He looked back over the history of occupation for health as a lead into the present in which he supported the concept of therapeutic communities. His paper, too, will be revisited later, in the section addressing rehabilitation in mental health, but here a brief note is included of one of his very interesting observations. He wrote about the need for meaning in order for occupation to be therapeutic:

> One of the most vigorous supporters for occupational work is Dr Pickford up in Yorkshire, but he has said some rather rude things about occupational therapy. For example: 'A patient can deteriorate just as fast sitting making a rug day in day out, as he can sitting unemployed in a ward.' The important factor is that he has ceased to have any interest in the task. The task has no meaning for him, and Dr Pickford believes that it should have meaning and has nothing against the patient making a rug. [32]

Apart from individual papers, reports of Association, Council and educational meetings were a strong feature of the Journals, along with descriptive pieces about personal experiences.

Advertisements in the Associations' Journals reviewed reveal that a fundamental interest in craft was either still apparent, or seen to be so in the minds of suppliers.[33] Apart from those for insurance, uniforms, stationery, and the SAOT Coffee Club, all the advertisements were from suppliers of materials and equipment for pottery, needlework, cane, stools, peg frames, rug making, lampshades, wool, weaving, artists supplies and, one in the SJOT, for sports and games equipment. In other issues, an advert appeared for a Hand Wire Brush Twisting Machine specially designed for remedial work in occupational therapy. (This was originally designed by Mary S. Jones and is discussed further, later in the Chapter.[34])

In one of the 1958 journals, it was reported that the Minister for Health, Mr Walker-Smith, was questioned about the number of occupational therapists employed in hospitals and other parts of the NHS, the number of unfilled vacancies, and what was being done about any shortfall. Walker-Smith told the House (of Parliament) that the equivalent of 1453 occupational therapists were employed in hospital service in England and Wales by December 1956. Figures were not available for the numbers employed by Local Health Authorities, or for those of unfilled vacancies. No mention was made of how any shortfall was being addressed.[35]

On that matter, in another journal Dr Harris, Consultant in Physical Medicine at the Devonshire Royal Hospital, Buxton, and the Royal Infirmary, Manchester, proposed that rather than there being an actual shortage of occupational therapists, they were wrongly distributed. Most occupational therapy at that time, he said, was for in-patients, with only one-twentieth of the eight million treatments given in 1952, being for out-patients.[36] Some two-thirds of occupational therapists worked in mental hospitals, and of the very few in physical rehabilitation most were concentrated on London. As the major part of rehabilitation work was to be found in out-patient services, occupational therapists were not taking a full part in it and departments must be re-organised. He wisely advised, though, that leadership in occupational therapy must come from people working in the field.[37]

The AOT recognised that the supply of trained workers was still below demand in mental hospitals, clinics, rehabilitation centres, and hospitals for treating disorders such as nervous diseases, tuberculosis, arthritis, fractures and paralyses, and moreover, that within the new Health Scheme further opportunities would arise.[38] That factor meant that issues of training remained of paramount importance.

# Training

The AOT had, from the start, taken a keen interest in education, and in 1948 Council inaugurated a Teachers' Diploma following the recommendation of the Education Sub-Committee. It was a two year in-service course, and required that those working in the physical field had to tutor in anatomy, and those in the psychiatric field in psychology. Their tutoring was assessed. They were also required to submit, for examination, a 6,000 word thesis or dissertation on a topic of their choice. Following assessment by an internal and external examiner, their performance was rated. Those who completed the Diploma were able to call themselves a Teaching Member of the Association of Occupational Therapists (TMAOT):

*Provision has been made for the admission without examination, for those with experience on training school staffs who fulfill certain requirements. Admission in this way is available until July 1950, after which the Teacher's Diploma will be gained by examination only. Fourteen members of the Association have been awarded the Diploma.*[39]
Only those holding a Diploma were eligible for the post of Principal of a training school.

The 1949 Annual report noted that two 'further schools were approved and welcomed at Botleys Park Hospital, Chertsey, Surrey and at Derby, the latter being the first NHS School, was run under the auspices of the Sheffield Regional Hospital Board.[40] The Liverpool School had already opened its doors due to the efforts of Constance Owens, and the School at the Retreat was closed during this decade. Their stories are found in Appendix A. Apart from those approved Schools, during the 1950s, candidates were also admitted to the examinations as external students, provided their application to sit as such was approved by a Selection Board appointed by the Council. In those cases there was a minimum of one month's probation, which had to be spent with a supervising Member of the Association.[41] From the earliest days students could be either awarded a diploma to practice in the psychological or physical field, or both. When the dual qualification was introduced, those with a single one could update following both study and extra clinical practice.

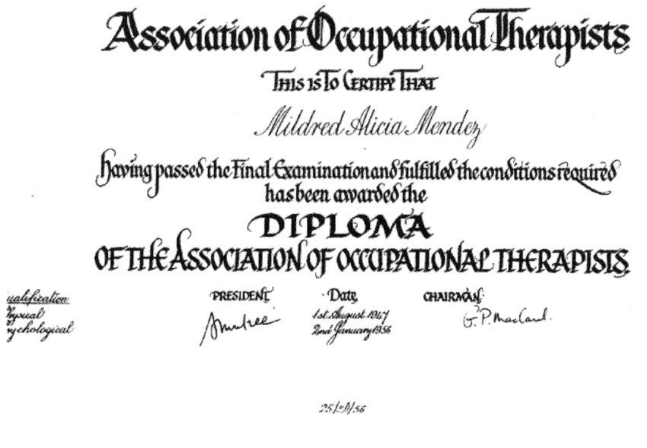

**Figure 2.7.2:** **Single Qualification Diplomas**
*(Courtesy of Alicia Mendez)*

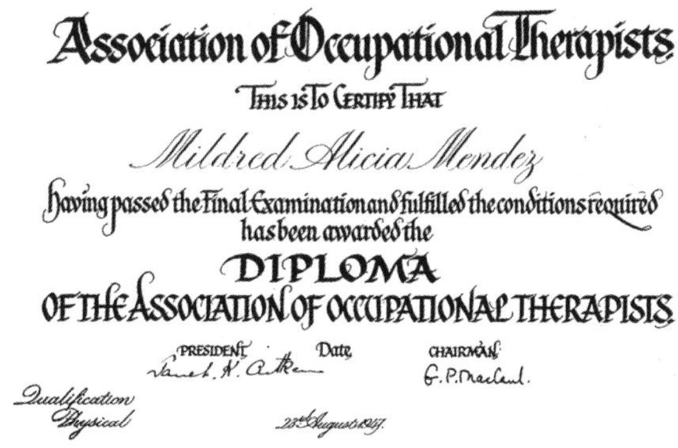

## The Syllabus

In order to appreciate why and how occupational therapists chose to concentrate on the issues and services that they provided after the war, it is important to look not simply at the places where their professional training took place, but also at what they learned and were assessed upon. Although some changes did occur, there was remarkable consistency in the requirements for many years until major changes took place in the 1980s. This was because the syllabus and regulations for the Diploma were set by the Association rather than by individual education institutions. The content descriptions provided below are taken from an undated but pre-1974 official publication. It provides a fairly accurate idea of how AOT training looked for several decades, give or take minor changes in requirements according to altered views as time went on of education or practice.

The three-year course of study was divided into four sections all of which had to be passed at predetermined intervals. As well, students had to reach a satisfactory standard in hospital placements with people experiencing mental or physical disorders. Placements had to cover 1440 hours, in situations where treatment of abnormality or adaptation to disability was the aim. The Diploma of the Association was awarded to candidates who successfully completed papers on Anatomy and Physiology, Psychology of Personality and Human Relations, Psychiatry, and General Medicine and Surgery including Orthopaedics. Apart from those foundation subjects, students had to also meet the practical examination requirements described as Occupations and Techniques, and formal examinations on the theory and practice of occupational therapy applied to Mental and Nervous Illness, Physical Disabilities, Industrial and Social Resettlement, and Administration of an Occupational Therapy Department. Viva Voce examination was a feature of the first two of those.[42]

Concessions in training were granted to those holding special qualifications such as physiotherapists, psychiatric social workers, state registered general, orthopaedic, and mental nurses, and physical education specialists. Exemptions were also available to people holding recognised qualifications in Drama, Physical Recreation, Dancing, Music, Engineering, Toolmaking, Carpentry, Domestic Science, Horticulture, Art and Craft.[43]

The syllabus was centred on the current knowledge of the body and mind in normal health. The structure and functions of the body were addressed with emphasis on the skeletal, muscular, nervous, circulatory, and respiratory systems, detailed systemic and regional anatomy and physiology, the physiology of exercise, and functioning of the body under different conditions.[44] The psychology of personality and human relations was addressed through the study of growth and development, maturity and decline, theories of behaviour and human motivation, learning and teaching, the individual and the group, informal assessment of personality and mental measurement, and social and therapeutic relationships.[45]

The second section of the syllabus addressed the current understanding of deviations from health by disease, deficiency and trauma. In 'Psychiatry' students learned about abnormal psychology, the causes and symptoms of mental illness and mental deficiencies, principles of mental hygiene, the laws protecting mental patients, and current theories and practices. In 'General medicine, surgery, and orthopaedics' students learned about the cardiovascular, respiratory, digestive, urogenital, nervous and locomotor systems, and blood and metabolic disorders. The syllabus aimed to give students an understanding of disease and reactions of the body to adverse factors, disturbance to function, signs and symptoms of disordered physiology, and the principles and application of modern methods of diagnosis and treatment.[46]

The study of 'Occupations and Techniques' which made up the third section of the syllabus was not confined to handicrafts, but covered a range of work, recreation or therapeutic activities, such as: Dance, Drama, Music, Gardening, Housecraft, Languages, Book-keeping, Shorthand, Typewriting, Footwear for Disabilities, Self Aids, and Splint-making. Students were expected to have 'knowledge of treatment value, application and teaching method…combined with a skill in technique.' They had to analyse them with particular reference to:
- disabilities involving loss of limb, poor sight and working positions
- the psychological and physical effects
- patterns of movement, good posture, and environmental factors
- social and recreational possibilities
- the establishment of patients in a job, the home, or with some interest
- intellectual and cultural needs
- study and training courses for the disabled.

The fourth section was of an integrative nature, combining and applying theoretical knowledge with the occupations and techniques learned, as well as subjects concerning social and industrial resettlement and administration of occupational therapy departments.[47]

As a result of their studies students were expected to adopt some general principles, which probably related to a largely unspoken philosophy of the profession. The principles referred to the scope of occupational therapy as a prophylactic measure, and as a means of restoring general health and function, assessment for work, and helping the permanently disabled become independent in activities of daily living (ADL) and adjust socially to their disabilities.

# Rehabilitation

In 1958 the World Health Organisation explained that 'medical rehabilitation has the fundamental objective not only of restoring the disabled person to his previous condition, but also of developing to a maximum extent his physical and mental function.'[48] In Britain, Dr James Sommerville, a medical rehabilitation authority, described it as 'the process whereby a man is made mentally, physically, socially, vocationally and economically equivalent to what he was before he became sick or injured.'[49]

The Standing Committee on the Rehabilitation and Resettlement of Disabled Persons described how the two world wars had given impetus to the establishment of rehabilitation services to meet the needs of people in peacetime. Generally, its purpose as part of medical care in Britain had been to assist people after accident, illness, or disability to resume, as far as possible, a normal lifestyle in regard to physical, mental, social, vocational or economic factors. It was also used to enable their independent resettlement in the community including the supply of necessary aids or appliances. In particular, because the value of paid employment for health as well as for economic purposes was recognised, rehabilitation programmes were aimed at people returning to former work, or preparing them for a different job according to their capacities.[50] Because of that, two aspects of rehabilitation were emphasised, namely medical or industrial, and the twin phrase of rehabilitation and resettlement was adopted. In the late 1940s and 1950s occupational therapists were mainly employed in medical rehabilitation services and not in industrial rehabilitation settings, as shown in Figure 2.7.3.

**Figure 2.7.3:    From Disability to Employment: The avenues of progress from disability to resettlement in suitable employment[51]**

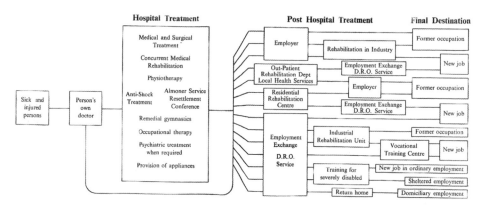

In *Rehabilitation After Illness And Accident* Dr C. J. S. O'Malley argued that separating rehabilitation into medical and industrial divisions was unrealistic. He supported the Piercy Report recommendation of the setting up of an experimental comprehensive centre that combined medical and industrial disciplines. He felt so strongly on that point that he stated:

> The problem of the rehabilitation, resettlement and retraining of the disabled has not yet been solved. It is one of the major problems of social medicine, in fact it is the therapeutic side of preventive medicine. Prevention having failed, society is faced with the problem of seeing that the patient lives to the maximum, not the minimum of his capabilities...[52]

Doris Sym explained that, even with many options, or perhaps because of them, there were gaps, the responsibility for rehabilitation and resettlement being shared by the Ministry of Health, Ministry of Labour, Local Authorities and independent bodies. This had the disadvantage of there being no uniform plan throughout the country. Independent or government sponsored schemes abounded, designed to suit the particular needs of the areas they served. They included:

1. *Physical Medicine Departments working within the acute hospital.*
2. *Convalescent Hospitals, accepting bed, ambulant, and out-patients.*
3. *Medical Rehabilitation Centres, which take ambulant, and out-patients, or only out-patients.*
4. *Medical Rehabilitation Units, designed for a particular type of patient, such as those in operation for the armed services, and for specialised industry.*
5. *Industrial Rehabilitation Units, run by the Ministry of Labour to condition men and women for employment.*
6. *Training Schemes…set up by independent bodies as well as by the Government.*
7. *Sheltered Workshops for men and women too disabled to compete in the open market.*
8. *Social Rehabilitation Centres…beginning to appear in the big cities to cater for the very severely disabled.*
9. *Domiciliary Schemes undertaking treatment for the home-bound in the English Counties.*[53]

Despite such comment, the concept and practice of rehabilitation continued to advance during the 1950s, being available to patients with either physical or psychiatric problems.[54] In the field of mental health, the introduction of the NHS in which medical officers were employed in salaried positions had allowed psychiatry to become established in ways that had been previously impossible. Rehabilitation services that narrowed the gap between mental hospital and community were started. These included hostels, domiciliary visits, outpatient facilities, and day hospitals. In 1951 the second day hospital in Britain was opened in Bristol, heralding the shape of services to come. By twenty or so years later there were 12,600 day-patients throughout Britain. The changing attitude led to the Mental Health Acts of 1959 in England and Wales, and in the following year in Scotland, which introduced two new principles. The first of those decreed that, as far as possible, the provision of treatment should parallel that of physical illness and, the second, that it be available in the community rather than in hospital, with patients being treated, whenever possible, as voluntary. Such changes were probably instrumental in the decreasing population in mental hospitals after a peak in 1954, even before the widespread use of the newer drugs. The decade, though, was also significant because of the introduction of the tranquillisers, Reserpine and Largactil, and later Librium and the tricyclic antidepressants that assisted the change to a rehabilitative rather than a palliative approach.[55]

The newness and importance of the rehabilitation concept was apparent in the frequency of educational visits arranged to centres as part of occupational therapy meetings. For example, at the second meeting of the Welsh Regional Group in 1951, members went on a visit to the Ministry of Labour Rehabilitation Centre in Cardiff, where 'cases' were 'being prepared for re-employment, and where each step in the rehabilitation process was carefully explained to them.'[56] In 1954, the Scottish Journal reported a lecture about medical rehabilitation given by Dr Sommerville to members. His views add some useful points to the discussion. For example he put it into perspective in terms of the range of medical interests. It was, he said, 'the fourth leg of medical practice, i. e.—prevention, diagnosis, treatment and rehabilitation.' Although hailed as a new field of medical activity it was merely the practice of principles which had been known for many years. He cited the work of, for example, 'Dr Moore at Crewe, Dr Griffiths at the Albert Dock Hospital and Mr Plewes at Luton,' as well as the work of Sir Robert Jones in the 1914–18 War.[57]

He talked of the need to recognise the patient's mental attitudes. Scant attention in the acute hospital, he felt, was paid to patients' fears of pain, deformity, financial hardship, industrial degradation and litigation, which all delayed recovery. However, in line with the thinking of the times, he believed that, 'All the effort applied in the physical, mental and social rehabilitation of a patient is dissipated if he is not placed in suitable work.' In that regard he was not in favour of 'placing the handicapped' in employment out of pity or sentiment, but on 'fitness to carry out a job once medical treatment has been completed.'[58]

In terms of welding a patient group into a working community he saw personality, particularly of the medical director, as, probably, the greatest single factor which determined whether a Rehabilitation Centre was a success. Even 'one inappropriate personality on the staff can cause tremendous harm.' He added:

*There is no such thing as a man alone. An individual must be orientated not only as regards himself, but as regards his place in society. An understanding of this basic concept provides one of the corner stones of rehabilitation, and must be understood by all who do this work. A specialist in rehabilitation is not a specialist at all. He considers himself a member of a team of workers, both lay and medical, directed towards the patient as a whole.*[59]

Like Sommerville, Harris from the Devonshire Royal Hospital, in Buxton, believed that teamwork between 'the medical man' and 'his auxiliary staff' was the key to rehabilitation.[60] He was speaking at a Northern Region occupational therapists' conference in 1956 at Hatfield College, Durham, where a series of talks was given around the theme of Rehabilitation and Resettlement.[61]

Rehabilitation was also the topic chosen by the AOT Council for a series of refresher courses during the week preceding the Annual General Meeting of 1955. It had long been their wish to promote opportunities for postgraduate study, and in November 1954, a Committee was appointed under the leadership of MacCaul, to initiate the process. Members able to attend the full five days were to be placed as 'graduate student observers,' at selected hospitals or treatment centres to note specialised modern forms of therapy. Others spent shorter times in observation. Everyone attended lectures given on the last day by rehabilitation specialists. Altogether 100 people attended, and, generally, hospital authorities appeared supportive of the initiative. An interesting snippet in the Report on the Course noted that over half of the departments in General Hospitals, but few Mental Hospitals, provided either rehabilitation or facilities for assisting with activities of daily living and for home visiting. Instead, at that time, Mental Hospitals generally offered good social programmes. In both the Geriatric and Tuberculosis field, occupational therapists had difficulty securing the interest and active participation of Medical staff, despite rehabilitation problems being dealt with by Local Authority services when referred to them.[62]

On 16 May 1958, another Association refresher course was held at the Medical Rehabilitation Centre, Camden Road, and details of the visit are worth recording. From its opening in 1955, some 80 patients had attended daily having been referred by medical practitioners from any location. The simple criterion for acceptance was that rehabilitation would be of value. Approximately half suffered from medical disabilities, and the others from orthopaedic and surgical causes of disability. The majority underwent six weeks of extremely intensive group and individual treatment.[63]

From Monday to Friday each week, from 9.00 a. m. until 5.00 p. m., life for the patients was hectic. Well over half of all patients were discharged to their previous job, and another 21% were discharged with greatly improved functional movement. About 18% were referred back to their own hospital for extra medical attention. Treatment was based on the understanding that the protagonist, antagonist, synergist and fixator muscles act in concert; that total movement patterns are involved and that movement is often initiated through proprioceptive and sensory feedback mechanisms. On touring the centre and observing treatment those who attended were impressed by a 'Pre-work' group of men in a gymnasium who were racing around an obstacle course built of ladders, planks and wall-bars carrying in turn rolled up mats and heavy medicine balls. Another feature was the 'stationary bus' to provide practice and confidence in coping with public transport. The occupational therapy section, run for much of the time by Wenona Keane, 'faithfully followed the total functional approach, and was admirably geared to the end result of full rehabilitation.' A clerical section was very busy and, in the adjoining 'heavy workshop', patients had themselves constructed the majority of fittings.

**Figure 2.7.4:** **An example of a stationary bus for practice and confidence in coping with public transport**

In the 1955 Ministry of Labour publication *Services for the Disabled* occupational therapy was described as being 'directed towards restoration of particular functions or aimed at maintaining general physical and mental well-being.' Whilst handicrafts were used to exercise fingers and hands when patients were in bed, 'a much wider field of activities was available.' Those exercised the 'limbs, legs, feet and body' and the most modern tendency was 'to encourage workshop activity such as woodwork and metal work, and for it to be carried out in a more realistic industrial atmosphere.' The account stressed what would now be described as a reductionist remedial focus suggesting that 'processes are also separated as much as possible, so that a patient may concentrate on that portion of a job which is of most benefit to him, instead of performing a job from beginning to end and in the process doing much that is of no particular therapeutic value to him.' Special developments along those lines were recognised at the Luton and Dunstable Hospital and the Birmingham Accident Hospital, where the occupational therapy was undertaken in an atmosphere very closely resembling that of a factory. Instruction in those cases, the writer explained, was by skilled tradesmen under medical supervision 'rather than by the ordinary occupational therapists.' That rather disparaging comment is worth noting because Alice Savage, the Head Occupational Therapist at the Birmingham Accident Hospital, was so well regarded, particularly in the sphere of the treatment of head injuries that she was made an honorary Fellow of the Institute of Accident Surgery. The rehabilitative function of occupational therapy in mental hospitals was also recognised. It was explained that even diversional occupation could be 'the first and even the chief factor in restoring mental health' if it was 'actively therapeutic'. In mental deficiency colonies, occupation was used to train patients in habits of industry, to co-ordinate muscles, to provide a steadying interest, and as the means of introducing something approaching industrial conditions.[64]

**Figure 2.7.5:**   **Cross-cut sawing as part of rehabilitation**

From that overview it is possible to extract a number of different functions which rehabilitation fulfilled. They are discussed according to several headings that have become apparent during analysis of rehabilitation practice during that decade. The headings are: remediation, reablement, independence, and industrial, domestic and social resettlement.

## Remediation

From 1940 a large number of occupational therapy departments had been opened in physical hospitals and rehabilitation centres. Typically, occupational therapists assessed patients at the commencement of treatment and at regular intervals throughout. They used a range of occupations, slinged and pulleyed apparatus, and adapted tools to improve range of movement, muscle strength, work tolerance, confidence and develop a positive attitude to the future.[65] In many ways that carried on the tradition of occupation as exercise as recommended by the Regimen Sanitatis centuries earlier, but with added specificity. Remediation, that is the restoration of physical and mental capacities after illness or accident as part of the medical process, was the starting place for rehabilitation programmes.

Sidney Lock was one occupational therapist who became very involved in rehabilitation programmes at that time. He has contributed an overview of the rehabilitation process with particular reference to some of the equipment that was especially devised for physical remediation, some of which he designed and built.

## Equipment for remediation
### By Sidney Lock

During the immediate postwar years one of the greatest needs was to boost all sections of the economy, but particularly manufacturing, in order to redress the years of neglect during the war. For the field of occupational therapy this meant that patients needed to return to work as quickly as possible—fit and sufficiently active to fulfill the requirements of their work in the home, construction manufacturing, or reconstruction such as the building industry. Rehabilitation Centres were developed in different parts of the country. They usually included occupational therapy, physiotherapy, and remedial gymnastics departments, frequently under the direction of a consultant in physical medicine. Where it was not possible to set up a full-scale centre, therapists in all disciplines were encouraged to apply rehabilitation attitudes within their departments.

In 1948, a register was instituted by the AOT for technicians who were working with occupational therapists, were supervising patients in carrying out therapeutic activities, and who ensured skilled maintenance of mechanical equipment. Engineers or craftsmen with industrial experience were engaged; eventually they were fully recognised and placed on the National Salary Scales. A grade of staff known as 'occupational therapy helpers' was introduced around this time. They were individuals with practical skills who could assist in the supervision of programmes set up by occupational therapists. They also received national recognition and were placed on the salary scales.

Occupational therapists became more specific in their remedial purpose. Different equipment was introduced, but past activities were not abandoned completely; instead a clearer link between the activity and the specific therapeutic needs of the patient were made. Interest in the work itself and in its contribution to the restoration of function was essential. John Colson made an extensive survey of the value of various items of equipment and materials being used at that time. His book was studied avidly and applied by occupational therapists working in the physical field. Some of the key principles that needed to be fulfilled were that:

(a)   the activity included the required degree of function and effort to meet the physical needs of the patient;

(b)   the work was of some interest; and

(c)   there was a finished product which could have a use.

Soon it became apparent that some equipment could have greater value if adapted. Some of the most used items in what was often known as the 'Heavy Workshop' were:

**Hand fretsaws.** These were useful to encourage elbow function and grip, and it was possible to improve their use if one fitted handles of different thickness to assist grip.

**Hobbie's Treadle Fretsaw.** This was often one of the first items of equipment used for the treatment of lower limbs. Usually, to hold the feet in position, occupational therapists fitted a wooden platform with a heel-stop and straps to the treadle. Although mainly used for mobilising the ankle joint and developing muscles of the lower limb it also had some influence on the knee joint especially if the height of the chair was altered.

**The Ankle Rotator.** Mary S. Jones devised this equipment. Basically it was a machine for fretsawing, but the driving wheel was set at right angles to the footpiece (instead of the usual in-line). A special footpiece was made incorporating straps to hold the foot in position. The patient made an imaginary O with the toes to drive the driving-wheel. The range of movement could be changed including the degree of inversion or eversion of the foot. Jones pioneered occupational therapy for lower limb injuries, working out graded programmes of treatment utilising treadle wood turning lathes and other foot-powered machinery. To widen the scope of treatment, as well as the ankle rotator saw, she designed, and her technician constructed, a bicycle fretsaw, a bicycle file, a foot-treadle drilling machine, and two bowl lathes.

**The 'Larvic' Rehabilitation Lathe.** This woodturning lathe was normally used during the later stages of treatment, particularly for mobilising the knee and hip joints and increasing work tolerance. To provide static exercise for the quadriceps a patient was seated on a 'Bicycle Saddle Seat', the 'good' leg treadled while the leg to be treated was suspended in a long sling under the bed of the lathe. This lathe and the Farnham Lathe owe much to Jones' influence.

**The 'Oliver' bicycle fretsaw.** This was named after the designer Edward ('Pim') Oliver. It became an essential piece of equipment in occupational therapy workshops. The patient sat on a bicycle saddle seat. In front were the table and the saw, which was driven by a belt linked to the pedals. The action of peddling helped to improve the range of knee, hip, and ankle joint movement. Later models had resistance facilities to develop muscular strength.

**The Quads Switch.** Designed by an occupational therapist and engineered by a technical instructor, this piece of equipment was used to maintain the tone of the quadriceps when flexion of the knee joint was contra-indicated. The patient's leg rested on a foot support at hip level and the switch, on a stand, was placed beneath the knee joint. To operate the switch, which then activated a piece of electrical equipment, the quadriceps were contracted, thus pushing the switch.

**Figure 2.7.6:**    **Rehabilitation machines designed by Mary S. Jones**

Another part of a department, usually set aside for 'cleaner' or quieter activities was referred to as the 'Light Workshop' although that was often a misnomer. Weaving in various forms was frequently used: partly because of the creative aspects of this craft but, also on account of the therapeutic benefits obtainable by using different types of loom and/or by the addition of adaptations:

**Two-way Table Looms.** These were used extensively as the weaving involved gentle hand, arm and shoulder movements. To help maintain a working position, the arm could be supported in a sling with helical spring suspension. Different adaptations were devised, many of which involved the use of pulley circuits to develop a range of movement and/or to add resistance. There were also adaptations for treating the lower limbs which included work for flexion and extension of the knee and the hip with added resistance when required.[66]

**Upright Rug Looms.** These were used in many departments, space permitting. Weaving on these looms was particularly useful in providing fairly strenuous activity for back strengthening and elevation, abduction and adduction of the shoulder joint.

**The Fletcher/Wiltshire Bed Loom.** This was originally designed by Jill Fletcher, an occupational therapist, and developed by a loom maker, Mr. Wiltshire. Patients with fractured shaft of femur were often in bed for several months, with their leg in traction. When active exercises were permitted, treatment on this loom could commence. The loom stood upright on the bed. Both legs were suspended, just clear of the bedding, to allow freedom of movement. Cords attached to the ankles and the loom mechanism were operated by abduction and adduction of the legs; the ranges of movement being determined by the occupational therapist. Flexion of the hip could be achieved by changing the direction of the cords.

**The FEPS (Flexion, Extension, Pronation, Supination) Adaptation.** For many years this adaptation, designed by me and made commercially, was exported throughout the world. A roller at right angles to the table edge had, at one end, a 3-inch wheel. This could be turned for pronation and supination exercise and, of course, for finger movements. The adaptation could be rotated through 90° and then the roller was turned by flexion and extension of the wrist.

**Hand Printing Machines.** Printing had been used for some time in psychiatric units but, precipitated by an article I wrote for the British Journal of Physical Medicine entitled Printing Adapted, in 1956 its use was extended to physical rehabilitation.[67] The printing press could be used in conjunction with the 'Therapeutic Table'. When mounted on the table, the press was operated by means of pulley circuits, which allowed graded and timed exercises to be carried out for a wide range of movements of hand, wrist, elbow, shoulders, knees and hips.

**The Therapeutic Table** was constructed in occupational therapy departments to plans supplied by the designer, and used widely, both in the UK and overseas, for many years.

**Figure 2.7.7:** **The FEPS adaptation designed by Sidney Lock**

A contributor to the field, Doris Sym, who worked at the Astley Ainslie Hospital during this period, started a discussion of recent trends in rehabilitation by a reminder that without the patient's co-operation 'all our skill is virtually useless.' That was achieved, she said, by 'bringing a patient into the busy confident atmosphere of a workshop where emphasis is not on disability but on productive work.' With that 'enablement' sentiment as a background, she elaborated in remedial terms so the profession could be seen to make a scientific 'reductionist' contribution. She argued that as certain aims of treatment were accepted universally by rehabilitation teams as restorative of function it was sensible to consider those in terms of provable occupational therapy gains. The implication was that it would also be politically expedient. The aims were:

1. To increase or maintain the range of joint movement within the limits of pain.
2. To increase or maintain the power or strength of a muscle group.
3. To establish or re-establish co-ordination between groups of affected muscles and restore their smooth or unconscious function.
4. To increase or maintain endurance not only in a specific muscle group, but also in the patient as a whole.
5. To increase or maintain the speed or reaction in muscle groups.

She went through each of the aims and, using the example of a 'knee joint', suggested how they might be accomplished within occupational therapy and recorded in hard facts which could be seen at a glance by the Doctor. She used an adjustable bicycle fretsaw as treatment for the first aim, and joint measurement using a goniometer to record progress. For the second, she suggested an adaptation on a four-way loom in which a spring balance was set in the adaptation to record progress. For the third, general woodwork, keeping capability and work tolerance records. For the fourth a foot powered lathe, for which time and repetition rate was clocked. And for the fifth, games that required speed of action, for which time and skill were clocked. To those very specific interventions, Sym added another. This was the manufacture of small and temporary splints to meet the immediate need of a patient during the course of treatment.[68]

Another occupational therapist who wrote about the use of remedial technique and its appraisal was Leonard Allbon. He queried the accuracy of methods used in departments to measure the range of joint movement. Like Sym, he urged the use of clinical goniometers or arthrometers believing that two sizes were required, the smaller 'Conzett' type for hand and finger measurements, and a bigger model for larger joints. He discussed in great detail where they could be purchased, how they could be made, and how they were used.[69]

Bearing those comments in mind it is of interest to view some examples of how, and with what type of patients, occupational therapists were using remedial approaches. One of the most common disorders currently treated by occupational therapists is hemiplegia as a result of stroke. Looking back almost fifty years to articles about treatment then, one by Dr H. Droller, a Leeds Consultant Geriatrician, discussed it as a medical issue in which the number of deaths was known to have comprised 14% of all those recorded.[70,71] In a later paper he described the rehabilitation of the stroke patient as:

> *Restitution of the ability to use the hemiplegic limb as far as the damaged nervous system will permit. Prevention and treatment of contractures of shoulder and legs by passive and active movement, heat and intra-articular injection of hydrocortisone…Constant encouragement is given to stand, balance and walk, first aided, later freely. Re-training for an independent existence is insisted upon during the later stages of rehabilitation.[72]*

Two articles outlining the therapy of a hemiplegic patient in 1953 and 1954 suggest that there was some congruency of treatment across treatment venues.[73,74] Miss A. K. Levin, an occupational therapist from Bangour Hospital in Scotland reported a programme aimed at re-education of gait with the patient 'wearing a caliper for spastic drop foot.' The patient should be encouraged to walk as much as possible by 'treatment being arranged in such a way that he has to move from place to place in the department.' The use of a bicycle fretsaw was recommended because of its rhythmic bilateral movement and co-ordination, which tended 'to overcome the spasticity of the affected leg.' (Interestingly, the use of the bicycle for that purpose was supported by research carried out by a group of North American Physiotherapists in the 1990s. In the interim it had been frowned upon, because it was thought to increase spasticity.) Games such as croquet, and floor draughts were used to improve movement control and balance. For the treatment of upper limbs the programme aimed at both the affected arm and sound arm, the latter to compensate for loss of function in the other, and helping it. Movement could be assisted by sling support to facilitate shoulder abduction and adduction, and by use of a narrow sling which supported the wrist with a thumb hole to 'counteract spastic flexion of the wrist.' With such assistance, patients often found grasping and releasing objects was easier. Simultaneous bilateral movement, swinging and rhythmic movements were encouraged. Unfamiliar occupations were recommended to prevent the discovery of the inability to carry out everyday tasks which may be depressing and discouraging.[75]

Those treatment aims and procedures were in line with the advice given by surgeon, Mr F. J. Gillingham, who, when asked what were the uses of slings in the treatment of hemiplegia—their types, the springs and counter balances used, and what were the uses of games, answered:

*A fact to remember in treatment is that movement starts at the shoulder— elbow and hand movements should not be attempted when there is only coarse movement at the shoulder. The use of reciprocal innervation with large rhythmical movements is recommended, e. g. in beating on a foot loom with the paretic arm in a sling and using the sound hand to assist; bicycling with the paretic foot strapped to the pedal and with the sound leg assisting. At this stage the limb is used as a single unit.*

*Frequent handling of objects graded from large to small gives practice in 'letting go' i.e. in relaxing flexors, e.g. big draughts, Chinese checkers and solitaire. Table tennis is valuable for co-ordination, and outdoor games such as croquet, where the mallet is of assistance in walking, give confidence.[76]*

Remediation for rheumatic patients was another area of wide concern. Virginia Fitch wrote in SJOT how a 30-bed Rheumatic Unit, first opened at Stracathro Hospital in 1945, had grown considerably by 1951 and had a waiting list. At that institution the occupational therapist and the physician in charge had compiled a programme of an experimental nature, and every day, as many of the patients as possible attended the department and those confined to the ward were visited. The prescription card was always filled with 'exact details of the regions affected and movements required.' It was determined that there were three essentials of treatment, which differed with stages of the disease:
- The acute period: regular contact to alleviate anxiety and restlessness.
- The sub-acute phase: use of carefully graded remedial craft work for exercise.
- Long-term treatment: satisfaction of the normal need for self-expression and independence.

With those essentials in mind the amount and type of work was strictly limited by pain, limitation of movement, and susceptibility to fatigue. Knitting, for example, was forbidden because it entailed 'a cramping movement and involves the contraction of muscles, defeating entirely the aim of our work, which is to obtain large easy movements graduated to smaller and more precise ones.'[77]

Wallace, the Scottish plastic surgeon discussed in the last chapter, saw occupational therapy as 'very personal: it is the therapy that takes possession of the individual' he said.[78] He found it useful because the majority of patients in a plastic unit, at that time, suffered considerable mental anxieties in addition to physical injury. He provided a Table (shown here as Table 2.7.1) illustrating several cases, the aims of therapy, and the occupations prescribed to meet them.[79]

## Table 2.7.1: Occupational therapy with plastic surgery cases c. 1950

| Case | Aim | OT Prescribed |
| --- | --- | --- |
| Civilian Pilot<br><br>Extensive Burns | 1. Morale<br>2. To assess skin loss of dorsum of hand<br>3. To improve grip<br>4. To assess resistance of skin to friction | 1. Reading frame used while both hands were in plaster (non smoker)<br>2. Cord Knotting, using wooden blocks of graded sizes to improve grip and give gentle exercise to upper limbs-use of leather punchers into which graded compression springs might be fitted-wood work in department<br>3. Finally, steps were taken to obtain a grant for school masters training |
| Hairdresser<br><br>Electrical burn to left Palm | 1. To improve grip<br>2. To prevent contraction of skin graft | 1. Graded sizes of wooden shuttle used for stool seating (patient worked in glove due to unhealed areas)<br>2. Large and small shuttles used alternately |
| Laundry Worker<br><br>Burn of Rt Hand. Loss of distal and middle phalanges of middle, ring and little fingers, and loss of distal phalanx of index | 1. Flexion of metacarpo-phalangeal joints<br>2. Opposition<br>3. To enable patient to become used to prosthesis | 1. Padded Perspex handles fitted to loom to give easiest possible movement. Resistance gradually increased<br>2. Table tennis with padded handle on bat<br>3. Games involving picking up small objects |
| House Wife<br><br>Burns of face & Rt. hand with amputation of all fingers | 1. To increase manipulative skill of thumb against prosthetic fingers | 1. Stitching, hooked rug making etc.<br>2. Special fixing for prosthetic limb made to improve cosmetic result |
| Gardener<br><br>Old burn scar on elbow – for excision | 1. To aid healing by stimulating the circulation, particularly venous return<br>2. To keep up muscle tone | 1. Arm in plaster after grafting: therefore exercises for hands and shoulder. Glove making involving stitching<br>2. Arm out of plaster: Arm resting on pillow – wrist and hand could only be used at first |
| Apprentice Marine Engineer<br><br>Severe burns, causing destruction of eyelids, eyebrows, nose, ears, and most of skin from face | Resocialisation to get:<br>1. Out of ward<br>2. Down to Workshop<br>3. To gain sufficient confidence to travel in buses to pictures etc.<br>4. To go back to ship yard | Long Term Programme<br>1. Recreational room for table tennis<br>2. OT department to work on motor bicycle, at first behind screens<br>3. By bus to cinema at nights only<br>4. Local garage, working all day<br>5. To shipyard (accomplished with success) |
| Schoolgirl—epileptic<br><br>Deep burns of hands with residual deformities | 1. To re-educate fingers, often finger by finger as they were released from plaster<br>2. To observe a number of fits (two fits in department, no warning) | Long term treatment with resettlement as aim:<br>1. Typing, useful finger exercise<br>2. Final assessment with surgeon and rehabilitation district officer found that present day competition would make typing impossible, *suggestion*: calculator machine which would require less speed |
| School boy<br><br>Car accident, admitted for ear repair | 1. Keep up Morale | 1. Work of a diversional nature, using one free hand. Vice used to hold leather for stitching |

| School boy | 1. Diversional while a bed patient | 1. Quadriceps loom adapted to give range of movement required |
|---|---|---|
| Burns of lower limbs | 2. Exercise for quadriceps and ankle movements of both legs. | 2. Ball games requiring kicking<br>3. Treadle saw for plantar and dorsiflexion- this was adapted to give inversion and eversion |

Four years later, in *The Rehabilitation of the Burned*, Wallace explained how, in the past, surgeons had paid little attention to a patient's return to work. Indeed, on the outer cover of old hospital case records was frequently written: 'Diagnosis, "Extensive Burns"; Result, "Cure"' when the end-result in most cases was severe crippling. He discussed, in some detail, problems associated with immobility, such as oedema, adhesions, shock, infection, deformity, and grafting, along with patients' fears of permanent disfigurement, disability, loss of employment and of income. Occupational therapy was a way to encourage patients to resume work by easy stages with rehabilitation starting, more or less, from the time of injury, however, the surgeon-in-charge made all final decisions, even in 'reconditioning':

> *The manual labourer requires physical endurance; the skilled worker, fine controlled movement for accuracy and drawings; the accountant, sustained mental effort. Measures in rehabilitation must be directed towards recovery of the parts essential for the functional needs of a particular injured man.*[80]

Squadron Leader C. B. Wynn Parry addressed the role of occupational therapists in lower motor neurone disease such as poliomyelitis and peripheral nerve injuries in a lecture he gave on electromyography. In the treatment of peripheral nerve injuries, it was, he said, 'to provide careful splintage to prevent deformity and allow maximum function and retraining of functional use' by craftwork suited to interests and work requirements. With polio the role was threefold. First, occupational therapy taught patients how to manage personal toilet and tasks of daily life; second, it provided splints, appliances, and gadgets to overcome disability; and third, it provided remedial treatment for recovery of movement and muscle power related to vocation. In his call for basic clinical research he suggested that the electromyograph would be a useful tool to appraise the true indications and limitations of occupational therapy practice and techniques scientifically.[81]

Wynn Parry is well known for *Rehabilitation of the Hand*, a book written in partnership with Natalie (Smythe) Barr. She, too, led the way in remedial techniques within occupational therapy in relation to hand therapy and splinting. During the early part of the 1950s, she was head occupational therapist at the new Etwall Rehabilitation Centre in Derby working with Guy Pulvertaft. With his encouragement her interest in hand therapy was nurtured, and was further developed at the Medical Rehabilitation Unit, Royal Air Force, Chessington, where she moved in 1954. Similarly to Jones at Farnham Park, and working with Wynn Parry, she developed dynamic, lively splints using the workshops at Chessington to produce metal hinges and springs for wrist and hand splints. Before then, most hand splints had been static. Hers, like Jones' were neat and close fitting, allowing the hand to function as normally as possible whilst preventing contractures.[82]

Even in programmes for children, occupational therapy of a very specific nature was advocated. For example, Jean Waterston drew up a table (presented here as Table 2.7.2) which categorized occupations for their treatment according to regions affected by disease or injury.

## Table 2.7.2: Occupations for Children of Different Age Groups[83]

| Age | Regions Affected | | General |
|---|---|---|---|
| | **Upper Limbs** | **Lower Limbs** | |
| <5 | *Toys*—plasticine, crayons, big bricks, toys on wheels, constructive toys, woolly balls, finger painting, paper-cutting | Toys mobilised by feet, e.g, tricycle, pedal car, hobby horse | Suspended ball for hitting and kicking |
| 5-10 | Weaving —tabby, card Woodwork – simple with no joints, sawing hammering and screwing Painting Other Minor Occupations: Embroidery, coarse canvas with wool or raffia (5-7); Simple stitches (8-10); Basketry or cord knotting (8-10) e.g. dog leads Sewn rugs, paper cutting, clay modelling, thonging, etc. Washing ironing and making dolls clothes, knitting and crochet  NB. Felt toys should not be given to children under 8. | Weaving—cottage loom or tabby loom with foot power adaptation with tabby upset. Floor loom with tabby upset (7-10) Woodwork—treadle or bicycle fretsaw can be used for all ages if the guiding of the object to be cut is done by the therapist for the younger children Sewing machine—can be used by younger children if machine is unthreaded and supervised. Much pleasure is derived from making patterns on a piece of paper instead of sewing cloth Games—foot draughts, snakes and ladders on a big board etc. | General play—croquet, ball games |
| >10 | Any occupations including quite complicated weaving and woodwork, plastics, pottery, book binding, metal work, puppets, darts, billiards | Lathe work, bicycle and treadle fretsaws, floor looms, foot dominoes and draughts, potters wheel, dress making with hand or treadle sewing machine | Rounders cricket, gardening, table tennis |

Waterson made some very practical observations: 'Small boys require more variety than girls'; better results were achieved by giving short periods of one occupation interspersed with others; girls liked doing 'boys' occupations; and boys were willing to do 'many so called feminine occupations, provided it is accepted as being the natural thing to do and that they are not laughed at, particularly between the ages 10 and 13.'[84]

Within child psychiatry, Dr J.G. Howells and occupational therapist, Miss D.K. Cooke, adopted a remedial approach to neurosis. They saw that the function of child psychiatry was to cure children's neurosis and so prevent the development of adult neurosis. In that process a fundamental change of parental attitude was sought.[85] Howells made the treatment of the parent his main work, and decided that the occupational therapist had exceptional qualifications for:

● **Play observation**
Here there were three aims: as a means of objective assessment; to reveal information about specific aspects of the case; and as an initial assessment of the child by which to judge progress. Such factors as appearance, adjustment, responsiveness, motivation, motility, attention, verbalisation, obvious physical defects or pathological signs were noted and recorded.

• **Diagnosis**

Children were encouraged to reveal what they felt about life at that particular moment. The most dynamic information was revealed through play. Of particular use for the task were:

—a variety of figures which could be used to represent people in the child's environment;

—a dolls house with 'little people';

—a box puppet theatre with a reflective mirror so the children could see their own actions,

—'headless' glove puppets for which children made their own cardboard heads;

—a collection of miniature toys representing objects in the child's world; and

—sand and water trolleys, clay, plasticine, paints and crayons etc for use in imaginative play. Assessment reports were based on:

1. Description of the play situation and the media used.

2. Description of the child's reaction to a specific play situation.

3. Discussion and interpretation of each reaction.

4. Conclusion, correlating the findings of each reaction and relating them.

• **Prescribed, supervised treatment of the child (Play Therapy)**

Play Therapy had four aspects:

1. Symptomatic Therapy, aimed at removing a socially inconvenient symptom like. stammering, a tic, or an inability to write. That was often the starting point. Toy telephones and puppetry were found useful.

2. Release or Cathartic Therapy, aimed at 'the release of dammed up emotion'. It was a palliative procedure with only temporary value. Clay, painting and puppetry were particularly applicable.

3. Supportive Psychotherapy, for the child's immediate difficulties, which went hand in hand with the treatment of the parent. For that, constructive and creative work and a close confiding relationship encouraged the children to speak of problems while success brought praise and encouragement.

4. Prolonged Psychotherapy, aimed at situations in the past to produce a change in present behaviour in which any of the occupations could be useful.[86]

The department at the Ipswich and East Suffolk Hospital where they worked offered one- or two-year training in child psychiatric practice.

In a totally different remedial set up for neurotic children at the Maudsley Hospital where Gillian Forward was known for her advanced and innovative occupational therapy programmes, two occupational therapists worked with younger children morning and afternoon between lessons. Two students, two nurses, and one male nurse worked alongside making a staff patient ratio of 1:2. An observer recorded at the time of her visit, '...there were about fourteen children who were given complete freedom and very little constructive occupational therapy.' This was to counteract the discipline the children experienced at school. In a large room with bare walls and no furniture the children were allowed '...to draw on the walls and rush around on roller skates and play football. They also have a clay room where they can, if they feel inclined, throw clay at each other and anyone who happens to come in.' There was no organized work, apart from paintings done on large sheets of paper with a thick brush. All the children's artistic efforts were kept for the psychologist.[87]

# Reablement

In recent years occupational therapists have adopted the phrase 'an enabling approach' to describe how they chose to go about the therapeutic process. An enabling approach accepts patient- or client-driven practice, which meets needs as they are perceived by the patients rather than by a therapist. Reablement has similar connotations, whilst also embracing the idea that earlier skills may need redevelopment. Reablement embodied the remedial idea, but was more than a 'reductionist' process of improving specific anatomical or psychological components, such as muscles or concentration. It made use of those components in necessary or desired occupations, which added meaning and purpose according to individual values, needs and interests.

Considering the rehabilitative process in terms of either reablement or resettlement, Dr Cooksey, who was in charge of the Physical Medicine Department of King's College Hospital, described reablement as the restoration of physical and mental function after illness including the regaining of independence in daily living activities and in coping with disability as well as work skills. It was carried out largely in hospitals by a closely knit highly organised team of doctors, nurses, physiotherapists, almoners, and occupational therapists.[88]

Mary S. Jones, known as Molly, chose to use the term 'reablement' in preference to physical rehabilitation. In 1940 she had started an occupational therapy department at the Rowley Bristow Hospital, Pyrford, working mainly with patients who had nerve lesions, and tuberculous spines or hips. During this period she did pioneer work on hand splints and devised a special high stool with a bicycle seat so that patients in hip spicas could work in a comfortable sitting position. She invented an overhead bed table that not only enabled bed patients to work in a good position, but also made it possible for patients spending months in plaster beds to do factory outwork, such as assembling cables for 'walkie-talkie' wireless sets, as part of their war effort.

**Figure 2.7.8:** **Bed patients at Pyrford**

In 1947 Jones was the founding Head Occupational Therapist at Farnham Park Rehabilitation Centre which attracted a constant stream of visitors, so that many of her ideas became utilised in other centres. Jones' paper, published in the Lancet in 1951, provides an indication of her approach to occupational therapy for physical reablement at the time.[89] The aims of reablement, she said, were:

> ...to improve a patient's capacities for living as normal a life as possible after disablement by illness or injury. In most communities, 'living a normal life' implies that a part of the day is spent in activities which are gainful; that is, they are directed towards obtaining necessities and something extra to provide amenities, while the rest of the waking hours are spent in enjoying those amenities. The capacities needed for an individual to live a normal life may be divided into those needed for earning a living and those for enjoying life.

Jones went on to explain further the basic philosophy on which she based treatment:

> People who earn a living in a way which absorbs all their interests and energies are to be envied, until the even tenor of their life is interrupted by ill health, or by forced retirement in old age; then their state becomes pitiable. There are others whose recreations are their paramount interest, perhaps some form of strenuous sport. After illness or accident they may be perfectly capable of doing their previous work, but they may be reluctant to return to a drab and monotonous job at the work-bench in factory or office, without the excitement of looking forward to playing in the football team on Saturday, or to the bicycle club tour on Sunday.
>
> At the moment in England, we are in the middle of an experiment in the development of the responsibility of society to the individual. Perhaps insufficient emphasis is being laid on the equally necessary responsibility of the individual to society. When the habits of life are grossly interrupted by ill health, this sense of responsibility is easily shed. The reablement team has been set up to expedite, or to make possible, the return of the patient to normal life. If success is to be other than passing, the patient must himself be enlisted as a full-time member of the team.[90]

In Jones' view, in order to restore or adapt function, occupational therapists aimed to stimulate and harness a patient's active or latent desire to create. Work was planned to attract and hold the patient's attention, whilst processes were graduated 'to develop grip, stability, and balance, both mental and physical', and to encourage independence. The chosen activity had 'to entail movements remedial to the disability', provide 'suitable supports to maintain correct posture', and tools or machinery were adapted 'to ensure the use of the affected muscles and joints', all without 'undue stress, fatigue, or pain'. Contrary to many later occupational therapists working in physical rehabilitation, Jones advocated that enticement to greater effort should be by 'increasingly rewarding results in the beauty, elaboration, or size of the object' just, but only just, within each patient's capacity for a high standard of work. That was of great psychological value. However, she conceded that 'both types of work—the modern industrial and the traditional handicraft—have their place in reablement', along with that of a more intellectual nature.[91]

Adding to the long running debate of whether to pay patients for work done, Jones had taken an experimental approach to the issue during the war. She developed procedures that allowed long-term patients, whether ambulant, or in 'plaster' or 'tilted' beds, to work at some small assembly work. Within two years about 170,000 assemblies were completed with an average of 4.5% rejects, which was lower than for the same work done at the factory bench. In that situation, patients responded well to the stimulus of doing work essential to the war effort, as well as to 'cash in the hand', the latter especially as many of the patients were anxious about their family's financial situation. After the industrial work was provided, handicrafts found favour as recreation and relaxation.' Later at Farnham Park, some light sedentary industrial work was used to encourage small finger movements, accuracy and manual dexterity. Without the stimulus of payment, patients soon found it monotonous, and became bored and careless.[92] Those experiments suggested, to Jones, that some personal interest in the resultant article must be aroused. Additionally she surmised that the industrial atmosphere of reablement workshops attached to factories cannot be genuinely reproduced without some use of the personal profit motive, or patients may well suspect they are being exploited. She envisaged occupational therapists in the future working in industrial situations, specifically to enlist help in finding suitable work for certain types of patient and, in return, providing assistance to employers through their understanding of the problems of work, and assisting the return to work process of people with disability. She appreciated that 'the bored factory worker becomes careless and "accident prone."' Pre-empting a preventive approach, Jones not only understood that the monotony of repetitive work could increase the incidence of industrial illness, but also the potential role of recreation to alleviate such problems. Accordingly, she recommended study of the recreation habits of industrial workers, and encouraged employers to establish a range of recreational facilities for handicapped as well as active workers.[93] Later again at Farnham Park, industrial outwork was used, enjoyed and preferred to creative work by some patients, particularly when working as part of a group of others.[94]

**Figure 2.7.9:    Reablement
                at Farnham Park**

One of Jones' greatest achievements as a therapist was to create such an enabling atmosphere in her workshops that the patients' morale was invariably high. They worked hard at any activity they were given and sometimes seemed to show improved function just by being there. She believed profoundly in the value of occupational therapy, and her personality was such that patients who had perhaps spent only a short time with her, would come back to visit and report their progress, often many years later.

Reablement was a central theme in the treatment of tuberculosis, which was still a major health concern despite progress made in latter years with the use of streptomycin, PAS, and nicotinic acid. The average stay of patients then was nine months. Only staff with positive Mantoux reactions or who had been treated with BCG vaccination were employed and all were X-rayed every three months. Dr William Murray, from East Fortune Sanatorium, East Lothian, talked to the SAOT at the summer general meeting of 1952, about their role as he saw it. He believed that patients should 'be trained to be able to stand up to work, mentally and physically' and not only 'for work on discharge.' He advocated art therapy as very beneficial for self-expression, and thought it should be carried out by occupational therapists rather than artists 'who worried too much about correctness of style.' All the work done by the patients was kept in the occupational therapy department for at least a week whilst the articles were treated under an ultra-violet lamp and left in sunlight before being wrapped and kept until collected by visitors. Patients were not taken off the follow-up list until their disease had been quiescent for from three to five years.[95]

An occupational therapy programme in an Old People's Home for Displaced Persons situated on the North West coastal plain of Germany reminds us of the holistic nature of illness and disability. The inmates, who represented a great variety of nationalities, suffered from chronic disease, mostly as a result of ill treatment, malnutrition and privation. In order to overcome the difficulties of a community made up of people with divergent language, national customs, prejudices, religion, and indigenous culture, as well as some very individual and traumatic reasons for their present placement, a reabling approach was vital. The occupational therapist who had journeyed there from the UK to work for two years, provided treatment in the form of resocialisation and rehabilitation through socialisation, rather than by a direct attempt to increase specific restoration of physical function. As they began to regard themselves as people again, confidences were divulged to work companions. As their mental condition improved an incidental physical improvement also took place.[96]

## Independence

Although some occupational therapists were already involved in assisting people with activities of daily living the first official adoption of the term was found in the 1955 government publication Services for the Disabled. Under that heading it is stated that:

> One of the first essentials of rehabilitation is that the disabled should be as independent as possible in the personal activities of daily living such as dressing, feeding and hygiene. Until recently, however, this important aspect of rehabilitation had received scant attention, except in the case of the limbless, the paraplegic and the blind.[97]

This publication of the Standing Committee on the Rehabilitation and Resettlement of the

Disabled recognised pioneer work in the field by the British Red Cross Society and the Central Council for the Care of Cripples, along with more recent interest in hospitals by physiotherapists who tailored exercise towards functional movement patterns, and occupational therapists who, the text stated, made necessary appliances and showed patients how to use them.

**Figure 2.7.10: Aids to enable independence**

Many appliances were, indeed, devised and made in occupational therapy departments as very little was commercially available in the 1950s. Sym suggested that a display of aids to daily living, both home-made and manufactured, was a stimulus worth having in all occupational therapy departments. However, she cautioned that such appliances were individual in their application and that indiscriminate handing out of 'gadgets', particularly by those with no knowledge of the aims of treatment, could delay recovery as well as being a waste of money.[98]

Barbara Stow set up one of the earliest rehabilitation kitchens and ADL units in Britain at St Thomas' Hospital and, like MacCaul, at Kings College Hospital, led the way in furthering occupational therapists' interest in independence in ADL. MacCaul had developed a particular interest in the production of equipment to enable people with disability to overcome their handicaps. Her flourishing ADL unit included, as Sommerville described, a complete kitchen especially adapted so that disabled housewives could be trained 'to return home to an independent life.'[99] In 1957, the first Functional Assessment unit was set up at the hospital.[100] Phyllis Howie, who joined MacCaul's staff in 1958, was engaged as a research occupational therapist to study the problems of disabled housewives in the kitchen alongside Margaret Stewart, a physiotherapist. They produced a joint report in 1961, and Howie, a few years later, published *A Pilot study of Disabled Housewives in their Kitchen.*[101]

Cooksey supported MacCaul's approach to make treatment more relevant to his patients' problems of daily living. He wrote, somewhat ahead of his time, that 'housewifery is certainly the largest industry in the country, and probably the most important.' He believed that the state was pre-occupied with the disabled wage earner, and saw that very little had been done to assist housewives, perhaps because there was no powerful trade union to further their welfare.[102] His concerns were echoed in *Services for the Disabled*, which suggested:

> It is, perhaps, surprising that whilst so much has been done to secure employment for the disabled on equal terms with the able bodied, so little attention has been paid to the need to make them independent in their private lives.[103]

Cooksey was a useful ally, because as a Consultant Adviser to the Ministry of Health he was called on when, for example, guidelines for building and equipping occupational therapy departments in new hospitals were required. In that capacity he advanced the acceptance of ADL as a valuable contributor to medical care.

Interest in aids to daily living to promote independence was also evident elsewhere. Hardy, in a 1951 Scottish Journal, explained that patients who had lost hand function through accident or disease could be helped back to 'a fair degree of independence by the use of appliances and gadgets to aid them in carrying out everyday tasks.' She described how two simple gadgets which took no more that fifteen minutes to make would give the patient the satisfaction of being able 'to "do" for himself, that is so necessary for his happiness.' One was a perspex holder for a spoon or fork which 'curled to fit the patient's index finger and thumb.' The other was a plaster of Paris hand rest, with a ball-bearing castor for writing. This was a prototype for a later model made of aluminium.[104]

## Industrial, domestic, and social resettlement

Some eminent authorities in the field held that rehabilitation was not complete, or could be classed a failure, if the recipient was not, ultimately, resettled. In most cases that meant returning to work, but in others it also applied to domestic or social situations. Sommerville was one who thought that return to paid employment was essential, and Harris, from the Devonshire Royal Hospital, was another. He said, with regard to failure: 'the most difficult problems arise where there is some grumbling disability left, such as with rheumatoid arthritis and the progressive disabilities of disseminated sclerosis.'[105]

At the May, 1955, Post-Graduate Study Course on Rehabilitation mentioned earlier, three experts—Dr Cooksey, Dr Pomryn, from the field of Psychological Medicine, and Mr Earl, from the Ministry of Labour—were invited to speak on resettlement. This was said to be the most difficult aspect of rehabilitation for occupational therapists to deal with. Perhaps that was because the profession had been largely excluded from the process by government action, except with regard to those patients not planning to re-enter the work force. That was to lead, ultimately, to more concern with the treatment of women, the elderly and children, and more responsibility for domestic activities of daily living than those of paid employment. How much, one wonders, was that to do with gender issues of the time?

Resettlement usually called upon a different group of experts from remediation or reablement. Resettlement required input from the Ministry of Labour, the disablement resettlement officer, and a mass of local and central statutory authorities and voluntary societies. The Local Authority provided care and after-care such as meals on wheels, home nursing or home help. The Local Welfare Authority was responsible for providing welfare officers, adaptations such as alterations in the home to assist with daily living activities, clubs and hostels for holidays, sheltered work, and transport between home and work, except for some specific groups such as the deaf. The Ministry of Health provided appliances and other commodities such as transport and petrol driven chairs, and Voluntary Societies did any of the things that the Government did not do.[106]

Whilst addressing those issues, Cooksey was the only one of the three experts who included occupational therapists in the 'resettlement team', which, at King's College Hospital, was also the 'reablement team'. A weekly case conference between the almoner, medical specialist, welfare officer, health visitor, physiotherapist and occupational therapist tackled the problem. Cooksey felt, however, that while statutory provision for full resettlement had been agreed by Parliament 'implementation still hung fire.' He identified the greatest needs as '(i) to make available to all areas what was already available to some, (ii) to provide occupation centres for those who are too disabled to go to the DRO [Disablement Resettlement Officer]; and (iii) to provide an efficient home workers' scheme.'[107]

After presentations from the experts, groups of occupational therapists at the Study Course continued discussions. Problems of the day regarding resettlement were aired. Exclusion from the process, and ongoing difficulties were experienced in the field of tuberculosis, in geriatrics, in mental health, sometimes in general hospitals and rehabilitation centres. Securing co-operation, interest and active participation with local authority services, medical staff, senior nursing staff, and DROs was often a problem. There was also some difficulty found in obtaining equipment, and generally, it was felt that more accurate means of assessing patients capabilities was needed.[108]

Despite overall limited opportunity, some rehabilitation centres and specialised hospital departments with a physical medicine/rehabilitation focus did expect occupational therapists to work on resettlement as they went through the process of remediation, reablement, and independence with patients. A prime example was the Astley Ainslie Hospital where, as an aid to speeding-up the resettlement of miners, a model coal face was designed, presented and installed by the National Coal Board (NCB) as part of the occupational therapy department. The hospital served an area whose population included 14,000 miners. One hundred and eighty-three of those were treated in 1958. Like authentic mines, the rehabilitation model had an arched roadway, two seams, one 3ft 6ins high and the other 4ft 6ins high, a bogie, stone packs, wooden chocks, props and rails, and was designed to reproduce the working positions and atmosphere of a coal mine. Patients were able to carry out a number of tasks similar to those required underground. The model coal face was used at different stages of treatment for the rehabilitation and assessment of the working capacity of injured miners under normal cramped conditions. An instructor from the NCB trained the occupational therapists.[109]

**Figure 2.7.11: Two faces of resettlement: developing work skills in a commercial wood yard and the Astley Ainslie Coal Mine**

At the same hospital, tests were developed for the guidance of occupational therapists in the resettlement process. Resettlement was threefold: independence in personal toilet, feeding, dressing, and getting to and from the place of work; work that was psychologically and economically satisfying to the worker and family; and the ability to participate in family and social life. Therapists were advised to consider the patient in terms of former or potential jobs in relation to physical and psychological capacities. They used work assessment to test physical and mental capacity; work testing to estimate physical and mental capacity within simulated work conditions; and job analysis to estimate the demands of an occupation within its authentic work environment. For assessment to be of value, the therapists felt it must be:

—asked for by the doctor in charge of the patient;

—recognised by the medical profession as a considered and scientific report;

—accepted by employers and work-mates as a fair test of employability; and

—introduced at the right time in the patient's rehabilitation.

Very precise requirements were recorded for a range of tests—some in simulated work conditions, from those of a cognitive nature to others suited to agriculture, industry, or mining. Final work-testing was carried out over a full day sometimes within the hospital utility departments or at the patient's place of work.[110]

However, just as legislation often restricted occupational therapists being involved in resettlement, some medical authorities, too, held that opinion. Dr P. J. MacLeod, who was well respected for his guidance of occupational therapists at Gleneagles and Bridge of Earn, felt strongly, for example, that 'occupational therapy should not start to take part in vocational training: the function of an occupational therapist is a therapeutic one, and not concerned with resettlement. This should never be forgotten.'[111] Interestingly, at Bridge of

Earn simulated working conditions of a coal face were developed very early, as Mary Loggie, who was employed there soon after the war, recalls. She went on to work at the Thistle Foundation in Edinburgh, which was a 'village' settlement for severely disabled people where they could live with their families.[112]

In contrast to MacLeod, orthopaedic surgeon Mercer predicted a future for occupational therapy in industry working in large firms like Vauxhall Motors where there were 12,000 employees, of whom 9,000 were 'manual workers subject to all the trauma of heavy industry.' That, he felt, would be 'quite a step forward from the occupational therapy prescription of ten years ago which was homeopathic in comparison.'[113] 'At Vauxhall Motors factory at Luton, and Austin Motors in Birmingham, production line work was adapted to provide remedial work as an integral part of rehabilitation.'[114] Many occupational therapists would have agreed with Mercer and with Harris, who suggested that the final assessment of rehabilitation, resettlement, and reintegration into the community should be in the hands of occupational therapists.

Harris pointed to the anomaly of:

*In the case of a miner with a fractured spine, the occupational therapist does not, at present, play a major role, though in the case of a hemiplegic housewife the final assessment of rehabilitation and resettlement possibilities is almost entirely in the hands of the occupational therapist.*

He added, how, in case of the housewife, while rehabilitation may present no problem, to resettle her and 'get the necessary household alterations carried out so that she may cope with her life as a housewife again' was a different matter. Legislation was at fault in that local authorities whilst empowered to do welfare work were not yet directed to do it. Their method of handling finances that involved capital expenditure was also unfortunate. That resulted in situations in which a local authority would 'not pay one sum of £25 so that a disabled housewife may have the necessary alterations made to her home but will continue, almost indefinitely, to pay £3 a week for a home help for her.'[115]

Sym, who would certainly have agreed with Harris, commented on the need for occupational therapists to carry out assessment of patients' work capacity not only for medical records but also as a basis for recommendations to the Ministry of Labour. She included in the 'work' category, the housewife in her kitchen, and other requirements of daily living.[116] The government, too, commented on the economic problem of the disabled housewife, obviously prompted by Cooksey, their advisor on such matters. They found 'surprising' the fact that 'very little had been done until recently to help the permanently disabled housewife resume her work':

*...for in a sense house wifery is the largest 'industry' in the country (although it is not employment within the meaning of the Disabled Persons (Employment) Act, 1944) and the housewife has little choice of other work. Housewifery is also of great importance since the health and efficiency of school children and wage earners depend so much on a well run and happy home.[117]*

The government's first approach to the problem was to provide welfare services such as home helps, day and residential nurseries and 'meals on wheels' to relieve the disabled housewife of difficult or impossible duties. The modern approach, it was argued, though in its early stages, was for occupational therapists to assist the housewife to regain her independence by suitable modification of tools and home layout. Recognition was given to the development of domestic sections within their departments for the assessment of residual function and vocational training. After assessment occupational therapists visited the disabled housewife's home, to determine what adaptation was necessary. Domestic appliances required were bought in the normal way and adapted in an occupational therapy department. Some Local Authorities were beginning to use their powers under the National Assistance Act, 1948, to make necessary structural alterations in the home.[118] In some parts of England, such as Surrey, Buckinghamshire, and Liverpool, occupational therapists were beginning to develop domiciliary services to disabled people in their own homes to help them be more independent with activities of daily living and to improve their quality of life.[119]

With regard to people, post stroke, Droller believed some effort to provide special dwellings or suitable hostel accommodation was required for those who could live outside a hospital. Additionally the planning of special hemiplegic units for their rehabilitation was necessary because some restoration of function could be expected even in seemingly hopeless cases for up to two years. For the last stages of rehabilitation, Droller said, group activities and daily home activities were most important. Thornely, the occupational therapist who worked with him, provided basic training in dressing and assisting people to live at home, with the help of simple gadgets if need be.[120]

Apart from domestic duties, resettlement began to include engagement in paid work in a domestic environment. In the early 1950s, in some places, occupational therapists began to provide this to homebound people in the community. Patients were paid the profit on any of the goods made by them and returned to the occupational therapist for sale. Some people criticised the policy, but the much abused 'profit motive' may have benefited a patient's health. Earning a little 'pin-money' was seen to make an enormous difference to many, enabling them to have some small comfort, as well as providing incentive to carry on with the work. The types of patients and the source of referral varied. General practitioners, hospital almoners, Ministry of Pensions, education authority, the University settlement, the Council of Social Services, and dispensaries such as the Royal Victoria Dispensary all referred patients to the scheme. Some patients had permanent or deteriorating conditions such as rheumatoid arthritis or disseminated (multiple) sclerosis, others were referred 'pre-hospital', and yet others had been discharged from hospital prematurely because of the shortage of beds.[121]

Whilst few homebound patients could carry out work on a production basis, there were many who could work for short periods. The Ministry of National Insurance allowed such people to supplement their benefits, but only minimally, which acted as discouragement. Sommerville suggested there was a wide field for providing some form of diversional occupational therapy for homebound patients. Although Local Authorities had permissive power to provide such facilities he believed that a Statutory obligation was required to be laid upon them to organise work for the home-bound disabled.[122]

With the field of mental health, at the North Wales Hospital in Denbigh, as elsewhere, the introduction of new drugs such as Largactil and Stelazine from 1953 made it more possible for patients with psychiatric problems to re-enter the community. That was particularly the case when the new medications were coupled with newer psychological and rehabilitation techniques. A more enlightened attitude 'enabled the gradual discharge of patients many of whom were suffering from the effects of institutionalisation more than mental illness.' That change of attitude was typified by the unlocking of the majority of the wards and villas.[123] Patients were still employed in all departments, with the kitchen having as many as 40 patients supplementing the staff. 'Unfortunately, in 1958, the farm, which throughout the history of the hospital had provided much of the patients' dietary needs and also offered suitable employment, was sold.' Recreation and entertainment continued to play an important part in the treatment. A sports and recreation officer was appointed.[124]

**Figure 2.7.12: Printing Department of North Wales Hospital in Denbigh**[125]
*Photograph courtesy of Clwyd Wynne*

# Palliative treatment and health promotion

Although the terms palliative treatment and health promotion were not in common use during the late 1940s and 1950s, these current descriptors suggest the intent of some aspects of occupational therapy at that time. *Palliative* refers not only to treatment with dying patients, but to intervention which is not curative  but will make patients feel better, mentally or physically, or the situation they are in easier to cope with. *Health promotion* encompasses not only the prevention of illness but also positive initiatives that have the potential to enhance health and well being. Together, they form a large part of programmes that would now be broadly grouped under the term 'quality of life'.

In many ways what was called 'general treatment' was of that ilk. *General treatment* was the preferred term for occupation used to prevent 'introspection, anxiety, boredom and other ill effects of prolonged hospitalisation, of loss of morale and loss of work habit.'

It was also used for progressive treatment programmes to 'prepare patients for return to work after debilitating illness and long periods of curtailed activity'.[126]

It was heartening to discover, in a 1954 issue of *Occupational Therapy*, an article detailing a preventive/health promotion approach to occupation with an elderly population. It was written by the medical officer and personnel manager of the Rubery Owen Engineering Co. Ltd at Darlaston in Staffordshire. Whilst it does not appear that an occupational therapist was involved in the process the article detailed, the fact that it was published implies some acceptance of the concept at a professional level. It aimed at providing men aged 70–86 years with 'essential work' suited to their mental and physical capabilities. It was based on an understanding that 'a man's conception of what is useful is doing something that is associated with the industry in which he may have spent his whole life.' Pay was, as is usual in an engineering industry, based on degree of skill. The need for time out or other adjustments was dealt with practically and empathetically.[127] Programmes with similar aims are probably needed nowadays.

When Walter Mercer, Professor of Orthopaedic Surgery at the University of Edinburgh, addressed the future of occupational therapy in the orthopaedic field, he did so by responding to questions put by the secretary when she invited him to the SAOT Annual General Meeting of 1951.[128] Contrary to the remediation directions discussed earlier, Mercer did not believe that occupational therapy was necessary in an acute orthopaedic ward, such as at the Royal Infirmary, Edinburgh, as stays were short. Nor did he think occupational therapy clinics were needed for outpatients. He did believe it had a place in the treatment of carefully selected patients. These might be found in chronic hospitals, such as sanatoria, the convalescent home, the Astley Ainslie Hospital, in a projected long-term hospital, and for the homebound even though that was 'fraught with many problems, legal, ethical, personal, and, not least of all, economic.' He also thought that occupational therapists would be of immense value to the Ministry of Labour by assessing long term patients' mental and physical abilities, and for laying the foundations of a new life for the disabled.[129] Those ideas suggest that at least one expert saw occupational therapy as having more value in helping people with health problems to improve their quality of life, a health promotion approach, than using occupation as exercise to improve specific disorder.

The rather negative responses to occupational therapy by medical experts in a position of authority, such as Mercer, must have been disappointing. He did, however, finish on a more positive and creative note, which contained some consideration for social preventive health initiatives in the future. Stimulated by a Dr Herford's letter to the Lancet, he had recognised that many people were occupationally dissatisfied. He proposed the establishment of well-equipped community centres under the care of experts where skills might be learned or practised, and the injured or sick, during convalescence, might continue what they had learnt in occupational therapy:

> *Stimulated on a national basis with strong community support, these centres might go far to restoring the sense of creative activity of the old craftsman, and assuage the unrest produced by repetitive work at dull routine jobs or semi-automatic machines—a factor of undoubted importance in producing industrial neurosis.*[130]

# Care of the elderly

Whilst care and treatment for older people is discussed in this section, no suggestion is made that it was not rehabilitative also. Indeed, it spans many aspects of practice. Specific geriatric care had been increasing since 1940. Residential or day hospitals and homes for the aged were available, and for some elderly who lived in their own homes there was local authority community care. Some attended rehabilitation centres, workshops or clubs, providing the journeys were possible or travelling provision was arranged.[131]

Dr L.Z. Cosin, Clinical Director of the Cowley Road Hospital, Oxford, was instrumental in raising awareness of the needs of the aged. He worried that while the quantity of old age pensioners had increased rapidly, the quality of their lives seemed to be deteriorating.[132] He explained that the increasing number of people reaching the age of sixty had revealed problems in the country's sociological fabric. The labour shortages of the war years had partially concealed the problem of a rapidly ageing population; a diminishing labour force would have to support a much larger population in the higher age groups and for a longer time.[133]

The British Medical Association reporting on the care and treatment of the elderly and infirm in 1947 recommended that Geriatric Units should be set up as part of General Hospitals. They would replace Chronic Sick Hospitals, which provided custodial care and the inevitability of total disability, and which were without appropriate facilities for rehabilitation. The function of Geriatric Units was to treat elderly patients as soon as possible in the natural history of their disease so that they were able to return to the family group or community, and not become psychologically isolated within an institution. Although many of the newly established Units succeeded in introducing modern methods of treatment and of rehabilitation, in many parts of the country they grappled with the problem of the 'chronic sick.' Cosin aptly described that term as 'an unfortunate euphemism which has concealed much obscure thought, confused philosophy, and sheer medical neglect.'[134]

Cosin raised the notion of social medicine, which still remains, in practice, on the backburner, but which is pertinent to today's problems and the future directions of occupational therapy. He said of social medicine, with reference to the special geriatric units, that the aim was to combine 'preventive medicine, medical treatment, and physical, psychological and social rehabilitation.' He advocated the replacement of the medical approach by what he called the 'Dynamic Quadruple Assessment', which had been used in a Geriatric Unit at Orsett Hospital in Essex in 1947 and 1948 under the Poor Law Acts. He chose the word 'dynamic' because any longitudinal study of or solution to 'the more than one problem' the elderly sick so often faced, must be varied. The Assessment could be subdivided into: the pathological, the psychological and the sociological to ascertain problems and resultant solutions in terms of medical treatment, helpful actions and therapeutic techniques. Following those a fourth assessment of the 'residual physical disability' provided direction for physical rehabilitation and compensatory requirements.[135]

In the early trial at Orsett Hospital about one-third of the patients over 60 years of age did not recover from their acute medical conditions. Of the remaining two-thirds over 60% were discharged and only 2% became permanently bedfast. The others whose social or physical problems prevented resettlement in the community, which was not always easy under the Poor Law, were termed Long Stay Residents. At Cowley Road, from 1950 to 1953 it was possible to extend the work; the tempo of rehabilitation and resettlement was increased with provision for adequate follow-up and continued care services after discharge. That called for 'the mobilisation of community resources and sharing the responsibility with the patient, the family group and the community.' A new initiative was the establishment of a Day Hospital.[136]

The Day Hospital in the Oxford Geriatric Unit aimed at maintenance of individual independence in the community whilst sharing responsibility with the family and the community for the frail elderly. It was housed in the occupational therapy department. There, patients were given a programme of activities consistent with their ability and disabilities, prescribed on an individual or group basis. Transport from and to their homes was provided by the Local Authority or volunteer Hospital Car Service. Cosin wrote that:

*The success of the Day Hospital within a Geriatric Unit depends upon the organizing ability and therapeutic approach of the occupational therapists. They cannot adopt the passive role advocated by some group psychotherapists; a more authoritarian approach is needed. When the larger Day Hospital we have planned is opened, it will be possible to arrange different organizational levels, some more permissive, some more hierarchical.*[137]

Margaret Mort was Cosin's Superintendent Occupational Therapist. She described the special problems in geriatrics as: more frequent occurrence of multiple disability; a slower rate of learning; long periods of unnecessary inactivity; loneliness and feelings of unwantedness; insecurity from loss of home surroundings; loss of self-respect with feelings of uselessness; and a lowering of standards. Mort differentiated between the psychological, physical and social cases, which she described as the main reasons for medical staff to prescribe occupational therapy. Despite the differentiation she explained how it was common for mental, physical and social problems to occur together. She used a wide range of occupations which fell into four main classifications: craftwork, self help, help to others, and social activities.[138]

**Figure 2.7.13: Elderly lady practicing writing at Cowley Road Hospital**
*(Reproduced courtesy of Dorset House Archives, Oxford Brookes University)*

Despite all the energy that characterised the decade, there was, apparently, some perception of a slowing down in the provision of occupational therapy facilities in civilian hospitals. According to Mercer, the slowing down may have been due to: post-war apathy; the poor location or inadequacy of occupational therapy facilities; lack of funds; lack of medical supervisors; lack of qualified therapists; and lack of advertising about the nature, purpose and value of occupational therapy. In the latter regard he thought 'one of your good speakers should seek every opportunity to set forth and speak about Occupational Therapy, its sphere, its methods, and particularly what you hope to—indeed do—achieve when you get the opportunity.' He added, 'New legislation is necessary for any satisfactory development to take place, so an Occupational Therapy Service Bill might be framed at a suitable opportunity.' Another of his ideas was that lack of research was a problem. Indeed, within occupational therapy there was a woeful lack of carefully controlled research to prove its value.[139] That concern leads to the ongoing story of the development of research within the profession told by Irene Ilott.

# The Beginnings of a research ethic
## By Irene Ilott

An early occupational therapist advocate for research in Occupational Therapy discussed the importance of the formulation, testing and revision of theory, in relation to psychiatric practice. 'Systematised observation' could lead to 'the formulation of hypotheses which can then be tested.' This, in turn, could provide 'more adequate theory upon which to base our future practice.' E. Foulds, the author, proposed that occupational therapists, in order to ensure a future for the profession, should 'discontinue demonstrations of our practical use and devote more of our energies to the discovery of exactly why and to whom we are of use.' With a note of caution that we should not 'embark unaided upon ambitious research projects,' Foulds argued that a more fruitful approach might be 'a series of well planned and systematic observations which at a later date may be welded into a cohesive body of knowledge.' Even to go that far, she felt, required help and guidance from people experienced in research method and technique.[140]

Jones was one of the first to become practically involved in carefully controlled research to prove occupational therapy's value. The Council of AOT gave her a research fellowship following an anonymous gift of £1,000, which had been donated, specifically, for research. They accepted Jones' proposal of a survey of 4,115 patients treated at Farnham Park between late 1947 and the end of 1955. Both observation and analysis of patient's records were used, and the results provided the foundation for her book An Approach to Occupational Therapy published in 1960.[141]

Another early study of a very different kind, researched the clinical effectiveness of power tools. A twelve-month experiment investigating the remedial and psychological value of using portable power tools reported that the 'interim conclusions appear to be that they are of great benefit in helping to train injured hands' and have 'great psychological value in providing a "normal" workaday atmosphere.'[142]

Apart from those examples, other research papers published in Occupational Therapy in the 1950s were by medical experts. Perhaps because of the rarity of research by occupational therapists, it was celebrated. The following headline, from August 1955, is a case in point: 'University honour for a founder member of the Association.' The article stated that:

> The degree of Bachelor of Letters (B. Litt.) has been conferred upon Miss E. Mary Macdonald, Principal of Dorset House School, by the Ancient House of Congregation of the University of Oxford for her thesis entitled 'The development of certain therapeutic services, their inter-relationship and their place in the social framework. The effect of these factors on recruitment, selection and training of personnel.' The Association offers very sincere congratulations upon this outstanding success. This is the first research thesis related to occupational therapy that has been accepted by a British University for a degree.[143]

Research issues were to become major concerns of the profession, although its implementation was slow to develop. As Professor Dott foretold at the first WFOT Congress: 'occupational therapy is a potent tool of research as well as an immediate benefit to the sufferer and his circle and community.'[144] The topic will be revisited in subsequent chapters.

---

**In summary**, in this chapter, the development of occupational therapy in the post war years has been told, following the establishment of the National Health Service. The Service assisted occupational therapy to develop more extensive and wide ranging programmes, so the 1950s proved to be a period of development and growth for the profession both in practice and in education. Whilst the predominance of rehabilitation straight after the war was aimed at getting people back into the workforce, later the importance of domestic work and independence for those with residual disability was recognised. Those latter themes which were to become dominant for many future decades are picked up in the next chapter.

[1]Bramwell DB. International Congress of Occupational Therapy. Scottish Journal of Occupational Therapy 1953; 14: 6.
[2]O'Sullivan ENM. Textbook of Occupational therapy: With Chief Reference to Psychologcal Medicine. London: H. K. Lewis, 1955; 15.
[3]The Chairman was Sir William Beveridge of the London School of Economics.
[4]Macdonald EM. World-Wide Conquests of Disabilities: The History, Development and Present Functions of the Remedial Services. London: Bailliere Tindall, 1981.
[5]Hepworth J. The Rehabilitation of the Disabled Worker in Heavy Industry. Occupational Therapy 1954; 17(1): 12–14.
[6]Report of the Standing Committee on Disabled Persons:. London: HM Stationary Office, 1946.
[7]Casson E. Occupational Therapy in Great Britain. Journal of the American Medical Women's Association 1947, 2 (6) 303–305
[8]It should be noted that in 1948, the title 'medical auxiliary' caused concern, but it was used to designate those persons (other than nurses) who assist medical practitioners in the investigation and treatment of disease by virtue of some special skill acquired through a recognised course of training.

[9]Macdonald. World-wide Conquests of Disabilities....

[10]Macdonald. World-wide Conquests of Disabilities....; 200–201.

[11]Report of the Council for the Period July to September. Scottish Journal of Occupational Therapy 1951; 7: 2.

[12]Jay P, Mendez A, Monteath HG. The Diamond Jubilee of the Professional Association, 1932–1992: An Historical Review. British Journal of Occupational Therapy 1991; 55 (7): 252-256.

[13]Report of the Council for the Period April to June, 1953. Scottish Journal of Occupational Therapy 1953; 14: 3.

[14]A.O.T. Proceedings of the First Conference of the Association of Occupational Therapists. London: June 15th and 16th, 1951.

[15]Mendez A. A Chronicle of the World Federation of Occupational Therapists. The First Thirty Years:1952–1982. Jerusalem. WFOT. 1986.

[16]Dott Prof N. Closing Address. Proceedings of the First International Congress. Edinburgh: WFOT, 1954.

[17]Mendez A. A Chronicle of the World Federation of Occupational Therapists....

[18]Paterson CF. The First International Congress of the World Federation of Occupational Therapists, Edinburgh, 1954. British Journal of Occupational Therapy 1994; 57 (4); 116–120.

[19]Dott Prof N. Valedictory Address. Proceedings of the First International Congress. Edinburgh: WFOT, 1954.

[20]See, for example: Jones MS. Uses of Occupational Therapy in Physical Medicine. Reprinted from Lancet 1951; 18th August: 308.

[21]Association of Occupational Therapists. Reprinted from The Lancet 1951; (further details of date unknown): 1.

[22]Association of Occupational Therapists. Reprinted from The Lancet 1951...; 1.

[23]The Scottish Association of Occupational Therapists. Scottish Journal of Occupational Therapy 1957; 30: 39-43.

[24]Bobath K, Bobath B. An assessment of the motor handicap of children with cerebral palsy and of their response to treatment. Occupational Therapy 1958; 21 (5): 19–34.

[25]Bobath B, Finnie N. Re-education of movement patterns for everyday life in the treatment of cerebral palsy. Occupational Therapy 1958; 21 (6): 23–30.

[26]Moncrieff A. Cerebral palsy today. Occupational Therapy 1958; 21 (5): 13–17.

[27]Woods GE. Cerebral Palsy in Childhood. Bristol: John Wright, 1958.

[28]Henderson DK. Reflections on Criminal Conduct and its Treatment. Scottish Journal of Occupational Therapy 1953; 14: 8–20.

[29]Baker KVW. Beauty culture in a mental hospital. Occupational Therapy 1958; 21 (5): 36–39.

[30]Smith-Rose M. The purpose and methods of teaching psychology to students in the professions allied to medicine with particular reference to Occupational Therapy. Occupational Therapy 1958; 21 (6): 30–35.

[31]Carstairs GM. Some new initiatives in occupational therapy. (Address: Ordinary General Meeting of the Association, May 1958. Occupational Therapy 1958; 21 (6): 14–19.

[32]Carstairs. Some new initiatives in occupational therapy....

[33]Occupational Therapy 1958; 21 (5); Occupational Therapy 1958; 21 (6); Scottish Journal of Occupational Therapy 1953; 14.

[34]Verinder & Sons Ltd. Occupational Therapy 1954; 17(4): xix.

[35]Questions in the House. Occupational Therapy 1958; 21 (6): 22.

[36]This statistic is as quoted in: Services for the Disabled. London: Her Majesty's

Stationary Office, 1955; 13–14.

[37]Harris R. Resettlement and Rehabilitation of the Physically Handicapped Patient. (Northern Region Conference Report: Rehabilitation and Resettlement. 13–15 January 1956) In: Regional News Occupational Therapy 1956; 19 (2). 65–66.

[38]Association of Occupational Therapists. Reprinted from Lancet (date details unknown) 1951.

[39]Association of Occupational Therapists. Annual Report. 1948: 4.

[40]Association of Occupational Therapists. Annual Report. 1949: 10.

[41]Association of Occupational Therapists Lancet....; 4.

[42] Association of Occupational Therapists. Syllabus and Regulations for the Diploma; 2, 35.

[43] Association of Occupational Therapists. Lancet....; 3.

[44] Association of Occupational Therapists. Lancet....; 8–9.

[45] Association of Occupational Therapists. Lancet....; 5,10–11.

[46]Association of Occupational Therapists. Lancet....; 13-17.

[47]Association of Occupational Therapists. Lancet....; 21-22.

[48]Cited in: Macdonald. World-wide Conquests of Disabilities....; 155.

[49]Sommerville J. Medical Rehabilitation. Scottish Journal of Occupational Therapy 1954; March: 30–43.

[50]Macdonald. World-wide Conquests of Disabilities....; 155.

[51]Standing Committee on the Rehabilitation and Resettlement of Disabled Persons. Services for the Disabled. London: Her Majesty's Stationary Office, 1955; 2–3.

[52]Ling TM, O'Malley CJS, eds. Rehabilitation After Illness and Accident. London: Bailliere, Tindall and Cox, 1958; 98–99.

[53] Sym D. Recent Trends In Rehabilitation. Scottish Journal of Occupational Therapy 1957;December: 31–36.

[54]Macdonald. World-wide Conquests of Disabilities....; 155.

[55]Pullen I, Hume C. Rehabilitation in Psychiatry. An Introductory Handbook. Edinburgh: Churchill Livingstone, 1986.

[56]Regional Group Reports. Occupational Therapy 1951; 14(1): 53.

[57]Sommerville J. Medical Rehabilitation. Scottish Journal of Occupational Therapy 1954; March: 30–43.

[58]Sommerville. Medical Rehabilitation....

[59]Sommerville. Medical Rehabilitation....

[60]Harris. Resettlement and Rehabilitation of the Physically Handicapped Patient....

[61]Northern Region Conference Report: Rehabilitation and Resettlement. 13–15 January 1956. In: Regional News Occupational Therapy 1956; 19 (2): 65–66.

[62]A Report on the Rehabilitation Post-Graduate Study Course, 2-6 May, 1955. Occupational Therapy 1955; 18 (4): 169–174.

[63] Allbon LG. Refresher Course: The Medical Rehabilitation Centre, Camden Road. Occupational Therapy 1958; 21 (6): 21.

[64]Standing Committee on the Rehabilitation and Resettlement...Services for the Disabled....; 13.

[65]Macdonald. World-wide Conquests of Disabilities....; 157–9.

[66]A booklet about this was published by Arts & Crafts (Doncaster) Ltd. (Now out of print)

[67]Lock SJ. Printing Adapted. British Journal of Physical Medicine 1956. (Presented as a paper at the WFOT Conference in Copenhagen in 1956. Later published by the Association of Occupational Therapists and revised in 1980)

[68] Sym D. Recent Trends In Rehabilitation....

[69]Allbon LG. The Measurement of Joint Angle. Occupational Therapy 1955; 18 (4): 141–145.

[70]Registrar General, 1952.

[71]Droller H. Deaths and Survivals of Elderly Patients Suffering from Hemiplegia. Occupational Therapy 1956; 19 (3): 85–86. (Reprinted by kind permission of the Author and The Medical Press.)

[72]Droller H. The Out-patient. Treatment of Hemiplegic Patients: Experience of a Follow-up Clinic. Occupational Therapy 1956; 19 November: 125–132.

[73]Heywood A. Occupational Therapy in a Geriatric Hospital. Occupational Therapy 1954; August: 104–107.

[74] Levin A. K. An outline of the treatment of a hemiplegic patient by occupational therapy. Scottish Journal of Occupational Therapy 1953; December: 20–22.

[75] Levin. An outline of the treatment of a hemiplegic patient by occupational therapy....

[76] Gillingham FJ. Discussion Following Lecture: Spontaneous Intra-Cranial Haemorrhage. Scottish Journal of Occupational Therapy 1953; December: 22.

[77] Fitch V. Occupational Therapy in a Rheumatic Unit. Scottish Journal of Occupational Therapy 1951; June: 8–10.

[78] Wallace AB. The occupational therapist in plastic surgery. Scottish Journal of Occupational Therapy 1950; September: (page unknown).

[79] Wallace AB. The occupational therapist in plastic surgery....

[80]Wallace AB. The Rehabilitation Of The Burned. Occupational Therapy 1955; (18) 1: 20–26. (Reprinted by permission of the Editor of Rehabilitation.)

[81]Wynn-Parry CB. Electromyography. Occupational Therapy 1954; 17(3): 86-93.

[82]Swan D, Jay P, Mendez A. Obituary: Natalie Barr (née Smythe), MBE, FCOT. 1910-1993. British Journal of Occupational Therapy 1993; 56(5): 189–190.

[83]Waterston J. Table of Occupations for Children of Different Age Groups. Scottish Journal of Occupational Therapy 1951; June: 18.

[84]Waterston J. Table of Occupations for Children....

[85]Howells JG, Cooke DK. The practice of occupational therapy in child psychiatry. Occupational Therapy 1956; (19) August: 113–116.

[86]Howells JG. Occupational Therapy 1951; 14: 250.

[87]Birnie T. Occupational Therapy In Child Guidance. Scottish Journal of Occupational Therapy 1951; December: 14–16

[88]Cooksey FS. Resettlement of the Physically Handicapped. (A Report on the Rehabilitation Post-Graduate Study Course, 2-6 May, 1955) Occupational Therapy 1955; 18 (4): 169–174.

[89]Jones MS. Uses of Occupational Therapy in Physical Medicine. Reprinted from Lancet 1951; 18th August: 308.

[90]Jones. Uses of Occupational Therapy in Physical Medicine....

[91]Jones. Uses of Occupational Therapy in Physical Medicine....

[92]Jones. Uses of Occupational Therapy in Physical Medicine....

[93]Jones. Uses of Occupational Therapy in Physical Medicine....

[94]Jay PE. Personal comment to author. 2001.

[95] Murray WA. Report of a talk on tuberculosis and occupational therapy. Scottish Journal of Occupational Therapy 1952; September: 4.

[96] Johns JA. Psychological Aspects Of Physical Disability In A Displaced Persons Camp. Scottish Journal of Occupational Therapy 1957; December: 27–31.

[97]Standing Committee on the Rehabilitation and Resettlement...Services for the Disabled....; 13.

[98] Sym D. Recent Trends In Rehabilitation. Scottish Journal of Occupational Therapy

1957;December: 31–36.

[99]Sommerville J. Medical Rehabilitation. Scottish Journal of Occupational Therapy 1954; March: 30–43.

[100]Jay P, Mendez A. Obituary: Griselda Patricia MacCaul, MBE, FAOT. British Journal of Occupational Therapy 1997; 60(1): 42.

[101]Howie PM. A Pilot study of Disabled Housewives in their Kitchen. London: Disabled Living Activities Group. 1967.

[102]Cooksey FS. Rehabilitation of the Disabled Housewife. Occupational Therapy 1954; 17 (4): 133–144. (Reprinted with permission from Annals of Physical Medicine 1952; 1(4).)

[103]Standing Committee on the Rehabilitation and Resettlement...Services for the Disabled....; 13.

[104]Hardy G. Hand appliances to aid limited function. Scottish Journal of Occupational Therapy 1951; (6) September: 6–7.

[105]Harris R. Resettlement and Rehabilitation of the Physically Handicapped Patient. Northern Region Conference Report....

[106]A Report on the Rehabilitation Post-Graduate Study Course, 2-6 May, 1955. Occupational Therapy 1955; 18 (4): 169–174.

[107]A Report on the Rehabilitation Post-Graduate Study Course, 2-6 May, 1955....

[108]A Report on the Rehabilitation Post-Graduate Study Course, 2-6 May, 1955....

[109]JW. A Model Coal Face Aids Rehabilitation. Scottish Journal of Occupational Therapy 1959; September: 17.

[110]Waterston J. Work Assessment, Work Testing and Job Analysis. Scottish Journal of Occupational Therapy 1959; December: 34–45.

[111]Macleod PJ. Therapeutic Occupations. Scottish Journal of Occupational Therapy 1950 ; December: 16–17. Occupational therapy was one of Dr Macleod's main interests. In planning the rehabilitation for the Fitness Centre he saw great possibilities for occupational therapy from early ward work to the later stages of rehabilitation to develop his belief in the power of work to restore confidence and prove to patients their ability to recover.

[112]Smith M. Notes from retired OTs' focus group. July, 1999.

[113]Mercer W. The future of Occupational Therapy in the Orthopaedic Field. Scottish Journal of Occupational Therapy 1951; March: 6–12.

[114]Jay P, Jones MS. An Approach to Occupational Therapy, 3rd ed. London: Butterworths, 1977: 58.

[115]Harris R. Resettlement and Rehabilitation of the Physically Handicapped Patient. Northern Region Conference Report....

[116]Sym D. Recent Trends In Rehabilitation. Scottish Journal of Occupational Therapy 1957;December: 31–36.

[117]Standing Committee on the Rehabilitation and Resettlement....Services for the Disabled....; 13.

[118]Standing Committee on the Rehabilitation and Resettlement....Services for the Disabled....; 13.

[119]Jay, Mendez, & Monteath. The Diamond Jubilee of the Professional Association, 1932–1992...

[120]Droller H. Deaths and Survivals of Elderly Patients Suffering from Hemiplegia. Occupational Therapy 1956; 19 (3): 85–86. (Reprinted by kind permission of the Author and The Medical Press.)

[121]Badenoch C. Occupational Therapy with the Homebound. Scottish Journal of Occupational Therapy 1951; December: 17–18.

[122]Sommerville J. Medical Rehabilitation. Scottish Journal of Occupational Therapy 1954;

March: 30–43

[123]Wynne C. The North Wales Hospital, Denbigh, 1842–1955. Denbigh: Gee & Son, 1995; 30.

[124]Wynne. The North Wales Hospital.…; 31.

[125]Wynne. The North Wales Hospital. . . ; 127

[126]Occupational Therapy.…; 23–25.

[127]The Sons of Rest Workshop. Occupational Therapy 1954; 17(1): 7–9.

[128] Mercer W. The future of Occupational Therapy in the Orthopaedic Field. Scottish Journal of Occupational Therapy 1951; March: 6–12.

[129] Mercer. The future of Occupational Therapy.…

[130]Mercer. The future of Occupational Therapy.…

[131]Macdonald. World-wide Conquests of Disabilities.…; 138–139.

[132]Macdonald. World-wide Conquests of Disabilities.…; 138–139.

[133]Cosin LZ. The place of the day hospital in the geriatric unit. Occupational Therapy 1956; 1: 13–22. (Reprinted in Occupational Therapy by kind permission of the Author and International Journal of Social Psychiatry.)

[134]Cosin . The place of the day hospital.…

[135]Cosin . The place of the day hospital.…

[136]Cosin . The place of the day hospital.…

[137]Cosin . The place of the day hospital.…

[138]Mort M. Occupational Therapy in a Geriatric Unit. Journal for Industrial Nurses. c. 1952–53: 132–141.

[139] Mercer. The future of Occupational Therapy.…

[140]Foulds E. Systematic observation in psychiatric occupational therapy. Occupational Therapy 1953; 16(4); 197–203.

[141]Jones MS. An Approach to Occupational Therapy. 2nd ed. London: Butterworths, 1964: ix, xi.

[142]No Author given. Results of a twelve month experiment. Occupational Therapy 1957; (20) 3: 36.

[143]Association Notices and Reports. University honour for a founder member of the Association. Occupational Therapy 1955; (18)3: 128.

[144]Dott Prof N. Valedictory Address. Proceedings of the First International Congress. Edinburgh: WFOT, 1954.

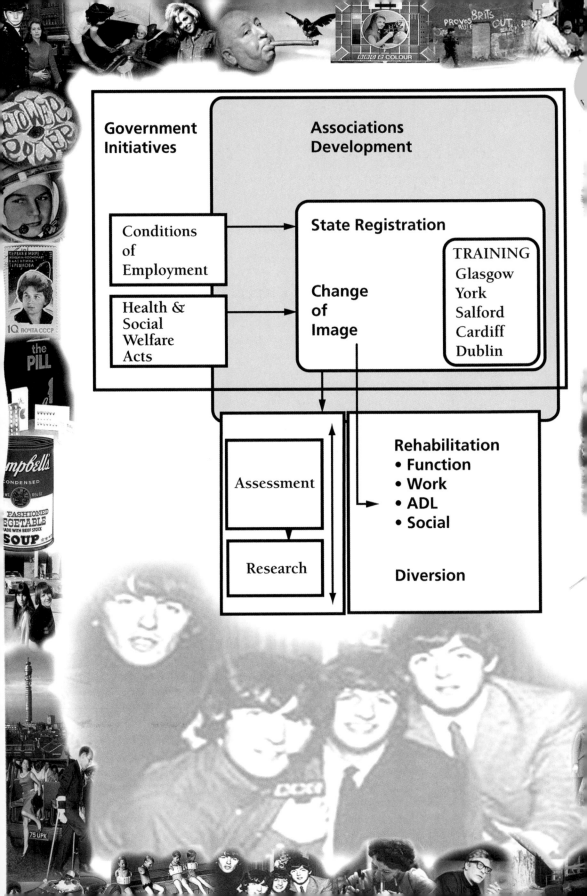

**Government
Initiatives**

**Associations
Development**

Conditions
of
Employment

Health &
Social
Welfare
Acts

**State Registration**

**Change
of
Image**

TRAINING
Glasgow
York
Salford
Cardiff
Dublin

Assessment

Research

**Rehabilitation**
• **Function**
• **Work**
• **ADL**
• **Social**

**Diversion**

# Chapter 8

# Activities of Daily Living: Towards Independence

## Contents

By Irene Ilott

The 1960s proved to be a time of both consolidation and diversification for occupational therapy. An ongoing debate about the primary concerns of the profession was central and noisy and, as will become clear in the chapter, resonated across various aspects of professional life. It was a watershed era in which the apparent preoccupation of the pioneers with creative aspects of occupation as therapy was seriously challenged by a movement towards functional activities and independence. The latter had been growing slowly as a result of attempts to overcome the individual devastation of war, and developed further partly because of a new ethos concerned with social health, social justice and rights of people with disability. Additionally medical advances, activated by the challenges posed by war injuries, eventually led to decreased lengths of stay for patients in hospitals and, subsequently, less time for extensive rehabilitation programmes for the majority of patients. As a result, domestic and individual issues concerned with personal care came to the fore in hospital discharge planning. As part of professional consolidation the issue of assessment also became paramount; this led to thoughts that the training of occupational therapists should be upgraded, perhaps to degree level. In the same vein there were calls for postgraduate education opportunities.

One fascinating outcome of the developments taking place was a very obvious substitution of the word 'activity' for 'occupation'. Although activity had always been used in occupational therapy as part of normal language, the most commonly used term to describe occupational therapy interventions and treatment media in publications up to this time had been 'occupation'. Perhaps the major impetus for change was the adoption of the term 'activities of daily living' (ADL), along with 'activity analysis' which, although of earlier origin, became more formally recognised as part of the assessment movement. As 'activity' took over from 'occupation' there were calls for a change to the profession's name along with the need to redefine its essence, despite the fundamental change of descriptor being largely unconscious.

# Context of the times: The sixties swinging towards independence

Occupational therapy was not the only thing undergoing fundamental change with its practitioners questioning previous values. The period was characterised by the beginning of a dominant youth culture with vibrancy and excitement the order of the day. The questioning of previous values resulted in a revolution in music, the establishment of 'hippie cults', 'flower power', communes, peace protests like 'ban-the bomb', and free love, made so much simpler by the advent of 'the pill'. Even at the time the decade was described as the 'swinging sixties', despite a falling off of full employment. The world, for the young, centred on London and California where 'it' was all happening.

Against that background a subtle change began to emerge in health care and the dominant flavour of rehabilitation. Whilst in the late 1940s and 1950s it had aimed, mainly, at getting people back to work, during the 1960s it was not only occupational therapists for whom personal and domestic independence in ADL (PADL and DADL), domestic work, and relationships between people assumed greater importance. The emergence of the Disabled Living Foundation and the types of services offered at places like Mary Marlborough Lodge typified the changes. The decade was also characterised by the advent of group therapy and therapeutic communities in many psychiatric hospitals and day centres, like the Henderson Hospital. Despite that, remedial and industrial rehabilitation remained important, with large purpose built centres like The Wolfson Centre at the Atkinson Morley Hospital being established, along with industrial therapy for long term psychiatric patients such as was offered at Downshire Hospital, south of Belfast.

During the decade a number of government initiatives took place followed by important reports. The Porritt Report of 1962 reviewed the country's medical services, and recommended change. The Ministers of Health, Enoch Powell and subsequently, Kenneth Robinson, published first A Hospital Plan for England and Wales in 1962, and later, an account of *The Administrative Structure of Medical and Related Services in England and Wales* in 1967. In a Green Paper, Robinson put forward tentative proposals for public discussion and consultation concerning possible revision of the administrative structure of medical and related services of the NHS and Scottish Health Services. The paper, which was reviewed in Occupational Therapy by Mirrey and Johnson, suggested that in order to achieve a good standard of treatment in all areas it was important that:

*i. The services throughout the country be alert to create and exploit new opportunities in treatment and prevention. The large resources of capital and skilled manpower involved need to be organized and managed at high efficiency...*

*ii. Men and women in all parts of the service should be employed wisely and well, without duplication of tasks and without confusion of function. Staff for highly specialised work must not be wastefully disposed.[1]*

Additionally, to reduce the problem of co-ordination of different services, Area Boards of which there would be approximately 40–50 in England and Wales would replace Executive Councils, Hospital Authorities and Local Authorities.[2] Richard Crossman, who became the first Secretary of State for Health and Social Services, in the newly established Department of Health and Social Security, which replaced the Ministry of Health, succeeded Robinson as minister in 1968.[3]

Another government report of particular interest to occupational therapists concerned Health and Welfare Development of Community Care. The objectives of the services were defined as promoting health and well-being and forestalling illness and disability by preventive measures. Unfortunately, occupational therapy was not mentioned[4]. Published in 1963, by Dr J. B. Meredith Davies, and submitted to the Ministry of Health, the report contained individual plans about all Local Authority services in England and Wales for the next ten years. It was the first time that such detailed information had been available but, to obtain a complete picture, it was clear that study of hospital and general practitioner plans for the next 10–15 years was required as well. Four groups of people requiring community care were identified: mothers and young children, the elderly, the mentally disordered, and the physically handicapped with most of whom occupational therapy was intimately involved. It was seen as necessary that care in the community and medical care given by the general practitioner, be co-operative.[5] Meredith Davies was later to become a supporter of occupational therapy.

Government initiatives also included the Salmon, Seebohm, and Tunbridge Reports. The Salmon Committee was established in 1963 to advise on the structure, administrative functions, and training of Senior Nursing Staff in hospitals. The report, published in 1966, touched on the relationship between therapists and members of the nursing teams. In psychiatric hospitals it appears that occupational therapists were concerned that nurses would take over their role, particularly in industrial workshops and social therapy. They were also concerned that advertisements for occupational therapists were being channelled through matrons. On both counts they fought to stress their individual capabilities, responsibilities, and rights to separate management. At a meeting to discuss difficulties it was recommended that the following action should be taken:

*1. The Council of the Association should produce a carefully prepared statement of the role of the occupational therapist in industrial therapy and social therapy (including day centres), and her relationship with members of related activities, and discuss this at top level with the Ministry of Health.*

*2. The Association should also take up with the Ministry the conflicting statements [included in the report], instanced at this meeting.[6]*

In 1965 a Committee to review the organisation and responsibilities of the Local Authority Personal Social Services was set up. It was chaired by Mr Frederick Seebohm and was responsible to the Education, Housing and Health Ministries as well as to the Home Office. The Seebohm Committee Report, which was published in 1968, advised on what changes were desirable for an effective family service in England and Wales. It called for a unified social service department to be organised by each Local Authority and for close links to be forged between local health and social services in order to care adequately for physically and mentally handicapped children, adults, and the aged. It was argued, within the profession, that whilst therapists working within those departments could accept advice from social services experts they also required contact with the consumer's medical advisers.[7]

A critical summary of the Seebohm Report appeared in Occupational Therapy. It complained that from the point of view of occupational therapy, it left a considerable number of points needing clarification. Throughout its chapters the committee seemed hazy about 'the true nature and range of occupational therapy.' In the chapter on services for the physically handicapped, for example, there appeared to be confusion about whether occupational therapy was a paramedical or social welfare profession. The important question, about whether occupational therapists, under the new scheme, might be working under the control of someone other than a doctor, remained unanswered. Indeed, the report questioned whether a doctor must be the leader of any team in which he was a member. There were staffing and salary questions, as well as service ones that needed clarification relating to occupational therapists' positions in day and geriatric centres, child guidance clinics, and domiciliary work.

The Social Work Scotland Act 1968 set out legislation for the development of Social Work Departments in Scotland, bringing together the former welfare side of Health and Welfare and Children's Departments. The new town of East Kilbride implemented the Act ahead of the rest of Scotland when it was big enough to get borough status - hence it was the first integrated social work department in the UK. Social Work Departments were part of, and managed by, local authorities. The 'health' component transferred to local NHS control.[8]

In May 1968, a Central Health Services Council subcommittee on Rehabilitation was set up, chaired by Professor, Sir Ronald Tunbridge. Its terms of reference were to consider the future provision, organisation, and development of rehabilitation services in the National Health Service.[9] A sub-committee to consider the pursuits and inter-relationships of the remedial professions was formed in 1969 under the same chairmanship. The process included a review of career pathways, lack of research opportunities and low salary levels of therapists, and the limited experience of many doctors to provide appropriate prescription and supervision. Another central issue related to overlap between occupational therapy, physiotherapy and remedial gymnastics. The committee's report was published in 1972, and had far reaching effects, which will be discussed further in the next chapter.

Some of the committees and reports encompassed conditions of work. For example the Zuckerman Committee report placed emphasis on the creation of an integrated organisation and the provision of adequate career, promotion and training prospects. Sir Solly Zuckerman, was a scientific adviser to the government and Chairman of a Committee of the Department of Health and Social Security that produced a report in 1968 on career structure. The Zuckerman Committee, who founded much of their report on research of dietitians, orthoptists and radiographers, proposed four tiers of professional personnel: scientific officers; technical officers; technical assistants; and technical aides. The report stated that a staffing organisation was required at national or regional levels to provide adequate career promotion and training prospects for a profession's purposes, as well as for the efficient deployment of trained staff.[10]

In *Occupational Therapy* Mayne commented on the Zuckerman report, by observing that the proposed career structure would almost certainly have repercussions when the professions supplementary to medicine were considered, because it was obviously based on the scientific and technical classes in the Civil Service. The level of Technical Officer with three grades, basic, senior and chief, was likely to be the closest parallel for occupational therapists.[11] The Zuckerman enquiry would undoubtedly cause repercussions for the Whitley Councils which in the 1960s were not thought to be satisfactory, as many salary scales appeared very low.

# The Associations

In 1960 the Professions Supplementary to Medicine (PSM) Act was passed, and a Council of Professions Supplementary to Medicine (CPSM) was set up the following year. That provided registration of members, and established boards and disciplinary committees for each profession. The Council and the Boards were not responsible for protecting professional interests, but for protection of the public, training standards and recognition of training centres. The Board gave approval of training institutions, courses, qualifications, registration and supervision of professional conduct for occupational therapists intending to work for the NHS, while keeping the Privy Council informed of considerations and intended decisions.[12]

Prior to the Professions Supplementary to Medicine Bill becoming an Act, all eight professions involved were each asked to nominate two representatives', to negotiate the terms of the new structure with the then Ministry of Health. Mary Macdonald and Barbara Stow were the AOT representatives. Joint Council was represented by its President, Doris Sym. The negotiations were lengthy and at times delicate and challenging, in order to ensure that the professions were treated fairly. Once the Occupational Therapists Board was set up under the Act all three occupational therapy representatives were elected members and Macdonald became the first chairman. The Annual Report of 1960 resonated with the jubilant statement, 'We are now "State Registered" and the years of protracted negotiations are behind us.' Registration did not, in reality, become fact until 1963, and on 1 October 1964 it became compulsory for NHS employees[13], and some time later for occupational therapists working in Social Services.

There remained an acute shortage of occupational therapists. The membership totalled 2358, plus 46 technical instructors, but a questionnaire sent to all hospital management committees and teaching hospitals had ascertained that towards the end of 1960 there were 655 vacant posts in the NHS. Additionally 436 unqualified personnel were employed because of the shortage. It was thought that unsatisfactory salary scales may be one cause of the shortage, so Lord Amulree, the President of the AOT met with the Under secretary at the Ministry of Health to discuss the dissatisfaction felt with Whitley Council negotiations.[14] Other action taken included the publication and distribution of a leaflet *A Career with a Future* in 1960, and five years later this was augmented by *OT Today* and *It Depends on You*.

**Figure 2.8.1:** **An illustration from *A Career with a Future***

From 28 January 1962, all those taking the Diploma examinations were required to sign a statement that they were aware of the Code of Ethics and Rules of Conduct drawn up in the previous year by the Joint Council and governing the conduct of both Associations. This was a prerequisite of taking the final examinations.

**Figure 2.8.2:** **Letter regarding Code of Ethics and Rules of Professional Conduct, 1961**

ASSOCIATION OF OCCUPATIONAL THERAPISTS

ALL COMMUNICATIONS TO BE
ADDRESSED TO THE SECRETARY

251, BROMPTON ROAD,
LONDON, S.W.3.

TELEPHONE: KENSINGTON 7458/9

Dear Member,

I am enclosing a Code of Ethics and Rules of Professional Conduct drawn up by the Joint Council of the Associations of Occupational Therapists in Great Britain, governing the practice of Occupational Therapy by members of the Association of Occupational Therapists and the Scottish Association of Occupational Therapists. The Council of this Association has adopted the Code and Rules, and has laid it down under Council Minute 7 of 10th November, 1961, that any breach of either the Code or the Rules will be held under Article 10 (D) of the Articles of Association to be an act, or practice, or conduct calculated to bring discredit on the Association, and the member concerned will be liable for the penalties for which Article 10 (D) provides. A copy of the Article is given overleaf.

The date of implementation is 28th January, 1962.

You will appreciate that it is essential that the Association should have recorded evidence that every member has received the Code and Rules, and is aware of the ruling by the Council of the Association which is quoted above. Will you therefore please sign and return the attached form of receipt immediately. A stamped addressed envelope is enclosed.

In future, all those who take the Diploma examination of the Association will be required to sign the Code of Ethics and Rules of Professional Conduct as a prerequisite for sitting for the final examination.

Yours sincerely,

Freda Sampson.

Chairman of the Association of Occupational Therapists
Vice-President of Joint Council of
Associations of Occupational Therapists in Great Britain.

For some time, the AOT, along with many occupational therapists, had felt the need for a central long-term plan. Occupational therapy had expanded and diversified to such an extent that a critical examination of the present state of development was called for to safeguard professional standards. Two surveys investigating psychological and physical fields of occupational therapy practice were conducted, followed by a special meeting of the Advisory Board, Council of AOT, the Board of Studies, and Principals of Training Schools in February 1963. On the recommendation of that meeting, the Council set up a Committee consisting of members of the Advisory Board and profession, chaired by Dr Francis Bach, 'to look into the basic problems with which AOT was faced.' Apart from Bach the members were Dr Bennett, Mr Birch, and six members of the profession: Winifred Hewstone, Wenona Keane, Grisel MacCaul, Mary Macdonald, Lynn Mirrey, and Barbara Stowe. Two co-opted specialists were Dr Brereton and Alicia Mendez.

The main findings in the Committee's report *Occupational Therapy, Present and Future (OT, Present and Future)* emphasised the changing role of occupational therapists. It called for a clear restatement of the aims and function of occupational therapy in the light of this changing role. The report suggested there was a need for re-orientation in practice and training; closer liaison with all allied workers; and use of industrial work as an important medium of treatment. To define the parameters of the scope and function of occupational therapy the following medical organisations were asked to express their opinion: Association of Industrial Medical Officers; British Association of Physical Medicine; British Orthopaedic Association; Medical Society for the Care of the Elderly; Royal College of Physicians; Royal College of Surgeons; and Society of Medical Officers of Health, along with the British Psychological Society and Royal Medico Psychological Association.

In terms of the scope and function of occupational therapy, it was recognised that there would be variations and differences according to the patients, their diagnosis, the place of treatment and the authorities under which treatment occurred. The need for treatment to be under medical direction was reinforced, which made it essential for doctors to understand the aims and functions of occupational therapy and be prepared to co-ordinate those services with others. Other differences were due to the availability of resources in departments; the approaches and standards of training schools; and adequate support from doctors and administrators.

In general, treatment responsibilities were to assist the recovery of patients from mental or physical illness, in co-operation with allied services. Training patients to use returning function or residual ability to gain maximum social and vocational re-adjustment achieved that aim. Re-adjustment was related to the patient's environment and mastery of practical functions and skills. It was dependent on 'equipment similar to that used in the home and workshop and on an overall "work atmosphere" in the department.' From referral on, activities related to each patient's 'life' situation, had to simultaneously fulfilll the aims of treatment. A smaller part of the work was with patients who had a specific need for diversion that must be satisfied 'realistically and without apology.' If necessary, occupational therapists were advised to enlist the help of experts in industrial and commercial subjects, languages, domestic science, and arts or crafts.

*OT, Present and Future* deemed that precise, regular and serial assessment was a necessary condition of treatment, because occupational therapists had to be able to relate their patients' ability to work, medical state, and social performance. It had to include: general level of ability; speed of performance; desire to work and general attitude to work; quality of relationships; understanding of capacities and limitations; degree of independence, and initiative, persistence and sociability. Before discharge, where resettlement was under consideration, the final assessment had to be realistic about plans for open or sheltered employment.

Prior knowledge of the demands of the home and work environment were seen as essential to those planning treatment and resettlement. Occupational therapists were expected to share such knowledge and to be able to advise on equipment or alterations needed in the home, alternative recreations or interests and social contact. An urgent need for research was recognised, particularly in the development of efficient methods of assessment, to be used 'as a basis for more precise application of treatment.' It was considered essential that occupational therapists 'become more conversant with the relevant areas of sociology, psychology and medical studies.'[15]

As a result of this report Council set up a Co-ordinating Committee of Dr Constance Owens, then Chairman of AOT Council, Naomi Duncan (later Fraser-Holland), Hewstone, MacCaul and Mendez. This, in turn, established eight Working Parties to enquire into issues related to the recommendations of OT, Present and Future. These considered equipment costs, designation of staff in departments, assessment and testing, treatment principles and trends, student selection procedures, post graduate courses and possible financial support, occupational therapists outside the health service, and recent graduates' views on the syllabus of training. The Co-ordinating Committee reported the findings of the Working Parties back to Council in 1968, and an Action Committee was set up to make urgent and practical suggestions for the implementation of the Co-ordinating Committees recommendations. Their suggestions, finalised in 1971, will be reported in the next chapter.

In line with many of these ideas were those of Rita Goble presented in an invited paper given at the 1968 Annual General Conference of the Association. She prefaced her paper by suggesting that the early pioneers 'were well aware that if occupational therapy was to survive, not merely as an institution but as a living and influential force,' it must be alert and recognise questions to which it could provide the answers. To do that it had to have a secure foundation, and she questioned that security:

> We refer to ourselves as a profession. However, if one considers that a profession must have a body of knowledge which is both identifiable and different from that of other professions, perhaps we could more appropriately be termed technocrats—who may be defined as persons conversant with the technicalities of a particular subject and skilled in the techniques or mechanical parts of an art, or, more simply, 'persons skilled in a practical art'.
>
> It is possible to argue that as occupational therapy is essentially a highly developed practical skill operating through another discipline such as medicine, we could be better defined in this way. However, to be called a technocrat casts certain aspersions upon our

*endeavours for it implies a certain narrowness of outlook and an ignorance of the broader issues at stake. But by calling ourselves 'professionals' do we immediately become more broad-minded?*

She added a challenge by arguing that the only effective way to ensure that the apprenticeship to becoming a profession was well served was for therapists 'to encourage the study, improve the practice and advance the knowledge of occupational therapy.'[16]

Demands were increasing on the Association to provide a wide range of services to the members. For example, probably as a result of the changing image of occupational therapists, there was interest in the design of new departments that would fit what was being done. At a Planning Day held in Leeds, it was agreed that AOT should make available information which 'would help members when they were asked, sometimes at short notice and with inadequate experience, to comment on plans and equipment lists for new departments. It was suggested that the Ministry Planning Note No. 9 in respect of occupational therapy departments, was in some respects now out-of-date and that revision of this should be the first priority.'[17]

In the middle of the decade, Jean Waterston, the then President, reported that Joint Council had begun preliminary discussions and investigations into the educational, financial and legal aspects of establishing a United Kingdom Association.[18] So it was that at the end of the 1960s as well as the start of them the Annual report carried a momentous statement:

*As a result of a referendum carried out by Joint Council, members of the AOT and SAOT, by an almost unanimous vote, have given a clear decision in favour of amalgamation in order to form a single professional association for the United Kingdom. The practical details are now under discussion between representatives of both Associations, particularly the legal, educational, and financial implications.*[19]

## The Fourth International Congress of WFOT

The mid-1960s was also the occasion for the United Kingdom to once again host an international conference. In 1966 the WFOT Council met in London in the week prior to its 4th International Congress which adopted the theme, *Through Youth to Age: Occupational Therapy Faces the Challenge.*

Owens, Chairman of the host Association, welcoming overseas colleagues to Congress, thanked the Congress Committee, centred in London under the able leadership of Barbara Stow, which was the focal point for organising it, and also the many other occupational therapists up and down the country, whose identity would never he revealed but who had worked with equal zeal. A programme of work and of play made up the structure of the Congress, but she explained 'as anyone who has been to a good Congress knows, once the programme goes into operation a Congress develops an entity of its own.'

*This entity is dynamic or stolid, gay or dreary, serious or frivolous, friendly or impersonal, according to the attitude and behaviour of the participants. Inevitably, since there are usually more participants drawn from home than from abroad, this entity reflects host rather than guest qualities.* [20]

Owens continued:

> *Professional enrichment is largely dependent upon effective interpersonal communication. Formal lectures and discussions, exhibitions and film shows are methods of communication which can be organised by a committee. A committee can also provide opportunity for informal contact and communication, but after this has been done the organisers' part is fulfilled and communication must be between individuals and between groups who come together because of their common interests. Visits to hospitals and social events arranged in conjunction with the Congress afford many openings for making new contacts. Let us cast away our traditional reserve and go out to make new friends in addition to enjoying the society of old ones.[21]*

A large exhibition was organised by the Congress Committee to run concurrently with the Congress Scientific programme which, true to its theme, progressed through papers grouped according to age groups. The topics provide an overview of interests at that time:

- **For children** topics included: congenital deformities, thalidomide, function, prosthetics, and psychosocial aspects; childhood autism; handicapped children, perceptual dysfunction; overt emotional disorders; and educational problems of physically or mentally handicapped children.
- **For adolescents** topics included: spina bifida; cerebral palsy; biochemistry and treatment of the subnormal; research into retardation; work; the Child Guidance Clinic; emotional disturbance; and tuberculosis.
- **For young adults** topics included: the psychiatric day hospital; pre-vocational services for psychiatric patients; pollicisation (surgical transposition to take the place of the thumb) of index and ring fingers; cultural and economic effects of poliomyelitis; leprosy; training the physically disabled; hand splints; psychotherapy versus physical treatment; ego function in schizophrenia; and psychopaths.
- **For middle age** topics included: paid work; industrial rehabilitation and techniques; personal relationships in rheumatoid arthritis; hemiplegia; disseminated sclerosis; work study; work retention; and preparation for retirement.
- **For old age** topics included: treatment in sheltered conditions and home; community care; routine methods of retraining disabled people; ADL and activities in nursing education; cultural and social activities; social work, and working in Israel.[22]

Other topics covered student education; architectural barriers; audio-visual aids; sheltered work centres in the Philippines; rehabilitation in a refugee community; and standardisation of therapeutic apparatus.

## The Journals

In the two British Journals during the 1960s there were a wide range of papers dealing with topics as various as decorating or venetian blind making as therapeutic activities,[23] child delinquency[24] and the care and comfort of the aged poor.[25] Several themes such as work and resettlement ran over from the 1950s,[26] others, such as spasticity and cerebral palsy, developed further,[27] and yet others became dominant during the decade, such as assessment[28] or industrial therapy.[29] Many such topics and themes were reflected in the book reviews and purchases made for the AOT Library. There was (occupational therapist) Allbon's Basic Basketry,[30] Morton's *Hobbies for the Housebound*,[31] McClurg Anderson's *Housework with Ease*,[32] Robinson's *Patterns of Care*,[33] Klare's *Anatomy of Prison*,[34] a Barnardo Technical Booklet about Cerebral Palsy,[35] and a government publication about seats for workers in factories.[36] Among a number of others were important acquisitions which heralded the trend of books relating directly to occupational therapy practice published in the USA.[37]

Advertisements for craft supplies still featured, such as those for The Silk Shop in SJOT, for Dryad or Crown Pressing Co. in *Occupational Therapy*, or for Nottingham Handicrafts in both. Those for rehabilitation equipment began to be more prominent. There were in *Occupational Therapy* across the decade, for example, advertisements for the Walker Andrews Rehabilitation rug loom; the Pollard Walker winder; the Thame wire twisting machine; and the Oliver machine. The Nottingham Handcraft Company, which had patronised the Journals' advertising spaces from the early days, tended to reflect the trends in practice. In this decade they followed the remedial image with, for example, an advertisement for Prenyl for the first time in the British Isles. They went so far as to describe how it was used, as well as stating the product's special properties:

> *PRENYL is easily cut with scissors or a knife when it is cold or warm, leaving a smooth edge...The splint is formed directly on the patient's hand and held in position for one or two minutes. Any area to be trimmed or reshaped can then be marked. Shaping may be continued after the material reaches room temperature.*[38]

In *Occupational Therapy* uniforms were discussed frequently. The 1960s saw changes in the official uniform to creations more in line with the times. Farnham Park occupational therapists were in the vanguard of that change when Peggy Jay wrote to inform AOT Council that her staff were wearing 'unfashionably loose bottle green ski trousers' in view of the nature of the work in that Rehabilitation Centre. Apparently Council laughed.[39] In another manifestation of a change of image, a new 'less amateur' journal cover for *Occupational Therapy* was decided upon by the Publicity Committee,[40] and was designed by artist Michael Smith. It depicted a stylised version of the phoenix which, as well as being 'a symbol of self-regeneration' was also one of a forward-looking and expanding organisation. A different colour was planned for each season befitting the time of year. It was launched before the WFOT Congress in July 1966.[41]

**Figure 2.8.3:** **A change of image: a new cover for *Occupational Therapy* and a new uniform**

In the quarterly SJOT details of study weekends, and reports from Joint Council, WFOT, and the links with Philadelphia (where the 1962 WFOT Congress was held) featured regularly. As well, during this decade, a number of themes were evident. One concerned discussions on reciprocity with AOT such as about a Teaching Diploma, another was the drafting of a Code of Ethics, and a third the shortage of occupational therapists and the associated issue of poor salary scales. Papers and reports covered wide ranging professional interests such as: guidance on evaluative research; the opening of the new Glasgow School; the introduction of Phenothiazines for the treatment of psychiatric patients; and debate about whether 'hospital industry' was appropriate treatment or exploitation of patients. By the end of the 1960s the future of occupational therapy in the community was emerging as an issue following the Social Work (Scotland) Act of 1968, and concern was being expressed, south of the border, about the apparent lack of awareness of occupational therapists' requirement of a medical referral before giving treatment. Discussion of earlier Parliamentary Acts such as of the Mental Health (Scotland) Act, 1960 also featured in SJOT. Prior to the passing of the PSM Act, the March 1960 edition included the script of a preparatory talk given in January and February of 1960 by Doris Sym, as President of the Joint Council, to AOT and SAOT meetings.[42]

Editorials in *Occupational Therapy* addressed various issues of professional concern. One in 1964, for example, considered the image of occupational therapy. The subject has remained an emotional one throughout the years and, at that time of major change, the debate was manifest by the conflict between advocates of creative or functional therapy. The former group seemed to attract particularly bad press within the profession from the 1960s on, although the opposite was the case in a letter from a patient to the Editor of SJOT:

> *I have been interested to hear of discussions about different kinds of occupational therapy—ADL, Industrial Activities and so on and that some people think that crafts are not needed any more. I want—as a patient—to say a word in support of diversional therapy...*
>
> *Somehow, if I had perhaps broken my leg, it wouldn't have seemed so bad, but here I have had to lie, just to get injections, feeling perfectly able to get up and go about, yet I must stay here worrying about my family. I brought in plenty of knitting, but that didn't keep me from thinking, and the more I thought, the tighter I grasped the pins and the faster I knitted until I nearly knitted myself into the jersey!...And so it went on; the days dragged and though we have television and plenty of visiting days and I had soon knitted the boys each a jersey I still felt pretty desperate. And then the therapist came and said she had a Referral Card for me...*
>
> *...she brought the thing I was to make...but was I nervous?...I have never known time to pass so quickly...The therapist can come only three days a week and if she has too many Remedial patients she cannot always spend a lot of time with us. We understand this— but I would like people—especially newly qualified O.T.s—to realise how much help they can give even to 'Diversional' patients. Believe me, we do not find our position a bit diverting! I can't understand people running down Diversional Therapy.*[43]

The 1964 editorial used the terms 'Pink Bunnies' and 'Basketry'. 'Mention those two words in connection with Occupational Therapy and exasperated voices will be raised.' It continued:

> *They have become a symbol, signifying misunderstanding by the medical and allied professions, as well as the lay public, of the real nature of this work. It is not that the value*

*of craft-work is being disputed, for wise occupational therapists see its value for certain*
*conditions. Rather is it the subtle implication that Occupational Therapy is slightly*
*frivolous work which at boarding school might be regarded as an 'extra'.*

The Editor suggested that '"feeling misunderstood" is said to be a sign of adolescence...'
and that the solution lay somewhere between ignoring such misunderstanding and
concentrating on improving the quality of service or tackling the issue head on. She
thought the profession was far too reticent and stressed that its image depended entirely on
practising occupational therapists being agents of their work with first-hand information of
new trends and developments. Their responsibility towards the public included potential
patients' right to know what services were available under the NHS.[44]

Another editorial in *Occupational Therapy*, a couple of years later, raised the issue of
married women in occupational therapy. Unlike earlier times, when they were excluded
from work after marriage, in the 1960s the government pleaded for them to return to their
professions. Occupational therapy vacancies caused by marriage were cataclysmic, said
the Editor. Training schools were constantly being asked to find staff to avoid
departments closing down. A survey about that time showed that 47% of full-time
practising members of the Association were married women, 58% of part-time practising
members were married women, and 82% of non-practising members of the Association
were married women. It was understood that to return to a career required careful
planning, and a willingness to be flexible on the part of employers and colleagues. Shared
positions, flexible or staggered hours, and work-place crèches were suggested
possibilities, along with the Association providing clinical refresher courses.[45]

November 1964 saw the appointment of Miss D. M. Whitlamsmith, BA, the first non-
occupational therapist to be appointed to the position of Editor of *Occupational Therapy*,
She was to be followed in the next decades by Anthony Bax, HGN Gore, and Upma
Barnett. The SJOT maintained occupational therapists as editors or 'journal convenors',
like Mary Cunningham and Miss J. Errington.

# Training

At an AOT Symposium held in 1963, Miss Rook, who was then the Director of
Training at the Liverpool College, spoke about *Education—What? and Why?* She
explained that she preferred the word 'education' to 'training' because the latter
implied technical training alone. Instead of that she favoured a stimulating and
progressive education programme. This, she believed, should be in a state of constant
appraisal so that obsolete ideas and practices could be discarded progressively and
courses did not get overloaded as new trends emerged. She suggested a more flexible
approach in the future, with less rigidity in the requirements imposed by AOT
examinations, believing this would enable adjustment to rapidly changing demands.[46]

*Training* remained the term commonly in use. *OT, Present and Future* also addressed
training issues. It reaffirmed that common basic preparation for all occupational

therapists should continue. However, it suggested review, research, and revision of selection criteria for admission, and re-appraisal of the training programme in view of potential and actual role changes.[47] That was timely as, by 1965, with the increasing numbers of schools and students it was noted that modifications were necessary because of the impossibility of examiners marking the number of papers or being able to carry out the administration required in the necessary period.[48]

On the topic of postgraduate work, *OT, Present and Future* advised the establishment of opportunities for research, the offer of advanced courses in clinical specialties, and grants to support occupational therapists undertaking formal postgraduate training. AOT Council took the recommendations further suggesting that the possibility of a degree in occupational therapy should be investigated. In the short term, the examination requirements in 'occupations and techniques' were liberalised to allow for modern treatment trends. Other potentially more radical revision of the syllabus was postponed pending further investigation. Long-term policy, it was agreed, should expect that increasing numbers of occupational therapists would read for advanced degrees.[49]

No mention was made of basing training on the American system of degree education, which had taken place there in Universities since the 1920s. Interestingly, on that issue, Constance Owens wrote in 1960:

> From the beginning it was evident that there could be no direct transfer either of the American system of training or of the method of using occupational therapy in the American hospitals to the United Kingdom. Modifications in relation to differing educational, social, cultural and economic patterns were accordingly made.[50]

A more practical and less academic path was continued with an expectation that students, during basic training, would develop a taste for advanced or specialised study along with the acquisition of knowledge of the basic sciences, and relevant professional skills. The basic sciences were specified as Anatomy, Physiology, Psychology and Social Studies as related to the characteristics of, and deviations from, health; an appreciation of human relations in differing environments; and appropriate aspects of social legislation, work study and administration. In contrast to earlier programmes, which detailed particular occupations in the requirements, the Committee explained a new way of looking at professional skills. They were of three kinds, namely:

> (i) Social skills—these cover the ability to make easy social contacts with people from a wide range of social, racial and economic backgrounds, and to maintain good rapport over extended periods of time. They also cover the ability to create and to share in group situations, and to lead group activities for therapeutic ends...
>
> (ii) Skills of communication—...to and with patients, and to and with medical directors and colleagues. They depend on facility in spoken and written (formal) expression, to ensure accurate interpretation of therapeutic procedures. They also include the ability to understand professional literature which is instrumental in achieving higher competence.
>
> (iii) Practical skills—...in the use and maintenance of hand tools and simple machines, ... and the use and manipulation of common materials. In addition, the student must study relevant aspects of activities of daily living and other factors essential to home rehabilitation. [51]

In the 1960s it was generally agreed that trainees should have a stable personality, an interest in people and their problems, be adaptable, have, at least, 'moderately high intellect and have some practical bent.' To develop, the profession needed more: an intellectual elite, ongoing research to verify theory and improve practice, and better education for its teachers. To that end postgraduate opportunities were urgently required.[52] The pioneer effort was the first PhD awarded to an Occupational therapist in the United Kingdom. That was to Constance Owens in 1963; she had resigned as Principal of the Liverpool School in order to undertake it, because part time PhD students were not admitted to study for the degree at Liverpool. Her research was based on her experience with students learning anatomy, which had shown that:

> ...imagery was of great practical importance. This is now widely recognised but at that time her ideas were regarded with scepticism by many psychologists...she produced one of the most massive theses in the history of the department.[53]

The one opportunity for advanced study within occupational therapy—the 'teaching diplomas' of England and Scotland—had also reached a point of change. Joint Council announced a United Kingdom diploma for teachers of occupational therapy. That had finally come to fruition due to the hard work of a Standing Committee under the Chairmanship of Miss Smith-Rose, when the Registration Board gave formal approval in July 1966.[54] In the 1970s there was a grave shortage of teachers. The DHSS was approached and they agreed to fund a 'crash course' at Garnett College. This not only increased the pool of teachers, but also enabled people who could not spend time away from their families doing the longer course to become teachers. There was some opposition to this from those who tried to uphold the traditional route.[55]

Four new training schools opened in the United Kingdom during the decade: at Glasgow in 1962, the second school to be situated in York in 1963, Cardiff in 1964, and Salford in 1967. Another started in Dublin. The 1962 Annual Report told how Council had agreed:

> ...that schools outside the UK should be allowed to train students for the Diploma of the Association, provided that the Schools fulfilll the Association's requirements, and are responsible for costs associated with travel of examiners.[56]

The Dublin School, with Miss J. M. Rook as Principal, was the only school outside the United Kingdom to be granted permission to train candidates for the Association's Diploma.[57]

# Practice: Function versus diversion

In *OT, Present and Future*, guidelines were put forward for current and future practice. To advance recovery from mental or physical illness, practice was aimed either at returning function using a remedial approach or training residual ability for personal independence, and social and vocational re-adjustment. Intervention was to: be related to the environment; be carried out in a 'work atmosphere'; utilise practical skills and everyday domestic or work equipment; and employ age-appropriate approaches. It would foster independence, initiative, responsibility, judgement and resettlement according to the demands of home and job, and provide advice on equipment, home alterations, avocational interests, and social contacts. Little was mentioned about earlier creative paradigms of practice.

In some ways that was associated with medicine becoming increasingly scientific. It had both expanded its boundaries and reduced the immediate focus of intervention. That is not the contrary statement it appears. Because, much of the time, medicine was able to effect better results at the seat of trauma, attention was focused there thus creating a 'reductionist' paradigm of treatment. However there were, at the same time, expanding fields of practice and an increasing number of trained auxiliary personnel involved in overall patient programmes. As part of both aspects, in order to achieve the most effective outcomes, careful assessment was called for to inform interventions and strategies of care. So, for occupational therapists too, the decade heralded a much more conscious attempt at assessment prior to, during and at the conclusion of treatment, and a more reductionist focus overall.

## Assessment

As assessment became regarded as essential, there was a proliferation of occupational therapy tools evaluating patients' medical state, ability to work, needs for open or sheltered employment, and social performance. It became a word on the lips of the majority of occupational therapists, whether working in psychiatric or physical fields. Strategies to assess a wide range of manifestations were devised along with a plethora of assessment forms. Some were so thorough and lengthy that they would take an age to complete, and eventually led to more attention being given to assessment than to treatment. Others were simply a place to record necessary information in a systematic fashion. In the last regard, an early ADL assessment form at Farnham Park Rehabilitation Centre had headings relating to general aspects of personal care such as 'dressing', 'food preparation', or 'bathing' which were addressed differently and individually according to person, diagnosis, handicap, social and occupational requirements.

Much discussion surrounded the use of assessment and assessment forms for the wide variation in type, method and scope of practice. Elizabeth Wright, in a thesis towards the SAOT Teachers' Diploma, argued that no other discipline could use such a wide range of media or activities in the assessment of a patient's 'emotional state, social interaction, work level and potential, diagnostic and personality evaluation.' She further argued that only when those factors were fully considered could the therapist be totally useful in patients' treatment. She cautioned that such advantages must be integrated with 'a common language, a standard and clear-cut assessment and effective staff relationships, without which the use of that potential would never be achieved.'[58]

Also in the field of mental health, Kathleen Hamilton argued for making use of observation, believing that the notion that 'good psychiatric O.T. is more of an instinct than a science', was insufficient excuse to waste the profession's 'potential value as a source of information to the treatment team.' She found that the process of compiling an assessment form designed to cover as wide a field as possible had led to clearer understanding of its need. Aware of the problems of lack of objectivity, Hamilton believed that even potentially subjective assessment would enable staff to get an all-round picture of a new patient, aiding diagnosis and treatment planning and preventing preconceived notions. For long-term patients such assessment may throw light on behaviour problems or response to drugs, provide greater awareness of capabilities, and be a stimulus to take a fresh look at their case. In her place of employment the doctor maintained that although 'the occupational therapist and the patient(s) being assessed should not be strangers to one another,' patients should be unaware of being specially observed and in no circumstances should the assessment be discussed with them.[59]

At the 1968 Annual General Meeting of AOT Rita Goble also talked about making use of observation. Like Wright, she ascribed to occupational therapists' diverse training, the facility to take on the essential job of assessment. She argued for 'improved treatment techniques based on scientific data' gathered by 'accurate assessment and measurement' and coupled with clinical judgment. Goble said that for occupational therapist's rehabilitation programmes to become an integral part of patient care, it was essential that their practice withstand critical analysis. That was dependent upon a foundation of physical, psychological, social or functional fact. She compared psychologists' assessment using objective measurement, standardised tests, training in test procedures and interpretation of test scores, agreed standards of recording data, and so forth with the 'subjective jottings' assessment used in occupational therapy and the diversity of forms, arguing that:

> Recording must be systematic, consistent and deliberate, requiring great concentration if it is to be accurate and effective. It is extremely difficult to describe patients simply so any appropriate techniques and systems that can assist us must be developed as tools to help us in any detailed scrutiny. [60]

**Figure 2.8.4:** **Assessment in occupational therapy departments using practical or theoretical tasks**

It will be clear as the discussion continues that assessment had become central to practice, no matter whether the methods met scientific criteria established by other professions. Indeed, in practice during the 1960s where rehabilitation remained the central theme, even that process was seen, by some, as also in need of constant appraisal. Along those lines, in a remarkably forward thinking paper, Owens described rehabilitation as a 'dynamic process directly geared to the attainment of a specific goal by an individual patient.' However, the concept of individual uniqueness implied that 'the process of rehabilitation must be subject to infinite variation of technique, and capable of endless adjustment to meet the needs of patients under treatment.' It 'must be deeply concerned with change; with change in self, and with such environmental change as is related to life and adjustment to living.' All that required constant evaluation and re-evaluation of the changing demands of educational, social, work or leisure factors in relation to individuals.[61]

## Rehabilitation and restoration of function

*OT, Present and Future* stated that part of the occupational therapist's role in the treatment of patients with physical illness or injury was 'to restore a sense of well being and maximum physical efficiency in the shortest possible time,' by restoration of psychological and anatomical function. To effect improvement related to the normal requirements of patients, occupational therapists needed to apply 'detailed knowledge of the working positions and actions that occur in the(ir) home and work environment.' Restoration of function was also understood to include adjustment to permanent disability in terms of maximising residual abilities, conserving energy, and building up general fitness. In most cases of physical rehabilitation there was an individual relationship between therapist and patients. Successful treatment depended on good communication with a doctor and mutual co-operation between members of the treatment team. Overlap in treatment was not deemed to be a problem as long as there was collaboration.[62]

There were numerous well-known centres apart from the London and district teaching hospitals in England, Scotland, Wales and Northern Ireland, which offered specialised occupational therapy for return of physical function. They included places like the rehabilitation centre for coronary patients at the Barnsley District General Hospital, Yorkshire; the Medical Rehabilitation Centre, Camden Road, London; the Cedars Unit at Nottingham University; the Crow Hill Rehabilitation Centre at Mansfield, Notts; the Etwall Unit at the Derby Royal Infirmary; Farnham Park Rehabilitation Centre near Slough; the Luton and Dunstable Hospital; the Passmore Edwards Centre in Essex; the Rivermead Hospital in Oxford; the Odstock Hospital, Salisbury; the Princess Mary Hospital, Margate; the Roffey Park Centre at Horsham; the Royal Hampshire County Hospital, Winchester; the Simon Square Centre, Edinburgh; and the Wolfson Centre at the Atkinson Morley Hospital, Wimbledon. Some were for people with particular vocational requirements, such as those for miners, run by the Miners' Welfare Commission, at Berry Hill Hall, Mansfield and the Bridge of Earn Centre at Perth, amongst several others; for railwaymen at Crewe; for seamen at Greenwich; for the RAF at Chessington; and for ex-service men and women the Star and Garter Home, and the Forces Help Society, in Kent, run by the Royal British Legion.[63]

At the Wolfson Medical Rehabilitation Centre, opened in 1967, which offered rehabilitation for brain damaged and neurologically disabled patients, Elizabeth Grove was the head occupational therapist, with a staff of three others and a technical instructor.

**Figure 2.8.5:** **The light and heavy workshops at the Wolfson in 1967**

It was to the Wolfson Centre at the Atkinson Morley that Stirling Moss, the famous racing driver, was sent to receive treatment following a head injury, fractured femur and fractured humerus received when his car crashed in a race in 1962. Grove recalls that his reactions were well ahead of the rest of the patients, that he took to a computer driving game developed by a psychologist, and that on a home visit she was faced with the problem of helping him access the bathroom, which was up a spiral staircase, with a rope hand-support whilst he was using elbow crutches.

**Figure 2.8.6:** **Stirling Moss takes his therapists out to dinner**
(*Courtesy of* The Daily Express)

## William Hickey

Moss says thank you . . .

STIRLING MOSS, grateful to be out of hospital only nine weeks after his Goodwood crash, last night took out the nurses who helped him back to fitness.

Smiling broadly as he walked on crutches, he led 10 pretty girls from Atkinson Morley's Hospital, Wimbledon, into the Criterion Theatre to see the revue "Four To The Bar."

He told me: "I can't remember the last time I was in a theatre that was not an operating one. It's wonderful to be back in the West End. As I lay there in bed I wondered how I could repay the kindness."

★ ★ ★

The party included Elizabeth Grove (leaving the mini-bus in the picture), the occupational therapist who trained Moss to use his damaged arm.

"Aren't they wonderful," Moss said, turning to the girls. "They all deserve a pay rise."

It was his first night out in the West End since the crash, but he left after the show to go home to bed.

Moss leads . . . followed by therapist Elizabeth Grove and nurses

Grove saw the 1960s as a time of change and expansion. Developing considerable expertise in the treatment of neurological disorders, in 1969 she wrote the chapter on head injuries in *Occupational Therapy in Rehabilitation*,[64] and presented a paper on the 'Assessment of Neurological Disabilities' at the 1970 WFOT Congress in Zurich. This was indicative of the increasing interest in treating neurological disorders, which was beginning to take precedence over the profession's previous concentration on orthopaedics.

In *A Fresh Look at Hemiplegia* Stella Mountford, who wrote two occupational therapy texts on rehabilitation in the 1960s and 1970s, discussed the processes of individuals regaining function after stroke. She linked the remedial process closely with ADL. Rehabilitation, she said, was the name given to the process by which 'transition from the institutional environment to the home is effected.' In occupational therapy the main emphasis, she thought, should be on 'neuromuscular dysfunction assessment and activities of daily living':

> *For women patients the latter would develop into domestic activities and for the men activities emphasising work tolerance and capabilities. At the ward stage attention would be given to personal independence—dressing, feeding, washing, writing, hair, make-up and shaving. Once out of the ward the patient would progress to activities involving balance and mobility—bathing, bed-making, washing and ironing, cooking and housework.*[65]

Interest and skill in splint making for hand injuries, and particularly lively splints, was also growing. Mary Jones, with her 1960 publication *An Approach to Occupational Therapy*,[66] and Natalie Barr (née Smythe), with her contribution to *Rehabilitation of the Hand*,[67] had a major influence on its development as an occupational therapy specialty. The London Hospital, too, treated a large number of hand injuries and conditions, and the increasing interest of medical staff there led that department to develop and use many different types of splints. Splints were made which were easy to construct, quick to put on and off, as unobtrusive and small as possible, and suitable for work requirements.[68]

**Figure 2.8.7:** **Treatment of median nerve injuries and a variety of early splints to enable occupation**

Colles fractures of the wrist are the most common fractures treated by occupational therapy. These mostly occur when elderly people fall on an outstretched hand. Devas and Tyrell wrote of an out-patient programme for those not capable of continuing their own treatment. Many patients could be treated at the same time in a group by various activities which enabled them to exercise wrist and fingers to best advantage and that attracted their interest. Following introduction of that system of treatment, no patients had experienced stiff fingers or wrists after Colles fractures or similar injury.[69]

Ingamells, in a thesis for her teaching diploma, presented an anthology of the methods of treatment used by occupational therapists for hand conditions and injuries. Personal experience, supplemented by that of twenty other occupational therapists, provided the data. She found some common sense reasons for why treatment varied such as the state of nutrition of the hand on admission; the age of the patient; the distance of the individual patient from the hospital, which influenced the duration of treatment; and the industries in the hospital district, which dictated the patient's requirements for hand mobility. Several points of controversy were uncovered such as surgeons who encouraged occupational therapists to treat individual joints involved, and others who wanted the hand treated as a functional whole.[70]

**Figure 2.8.8:   Remedial games used to treat hand injuries**

Rehabilitation aimed at return of function was not restricted to institutional care. Indeed, at that time, the aims of domiciliary work were the same as in hospitals, even though some different types of patient were seen. At a Liverpool Refresher Course in 1961 it was explained that although domiciliary work had more responsibility for treatment of the chronically handicapped for whom the outlook was poor, it was also sometimes concerned with rehabilitation of the ill and the acutely injured who had some chance of recovery. The objective of the domiciliary service was to take specialists to the home in preference to taking the patient to the hospital. Previously a necessity in country areas it was being recognised as an important service to establish more fully in urban areas. Dr J.B. Meredith Davies, Liverpool's Deputy Medical Officer for Health, prophesied that in the future, domiciliary work would become more and more important and that 'while domiciliary health services remained with Local Authorities, occupational therapists must remain with them, too.' To get patients to as near to normality as possible, it was considered essential that they should be 'fired with enthusiasm for life', and for therapists to have 'an unconquerable belief in the patient's ability to win through and to convince the patient of this.'[71]

Within the field of mental health, *OT, Present and Future* recommended strengthening patients' residual function as well as developing the assets of patients' personalities through resocialisation and remotivation. 'In many cases, these aims may best be served if the patient is treated in a group situation.' To do that:

> *Occupational therapists must understand the principles of social psychology and utilise the potential inter-relationships that occur in any group situation, so that patients will benefit from each other's influence as well as from relationships with other staff members and the occupational therapist.*[72]

*OT, Present and Future* made some potentially controversial recommendations, such as:

> *The occupational therapist should always maintain treatment at a level slightly in excess of the patient's wishes, although the demands of the therapist must be reasonable. Treatment should not be geared to tolerant acceptance of the patient's illness and tactful moderation of demands.*
>
> *The occupational therapist must be willing to work with very disturbed patients, assisting in the social control of their behaviour. This is frequently difficult but has been successfully achieved in some hospitals.*[73]

Because of the increasing emphasis on relationships in remediation of psychiatric disorder not only group work, but the concept of therapeutic communities, as envisaged first by Maxwell Jones, grew apace. Alison Perks explained how she had become aware of the changing nature of occupational therapy in the psychiatric field after working for a year in a small psychoneurotic unit for early recoverable cases. Despite many large mental hospitals still being places for long-term custodial care of chronic deteriorated patients, improved methods of treatment and earlier diagnosis had resulted in many more patients being treated in the family or wider community. She saw mental hospitals developing gradually along democratic rather than authoritarian lines, and becoming 'places of education in basic attitudes to life and community living.'[74]

In developing to keep pace with such changes occupational therapy had to fulfill realistic needs within the community. Typically of many programmes, the role of the occupational therapist was almost inevitably determined by her view of herself and her approach:

> *The degree of involvement required places a good deal of pressure on the occupational therapist's personality, her own view of life, individual attitudes and opinions, if there is to be any more than a superficial exchange between patients and herself.*
>
> *The community involves the staff equally in their relations with one another. If the patients are expected to question their own prejudices and ideas, then members of staff must be prepared to do likewise, if they are to have understanding and establish rapport. Occupational therapists, by the very nature of their work, are often brought a good deal closer to the patients' immediate needs and problems than other members of staff. They must be able to draw on their own inner resources to help the patient cope with the dilemma rather than resort to a book. The occupational therapist, then, has to learn to adapt and become part of a community.*[75]

Additionally the prospect of fairly early return to home and the wider community implied that patients must be enabled to remain in touch with life outside the hospital.

Programmes aimed at involvement in current events, use of public rather than hospital facilities, outings to community events, and clubs within the catchment area of the hospital were useful to enable patients to continue their interests after discharge.[76] Changes supporting such programmes had been facilitated by the Mental Health Act of 1959 which, whilst holding hospitals responsible for treatment, had put responsibility for care and aftercare with the local authority. This had resulted in the growth of mental health centres around the country, and of co-operation between the hospital and the local authority. Instead of remaining as in-patients for years, some patients were beginning to live outside as members of families, in group homes, or in hostels.[77]

The treatment of disturbed and delinquent children also used group methods. Manley reported on children of primary school age with a variety of emotional and psychiatric disorders, psychoses, neurotic disorders, organic brain damage or disease, reactive behaviour disturbances, epilepsy, psychosomatic and personality disorders. The children often came from deprived and disturbed backgrounds and had deep-seated maladaptive patterns of behaviour such as stealing, truancy from school, running away from home, telling lies, arson, housebreaking, and excessive aggressiveness and destructiveness. Their relationships were distrustful and actively hostile. The occupational therapists were entirely responsible for the group therapy in which the children were given opportunities to form close and meaningful relationships with others with a free range and choice of activity. Groups were kept small, very natural, and as close as possible to a family situation so that the children regained lost confidence in abilities and self, and learnt new patterns of behaviour which gained approval. The close relationships that were established made it possible to help them to modify behaviour according to the demands of society.[78]

## Rehabilitation and work

The 'return to work' ethos of the 1950s did not disappear overnight, and a great number of rehabilitation programmes, particularly for male patients, were aimed towards that goal in both physical and psychiatric services.

In the physical field the continuing interest was typified by the provision by the Ministry of Labour of special tools and equipment to more than 250 disabled workers in 1966, so that they might obtain or keep jobs or become self-employed. The grant included: Braille micrometers and textbooks, shorthand and dictation machines, typewriter scales and special typewriters for those with paralysis, electronic devices, tape recorders, measuring tapes, calculating machines, sewing machines, draughtsman's boards and equipment, shoe and watch repair tools, and equipment for blind physiotherapists.[79] Another sign of the interest was the theme *From Disability To Work* of the first European International Study Course which, under the auspices of the British Council for the Rehabilitation of the Disabled, was held at Cambridge in 1962. The list of 42 speakers included Dr Kessler from the USA, who was regarded as the Father of Rehabilitation, and two British occupational therapists. Alicia Mendez provided a very thorough overview of the profession in a paper titled 'Residual Abilities' and discussed assessment of work capacity and prevocational training.[80] The other, Caroline Henderson, spoke on occupational therapy in the rehabilitation of psychiatric patients.[81]

Although interest in vocational rehabilitation had gained ground in the previous decade it was in the 1960s that a major change occurred in psychiatric hospitals, particularly in the use of industrial rehabilitation. People with psychiatric disorders, at that time, constituted the largest disability group in Industrial Rehabilitation Units (IRUs). Added to those with organic nervous disorder, who often had secondary psychiatric handicap, they made up about one-third of the population. An Inter-departmental Working Party on Industrial Rehabilitation in 1966 recommended that psychiatric services and IRUs should act in concert.[82]

Apart from IRUs, industrial therapy was part of the occupational therapy programmes of many departments in psychiatric hospitals throughout the country. It was so popular that rivalry developed between occupational therapists and nursing staff about their role in its organisation and management. Without doubt, it embodied many of the 19th century notions about the importance of work as therapy for psychiatric patients, but the mass resurgence of industrial therapy has been attributed to Maxwell Jones. In his book Social Psychiatry he described a system inaugurated at the Belmont Hospital, Surrey, in which patients worked in factory-like conditions.[83] Other British pioneers, Tizard and O'Connor had, in 1952, initiated carefully planned projects among high grade male adolescent 'defectives' in a Kent institution, and four years later O'Connor and colleagues initiated an experimental workshop for male patients with chronic schizophrenia in a Surrey Mental Hospital. The hospital kept the workshop going to activate long-stay patients and some of the workers had found employment after discharge. These workshops were copied in other institutions and hospitals.[84]

The growth of factory-type work largely occurred where staff made determined efforts to contact local industry; this resulted in workshops where patients, in the main, assembled relatively simple industrial products. At Highcroft Hall, in Birmingham, for example, about 300 patients were so employed, and at Bristol the manufacture of ballpoint pens was used alongside the commercial washing of motorcars. In 1960 some fifty hospitals demonstrated their types of production when the Cheadle Royal Hospital, a leader in the field, organised an exhibition. Experiments conducted at the Cheadle Royal Factory compared the working capacity of patients with chronic schizophrenia with normal employees. Although there was little difference in time lost between the two groups, the patients responded more to the incentives of special appeals or a graphical record of performance, and they acquired skill much more slowly. Patients' output improved when both groups worked together, and their performance was found to be related more to IQ than to other clinical features of illness.[85]

Experience with occupational therapy of this type led Affleck to the recognition that:
> The principles on which the organisation of therapeutic occupation should be planned include the conception of a system of activity pervading the whole hospital and the abandonment of the idea that only one room should be reserved for occupational therapy...The essential problem in the large mental hospital is the provision of occupation for hundreds of patients: this is a very big undertaking.

He went on to explain about money used as an incentive:
> The National Health Service encourages the use of money in rehabilitation by providing pocket-money, incentive money and arrangements whereby patients can live in

*the hospital while earning money outside the hospital and paying for their board and lodgings in an hostel-like arrangement: or can earn up to £2 per week without interfering with their National Health Insurance payment. These financial mechanisms can be therapeutic weapons and of great value.*[86]

Industrial therapy, in some places was but one aspect of work therapy. Rhoda Begg reported that work therapy with payment incentive, at the Crichton Royal Hospital, included telephone dismantling, rubber mat making, occasionally book-keeping or other study courses, and a poultry farm, with a poultry expert to give training in modern methods. The industrial unit in the hospital engaged patients in printing, packaging, making Christmas crackers, picture framing, and other woodworking tasks for which they drew wages. Known as the Solway Industrial Unit it was featured in a television documentary programme in 1968 highlighting the concept and benefits of work and the basic right of disabled people to meaningful employment.[87]

In like vein, industrial therapy was the main feature of the new occupational therapy department at Carlton Hayes Hospital, in Leicester. However it was just one of the types of work therapy given to patients daily. Apart from the industrial therapy, many activities such as bookbinding, concrete slab making, and wood machining featured in the therapeutic programme.[88] Similarly, at the Royal Edinburgh Hospital in addition to regular classes of simple occupations for patients who were unable to leave the wards, every utility department, from the piggery to the administrative offices, employed patients, full time, on pre-vocational assessment and work. Whilst short-term patients were treated with occupations such as printing the monthly magazine, cooking, wood carving, beauty culture, games and sports, long-term patients were doing contract work for local firms. That ranged from stringing labels, dismantling telephones, and turning kipper boxes into seed-boxes, to copy typing, supplying kindling, and joinery work to order within the Hospital. A further group was employed in jobs in Edinburgh and at the IRU, preparatory to discharge.[89] At Rosslyn, Agnes Cook also described how usual hospital industries still provided employment to some patients. Others were referred to the Laundry, which dealt with contract bag-washing, being paid a regular weekly sum which provided incentive as well as the opportunity for assessment. At Bangour Village Hospital patients could be offered clerical and secretarial rehabilitation. Previously ward-bound and unemployable patients participated in experiments in productive employment carried out in the occupational therapy department, such as cracker-making and mop assembly.[90]

**Figure 2.8.9:   Industrial work**

Industrial work also featured in rehabilitation centres, in rehabilitation departments of general hospitals, in special and geriatric day centres. An example is provided by Sherrards, an industrial rehabilitation unit for people with cerebral palsy. This had the object of training and assessing them for work in open employment, sheltered employment, or work centres. Candidates were selected by the Social Work and Employment Departments of the Spastic Society at 12-day assessment courses involving manual, intellectual and social tests and activities. At Sherrards, where the maximum length of stay was one year, 70 trainees ranged between 17 and 24 years. Two-thirds of them were males. The scope for training was from simple assembly to repetitive machine operating with the emphasis on mass production, and simple office work.[91] Joanna Pitts, the occupational therapist explained:

> We are not preparing the disabled for life unless we demand a high standard of performance discipline and work. Sooner or later they will meet the normal world, so let them be prepared to learn and face their disabilities now.[92]

Some other return to work initiatives, whilst emanating from the same ethos, were separate from industrial or work therapy per se. 'Work Adjustment as a Function of Occupational Therapy' was the topic of a study course held at the New York Institute for the Crippled and Disabled in connection with the Third WFOT Congress. Jean Colburn reported on that meeting and discussed what was suggested as the final steps towards resettlement. In relatively new 'language' that was to become much used in the following decades, she introduced concepts in terms such as job sampling, work adjustment, work evaluation, prevocational testing and vocational training.[93]

In more familiar terminology, Jean Waterston discussed resettlement in three stages in the scheme of health care, namely, the treatment, work, and Local Authority (LA) stages. In the treatment stage, occupational therapists explored the physical and psychological demands of previous employment, and whether return to it was possible. If not, new possibilities and patient capacities were explored; work visits, and contact with foremen, trade union officials, work-mates, and medical advisers, were made. Patients were assisted with practice of old or new skills to develop or redevelop competencies.

In the work stage occupational therapists, in teams with medico-social workers and DROs, prepared patients for IRUs, Government Training Centre or Remploy. They simulated activities so that patients were able to hone their work skills. Waterston provided an example of a very nervous and apprehensive bus conductor being treated for a fractured femur. His 'final pre-work preparation was on a double-decker bus' where 'he spent the time running up and down the stairs with the bus in motion, until his confidence was regained.' Waterston advocated that the most realistic work situations were best like the model coal face at the Astley Ainslie Hospital. But because it was impossible to simulate the great variety of work, trades and professions, common activities which provided a reasonable basis for pre-work rehabilitation and work-testing were useful. Whether industrial rehabilitation or direct return to work was planned the occupational therapist also ensured that patients could attend to personal ADL, and use public transport.

**Figure 2.8.10: Pre-work and resettlement**

The local authorities stage was when patients were unemployed or unemployable, and occupational therapists working for the LA provided suitable activity at home or in the Work Centre. In those cases they worked with general practitioners, medico-social workers, health visitors, case workers and voluntary organisations. If patients were discharged prior to ultimate resettlement, Waterston saw it as the occupational therapist's job to maintain them, 'within her hospital department or in the LA Work Centre, at the peak of physical and mental fitness.' LAs were implementing their powers to make provision for people with handicap who were unable to work in the open market. Occupational therapists, with the help of many voluntary organisations, supervised any form of occupation and recreation within the handicapped person's capacity, which gave some small financial incentive up to the limits allowed by the Authorities.

In line with those views, Waterston enunciated a central philosophy of the profession which is often overlooked, but is a major part of the relationship between occupation, health, and well-being, namely, that:

> ...*every person, however handicapped they may be, has a potential talent which must be developed to the maximum, whether it be by the occupational therapist or by any other person with whom he comes in contact.*[94]

## Rehabilitation aimed at domestic resettlement and independence

According to *OT, Present and Future*, as well as remediating function, and enabling return to work, the other major role of occupational therapy was assisting patients to carry out activities of daily living. Although, in some places, ADL had been important in earlier decades, in the 1960s it was an expanding and exciting field generally. Indeed, the term ADL was coming to the forefront in the reablement of patients suffering from a variety of disabilities, such as for those Binnie describes with stiff hips or knees, stiff or painful shoulders, weak grip or stiff or painful hands, and the loss of or lack of use in arms or legs.[95]

One of the leaders in the ADL field was Betty Hollins who was the Head Occupational Therapist at Mary Marlborough Lodge. At a Liverpool Domiciliary Refresher Course, Hollings provided an insight into the work being carried out there. She explained that the Lodge was not a rehabilitation unit in the accepted sense but, rather, a place where patients and families could learn to cope with life. The building was designed to take 12 residents, which could include relatives learning to look after a disabled member of the family. The Lodge offered them the help of an experienced team to assist with problem solving along with the opportunity to try out a variety of equipment and furniture. A technician was available to make special aids or individual equipment. The Lodge was in the grounds of the Nuffield Orthopaedic Centre—close enough for its facilities to be available, but just far enough away for it to be considered an entity in its own right, and to be a step nearer home for patients. Mary Marlborough Lodge had been built and equipped by a grant from the National Fund for Research into Poliomyelitis, which had widened to cover other crippling diseases. Each patient's programme was planned individually and timing was flexible, so that if someone wanted to learn or practice something, and it took all day then that time was available with the staff to help when needed. Staff visited homes within reasonable distance, and made contact with domiciliary services if required when patients went home.[96] When the Birmingham Regional Group visited Mary Marlborough Lodge in 1968, Dr Ann Hamilton made clear it was the ability to assess the capabilities of patients who were temporarily or permanently disabled which was particularly valued at the Lodge. Skill in appreciating the gap between capabilities and performance demand, fitted those working there to be 'the Geiger counters of the Health Service.'[97]

The Stoke Mandeville Hospital, in Buckinghamshire was another recipient of a Polio Research Fund grant for the development of the equipment known as 'Possum', an invention by RG Maling and DC Clarkson. This 'first' of electronic environmental controls allowed a disabled person to work 10 items of equipment in the immediate environment. Its genesis was followed by requests from people with disability for more devices to provide even greater independence and, in some cases, a means of earning a living.[98]

The 'Disabled Living' movement also made its debut in the 1960s. Shirley Smith described how the Disabled Living Activities Group (DLAG) of the Central Council for the Disabled was formed in 1963 when it was obvious that:

> ...the majority of disabled people did not have the same opportunities in life as the able-bodied, due to problems connected with housing design, accessibility of public buildings, equipment for the home, clothing, employment, and lack of recreational opportunities, etc.[99]

The philosophy of the Group was that conditions could be improved; and that careful study of the environment, in the widest sense, could provide access to some of the opportunities in life which disabled people had lost. Their approach was essentially practical and aimed towards direct application. The Director of the Group was Barbara Stow, and the Chairman, Lady Hamilton. The women had first met two years earlier when the latter was working on the 'Towards Housing the Disabled Exhibition, which consisted of a model bungalow fully furnished with items useful to disabled people' and on which Stow had advised. Lady Hamilton explained:

> The Design Council were interested in the selection of items and for some time after that Barbara and I were two members of the team which went to the viewing panel of the

*Design Council to consider any special suitability for disabled people of items submitted for the Design Index.*[100]

The DLAG Office in Victoria Street opened in January 1964, and almost immediately project work developed and advisory panels were established. The first study grant for a survey resulted in the first DLAG book—*Problems of Clothing for the Sick and Disabled* by Gamwell and Joyce in 1966. The following year the Group showed a garden for people with disability at the Chelsea Flower Show which won the Silver Gilt Lindley Medal. In 1968, a grant from the King's Fund enabled preparatory work for an Information Service for the Disabled to be undertaken. It started officially in 1968.[101]

An Editorial of a 1968 issue of *Occupational Therapy* posed some questions to readers to inform them of the new service. It asked:

*Are you familiar with the stair-climbing aids at present in production? Do universities ever accept students confined to wheelchairs? Is there a spoon which would stay upright even if the hand turned? Is there a wheelchair which will go into the boot of your patient's mini-car? Where can the answers to such questions be found?*[102]

It described the Service as a central resource for people with disability, occupational therapists and others to consult in order to find out, not only about new equipment, but also about new laws and ideas. The Editorial went on:

*Subjects at present included in the Service are aids to mobility and movement e.g. wheelchairs, transport, tables, beds, hoists and lifting equipment, besides small aids. Details of all these aids are available, with the laws relating to their supply and other relevant comments.*

*Some of the most common inquiries concern special facilities such as holidays, voluntary helpers, and education (particularly at university level). The Group is sponsoring an investigation into education, and it is hoped it will soon be fully covered.*

*Inquiries about the design and construction of private homes and special centres are mainly dealt with by the consultant architect to the Disabled Living Activities Group.*[103]

Hamilton explained that in 1969 the preliminary work for the Aids Centre began, at which time the DLAG had around 50 voluntary and salaried staff. An offer of a separate endowment enabling it to become 'the Disabled Living Foundation, an independent charitable trust, was received, conditional on the terms of reference covering disability no matter what its origin.'[104] The Foundation, which housed in one place a variety of equipment that could be tried out, was established in January 1970 with.Stow as the first Director. Initially it was staffed almost entirely by occupational therapists. The Foundation flourished and was the forerunner of Disabled Living Centres and Independent Living Centres in Britain and overseas. The Information Service set up within the Foundation was also a first of its kind in the United Kingdom.[105]

Within the DLAG each particular field of study was carried out on an 'ad hoc membership basis' in order to utilise the services of eminent specialists in those spheres. Advisory panels of distinguished experts were set up to consider specific topics such as clothing, gardening, and the environmental problems of disabled people in the community. Projects were financed by some grants, charitable trusts, and the Central Council itself. The Group was instrumental in persuading the Ministry of Health to approve a study of the numbers and characteristics of physically disabled people. Without reliable statistics it was difficult to plan services at national and local levels to meet needs, to determine resources or cost to minimise the effects of disability.

Throughout Britain, occupational therapy departments were establishing 'home units' or 'ADL sections' which replicated domestic facilities where they could train, retrain, or assess patients prior to domestic resettlement. The Astley Ainslie Hospital pioneered the trend in Scotland when a 'Home Unit' was set up in Canaan Park as part of the occupational therapy facilities in May 1960. This comprised a bed-sitting room, bathroom, and kitchen in which were various aids and specially designed types of furniture installed to help handicapped people prepare for their return to household tasks. The 'Home Unit' staff also undertook home visits. Many of the aids available then, along with later inventions, were subsequently displayed in the Astley Ainslie's Hospital's 'Disabled Living Centre.'[106]

**Figure 2.8.11: ADL Units and adaptations of the 60s**

The Simon Square Centre in Edinburgh, too, followed the trend. Berendean Anstice tells how, as the Centre developed, it became possible to extend the services to include ADL. The number of cases referred continued to increase over the first two and a half years reaching 250 people needing continual treatment, whilst the overall number was higher with some attending only once for particular advice.[107] ADL training also occurred at Cowley Road Hospital, Oxford, for Geriatrics. There, elderly patients were discharged from the main hospital as soon as possible, afterwards often attending the Day Hospital from their own homes. To keep their period in hospital short, emphasis was given to early and regular ADL training, notably to dressing and cooking.[108]

Sometimes particular attention was given to the needs of a specific group such as those with arthritis, or stroke. In the latter case, a handbook for hemiplegics and their families, *Help Yourselves*, sponsored by the British Council for Rehabilitation of the Disabled, was published in 1966.[109] However, ADL training was not confined to physical rehabilitation. It took place in the majority of psychiatric hospitals throughout Britain. In Scottish hospitals, such as Bangour Village Hospital, Crichton Royal Hospital and Woodilee Hospital, for example, practical cookery sessions and shopping for provisions were regular features particularly for the benefit of long-term female patients whose discharge was under consideration.[110]

As domestic resettlement became an increasing concern of the government the role of the Local Authority Welfare Services (LAWS) in patient resettlement changed accordingly and occupational therapists became increasingly associated with those services. The extent and pattern of the roles undertaken by welfare departments varied throughout the country, but the duties, according to the National Assistance Act of 1948, were concerned with providing appropriate residential or temporary accommodation. The clients were elderly, infirm, and disabled people, and those temporarily homeless because of unforeseen circumstances for all of whom all reasonable needs were to be met. LAWS were also concerned with the welfare of disabled people and the provision of meals, other domiciliary services, and recreational facilities for old people.[111] The services were the province of the Ministry of Labour, the Ministry of Social Security and some voluntary organisations, often working together, as well as the Local Authority Health and Welfare Departments. Together those provided social and work centres, day care centres, clubs, classes, assisted holidays, provision for aids, and adaptations to homes.[112]

The Director of Welfare Services in the City of Leicester, K. J. Powell, stated that in the past hospitals and LAWS as separate organisations had, with some exceptions, tended to work to their own ends without consultation or co-ordination. That had resulted in a lack of forward thinking, and inadequate provision to meet the total needs of patients and their families. He called for co-ordination and clear understanding between services and for the establishment of flexible arrangements and a team effort by doctors, administrators, social workers, and occupational therapists.[113] Margaret Chitty, an occupational therapist who worked within LAWS, believed like Powell that co-operation between available services was important. In that connection she welcomed the Seebohm Report which, in her view, pointed the way to break down barriers between agencies. She described how occupational therapists working in the community continued the hospital rehabilitation team's treatment and particularly concentrated on assessment. This was despite often recognising a need for diversional and therapeutic activity that was commonly beyond the limits of available resources.[114]

Chitty also described working with the borough architect's department to help plan adaptations, which seems indicative of some occupational therapist's emerging interest and practice in architectural modification. Also indicative of the trend, at an AOT Symposium, Anne Cavaye, the Warden of Mary Marlborough Lodge, gave a paper on *Research into Housing and Equipment for the Disabled*. She asked, pertinently, whether there was any reason why new developments in housing could not be planned with the needs of disabled people in mind so 'that disabled and able-bodied could live congenially together.'[115]

Both the AOT and the Central Council for the Care of Cripples recognised that many disabled people, if provided with suitable accommodation within reasonable reach of places of employment, could be self-supporting individuals leading independent lives. The lack of suitable housing was, in fact, a major reason why many people, confined to a wheelchair, could not leave hospital or hostel accommodation. The movement towards domestic resettlement led therefore to an awakening interest amongst occupational therapists and others in access to public and private buildings that would meet the requirements of disabled people. It was in this decade that serious action began towards altering the consequences of inaccessible buildings, whether for education, employment, leisure, or any other sphere of life. To that end, an accessibility Guide to London for people with disability was published,[116] and Selwyn Goldsmith published his classic text *Designing for the Disabled*.[117]

## Rehabilitation, avocational, personal and social needs

Despite the overwhelming interest in work and domestic rehabilitation, some occupational therapists in the 1960s sustained a particular interest in practice which met avocational, personal, interpersonal, and social needs as well. Owens, for example, who had from the start taken an holistic approach, sounded a somewhat cautionary note about current trends. She argued that progress gained in the course of rehabilitation would fail to survive the difficult transition from care to independence unless those concerned took into consideration the needs of the patient as a whole person. She saw rehabilitation as a changeable process according to age related needs within the social context and recognised that it was a 'total preparation for re-instatement in society as an individual equipped to lead a full, useful and satisfying life.' Whilst changes in social, educational, technological and medical practice impinge upon everyone, Owens felt 'they press most hurtfully upon those least well equipped to cope with new ideas and new patterns of behaviour,' a category into which many patients fell. She recommended 'a knowledge of research findings from studies of age-related changes in behaviour in regard to motivation, abilities, habits, speed of reaction, speed and method of learning, level of arousal and amount of social involvement,' and advocated for 'a more energetic search for knowledge of cause and effect within the field of rehabilitation itself.'[118]

So much do social factors interact with physical and mental health and illness, and therefore therapeutic processes, that Margaret Heathcote was driven to suggest in 1961, that 'much of the most modern development in Occupational Therapy seems to belong as much to sociology as to medicine.' Her report of a weekend conference on *Delinquency and Social Patterns* had relevance to some of her patients moving to new satellite towns. These, she said, had 'peculiar problems' with new industrial and social patterns appearing. On a practical note, she suggested there was great scope, particularly for young male occupational therapists to work in 'virile Occupational Therapy' put in action by police in British cities such as Norwich and Liverpool.[119]

In the field of mental health Miriam Plummer, too, argued for a wider role. She, like Owens, was conscious of the emphasis on preparing patients to care for themselves outside hospital, and saw the need to help patients develop personal strengths and potential. Claiming that the role of the occupational therapist was a complex one that was not fully understood by doctors and other members of the team, she said occupational therapists:

> ...are trained to make use of scientific knowledge, and express themselves in medical terms when communicating with their colleagues. Their effectiveness in day to day work is primarily based on the quality of the interpersonal relationships they are able to establish with individual patients, on their ability as group leaders, and on the imaginative use of the techniques and facilities at their disposal.

Reminding readers that creativity is not restricted to arts and crafts, or even to the production of original ideas in science and philosophy, Plummer, argued that, in the first instance, occupational therapists' most important function was to form a bridge between self and patient. Next it was to assist by finding a means for each individual to interact positively with the environment. She argued that this required 'some creative ability on the part of the occupational therapist.' This was so because 'it is not in the materials, but in the way they are used that the skill of the Occupational Therapist lies…It is always associated with being involved with, and responding in, a constructive way to the environment.' In mental illness, she said, 'a patient's interaction with the environment becomes disturbed…To the already well-known list of symptoms of mental illness, deficiency in the sphere of creativity should be added.' In the treatment of mentally ill patients, an occupational therapist's task is to assess the resources left to the patient and to encourage and develop any potentials.[120] Another creative approach becoming known as 'projective techniques' was aimed at stimulation and self-expression. A programme at Royal Dundee Liff Hospital was representative of many others taken throughout Britain. There Viki Glover, working in conjunction with a qualified music teacher with experience in the field of amateur dramatics, introduced music along with other creative activities. She explained the programme, for a group of long-term female patients:

> *A wide variety of activities is covered with a view to encouraging individuals to think subjectively and express their personal feelings and ideas freely. This includes associating pieces of music with colours, shapes and textures or drawing an object or scene which is suggested by the music.*

Mixing feeling states with physical experience, movement to music was included to facilitate a state of physical relaxation preliminary to mental relaxation, and to overcome difficulty in 'slackening muscle groups.'[121]

As the decade went on, psychiatric services of various sorts were established increasingly in the community outside the hospitals following the publication of the Hospital plan for England and Wales (which) proposed that 'psychiatric units should be attached to District General Hospitals and community care was to be increased.'[122] That initiative was partly a response to modern drugs, such as injections of long acting tranquillisers, which enabled those who were forgetful or unreliable to remain in the community for longer periods, and partly because of a change in public attitudes. In 1960 Enoch Powell, the Minister of Health, had toured the North Wales Hospital and announced its eventual demise. This was to occur in psychiatric hospitals all over Britain, and as patient numbers declined so did recreational programmes and employment of patients.[123]

Day Centres and hospitals in the community began to take the place of the larger psychiatric institutions. At the AOT Symposium held in 1963, Miss M.M. Smith explained some of the programmes and the problems she faced in learning how to adapt practice to the different environment and needs of a day centre. Initially she had established a five day a week programme, providing as balanced a day as possible with the ingredients of work, play, group and social activity and exercise. That was followed by experimental group work, and then a survey of medical and nursing staffs using a questionnaire. The latter showed them favouring reality-based activities rather than craftwork as most suitable, followed by social activities, then group activities and discussions. Her own conclusions from those experiments mirrored many of her earlier ideas. She decided on a dynamic well-structured programme which included work, play, exercise and socialisation approximating the patient's usual cultural, social and work environments and providing 'opportunities for them to exercise initiative and to organise themselves when possible.' Because of patient turnover, programmes could be repetitive.[124]

By the second half of the decade, many more day facilities were being set up by Local Health Authorities as part of a comprehensive community service. A Day Centre at Sutton-in-Ashfield in Nottinghamshire, like others, was designed to provide intensive rehabilitation and socialisation after hospital treatment, serving as a halfway house, or before patients deteriorated to the point where hospital admission was unavoidable. It provided a sheltered, supportive environment for the chronically ill who no longer required in-patient treatment, and for an adolescent group with behaviour disorders and difficulties in socialisation.[125]

## The diversion battle

The diversional issue versus the functional issue posed the major conflict dividing therapists in the 1960s. Often, the correspondence section in a journal can provide an indication of matters of concern or issues about which people feel strongly, particularly when one letter or article triggers a chain response. Such was the case in 1961 regarding the much maligned 'diversional therapy' versus the newer specialty—ADL. Excerpts from that series are fascinating. K.S. Pollard, the Head Occupational Therapist at Frenchay Hospital, was moved to write on 18 July 1961:

> I was deeply disturbed to read the article by Miss Castle: 'Mobile Occupational Therapy—A Personal Account' in the July issue of the Journal.
>
> ...She asks for suggestions as to what anyone can offer her in place of 'diversional' Occupational Therapy. Has she not heard of Aids to Daily Living and training for independence? The wives of the disabled men and the mothers of the disabled children to whom she refers would surely welcome such practical help. Has she not heard of the advice and help that can be given to disabled housewives?
>
> My sister is a Health Visitor...Over a year ago she had occasion to refer a patient, through the appropriate channels, to the Domiciliary Occupational Therapy Service. The patient was a young woman, aged about 35, suffering from Rheumatoid Arthritis with a husband and family of four, who particularly wanted advice and help to enable her to run her home in spite of her disability. The domiciliary occupational therapist visited in due course, complete with mounds of cane. She told the patient that she was not there to think out aids and gadgets and, in short, did the woman want to make a basket or did she not? When told 'No,' the case was referred to the Red Cross, and at the end of another period of waiting she was issued with a Helping Hand Stick. Since then she has remained unvisited. This sort of experience does nothing to further the aims of our Association...[126]

A letter from domiciliary occupational therapists of a Welfare Department in Birmingham, found Miss Castle's article 'spirited' and appreciated the difficulties and compensations of travelling by car to visit patients. They added:

> Our colleagues in hospitals cannot imagine the trials of carrying stores around everywhere and of having to keep precise records of issues made over a vast area in all weathers...Our visits take us round the crowded city slums and we must learn patience the hard way. Traffic queues, with dreary vistas of squalor, dirt and dust are our daily lot. We have to carry all our stores, sort out individual deliveries with grubby inquisitive children

*climbing over the car and neighbours assembling as if by magic to offer advice and help. Certainly the domiciliary occupational therapists meet their patients not in a sterile artificial hospital department but in their own environment and family group. Frequently it is not one patient but a whole family with all its influence and problems that must be considered. Surely our job is not all handicrafts. The issue of aids to daily living is to us a major task. The 'text-book' bath and toilet aids are of little use to the handicapped person whose bath hangs on a nail in a yard and whose toilet serves not only his family but six others down the street. With the large amount of slum clearance and rebuilding in this and many other cities the occupational therapist can play an important part in an advisory capacity to the Housing Management Committees when rehousing or reconditioning are necessary. Grateful as one is for a well equipped Rehabilitation Kitchen it is of little use if there is no guarantee that the independence gained during a disabled persons attendance will not be maintained by the necessary adaptations in her own home.*

*...Whereas one must congratulate Miss Castle in pointing out the need for Diversional Therapy it is felt that this may in many instances be carried out by technical or craft instructors working under a qualified occupational therapist's directions. Furthermore it is becoming increasingly obvious that the majority of men are more grateful for the provision of industrial outwork than for the traditional handicrafts. However, this may be more easily organised in a densely populated city than in a large rural area. Help from voluntary organisations can be utilized when forthcoming especially where social centres are established. An occupational therapist with initiative and ingenuity has great scope for her activities in the rehabilitation of the handicapped person in the environment in which he lives. She can dispel the idea that all she can do is give craft instruction, but can fill the role for which she was trained, namely, the rehabilitation of the substantially and permanently handicapped by idleness, injury or congenital deformity. One is hearing constantly of occupational therapists from hospitals taking on this specialised field work but seldom of any returning. It would be interesting to hear from those who do return and the reasons why they relinquished the challenge. It would also be interesting to hear from those who plod on.*[127]

Miss M. Burden, a teaching member of AOT and Head Occupational Therapist for the area in which Miss Castle worked, attempted to 'put Mrs. Pollard right on one or two matters on which she appears to be uninformed.':

*The referral of patients is initiated by a visit of the Head Occupational Therapist to the patient concerned and is then reviewed by a medical board and also receives the assent of the local doctor. The scope of Occupational Therapy for patients in this area includes, not only the more traditional treatment through the use of handcrafts, but also helps and advises on matters concerned with 'Aids to Daily Living' and in connection with vocational training and resettlement. In a rural area such as this, part-time light jobs and factory outwork are not available as they would be in a more densely populated area, and the provision of suitable home work, usually a handcraft of some sort is, in my opinion, a suitable substitute and in keeping with this area's reliance on its tourist trade since this is the main source of disposal. With regard to Mrs. Pollard's account of the handling of a case suggested for Occupational Therapy, I can only conclude that her information is incomplete, and if I can be supplied by Mrs. Pollard with accurate details of the case mentioned I will endeavour to put her right on a confidential level on the true state of affairs.*[128]

Ella Targett, a head occupational therapist from Oxford, joined the debate:

> *Referring to Mrs. Pollard's letter in answer to Miss Castle's article published in the July Journal, is there the remotest doubt that Miss Castle's letter was meant to he humorous?...I am rather tired of this attitude of occupational therapists smugly hanging on to the peg of 'Aids to Daily Living', 'Assessments' and all the other grand names... But Occupational Therapy has many facets and it ill becomes one to judge the other, I find it extremely difficult to believe Miss Pollard's story of a patient referred to the domiciliary occupational therapist by her sister a health visitor. No qualified therapist surely would approach a patient in the way referred to in Miss Pollard's letter, and I can only charitably assume the story is part legend!*
>
> *In Oxford the domiciliary occupational therapist works in close cooperation with all hospital departments. Cases are referred to her when 'Aids to Daily Living,' 'Assessment' etc., are needed, but the work does not stop there. A great deal of social work in connection with the patients inevitably falls to the lot of the domiciliary occupational therapist. Visiting the same patients over a long period should create a relationship of trust and understanding with the whole family and I venture to say that this relationship is unusual if not impossible for the therapist running a hospital department. I enjoyed Miss Castle's article in the spirit in which it was written and I do agree with her that 'from the very first we treat the whole person.'*[129]

Finally, Castle, another teaching member of AOT, responded:

> *...I made no attempt to write a straight article on domiciliary work. Indeed I could hardly do this on two years experience in one place. Aids to Daily Living need no champion. On the other hand wretched diversional therapy is in process of being elbowed out to the status of a poor relation whom many would like to see buried. I did part of my clinical practice under a very fine Head Occupational Therapist —it would be impossible to praise her too highly, yet she could hardly be brought to pronounce the word and this does seem to be the prevailing progressive acute angle!*
>
> *It's just that the home-bound chronic patient presents a different problem. Here, I see daily our much-maligned poor relation's inestimable good. My patients include severely disabled men whose self respect rests on regular work making rugs. 'I don't know what I'd do without it! It isn't the payment.' And they're so right: to struggle to do is to continue to live. For these men, their occupation does more than divert, it nourishes and sustains. Referring back to my article: 'Or if not then what?'...I have never rammed mounds of cane down the throat of a patient who only wanted to pick up her hanky. (What a terrible picture.)*[130]

Towards the end of the decade, in an article Therapies Galore, Drouet pointed to some of the issues requiring careful thought which resulted from the rejection of diversion. Starting with allusion to 'the "basket lady" from whose image we have tried so hard to shake ourselves free', she argued that, at least in skilled use of crafts, occupational therapists were considered specialists and 'different.' But, she asked '...is what we have put in its place as demonstrably clear? I think not.' She suggested that diversifying too widely when the professional population was so comparatively few in number, could result in not having any kind of recognisable role at all.

> *The wide diversification of treatment undertaken these days by occupational therapists makes the job very worth while, and those engaged in new and specialised undertakings have thrilling opportunities...(but)...We are still **occupational** therapists and the*

*outward forms we use must still be occupations of some kind, whether they be cultural, educational, recreational, or work.*[131]

So, the ever widening diversity of practice was becoming a seeming source of conflict between therapists. It was increasingly possible for each practitioner to take a different path. But without a clear unifying philosophical belief that fitted each path into a total picture, and without evidence to support the value of one over the other it was possible to overlook the value of some approaches and overstate the value of others according to environmental context. In the USA the same process was beginning to give birth to philosophical questioning, and on both sides of the Atlantic to a realisation that research was indeed required to begin to answer some of the vexed questions.

Against that background, a request was made to Alistair Heron, Director of the Medical Research Council Unit for Research on Occupational Aspects of Ageing at the University of Liverpool for a straight forward, down-to-earth bit of guidance. The immediate 'problem' which had precipitated the request was the need for an objective evaluation of the relative merits of 'traditional' versus 'industrial' therapy. His paper *Occupational Therapists and Evaluative Research* was published in SJOT in 1962. He was clear that 'the therapeutic merits of various types of occupation will never be firmly established without research' which alone could 'lift the matter beyond the present unsatisfactory, level of impressions and opinions.' Heron suggested that, 'with a few notable exceptions in every field, those gifted in clinical practice and in scientific research are very, very rarely the same people.' He stated, though, that occupational therapists should become involved in research only if they were prepared 'to submit themselves to the demands inherent in the methods of research', and if they could find 'interested advisers and the cooperative consultants.' A possible solution was to work in close co-operation with a university department of social scientists such as psychologists, with interest and guidance from a medical statistician.[132]

# Research: Does OT make a difference?
## By Irene Ilott

Calls for research that would support occupational therapist's claims and directions were made throughout the decade. In the same year as Heron's paper was published in SJOT, *Occupational Therapy* featured a request from WFOT for information about any professional research projects being carried out at that time.[133] A year later there was a report of a paper given by Dr Greenblatt of Harvard Medical School and Massachusetts Mental Health Center, *Research and the Future of Occupational Therapy as a Profession*, at a WFOT study course:

*...occupational therapy has much face validity, testimonials as to its merits, acceptance as a form of treatment, but is it inclined, perhaps to 'engage in repetitive practice as against scrutinizing basic concepts and theoretical problems?' Should it remain the handmaiden of psychiatry or should it take the longer and more difficult way to professional maturity by means of research, using the best consultative advice, training suitable individuals, re-orientating the training curricula and pressing for grants to carry*

*out research projects? What are its limits and potentialities? And can it take on the task of scientific validation?*[134]

Editorials in *Occupational Therapy* implicitly criticised the little 'serious research into the techniques and practice of occupational therapy' that had been undertaken in the 34 years since the first training school, at Dorset House, opened.

> *How much more do we now know than we knew then, as to why certain methods and certain devices are superior to others in the treatment of particular patients?—have we proved beyond reasonable doubt that this apparatus was wholly advantageous to the patient? That it was unrivalled by other means in achieving the specific aim of treatment?—what steps are we taking to establish our premises on the firm ground of careful and critical research rather than on the sands of complacent surmise? NOT MUCH AND NOT ENOUGH must be our answer if we face the facts with honesty and courage.*[135]

Owens who, was responsible for that Editorial suggested that the following series of questions required answers:

> *Is occupation therapeutic? Is occupation always therapeutic? Is the therapeutic effect of occupation dependent upon the environment in which the treatment is given? Or does it depend upon the nature of the activity used? Or does all depend upon the therapist? Is the therapeutic quality of occupation significantly associated in some way with the sex of the patient? Is the age group to which the patient belongs of prime importance? Or is diagnosis the critical factor? Or length of illness? Or former occupation? Or socio-economic status? Or is it a question of prognosis?*[136]

In another editorial Howie, too, emphasised the need for inquiry and research, asking 'How scientific are we as a profession? How scientific are you as a member of it?' and suggesting that 'our professional life should be both questing and questioning, absorbing new techniques and discarding those which are no longer of value.'[137] Three years later yet another editorial recommended looking with a critical eye and asking awkward questions because 'opportunities for original research lie all around us in our day to day work.'[138]

From the early 1960s, AOT sought not only to establish research itself, but also research priorities, and to gather intelligence about who was researching what. Council formed a small group to consider the need for special studies and research and assuming that little had been done, called for information about any investigations. In a 1964 editorial, Owens announced that a Special Studies Standing Committee had been established 'charged with the duty of fostering research in relation to practice.' The Committee selected handedness and application of programmed learning and use of teaching machines as key areas for investigation.[139]

Such calls and initiatives did not fall on deaf ears. Some research was carried in mental and physical occupational therapy practice areas, in staffing and recruitment, and in education.

In mental health, one of the first intervention trials of occupational therapy was published in 1960. Two groups of patients with chronic schizophrenia received a twelve week, intensive programme of craft, recreational and social activities, without chlorpromazine and then twelve weeks of routine (as distinct from intensive) occupational therapy with chlorpromazine. A psychologist compared rating scale scores on the initial and later programmes and found significant improvement following the 12 weeks intensive programme at 0.0005 level. The results demonstrated that 'an intensive programme of occupational therapy is capable of producing a considerable behavioural improvement in a small group of chronic schizophrenic patients.'[140] In an evaluative study of chronic psychotic patients by psychologists, a handicraft group with an occupational therapist, industrial work, and domestic work were compared. No differences between the groups were noted, but the author highlighted the importance of choice, concluding that 'greater effort should be made by nurses and occupational therapists to explore individual preferences and aptitudes in each case.'[141] The importance of choice was also highlighted in one of the first single case studies to be published. This explored the relationship between emotional stress and choice of media in play therapy in a 16-year-old girl. A correlation was found between her emotional state, distress, and decrease in choice of media.[142]

In 1966, the question of seamless care across health and social care was raised. A questionnaire surveyed head occupational therapists in psychiatric and general hospitals about follow-up of patients in the community. Two-thirds stated that it was not their responsibility; they did not have the time or staff. They considered that research into the topic was unnecessary, and most identified that follow-up was the responsibility of the almoner.[143]

Within the physical field, a series of articles in *Occupational Therapy* by Rosemary Hagedorn, extending between 1969 and 1975, reported the outcome of the work of the Panel for the Evaluation of Rehabilitation Equipment Design. The series demonstrated the connection between research, development, and application. The articles started with an expression of frustration regarding the 'inadequacy of the usual apparatus and techniques used in the physical treatment of the patient,' calling for the development of new treatment media appropriate to the technological age, and for research to provide a more scientific basis for our work.[144] In 1967 Mendez reported on a survey that questioned and informed parents of 61 children with bilateral upper limb difficulties about specialised assessment and treatment at the Children's Prosthetic Unit at Queen Mary's Hospital, Roehampton. She noted that the benefits of the survey had enabled the improvement of treatment techniques, and facilitated a treatment service to a further 23 children.[145] Most early studies used return to work or discharge home as outcome measures. However, it was during the mid-1960s that the imperative for specific, objective measures and records began to be noted and, occasionally, used. Howie's 1967 book *A Pilot study of Disabled Housewives in their Kitchen* was a case in point. She examined and compared the work routine of 30 able-bodied and disabled housewives to investigate norms, problems and needs.[146] Mountford, who reviewed the work for *Occupational Therapy*, described the author as one of the first occupational therapists to be employed to do research.[147] Similarly, Goble described an extensive follow-up study of patients, two years after discharge from Mary Marlborough Lodge. The aims were to assess the degree of success or failure of comprehensive rehabilitation and resettlement. She emphasised that the results of planned observation can provide information when developing new methods or proving why existing ones are pursued.[148]

The involvement of consumers and carers in occupational therapy research also started in the 1960s. This is now policy within the UK. An example of that practice was provided by Beeston, who described how a questionnaire in a survey intended to share knowledge, benefits and limitations of the 'Possum' equipment amongst patients was designed with 'one of the tetraplegics'.[149] Another, by Howie and Stewart, was one of the first collaborative evaluations of a service provided by occupational therapy and physiotherapy. The paper reported the outcome for 463 patients treated over a two-year period in a functional assessment unit. It reported how the 'gap between hospital and home life has been bridged for in-patients by forward planning of home arrangements and the provision of related training in the department.'[150]

Two psychologists, in collaboration with J.R. Chick, an occupational therapist, investigated the personality attributes of occupational therapists working in therapeutic communities and general hospitals in the context of providing guidance when recruiting staff. Using the Kuder Personal form, statistically significant differences were found between the two groups of therapists regarding preferences for working with ideas rather than with concrete things[151] In 1969 a survey of recruitment and training between 1963 and 1966 in five of the professions supplementary to medicine found that a typical recruit to occupational therapy was a middle class girl, educated at a grammar or private school, possibly having one or two subjects at advanced level, with relatives employed in the health services and attracted to the profession by the scope for meeting and helping people.[152]

Staff and students in training schools were expected to be research aware and active. A 1965 editorial urged staff of new training schools to find more ways of encouraging students to produce more original work at all levels of training and commented on the need for research.[153] In one of the first studies in occupational therapy education a survey was undertaken to find whether the knowledge of anatomy, physiology, and kinesiology acquired in training had been retained and applied in professional practice. The reasons for differences were considered, and modifications to instruction methods were recommended.[154]

Those early studies showed a willingness to attempt to go to the heart of matters that were in need of proving. Research inquiry grew slowly and surely from this time on, but the issue of applying results and making research known which was discussed in IRs Editorial of 1967 still remains a problem in the 21st century.[155]

**In summary**, the 1960s was a watershed decade. The movement towards functional activities and independence seriously challenged earlier paradigms of treatment, resulting in quite heated debate. The energy generated resonated across aspects of professional life so that both consolidation and diversification occurred. The new paradigms that advanced and changed practice were influenced by medical advances leading to decreased hospital stays. ADL, domestic resettlement, and independence became catch cries of the new direction in physical rehabilitation, whilst industrial therapy, group treatment, and therapeutic communities were trendsetters in psychiatry.

The importance of assessment, calls for research, and degree level and postgraduate education opportunities were signs of the decades to come.

[1]Mirrey LM, Johnson B. The Green Paper. Occupational Therapy 1969; (32)1: 17.
[2]Mirrey & Johnson. The Green Paper...
[3]Macdonald EM. World-Wide Conquests of Disabilities: The History, Development and Present Functions of the Remedial Services. London: Bailliere Tindall, 1981.
[4]Despite that omission Meredith Davies was later to become a supporter of occupational therapy. See later in this chapter and Ch. 9.
[5]Meredith Davies JB. Survey of the Government Report: Health and Welfare Development of Community Care. Occupational Therapy 1963; (26) 9:10.
[6]The Salmon Report: Members Discuss Difficulties. Occupational Therapy 1969; (32)2: 38.
[7]Macdonald. World-Wide Conquests of Disabilities...
[8]Richards S. Personal Communication to AAW, 2002.
[9]Macdonald. World-Wide Conquests of Disabilities...; 160-163.
[10]Macdonald. World-Wide Conquests of Disabilities...
[11]Mayne S. What is Zuckerman? Occupational Therapy 1969; (32)3: 23, 24.
[12]Macdonald. World-Wide Conquests of Disabilities...; 192-193.
[13]Association of Occupational Therapists. Annual Report and Balance Sheet. 1960, 1963, 1964.
[14]A.O.T. Annual Report and Balance Sheet. 1960.
[15]Dunkin EN. Summary of the Report —Occupational therapy, Present and Future—to the Council of the Association of Occupational Therapists from the Advisory Board of the Sub-Committee. Occupational Therapy 1966; (29) 8: 9,10,13.
[16]Goble REA. Planned Observation. Occupational Therapy 1968; 31 (7): 23–30.
[17]Planning Occupational Therapy Departments: Report on a one-day study course held by the Leeds Group at St. James's Hospital, Leeds. Occupational Therapy 1966; (29) 12: 42.
[18]Busy Year for Joint Council. Occupational Therapy 1967; 30 (1): 35.
[19]A.O.T. Annual Report and Balance Sheet. 1969; 5.
[20]Editorial. 1966 WFOT Congress Welcome to England. Occupational Therapy 1966; (29)6: 1.
[21] Editorial. 1966 WFOT Congress...
[22]World Federation of Occupational Therapists Fourth International Congress. Occupational Therapy 1966; 29(5):17–19.
[23]Decorating as a therapeutic activity, or Danger—Women at work, or Scrape, scrape, scrape. Occupational Therapy 1961 24 (8): 333; Venetian Blind Making in a general hospital. Occupational Therapy 1961; 24 (9): 22–24.
[24]Delinquency in Children and Occupational Therapy. Scottish Journal of Occupational Therapy 1968; June: 23–35.
[25]Farrer Brown L. The care and comfort of the Aged poor. Occupational Therapy 1962; 25 (9): 27–32.
[26]British Council for Rehabilitation of the Disabled. Report on a three day conference on Resettlement of the Disabled in a Changing Society. Occupational Therapy 1961; 24 (10): 28–30; Waterman J. Occupational Therapy and Resettlement. Scottish Journal of Occupational Therapy 1960; September: 18–27; Anon. From Disability to Work. Scottish Journal of Occupational Therapy 1962; September: 24–5.

[27]Moncrieff A. Cerebral palsy today. Occupational Therapy 1958; 21 (5): 13–17; Bobath K, Bobath B. An assessment of the motor handicap of children with cerebral palsy and of their response to treatment Occupational Therapy 1958; 21 (5): 19–34.

[28]Howie PM, Stewart MA. The functional assessment unit. Occupational Therapy 1962; 25 (5): 11–17; Fairley R. Assessment. Scottish Journal of Occupational Therapy 1969; December: 8–9; Geriatric Services and the Community: The domiciliary assessment of social problems Occupational Therapy 1962; 25 (7): 18–21.

[29]Bardon DT. Out factory work in mental hospitals. Occupational Therapy 1961; 24 (10): 18–20; Collins M. The development of an industrial unit. Occupational Therapy 1961; 24 (10): 20–26; Cullen GH. Vocational training and industrial rehabilitation. Occupational Therapy 1961; 24 (12): 12–20.

[30]Allbon L. Basic Basketry. London: Max Parrish, c1961.

[31]Brenda Morton B. Hobbies for the Housebound. London: Mills and Boon, c1961.

[32]McClurg Anderson T. Housework with Ease The Art of Movement in Education, Work and Recreation. Edinburgh: Scottish Council for Rehabilitation, 1957.

[33]Robinson K. Patterns of care. London: National Association of Mental Health, c1961.

[34]Klare H. Anatomy of Prison. Hutchinson, 1960.

[35]Cerebral Palsy—A Case Study. A Barnardo Technical Booklet. c1961.

[36]HMSO. Seats for Workers in Factories. London: HMSO, c1961.

[37]For example: Linn L, Weinroth LA, Shamah R. Occupational Therapy in Dynamic Psychiatry. Washington: American Psychiatric Association, c1961; Lucas C. Recreational Activity Development for the Ageing in Homes, Hospitals and Nursing Homes. Charles C Thomas, c1961; AOTA. Occupational Therapy Reference Manual for Physicians. Dubuque, Iowa: Wm C. Brown Book Co., 1961.

[38]Nottingham Handcraft. Occupational Therapy 1966; 29(11): 9.

[39]Jay PE. Personal communication to Author. December 2001.

[40]Jay PE. Personal communication to Author. December 2001.

[41]WDM. Journal Cover. Occupational Therapy 1966; 29(6): 3.

[42]Sym D. Professions Supplementary To Medicine Bill. Scottish Journal of Occupational Therapy 1960; March (pages 6-9).

[43]Connochie M. Letter to the Editor. Scottish Journal of Occupational Therapy 1962; June: 41–43.

[44]Editorial. Occupational Therapy 1964; 27(1): 1.

[45]Editorial. Occupational Therapy 1966; 29(10): 17.

[46]Rook JM. 1963. Education —What? and Why? Looking Ahead to the Future. Occupational Therapy 1963; 26(7): 3–19.

[47]Dunkin. Summary of the Report—Occupational therapy, Present and Future...; 9,10,13.

[48]A.O.T. Annual Report and Balance Sheet. 1965.

[49]Dunkin. Summary of the Report—Occupational therapy, Present and Future...; 9,10,13.

[50]Owens AC. Selection for Training as an Occupational Therapist—A Survey of Selection Procedures used at the Liverpool School of Occupational Therapy, 1946–1959. Unpublished MA thesis. Liverpool: University of Liverpool, 1960: 14.

[51]Dunkin. Summary of the Report—Occupational therapy, Present and Future...; 10,13.

[52]Dunkin. Summary of the Report—Occupational therapy, Present and Future...; 9, 11-13.

[53]Professor Hearnshaw. In: Alice Constance Owen 1906–1976, remembered by her friends. British Journal of Occupational Therapy 1977; 40(1): 7–9.

[54]Busy Year for Joint Council. Occupational Therapy 1967; 30 (1): 35.

[55]Jay PE. Personal communication to AAW. 2001.

[56]A.O.T. Annual Report and Balance Sheet. 1962; 5.

[57]The Association and its members. Occupational Therapy 1963; 26 (8): 1.

[58]Wright EM. The Value of Occupational Therapy in the Assessment of Psychiatric Patients. Scottish Journal of Occupational Therapy 1963; September: 4–17.

[59]Hamilton KM. Patient Assessment. Scottish Journal of Occupational Therapy 1962; June: 29–31.

[60]Goble REA. Planned Observation. Occupational Therapy 1968; 31(7): 23, 24.

[61]Owens AC. Re-appraisal From Youth to Age: A contextual and age-related approach to rehabilitation. Occupational Therapy 1967; 30(2): 19, 20.

[62]Dunkin. Summary of the Report—Occupational therapy, Present and Future...; 10,11.

[63]Macdonald. World-Wide Conquests of Disabilities...; 160–3.

[64]Macdonald EM, ed. Occupational Therapy in Rehabilitation. London: Bailliere, Tindall & Cox, 1960.

[65]Mountford SW. A Fresh Look at Hemiplegia. Occupational Therapy 1966; 29(10): 19, 20, 21.

[66]Jones MS. An Approach to Occupational Therapy. London: Butterworths, 1960.

[67]Wynn Parry CB, assisted by Smythe NR & Baker LE. Rehabilitation of the Hand. London: Butterworths, 1958.

[68]Cross H. Some New Ideas in Hand Splints. Occupational Therapy 1966; 29(11): 25.

[69]Devas MB. Tyrell M. Rehabilitation of Patients with fractures near the wrist. Occupational Therapy 1967; 30(9): 24.

[70]Ingamells KM. Extracts from Occupational therapy for Hand Conditions. Occupational Therapy 1966; 29(7): 8, 16, 28, 29.

[71]Liverpool Domiciliary Refresher Course. Occupational Therapy 1961; (24) 11: 19, 20, 21

[72]Dunkin. Summary of the Report—Occupational therapy, Present and Future...; 9,10.

[73]Dunkin. Summary of the Report—Occupational therapy, Present and Future...; 9,10

[74]Perks AM. The Place of Occupational Therapy in a therapeutic community. Occupational Therapy 1968; 31(12): 32.

[75]Perks. The Place of Occupational Therapy in a therapeutic community...

[76]Perks. The Place of Occupational Therapy in a therapeutic community...

[77]Fisher JDW. Progress towards a network of mental health centres. Occupational Therapy 1967; 30(1): 44.

[78]Manley ID. Delinquency in children and the method of treatment in a child psychiatric unit. Scottish Journal of Occupational Therapy 1968; June: 23–32.

[79]Macdonald. World-Wide Conquests of Disabilities...; 153–4.

[80]Mendez MA. Residual Abilities. Occupational Therapy 1962; 25(8): 11-16.

[81]Anon. From Disability to Work. Scottish Journal of Occupational Therapy 1962; Sept: 24–5.

[82] Industrial Rehabilitation of the Mentally Disabled. Occupational Therapy 1966; 29(12): 17. (republished from Ministry of Labour Gazette Nov. 1966)

[83]Jones M. Social Psychiatry. London: Tavistock Publications, 1952.

[84]Heron A. Occupational Therapists and Evaluative Research. Scottish Journal of Occupational Therapy 1962; March: 5–8.

[85]Affleck JW. Social Psychiatry. Scottish Journal of Occupational Therapy 1962; Sept: 12–19.

[86]Affleck. Scottish Journal of Occupational Therapy...

[87]Williams M, Health Board Archivist. History of Crichton Royal Hospital 1839–1989. Dumfries and Galloway Health Board, 1989; 39.

[88]Hetherington K. Opening of new OT Department Carlton Hayes Hospital, Narborough Leics. Occupational Therapy 1963; 26(9): 22–3.

[89]Henderson C. Royal Edinburgh Hospital. In: Notes From The Mental Hospitals.

Scottish Journal of Occupational Therapy 1960; June: 26–31
[90]Notes from the Mental Hospitals. Scottish Journal of Occupational Therapy. 1960; June : 26–31.
[91]Pitts J. Assessment and treatment of cerebral palsied hemiplegic patients. Occupational Therapy 1968; 31(4): 19.
[92]Pitts. Assessment and treatment of cerebral palsied hemiplegic patients..; 26.
[93]Colburn J. Some Methods of Work Evaluation. Occupational Therapy 1963; 26(8): 11.
[94]Waterston J. Occupational Therapy and Resettlement Scottish Journal of Occupational Therapy 1960; September: 19–26.
[95]Binnie E. Occupational Therapy and Activities of Daily Living. Aberdeen Royal Infirmary Nurses League Journal. 1960: 44.
[96]Hollings EM. Liverpool Domiciliary Refresher course, Monday 18 September, 1961 Mary Marlborough Lodge Nuffield Orthopaedic Centre, Oxford. Occupational Therapy 1961; 24 (12): 23, 27.
[97]Hamilton A. Wider concept of occupational therapy. Occupational Therapy 1968; 31(1): 16.
[98]News from home and abroad: Teaching the paralysed (Possum) Occupational Therapy 1962; 25(7): 28.
[99]Smith S. The Disabled Living Activities Group of the Central Council for the Disabled. Occupational Therapy 1967; 30(4): 36.
[100]Hamilton Lady. Pioneer of the Disabled. Occupational Therapy 1977; 40(1): 16.
[101]Hamilton. Pioneer of the Disabled....
[102]Editorial. Information Service for the Disabled. Occupational Therapy 1968; 31(4): 17
[103]Editorial. Information Service for the Disabled...
[104]Hamilton. Pioneer of the Disabled...
[105]Hamilton. Pioneer of the Disabled...
[106]Smith C. Between the streamlet and the town: A brief history of the Astley Ainslie Hospital. Printed and bound by Polton House Press, 1988; 54.
[107]Anstice B. Training in Daily Living Simon Square Centre, Edinburgh Cripple Aid Society. Scottish Journal of Occupational Therapy 1966; (84): 21.
[108]Liverpool Domiciliary Refresher Course, Tuesday, 19 September, 11.15am. Occupational Therapy 1962; 25(2): 21.
[109]Jay P, Walker E, Ellison A. Help Yourselves: A handbook for Hemiplegics and their Families. London: Butterworths, 1966.
[110]Notes From The Mental Hospitals. Scottish Journal of Occupational Therapy 1960; June: 26–31.
[111]Powell KJ. The Role of the Local Authority Welfare Services in Patient Resettlement. Occupational Therapy 1969; 32 (6): 37–40.
[112]Report of the Central Council for the Disabled Conference. Bournemouth: 1965.
[113]Powell. The Role of the Local Authority Welfare Services in Patient Resettlement...
[114]Chitty M. An occupational therapist's collaboration with social workers in a welfare department. Occupational Therapy 1968; 31(11): 19,24.
[115]Cavaye AH. 1963. Research into Housing and Equipment for the Disabled. Looking Ahead to the Future. Occupational Therapy 1963; 26(7): 3–19.
[116]Smith S. The Disabled Living Activities Group of the Central Council for the Disabled. Occupational Therapy 1967; 30(4): 36.
[117]Goldsmith S. Designing for the Disabled: A Manual of Technical Information. London: Royal Institute of British Architects. 1963.
[118]Owens AC. Re-appraisal from Youth to Age...; 19, 20.
[119]Heathcote M. Social Patterns. Occupational Therapy 1961; 24(12): 22.

[120]Plummer M. Creative Aspects of Occupational Therapy. Scottish Journal of Occupational Therapy 1969; June: 35.

[121]Glover V. The therapeutic use of music. Scottish Journal of Occupational Therapy 1969; September: 13.

[122]Wynne C. The North Wales Hospital, Denbigh, 1842–1955. Denbigh: Gee & Son, 1955; 32.

[123]Wynne. The North Wales Hospital…; 32, 34 .

[124]Smith MM. Experimental Approaches to the Treatment of Short-Stay Psychiatric Patients. In: Looking Ahead to Future Developments. Occupational Therapy 1963; 30(7): 7–11.

[125]Back SA. Developing the work pattern in a purpose-built day centre. Occupational Therapy 1967; 30(4): 33.

[126]Pollard KS. Correspondence. Occupational Therapy 1961; 24(8): 28.

[127]Occupational Therapy Section. Correspondence 'Mobile Occupational Therapy'. Occupational Therapy 1961; 24(9): 15.

[128]Burden M. Correspondence. Occupational Therapy 1961; 24 (9): 16.

[129]Targett E. Corresondence. Occupational Therapy 1961; 24(9): 16.

[130]Castle P. Correspondence. Occupational Therapy 1961; 24(10): 17.

[131]Drouet VM. Therapies Galore. Occupational Therapy 1968; 31(2): 25.

[132]Heron A. Occupational Therapists and Evaluative Research. Scottish Journal of Occupational Therapy 1962; March: 5–8.

[133]Notices. Occupational Therapy 1962; 25 (4): 14.

[134]Smith MM. WFOT Study Course 2: Transitional programmes in psychiatric occupational therapy. Occupational Therapy 1963; 26(8): 20–23.

[135]ACO (Dr Owens). Editorial. Occupational Therapy 1964; 27(2): 1–2.

[136]Owens AC. An occupational therapist's approach to research. Part 1. Occupational Therapy 1964; 27(6): 11–12.

[137]Howie PM. Editorial. Occupational Therapy 1966; 29(5): 1–2.

[138]IR. Editorial: Research—can it help us. Occupational Therapy 1967; 30(4): 19–20.

[139]ACO. Editorial. Occupational Therapy 1964; 27(2): 1–2.

[140]Fransella F. The treatment of chronic schizophrenia. Intensive occupational therapy with and without chlorpromazine. Occupational Therapy 1960; 23(9): 31–4.

[141]Hutt SJ, Crookes TG. An evaluative study of occupational therapy. Occupational Therapy 1964; 27(2): 13–16.

[142]Waller G. The relationship between emotional stress and choice of media in play therapy. Occupational Therapy 1968; 31(7): 17–21.

[143]Sutherland M, Searle KF, Smith MM. Should we follow-up our patients? Occupational Therapy 1966; 29(12): 28–9.

[144]Hagedorn R. Our apparatus and techniques. Occupational Therapy 1969; 32(12): 18–19.

[145]Mendez MA. Survey by the occupational therapy staff of the Children's Prosthetic Unit at Queen Mary's Hospital, Roehampton. Occupational Therapy 1967; 30(5) 19–24.

[146]Howie PM. A Pilot study of Disabled Housewives in their Kitchen. London: Disabled Living Activities Group. 1967.

[147]Mountford SW. Book Review. Occupational Therapy 1968; 31(9): 31–5.

[148]Goble REA. The role of the occupational therapists in disabled living research. Occupational Therapy 1968; 31(2): 32–4; Goble REA, Nichols PJR. Rehabilitation of the Severly Disabled 1: Evaluation of a Disabled Living Unit. London: Butterworths, 1971.

[149]Beeston EM. Personal communications report on a POSSUM questionnaire. Occupational Therapy 1968; 31(8): 13–18.

[150]Howie PM, Stewart ME. The Functional Assessment Unit, Department of Physical Medicine King's College Hospital. A report of two years' work. Occupational Therapy 1962; 25(5): 11–17.

[151]Caine TM, Chick JR, Smail DJ. Personality attributes of occupational therapists. Occupational Therapy 1967; 30(8): 25–7.

[152]Martin EM. Recruitment and training. Occupational Therapy 1969; 32(10): 31–3.

[153]JMR. Editorial. Occupational Therapy 1965; 28(1): 1–2.

[154]Dunkin EN. A survey concerning the principal applications of anatomy, physiology and kinesiolgy for occupational therapists. Occupational Therapy 1965; 28(5): 18–22.

[155]IR. Editorial: Research—can it help us. Occupational Therapy 1967; 30(4): 19–20.

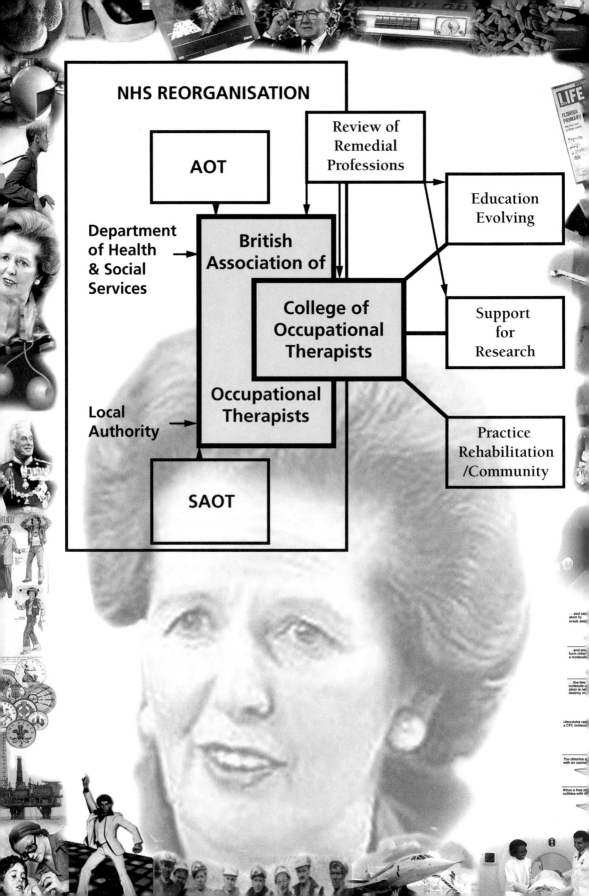

**NHS REORGANISATION**

AOT

Review of Remedial Professions

Department of Health & Social Services →

British Association of

College of Occupational Therapists

Education Evolving

Support for Research

Occupational Therapists

Local Authority →

SAOT

Practice Rehabilitation /Community

# Chapter 9

# Into the Community: New Look Social Services

## Content

In this chapter, the story is told of how the changes that dominated the profession during the 1960s escalated in the next decade. The 1970s saw significant developments towards community rather than institutional care as part of government initiatives. Changes within Health and Social Services resulted in Local Authorities becoming largely responsible for care of people within their own environments, and more and more occupational therapists working within those services engaged in functional assessment and helping people with activities of daily living.

Within the professional body itself, exciting changes were the order of the day. It was the decade when, from its two antecedents, the British Association was formed, and the journal of AOT and SAOT were combined. Later in the decade, the Association was to become a trade union, and the College of Occupational Therapists was established as a wholly owned subsidiary in order to retain charitable status for professional and educational concerns. New headquarters were acquired, and earlier models of training gradually began the metamorphosis towards mainstream tertiary education. Yet, despite all the positive activity, it was a decade of professional self doubt which manifested itself in feelings of being misunderstood by both the medical fraternity and the general public. Even today this has not been eliminated completely.

## Context of the times: Restructuring, resources, human rights, and community care

The 1970s was a decade when the socio-economic aftermath of World War II finally settled down. Mass media interest in issues across the globe, resulted in a dawning of appreciation that problems thousands of miles away could have serious consequences for the rest of the world. So it was not only the ongoing Cold War between communist and capitalist societies which concerned political thought and the masses, but issues such as the rapid growth of populations in developing countries, and human rights. At home as elsewhere, the issue of human and civil rights led to change, including an intensification of the women's movement culminating in 1975 being nominated 'International Women's Year'. On the economic front, intervention became increasingly worldwide with a rise of development economics and the attempt to control currency exchange rates. Oil prices escalated in 1973 and serious inflation spread to all the industrialised nations. The European Economic Community (EEC) expanded to include Britain, Ireland, and Denmark. In contrast to those economic growth initiatives, environmentalists and the conservation movement argued that to continue down the same materialistic track in the same way was incompatible with preservation of the natural world and they predicted the imminent disappearance of natural resources. Despite such warnings, the development of resource expensive technology continued apace with, for example, numerous space probes following the moon landing in 1969, and the birth of the first test tube baby in England in 1978.[1]

An immediate, but not devastating, effect on occupational therapy was felt from the strikes, and the power cuts which resulted from the economic difficulties experienced during the decade. In 1974, *Occupational Therapy* apologised that, owing to the difficulties caused by the three-day week and transport hold-ups, it had to bring forward the latest time for accepting advertisements until conditions returned to normal.[2] In the same year a shortage of paper in Britain, as well as an increase in its cost, led to a thinner, but not necessarily cheaper variety being used for the Journal.[3]

In the National Health Service (NHS), as elsewhere, economic conditions were tight. Nigel Weaver, a co-author of *A Unified Health Service*, provided an overview in *Occupational Therapy* of problems, resources, and predictions for the NHS as he saw them. He raised first a relevant but philosophical problem which has often been addressed in the following decades, but which seemed not to have attracted much attention prior to that time. How does one recognise a healthy person who meets the World Health Organisation definition of complete physical, mental and social well-being? He suggested that Beveridge at the end of the second world war equated better health with decreased morbidity and illness, which is perhaps why he claimed the NHS would soon pay for itself. However, commonly accepted standards of good health vary, and in the 1970s notions of ill-health had changed from the, mainly, acute infectious disorders which were prevalent in Beveridge's period of office, to chronic progressive diseases and 'obesity, alcoholism, depression, sexual deviations and even strained family relationships.'[4]

Apart from the primary question about the nature of health, there was another about what the country had expected to achieve from the NHS. The lack of a real definition had resulted in virtually unlimited demands on it. Weaver pointed to the problem of the elderly. The number of people over 65 was rising, and already that age group occupied 35% of hospital beds; many needs were unmet, and there was no immediate likelihood of increased services, health visitors, or accommodation. Weaver thought that the solution might lie in other than institutional care. Family support services had been calculated as costing less than one-third of institutional care, and it would make sense to increase that option. That would require more routine visiting, primary prevention, and 'bolder plans' such as provision for heating each winter. Weaver predicted that prevention of illness would assume greater importance in the future with concerted planning, and increased public education and involvement.[5]

The stimulation of interest in and discussion of preventive medicine in all relevant sections of the community was the aim of the Health Department's publication of *Prevention and Health: Everybody's Business* in 1976. Its object was not to recommend specific programmes of activity but to stimulate greater awareness of the possible contribution of preventive measures towards the solution of the country's health problems. The Department was aware that opportunities for developments would be limited by constraints on available resources of money and manpower. However, as not all preventive measures necessarily required additional or substantial resources, a large portion of responsibility for preventing disease could lie with individual practitioners, health service authorities, and individual members of the public.[6,7] A comment in the *British Journal of Occupational Therapy* about the publication welcomed the initiative 'as the first step in a long overdue process...(to)...a more health conscious public taking sensible steps designed to improve their own health.'[8]

Similarly, the government publication *Priorities for Health and Personal Social Services in England* took a cautious approach to spending. Limited national financial resources made it clear that growth in any service could be afforded only if economies were made elsewhere. The emphasis was on caring for more people in the community, and the development of services to meet the most urgent needs of elderly, mentally ill and mentally handicapped people. The main objective of services for elderly people was 'primary care', that is, 'care mainly provided by general practitioners' which was to help them remain in the community for as long as possible. A secondary objective was to improve hospital facilities for early diagnosis, intensive treatment, and rehabilitation. Emphasis was given to:
- the development of primary health care teams
- preventive activities and family planning services
- preventing pharmaceutical costs from rising unduly.[9]

A preventive measure of particular relevance to occupational therapy was a warning provided by the World Health Oganisation that boredom and loneliness may be overlooked as a cause of patients' dependency. The warning came as a result of a working group on rehabilitation in long-term and geriatric care. The working group considered rehabilitation as a service rather than a speciality which should be aimed at each individual using 'his full abilities', and that 'experience clearly shows that training and activation are valuable.'[10]

The cries for a return to earlier preventive paradigms of care, whether prompted by good sense or economics, had little impact on the custom of striving to update policy to both decrease the cost and improve the offerings of social and ill-health services in the realm of national politics. The 1970 Chronically Sick and Disabled Persons Act, sponsored by Alfred Morris, Parliamentary Under-Secretary at the Department of Health, and the Local Authority Social Services (LASS) Act of the same year, were cases in point. As a result of these Acts, and the Social Work Scotland Act 1968 occupational therapists began to work in social work/social services, when, prior to that time they had been employed mainly in the NHS.

The LASS Act, which was aimed at providing a unified system of personal social services, set up committees in the major local authorities with a director of social services to administer them. Those bodies took over some of the functions previously administered through earlier legislation. This included: 1946 NHS Act; the 1948 National Assistance Act and Children's Act; the 1958 Disabled Persons Employment Act; the 1959 Mental Health Act; the 1962 Health Visiting and Social Work Training Act; the 1966 Ministry of Social Security Act; the 1968 Health Services and Public Health Act; and some of the functions of the 1970 Chronically Sick and Disabled Persons Act. Local authorities began speedily to apply the Act, and because of differing socio-economic needs across regions there were understandable concerns about, for example, the varied range in money available to be spent on disabled individuals each year. The difference could be as great as £7–£70.[11] Occupational therapists working in social services became aware of their mandatory responsibility to inform clients about any services or benefit to which they might be entitled. Many local health authorities had already employed occupational therapists in their community health services, and whilst most therapists transferred over to local authorities, in several areas, they elected to stay in local health as was the case in Northamptonshire, Buckinghamshire, Bedfordshire and Oxford city, for example. Most local authorities became providers of occupational therapy services at that time but some, such as in Lancashire and many of the metropolitan authorities around Manchester, never planned or developed them relying, instead, on the local NHS provision.

Sir Keith Joseph became the Secretary of State for the DHSS in 1970 and the following year issued a *National Health Service Reorganisation Consultative Document*, which was enacted in 1973 and implemented in 1974. The administrative reorganisation of the NHS was planned to link closely with Local Authorities to provide better services for all. It stressed the importance of intensive rehabilitation. In preparation, the Local Authorities had set up a Management Study Steering Committee in 1972, which proposed management structures for the reorganised NHS including the 'Organisation of Skill Groups' such as paramedical therapy services.[12] Because there was not always parallel linkage with LASS (known as co-terminosity) difficulties resulted for some NHS based occupational therapists having to work with more than one local authority.[13]

With the publication of *National Health Service Reorganisation and Management Arrangements* for the Reorganised National Health Service there was an increased demand for community occupational therapists and more started to work in LASS Departments which were taking over responsibility for the problems of disabled people in the community. It was 'the name of the employing authority and the disappearance of the existing management structure that had been used in hospitals since 1948' that was the main change for most therapists.[14] To administer the new service there were 14 Regional Health Authorities and approximately 90 Area Health Authorities. What remained outside the triumvirate of hospitals, local authority services, and general practitioners included residential accommodation, community mental health services, home help services, the social services departments.[15] Additionally, in terms of rehabilitation and resettlement, the provision of industrial rehabilitation and vocational training remained with the Secretary of State for Employment. By the 1970s there were some 23 industrial rehabilitation units (IRUs) but only one, Garston Manor, combined industrial and medical rehabilitation on the same site. Disappointingly these remained separate. There were 42 government training centres providing mostly six-month courses in skilled trades. The Department of Employment also paid for courses at some residential training centres for disabled people run by voluntary societies such as: Finchale Abbey in Durham; Portland Training College in Mansfield; Queen Elizabeth's Training College in Leatherhead; and St Loyes College in Exeter.[16]

A change of government on the eve of NHS reorganisation in 1974 did cause some concern that this might be abandoned. It was not. However, the new Labour minister of the NHSS, Barbara Castle, rejected more organisational upheavals, except to make the bodies more accountable to the public. To do that she proposed, for example, that there should be more staff representatives on statutory bodies.[17]

In Chapter 8 the establishment in 1968 of the Standing Medical Advisory Committee on Rehabilitation known as the Tunbridge Committee was described (the Mair Committee was the Scottish equivalent[18]). Their terms of reference were to consider: the future provision, organisation, and development of NHS rehabilitation services; the function and inter-relationship of the three remedial professions—occcupational therapy, physiotherapy and remedial gymnastics, and their relation to other personnel concerned with rehabilitation; and the broad pattern of staffing required.[19] In July 1971, the Secretary of State for Social Services asked if he might receive the Tunbridge Committee's advice as soon as possible. The Chairman, to avoid further delay, submitted a brief statement of the Committee's views in place of a formal report which was later published, in February 1972, for consideration by bodies like the Council for the Professions Supplementary to Medicine (CPSM) and the NHS Whitley Council. The fact of publication was not a commitment to the contents, many of which were to be considered afresh in other forums.[20,21]

The Statement began:
*After careful review of the work of the three professions we accept that whilst there are spheres of activity common to all three, special aptitudes and skills are required for each of the three and they attract different candidates. We anticipate that the further development*

*of the rehabilitation services and the establishment of integrated training schools will encourage the professions to work more closely together and will increase the range of common activities.*

The Committee identified four principal areas of difficulty:

1. Remuneration was low in comparison with other professions of equivalent responsibility and educational background. That was aggravated in the case of occupational therapists by differences in salary scales between the NHS and LASS. The remedial professions were seen as particularly vulnerable to loss of skilled staff because they were predominantly female. Better salary scales were recommended to encourage more men into the profession.

2. Career structures were a source of difficulty in their own right. There were insufficient senior posts at a sufficiently high level for clinical, teaching, or research responsibilities.

3. Each of the remedial professions had an important role in rehabilitation despite some areas of common activity. In the immediate future, it was deemed in the best interest of patients that each continue to contribute its own special skill. In this section of the statement some controversial points were raised, namely: despite doctors' responsibility and prescription of rehabilitation, more scope could and should be given to therapists in its application; the domiciliary role of NHS employees should be primarily to advise and instruct, rather than to give treatment.

4. There was a serious lack of research into the effectiveness of various forms of remedial and rehabilitation treatment. The setting up of a special research advisory body or council to promote research in the field of rehabilitation was advocated strongly.

The Statement recommended:

*(a) A complete review of training syllabuses both independently and jointly...and consider(ed) it would be possible to have a first year (and possibly more) with much training in common...*

*(b) Common entrance requirements.*

*(c) Acceptance of candidates at the age of 17.*

*(d) The integration of existing schools...students sharing common room, library, catering and other amenity conditions.*

*(e) The concentration and rationalisation of centres for training and the association of training schools with other centres of further or higher education...limit(ing) the (number of) training centres in the United Kingdom to twenty...within the next ten years.*

*(f) Teachers should receive further and higher training in educational methods...*

*(g) Urgent attention must also be given to the training of clinical supervisors...*[22]

A copy of the Statement was enclosed in the February 1972 issue of *Occupational Therapy.*[23]

The Tunbridge Report and the Statement by the Committee on the Remedial Professions were great disappointments to the members of these professions. At a conference held in July of that year the professional organisations made it clear to Sir Keith Joseph that having waited for some years 'for constructive proposals for their future, they felt they had been let down. They saw no prospects of progress in the development of their professions or proper recognition of the skills and service they had to offer to the community.'[24] The Secretary of State called a meeting early in 1973 of representatives of the three professions together with the CPSM. He invited them to form a small working party with officers of the DHSS, under the chairmanship of Mr EL McMillan, with the objective of considering how best to construct an effective remedial service. Elizabeth Grove represented occupational therapy. It was noted that the Chartered Society of Physiotherapy and the Society of Remedial Gymnasts were considering amalgamation, and such an amalgamation was seen as a pointer to the future. It was recommended that 'ultimately all three professions should unite' to form a comprehensive one within which 'there would be scope for specialisation.' Apart from that, the McMillan Committee put forward a further five basic recommendations: increased professional and managerial responsibility; a new career and salary structure reflecting the new responsibilities; new methods of training; increased use and recognition of aides, and other supporting staff; and recognition of the need for research. The Report concluded:

> We believe that if this opportunity is missed the work of the remedial professions could in many aspects degenerate to the level of mechanical application of simple techniques; there could be no development of the rehabilitation services; no sense of service; and desperate problems of recruitment. The person who would suffer most would be the patient.[25]

An interesting ancient quote attributed to Arbiter Petronius[26] used by 'Agag' in *Occupational Therapy*, in the same year, suggests a more cautious approach to reorganisation might be have been advisable:

> We trained hard, but it seemed that every time we were beginning to form into teams we would be reorganised. I was to learn later in life that we tend to meet any new situation by reorganising and what a wonderful method it is for creating an illusion of progress, while producing confusion, inefficiency and demoralisation.[27]

Agag was the name chosen for a regular feature in *Occupational Therapy* of the political, health and welfare scene. 'Its aim (was) to be a commentary and not a soap-box and as the author's name implies it will try to tread delicately.'[28] Agag was King of the Amalekites who when brought to Samuel, it is written, came 'delicately'.[29]

It was obvious from some of the consultative processes of the Tunbridge, Mair, and McMillan Committees that career structures and conditions of work, along with delays in negotiations, caused considerable concerns for occupational therapists during the first few years of the decade. For example, at a meeting of head occupational therapists in 1974, concern was expressed about the disparity in the remuneration between health and social services based occupational therapists. Better pay, in part, resulted in a drift of qualified staff into social services where other attractive conditions included better prospects, a car allowance, more autonomy, less control by the medical profession, and more convenient, flexible hours of work.[30]

In 1974, the Halsbury Committee of Inquiry was appointed by the DHSS to inquire into pay and conditions of service of the Professions Supplementary to Medicine[31]. The Management Unit of the Whitley Council provided general background information, and each of the professional associations submitted written evidence about roles and educational requirements. In addition, Committee representatives made visits to hospitals and community health centres. Its final report was published in 1975. The positive result of the inquiries encouraged the Whitley Council to deal with the graded salary proposals, and to accept and fulfill the recommendations, with the provision that the professions negotiated according to Trade Union approaches.[32,33]

Lord McCarthy, an acknowledged expert on industrial relations, was appointed by the Secretary of State for Social Services in April 1975 as a special adviser to the Department of Health. He was charged with the task of reviewing the workings of the NHS Whitley Council. His long awaited Report was published in 1977. He proposed that Regional Councils should negotiate local conditions, provided there were improved methods of consultation. It was considered valuable to have a steward nominated for each English and Welsh Area Health Authority, and for the Scottish and Northern Ireland Health Regions. At that time, some therapists belonged to trade unions, and the unions considered that they could provide stronger negotiations on important matters, but this was not enforced. Although the Management section of the Whitley Council was pleased to deal with them, it also recognised professional associations. As a response to the general direction towards unionism, the latter investigated the possibility of setting up their own unions whilst retaining their Associations to deal with professional responsibilities. Occupational therapists were one group to do so.[34]

In Professor Cairns Aitken's 1976 Casson Memorial Lecture *Rehabilitation: Facts and Fantasies about Occupational Therapy* he referred to the political context. 'No subject,' he said 'more than rehabilitation has had such a plethora of reports in recent years advocating what should be its future.' He referred to reports in the early 1970s which addressed the nature of educational requirements; to the 1974 National Health Service, the 1968–69 Social Work, and the 1970 Chronically Sick and Disabled Persons Acts which reorganised local government;[35] and particularly to the Tunbridge, Mair, and McMillan Reports which endeavoured to alter the whole direction of services and the nature of professional arrangements. He noted with some concern that many of the new measures to help people with disability provided substantial cash benefits, while not being accompanied by increased provision for complementary professional services, which he believed would have detrimental effects on disabled people in the next decade.[36]

He went on to talk about occupational therapists' concern about insufficient recognition being given to 'practical skills and personal relationships' within the rehabilitation of patients. He talked with admiration of how occupational therapists had pioneered attention to the real needs of patients, approaching them as people who wish to do things in life irrespective of their diagnosis—psychiatric or physical. Aitken appeared to be encouraging occupational therapists to continue in that way despite the direction of recent legislation. He said:

*Over the centuries there has been ample evidence proving the effects of social circumstances on the pattern of disease. Evidence is accumulating on the importance of psychological state on current morbidity and even mentality. Many of the principal disorders in our society are known to be influenced by our behaviour, such as in relation to drug addiction (tobacco, alcohol and barbiturates), violence (accident and aggression), and habit (diet and exercise). Psychological factors seem to determine presentation of somatic complaint as often as simply the physical pathology...So often it is not the 'what' we do but the 'how' which matters.[37]*

# British Association of Occupational Therapists

Joint Council, which had been formed to deal with matters related to the World Federation of Occupational Therapists, had forged closer links between SAOT and AOT. It began taking a leading role on issues such as the preparation of a code of ethics for the United Kingdom and negotiations for State Registration. The need for a national body became increasingly obvious. SAOT was a small organisation and would benefit from having access to the facilities and wider membership of the AOT. At the same time, their members did not want to lose their identity and be swallowed up by the bigger organisation. A document was prepared setting out the advantages and disadvantages of amalgamation. A referendum was held in 1969 and the results were: AOT 525 for, 1 against; SAOT 81 for, 10 against. This mandate enabled the two Associations to go ahead with detailed work to set up the British Association of Occupational Therapists (BAOT).

**Figure 2.9.1: The formation of the British Association of Occupational Therapists**

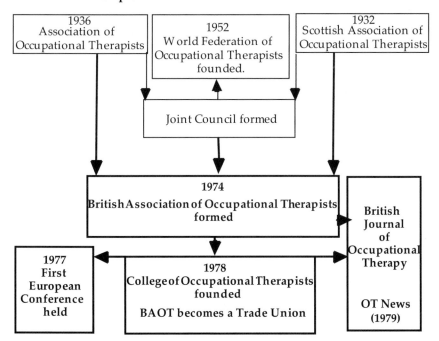

It was in 1974 that the BAOT formally came into being, following an extraordinary general meeting to pass the necessary resolutions. Despite a rail strike, members travelled to London from Scotland, Wales, and distant parts of England to vote for the merger. The first Chairman of the new Association, Peggy Jay, announced:

*THE AMALGAMATION between the Association of Occupational Therapists and the Scottish Association of Occupational Therapists took place on May 10. We have been looking forward to this event for many years. Although the negotiations have been prolonged they have given us an opportunity to get to know many of our colleagues north of the border and mutually to exchange ideas. This will surely help us to make a smooth transition into the British Association of Occupational Therapists....It is also appropriate at this time of re-organisation in the Health Service that we should be able to speak with one united voice. Although Scotland comes under the Scottish Home and Health Department, many of the problems facing occupational therapists are the same throughout the country. We are all seeking adequate representation at appropriate levels so that we can have some say in the development of rehabilitation services. We all face the prospect of more occupational therapists leaving the hospitals to work with local authorities. We all have salary problems. We hope that this union will strengthen the impact of any representations we may make.*[38]

When the President of the newly formed Association, Sir Alan Hitchman, welcomed delegates to Newcastle for its first Annual Conference in 1974, he did so with a similar message: '...It is extremely desirable that your profession should be able to make its united voice heard, for only in this way will it carry the fullest weight.' He went on to report that the Association had found new premises for its headquarters. The Council had purchased a 20-year lease of offices at 20 Rede Place, Bayswater, London.[39] Apparently the move to Rede Place was accomplished with remarkably little disturbance with 85 tea chests and five iron baskets.[40]

At the official opening ceremony of the Rede Place offices, the speakers paid tribute to members who collected more than £20,000 towards their new Headquarters by a succession of small events and contributions. The new President of the Association, Lord Byers, expressed his pleasure that so many of the Development Fund Committee were able to be present on this occasion and paid a special tribute to Hitchman who had chaired it. Lord Byers then presented the Secretary, Sir Christopher Nixon, with a golden key. He too paid tribute to both the faith and practical nature of the members as 'there were few things more difficult than trying to raise funds when the overall economic climate in the country was in a state of depression.'[41]

**Figure 2.9.2: New Headquarters: Rede Place**

The professional practice issue that demanded most attention of the associations during the decade was the change, for many therapists, from working within health services to working within local authorities. That raised fundamental questions about the strong ethic of working only under medical prescription, which had been held since the profession's inception. That requirement began to change, although the Council of the AOT believed that 'it was impossible to draw lines between health care and social support.' In Clause 18(4)(b) of the NHS Reorganisation Circular it was proposed that:

> ...occupational therapists should transfer from local authorities to the new health authorities if they are engaged wholly or mainly in providing occupational therapy services under medical supervision for people with a condition for which they are receiving, or have received, medical treatment under the health service. They should remain in local social services departments if they are engaged wholly or mainly in providing social rehabilitation for conditions not requiring medical supervision.[42]

The McMillan report was another of major importance for the Association about that time as it was the first that the government produced dealing specifically with the needs of the remedial professions.[43] The report had recommended the immediate amalgamation of physiotherapists and remedial gymnasts and that, eventually, all three professions should combine. Also recommended was the appointment of members of the remedial professions as district therapists. They would have overall management responsibility for the remedial therapy services provided in their district. Following some debate,[44] both physiotherapists and occupational therapists were appointed to manage their own professions, which had the advantage of eventually removing both from the yoke of medical administration.[45] Elizabeth Grove, who had been a member of McMillan's working party in 1973, was appointed to the Co-ordinating Committee to implement the accepted recommendations of the Report and review those which were not.

McMillan recommended the appointment of an Officer for the Remedial Professions at the DHSS. It could be one full time or two part time people. The Chartered Society of Physiotherapists and the Remedial Gymnasts favoured a full time position. Occupational Therapists favoured a shared appointment because as a smaller organisation they had more chance of a voice, and because they held concerns about representation covering psychiatric as well as physical domains. The latter view prevailed.[46] In 1976, Grove was appointed Occupational Therapy Officer at the DHSS.[47] She continued, in the other half of her time, as Sector Occupational Therapist based at The Wolfson Medical Rehabilitation Centre. The half time position was shared with Lois Dyer, a physiotherapist, who had been another member of the McMillan working party. As Grove's was the first official appointment to the Department, the Association's Council and its Chairman recognised it as a most important event, of potential benefit to both the profession and government. Arrangements were made for her to attend BAOT Council meetings as an Observer so that she could be fully informed on current business.[48]

Initially, Grove and Dyer were seconded to the DHSS to see if such an appointment was successful, and when that proved to be the case the positions were advertised formally and made full time in 1979.[49] Grove was the successful applicant for the full time position of Occupational Therapy Officer, Adviser to the Secretary of State and DHSS.

This was established as a full-time permanent civil service position in 1980, and Grove was to continue in that role until 1988. Later, part time staff were seconded to help her. She described the job as advising on matters which related to occupational therapy and rehabilitation, including various policy decisions in the Department. It involved answering parliamentary questions, liaising with the profession and the CPSM, and addressing issues about clinical services, training, research and development, and health planning.[50]

New Articles of Association of the BAOT Ltd were adopted by a Special Resolution passed at the Annual General Meeting on 13 May 1978. These outlined the functions of the Association's Council of Management, and of a newly created College of Occupational Therapists Ltd linked to the Association. The BAOT became a Trade Union responsible for organisation and negotiation in relation to employment, with a 'Stewards Scheme' set up in the regional areas. It accepted the Members and Fellows of the College of Occupational Therapists (COT), which was established as a registered charity and a wholly owned subsidiary of BAOT, to maintain educational and professional aspects of occupational therapy.[51] Occupational therapists can only be members of BAOT, COT, as its subsidiary, has no independent members. Instead, its members are the share holders - BAOT Ltd and a nominee of BAOT. Through their elected Council, members of BAOT have the controlling interest in the College. As a result of BAOT becoming a trade union and losing its charitable status, technically, subscriptions ceased to be eligible for deduction against income tax, but following negotiations with the Inland Revenue, 70% which represented BAOTs involvement in educational matters and the percentage of all subscription revenue directly transferred to the COT was deemed to be tax deductable at that time. The College energetically continued the processes of critical enquiry that had characterised its predecessor, anticipating many topical issues, and establishing investigative working parties towards the achievement of professional goals. One such was formed in 1979 to review the profession. Its findings were published two years later in *The Way Ahead*, which is discussed in the next chapter.

In 1971, The Casson Memorial Lecture was established with money donated by the Casson Trust to honour the memory of Dr Elizabeth Casson. The list of lecturers so honoured and their subjects is provided in Appendix D. The first occupational therapist to give the lecture was Alicia Mendez in 1978. She had developed occupational therapy services at Queen Mary's Hospital, Roehampton, initiating and continuing specialised work in the field of prosthetics, which she loved. Mendez, who had been Chairman of AOT 1959-60, recalls how, when elected, she was not only young but also naïve. She attributed her successful election and term of office to the awe felt by most of Council towards Owen, Macdonald, and Tarrant, who all sat on Council and who seldom agreed with each other. Mendez says despite her awe of them they were 'nice to her.' Mendez, herself, inspired awe and respect. Beryl Steeden, current Head of Membership and External Affairs at COT, recalls that 'the palmar arch' was forever etched in her memory after a particularly harrowing 'teaching session' when Mendez was her fieldwork tutor.[52]

In her 'Casson Lecture' which addressed *Processes of Change: Some Speculations for the Future* Mendez talked of the changing times:

*We are liberating the training system and welcoming experimental courses…that run outside the national pattern…We are beginning to recognise that competence to practice is not necessarily the same as educational performance and therefore need a separate set of criteria to be worked out to match service requirements. This is particularly relevant in a profession such as ours, where practice shifts its emphasis continually to meet clinical needs…These are challenging and exciting times. The 1950s and '60s set a new pattern— the 1970s questioned and promoted change—what will the 1980s hold?*[53]

## British Journal of Occupational Therapy

The *British Journal of Occupational Therapy* metamorphosed from the monthly *Occupational Therapy* and the quarterly *Scottish Journal of Occupational Therapy*. The first issue appeared in May 1974. In 1978 it became the official publication of the College rather than of the Association. The following year OT News made its debut as an insert to cover activities of BAOT. A silver covered special issue of the Journal in 1977 celebrated the Queen's Silver Jubilee. It held a full size coloured plate of the Association's Council for 1977–78.[54]

**Figure 2.9.3:** **The Association of Occupational Therapists Council for 1977–78**

The number of papers written by occupational therapists in the journal continued to grow, although the past trend of eliciting or reporting the comments of other professionals, especially doctors continued, although to a lesser extent. By this decade the books reviewed in the Journal were much more concentrated around medicine, psychology and social issues than previously. One that was reviewed in BJOT, December 1975, *Rehabilitation and the General Practitioner: Educational Needs*, urged GPs to learn more about occupational therapy, and recommended that a period of attachment or visit to a department was included in their vocational training period. The reviewer, S. White, was prompted to sidetrack from the text reflecting on people who could be helped by occupational therapists if GPs were more aware of their skills. These included: 'emotionally disturbed children, the elderly impaired, and the battered wives'.[55] The Editor described an enlarged book review section in BJOT, December, 1977, as an experiment. A number of books from one publisher—Penguin—were reviewed in one edition. It was an interesting selection presaging, to some extent an emerging interest in sociological issues with four texts, *Sociology of the Family, Modern Sociology, Introducing Sociology, and Racial Disadvantage in Britain* being the first to be discussed. There were yet others in the review, *Social Administration, Family and Kinship in East London, Sociology and Social Policy*, and a best selling study of a Suffolk village, *Akenfield*. They were accompanied by reviews of a selection of books about psychological, psychiatric and medical issues, including the classic A.R. Luria text *The Working Brain*.[56] In relation to the growing interest in matters sociological, an interesting question was posed in the June BJOT a couple of years earlier in a report of conferences:

> *Are we as a profession, or as individuals, prepared to do anything about social injustice towards our clients, and if so, how?*[57]

The change that had started in the 1960s in the nature of the advertising became significant. Advertisements for aids to daily living, splinting materials, and remedial equipment such as lathes and adjustable work tables replaced, in large part, those for crafts. KG Garrold of Nottingham Handicaft Company recognised that 'as a generalisation…virtually every piece of equipment emanates from designs originated by occupational therapists.'[58]

**Figure 2.9.4:** **Advertisements in the Journal during the 1970s**

References to electronic technology were also beginning to appear in the Journal. Most occupational therapists had been using a wide range of technology since the beginning of the profession, making their own equipment with or without the help of technical staff. During the 1970s advertisements for increasingly sophisticated electronic machines appeared, like those for the Meyra Rehab power wheelchair, a high rise power wheelchair for children with spina bifida, Tutormatic power beds and page turners, the Canon Communicator, and the Sigtron Personal Alarm. Computer technology was beginning to make its presence felt. Another technological note in the Journal came in a review of Keith Copeland's book *Aids For The Severely Disabled*. This mentioned as well as Possum, electronic devices such as Pilot, System Seven, Lightwriter, and Talking Brooch.[59] In the September 1977 Journal the story of Roger Jefcoate was told. A lecturer and consultant assessor of electronic equipment for severely disabled people, and one of the original trio who pioneered Possum, he was personally involved in installing 500 electronic systems in Britain. In 1974 he had established ACTIVE, a group of professional and amateur technicians, therapists, teachers and parents to help handicapped children to use toys and therapeutic developmental games. Three occupational therapists were members.[60]

The effects of free exchange of trained personnel between member states began to be debated as the EEC developed. 'A group of occupational therapy representatives from EEC countries was set up informally in 1972 under the aegis of the World Federation of Occupational Therapists (WFOT) to consider the implications of this free exchange on education and practice.' In 1974, at the first meeting of the Council of BAOT, it was agreed that 'the annual seminar in 1977 should be extended to include colleagues from Europe.'[61] This idea developed into a European Congress hosted by Scottish occupational therapists just as they had hosted the first WFOT Congress.

## First European Congress

The first European Congress, with the theme 'To exist—or to live', was held at the Assembly Rooms in Edinburgh from 10–13 May, 1977. There was a bomb scare on the first evening but, as no bomb was found, the Chairman of Congress, Professor Cairns Aitken, continued his welcome. There were over 540 delegates, 130 of them from 24 other countries. The Organising Committee put in an immense amount of work over two years to ensure that the Congress would run smoothly and efficiently. The opening session given by the Parliamentary Under Secretary of State for Scotland, Harry Ewing, stressed the vital role that occupational therapists played in the rehabilitation of disabled individuals in the community, to whom the Government had paid particular attention. The government's general aim, he said, was to integrate chronically sick, geriatric, and disabled people into the community by creating as far as possible a barrier-free environment.

Lord Byers, who spoke next, said that the European Congress was important not merely historically, but because it marked the beginning of a much closer association with European and overseas occupational therapists. He stressed that the 'European dimension is a natural and important development for those of you who are members of this great healing profession,' before complimenting occupational therapists for their contribution which played 'a vital part in remedial medicine.'[62]

The range of sessions is always indicative, to some degree, of developments at a particular time. Therefore, it is interesting to note the topics addressed. They included: 'hidden disabilities' such as chronic bronchitis and cardiac disorders; the cognitive, emotional and social effects of head injury, deafness, and dementia; brain injury and disease, such as epilepsy, progressive neurological diseases and strokes in adults and children; mental handicap; rehabilitation of fractured femurs; the implications for occupational therapy of an ageing population; quality of living; home aids and equipment; and future trends in education. Numerous study tours covered a wide range of services to most of the large general, psychiatric and rehabilitation hospitals nearby, social work departments, community domiciliary services, community employment services, paediatric facilities, and schools. The social programme, too, was extensive and included receptions given by the

Lothian Regional Council, HM Government at Edinburgh Castle, The Royal College of Surgeons of Edinburgh, and The Royal College of Physicians of Edinburgh.

Despite the celebratory feel of the Congress, Grove chose to sound a cautionary note on the final day. 'I want to look at the other side of the coin, for not everything in the garden is rosy,' she said. She pointed to the difficulty occupational therapists were experiencing in defining their role, and indeed the profession itself. She told how 'on one of those hot June days last summer in Paris during the WFOT Council meetings', a small international group sat 'with wet towels round our heads and arrived at the following definition—more of a short story really—of Occupational Therapy':

*Occupational Therapy is assessment and treatment through the specific use of selected activity. This is designed by the Occupational Therapist and undertaken by those who are temporarily or permanently disabled by physical or mental illness, by social or developmental problems. The purpose is to prevent disability and fulfill the person's needs by achieving optimum function and independence in work, social and domestic environments.*

The inclusion of social problems, and optimum function in social environments as well as the traditional notions of mental and physical illness is of interest in terms of present day directions, when it can be queried how adequately that is happening. So it is not surprising that Grove went on to query whether that very extensive role was being fulfilled at that time.[63] That seems to fit in with a self-doubting, 'misunderstood' phenomenon that began to emerge, seriously, during the 1970s. Indeed, Margaret Smith called the 1970s the 'Age of Doubt' following the 'Age of Confidence' of the 1960s.[64] Such feelings may have prompted the 'spontaneous reaction' following a comment on the BBC's Morning Current Affairs Programme on May 16, 1974. Dr Donald Gould described an occupational therapist as 'one who stops people going crazy from boredom in hospital and also works in long-stay geriatric hospitals and with children.' In its apology the BBC spokes-person, Alistair Osbourne, said the item had provoked 'a deluge of letters'.[65] A different idea about the causes of feeling misunderstood or of doubt was raised in a letter written by an occupational therapist returning to practice after a break. She blamed staff shortages as 'one of the causes of the deterioration of so many departments all over the country', adding that she was 'working in a hospital bursting with potential, but which at this time is sinking faster than the Titanic.' She also pointed to newly qualified therapists lack of 'stamina' to stay in a job if things did not go their way, explaining that relationships need to be established before suggesting change. She wrote 'the barriers are almost as great now as they were in the early days of occupational therapy. We have got to sell ourselves all over again and we are not succeeding by our present image.'[66]

## Fellowships

Under Grove's chairmanship, the Association in 1972 set up a scheme to recognise and honour the work of outstanding members by awarding them Fellowships, later to become Fellowships of the College of Occupational Therapists. No criteria were drawn up at the start because AOT was honouring its pioneers. Later COT guidelines were established to include local, national, and international contributions to occupational therapy. Initially honoured, in 1972, were: Nathalie (Smythe) Barr; Mary S. Jones; Mary Macdonald; Grizel MacCaul; Constance (Tebbit) Owens; Angela Rivett; and Muriel Tarrant. Two years later Betty Hollings, Alicia Mendez, and Barbara Stow were awarded

Fellowships, and in 1977, Betty Collins, Elizabeth Grove, and Jean (Waterston) Blades. During the 1970s three others were awarded Fellowships by examination. They were Margaret Smith, Averil Stewart and Diana Whysall.

The Association set up a scheme for members to attain a Fellowship by Examination. This was, in part, to offer some recognition and incentive for further education, which was not available by any other means at that time within the profession in the UK. It was also an endeavour to stimulate some serious research in 'the belief that it is part of the duty of all professional people to contribute to the advance of the theory and practice of their profession.' The Fellowship award was based on an approved programme of attendance at recognised courses and the preparation and submission of a thesis about occupational therapy upon which the candidates could be orally examined. Because the Committee was aware of the limitations of both time and resources, a relatively modest study was recommended. Its length could vary according to the nature of the subject and the method of addressing it. For example, a thesis as the outcome of philosophical reflection would usually need to be longer than one using research techniques with results in tabular form. Doris Sym, the Chairman of the Fellowship by Examination Sub-Committee, informed members that, for a limited time, recently published work, or that prepared for other purposes would be considered in lieu of a thesis. The Sub-Committee stipulated that any such work should be of outstanding quality.[67] The Fellowship by examination was one response to the evolving view of a need for ongoing education, and only ceased when more regular higher qualifications became available.

**Figure 2.9.5:** **Fellowship by Examination: Calendar and Work Timetable**[68]

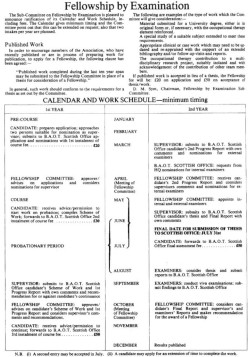

The Action Group, which had been set up as a result of the Co-odinating Committee Working Parties which followed the report Occupational Therapy: Present and Future, had finalised the following by 1971:
1. A re-edited version of the Manual of the Diploma Course.
2. Appointment of National Assessors to training Schools.
3. Clinical practice memorandum leaflets for head occupational therapists and students.
4. It was agreed that occupational therapists should be considered medical personnel with an educational bias.

The following year when it disbanded having fulfilled its remit its recommendations included the following:
1. Modification of the present Board of Studies.
2. Basic training course for occupational therapy helpers.
3. The organisation of Post Registration study courses.
4. Courses for clinical supervisors.
5. Shortened occupational therapy diploma courses for people with other qualification.
6. Refresher course for married women.
7. Degree courses.
8. Advanced diploma in specialised studies which should lead to a 'Working Fellowship of the Association.'
9. Revision of the Diploma syllabus as deemed necessary by a merger between AOT and SAOT, carried out by the Board of Studies.[69]

Most of those were acted upon in some way during the decade.

# Education evolves

Education blossomed during the 1970s. Up until 1976 grants to assist students with undertaking occupational therapy education had been at the discretion of local education authorities and the limitations of their particular resources. To increase student numbers the DHSS took over the provision of grants, awarding 440 in the first year of central funding.[70] Five new schools started, widely dispersed across the British Isles, in Northern Scotland, Northern Ireland, Northern England, the Midlands, and Essex. There were also initiatives which began to open up opportunities for postgraduate education in response to a growing demand. This was in line with the increasing interest in a need to change the basic qualification to degree level. As a result of the interest, discussion, working parties and consultation, and, in part, because ever increasing student numbers made it logistically difficult to provide examiners, this was to be the last decade of a national examination system.

The timely reviews of training and education policies commenced in Scotland where the Association started the process in 1971 with regard to its own courses. In that same year, in the rest of the United Kingdom, a number of committees were busy, one commencing a long term review of educational policy, and others considering the organisation and planning of post-registration, refresher, clinical supervisors', 'return to practice', and degree courses.[71] The coming together of the Associations had led to serious discussion and a working party being established to deal with combining their education systems. The working party under the chairmanship of W. Allen Gay, with joint representation from the AOT and the SAOT published its report—known as the Gay Report, in 1973. It recommended giving more autonomy to the schools, along with considerable liberalisation of the syllabus, internal examination during the first two years, and external examinations only at the end of training.[72] Neither party was totally satisfied with what was seen as a compromise.[73] Peggy Jay, as Chairman of Council put the report aside at that time.[74] Later, many of its recommendations eventuated, and its findings were used to support education papers and reports, such as the Council comments on the report of the Remedial Professions Working Party.[75] It was only when the whole educational system was liberalised by what was to be called Diploma '81 that the two systems of education became one.

In May 1974, the former Joint Council Teacher Training Committee was reconstituted and its functions were reappraised. Its plan for a restructure which was much more flexible than earlier models was approved by Council. In the same year Catherine F. Paterson, an occupational therapist, and Helen Johnson, a physiotherapist, were appointed by the Kings Fund to research the training needs of the remedial professions. Three hundred and one questionnaires were distributed randomly to students and the researchers concluded from their responses that most were 'not so much concerned with the content of the courses as with the place and methods of training. Students want to learn and work together.' Occupational therapy students liked 'the variety of subjects, the balance of theoretical and practical work and clinical practice.' They disliked 'the isolation of their training courses from the clinical situation and from other students.'[76]

In view of that finding, a paper by Joy Rook, a few years later, holds particular interest. She discussed the gradual decline of establishing occupational therapy education in separate schools in favour of colleges of higher education and polytechnics. Whilst seeing many advantages Rook also saw disadvantages in the trend. In particular she listed: students being taught by other disciplines, being a small group amongst many others, limitations on the number of contact hours, expectations of self-directed learning, meeting the expectations of clinicians, and the senior staffs' fairly lowly status in the institution's hierarchy.[77] Many current day educators will recognise that she anticipated many real problems which continue to be faced.

In August 1977, the Council reported that, at the Board of Studies' request, they were considering the possibility of 'awarding concessions to people holding certain degrees and diplomas.' It was recommended that 'a "let-out" clause should be included in a schools' entry requirements' for candidates holding appropriate qualifications.[78] It was during that year that the Board had started to consider seriously the restructuring of the basic diploma syllabus. The Council had requested that the Board give consideration to the Gay report and to the recommendations of the 1972 CPSM report Future Education and Training of Occupational Therapists. Both supported greater flexibility, freedom and autonomy, and allowed a 'variety in their educational patterns...bearing in mind the movement towards…higher educational establishments and the possible development of degree courses.'[79] The end of the 1970s culminated in the establishment of a joint Steering Committee for the Remedial Professions Post Registration Education, assisted by a grant from the DHSS.[80]

Naomi Fraser-Holland in her 1990 Casson Lecture explained, from an educator's perspective, what was occurring in the schools during the 1970s:

> *The schools of the sixties and seventies owed much to the enthusiasm and foresight of their principals who encouraged their staff to explore the variety of teaching methods being developed in higher education on a national and international basis. Peer teaching, small-group instruction and problem-based learning became the currency of occupational therapy educators. The aim was to provide the best possible conditions for learning. This pursuit of excellence moulded our teachers into facilitators. As a consequence, occupational therapy benefited from the best of educational advances while the rest of higher education was still thinking about the 'new methods'.*[81]

Fraser-Holland recognised that, during the 1970s, the COT formalised its interest in widening the access to qualification and increasing the flexibility of professional education. Council approved the recommendations of a Working Party that explored 'Alternative Routes to Training.' They included the day-release in-service route to the COT Diploma established first in Essex, shortened courses for psychology graduates, and 2 year graduate-entry accelerated Diploma courses. She also described how the debate on aiming towards an occupational therapy undergraduate degree was renewed, being seen by many, but not all, as advantaging occupational therapists in terms of research and the pursuit of higher degrees.[82]

In line with many of those ideas, and continuing the trend begun during the 1960s, all of the five new schools, at Ulster, the West Midlands, Newcastle, the Grampians and Essex were associated with other institutes of learning. Their stories are told with those of the other schools, in Appendix A; however, the Essex School was such a different model to the others that it requires comment here. The school was the first four year, part time, in-service course which would enable local assistants to qualify. Approval for one intake of students was granted in 1979 following three years' of research by Mavis Wallis whose brainchild it was and a report to the CPSM and the BAOT. Setting the pattern for part time education in occupational therapy the first group of 18 students enrolled in the course at Colchester Institute sponsored by the five Districts within the local Health Authority. Tutorials were held in the students' workplaces and Summer School took place at St Loye's School in Exeter.[83]

## Post-registration training

Reorganisation of the NHS in 1974 led to the development of regional training centres and post registration courses for both occupational therapists and others. In 1974–5 for example those which were planned or approved by the Association included: technical study days; 5 day courses on local authority work, geriatrics, PNF as applied to OT, and an intermediate clinical residential course; a two day course for clinical supervisors; one day courses on kinesiology, drug side effects, and wheelchairs and aids; Others with length not specified were aimed at administration and departmental management, paediatrics, head injuries, amputees, rheumatoid conditions, and ADL and functional assessment. They were held in many places about the country as well as London, such as Manchester, Birmingham, Cambridge, Leeds, Chessington, Guildford, and Wokingham.[84]

These shorter post registration courses were organised according to perceived need. A more extensive one followed a questionnaire sent in 1977. Grisel MacCaul with Lalage Dawson Jones, District Occupational Therapist at the Bexley Hospital, ran a pilot course for occupational therapy helpers and technicians. This in-service training was organised as a day release programme running for 36-weeks. It was supported by COT and attracted 16 helpers and 9 technicians. They came from a variety of settings, chiefly from the SE Thames Region, and worked in psychiatric or physical units, geriatric centres, or with young chronically sick patients.[85] Another approved course, which was to continue until the next century, was on psychological testing, initially set up by Bruce Crowe, of the British Psychological Association,[86] in consultation with Peggy Jay.

## AOT psychological testing course
### By Bruce Crowe[87] and Peggy Jay

In 1972, the AOT, through Peggy Jay, began discussions with Bruce Crowe, an occupational psychologist, about training occupational therapists in psychological testing. The AOT was seeking the benefits of using assessment procedures that were consistent and transferable, and related to observable outcomes because of their technical features of reliability and validity. It was thought that training in psychological testing would be helpful to occupational therapists when conducting assessments; when needing to understand the results of psychological tests conducted by others; and when developing, evaluating or interpreting their own assessment tools.

Approaches were made to the British Psychological Society (BPS) Test Standards Committee (TSC) and NFER to find out what needed to be done to train and accredit occupational therapists to purchase and use psychological tests. Following a formal submission and approval of the BPS TSC a five-day course in cognitive psychological testing was approved, and the first one was scheduled for mid-1974 at Leicester University.[88] The initial course, run by Crowe, covered general reasoning and examination and practice of specific aptitude tests. Assessment reports were evaluated by psychologists involved, and Dr Ken Miller, the Chair of the BPS TSC. Each successful participant received a personal certificate, which could be shown to a test publisher when they sought to purchase tests. When tests of direct relevance to occupational therapists, such as the Chessington Occupational Therapy Neurological Assessment Battery (COTNAB) and the Rivermead Perceptual Assessment Battery, came on the market they were incorporated into the course and one of the participating occupational therapists was invited to demonstrate them. As more tests became available, hands on sessions were included where course participants could examine a much wider range of material.

By 1995 there was so much relevant test material available that generic courses were replaced by specialist ones, at first for paediatric and neurological occupational therapists, and later for those working in adult mental health. Specialist occupational therapists took over one and a half days of the course to introduce participants to some of the tests in detail. There were also requests for Regional courses and these were run in Belfast, Trent, South Wales, Birmingham, and Glasgow. So instead of running one course a year there were two or three. Jay was involved throughout until the last course was run in 2001.

One post registration course, run by Dr John Marsden in conjunction with Ann Murdoch at the London School, was held at the Central Polytechnic in London.

Pre-empting the move towards degree and postgraduate degree opportunities, Dr A. Balfour Sclare, in his Address on Diploma Day, 5 November, 1971, at the Glasgow School of Occupational Therapy, said he would like to see 'more postgraduate courses and more opportunities for postgraduate advancement in occupational therapy.' Another wish reflected the emerging interest in community, when he envisaged 'occupational therapy become(ing) integrated into the new specialty of community medicine when the health service becomes reorganised under Area Health Boards.'[89] In a similar vein, Professor Hugh Glanville, who had been appointed to the inaugural Europe Chair of Rehabilitation, hoped that Southampton University would soon be able to offer post registration training. The aim, he said, would not be to produce better occupational therapists but 'to broaden their base by exposing them to, for example, formal teaching in sociology and social administration, the law in relation to matters in rehabilitation, principles in engineering and architecture as applicable, and methods of teaching.'[90] Two years later his plans came into being.

Southampton University pioneered a 'totally new concept in post registration training' for occupational therapists, and others in the field of rehabilitation. Until that time, the only post registration courses available in Britain were the very short ones devoted to specific topics, as mentioned above. At Southampton, a twelve month, full-time Diploma in Remedial Therapy offered by the Faculty of Medicine was launched in October 1978. Additionally, the first British MSc. Degree was offered to outstanding students who wished to pursue their studies to a more advanced level, if they achieved a high standard in the Diploma.[91]

Other important initiatives were taking place in established schools. For example, in Exeter, Dr Rita Goble 'harnessed the collective energy of enquiry that was growing in the region,' setting her sights on continuing education within a multidisciplinary setting. A post-registration studies scheme for occupational therapists, along with other remedial professionals, was pioneered. The scheme developed from a series of evening lectures in each term of the academic year, to a day-release course, an advanced trainers' course, and, eventually, to an MSc. in health care.[92]

# Practice

In the middle of the decade the Annual Conference was held in London at the Middlesex Hospital Medical School. Although some members complained of too little time given to the business side of the AGM, there were some excellent papers and the topics of some are included to illustrate changing practice within the profession.[93] Splinting, a topic often addressed previously sat alongside others such as projective techniques, sexual problems of the disabled, training the GP in relation to occupational therapy, behaviour therapy, and computers and research. Most of these topics surfaced as central concerns of the decade. One appealing title, which presented a slightly different view of disease very applicable to occupational therapy and to the 21st century, was that of Dr JA Muir Gray's paper *You Must Be Revolutionaries*. In answer to his own question, 'Which way should occupational therapy change?' he said:

> The diseases doctors diagnose cause disability, but handicap is diagnosed by the patients when they are unable to do what they want, to be at ease—handicap is disease...A study of the diseases will illuminate the areas into which occupational therapy must go and reflect what must go into their training.
>
> People who are physically disabled have five main diseases—poverty, bad housing, being cold, independence in the home, isolation.

He concluded by recommending a change of 'ammunition.' Occupational Therapists, he said, 'must be revolutionaries, changing society to prevent handicap being caused for people with disabilities who are often unable to effect change themselves.'[94]

Also indicative of practice during the decade was Professor Hugh Glanville's 1975 Casson Memorial Lecture. He told how he had asked the occupational therapists at Odstock (who had particular interest in hands and brain function) to tell him what changes they saw in 'occupational therapy over the last 20 years and how they saw their role in the future.' They identified four main changes:

- Assessment. They described 'assessment' as becoming more repeatable through standardisation of testing and recording.
- Different activities. They noted increased involvement in ADL and in interventions in which they worked with physiotherapists. They also described some reintroduction of craft work, which a few years earlier had practically disappeared. For example, they found crafts were useful for retraining concentration after acquired brain injury, for manipulation following nerve lesions, or for preparation for work.
- Altered demands. They described altered demands in the growth of domiciliary services and the type of patients referred. As an example, they pointed to the development of geriatric services to keep 'elderly people independent and capable of remaining in their own environment.' This was also seen as indicative of the trend to keep patients at home rather than treating them in hospitals.[95]
- Increasing involvement in teaching.

Similarly, Dr Meredith Davies, mentioned in the previous chapter and by this time Director of Social Services for the City of Liverpool, had predicted a great increase in occupational therapy carried out in the community in line with trends in all medical and social work practice. Rapidly developing community based caring services characterised the mid-1970s. It was, Davies said, the age of the day-centre, and supportive services designed to be undertaken without removing the patient/client from home. He saw occupational therapists as the best profession to concentrate on what he described as the urgent task of functional assessment.[96]

In line with those ideas practice will be discussed in this chapter under the headings: Functional assessment, Rehabilitation in a reorganised NHS, and Into the community.

## Functional assessment

The College took a role in trying to get standardised functional assessment established just as it had with research. Dr Philip Nichols, a rehabilitation specialist, reported how the COT, in the interest of standardisation, had developed four inter-related forms for recording ADL assessment and distributed them to a large number of hospitals for trial. Most hospitals preferred their own. In a talk given at a COT Workshop at Mary Marlborough Lodge, Nichols suggested that was, in part, because of the commitment that staff put into the development of such an assessment tool and the understanding they reached during the development process. It was also because the tools were tailor made to fit specific environments and patient needs. With that in mind he recommended that the purpose of ADL testing in functional terms was aimed at:

1. *Defining areas of difficulty.*
2. *Defining particular activities for further training or treatment.*
3. *Establishing categories of needs, care and management (in the community)*
4. *Indicating possible potential for further independence.*
5. *Providing an early warning of change, particularly deterioration, and thus alerting other health care services.*

To do that effectively required assessment be carried out in context, using ADL indices (checklists), and taking into account full personal and social biographies. He added that there was no point in doing functional assessment unless there was some hope of finding solutions.[97]

Assessment units began to be established. In 1977 Margaret Smith, and her colleagues wrote about the unit established in Edinburgh as part of a study to measure specifically the outcome of stroke rehabilitation. With yet another purpose to those already mentioned for ADL assessment, the study adopted a specific version as the outcome measure to compare two different ways of organising stroke rehabilitation. In the interest of objectivity all patients were assessed in the unit that was set up the replicate the home environment one week prior to discharge. Activities that could use outside assistance like bathing, preparing main meals, shopping or doing the laundry were excluded. Only the basic daily activities essential for an elderly patient to maintain life alone were measured. These consisted of bed and chair transfers, dressing for warmth and safety, mobility including internal steps, using the toilet and washing, making a hot drink and snack, feeding, and controlling the environment such as heating, lighting, switches and so forth.[98]

In *Occupational Therapy: A Modern Approach*, Andrew Zinovieff, Consultant Rheumatologist in charge of Rehabilitation Services at the Durham and North West Durham District Hospitals, stated that 'undoubtedly, the most important contribution of occupational therapy is in various forms of assessment.' He discussed 'functional assessment' in considerable detail describing many facets like 'assessment of movements such as dressing…using the bath or toilet…getting in and out of bed…walking, and so on', to provide useful information about a patient's independence and the degree of residual ability. 'A number of assessments conducted at intervals' he said 'will show improvement or deterioration.' Zinovieff also discussed other types of functional assessments such as kitchen, work and prevocational preparation, wheelchair, hand, sensory, and fitness to return home.

In the case of fitness to return home, he noted how occupational therapists evaluated what he described as the social situations. That included: the type of house; the number of relatives living with the patient; the availability of assistance from neighbours/friends; the location of the bathroom and the toilet, and heating arrangements; the cooking facilities, and patient's ability to prepare and carry meals and drinks; and accessibility of storage cupboards and doors. He then turned to the assessment of the need for after care service such as meals on wheels, home help, or district nursing. In addition to self-care assessment, he included assessment of psychological state and activity tolerance. Outcome measures from the functional assessment he described were recorded in terms of suitability for return home, or the need for a domiciliary visit, or further training.[99]

Investigating whether occupational therapists could provide fast and effective functional assessment, Rita Goble, with another occupational therapist and a general practitioner, carried out a survey in 1979. It sought answers to questions regarding occupational therapists working with older people living in the community. In particular they investigated whether following assessment occupational therapists could make relevant medical and social recommendations based on that information, and whether the results led to improvement in patients' function and quality of life. They described the need for functional assessment in terms of: 'the projected increase in the number of elderly people in the community;' a growing 'interest in methods of identifying unmet needs in this age group'; that previous community assessment had concentrated on medical needs, disability and dependence; and the length of previous assessments 'which would make the procedure unacceptable as a routine in general practice.'[100] It was surmised that a simple assessment 'which combines functional and medical elements might merit a place in the routine surveillance of this group of patients in general practice.' The results indicated that occupational therapists could administer a 'rapid but effective functional assessment and follow this up by making relevant recommendations that may improve functional ability or "quality of life."'[101]

At the start of the decade work-oriented functional assessment was described by Orr and Philips with regard to 'adult spastics'. The assessment used at the Scottish Council for the Care of Spastics Work Centre, in Glasgow, was based on that used at the National Spastics Society's Assessment Unit. The Centre ran a multidisciplinary assessment course aimed at: cerebral palsied adults to determine their suitability for employment—whether open, sheltered workshop, work centre, or senior occupational centre; for those who were unemployed but had been in open employment, were already in a Work Centre, or, if the need arose who had been placed elsewhere; and cerebral palsied school children during their final school term. The three-day Assessment Course provided a comprehensive initial work assessment and enabled the most suitable placement for individuals to be made.[102]

Spasticity was but one neurological disorder for which assessment was developing. Another area of practice which was fast unfolding into a central issue of interest was the assessment of visual-perceptual or perceptual-motor deficits following damage to the central nervous system. One of the earliest papers in BJOT detailing assessment of visual-perceptual problems did so in relation to self care activities. Patricia McMenamin hoped that this might encourage more accurate and realistic treatment goals.[103] Another assessment of similar problems was developed at the Leon Gillis Unit, Queen Mary's Hospital, Roehampton, for children with spina bifida. It was described as an easily applied and comprehensive assessment of pre-school abilities. It included many visuo-motor-perceptual tasks under the functional headings of eye-hand coordination, and pre-writing and reading skills. Standardised psychological tests run in conjunction with functional non-standardised activities were suggested as useful.[104]

Functional assessment of the hand was also a topic of much discussion during the 1970s. Ian Fletcher, a surgeon who began a paper on the subject by considering the hands evolutionary significance and relationship to the brain, wrote:

> When confronted by a hand for assessment…account should be taken of the person's occupation and pastimes. For example a musician and a conjurer are both capable of a high degree of dexterity but their respective muscle group movements are not comparable…

Although he described the hand as the least specialised part of the body:

> It is capable of an astronomical number of activities. Consider the many complex movements performed by the hands and arms as a daily routine…They are group movements which have to be learnt gradually…The greatest attribute…is not, however, its ability to perform fine and delicate movements but its exquisite sensitivity.

His recommendations for functional hand assessment included measurements using dynanometer and goniometer, appearance, observations of attitude towards the hand, comparison of both hands, handedness, sensibility and stereognosis, and group movements.[105] Another functional hand assessment that was consistent, accurate, not lengthy to complete, and with the results easy to read, was described by Mary Green, an occupational therapist. That assessment had been first devised to compare Swanson and Calnan-Nicolle metacarpo-phalangeal replacements in patients with rheumatoid arthritis, but was found useful for other disorders. Using simple tasks the test assessed pulp to pulp pinch, lateral pinch, spherical grip, and cylindrical grip pre-operatively and twice post-operatively. Power was assessed separately.[106]

In the field of mental handicap Richard and Christine McKeown worked on a rigorous assessment tool for use with adults going into the community to live independently away from full-time support of caring staff. Without such a tool, decisions about suitability for independent 'community house' accommodation were made by trying to translate a patient's achievements within hospital or hostel to a home setting.

Assessment replaced assumptions by testing whether patients could perform tasks. Each task was broken down into a series of stages. For example in the case of managing electric plugs, seven stages were identified—from 'Check that socket switch is off' to 'Switch on the implement.' Individuals did not have to be competent in all tasks when a group living together in a community house could share them. Leisure was considered separately. The process highlighted training needs and tasks that required concentrated training.[107]

Assessment of disturbed children being treated within inpatient units was the topic of a paper in 1979 by Dr Michael Field. Inpatient units were a relatively new development, three pioneer facilities being established in Scotland at Crichton Royal Hospital, the Edinburgh Sick Children's Hospital, and the Royal Dundee, Liff Hospital in the early 1950s. Occupational therapists were engaged in habilitation for life and school in which assessment and treatment were intermingled, and the language of paediatrics and psychiatry existed side by side. A summary of the occupational therapist's functions in terms of assessment and observation included:

> *Motor function, including motor behaviour; Sensory capacities; Capacity to work in a small group, and to share attention, tools and activities with others; Particular interests and aptitudes; Speech and vocabulary; Persistence and ability to concentrate; Relationship capacity; Frustration tolerance; Mood; Fantasy Life.*[108]

The Glaister Work Aptitude Battery (GWAB) plus a period of controlled observation of psychiatric patients in different work situations over a week, provided the substance of pre-work assessment at Netherne Hospital. Five patients could be accepted each week if they had no work history, were in their first admission, showed a disturbed work pattern, appeared able but failed in what seemed to be appropriate work, were unable to return to previous work, or if they had reached or fallen back to a plateau of achievement in treatment. The GWAB included a number of standardised tests of perceptual, motor, and intellectual performance, some of which required a psychologist to administer, and others could be completed by an occupational therapist. Observations of a negative nature only were recorded on what was called the Netherne Critical Incidence Scale 111 (NCIS 3).[109] A much less formal method of assessment was described by Jean Castle for the 40 bed psychiatric unit she worked in at Kingston Hospital. There a continual assessment of patients took place as each was engaged in a programme she described as 'The Middle Way'. 'It was neither the old style mainly craft orientated type of treatment, nor the group emphasized type found in therapeutic communities, but an amalgamation of the two.'[110]

## Rehabilitation in a reorganised NHS

Aspects of the NHS reorganisation were discussed at a 1974 conference of more than 100 head occupational therapists from most parts of the United Kingdom. Mr. S. Argyrou, of the City and East London Area Health Authority explained that the debate had been so 'red hot' that the resultant Act was 'a glorious compromise.' Despite many professional groups having undoubted victories, he had seen little in the statute for the paramedical professions. Asked to say something about the role of occupational therapists in the new system, he anticipated a battle with social services who, he thought, might appoint their own staff under an obscure title. He contended that an occupational therapist was 'one of the rarer birds whose work must not be confined to the hospital alone and if used well, she could be an excellent integration ambassador.' He saw them contributing to the function of management, planning, and to the organisation of the health care services. Recalling Enoch Powell's words, 'the growth of community care and after care; the development of preventive and remedial measures; more intensive and efficient use of hospital facilities,' would he argued involve 'dozens of independent professions…brought into harmony, and…direct involvement.' In consultation with Margaret Ellis, a Vice-Chairman of Council, he supported a working party of paramedical professionals to assist that process.[111]

At that time, it was estimated that physical disability affected 3–6% of the population, which suggested there were about 3 million people with a physical disability in the United Kingdom. Of those, 6–700,000 required some support, about 386,000 needed considerable support, and 157,000 were very severely handicapped. Those were the figures supplied by Philip Nichols in *Rehabilitation in the reorganised National Health Service*, a paper published in BJOT. Going on to discuss that topic he suggested that the definition of rehabilitation was so wide that it included 'virtually the whole of clinical medicine except for acute intensive care on the one hand and terminal care on the other.' Despite the width it was an appropriate term, he thought, to embrace the many physical, social and organisational aspects of the after care of patients. Whilst those with a temporary disability required immediate intensive programmes aimed at rapid return to work and home, the keys to rehabilitation for those with chronic disability were independence, social resettlement, maintenance and support. Nichols recognised that the remedial professions were the 'practitioners' of rehabilitation. They were in short supply and in disarray because, he said, 'their "role" has been ill-defined and their contribution under-valued or misapplied.' He argued that the considerable confusion regarding the role of therapists in hospital and community derived from an inability to separate the remedial and social components of rehabilitation. In addition he thought it was unfortunate that often community services tried to mirror those of hospitals. Local authorities had a statutory requirement to identify and to assess the requirements of handicapped people. They were in direct competition with hospital services for key personnel such as occupational therapists who could provide both intensive rehabilitation for temporary disabilities and community services for people with chronic disabilities. There was mounting evidence of the invaluable role which good domiciliary occupational therapists could play in identifying and assessing individual needs of disabled people and their families.[112]

Misunderstanding of the part the profession could play was also mentioned in Kathleen Moses' 1975 discussion on the role of occupational therapists in rehabilitation. She blamed the misunderstanding, rightly or wrongly, on lack of education aimed at 'professional circles and among the general public' and on 'insufficient pressure at national level in providing adequate training facilities which has resulted in an acute shortage of manpower.' Even so she found the misunderstanding surprising, especially as expanded venues had allowed occupational therapists to work towards the best possible outcome in the environs of the home, out of doors, at school, at work, or in recreational and social activity. In recent years, she claimed, social service departments had recognised the part occupational therapists could play in the assessment and provision of aids and adaptations, but health departments had not. Such difficulties, she said, 'hindered the development of a total occupational therapy service.' The reorganised NHS provided for co-ordinated hospital and community programmes and to avoid duplication, she suggested that district general hospital resources, such as ADL, remedial, and vocational workshops, should be available to community therapists. She considered patients, who needed to be involved in planning their own treatment programme, as the most important members of a rehabilitation team, and advocated family counselling and the use of family support groups.[113]

Within physical rehabilitation of a remedial nature, the development of specialised equipment had been ongoing for over thirty years. In 1971, Rosemary Hagedorn conducted a small survey, which appeared to indicate that there was some dissatisfaction with such equipment, but which left many questions unanswered. A second survey, reported in 1974, addressed such questions as: How many departments used each item of equipment? What types of patients were most frequently treated? Did everyone have the same equipment, or use it in the same way? Some of her findings are presented in Table 2.9.1 as they indicate particular aspects of the nature of occupational therapy in physical rehabilitation during the seventies.[114]

**Table 2.9.1:** **Frequency of activity and equipment use and conditions treated**[115]

| % Departments Using Activity | | Frequency of Treatment | Many Y | Seldom M |
|---|---|---|---|---|
| Activity | % | Condition | % | % |
| Remedial games | 90 | Hemiplegic | 90 | 5 |
| Stoolseating | 90 | Rheumatoid | 78 | 9 |
| Sanding | 88 | Geriatric | 77 | 17 |
| Woodwork | 83 | Orthopaedic | 59 | 19 |
| Printing | 79 | Fractures | 56 | 23 |
| Treadle sewing machine | 68 | Neurological | 53 | 21 |
| F.E.P.S. | 68 | General medical | 40 | 35 |
| Rug Loom | 63 | Heart conditions | 38 | 37 |
| Oliver cycle | 58 | Head injuries | 28 | 35 |
| Metal work | 52 | Leg amputees | 27 | 39 |
| Box loom | 50 | Nerve lesions | 26 | 36 |
| Thame | 50 | General surgical | 9 | 62 |
| Hobbies fretsaw | 46 | Upper limb amp. | 9 | 68 |
| Treadle lathe | 45 | Burns | 7 | 79 |
| Gardening | 43 | | | |
| Camden fretsaw | 26 | | | |
| Larvic lathe | 23 | | | |
| O.B. Help Arm | 23 | | | |
| Ankle rotator | 22 | | | |
| Electric lathe | 17 | | | |
| Industrial work | 17 | | | |
| Pottery wheel | 16 | | | |
| Camden cycle | 15 | | | |
| Electric cycle | 8 | | | |

Whilst the Table provides an indication of what therapists used and for whom, apparently there was great variation between them, such that Hagedorn concluded that 'occupational therapy departments, as much as the therapists who organise them, are highly individual.' Indeed, such was the variety of equipment and patients that Hagedorn was driven to proclaim that they were too variable. There ought, she said 'to be some room for standardisation, or we run the risk of being unable to guarantee a consistent standard of service to the patient, irrespective of the size or location of the department to which he is referred.'[116]

From that survey, it appears that remedial games were used extensively in occupational therapy departments during the 1970s. In treatment venues about the country patients often designed and constructed them as part of their therapy. Such was the case at Princess Margaret Rose Orthopaedic Hospital, where a marked improvement was noticed in the hand function of patients who used remedial games regularly as part of their treatment for tendon grafts and repairs, nerve lesions, or synovectomy operations. Perhaps the popularity of games as therapy was because almost any required movement could be accomplished by adapting a game like skittles, draughts, bagatelle, quoits, or solitaire.[117]

Games were also used in the treatment of sensory motor and perceptual dysfunction which could be a problem for people following strokes and other neurological disorders. That area of dysfunction had begun to take a major place in physical rehabilitation as work with orthopaedic problems decreased. In sensory motor rehabilitation, the use of Bobath's techniques to treat adult hemiplegia was particularly popular. Downing for example, wrote about them applied to woodwork as used at the Rivermead Rehabilitation Centre in Oxford.[118] The Bobath techniques had been a central aspect of treatment with children with cerebral palsy for years. Some departments also used a Proprioceptive Neuromuscular Facilitation (PNF) approach in the treatment of neurological disorders.[119]

Therapy for children was moving to the forefront in both physical disabilities and psychiatry. It too owed much to a growing awareness of sensory-motor problems and the difficulties caused by perceptual dysfunction. In terms of children with physical disorder, Lorraine Burr, at Northwick Park Hospital, discussed the treatment of the child with dyspraxia. That aimed at 'total cerebral integration to reinforce body awareness, recognition of body relationships to external form and spatial judgement.' Occupational therapy used as a back up to remedial educative techniques, progressed 'through body awareness and proprioceptive recognition to symmetrical organisation and eventually to cerebral integration.' Gross body tasks were later related to the 'academic situation through pencil games, drawing and writing.'[120] It was in this decade that the theory and treatment of sensory integrative dysfunction as developed by A. Jean Ayres at the University of Southern California in the USA began to appear. Courses were held in Dundee and London in 1979, and at the first, Dr J. A. Young, a consultant paediatric neurologist who felt generally sympathetic to the treatment, suggested careful, controlled studies were required in the UK before people began to 'dabble' in it.[121]

In the psychiatric field Dr Michael Field, mentioned earlier, provided a summary of the occupational therapist's treatment with behaviourally disturbed children. It was, he wrote:

*Promotion of: Construction and creative work to the benefit of the child's self-*
*assurance and view of himself. The release of tension and aggression, which can be*
*expressed in joinery, modelling, dressing up and acting, puppetry, percussion and so on.*
*A helpful relationship between therapist and child the therapist being a person with*
*confidence in the child's capacity to achieve creative ends, and also one willing to accept*
*the child's limitations and sometimes negative behaviour.*[122]

Rosemary Huggins held concerns about practice in the field of mental health. She was troubled by the difference between the rehabilitation of physically disabled people and of those with 'damaged minds and personalities.' The physical rehabilitation model was frequently used as a measure of expectation that was inappropriate for those with mental breakdown, and could have disastrous results. She said that therapeutic workshops in psychiatric hospitals were filled with individuals able to work at a 'high standard of efficiency and intricacy, but who have become "stuck" there because they are unable to take their place in society as well-adjusted human beings.' In contrast to that model, Huggins supposed that in psychological medicine the term 'rehabilitation' was perhaps best applied to a return to good basic living habits after prolonged mental illness. This would be followed by resocialisation, work skills, and then return to home, hostel or group home. The increasing number of day hospitals, she thought, helped to maintain normal ways of life in the community.[123]

In order to illustrate the essential elements of successful rehabilitation in psychiatry, 'remotivation, unhurried preparation and concerted teamwork between hospital and community', Huggins told the story of Eastern European refugees who came to England during or after World War II. 'Past the acute stages of their illnesses, without friends, relatives or any place to go, they become the passive recipients of an institutional way of living.' An experimental group of such refugees was given the opportunity to try living on their own in a three-roomed detached cottage in hospital grounds. It took them six months to agree. Under the observation and with the support of an occupational therapist, the group took up residence. They had their own latch keys, and relearned the art of living as a family whilst continuing to attend the hospital workshops during the day, as they had done before. It took many months before they could accept responsibility for themselves and each other. While this process of resocialisation was proceeding, negotiations opened with the British Council for Aid to Refugees to find a house in the community for them. They saw it as a possible pilot scheme for the future, and its executive committee completed the purchase of a semi-detached three bedroomed house for the group's use at a rent they could afford. The house was voluntarily redecorated by hospital nursing staff, and furnished through goodwill gifts. The hospital secretary agreed to act as landlord, and a home help was found. Local Eastern Europeans were encouraged to befriend the group and to make them welcome amongst compatriots. The refugees continued to attend the hospital workshops as day patients.[124]

Occupational therapy for rehabilitation in psychiatry continued to play a personal curative role in the 1970s. At the beginning of the decade, occupational therapists recognised the changing emphasis of their work. Batchelor was saddened that programmes emphasising the psychological interaction between patient and therapist were daunting for some therapists. Referring specifically to psychotherapeutic aspects of occupational therapy aimed at reinforcing healthy aspects of the patient's self by engagement in new interpersonal transactions, she argued that patients' distress often sprang from disorders of their self-systems. When that was the case, the main therapeutic tool was the self of the therapist. The therapeutic role was to help patients to modify expectations of the activity being done, in the belief that modifications would generalise to other areas of the patient's life. Within those limits, the therapeutic goal was to strengthen healthy aspects of the patient's self-picture and weaken unhealthy ones. To differentiate between occupational therapists and other psychotherapists, Batchelor contended that:

> ...the presence of objects (ready made and offered, or created), the setting of tasks, the fostering of manual dexterity and competence and the emergence of talents, problems, conflicts and personal relationships in a working environment, should be taken as distinguishing occupational therapy from individual or group psychotherapies. The dynamics of individual and group psychotherapy operate also in Occupational Therapy, but the presence of objects, which can be manipulated according to the emergence of internal psychological happenings, marks the point of emphasis and of distinction in the Occupational Therapy setting. In psychiatric psychotherapy the individual is in a situation where he can verbalise, but he cannot 'do' things to objects and is thus isolated from the stimuli and constraints of occupation.[125]

As well as using self therapeutically, the use of projective techniques was popular. Sheena Blair described projection as learning about personality by examining thoughts and feelings about another person or object. Marshack explained that the term 'Projective Technique' had only recently been adopted for many of the media used in occupational therapy, such as art, pottery, music and drama. It was used at Claybury, in Essex, where occupational therapy was an integral part of the total psychotherapeutic programme within a 'Therapeutic Community'. There 'the latest', and Marshack suggested 'potentially the most effective method of barrier and inhibition break down', was the technique of 'Physical Encounter, that we at Claybury call "Contact Groups".' Based on the link between body image and affective state, and drawing on the experiences and conclusions of the Esalen Institute in California, they began to incorporate 'body talk' into the programme. She explained that every Monday morning, the weekly programme began with a Contact Group involving as many members of the ward team as possible—patients, nurses, social workers and doctors. The occupational therapist acted as a facilitator of movement patterns for people to experiment with. The contact group was always followed by a group discussion to enable people to share and gain greater insight into the feelings they experienced during the session and to relate their nonverbal physical side to the intellectual thinking side. Contact groups were used to enhance and extend individuals' awareness of self, of personal potential and as the essential integrating factor in bonding relationships with others.[126]

Marshack's paper was given at the Scottish Association's Study Day in October 1973, when over 60 participants also rotated through three groups to experience different media used projectively. Pottery and poetry were the media of one group, a variety of sociodrama 'warm-ups' and role playing situations of another, and art and music were the media of the last group. All were designed either to promote discussion or to instigate expression of emotional subject matter.[127]

At the same study day, Sheena Blair talked about occupational therapy using group psychotherapy at the Royal Edinburgh Hospital. It was difficult, she said, to divorce any one discipline involved in treating people in groups, as all treatments must complement the overall approach. Basically, group psychotherapy was about: improving relationships and communications with others; providing motivation for further improvement; recognising emotional patterns of behaviour due to anxiety, and defensive patterns of behaviour; and providing patients with a situation for reality testing in which to try out new roles and new responses to assess their own progress. Occupational therapy, in the ward in which she worked, could be divided into projective techniques, which were allied closely to the other psychotherapy groups, and recreational or project activity groups which dealt mainly with assessment and treatment of relationships. They used music, art, pottery and poetry sessions in projective sessions which were regular and accepted groups. Some advantages of their use were:

1. The projective group acts as a prop, an assistant to psychotherapy, in many cases making the expression of strong feelings easier for the patient.
2. A visual aid—painting or piece of sculpture—gives the group more of an insight into the verbally slow patient.
3. Maximum participation is possible whereas in other large or small groups the focus of participation is less often concentrated on the most vocal members.
4. Provision of a different approach to exploring problems and conflicts and for ventilating feeling.
5. Within the psychotherapy situation, the projective group acts as a supplement to our understanding of the person.

In contrast, recreational sessions included exercise and relaxation, indoor or outdoor games, and sports. They were used to create awareness of physical changes and postures while under stress, and as simple procedures of physiological relaxation; as a means of assessing relationships; and as a source of social contacts.[128]

Despite the exciting picture which is apparent from those articles, some of the problems faced by occupational therapy practitioners in psychiatry were alluded to in a paper published inBJOT mid decade. In it the notion of 'Frames of Reference' and 'Models' in psychiatry made their debut. Miss McClean, an American trained occupational therapist working as tutor in psychiatry at the Dorset House School, defined them as:

*A frame of reference is based on theories of personality development and is information gathered together into a structure or conceptual framework that gives meaning upon which therapy is based.*

*A treatment model is a definition of that framework into a workable and researchable identity or programme.*

McLean argued for their use because financial presures were forcing non essential services from psychiatric hospitals, and 'the day when occupational therapy's contribution to treatment was accepted because people enjoyed it is no longer with us.' Frames of reference and models, she stated, would enable occupational therapists to evaluate clinical programmes and validate the service through research. That she felt was vital pointing to the many other professionals taking over the roles that had formerly been those of occupational therapists like recreational, dance, art, group, music, relaxation, and drama therapists. Anticipating reaction from readers relating to belonging to a profession of 'doers' rather than theorists, she suggested that the vast amount of knowledge held by occupational therapists was disorganised to the extent that it was impossible to explain a clear and definite service.[129] The use of frames of reference and models to describe and define treatment evolved gradually.

By the end of the decade, some therapists saw that 'expansion into the community' was having both positive and detrimental effects on psychiatric occupational therapy. Its future, said Jo Sackett in 1979, was 'in the melting pot…It could be good: on one hand, we have altered and expanded crafts, art, music and group therapy; on the other hand, there is bureaucratic muddle, which impedes progress.' There was a 'crying need' for 'a cohesive national development plan…carefully devised by those actively concerned at grass roots level', rather than by government officials. Pre-empting much of the concern that was to come later as psychiatric treatment institutions closed their doors, Sackett worried about the future of occupational therapy in psychiatry. She was concerned about potential subdivision into specialised areas of treatment, and the 'tremendous emphasis being laid on the fact that the mentally ill should be treated in the community' with insufficient thought being given to the families who have to cope. She argued that Area Health Authorities should accept that the mentally ill, the physically disabled, and the mentally handicapped all needed different treatment and facilities, and that the mentally ill need a wide range. Occupational therapy, whether it be part of a large hospital, a psychiatric unit, a day hospital or day centre, was aimed at helping patients to become members of the outside community as efficiently and quickly as possible. Sackett said that was achieved by helping patients to understand themselves, to come to terms with their illness, to establish or re-establish a work-pattern, and to build bridges between the themselves and the community.[130]

## Into the community

Community occupational therapy services in the United Kingdom had first started in 1938, but the 1939–45 war delayed further development until post-war legislation required local authorities to provide community services. Local authorities had employed occupational therapists to perform duties according to the National Health Service Act, 1946, to provide 'prophylaxis, care and after care', and the National Assistance Act, 1948 to provide 'occupation'. Despite that early start, wide scale expansion into community practice characterised the 1970s.

As described earlier, when departments of social services were created in 1971, the majority of community-based occupational therapy services had transferred to them.[131] Authorities were directed by the DHSS to decide at local level on the administrative framework within which occupational therapy should be continued.[132] This led to responsibility falling in either health or social services departments.

John Chick, Head Occupational Therapist for Buckinghamshire County Council where a Community Occupational Therapy Service had started in 1950 and remained with health services, argued that the development of community rehabilitation had created a demand for skills and manpower resources of crisis proportions. Commenting on a postal survey of county Medical Officers of Health in England and Wales in the autumn of 1972, he advised that, of the replies from 52 of 58 county authorities, 71% provided an occupational therapy service. There were 193 posts for qualified staff and since then, the figure had increased. Chick's survey had tried to identify occupational therapists' role. Approximately 41% offered a diversional service, 35% therapeutic and/or ADL, while 20.6% were inconclusive.[133] The following year Chick analysed advertisements in *Occupational Therapy* for posts within local authorities in England and Wales during a three month period. Generally, he found it alarming that 50% of the newsprint of the journal was taken up with job advertisements. Many of them were for employment within local authorities. Although there were 3850 registered practitioners in the United Kingdom, he argued that the profession could not meet the manpower demands. Also disturbing was a range of salary scales so wide that it suggested to him there were widely differing views amongst employing authorities regarding the role. Cautioning that care must be taken to ensure that scarce skills were not wasted, he called for a definition of therapists' roles in the community. He described them as threefold:

*a) Skilled assessment of occupational and environmental needs of patients at the initial, intermediary and final stages of treatment to meet the needs of a wide spectrum of impairments.*

*b) Analys(is) and modif(ication of) a wide range of complex activities to meet the needs identified.*

*c) The use of psychological skills to encourage the re-motivation of patients who have sustained temporary or permanent limitation of function.[134]*

The same year Sidney Lock undertook a survey amongst members of regional groups. Twenty percent responded that they were leaving hospital posts to take up positions with a local authority. That reason for leaving scored the largest response, above pregnancy or moving.[135] The Scottish statistics on the employment of occupational therapists from 1971–73 shown in Table 2.9.2 reflect the trend.[136]

## Table 2.9.2: Employment of occupational therapists in Scotland 1971–73

| Type of Department | Establishment | | | WTE staff | | | Vacant | | | %Posts vacant | | |
|---|---|---|---|---|---|---|---|---|---|---|---|---|
| | 1971 | 1972 | 1973 | 1971 | 1972 | 1973 | 1971 | 1972 | 1973 | 1971 | 1972 | 1973 |
| NHS | 263.5 | 272.5 | 285.5 | 172 | 198.5 | 193.5 | 91.5 | 74 | 92 | 35 | 28 | 36 |
| L. Authority | 38.5 | 62.5 | 102 | 30.5 | 50 | 70.5 | 8 | 12 | 31.5 | 21 | 20 | 31 |
| Independent | 33 | 31 | 39 | 30 | 25.5 | 30.5 | 3 | 5.5 | 8.5 | 9 | 18 | 22 |
| Totals | 335 | 366 | 426.5 | 232.5 | 274 | 294.5 | 102.5 | 92 | 132 | 31 | 25 | 31 |

Also in 1973, a statement on problems affecting occupational therapists working in the Local Authority service with a summary of actions to that date by AOT was published in *Occupational Therapy*. It reported:

*...anomalies in salaries and conditions of service between occupational therapists working for different local authorities; lack of a properly defined hierarchical career structure for occupational therapists working in this field, the failure of the National Joint*

*Council to reorganise the educational and training qualifications of occupational therapists by not having their qualifications written into the Purple Book; discrimination against certain occupational therapists by their being paid at lower rates than other disciplines employed by local authorities who have to complete an equivalent two/three year training prior to practice; and finally inadequate training facilities for occupational therapists working in Local Authorities. The Association is in close touch with grass root opinion all over the country on the issues involved but is not in a position at the moment to give definitive answers to a number of problems under debate because solutions to these problems are still being discussed at the highest level in the Ministry.*[137]

A year previously a report of a subcommittee of the Standing Medical Advisory Committee on Rehabilitation indicated that many local authorities were failing to provide the necessary facilities for disabled people and that if those were not available, much of the intensive rehabilitation undertaken in hospital was rendered all but useless. Without such support, patients were likely to deteriorate, and lose incentive to live as full a life as their disabilities would allow.[138]

It seems that some of these concerns were justified. In October 1975, nearly 40 heads of occupational therapy departments attended a conference at the Southern General Hospital in Glasgow. At that meeting, Jean Waterstone, with support from others present expressed anxieties about local authorities using occupational therapists 'merely to provide aids for the disabled' which 'was too confined a role'. Indeed, virtually no treatment was given at some centres for the elderly and middle aged. There was considerable agreement that many long term patients needed work centres and day centres where treatment or training took place as part of occupational therapy.[139]

The BAOT, in 1976 published the results of a national survey into the number of occupational therapists working in social service and social work departments. The results are shown in Table 2.9.3.[140]

**Table 2.9.3:    Number of occupational therapists working in social service and social work departments in 1976**

| Country | Establishment | In post |
|---|---|---|
| England and Wales | 777 | 602.3 |
| Northern Ireland | 15 | 14 |
| Scotland | 155.5 | 114.5 |
| **Total** | **947.5** | **730.8** |

Section 2 of the Chronically Sick and Disabled Persons Act required social services departments to assess the needs of handicapped people who were referred to them. That included whether they needed assistance with carrying out adaptations to the home. Assessment of a person's requirements was made by a social worker or an occupational therapist in conjunction with other staff if considered appropriate. Assessing priorities for expenditure on adaptations for disabled people differed between social services departments. The most common disorders associated with prolonged physical disability and subsequent need for assistance under the Chronically Sick and Disabled Persons Act and the Housing Act 1974, in approximate order of incidence, were osteo- and rheumatoid arthritis, multiple sclerosis, hemiplegia, respiratory infections, cerebral palsy, paraplegia, spina bifida, tetraplegia, other neurological disorders, particularly muscular dystrophy, amputation, and the results of trauma, particularly fractures of femur. An application for grant aid was made to the social services department and possibly the environmental health department of the district council, or other voluntary bodies.

The Housing Act of 1974 provided for improvement and intermediate grants to be payable in a wide range of circumstances. Three words within the act *accommodation, welfare or employment* appeared to enable most disabled people to apply for an improvement grant under a very wide range of circumstances. Holmes and Peace suggest that, despite some unfortunate anomalies and shortcomings, that 'may make the Housing Act 1974 a Disabled Person's Housing Rights Charter.' Adaptations to a home might require relocation of standard amenities and increased space to improve access to amenities or assist the person's 'welfare or employment.' They might include other provision such as central heating, power points at convenient heights, low level food preparation and cooking facilities, or ramps.[141] Building Surveyor for the Surrey County Council, Terence Lockhart, pointed to the need for close association between architects or surveyors and occupational therapists. Assuming that sufficient financial resources were available, he argued that success depended largely upon the knowledge and skill of the architect or surveyor and the occupational therapist. He recommended that aesthetic as well as pragmatic considerations needed to be incorporated when designing adaptations, and that feedback from the disabled occupant and occupational therapist was essential. He noted that 'even after the most assiduous research, contemplation and discussion, irritating faults can manifest themselves over a period of months.' Learning from each experience and from feedback was important for increasing success in future work.[142]

So, during the 1970s much of the role of occupational therapists became centred on the prescription of equipment to help people remain independent, and to ensure that where possible a disability did not become a handicap. Hyland suggested that was sometimes as simple as providing the correct chair, instruction, or advice to the family on how to help clients to stand up or sit down. Adaptation was recommended as a cheaper and often preferable option to specially made equipment. For example, adjustments to chair height and seat angles, or the provision of an ejector device, often meant that clients could keep a favoured chair and its chosen position in the room.[143] The prescription of wheelchairs also became an important aspect of community care and Journal articles about selection appeared. One by Crewe stressed that a wheelchair should increase mobility, comfort and independence. As well it should promote as near normal a life as possible, while reducing pain, joint stress, fatigue or family dependence. Its prescription followed clinical and functional assessment to ensure that a wheelchair was required and that the most appropriate model was supplied.[144]

The Disabled Living Foundation continued to pioneer and sustain many projects concerning advice about aids and equipment prescribed by community based occupational therapists. It produced audio-visual programmes, and held annual study days on practical subjects such as the frequently demanded 'Selection and Use of Wheelchairs' and 'Lifting and Hoisting.' A Disabled Living Centres Council was established promoting a network of DLCs throughout the UK. Other permanent centres where disabled people could visit and seek help without a medical referral or a Social Service recommendation were springing up for those living far from London. The Merseyside Aids Centre in Liverpool, and the National Demonstration Centre, Pinderfields were purpose built. The Medical Aids Department, Leicester, was a converted Victorian school. The Disabled Living Centre, Birmingham, was a converted commercial building. The Aids Centre, Newcastle Upon Tyne, was housed temporarily, as was the Wales Council for the Disabled Aids & Information Centre, at Caerphilly, the Hampshire Area Health Authority at Southampton, and the Aids/Assessment Unit at Stockport. The Family Service and Assessment Centre in London was unique as the only Centre with residential accommodation. Whilst all differed in size, funding, methods of establishment and premises, all shared common aims. They acted as a reference source for those professionally involved with disabled people, and as a teaching source for students, as well as a support for Social Services and Area Health Authorities. The great majority of the staff of such centres were occupational therapists who were 'prepared to tackle anything and be master of many trades' such as 'advertising, publicity, showmanship, display and design'. Some of the Centres had an information service with up-to-date easily retrievable information, which was growing rapidly. Larger provincial Centres had many on-going community projects, uniting in voluntary and professional effort in endeavours like wheelchair clinics; stroke clubs; mastectomy and stoma clinics; counselling training; and facilities for incontinence and sexual/personal relationships.[145]

The National Aids for the Disabled Exhibition (NAIDEX)[146] started in 1973 as a market place showing disabled people, their relatives and carers, and professional people concerned with their welfare something of the range of equipment that was then becoming available. It provided an opportunity to try out the various products, to compare similar items under one roof, and to order equipment direct from the suppliers. In 1978, and for the following four years, the BAOT Annual Conference was held jointly at the same venue with NAIDEX, to enable the delegates to see for themselves what equipment was available and what was new on the market. The Annual Conference grew and needing a venue to suit its requirements it was decided that in future it would be held at a venue of COT choice, and that the concurrent exhibition would be extended, subsidising, to some extent, the costs of the Conference.[147]

Mobile centres, such as the Travelling Exhibition of Aids, the Visiting Aids Centre, London, and the Mobile Aids Centre (MAC), Edinburgh, were also being established to demonstrate equipment and publicise services for people with disability. They visited anywhere they could reach. MAC was a gift to the Scottish population from the Scottish Gas Board. It was a 22-foot long Bedford truck, easily recognised with blue and white livery depicting the wheelchair logo. Access to the vehicle was either by fold-down steps or by hydraulic lift for the non-ambulant. The Officer-in-Charge was an occupational therapist, assisted by an organising secretary, and a driver. Operational costs were met by the Secretary of State for Scotland. The Mobile Aids Centre was packed with information and aids which people tried out for themselves with guidance and advice, and in the eighteen months following MAC taking to the road, it visited all twelve regions of Scotland, including the Inner and Outer Hebrides, Orkney and Shetland.

Apart from ADL, it appears that the community concept embraced voluntary as well as paid work for some occupational therapists. Horse riding for the Disabled was one sphere that attracted volunteers. An article in BJOT late in the decade described another—the voluntary activities of two community-based occupational therapists in the 'intermediate treatment' of young people. Intermediate treatment, as defined in the 1969 Children and Young Persons Act,[148] was a community-based programme for children and adolescents who had appeared before the Courts or were at risk of getting into trouble. The concept came from a 1962 Home Office report which discussed alternatives to residential treatment for young offenders and the need to provide an 'intermediate' solution which could include preventive and curative elements. The early development of intermediate treatment included vigorous activities such as mountain climbing and canoeing to provide 'alternative ventures and physical outlets for the misdirected adolescent.' It was gradually realised that often the social problems of such adolescents required activities structured to develop personal relationships and social skills. Media such as creative art, cookery, drama, group games, claywork, macramé, tie-dyeing. batik, woodwork, and photography, were recognised as useful, along with the concept of group skills and the use of various group models. In Peterborough Social Services two community occupational therapists became involved. They recognised an interesting historical similarity between the development of intermediate treatment and occupational therapy, and were ready to demonstrate their skills in group therapy.[149]

That community story reflects the growing attention to paediatrics, not least within the Local Authority services. The Buckinghamshire County Council, which appears to have been very pro-active in developing extended services in the community, started to consider the treatment of disabled children. With the College of Occupational Therapists, it published *A Report on Occupational Therapy for the Disabled Child*.[150] The Report recommended that the role be recognised as providing a pre-conditioning programme before school; advice and guidance to schools, welfare assistants, and careers officers; to parents regarding the use of toys as well as ADL; and to planners about building design and equipment. Interestingly, and perhaps reflecting the newness of the paediatric concept to occupational therapists, at a follow up study day at Milton Keynes, most of those who attended felt that their basic training did not prepare them for specialist child care.[151]

The *Calendar of Coming Events* two years later revealed that paediatrics provided a theme at the Oxford Region AGM covering topics on autism, paediatric assessment, and toy libraries. Similarly at the East Anglia AGM paediatric issues were central and dealt with learning difficulties at school, and rheumatoid arthritis. The Welsh Region chose Spina Bifida as a topic at one of its meetings, and the Scottish Eastern Region chose Children in the Community for one of theirs. The Wolfsen Centre held a 5-day course on the Motor Problems in Multi-Handicapped Children, which was followed by 10 day releases of practical work at South Ockendon Hospital, Essex. In the same year there was also a course on Special Education as well as the Bobaths' Cerebral Palsy training course.[152]

The Toy Libraries Association was formed in 1972 as a charity that disseminated information, not only to toy libraries themselves, but also to manufacturers, designers, and therapists. In the Newcomen Toy Library, attached to a district and regional assessment centre, the choice of toys was shared between the librarians and occupational therapist. Constant appraisal of the use and quality of specific toys was made, and occasionally a particular toy was assessed for a manufacturer.[153] B. D. Dasari, occupational therapist at the Bangour Village Hospital, recognised that the contribution of occupational therapists in the running of toy library centres was increasing. Such centres, she said, were needed in all counties. The challenge for those working with handicapped children was to increase the awareness of the local authority and educational department of their specific play needs. She explained 'all children need to play, and toys are their tools.' Through fun children learn about the nature of the world, about themselves as part of it, about relationships; and about qualities and features of their environment. It was becoming increasingly recognised that, as far as possible, handicapped children should be provided with toys of every kind to foster such learning. Without play, Dasari said, a child was 'shut off from reality. All handicapped children whatever their disability, share the same basic disadvantage: an impaired ability to interact with their environment. This leads directly to the distortion or deprivation of learning.' Dasari went on to discuss how, despite activities used in occupational therapy being selected for their therapeutic value, 'children's normal development should be considered and activities be chosen which will encourage this.' Many occupational therapy departments were engaged in the production of special toys for individual problems. At Queen Mary's Hospital for children in Surrey, Linda Routledge, the Senior Occupational Therapist, did so as part of a team with the medical engineering research unit and the orthopaedic consultant.[154]

Other interesting 1970s community initiatives for children included the establishment of an Opportunity Playgroup in 1974 in which the Paediatric Occupational Therapist at Northwick Park Hospital became involved. By definition this was: a pre-school group for children with any form of handicap; a place where handicapped and normal children could meet together; and a place where mothers of handicapped children could meet together. Following discussions with community physicians, paediatricians, physio- and speech therapists, community nursing officers and health visitors, an occupational therapist was employed to work in the playgroup and children in the area were referred to it, especially those who were socio-economically disadvantaged.[155] Another initative was an Occupational Therapy Summer Play Scheme to which medical staff of the Institute of Family Psychiatry referred children aged 6–17 years. Each child could attend for up to ten hours a week, and the scheme catered for the needs of 83 children and their families. Primarily, it provided support to both child and family, aided in diagnosis of the family situation, and in the future treatment programming. It was also of a preventive nature in that it provided children 'at risk' with supervised play schemes over the school holidays.[156]

Just as the developmental and play needs of children took a long time to surface as a separate issue in occupational therapy, so too did another topic of fundamental importance – sexuality and sexual problems of handicapped people. It, too, can be seen to be associated with initiatives towards the community and concomitant recognition of the right of disabled people to have normal living experiences. The Committee on Sexual Problems of the Disabled, (SPOD) a body set up by the National Fund for Research into Crippling Diseases, sought to remedy the lack of understanding. Intensive research during 1973–75 revealed the prevalence of, the widely varying nature of, and many solutions to sexual problems among those with disability. Afterwards, in a period of just two years, the Committee was called upon to provide speakers for some 400 occasions at international or local level. SPOD 2-day courses for workers with disabled people provided grounding in the sexual problems of disability and their solutions. Occupational therapists, together with social workers, were in the forefront of those requesting and receiving training.[157]

With so many changes, and so many new directions for practice, there were numerous and fundamental problems which needed to be evaluated or researched. To many, research was the obvious way forward, but daunting. Cairns Aitkens encouraged 'all occupational therapists to become involved in measurement. Only then will there be advance in your area of concern, such as in better assessment for aids and appliances.' Recognising how hard it was to get started he advised that 'it need not be with sophistication, the primary need being simply to record in a meaningful way what you do.' Additionally, he encouraged 'perhaps only a few—to obtain specific training in research methodology in order to promote some more intensive studies.'[158] Jay, Mendez, and Monteath discussed how 'research into the validity of the techniques used by occupational therapists' as well as 'opportunity for personal professional development' was seen by the Association as a growing need. To help facilitate this in 1975, COT:

> ...set up a Research and Development Committee whose remit was to help members to become research orientated as well as to identify opportunities for research. The DHSS also supported this endeavour and held joint study days in different parts of the country for both occupational therapists and physiotherapists in collaboration with their professional associations. A few research bursaries were made available by the DHSS, initially in England and Wales, Scotland being included later. [159]

The following year, the College made plans to establish a research register, and to that end, Margaret Ellis asked for news of research projects being done, 'either research or evaluation in connection with occupational therapy.'[160]

Margaret Smith, one of the first fellows by examination, was awarded honours for her thesis *The Use Of Familiar Daily Activities In The Assessment Of Neurological Deficit Following Stroke*. She had an occupational therapy career somewhat different from most, in that research became her major interest and contribution to the profession. Returning to the work force when family commitments allowed she became involved in a research position studying the problems of mentally handicapped school leavers in Edinburgh. Following that, she became the first occupational therapist to be employed in full-time research by a Scottish University. As a Research Fellow in the Department of Community Medicine in Edinburgh under the direction of Cairns Aitken, she was engaged in computer analysis of data. As well as the effectiveness of stroke units mentioned earlier, the research included projects for hand surgeons in training, and the outcome of severe injury with particular emphasis on legal compensation. She was a founder member and on the Council of the Society for Research in Rehabilitation (SRR).[161]

The SRR was a multidisciplinary society founded in 1978 to promote research about rehabilitation and its application to practice. Of the hundred researchers initially invited to become members, eight were occupational therapists. During the next 20 years they made up 14% of the Council, and Alicia Mendez was one of the 12 Presidents. Mendez believes that the SRR helped many occupational therapists become more involved in research. The early meetings were very exciting for occupational therapists, but Cairns Aitken recalls concern before the first that the standard of presentation of non-medical members might fall short of what would be acceptable. That was not to be the case, and a small monetary prize, given in the early days, for the best free paper decided by ballot by members present was awarded three times to occupational therapists, and once only to a physician, a bio-engineer, and a social planner.[162]

Irene Ilott continues the story of occupational therapy research in the 1970s as told in *Occupational Therapy* and BJOT.

# Research in the 1970s
## By Irene Ilott

During the 1970s, occupational therapists began to have their attention drawn to research posts, funding schemes and training courses. For example, positions advertised included those for two staff at the Possum Research Foundation,[163] and an opportunity for research into occupational therapy in the early treatment of brain damaged patients and in the fields of perceptual and sensory-motor training.[164] Funding opportunities to undertake research training ranged from private, charitable trusts to national R&D schemes. For example, there was a £500 scholarship for research from the Sedwood Charitable Trust for people working in the field of prosthetics and orthotics.[165]

A number of research studies validated the use of occupational therapy in a range of different areas of practice. Simpler designs such as recommended by Cairns Aitken were the chosen method of some. In 1971, Grove published a retrospective study of 100 patients with head injuries discharged from the Wolfson Medical Rehabilitation Centre. Its purpose was to 'to see if any particular factor is significant in resettlement and what sort of results have been achieved.' The results indicated that 48 were employed, 44 were unemployed, and 8 were not known. Younger patients had a higher success rate, with personal contacts and family firms employing the more severely disabled people. Grove noted that government training schemes demanded higher physical and intellectual agility than patients were able to attain; and that the service could be improved with provision of sheltered workshop and hostel facilities.[166]

Similarly, Campbell carried out a 10 year, retrospective study of the pattern of attendance and discharge from the rehabilitation workrooms and groups at the Simon Square Centre since 1960. The Centre had provided Services for nearly 1900 physically disabled persons in Edinburgh. She analysed particularly those patients with additional or associated problems of behaviour or perception. In the discussion, she highlighted two important principles related to data collection and dissemination. These were: record keeping for forward planning for longitudinal studies; and access to existing medical and psychological research.[167]

Reports of studies evaluating the effectiveness of equipment to assist ADL became a regular feature in the Journal from the mid-1970s. One of the first was an evaluation of the prescription, supply and use of aids and equipment for the bath and toilet.[168] Another was a study about adults with Friedreich's ataxia which involved visits to 58 patients and a questionnaire about all aspects of personal ADL, independence, wheelchairs, transfers, outdoor transport, housing, schooling, Further Education, employment, and hobbies. The study resulted in a booklet for patients and relatives about the problems encountered.[169]

Hagedorn, whose study collecting information about equipment was referred to earlier, suggested that research thinking was still rare amongst the practically trained therapists. She reported, '…it was noticeable, however, that few attempts were made to be really analytical in examining how well apparatus achieved the treatment aim for which it was used.' She noted how discouraging it was to receive so few replies and that the lack of research into equipment and treatment techniques was disappointing. Hagedorn excused those traits by reference to lack of time and facilities, and also, that the AOT 'is not at present geared to organise research and the training schools are struggling with the problems of finding tutors and producing enough students to meet the increasing demand.'[170] The results of Hagedorn's survey were coded using a computer programme at Brighton College of Technology Computer Centre.[171] The following year, she described working with the manufacturers on the prototype and manual about the Larvic Rehabilitation Lathe, which was the First Report of the Panel for the Evaluation of Rehabilitation Equipment Design.[172]

Smith's Edinburgh Stroke Rehabilitation Study was another evaluative investigation. A randomised, controlled trial, it tested the hypothesis that, following acute strokes, a stroke rehabilitation unit could discharge home a higher proportion of patients functionally independent than could general medical wards. The paper focused on measuring the outcome of rehabilitation, especially activities of daily living. [173]

In one of the first clinical trails of paediatric occupational therapy, a complex study design was used. A 'double-blind cross over technique' of Tetrabenazine and occupational therapy studied 30 children with athetoid cerebral palsy. It was found that 'Tetrabenzine did not produce obvious clinical improvements but the endorsement of occupational therapists value was an important result of our study.' The results suggested that it was practice provided in occupational therapy that improved hand function and the study recommended that 'occupational therapy should be practised at school and at home as well as on infrequent visits to clinics.'[174]

Another study compared occupational therapy with operant conditioning techniques in the treatment of long term psychiatric patients. It was noteworthy because it was one of the first to include detailed statistical analysis. There were positive results from both interventions, but 'the group receiving occupational therapy significantly improved in the areas of social interest and overall behavioural level in off-ward situation.'[175]

In conjunction with the Biomechanics Unit of Imperial College, London, Margaret Ellis published one of the first articles reporting the outcome of a splint making technique—cast bracing of femoral fractures. The paper described the outcome with 37 patients: the time between commencement of traction and fitting the brace had been reduced and there were encouraging results in consolidation.[176] A small-scale study published the following year also investigated the effects of splinting. The study involved 20 children with Still's disease. Writing tests were carried out with and without wrist splints. The splint was found to be useful in maintaining wrist position when writing, and was not detrimental to performance.[177]

Apart from the research discussed earlier, Rita Goble reported on an early rehabilitation study of heart disease. It was a follow-up of patients treated with artificial cardiac pacemakers, using psychological tests, return to work, and social activities as measures. The methods included interviews at the time, 3, and 6 months later, and a postal questionnaire 12 months later. The conclusion was that 'there seems to be a place for trials to determine which areas of rehabilitation are important, and to examine further the characteristics of patients who will require extra help in their return to a normal life.'[178]

Although only a few studies were published, the range of methodology was impressive, from making use of standard, but meticulous record keeping to the most complex double-blind cross over technique clinical trial. All those reported appeared to support the practice of occupational therapy, and it is disappointing that promulgation of the benefits were not more widespread.

In summary the 1970s was a time of great development and excitement. The British Association of Occupational Therapists and, later, the College of Occupational Therapists were formed from an amalgamation of the Association and Scottish Association of Occupational Therapists. The BAOT became a trade union, new headquarters were acquired, and varied models of education began to evolve. They including opportunities for helpers to upgrade their qualifications and for trained occupational therapists to engage in post registration courses. There were opportunities, too, for some to engage in research, as therapists were being urged to do. Government initiatives led to debate about the future of the remedial professions, and to an occupational therapy presence in government. The reorganisation of the NHS produced a significant shift towards community rather than institutional care. The profession was growing and there was a fairly rapid expansion of occupational therapists in social and local authority services, where, in the main, they were involved in functional assessment and assisting people to engage in daily life.

The question remains. What caused the professional self doubt that emerged, along with concerns about not being understood by the medical fraternity and the general public? Could it have been the result of a too rapid transition from remediating illness by the use of craft work, recreational and vocational employment within a hospital environment, to assessing and advising on the use of aids and equipment in home environments in the community? Could the change have been too rapid for others to recognise that both types of activities were integral to the relationship between occupation and health? Could it have been too total a rejection of former practices which left the majority of the profession without a historical foundation? Or could it have been a result of all those factors in combination with a loss of philosophical base?

[1]Random House. Timetables of History. New York: Random House, 1996.
[2]Occupational Therapy 1974; 37(2): 28.
[3]Comment. British Journal of Occupational Therapy 1974; 37(8): 134.
[4]Weaver NDW. Health service problems resources and predictions. Occupational Therapy 1973; 36(11): 535, 536, 537.
[5]Weaver. Health service problems resources and predictions....
[6]Health Department of Great Britain & Northern Ireland. Prevention and Health: Everybody's Business. London: H.M.S.O., 1976.
[7]N.W. British Journal of Occupational Therapy 1976; 39(6): 153.
[8]Comment. Preventive Health. British Journal of Occupational Therapy 1976; 39(7): 170.
[9]Government priorities for health. British Journal of Occupational Therapy 1976; 39(5): 123.
[10]W.H.O. warns health workers: Boredom and loneliness, the cause of dependency may be overlooked. British Journal of Occupational Therapy 1974; 37(9): 154.
[11]Randle APH. Rehabilitation and Society. Occupational Therapy 1974; 37(1): 15–17.
[12]Macdonald EM. World-Wide Conquests of Disabilities: The History, Development and Present Functions of the Remedial Services. London: Bailliere Tindall, 1981; 146–9.
[13]Mendez MA. Personal communication with AAW. 2001.
[14]Weaver NDW. 1974 and After. Occupational Therapy 1972; 35(12): 961.
[15]Weaver. 1974 and After...
[16]Randle. Rehabilitation and Society....
[17]A wider view by Agag: The political, health and welfare scene. Occupational Therapy 1974; 37(4): 59.
[18]Scottish Home and Health Department. The Mair Report: Medical Rehabilitation: The Pattern for the Future. Edinburgh: H.M.S.O., 1972
[19]Macdonald. World-Wide Conquests of Disabilities....; 160–3.
[20]Rehabilitation. Report of a Sub Committee of the Standing Medical Advisory Committee. London: H.M.S.O., 1972.
[21]Dept of Health and Social Security Scottish Home and Health Dept Welsh Office. Statement by the Committee on the Remedial Professions. London: H.M.S.O., 1972; v.
[22]Dept of Health and Social Security...Statement by the Committee on the Remedial Professions....; 1–5.
[23]Comment. Remedial Professions Committee Statement. Occupational Therapy 1972; 35(3):151.
[24]Department of Health and Social Security. The Remedial Professions: A Report by a Working Party set up in March 1972 by the Secretary of State for Social Services. London: H.M.S.O., 1973.
[25]Department of Health and Social Security. The Remedial Professions...; 21
[26]There is a great deal of controversy about the origin of the quote. Agag quotes the year as 6 AD, but the most favoured dates appear to be 210 BC or 66 AD.
[27]A wider view by Agag: The political, health and welfare scene. Occupational Therapy 1974; 37(4): 59.
[28]A wider view by Agag: The political, health and welfare scene. Occupational Therapy 1974; 37(1): 10.

[29]Old Testament. Samuel 1, 15: 32.

[30]Why OTs leave hospitals. Occupational Therapy 1974; 37(2): 26; Conferences. Head O.T.s discuss their place in rehabilitation team. British Journal of Occupational Therapy 1974; 37(6): 101–3.

[31]Department of Health and Social Security. Report of the Committee of Inquiry into the Pay and Related Conditions of Service of the Professions Supplementary to Medicine and Speech Therapists. London: H.M.S.O., 1975.

[32]Macdonald. World-Wide Conquests of Disabilities….; 201–2.

[33]Initial BAOT evidence for Halsbury Committee. British Journal of Occupational Therapy 1975; 38(1): 9–10.

[34]Nixon C. Lord MacCarthy recommends major overhaul of Whitley Council System. British Journal of Occupational Therapy 1977: 40(1) : 3,6.

[35]See also: A Report on the Joint Working Party of the Nursing and Remedial Professions. Health Circular HC(77) 124 , London: DHSS, 1977; A Health Circular on the Relationship between the Medical and Remedial Professions. Health Circular HC(77) 33, London: DHSS, 1977; Training of Teachers of Occupational Therapy, Physiotherapy and Remedial Gymnasts. HN(77) 90, London: DHSS, 1977; Management of the Remedial Professions in the NHS. HC(79)19, London: DHSS, 1979; and Central management Services Study on Staffing Levels in the Remedial Professions, London: DHSS, 1979.

[36]Aitken C. The Casson Memorial Lecture: Rehabilitation: Facts and fantasies about occupational therapy. British Journal of Occupational Therapy 1976; 39 (7): 172–3.

[37]Aitken. The Casson Memorial Lecture….

[38]Jay P. Editorial: Into the Future United. British Journal of Occupational Therapy 1974; (5): 70.

[39]Hitchman A. Unique Conference. British Journal of Occupational Therapy 1974; 37( 6): 90.

[40]Comment. British Journal of Occupational Therapy 1974; 37(12): 214.

[41]Association's new Headquarters opened: Members' hard work and ingenuity praised. British Journal of Occupational Therapy 1975; 38(3): 58.

[42]Clause 18(4)(b). NHS Reorganisation Circular HRC(73)25. In: Occupational Therapy 1973; 37(2): 25.

[43]Department of Health and Social Security. The Remedial Professions: A Report by a Working Party set up in March 1972 by the Secretary of State for Social Services. London: H.M.S.O., 1973.

[44]See for example: BAOT Council. Council comments on the report of Remedial Professions Working Party. British Journal of Occupational Therapy 1974; 37(7): 117–19.

[45]Jay P. Personal communication to AAW. 2001.

[46]Jay P, Mendez MA. Personal communication with AAW. 2001.

[47]Advisor to Department. British Journal of Occupational Therapy 1976; 39(8): 209.

[48]Comment. Our Profession has a splendid representative. British Journal of Occupational Therapy 1976; 39(9): 218.

[49]Grove E. Casson Memorial Lecture: Working Together. British Journal of Occupational Therapy 1988; 51(5): 150-156.

[50]Grove E. Personal communication with AAW. 2000.

[51]Macdonald. World-wide conquests of disabilities….204–5.

[52]Mendez MA, Steeden B. Personal reflections to AAW. December 2000.

[53]Mendez MA. Dr Elizabeth Casson Memorial Lecture. Processes of Change: Some speculations for the future. British Journal of Occupational Therapy 1978; 41(7): 225–8.

[54]British Journal of Occupational Therapy 1977; 40(9): opposite page 218.

[55]White, S. Doctors urged to learn more about occupational therapy. British Journal of Occupational Therapy 1975; 38 (12): 267–8.

[56]NW. Book Reviews: Special edition. British Journal of Occupational Therapy 1977; 40(12):314–15.

[57]IM. Conferences: What should O.T.s do about social injustice? British Journal of Occupational Therapy 1975; 38(6): 137.

[58]Garrold KG. Letter. Occupational Therapy 1972; 36(11): 874.

[59]Stewart H. Review of technology in BJOT. Unpublished, 2001.

[60]Orriss HD. Rehabilitation Catalyst Extraordinary. British Journal of Occupational Therapy 1977; 40 (9): 219.

[61]Jay P, Mendez A, Monteath H. The Diamond Jubilee of the Professional Association, 1932–1992: An Historical Review. British Journal of Occupational Therapy 1991; 55 (7): 252–6.

[62]BAOT. 1977 First European Congress and Exhibition Delegates attended from 24 countries. British Journal of Occupational Therapy 1977; 40(6): 132.

[63]Grove E. Occupational Therapy in the United Kingdom. Ist European Congress, Edinburgh, May, 1977.

[64]Smith M. Why research? Tales of the unexpected. Keynote Address. 15th Federal Conference of the Australian Association of Occupational Therapists. Sydney, Australia, 1977. Australian Occupational Therapy Journal 1989; 36(1): 4–13.

[65]BBC apologises for that comment in "Today". British Journal of Occupational Therapy 1974; 37(9): 127.

[66]Barker J. Yesterday's student looks at Today's. British Journal of Occupational Therapy 1974; 37(6): 106–7.

[67]Sym DM. Fellowship by Examination. British Journal of Occupational Therapy 1977; 40(11) : 279.

[68]Fellowship by Examination. British Journal of Occupational Therapy 1977; 40(12): 298.

[69]The Action Committee chaired by Gordon Marsh, a hospital administrator, included an orthopaedic sugeon, and 7 occupational therapists–Grove, Hewstone, Huggins, Jay, MacCaul, Macdonald, and Mendez, plus 3 co-opted OTs and 2 observers from SAOT. Précis of recommendations provided by Peggy Jay, 2001.

[70]Grove. Casson Memorial Lecture: Working Together.…

[71]CN. Council discusses Future Needs: Will two more schools be opened? Occupational Therapy 1971; 34(8): 21–2.

[72]BAOT Teacher Training Policy. British Journal of Occupational Therapy 1975; 38(5): 109.

[73]Jay PE. Year of Great Achievement. British Journal of Occupational Therapy 1974; 37(6): 90–91.

[74]Jay PE. Personal Comment to AAW. 2001.

[75]BAOT Council. Council comments on the report of Remedial Professions Working Party. British Journal of Occupational Therapy 1974; 37(7): 117–19.

[76]Johnson H, Paterson CF. Research into training for the remedial professions: A summary of a report on student's attitudes. British Journal of Occupational Therapy 1975; 38(11): 237–9.

[77]Rook JM. Occupational Therapy education—monotech or polytech. British Journal of Occupational Therapy 1977; 40(10): 235–6.

[78]Council Report. British Journal of Occupational Therapy 1977; 40(8): 181.

[79]Collins BG. Diploma diplomacy: Progress towards a new educational syllabus for the basic O.T. Diploma. British Journal of Occupational Therapy 1977; 40(12): 305.

[80]HG. Comment. British Journal of Occupational Therapy 1979; 42(9): 206.

[81]Fraser-Holland EN. The Casson Memorial Lecture: Moving Targets and 20:20 Vision. British Journal of Occupational Therapy 1990; 53(8): 326–7.

[82]Fraser-Holland. The Casson Memorial Lecture....

[83]Askham L. Essex School. 1999. See Appendix A of this History.

[84]Post Registration Courses Planned. British Journal of Occupational Therapy 1974; 37(5): 83.

[85]MacCaul CV. Pilot Scheme for O.T. Helpers/O.T.T.I. combined course 1977/78. British Journal of Occupational Therapy 1978; 41(11): 374.

[86]Prospects for advanced work are brighter. Occupational Therapy 1973; 36(6): 3825.

[87]Bruce Crowe is an Associate Fellow of the British Psychological Society, a Fellow of the Australian Psychological Society (APS), and a past President of the APS.

[88]See Report: Advantages of psychological testing. British Journal of Occupational Therapy 1974; 37(6): 104.

[89]lSclare AB. Address on Diploma Day Glasgow School of Occupational Therapy. Scottish Journal of Occupational Therapy 1972; March: 17.

[90]Glanville H. From pioneer O.T. school to Chair of Rehabilitation. Occupational Therapy 1975; 38 (6): 127–8.

[91]Announcements. Southampton University launches first British Diploma and MSc Degree Courses. British Journal of Occupational Therapy 1977; 40(12): 317.

[92]Fraser-Holland. The Casson Memorial Lecture. 1990....

[93]Letters to the Editor. British Journal of Occupational Therapy 1975; 38(6): 130.

[94]Muir Gray JA. You must be revolutionaries. British Journal of Occupational Therapy 1975; 38(6): 126.

[95]Glanville H. From pioneer O.T. school to Chair of Rehabilitation....

[96]Davies BM. Organisation of O.T. in the new Health and Social Services with special reference to Liverpool. Occupational Therapy 1974; 37(4): 53.

[97]Nicholls PJR. Are ADL indices of any value? British Journal of Occupational Therapy 1976: 39(6)160–63.;

[98]Smith ME, Garraway WM, Akhtar AJ, Andrews CJA. An assessment unit for measuring the outcome of stroke rehabilitation. British Journal of Occupational Therapy 1977; 40(3): 51–53.

[99]Zinovieff A. Occupational Therapy: A Modern Approach. World of Medicine 1977; April: 213–16.

[100]Goble REA, Harper J, Jones RVH. Functional Assessment of the Elderly: Occupational therapy in General Practice. British Journal of Occupational Therapy 1979; 42(9): 207–10.

[101]Goble REA, Harper J, Jones RVH. Functional Assessment of the Elderly....

[102]Orr A, Philips A. Assessment Unit for adult spastics. Scottish Journal of Occupational Therapy 1970; September: 19–25.

[103]McMenamin P. Assessment of visual perceptual problems in relation to self care activities. British Journal of Occupational Therapy 1976; 39(1): 6–8.

[104]Pouw RM. An easily applied and comprehensive assessment of pre-school abilities based on spina bifida children. British Journal of Occupational Therapy 1977; 40(3): 61–3.

[105]Fletcher I. Functional Assessment of the Hand. British Journal of Occupational Therapy 1975; 38(8): 173–4.

[106]Green M. Hand Assessment. British Journal of Occupational Therapy 1974; 37(12): 215–18.

[107]McKeown R, McKeown C. Who Can Live Independently at Home? Assessment of Mentally Handicapped Adults. British Journal of Occupational Therapy 1976; 39(4): 100.

[108]Field MAS. The residential assessment of the disturbed child. British Journal of Occupational Therapy 1979; 42(2): 31–3.

[109]Freeman J, Glaister B. Assessment of patients for work in a psychiatric hospital. Occupational Therapy 1971; 34(4): 11–15.

[110]Castle J. Middle way for continual assessment. British Journal of Occupational Therapy 1975; 38(12): 263–4.

[111]Conferences. Head O.T.s discuss their place in rehabilitation team. British Journal of Occupational Therapy 1974; 37(6): 101.

[112]Nichols PJR. Rehabilitation in the reorganised National Health Service: A King's Fund Centre talk. British Journal of Occupational Therapy 1974; 37(7): 113–14.

[113]Moses KM. The Role of the Occupational Therapist in Rehabilitation. Health and Social Service Journal/Hospital International 1975; 12–13.

[114]Hagedorn R. Survey of occupational therapy equipment and techniques. Occupational Therapy 1974; 37(1): 11–12.

[115]Hagedorn. Survey of occupational therapy equipment and techniques....

[116]Hagedorn. Survey of occupational therapy equipment and techniques....

[117]Bradshaw A. Princess Margaret Rose Orthopaedic Hospital remedial games. Scottish Journal of Occupational Therapy 1974; March: 20–27.

[118]Downing V. Bobath Techniques applied to woodwork: As used at Rivermead Rehabilitation Centre, Oxford. British Journal of Occupational Therapy 1978; 41(8): 272–3.

[119]Hurd S. Survey of occupational therapy for the hemiplegic patient: Trends in treatment methods and media including the use of PNF and the Bobath approach. British Journal of Occupational Therapy 1975;38(4): 81–3.

[120]Burr LA. Treatment of the child with dyspraxia. British Journal of Occupational Therapy 1979; 42(2): 34-39.

[121]Stephenson EA. An introduction to the theory and treatment of sensory integrative dysfunction. British Journal of Occupational Therapy 1979; 42(2): 48–9.

[122]Field MAS. The residential assessment of the disturbed child. British Journal of Occupational Therapy 1979; 42(2): 31–3.

[123]Huggins R. Resettlement After Mental Illness. Rehabilitation, Health and Social Service Journal 1975; 33–4.

[124]Huggins. Resettlement After Mental Illness....

[125]Batchelor LJ. The occupational therapist as a therapeutic medium. Scottish Journal of Occupational Therapy 1970; December: 16–29.

[126] Marshack P. Contact as an adjunct to group psycho-therapy. Scottish Journal of Occupational Therapy 1973; December: 7–14.

[127]Stephens H. The use of projective techniques in psychiatry. Scottish Journal of Occupational Therapy 1973; December: 6–7

[128]Blair S. Occupational therapy: Its role in treatment using group psychotherapy. Scottish Journal of Occupational Therapy 1972; Sept: 18–22.

[129]McClean H. Towards developing a frame of reference and defining a treatment model in occupational therapy as applied to psychiatry—An object relationship base to a developmental model. British Journal of Occupational Therapy 1974; 37 (11): 196–8.

[130]Sackett J. What of the Future. British Journal of Occupational Therapy 1979; 42 (2): 46-47.

[131]Chick J. Working in the community in a remedial and social role in 1974. Occupational Therapy 1974; 37(2): 24–25.

[132]Department of Health and Social Services. I.S. W.G. Circular 5/70.

[133]Chick. Working in the community in a remedial and social role in 1974....

[134]Chick. Working in the community in a remedial and social role in 1974....

[135]Lock SJ. Why O.T.s leave hospitals. Occupational Therapy 1974; 37(2): 26.

[136]Scottish Association of Occupational Therapists. Report of the 1973 Survey. Scottish Journal of Occupational Therapy 1973; Spring.

[137]Problems affecting occupational therapists working in the Local Authority Service with a summary of actions to date by the Association. Occupational Therapy 1973; 36(5): 342.

[138]Kimmance KJ, Chick JR. Occupational therapy in the community. Occupational Therapy 1973; 36(1): 33, 36

[139]Conferences: Some day centres neglect treatment. British Journal of Occupational Therapy 1976; 39(1): 21–2.

[140]BAOT survey of O Ts working in community. British Journal of Occupational Therapy 1976; 39(3): 77–80.

[141]Holmes P, Peace C. Disabled People and Grant-aided Housing Adaptations. British Journal of Occupational Therapy 1976; 39(11): 270–72.

[142]Lockhart T. Designing Adaptations for the Disabled Part 1. British Journal of Occupational Therapy 1978; 41(1): 19–20. (This article appeared in the June issue of 'Contact' and was reproduced by kind permission of the editor.)

[143]Hyland PA. Chair assessment and three methods of raising chairs. British Journal of Occupational Therapy 1979; 42(11): 269.

[144]Crewe RA. Wheelchair choice or the biomechanics of wheelchair selection. British Journal of Occupational Therapy 1979; 42(11): 272.

[145]Jeff O, Chamberlain MA. Survey of Aids Centres 1978-1979. British Journal of Occupational Therapy 1979; 42(12): 308-312.

[146]National Aids For The Disabled Exhibition. Account provided by Peggy Jay, 2001.

[147]Hogg J. From Gas to Grabrails. British Journal of Occupational Therapy 1979; 42(6): 142.

[148]The 1969 Children & Young Persons Act defined the need for treatment intermediate between home and care, with a provision of 90 days residential care, or attendance at an l.T. Centre. I.T. orders are a clause within a Supervision Order.

[149]Wheble JE. The contribution of Occupational Therapists in the intermediate treatment of young people. British Journal of Occupational Therapy 1979; 42(10): 239.

[150]Working Party Report. Occupational Therapy for the Disabled Child. British Journal of Occupational Therapy 1975; 38(2): 25–7.

[151]Conferences: OT in the community for Disabled Child. British Journal of Occupational Therapy 1975; 38(5): 116.

[152]Calendar of coming events. British Journal of Occupational Therapy 1977; 40(2): 45–7.

[153]Toy Library attached to a district and regional assessment centre. British Journal of Occupational Therapy 1975; 38 (2): 30

[154]Dasari B. The Role of Recreation for the Handicapped Child. British Journal of Occupational Therapy 1977; 40 (2):40,41.

[155]Andrews GM. Occupational Therapy in an Opportunity Playgroup. British Journal of Occupational Therapy 1977; 40(4): 83.

[156]Hindmarsh WA. Occupational Therapy Summer Play Schemes. British Journal of Occupational Therapy 1978; 41(8): 268.

[157]Stewart WFR. Sexual Advice and Counsel for Handicapped People. British Journal of Occupational Therapy 1978; 41(3): 95.

[158]Aitken C. The Casson Memorial Lecture: Rehabilitation: Facts and fantasies about occupational therapy. British Journal of Occupational Therapy 1976; 39(7): 172-173.

[159]Jay, Mendez & Monteath. The Diamond Jubilee of the Professional Association, 1932–1992...; 255.

[160]Ellis M. Committee needs news of research projects. British Journal of Occupational Therapy 1976; 39(7): 178.

[161]MacKenzie L, Monteath H. Retirement: Margaret Smith: An Appreciation. British Journal of Occupational Therapy 1992; 55(2): 79.

[162]Jay PE, Mendez MA. History of the Society for Research in Rehabilitation (from extract provided by authors)

[163]Advertisement. Possum Research Foundation. British Journal of Occupational Therapy 1978; 41(3): 258.

[164]Advertisement. Senior Occupational therapist for department of Neurology and Neurosurgical Surgery, Addenbrooke's Hospital, United Cambridge Hospitals. Occupational Therapy 1970; 33(8): 38.

[165]Notice. Sedwood Charitable Trust. British Journal of Occupational Therapy 1975; 38(2): 33.

[166]Grove EM. Occupational therapy in the rehabilitation centre. Occupational Therapy 1971; 34(3):11–20.

[167]Campbell CM. Rehabilitation of selected groups of patients at Simon Square Centre 1960-70. Occupational Therapy 1972; 35(9): 660–65.

[168]Thornley G, Chamberlain MA, Wright V. Evaluation of aids and equipment for the bath and toilet. A report on the findings of a survey funded by the DHSS into the prescription, supply and use of aids and equipment for the disabled when bathing and toiletting. British Journal of Occupational Therapy 1977; 40(10): 243–6.

[169]Langton Hewer R, Rogers EE. Friedreich's Ataxia: A study of major problems encountered by patients. Occupational Therapy 1972; 35(10): 764–5.

[170]Hagedorn R. Therapists are dissatisfied with rehabilitation equipment. Occupational Therapy 1972; 35(9): 655–7.

[171]Hagedorn R. Survey of occupational therapy equipment and techniques. Occupational Therapy 1974 ; 37(1): 11–12.

[172]Hagedorn R. First Report of the Panel for the Evaluation of Rehabilitation Equipment Design. British Journal of Occupational Therapy 1975; 38(4): 84–5.

[173]Smith ME. The Edinburgh Stroke rehabilitation study. British Journal of Occupational Therapy 1979; 41(6): 139–42.

[174]Wright R, Heggarty HH, Birch P, Marshall P. Occupational therapy in athetoid cerebral palsy. Occupational Therapy 1972; 35(10): 757–9.

[175]Saunders WM, Miller A. Occupational therapy versus operant conditioning techniques in the treatment of long term psychiatric patients. British Journal of Occupational Therapy 1975; 38(4): 103–7.

[176]Ellis M. Cast bracing of femoral fractures. British Journal of Occupational Therapy 1975; 38(4): 73–5.

[177]Renn G. Initial investigation into the effects of wrist splinting in children with Still's Disease. British Journal of Occupational Therapy 1976; 39(1): 9.

[178]Goble RAE, Morgan DC, Shaw DB. Rehabilitation in heart disease a study following patients after myocardial infarction and brady arrhythmias treated with artificial cardiac pace makers. British Journal of Occupational Therapy 1976; 39(11): 281–4.

# Part 4

# Modern Trends, Self Health and Future Global Visions

**Ch. 10**
**Degrees of Excellence and Specialisation**
**Ch. 11**
**Enabling Occupation and Client Centred Practice Towards Self Health**
**Ch. 12**
**Serpent and Phoenix: Self Health and Revitalisation**

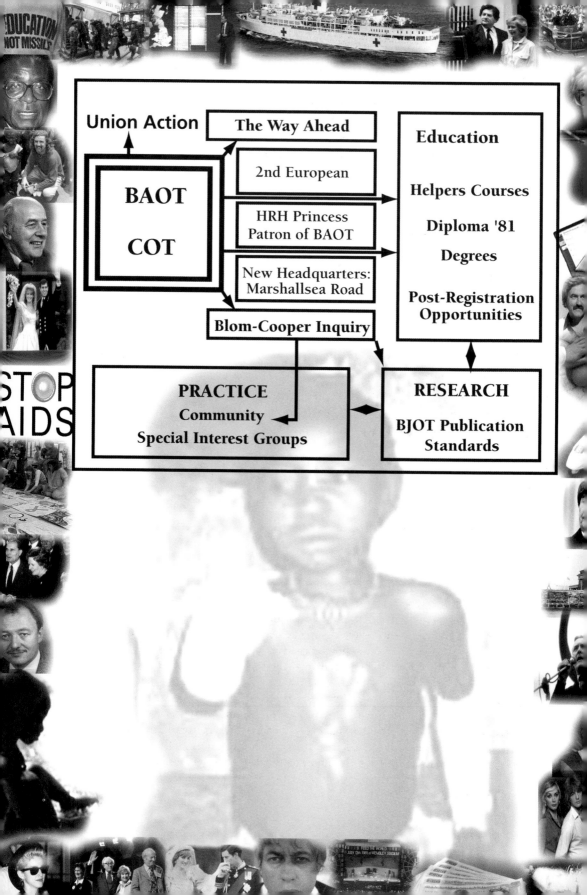

**Union Action**

**BAOT COT**

**The Way Ahead**

**2nd European**

**HRH Princess Patron of BAOT**

**New Headquarters: Marshallsea Road**

**Blom-Cooper Inquiry**

**Education**

**Helpers Courses**

**Diploma '81**

**Degrees**

**Post-Registration Opportunities**

**PRACTICE**
**Community**
**Special Interest Groups**

**RESEARCH**

**BJOT Publication Standards**

# Chapter 10

# Degrees of Excellence and Specialisation

## Contents

This chapter tells the story of how major changes in occupational therapists' education epitomised the period. Scarce resources, partly as a result of more and more expensive technical fixes for health problems, made 'proof' of effectiveness appear even more desirable to occupational therapists. As would be expected in such a climate, involvement in research grew and this was observable in the type of articles published in the BJOT. Of similar ilk was the apparent need of the College of Occupational Therapists to explore its directions to ensure that it, too, was based on firm foundations. That can also be seen as an indication of continuing concerns about being misunderstood, which had manifest in the preceding decade. Whatever the probable mix of causes, it resulted in the College initiating two major reviews during the 1980s. Those reviews provide the background to much of the story told. It was a time of unrest, a time of industrial action and challenge, which was manifest within occupational therapy as it was in the community at large.

# Context of the times: A challenging decade

The 1980s was a period of major socio-economic and political change, as well as being the time when technological wizardry began to assert its power over simpler 'human-based' interventions. In 1979, for the first time in British history there was a woman Prime Minister. Margaret Thatcher's 'hard right' approach was anything but conciliatory, and resulted in what has been described as 'one of the most tumultuous, disturbing, and dramatic periods in post war history.'[1] The tragic and demoralising civil war in Ireland dragged on with major incidents like the bombing outside Harrods amongst the Christmas crowds. For a while that conflict was overshadowed by the Falklands War, which led to 'resurgence in Britain of old-style patriotism and national pride.' Patriotism and pride were also fuelled by the marriage of the Prince of Wales to Lady Diana Spencer in 1981. Despite such stirring events, the bottom fell out of the economy: and 'whole sections of Britain's industrial heartlands became deserts.' There was a north-south economic divide, and inner cities experienced unemployed youths rioting, looting, setting fires and battling with police.[2] Department of Employment figures for October 1981 recorded that there were 2,988,600 unemployed people in the United Kingdom.[3] Automation had resulted in many unskilled and semi-skilled jobs being lost; steel and textiles manufacturing had declined; and a worldwide recession had caused major cutbacks in many spheres. Redundancies resulted in stress related disorders in workers and families, which in turn increased pressure on the psychiatric and social services.[4]

The Prime Minister was determined to cure the British malaise, to restore the nation to what she considered was its rightful place, and to recreate, in 1980s Britain, attitudes of Victorian England when there was 'acceptance of personal responsibility' and 'freedom of choice.'[5] From the start of the decade, concerns were being expressed about the NHS within the Association. In 1980, the Chairman, Betty Collins, wrote to Margaret Thatcher to urge consultation with bodies like the BAOT when policy decisions were being made about the nation's health. The Prime Minister was informed of the BAOT decision that a secret ballot of members would precede any industrial action should concerns reach that level, and that the latter action would be taken with great reluctance especially if likely to affect patient care.[6] By 1983, the government was giving notice of cuts, and there was privatization of some services, despite pre-election claims that 'the NHS is safe in our hands.' Two thousand doctors were in the ranks of the unemployed, and there were plans for a two-tiered, public and private health service. Indeed more people were turning to private health funds, and insurance firms experienced a sharp upturn in business.[7] The trend continued, and later in the decade some occupational therapists showed their concerns about cuts being made to the NHS and social care.

Yvonne Cleary, BAOT Industrial Relations Officer, described how members from all over Britain took part in demonstrations in London, Birmingham, and Stirling on Saturday 5 March 1985. They called on the Chancellor of the Exchequer, Mr Nigel Lawson, to 'Make Budget Day NHS Day' by announcing that money set aside for tax cuts would go to the NHS instead.

**Figure 2.10.1: Margaret Ellis, Chairman of BAOT/COT demonstrating with members in central London 1985**

Despite short notice from the TUC, over 200 BAOT members supported the demonstration, including Margaret Ellis, Chairman of Council, and almost half of Headquarters staff. With about 100,000 representatives from all sections of the NHS, members with placards marched under the BAOT banner near the front of the demonstration, from the Embankment to a rally in Hyde Park. There, the leader of the TUC, Norman Willis, welcomed 'The British Association of Occupational Therapists, for the first time on a TUC event.' Commenting on the march, Ellis said, 'We are worried about cuts in the NHS. We are also concerned about the fact that there is a national shortage of occupational therapists and the Government seems to be taking inadequate measures to resolve the problem.' The march in Stirling, Scotland, was less well attended possibly because of the short notice given by the Scottish TUC organizing the event. However, fifteen BAOT members braved inclement weather by marching to a rally in a very exposed King's Park, Stirling. Cleary finished her report: 'We must do everything possible to make people outside the NHS aware of the inadequate support from the Government for this vital service. It would be too easy and a betrayal of all that the NHS stands for to give up now.'[8]

Correspondence in BJOT in June 1988 provides more evidence of the political militant spirit developing within the profession. In Letters To The Editor a group of occupational therapists from Manchester triggered by an earlier one from an occupational therapy student, Jasper Gripper,[9] complained of cuts affecting their work, and called for action:

> *Congratulations to Jasper Gripper for breaking the notable silence regarding the current crisis in the NHS! How shameful that we have to rely on our students for a response which is so late in the debate.*
>
> *...we have two major concerns regarding the NHS. The first and most immediate is the current financial crisis...*

This is a brief outline of how Central Manchester has been affected:

> *...£180,000 to be found from existing Department of Psychiatry budget after RMN training funding axed. 16% cut in occupational therapy budget. Crisis management, for example, non/delayed bill payment resulting in loss of discounts, financial penalties and firms refusing to do business with NHS.*

*OT Physical. —5% cut in occupational therapy budget. —3 basic grade posts frozen (occupational therapy establishment already grossly understaffed). —Unable to provide service to orthopaedic and surgical patients. —Many patients have to spend longer in hospital due to limited occupational therapy service. —Unable to provide any outpatient treatment or follow-up. —Unable to accept occupational therapy students for long practices...and (waiting time for aids/adaptations can be up to 5 months).*

*As an interim measure, we would like to invite colleagues throughout the country to write to us with details of how the cuts/changes are affecting them and their patients/clients...This will be the first step towards developing a collective voice —our only real chance of being heard...*

*While it is gratifying to see pictures in the BJOT of our senior officers demonstrating for the NHS, something more substantial is needed. It is difficult to fight for a cause, however just, without being able to provide relevant data. We propose that the BAOT institute a survey of members to assess the nationwide effects of the current NHS cuts, as an adjunct to the timely staffing levels survey.*

*Our second concern is the insecure future of the NHS. The secrecy surrounding the current government review is not helpful. It seems likely that severe and radical changes are imminent, where the priority will be financial, not quality of care. All this at a time when disadvantaged people are hit by the budget, social security reforms and the poll tax. This is a crucial time to maintain a high profile of action. We are not claiming that NHS reforms are not necessary, but that different standards of health care should not be the result.* [10]

Ellis responded to the letter:

*Heather Kirby and colleagues comment on the cutbacks in their local NHS and the apparent lack of activity of BAOT about this nationally.*

*I do not believe the Manchester experience to be an isolated case. However, the Jasper Gripper and Heather Kirby letters are the only ones I have seen either to the Journal or to me as the Chairman of BAOT. Maybe members of BAOT are so busy trying to cope with the cutbacks that, they have overlooked the need to be involved with a national response.*

*We know that a recent study undertaken by the King's Fund about the four Metropolitan Regional Health Authorities shows that the bed reductions have already met targets set for 4–5 years ahead. However, the resulting savings are only one-third of those predicted and expected. Such discrepancies and reductions cannot be good for the service. The general public and BAOT members frequently seem unaware of the national deteriorating picture of the NHS. Equally, it is possible to demonstrate cuts in the social services departments of local government. Such difficulties caused some of us to join the 5 March demonstration to Hyde Park. However, this is not the only action taken by BAOT.*

*I wonder if the authors were present at our recent Annual General Meeting at the University of Warwick? If they were, they would have heard more detailed reports of comments submitted to Len Peach and to Sir Roy Griffiths.* [11] *More recently, we have commented on the review of the NHS.*

*One of the main reasons for setting up the Independent Commission into occupational therapy is the pent-up frustration at knowing we are short of manpower, constantly attempting to meet demands under increasing difficulties.*

*Sadly, when we ask for comments or views from members directly or via their Council Members there is little response. A recent example demonstrates the typical picture. We*

*circulated to all Council Members a DHSS paper on the effects of early discharge of patients*
*from hospital, asking for a reply by 20 April. At that time, only three people had responded.*
*So I wish Heather Kirby and colleagues better joy in their request for information. I*
*certainly look forward to having any information they receive. I also suggest that all members*
*pass their views on to their Council Members so that the topic can be discussed nationally.* [12]

At a different level, concerns were expressed about the 'general management'
approach that was introduced into the NHS in 1985 to ensure that:

*...the concern shared by all working in the Health Service for the quality and efficiency*
*of patient services will be more easily translated into effective action; the available resources*
*will be better used and those working in the Service will obtain greater satisfaction from their*
*work. The patient, the community, the taxpayer and the employee will all benefit.*[13]

Stephanie Correia reported in BJOT that, although the approach had produced some
positive results such as clearer directions, precise decisions, responsibility taken for
action, availability of information, and use of quality assurance measures, there were also
some worrying effects. There appeared to be a trend to treat all professional groups in the
same way. 'Locality' or 'patch' management, and the establishment of managers within
local multidisciplinary teams were thought to be threatening patient care, whilst not
providing junior staff with appropriate support and guidance. There was concern that if
team members became 'generic in their attitude,' that would disadvantage the needs of
individual patients. Correia explained how 'past experience shows that a dominant
model, such as the medical model, led to reinforcing a particular professional approach
rather than responding flexibly to individual needs.' Junior staff, particularly, she
suggested, benefited from having a manager of their own profession, which also enabled
the fostering and maintenance of a broad theoretical perspective and clinical approach
needed in a multidisciplinary team. It was suggested that some occupational therapists
working in local authorities had already experienced a lack of strong professional
management, which limited their contribution. She queried whether the profession
should launch a campaign to alert the general public to the consequences of
implementing general management at team level.[14]

Similarly pro-active, following the setting up by the government of the Disablement
Services Special Health Authority (DSA) Beryl Warren (a member of the DSA), advised
occupational therapists to be aware of the systems proposed or planned within their
region, to be vocal about any concerns, and to ensure that their voice was heard in the
decision making process. The establishment of the DSA, which was directly responsible
to the Minister for the Disabled, was a consequence of the publication of Professor Ian
McColl's Working Party Report on the Artificial Limb and Appliance Centre Services in
1986. The McColl report had stressed the importance of rehabilitation and involvement
of therapists in the treatment of amputees, and in assessment and prescription of
wheelchairs. Therapists were appointed to the Disablement Services Centres at Exeter,
Kingston and Newcastle on an experimental basis to work with the staff and advise on
the prescription of wheelchairs, cushions and seating.[15]

Disabled people were also becoming increasingly articulate about their needs and
concerns and began to take a more active role in organising and representing themselves.

*The Disabled Persons Act* of 1986 recognised their fundamental right to be consulted and to be in control of the services offered. The Act required local authorities to inform disabled people about the services it and other authorities and agencies provided, and of their right of access to necessary services whether or not they were currently available.[16]

Continuing that more positive note was the Government White Paper *Promoting Better Health* published, in November 1987, as a result of consultation and of a comprehensive review of the care services.[17] Aiming at a healthier nation by raising standards of care, promoting better health and preventing illness and disease, the Government focused on Family Practitioner Services and becoming responsive to the needs of the consumer. While the growing interest in the enhancement of public health and reducing the incidence of disease was timely, the paper was conservative. Particular mention was made of services for the elderly population and during the early years of childhood. For those services there was an expected growth of expenditure of 11%. Even so, the Government ensured that for some of these services, those who could afford to pay would do so, and doctors were encouraged to prevent ill health by the offer of various remunerative incentives. Restrictions on the type and number of staff that doctors could employ were relaxed, and the White Paper suggested that physiotherapists, nurses and chiropodists might be appropriate. Occupational therapists were not mentioned, which was sad in the light of the emphasis on monitoring, maintaining, and assessing elderly people regularly, and preventing deterioration of ability by prompt intervention. Eve Evans, a member of the Community Occupational Therapy Committee, who reviewed the paper, suggested that occupational therapists might bring that omission to the attention of their Members of Parliament.[18]

The emphasis on the elderly in *Promoting Better Health* was in line with demographic change. The Royal Commission on the NHS at the end of the previous decade had reported that 'the greatest single influence on the shape of the NHS for the rest of this century is the growing numbers of old people and particularly those over 75.'[19] Indeed the Office of Population and Census and Surveys predicted that by 2018 there would be a 10% increase in the number of people over retiring age—approximately 9.5 million, 17% of the total population; and those aged 75 and over would have increased by 20% to 3.2 million.[20] Additionally, it was predicted that the number of the elderly people living at home would rise rapidly.[21] Appropriately, in 1981, the DHSS published *Report of a Study on the Respective Roles of the General Acute and Geriatric Sectors in Care of the Elderly Hospital Patient, and Care in Action*, a handbook of policies and priorities for health and personal social services in England.[22,23] Four groups of clients whose needs should be given priority were identified:

(i) *Elderly People, especially the most vulnerable and frail. This group includes those living within the community and requiring both specific primary care and more general support, those within acute units of hospitals who are to be returned to the community with as little delay as possible and those already in receipt of long-term institutional or residential care.*

(ii) *Mentally Ill People. Emphasis is given to close liaison between the N.H.S. and Social Service departments. The provision of easily available treatment in local hospitals or in the community is preferable to maintaining large and inconveniently placed mental hospitals. Suitable accommodation needs to be provided within each district for the care of the elderly mentally infirm. Regional secure units remain an important part of the service for those requiring such an environment.*

*(iii) **Mentally Handicapped People**. Provision for support, day care or residential care should be a local facility and not a function of large asylums. Again there is an emphasis on the need for rehabilitation or training and on liaison between health and social services.*

*(iv) **Physically Disabled and Sensorily Impaired People**. Particular attention is paid to the problems of the permanently disabled. The needs for day care and for rehabilitation training in skills required for independence are stressed.*[24]

Early in the decade the significance of such changes to occupational therapy was recognised and articulated. It was recommended, for example, that more emphasis and training should be available on community care, and the needs of the elderly. Also noted was the belief that the number of patients suffering from stress-related diseases would increase, because of the economic uncertainties of the times, and that 'a lead' should be taken on the use of leisure time.[25]

Apart from, and associated with, the increasing age of the population, other demographic and social changes were apparent. A dramatic drop in birthrate, evident from the mid 1960s, had resulted in school closures, cutbacks in teaching, fewer school leavers and eventual pruning of higher education. Women were deferring starting families, staying at work longer after marriage, and more were returning to work after child rearing.[26] Together, those factors, amongst other sociological changes and the increasing impact of technology, resulted in a need for many to access re-training, recurrent and continuing education, part-time and day-release courses, and longer periods of paid educational leave from employment.[27] A cut back in university places, led to demand for places in polytechnics and colleges of higher education. That, in turn, impacted on occupational therapy applicants. For example, in September 1981, when 742 students started the course, the COT Clearing House received over 2,988,600 applications from people eligible for entry.[28]

The Department of Health established a second Occupational Therapy Officer position in 1984. Readers will recall that the Officer helped, informed, advised and supported Ministers and DHSS across the range of their responsibilities, supported the Secretary of State in the implementation of legislation, advised the DHSS on professional practice, influenced Government and DHSS policy, and interpreted professional views to them. Additionally the Officer interpreted Government and DHSS views to the profession, assisting the implementation of policies. Some of the positive outcomes of the 1980s were provision of funding for research training and research training fellowships; an occupational therapy use of microcomputers research project; and clinical and management systems for occupational therapists and physiotherapists. Elizabeth Grove found that an essential feature of the job was communicating with the CPSM Occupational Therapists' Board; with BAOT/COT, and occupational therapists in the field in the NHS and LASS; and with occupational therapists internationally.[29] Grove's diagram detailing the support and advice network is shown as Figure 2.10.2. When Grove retired, Rosemary Bowden took her place and, later, Sheelagh Richards.

HAP = Health Authority personnel; MPAG = Manpower Planning Advisory Group; NHSTA =NHS Training Authority; HAS = Health Advisory Service; DSA = Disablement Services Authority; NDT = National Development Team

**Figure 2.10.2: Department of Health Occupational Therapy Officers' network 1988**[30]

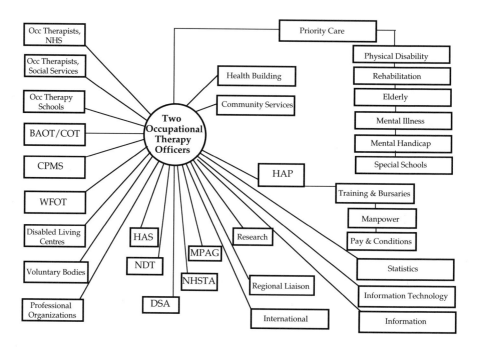

# The British Association and College of Occupational Therapists

By the 1980s the British Association and College of Occupational Therapists was the second largest occupational therapy organization in the world with over 8000 members. Analysis of the membership figures shows that well over three-quarters of these practised in the NHS, nearly 1000 were employed in the community by local authorities, and more than half that number worked in charitable bodies of some kind. The committee and organisational structure of BAOT and COT had become more complex. The various functions carried out by a range of industrial relations and professional committees which had developed over the years, and which were answerable to Council and the Executive, are as illustrated in Figure 2.10.3. The organisation's secretariat was assisted by general, financial and industrial relations staff as well as by those designated to deal with membership, education and publications, as is shown in Figure 2.10.4.

### Figure 2.10.3: Committee structure

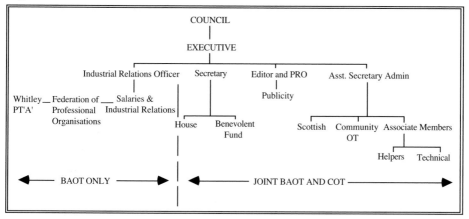

### Figure 2.10.4: Organisational and staffing structure

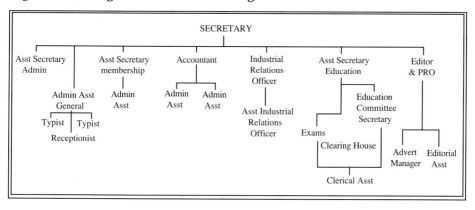

The policy and activities of BAOT were formed and directed by its Council, which comprised some thirty elected members and, usually, a few co-opted members such as: the Whitley delegate; the DHSS Adviser; and a representative of the Occupational Therapy Board of the CPSM. Most Council members were occupational therapists elected by postal ballot from members of twenty regions in the country, six were elected nationally, and one represented the Training Schools. The Council year began on 1st October and the Annual General Meeting was usually timed to coincide with the COT Annual Conference, and Council met for meetings twice a year. Normally no member served for more than three years, so there were always new faces and fresh energy; and the difficulties, which might result from entrenched members remaining on Council and dominating its policy, were avoided. The Council of COT had the same membership as BAOT. It elected and appointed committees to carry out details of its business. These included committees concerned with Scotland, Northern Ireland, Wales, education, community occupational therapy, district management of occupational therapy, helpers, technicians, salaries and industrial relations, professional and ethical matters, publicity, the benevolent fund, and one for Headquarters matters. Additionally, an Editorial Board supported the publication of the Journal. There were twenty-five Headquarters staff employed to enable Council and its committees to implement their decisions.

Regional groups were responsible for organising and promoting the work of BAOT and COT, making policy matters known, supporting, and providing continuing education for members within designated geographical areas. The work was organised and carried out by a regionally-elected Executive Committee. In 1987 the regional group structure and constitution were redefined, and their Executive Committees were required to meet at least six times each year. In addition, a network of over 250 members acted as BAOT union stewards throughout the country. Their role was as the first point of contact for members with queries over conditions of service, grievance or discipline. They also sought members' views on industrial relations problems that affected them directly, kept members informed of industrial relations matters, and recruited new members.

In 1985, in order to provide better representation for its members working in LASS and social work departments, the BAOT formed a link with the Managerial, Administrative, Technical and Supervisory Association (MATSA), a section of the General and Municipal workers (GMB), Britain's second largest general trade union. The GMB amalgamated with the Association of Professional, Executive, Clerical and Computer Staff (APEX) in 1989 and the white collar section of the GMB became the Apex Partnership. All members of the BAOT working in local authorities had dual membership of the Association and the Apex Partnership. Readers will recall that when the BJOT became a publication of the College, a separate newsheet BAOT News was inserted in each Journal. This was partly because the Journal could no longer include information about Trade Union activities.[31] BAOT News had proved popular and widely read. Consequently in August 1981 it was expanded into the BAOT and College News to ensure that a balance of topical information between Educational and Union matters was made available to members.[32]

In 1987, the Manpower Planning Advisory Group (MPAG), which had been established to advise the NHS, commissioned the NHS Training Authority (NHSTA) to undertake the development of guidelines on long-term demand forecasts and skill mix of various professions. The study on occupational therapy examined the number of staff and the work appropriate to, and needing to be done, by occupational therapists. Chaired by Dr Peter Horrocks, the group involved senior members of the profession along with NHS and medical personnel. The project included analysis of the level of skills necessary for an occupational therapy department to operate effectively and economically, which was then related to the framework of the National Council for Vocational Qualifications (NCVQ).[33]

Increasingly it was becoming accepted that research held an important key to the future. As the first major event of the Golden Jubilee Year, the COT Research and Degree Committee, with support from The King's Fund Centre and RADAR, convened a special meeting on Research and Occupational Therapy in February 1982. It was aimed at bringing together a multidisciplinary group interested in research and to establish where occupational therapists have or might contribute. Professor Cairns Aitken spoke to that theme, and he was followed by presentations of projects demonstrating contributions by occupational therapists. Informants and topics included: Margaret Smith on the assessment of deficit following stroke; R. Howorth on total hip replacement; J. Martin on perceptual tests with anorexia nervosa patients and occupational therapy students; S. Wells on work preparation for psychiatric patients; and L. Bradshaw on food preparation aids with rheumatoid patients. The afternoon included discussion of priorities and future directions with input from Dr N. Dunkin, a tutor at St Loyes School of Occupational Therapy.[34]

Excellence and research were recognised during the 1980s by the people who were made fellows of the College of Occupational Therapists. Honorary Awards went to Sidney Lock, Doris Sym, Lily Jeffrey, Lalage Dawson Jones, Phyllis Howie, Margaret Ellis, Peggy Jay, Hester Monteath, Lyndia Jones, Julia Robbins, and Mary Loggie. Fellows by examination were D. Hughes, C.M. Campbell, E.E. Bumphrey, Dianna Whysall, Joan Martin, and Susan Woodward. Mention of the work of some of these Fellows has already featured in the history, but the stories of all are told briefly in Appendix B.

## 'The Way Ahead'

An internal working party was set up early in the decade to provide Council with a basis on which to determine policy over the next ten years. Betty Collins, then Chairman of Council, felt a clear view of the current situation and probable future developments would enable it to give more considered responses to events within and outside the profession. The reviewers were occupational therapists—Leigh Atkinson, Averil Stewart, Carol Underwood, and Moya Wilson. Council in its introductory statement said that their report, *The Way Ahead*, gave 'relevant history and a valid picture of the present situation of the Profession.' The reviewers' terms of reference were:

> Using the baseline of known current practice in occupational therapy the Working Party aims to consult colleagues and other professionals in addition to examining relevant published reports to enable all views to be co-ordinated into possible future policy for the British Association of Occupational Therapists Ltd.[35]

*The Way Ahead* covered, first, internal and external trends that affected the profession, such as specific techniques, social/economic/medical developments, and inter-professional relationships. Secondly, it considered conditions of service and fields of work. Thirdly, it looked at industrial relations; and lastly, at basic and further education.

**Figure 2.10.5:** *The Way Ahead* **working party 1986**

*From left to right: Moya Wilson, Averil Stewart, Leigh Atkinson and Carol Underwood*

Council explained that although the Report would form the basis of urgent debate on many policy issues it did not necessarily reflect their opinions or policy. However, they urged members to read it, emphasising that it was written mainly for them, prompted by the Working Party's finding that a surprising number of occupational therapists, from whom they gathered data, were poorly informed about the Association and College and of current issues facing the profession. Council thought the Report's most significant recommendations lay in Education, and this will inform later discussion. They were however disappointed at the brevity of the recommendations on the economic constraints facing the profession, which they considered a very high priority.

In terms of policy the report recommended that:
- *Information on and literature about Occupational Therapy should reflect that, increasingly, work will be with the elderly and mentally handicapped.*
- *The use of activities should remain as an identifying feature of Occupational Therapy. Emphasis must be placed on the analysis of activity and its appropriate selection.*
- *Occupational Therapists should make greater efforts to inform others of the potential use of Occupational Therapy.*
- *Newly qualified staff should be better prepared for working with Helpers and Technical Staff*
- *The appointment of managerial District Occupational Therapists should take place before or as near as possible to 1st April 1982.*
- *The professional structure in the community should allow supervision of clinical work from within the profession.*[36]

In terms of BAOT and COT they thought:
- *Fees are unrealistic for the services required, and they should be increased if members wish the present level of services to be maintained and developed. A resource centre inclusive of library, audio-visual material and publishing service is required.*
- *All Occupational Therapists should be encouraged to join the B.A.O.T.*
- *There should be a continued rationalisation of committee structure in C.O.T. to meet future demands.*
- *Special Interest Groups should identify the primary tasks of their members as a contribution to clearer definitions of roles in Occupational Therapy.*
- *The C.O.T. should appoint a Clinical Development Officer to study and support standards of practice nationwide, but particularly in areas of need.*
- *That C.O.T. and C.P.S.M. continue to work closely together through the Liaison Committee.*
- *There should be recognition by Whitley Council of clinical expertise beyond that of Senior I; and similarly in the local authority.*
- *That Occupational Therapists working in local authorities should be State Registered.*
- *The B.A.O.T. should press for legislation to alter the 1960 Act, so that it can be used equally in Social Service Employment regulations. This is considered a priority.*[37]

In terms of manpower they explained:
*It is widely accepted that there is a shortfall of over 31% and that at least a further 1,236 individual Occupational Therapists are required to meet demand for staff in the NHS; when the College discussed manpower with the DHSS in April 1981 at that time it was estimated that the shortage was well over 1,000 in local authorities.*[38] *Despite tight cash limits it was expected that there would be an estimated growth of 6–7% compared with 1.2% for the N.H.S. as a whole. This would mean an increase of some 200*

*Occupational Therapists each year over the next few years.*[39]
Those figures did not reflect the potential 'need' for staff then or in the future.[40]

Other sections of *The Way Ahead* will be considered in relevant parts of the chapter.

## Conferences

The Annual Conferences began to assume a greater importance, not only to the growing membership, but also as a means of demonstrating a national cohesiveness and image. To that end, at the dawn of the decade Wales was chosen in 1980 as the venue of the first BAOT annual conference to be held outside England. Two years later, the Golden Jubilee year of the first Association in Britain was appropriately celebrated in Scotland, by holding the annual conference there. It was the first to be held in Scotland. The last national conference of the decade was also held in Scotland, at the University of Strathclyde in Glasgow. It had the theme of 'Human Occupation', presaging a return to the use of the word 'occupation' within the profession in Britain. Sharon Green picked up what was to become an ongoing debate about occupation in the BJOT. She proclaimed:

> *Oh, how we avoided the knotty topic of defining occupation. We currently measure the efficacy of 'it' (quality assurance) and keep statistics about 'it' (for example, Korner), yet still we cannot define 'it' with any degree of unanimity. Maybe our energies should be employed here?…We know that what is essential or meaningful to one of our clients may equally well be rejected as irrelevant by someone else. I suggest, therefore, that long may this core debate into 'occupationology' continue, both at meetings and seminars and through the pages of our journal. For meaningful occupation defies definition; it must be a unique choice available to us all.*[41]

In 1985 the second European Congress was held at Imperial College, in London, during a heat wave. The event, convened by Peggy Jay, was attended by over 800 people from 27 countries. The opening ceremony was chaired by Lord Ennals, President of the COT, and it was formally opened by HRH the Duchess of Gloucester. It was a sign of the times that, when she arrived, there was heckling from some occupational therapists and other paramedical professionals, who were demonstrating against the inclusion of South African delegates. Interestingly, many South African occupational therapists worked in Britain, filling posts that would otherwise have remained empty.

**Figure 2.10.6: Second European Congress 1985**
*From left to right: HRH the Duchess of Gloucester, Lord Ennals and Peggy Jay*

As the Congress was held in lieu of the usual annual COT Conference, the Casson Memorial Lecture was given during its opening session. Professor Lindsay McLellan, the honoured lecturer, talked about Training for a Rehabilitation Team.[42] Although McLellan was not an occupational therapist, at this second European Congress 75% of the papers were presented by occupational therapists, a reversal of the situation in 1977 when a similar proportion was presented by people of other professions. The papers covered the work of occupational therapists in a variety of fields. In a session where research was discussed, papers were given on: investigation, using control groups, of the effects of rehabilitation on patients with chronic obstructive airways disease; the role of occupational therapists in clinical measurement linked to impairment, disability and handicap; a DHSS Aids Assessment Programme based on trials of equipment by and the opinions of disabled people; and a comparative study of people with epilepsy which established that social skills training is of greater benefit than drama therapy or non-intervention. There were sessions on chest, heart and stroke rehabilitation, neurology, paediatrics, psychiatric rehabilitation, and mental handicap. There were also some papers grouped under more generic categories, such as: employment and leisure; the elderly; counselling; community; and international community services.[43] In 'Reflections on the Congress' published in BJOT the recurring concern about the core of occupational therapy was revisited, albeit briefly, with the comment:

> ...it was disappointing that certain papers looked at the skills some occupational therapists were using which did not involve the use of activities as treatment media. It is not surprising that some of us are confused about our professional identity and that our skills are being eroded by other professional groups.[44]

Study visits to specialised centres in London and the Home Counties took place in the hot weather that had favoured the Congress. The reports suggest an international camaraderie was beginning to develop between occupational therapists throughout the EEC. Sharing of ideas, and professional skills, a formal reception of the Royal College of Physicians, and a trip on the Thames assisted that process. And in the following year the Committee of Occupational Therapists for European Communities (COTEC) was established, initially with six participating countries.

Despite such auspicious occurrences, the 1980s proved to be years of internal industrial dispute and financial difficulty for the BAOT and COT, just as it was for many other groups within the community. As an example, Beryl Warren, Chairman of Council, 1986–87, shares her story of the difficulties and joys of that time.

# 1986–87: A chairman's perspective
## By Beryl Warren

My year of office covered a very unsettled period for BAOT. An industrial dispute already affecting Headquarters staff was causing great unrest, anger and confusion amongst the members, and almost destroyed the Association. The dispute cost the organization many thousands of pounds, undermining an already fragile financial situation, and overshadowing the work of BAOT and indeed COT for the whole year.

I had known of the problems when I became Chairman and I set out in very uncertain circumstances feeling that the best I could achieve was to act as a conciliator—to damp things down, to talk to everybody and to be available—with the hope that at the end of the year the Association would be still functioning. At its meeting in York, Council accepted in principle the recommendations of a Management Report it had commissioned to address the problems highlighted by the dispute. The report's aim was to make the organization more open and accountable to the membership and improve the management structure at Headquarters. However, many members were angry about the circumstances surrounding the dispute, and one of the worst experiences of my year as Chairman was the Special General Meeting at Aston University convened to discuss the findings of the Management Report. It was a very fraught occasion with anxious, upset and angry members speaking from the floor. The debate rumbled on for the whole year and changes to the organization were not achieved until some time later.

The death of Tilda Lloyd (Alexander) the Assistant Secretary (Admin.) in January 1987 was an enormous blow, to me personally and to the Association, as she had been 'the fount of all knowledge' within HQ for many years. However, little of her vital information about every conceivable facet of COT organization was written down, and at a time when the staff were severely overstretched the gap left by her loss was tremendous. At this time the staff at Headquarters were physically divided in two buildings in Notting Hill about 400 yards apart, where you had to walk round the corner and cross a busy road. This was not an ideal situation and did not help overall management. We started to look for more suitable premises that would be large enough to house all the staff under one roof, and after several other possibilities proved unsuitable we found a derelict building in Marshalsea Road just off the Borough High Street in South London. We thought that, with a lot of vision and faith (to say nothing of the finance), it could be renovated to provide suitable accommodation for all the staff.

During this period of unrest and bad feeling it was a marvellous boost when HRH, Princess Anne agreed to become the Patron of the College of Occupational Therapists, and as a result of our new patronage the College was allotted tickets for one of the summer 1986 Buckingham Palace Garden Parties. The immediate past Chairman Loreen MacKenzie (Scotland), Christine Court, PTA Whitley Council Delegate (Wales), Nuala McArdle (N. Ireland), and I donned our finery on a beautiful summer afternoon to enjoy the delights of the Buckingham Palace Gardens. Princess Anne's Private Secretary, Peter Gibbs, introduced us to HRH who, as always, was knowledgeable, well informed, and interested in occupational therapy. In early December 1986 COT invited her to an evening Reception at the RAF Club in Piccadilly, London. One hundred and fifty members representing all the Regions and staff from headquarters were present. We had commissioned Nigel Bumphrey, a goldsmith and husband of past Chairman Eileen Bumphrey, to design and make a gold brooch depicting the COT logo which I presented to HRH at the reception. It was a very happy occasion and Princess Anne spoke to everyone present and in her doing so we were delighted but also somewhat worried that she overstayed her allotted time by about one and half hours![45]

## A Royal patron, and new headquarters

When HRH, the Princess Royal, became the Patron of the College of Occupational Therapists in 1986, Beryl Warren welcomed her at a Special Reception. She said, the COT was:

*...delighted and honoured that you have graciously agreed to become the very first Patron of the College, particularly since we know of your interest in people with disabilities and, of course, children.*

*As you are aware, occupational therapists have special skills to offer in the habilitation and rehabilitation of people suffering from a wide variety of disabilities, and in ages ranging from the very young to the very old, to ensure that all of our patients or clients, whatever the problems, are equipped to cope with the practicalities of daily life, leisure and work, to the very best of their abilities.*

*We think that the input we make in the health care and social services scenes is inversely proportionate to our relatively small numbers. With the present moves towards care in the community, the closure of large, long-stay hospitals and the increase in bed turnover rate in acute medicine, the contribution occupational therapists can make in effecting these changes is being increasingly acknowledged and requested. It is indeed unfortunate that we cannot fulfill these demands made for our services due to shortage of staff.*

*Ma'am, we hope that in the future you will be able to visit occupational therapy departments up and down the country to see at first hand the wide variety of work in which we are engaged. Indeed I think that you have already visited several occupational therapy departments during recent hospital visits.*

Her Royal Highness took her duties seriously, and attended many different functions as well as occupational therapy departments. In much the same spirit as Warren had welcomed her, towards the end of the decade, in the Foreword to the Blom Cooper Report, she wrote:

*In these days when more and more hospital patients convalescence at home and there is greater and greater pressure on institutional resources, the role of occupational therapy is becoming increasingly important.*

*Occupational therapy is still too often associated in the public mind with basket-making. In fact it has been revolutionised in recent years, along with all other medical facilities, and its members provide a wide range of caring and rehabilitation services within the community. One can hardly exaggerate the value of the work in restoring patients' ability to return to paid employment and regain personal autonomy and independence.*

*This excellent report is the first attempt to evaluate the profession as a whole. Its analysis of problems, and recommendations for future developments, are essential reading for all who care for our health services.* [46]

**Figure 2.10.7: Her Royal Highness, the Princess Royal, becoming Patron, and taking an active interest in the profession's affairs**

The new headquarters acquired at 6–8 Marshalsea Road in Southwark, London SE1, was officially opened by HRH, The Princess Royal, in 1989. As Warren intimated, the organization had outgrown the Rede Place premises, despite additional office space being purchased in nearby Needham Road at the beginning of the decade for the COT Educational and Journal staff. Before that they had worked in rented accommodation above Whiteley's Store in Queensway.[47] The closure, in 1981, of the office in Edinburgh, previously the SAOT headquarters, had been but one of the dimensions added to the work undertaken in the bulging Rede Place HQ.

Jay, Mendez, and Monteath recall of the Marshalsea Road HQ that it was a source of great pride to the membership that it was in a position to purchase and reinstate a building with facilities that reflected the current status of occupational therapy. It included meeting rooms generous enough to house all committees, including Council, and the Disability Information and Study Centre (DISC) which incorporated a library.[48] Ann Carnduff and Sheelagh Richards, vice-chairmen of Council, when describing the opening told how an 'amazing staff' had worked late even at weekends (along with some spouses) to get all ready for the Royal opening only two weeks after the move. It was obvious to all who attended that it was a headquarters to be proud of and one which disabled consumers could use with ease. Both the Princess Royal, and the Chairman of Council, Margaret Ellis (1987–89), reflected on 'our modest beginnings in the 1930s and our growth to an Association with 10,500 members.' Her Royal Highness also remarked how 'the fund-raising appeal was launched at Buckingham Palace in June last year.'[49] Carnduff and Richards completed their report with an appeal for continued generosity:

*Headquarters looks beautiful, but if it is to become not only a headquarters but also an information study centre that can be used by people as far away from London as Shetland or the Channel Islands, there is still a lot of work to be done. Technology is needed, software is needed and books are needed, just to give a few examples. Fundraising must go on if work is to continue to make sure our headquarters becomes a centre of excellence, not only for occupational therapists, but also for members of other professions and people with disabilities.*[50]

## Figure 2.10.8:  Opening of Headquarters, Marshalsea Road 1989[51]

# The Blom-Cooper Inquiry

In 1987, the College of Occupational Therapists appointed an Independent Commission of Inquiry under the chairmanship of Louis Blom-Cooper, QC, to study the present state of the profession and its future role. The terms of reference of the Commission were:

> To review the existing activities and future demands upon, and the resources available to, the profession of occupational therapy, having regard to the social, demographic and epidemiological trends into the twenty first century, and to report with recommendations.

The report, which was entitled *Occupational Therapy*: an Emerging Profession in Health Care, highlighted the need to continue educational development towards degree status, to raise the public profile and increase the workforce of the profession, and to re-deploy occupational therapists into the community.

Members of the Commission found it unusual 'for a professional association voluntarily and at considerable cost to expose its present and past activities, and its future existence, to the scrutiny of a group of people from disparate disciplines.' That circumstance made them 'conscious that it was embarking upon its task in extraordinary circumstances' and that the process was more than a stereotyped review. With observers from the COT and DHSS, the Commission met in various parts of the country on eight occasions during 1988 to carry out its task.[52] They started by considering the definition of occupational therapy. They found the one used by COT 'too broad and unfocused to be useful as a description of the role' and coined and recommended the following instead:

> Occupational therapy is the assessment and treatment, in conjunction and collaboration with other professional workers in the health and social services, of people of all ages with physical and mental health problems, through specifically selected and graded activities, in order to help them reach their maximum level of functioning and independence in all aspects of daily life, including their personal independence, employment, social, recreational and leisure pursuits and their inter-personal relationships.[53]

Their reading of an occupational therapist's core knowledge and skills based on detailed curricula of the profession's schools, was 'roughly' categorised as:

> *(1) Knowledge of the intelligence, physical strength, dexterity and personality attributes required to perform the tasks associated with a whole gamut of paid and unpaid occupations and valued leisure pursuits.*
>
> *(2) The professional skill to assess the potentialities and limitations of the physical and human environments to which patients have to adjust and to judge how far these environments could be modified and at what cost to meet individual needs.*
>
> *(3) Pedagogic skills required, first to teach people how to acquire or restore their maximum functional capacity, and second to supervise and encourage technically trained instructors and unqualified assistants in their tasks of implementing and monitoring therapeutic recommendations.*
>
> *(4) The psychological knowledge and skills to deal with anxiety, depression and mood swings, which are the frequent aftermath of serious threats to health or of continuing disability, and to motivate, or remotivate, those with temporary or persistent disabilities to achieve their maximum functional capacity.[54]*

Other elements were recognised, but they were also evident within other professional groups. However, the Commission found no other professional group had the same specific combination of knowledge and skills.

Four other crucial questions the Commission considered were:

*(1) Whether the activities undertaken by occupational therapists and their helpers are essential components of modern health care, or whether, in straitened economic circumstances, they could be dispensed with altogether or in part without harming individuals.*

They concluded that 'occupational therapy is needed as an integral part of health and social service provision.'

*(2) Whether any of the activities currently undertaken by occupational therapists could be adequately performed by less highly qualified professional workers.*

They concluded that 'although there is room for a devolution of some of the work at present performed by trained occupational therapists to their helpers and clerical staff, there will be a continuing and expanding need for fully professional occupational therapists.'

*(3) Whether there is a case for a generic rehabilitation worker in place of the various professions whose work may possibly overlap with that of the occupational therapist.*

They concluded that 'further consideration should be given, in the long-term if not in the immediate future, to the creation of a united profession of rehabilitation therapists, permitting post qualification specialisation.'

*(4) Whether the greater concentration of occupational therapists in the hospital-based specialties, as opposed to the community services of the NHS and local government, can be justified, or whether the time has come for an organisational re-alignment of the profession towards the community.*

They concluded that in 'the next decade and increasingly into the twenty-first century occupational therapy should be largely relocated in community care services.'[55]

Recalling the 'misunderstood' feeling of the previous decade, it is of interest that the Commission's investigation found occupational therapy 'something of a submerged profession.' To them it appeared difficult to eliminate an outdated image. They were so concerned by those findings that they, as many have before and since, discussed a change of name for the profession. They also recognised the profession's long and continuing struggle to establish and maintain an autonomous practice, and saw several factors that contributed to its problems. These were:

- *The dominant position held by the medical profession in the division of labour in the health service, and the similar domination of the social work profession in the local authority domiciliary social services...*
- *...The dependence of occupational therapists on doctors and social workers for access to their clients. Those who can benefit from the knowledge and skills of occupational therapists are not able, let alone likely, to approach them directly. Client-support for their claims through the market is therefore not forthcoming, as it is for some of the other occupations which live in the shadow of medicine.*
- *A...false and damaging stereotype of their function, derived unmodified from the very earliest preoccupations of do-gooding volunteers...*
- *The pronounced female composition of the profession.*

- *The new managerialism called for in the National Health Service and—to a lesser degree— in local government...and restricted resources...*
*Given the difficulty of measuring the outcomes of occupational therapy procedures, and the competition for resources from users of high technology, the professional activities of occupational therapists are likely to be seen as peripheral to the main medical and surgical objectives of cure. They may even be judged as luxuries.*[56]

Shortages of occupational therapists were seen as the result of 'a variety of pressures exercised on employing authorities' such as population-ageing and changing perceptions of patients' potential for rehabilitation. Despite continuous expansion there remained an inability to meet the demand for qualified occupational therapists in the NHS and local authorities. This was regarded by the Commission as a major problem accounting for much of the malaise felt among its members because it had the potential to create dilemmas in:

- departmental organisation
- recruitment, training and retraining
- long-lasting conditions of 'boom and slump in promotion prospects'
- higher rates of leaving.[57]

By and large, no drastic changes were suggested, and many recommendations reinforced decisions already taken or under active consideration. The Commission's overriding recommendation to COT was to prepare its members for an exciting future in the practice of occupational therapy. 'In the process of achieving that object occupational therapy will cease to be the submerged profession of today. Tomorrow occupational therapists should emerge as major practitioners in community care.'[58] To that end they recommended that COT should:

- aim for an 80% expansion in the number of qualified occupational therapists by the end of the century;
- put pressure on the Government to establish national norms of the number of posts for qualified and assistant occupational therapists;
- provide greater help to young Basic Grade therapists; institute or improve courses for re-entrants; and investigate the discrepancy between the numbers qualifying annually and Basic grade recruits in post;
- accelerate the pace of change from hospitals to the community;
- intensify efforts to attract graduates from other disciplines into accelerated courses;
- continue suspending minimum entry requirements for mature applicants whilst sustaining those for school leavers;
- review the advantages and disadvantages of joining forces with physiotherapists to form a single therapy profession, with post-qualification specialisation;
- regularly consider the desirability of finding a new name for the profession;
- seek to validate claims to professional status by measuring and monitoring at all levels of the profession, by annual appraisals, by raising the profession's public profile through multi-disciplinary events considering common health and welfare objectives, and by 'marketing', creating and maintaining a buoyant demand for its services.[59]

**Figure 2.10.9. Louis Blom-Cooper QC and Dr Farrer-Brown, Vice Presidents of COT, discuss the Report 1989**

Whilst the report was generally well received there was some immediate questioning of a few points, such as the numbers who, following qualification, did not take up employment. It was felt that the large number cited in the Report may be an artefact of a number of circumstances, and that further research was needed.[60] Christine Craik outlines some of the action that followed:

> *The veracity of the figures presented and their subsequent interpretation was challenged as early as 22nd September 1989 at the Conference which launched the Report. Geoffrey Claridge, Secretary of COT, questioned the figures as they did not reflect the situation as reported by the Heads of occupational therapy schools. The potentially negative effect of this aspect of the report concerned Council and in an issue of the BJOT in the following year an announcement was made to clarify the question. It noted that the CPSM had conducted a short research study into the leaving rates from the profession over the same period as those quoted by the Report. The figures they obtained were vastly different indicating that 99% of the 679 students who graduated in 1988 had registered with CPSM and that of them 664 (94.3%) had paid a retention fee to remain on the CPSM register the following year.[61]*

# Education: Helpers, Diploma '81 and degrees

More than just the structure of BAOT and COT was becoming complex in occupational therapy. It was also the case in education where the socio-political context was a driving and changing force. Occupational therapy education was expanding in three spheres: to meet the needs of support workers; to equip beginning practitioners with the basic values, knowledge and skills of occupational therapy; and continuing to try to meet the needs of those in the profession for further and ongoing education.

The role of COT covered a range of activities, from enquiries by would-be applicants for training, through to post registration education. A clearing house system had been established to handle applications from England, Scotland and Wales for entry to occupational therapy training. An Education and Research Board formulated education policies and reviewed and co-ordinated educational development. After the start of Diploma '81 (see shortly) a Validation Board had the delegated responsibility of recommending approval of each School's syllabus submission to the Privy Council, through the CPSM.

At the start of the decade The Way Ahead suggested some of the external factors to be considered in future planning of education. These included the prediction that universities, colleges of higher education, and polytechnics would be competing for students to fill their courses, that there would be an increase in mature entrants because of the trend of married women to seek a career, and the need for redundant workers to re-train. Because of such factors it was suggested that, within occupational therapy education, flexibility was needed along with more day release, part-time, and "sandwich" courses, further four-year in-service diploma courses, and that a feasibility study should be carried out regarding the provision of shortened training for those with other qualifications.[62]

Towards the end of the decade Grove, in the Casson Memorial Lecture of 1988, illustrated the impressive range of opportunities in education and training available within occupational therapy in the UK as shown in Figure 2.10.10. Her three divisions: Support Staff; State Registered OT; and Advanced, will be discussed under two headings: Helpers, Instructors and Assistants; and Pre- and Post-Registration Education.

**Figure 2.10.10: Opportunities in education and training in occupational therapy (Elizabeth Grove, 1988 [63])**

| ADVANCED | Clinical | Teaching | Management | Research |
|---|---|---|---|---|
| **STATE REGISTERED OT** | 4 year degree | | | |
| | 3 year degree | | | |
| | 3 year diploma | + 1 year degree | | |
| | 2 year diploma for graduates | | | |
| | 4 year in-service OT Helpers /Technical Instructors ➤ Diploma/SROT | | | |
| **SUPPORT STAFF** | OT Helpers /Technical Instructors COT In-service 300 hours | | | |
| | OT Helpers/Technical Instructors | | | |

## Helpers, Instructors and Assistants

Before considering the specific educational needs of helpers, it is important to appreciate their role. Helpers and instructors constituted a major force in the profession, as there were, for example, approximately 77 helpers, helper technical instructors, or technical instructors for every 100 NHS positions for qualified occupational therapists. There was little difficulty in recruiting them and many were considered invaluable. COT provided an overarching and broad job description of their work:

> An Occupational Therapy Helper shall be a person appointed to work only under the guidance and supervision of a qualified occupational therapist to assist in carrying out duties, in the treatment of patients and in administrative functions.[64]

Under the Articles of the Association, Associate Membership was open to anyone interested in occupational therapy. At that time the voting rights of technical instructors and occupational therapy helpers for Council were restricted to electing one representative from each, but that clause was being reconsidered. All practising professional and associate members had equal voting rights on BAOT ballots concerning issues such as salaries and conditions of service.

Helpers were often 'a self selected and mature group of people', capable of making a contribution in various roles, especially in departments with adequate supervision and support, and clear job specification. That their roles varied was recognised at the time in the Whitley Council Grades of Helper and Technical Instructor III, II and I.[65] Often in the psychiatric field, helpers were employed with specific skills such as in art, drama and music,[66] carpentry or printing, although occupational therapists remained the overall managers of activity programmes.[67,68]

The shortage of qualified staff influenced the recruitment of helpers. It is worth noting that, even with helpers, in some places like the North and the West Midlands staffing remained well below the national average. Sometimes helpers provided most of the patient contact because the sole qualified staff had to deal with a mass of paper work. There were even places where untrained staff were unsupervised, or they filled posts established for occupational therapists. Within the NHS there was a difference in the numbers of qualified and unqualified staff working within practice specialties. Paediatric and community services were provided mainly by occupational therapists, whilst in services for mentally ill or handicapped and elderly people there were more helpers and instructors.[69]

In 1984, Lady Hamilton, the Chairman of the Trustees of the Disabled Living Foundation, highlighted the shortage of occupational therapists when she discussed differences in staffing levels in Health Service Regions on the occasion of her being presented with the Harding Award for services to disabled people. She was also concerned about the uneven distribution of helpers throughout services and regions, and suggested that a survey be undertaken to investigate the role and ratios of helpers in the NHS and LASS. In 1987 the Nuffield Provincial Hospitals Trust agreed to fund two occupational therapists, Peggy Jay and Peggy Davies, to study the role and deployment of occupational therapy helpers. The terms of reference were:

> To investigate the previous experience, duties, training and supervision of OT Helpers in the NHS and in Local Authority employment. To identify, if possible, reasons for the wide variation in ratios of Helpers to OTs in different locations and to make suggestions for more appropriate and efficient use of the time of both OTs and their Helpers on the basis of the work that helpers might be in a position to undertake with appropriate training and supervision.[70]

It was found that in both the NHS and local authorities, helpers and assistants were predominantly female, over half were more than forty years of age, and many had been in post for some years. Many worked part time. Of those in the survey, only 1% in the NHS, and 3% in LASS were from ethnic minorities. Their previous experience varied greatly, encompassing vocational qualifications such as teaching, nursing, clerical, and business studies, and practical skills in arts and crafts or social services, or with children, elderly or disabled people. Job descriptions were found to be broad reflecting the wide range of activities in which helpers and technical instructors could be engaged.

They found there was a need for more training for helpers, as about a quarter had not even received minimal training during the past three years and most expressed interest in further training. It was recommended that:

- employing authorities be responsible for requiring and supporting their occupational therapists to provide induction and regular, on-going training for helpers;
- COT continue to participate in the development of National Vocational Qualifications (NVQ) based competencies, and that it extend existing paths to a professional qualification.[71]

*The Way Ahead* reported how the COT Education Board had devised a 216 hour in-service, Helpers Course run by District or Head Occupational Therapists.[72] As well, the College provided a Manual for courses with comprehensive lecture notes,[73] guidelines for course organisers, and a visiting panel to facilitate standardisation of courses throughout the country.[74] In less than a decade over 200 courses had been held, for more than 1700 helpers since they had been approved and initiated in 1972. Both Inquiries recommended that 'in-service' courses for helpers and technical staff should be validated and remain under the control of the COT, and that the profession should support the development and use of Social Services Courses for Helpers and Technical Staff employed within local authorities.[75]

Helpers and instructors, for whom the Blom-Cooper Inquiry recommended the single designation of 'Occupational Therapy Assistant', were also a source of recruitment of mature people to the profession itself. In Crawley, Bristol and Brent as well as in Essex, there were, by the end of the 1980s, courses organised over a four-year period, designed for Helpers to become registered practitioners.[76] Details of these are found in Appendix A.

## Pre- and post-registration education

During the early 1980s high numbers of students continued to be attracted to occupational therapy pre-registration courses; attrition rates were low, and most completed the programmes of study and found employment. Although by mid-decade the DHSS was increasingly looking to health authorities and local authority employers to take responsibility for student grants, the DHSS remained the major source of funding them. In 1987, for example, it provided for 623 students out of 744 in England and Wales, and for 28 out of 31 in Northern Ireland. In Scotland, that year, the major fund granting body was the Scottish Education Department.[77]

There was beginning to be considerable variation between schools, although all had to meet the COT requirement for 1200 hours of clinical practice, and students, at the start of the decade, were still prepared for national examinations. In Scotland, internal assessment was used, except for final examinations.[78] Students were taught in sixteen occupational therapy schools across the country by about 95 occupational therapy tutors of whom about three-quarters had teaching diplomas and the others were student teachers.[79] Apart from the four year part-time in services courses already mentioned, a new school at Canterbury had a first intake of students in 1987, and the school based at Wolverhampton moved to Coventry in 1988. A different model was adopted at another new school established as part of the London Hospital Medical College in 1989. It offered an alternative student-centred and accelerated curriculum for graduate learners over a 25-month period arranged as 46 weeks per calendar year with periods of fieldwork placement interspersed throughout.

That course was indicative of major changes that the decade heralded. The COT, giving due consideration to reports on education, was 'revising its strategies for professional qualification, taking into account advances in the methods and theories of adult education.'[80] In June 1980 the Council had approved the new syllabus of COT, known as Diploma 1981 (Diploma '81), which phased out national examinations devolving responsibility to the schools. Instead, schools had their courses validated by a 'Validation Board', and a subcommittee of Council. The Validation Board, with at least one member from England, Scotland, Northern Ireland, and Wales, was made up of four principals of occupational therapy schools; four representatives of practising occupational therapists; four representatives of the medical profession; and three higher education representatives.

This major development allowed schools flexibility in the design of curricula and assessment, and encouraged innovation and much easier adaptation to new ideas. However COT still provided the objectives and syllabus of training. The objectives were:

*To give the students sufficient appreciation of the normal and abnormal development and function of the body and mind to enable them to interpret referrals, to determine appropriate treatment and to carry out and monitor progress of treatment. Consideration should be given to the problems of the young and the old and the processes of development and ageing.*[81]

The syllabus remained traditional in subject requirements. They were anatomy, physiology and kinesiology, psychology and sociology, medical sciences, study of occupational therapy, practical skills, management skills, and clinical practice.[82] Naomi Fraser-Holland in the 1990 Casson Memorial Lecture explained that the new syllabus meant that:

*...subject to a system of external moderation, the schools of occupational therapy had the freedom to propose courses within the revised, general syllabus of 'Diploma 1981'. This freedom was accompanied by challenges and great responsibility for the future excellence of the profession...*

*In consequence, from the point of view of critical thinking and familiarity with research processes, people studying in the new Diploma courses became indistinguishable from those reading for first degrees. This parity in intellectual and scientific development led many educators to support the view that the Diploma of the College of Occupational Therapists stood shoulder to shoulder with a bachelor's degree.*[83]

The Blom-Cooper Report was in agreement with that opinion:

> *...the present curricula and practical training offered in schools of occupational therapy are about right, and (that) they are of general degree standard. In our view future recruitment would be easier and justice would be done if the present diploma was recognised by degree awarding bodies as the equivalent of an ordinary degree.*[84]

The Salford School was the first to submit a course for approval, and commenced Diploma '81 in September of 1981.[85]

The Research and Degree Committee of COT recognised that the 'new flexible syllabus for the Occupational Therapy Diploma will enable the development of degree courses.'[86] Other major factors supporting a move to degree programmes were the shift of occupational therapy schools towards institutions of higher education, a recognised need to entice university orientated students into vocational courses, and for courses to be attractive to mature students. Both the Research and Degree Committee which reviewed the need for entry level degree programmes in 1981, and The Way Ahead working party agreed that COT should facilitate and implement a first degree in Occupational Therapy as soon as possible. Both recommended that a vocational degree course should be of four years' duration.[87] The Committee recommended: COT's active commitment to its degree policy; immediate discussion with universities, polytechnics, and occupational therapy schools; and formal approaches being made to government departments and regional health authorities.[88] The COT took this on board, and urged individual schools to affiliate with institutes of higher education. Then, together with the CPSM and the host institutions the COT sought to ensure professional standards and academic excellence.[89]

Margaret Ellis as the then Chairman of the Degrees Committee recalls that in the early 1980s:

> *...it was a very ponderous process to achieve any change. Just before Lord Byers (then President of COT) died, I remember a crucial meeting at the House of Lords when we met the then Minister of Health to discuss the Department of Health objections to degrees. This meeting resulted in the vital (but at the same time delaying tactic) setting up of the Ministerial Committee to evaluate whether it was better to have a straight forward occupational therapy degree or a diploma in occupational therapy followed by an opportunity to do an extra year to obtain a degree. Eighteen months later the Committee reported to the Minister that the Degree would be cheaper, speedier and more satisfactory. The next stage was persuading institutions to actually change to a degree. That was just as difficult!* [90]

The first full time degree programmes to start, in 1986, were a 3-year degree course at Queen Margaret College in Edinburgh and a 4-year honours degree course at the University of Ulster at Jordanstown, just as the last schools to implement Diploma '81 were about to commence their first year on that new system.

The changes occurring in occupational therapy pre-registration education were not all related to its status, nor of a structural nature, and the COT in instigating Diploma '81 had been responsive to common educational trends being implemented in various ways throughout the world. In 1988, Mary Green, for example, pointed to Canada's McMaster programme of problem-based learning in medicine in her discussion of some of the important changes in educational theory. Quoting Jarvis, she supported the notion that:

> *Competency to practise is not a legitimate aim in professional education. Rather, producing in the learner the ability to recognize good practice and the determination to ensure that his own future practice will not fall below this standard is a major aim.*[91]

Notwithstanding that philosophical stance, the issue of 'competent practice' was central to much of the thinking and debate of the time,[92] competence having already been defined by the CPSM as:

> *...possession of the knowledge, skills and attitudes enabling an individual to perform fully in a basic professional role. It includes performance of tasks and relationships with patients and co-workers which meet specific objectives of safety, effectiveness, efficiency and social acceptance in the environments normally encountered.*[93]

As well as challenging the value of competency as the aim of professional education, Green also pointed to new ways of thinking about professional interventions in terms of models. Emerging theoretical bases for practice, such as Keilhofner's Model of Human Occupation[94], and Reed's Models of Practice in Occupational Therapy,[95] were leading therapists away from the old 'medical model' of earlier curriculums.[96] Other changes in educational theory which she discussed were those which:

1. Emphasized the learner as an individual;
2. Directed attention to the essence of a subject to overcome the problems of increasing amounts of complexity of knowledge;
3. Met each individual's different learning needs.

Green explained how because of change within occupational therapy itself, in the 1980s 'highly motivated individuals, who can and will think for themselves' were required. All, rather than a few leaders, had to be able to argue:

> *...back to first principles and indeed to the ultimate uncertainties at the centre of disciplines—in short, to the point of authoritative uncertainty where what is not known, nor even knowable, is even more important than that which is known.*[97]

To do this, she said, students needed a grounding in:

1. The knowledge base which underlies practice;
2. Patient/client need;
3. Techniques to be learned by the developing therapist;
4. The role of the practising therapist.

In terms of post-registration opportunities, increasing numbers of occupational therapists were working towards qualifications such as a COT Fellowship, degrees through the Open University, Southampton University or the Polytechnics of Central London and Loughborough. Opportunities seized by a few encouraged others to undertake further training whether for research purposes or continued professional development. In an encouraging vein, also, BJOT published advertisements and marked achievements. For example, in December 1983, there was announcement that two occupational therapists (not named) had successfully completed research projects for an Honours Degree in Science for the Remedial Professions from the Polytechnic of Central

London.[98] Two years later a triple celebration of academic achievement was reported at St Loye's. Rita Goble had been awarded a doctorate from the University of Exeter; Naomi Fraser-Holland, who had been awarded a PhD in 1971, was appointed a Research Fellow at the University, and Joan Martin gained an MA.[99] In February 1988 the first PhD awarded from a Scottish University was announced. This was to a Nigerian Occupational Therapist, Francis Olatokuunbo Osikoya, who was the first recipient of the WFOT Foundation Award and had studied at the Department of Education at the University of Stirling.[100]

**Figure 2.10.11: Naomi Fraser-Holland, Connie Henson and Rita Goble celebrate post-graduate awards**

The COT showed its commitment to the establishment of ongoing study with a conference at the University of Warwick in 1981, and a dedicated session at the 1985 European Congress, both of which explored Post-Registration Education. At the latter, Rosemary Barnitt began the session with a paper entitled *Post-Registration, Education in the UK: Staying Alive Practically and Intellectually*. Such education, she claimed, would enable an improved standard of care and treatment for patients. To that end, she called for increased competence, evaluation, research approaches and degrees, and declared that the problems in providing post-registration training must not be used as lame excuse not to seek their establishment.[101]

In other papers at the Congress, the issue of post-registration education was tackled variously, not simply in terms of what degree granting authorities had to offer. J. M. Holder, for example, suggested structured self-help groups to identify and clarify goals. Such problem solving could enable therapists to overcome many of the problems caused by burnout, which she claimed was a critical problem among health professionals. Another way forward was described by Vivien Hollis, who combined her roles as a District Clinical Supervisor with post-registration training responsibilities in East Dorset. There, a '3-year staged development/training programme planned to meet immediate needs, extensions of other courses, such as basic clinical courses, and training in skills for different grades of staff' was part of an economic and practical approach. Hollis explained the importance of tapping 'local expertise and resources in order to meet local needs and develop specialized expertise' because education of any sort was expensive. To that end the District had developed an 'OTLINE' for the distribution of educational information about package courses, special interest groups and workshops. Rita Goble, by then Principal of the Exeter School and Director of the Continuing Scheme at Exeter University, rounded the session off by recommending that occupational therapists needed to 'dream daringly' and use all the resources available such as 'postgraduate medical centres, distance learning and research.'[102]

# Practice

The 1980s could be regarded as the time when modern trends towards specialisation became significant. There was a marked increase in the number of textbooks being written or edited by British occupational therapists, and treatment was becoming based on evidence of a formal nature rather than on trial and error. There were moves towards early (and sometimes only) therapeutic interventions using basic communication, counselling, perceptual, sensory and physical modalities in preference to a range of complex activities and use of the therapeutic machines of previous decades. Leigh Atkinson, in the Casson Memorial Lecture of 1980, talked of the changing trends noting as evidence that rehabilitation equipment like the Larvic Lathe was no longer being made.[103]

The principle employers of occupational therapists in the 1980s remained the NHS and local authorities. The main recipients of occupational therapy within social care in 1981 were the elderly, mentally ill or handicapped, physically disabled, sensorily impaired, and children undergoing treatment or 'at risk', which accorded well with those identified by the DHSS as requiring the most treatment.[104] More were employed within the NHS, a 1986 census calculating the number of its occupational therapist positions as 7770.[105]

Jean Edwards, as part of a study completed in 1980 towards an MSc found that the greatest percentage of NHS occupational therapists' time was spent treating people with psychiatric conditions, followed by neurological, then general medical conditions, followed by orthopaedic conditions, and then mental handicap. The majority of patients were elderly, often with multiple problems. Edwards found the most commonly observed interventions of occupational therapists were: teaching improved methods of functioning; advising and implementing activity programmes and running work centres and clubs; assessing patients' functional ability; providing suitable environments and simulated conditions; providing information on aids and local provisions; treatment to ameliorate symptoms; making splints, aids, and designing adaptations; and supplying aids and craft materials.[106]

In *The Way Ahead*, the skilled use of 'realistic activity' was still seen as the special contribution of occupational therapists in assisting patients or clients to function as a 'whole' person. However, it was suggested in that review that, despite the diverse, holistic, and problem-solving approach of occupational therapists, the relinquishing of some areas of work may be necessary. Apparently many of the occupational therapists consulted by the reviewing team questioned particular aspects of the work because there were other skilled people able to do it, or because they felt that an 'unreasonable proportion of the Occupational Therapist's time was being taken up.' Those included orthotics; excessive administrative duties; counselling; non-productive mobilisation (more suitably achieved through physiotherapy); general recreation or entertainment; and the routine provision of certain aids. (It was thought that such tasks could still be appropriate, in some cases, because of local needs or the lack of other skilled personnel). The Review also alluded to the fact that contributions aimed at return to work required careful consideration in the light of the economic situation.[107]

The *Practice of Occupational Therapy*, the textbook edited by Ann Turner, made its debut in 1981. A very practical book, the first section provides another idea of the range of treatment common in the treatment of physical dysfunction at the start of the decade. It includes chapters on assessment, measurement, activities of daily living, transfer techniques, walking aids, wheelchairs and outdoor transport, home visits, domiciliary occupational therapy, remedial games, splinting, work resettlement and rehabilitation equipment (even if that was reducing in popularity.) The chapters of the book also provide an idea of the kinds of dysfunction and specific patient groups commonly treated at that time. They covered amputations, burns, the elderly, hand injuries, head injuries, hemiplegia, lower limb injuries, multiple sclerosis, osteoarthrosis, paediatrics, parkinsonism, peripheral nerve lesions, rheumatoid arthritis, spinal cord injuries, and upper limb injuries.[108]

The European Congress provides another insight into practice in the 1980s. Cardiac programmes included counselling as part of rehabilitation along with graded exercise, lifestyle education, and group discussion. *Counselling in the Community Setting* was addressed by Gaynor Sadlo of the London School; and The Importance of *Counselling Skills for Occupational Therapists* was discussed by Louise Jay of Queen Mary's Hospital, Roehampton. The difference between 'counselling' and 'counselling skills' was another topic, and it was suggested that although occupational therapists could not avoid counselling patients, they needed to avoid doing more than their training prepared them for. The counselling aspect of practice was discussed alongside other papers about *Psychosocial Change in Illness and Disablement and Sexuality in Health Care.*[109]

It was noted in an earlier chapter that practice in the neurological field was increasing. At the Congress the neurology session was so oversubscribed that it had to be repeated. Among the papers which addressed neurological issues, the treatment of multiple sclerosis, motor neurone disease, and stroke featured. On stroke there were presentations about the eclectic use of sensorimotor techniques; simple aiming tasks to explore recovery of movement control; apraxia; and the place of stroke clubs. Neuro-developmental treatment (NDT) and sensory integration (SI) techniques were described as part of an infant stimulation programme and to assist in early developmental screening. SI proved to be a common theme running through the papers in the paediatric session. Paediatrics was recognised as a growing area of interest within psychiatry as well as in the neurological and developmental fields. The treatment of deprived children and those with emotional disorders featured in Congress papers. So too, was the Communication Aids Centre at the Wolfson Centre where occupational therapists were involved in assessing the needs of children with communication difficulties.[110]

The growing interest in paediatric occupational therapy was evidenced by a text on the subject in 1987. Dorothy Penso, the author, attempted to look beyond individual impairments to the basic approach taken by occupational therapists. Penso considered the environment of the child with disability, the family and the therapist as 'transmitters of stimuli,' and therefore as appropriate sources of input to use for the child's treatment. The book discussed assessment and treatment based on solving the problems of a particular child's everyday life.[111]

In terms of employment, Mr P. E. Daunt at the European Congress told how the EEC had 16 linked projects in Europe testing out new ways of enabling physically handicapped, mentally ill or mentally handicapped people to integrate better into employment and the local community. One of these was *Lambeth Accord: Europe's New Approach to Economic Integration of Disabled People* described by Hilary Schlesinger. Accord was run by its disabled members. It differed from 'traditional services in that assessment and treatment are related to local opportunities and employers' requirements; clients apply to come to Accord; they assess themselves with guidance; they respond positively to the staff's high expectations; and 50% of the staff are disabled.' The self-help theme continued with a paper on *Self-help Firms for the Psychiatrically Disabled—a Movement in West Germany in Times of Increasing Unemployment*. Thirteen firms had been established in Germany since 1979 with funding from church and industry.

In contrast to the progressive ideas reflected in those papers, a reflection by Gwilym Roberts on the relatively late development of occupational therapy in the County of Gwynedd, in North Wales, illustrates how practice and opportunities differed throughout the country even as late as the 1980s.[112]

# Occupational Therapy in Gwynedd
## By Gwilym Roberts

Up until 1984, occupational therapy in Gwynedd was focused primarily on social services from the headquarters in Caernarfon under the leadership of Eryl Roberts and Christine Salisbury, on learning disability in Llanfairfechan under Jan Ingham, and on medicine for the elderly at St David's Hospital under the leadership of Margaret Gauge, one of the founders of an occupational therapy service in North Wales. Historically, mental health services were not provided in the county. Patients had to travel up to 100 miles for the occupational therapy service at the North Wales Psychiatric Hospital in Denbigh under the management of Jennie Roberts and Pauline Badger.

In 1984 the opening of the new Ysbyty Gwynedd General Hospital in Bangor included occupational therapy facilities that consisted of a Day Hospital for the elderly, heavy and light workshops, and activities of daily living units under the management of the county's first District Occupational Therapist, Sian Griffiths. In addition an in-patient and day hospital for mental health clients opened under the management of Julie Owen. The new occupational therapy teams served a predominantly rural Welsh speaking community in the county of Gwynedd. This identified a need to recruit and promote occupational therapy as a career amongst the Welsh speaking population in Wales. It was at this time that discussions began in relation to the potential for a school of occupational therapy in either Cartrefle College in Wrexham or the University College of North Wales in Bangor.

In 1987 the mental health service expressed a need to be more community focused and as a result Wales' first Mental Health Resource Centre opened its doors at College Road in Bangor. Amongst the services on offer were community based occupational therapy initiatives, which I managed. These projects included Wales' first GP liaison schemes in which professionals, including occupational therapists, were semi-based in GP practices offering crisis intervention services and community based rehabilitation projects. Within four years the mental health services in Gwynedd employed ten state registered occupational therapists in addition to a team of support workers.

---

Roberts' reflection on the Gwynedd scene of the 1980s is complemented by a glimpse of practice in the Edinburgh City Hospital, provided by Finola Meikle. When she became Head of the Department in 1986 there were 5.5 occupational therapists working there. She followed in the footsteps of Liz Davies, Margery Helm, Rosemary Crewe, and Avril Gardiner, a red-haired, larger-than-life lady who, although not qualified, had provided diversional therapy for the war wounded. Meikle described how 'the full range of OT skills should be applied and that, where appropriate, the sometimes despised diversional therapy—weaving baskets and making teddy bears—could be incredibly valuable. For example she had found that frail aged patients often 'pitch forked' into the infectious diseases ward by overworked GPs, without a minimum of diversional therapy to stimulate them, would soon become totally dependent. Apart from that service a full range of functional assessment and ADL services were standard, and the patient load included an increasing number of those who were HIV positive and intravenous drug users. It was a far cry from earlier times at the City Hospital, and Meikle recalls that only the decade earlier, because there was no crèche, occupational therapy and physiotherapy staff took their babies with them to the hospital in carry cots.[113]

Once more that vexed issue of diversional therapy has been raised. In 1987, Debbie Williams, Jane Harrison, Catherine Newell and Jo Holt dared to address it also, as a third year research project titled *Crafts: A Criminal Offence?* The project was aimed at establishing the way in which the traditional crafts of basketry, stool-seating, pottery, weaving and macramé were used in the treatment of various groups of hospital psychiatric patients, and whether occupational therapy staff felt that these activities still had a role to play in the therapeutic process. They had found that 'some therapists regarded crafts as an anachronism' and their use 'almost a criminal offence.' They had also encountered 'occupational therapists who felt that crafts still had a valid and valuable place in therapy.' They concluded in favour of the use of crafts, suggesting that explanation rather than guilt was the way forward.[114]

Electronic technology is perhaps the antithesis of the craft image. In an article describing *The OT's role with the Younger Disabled Child,* interestingly, two students with cerebral palsy used Possum typewriters, and published a Unit magazine, alongside engagement in printing, stool seating, basketry and weaving.[115] By 1980 electronic equipment was being advertised in BJOT, and apart from the Possum communicator, there were also advertisements for items such as the Possum Text Processor, the Ports scoot electric scooter, and the Egerton EduCom Unit. The Journal also reflected growing involvement in other technologies by including more adverts for thermoplastic splinting material and pressure garments, along with discussion within articles about equipment such as stair lifters, power chairs and alarm systems. At that time, the first personal computers were just becoming available and their application in the wider community was not clear. In *The Use of Technology in the Care of the Elderly and Disabled* the authors claimed:

> *The silicon microchip could be of much benefit to many disabled people but its potential is little understood by the caring professions. The applications of modern electronics have been slow because many people have not yet grasped their significance. The Occupational Therapist needs to understand the value of electronics as communication aids for disabled people, their potential as a provider of jobs for disabled workers and as aids to research and departmental administration.[116]*

## Community practice

The issue of occupational therapists working more and more in the community rather than in acute care settings featured largely as a desirable aim in the Blom-Cooper Report, so a review of some of the material relating to such practice is relevant. In 1987 Eileen Bumphrey edited a book on occupational therapy in the community. At that time, and still today to a large extent, it was concerned mainly with helping disabled and elderly people 'to become members of the community' instead of being 'relegated to an institutional life.' Bumphrey provides an indication of an approach which is facilitatory rather then authoritarian, and is therefore in line with other community development values:

> *The family, of course, is the primary support for all those we are asked to help, and it is essential that they too are cared for…For those well motivated, little call will be made on the professional services: however the majority of disabled people will need the services of an occupational therapist to help them over hurdles from time to time…the emphasis has been on the therapist working with the disabled person to achieve what he or she wants to do…Rehabilitation therefore is a process in which the disabled and handicapped person is the key figure and the occupational therapist's input is seen as one of the many catalysts or facilitators who enables him or her to achieve these. It is a process of solving problems…[117]*

Bumphrey, who worked for the Norwich Health Authority, described in a later article practice within a Primary Health Care Team in which service in the community was integrated with that provided by hospitals. Centred on the patient, it was based on a continuum of care with the objectives of promoting good health; wide-ranging and easily accessible non-hospital health care; a unified and cooperative approach between agencies and interested parties; and experience, training, and job satisfaction of health workers in the community. Community Care Groups (CCGs) were instigated as part of primary health care and community services. These included: community, psychiatric and mental handicap nurses; chiropodists; clinical psychologists; dietitians; health educators and visitors; midwives; occupational, speech, and physiotherapists. Each CCG had an administrator and all the activities were co-ordinated through a patient care manager. Occupational therapists proved to be key members of CCGs, working with patients of many diagnoses in assessment and rehabilitation programmes towards maximum independence and integration into the community.[118]

Sue Smith's 1989 findings, from a survey of how 157 occupational therapy staff working in Southampton and South West Hants Health Authority spent their time, pose some questions about work in the community at that time. Exploring the treatment and treatment-related activities used during one working week, she found that 48% of work time was spent in direct treatment, 32% in treatment-related work, and 20% in other kinds of activities. Staff members' use of, or involvement in, different types of treatment activities tended to differ according to their employment grade. Actual treatment was carried out largely by technicians and helpers, while trained therapists spent more of their time on treatment-related activities. Apart from those findings, which raise one type of concern, Smith's study also led her to query 'the adequacy of occupational therapy provision to patients living in the community, particularly in the fields of general psychiatry and mental handicap.'[119]

Lesley Ford, who contributed to Bumphrey's text, wrote about maintaining mental health in the community. She described this aspect of occupational therapy as the newest field of practice in the 1980s. It had evolved through the introduction of new drugs, and the Mental Health Acts of 1959 and 1983, which directed services away from institutional care towards prevention, treatment and rehabilitation within the community. The 1983 Act reinforced the statutory duty of the DHSS to provide aftercare, preventive care, and treatment in the community.[120]

A letter to BJOT from Stephanie Phipps, a Senior Occupational Therapist with Holderness Community Mental Health Team, discussed some of the issues she thought difficult. Her role included 'acting as a key worker for clients, family work, crisis intervention and establishing group-based services on both a formal referral-type basis and an informal self-help pop-in basis.' She found that:
> ...as the service develops and is encouraging self-referral into the Mental Health Unit,
> I am restricted in the service I can offer as part of a multidisciplinary team.
> The BAOT's Code of Professional Conduct states: 'call for its members to discharge

*their duties and responsibilities in a manner which professionally, ethically and morally compromises no individual with whom they have contact'. And, further on, 'occupational therapists shall undertake treatment either when the patient has been referred by a medical practitioner or where occupational therapists have direct access to a patient's doctor'. On occasion, I feel that I would be compromising the clients to whom I offer a service if I were to have access to their GP. The client may not want his or her GP to know because a group may be non medical in approach and it would not be appropriate to ask for access.*

*As we hope to develop services to offer 7-day access and an out-of-hours crisis response, I also find that I am limited in the service that I can offer both the team I work with and the clients I work for: Whitley terms and conditions of service appear confusing regarding the remuneration they offer occupational therapists for overtime or on-call services and, once again, I may not be in a position to have direct medical access if a client were seen at a weekend or as part of an on-call service.*

*As occupational therapy services are, it is hoped, developing as an integral part of Community Mental Health Services, and rightly so with the skills we have to offer, I wonder if any other occupational therapists are experiencing similar difficulties in trying to work equally alongside other mental health professionals? I should be grateful to hear if anyone else has come across similar hurdles to cross, or found a way forward.*[121]

Local Authorities also ran more institutional services in the community. One such was the Netherne Rehabilitation Unit at Wingfield; staffed by nurses and occupational therapists it was aimed at:

*...assessment, preparation, resettlement and follow-up of mentally ill people, achieved through moving away from the medical model and providing a realistic work environment. The emphasis is not on training for a particular skill, but on establishing and maintaining the work habit.*

It accommodated 30 day patients attending for a 35 hour week, and gave support to about 100 discharged patients. Rehabilitees were able to draw their benefits, which were supplemented by 'therapeutic earnings.' Light assembly, clerical, printing and domestic work reflected the local job market with individually tailored programmes including a work-orientated social skills group, self-care and communication skills, counselling, family support, vocational guidance, regular visits to the job centre, and help with finding a job. Unpaid work experience, during which rehabilitees continued to receive therapeutic earnings from Wingfield, enabled easier transition to employment. A 1981 study noted that placement from Wingfield into open employment remained high[122] when compared with the national average.[123,124]

In a paper on alternatives to open employment in the community, Sue Gilman, described how staff of a psychiatric rehabilitation unit tackled the problem of work opportunities for patients at a time of wide-scale unemployment. She explained that although work is often seen as being synonymous with employment, many experts had found that, for patients, its real value is therapeutic rather than as a means of obtaining a job, because it 'provides a normal social role, gives a structure to the day and helps to prevent deterioration or relapse.'[125,126,127,128,129,130]

Multidisciplinary teams have featured in the discussion of practice, and were the topic of a BJOT paper by Anne Joice and Denise Coia. The paper, prompted by the Blom-Cooper Commission of Inquiry, noted the appropriateness of the Inquiry at a time when the authors perceived occupational therapists questioning their professional role, 'seeking to quantify its achievements and to further its development.' The Commission's request for information on current practice had led them to review the skills contributed by occupational therapists to a multidisciplinary team in the field of psychiatry. In turn this led them to the belief that occupational therapists were not bound by statutory requirements to the same extent as other professionals, allowing them greater flexibility in applying their skills within multidisciplinary teams and setting priorities for their work. On the downside they recognised a limiting of occupational therapist's skills, 'in particular mental health skills,' within local authority community services. In the interest of team harmony they debated whether occupational therapy practices should be restricted in some defined ways. They argued that respect for each other's core skills is essential to the effective functioning of a multidisciplinary team. They believed literature stating the core skills of occupational therapists was ill-defined and sometimes patronising, and identified what they believed the core skills to be:

- Use of selected activity as a treatment medium.
- Activity analysis, and application to meet the needs of the individual.
- Assessment and treatment of functional capabilities.

They described the common skills shared by most professions working in mental health, such as a basic knowledge of psychopathology, models of psychiatry, group therapy, observation, counselling, and management. They concluded that occupational therapy appeared to be an underused source due to some degree of ignorance as to the full extent of the skills that can be provided, a lack of confidence on the part of occupational therapists, a need to examine their own skills and capabilities, a lack of adequate evaluative research, and financial restraints in the NHS which reduced advanced training opportunities.

## Special Interest Groups

Specialisation is largely recognised as one of the steps along the road of developing professions. A number of special interest groups heralded the era of specialisation for occupational therapy, and indicate particular areas of clinical expertise that had developed. *The Way Ahead* reported that COT listed a number of such groups: Care of the Elderly, Orthotics and Prosthetics, Mental Handicap, Remedial Gardening, Research, and Paediatric Interest People, as well as two Scottish regional groups interested in paediatrics.[131] Some of their stories will be told briefly to provide a flavour of this aspect of the profession's growth, starting with the group concerned with orthotics and prosthetics, one of the earliest to be established.

# Special Interest Group in Orthotics and Prosthetics (SIGOP)

## By Sue Kennedy[132]

A group of 20 BAOT members met at the London Hospital in April 1977 with the intention of forming a special interest group. The name of the group, Special Interest Group in Orthotics and Prosthetics (SIGOP), was decided upon, and it was agreed to develop the orthotics area first and prosthetics in the following year. From the beginning there was a commitment to serve both those who were experienced in orthotics and prosthetics and those who wished to maintain or cultivate an interest in the subject. The annual subscription cost was £2 for members of BAOT, and the first elected officers were:

**Chairman:** Mrs Maggie Ellis (The London Hospital)
**Secretary:** Miss Lynn Cheshire (Farnham Park Rehabilitation Centre)
**Treasurer:** Mrs Carolyn Rutland (City Hospital, Nottingham)

At the first meeting Alicia Mendez displayed samples of pressure garments, which she reported were giving successful results in the treatment of burns hypertrophy. Sheila Lawton (Canadian Red Cross, Taplow) showed slides of orthoses she had made for children suffering from juvenile chronic polyarthritis, and a new splint materal, Polyform, was discussed.

American hand therapist, Maude Mallick was instrumental in supporting the group to commence on a sound practical and financial backing. She had hosted Lynn Cheshire on her Churchill Fellowship in the U.S.A. at Harmarville Rehabilitation Centre and Burns Unit in Pittsburg. Subsequently Mallick offered SIGOP a shipping of her manuals on hand splinting to sell for fund raising purposes. She also introduced Carolyn Jobst-Gottfried, the President of the Jobst Pressure Garment Co., USA, who funded, supported and was present at the group's Burns conference in Leeds, and three workshops held around the UK. This ensured that UK occupational therapists were prepared for treating burns by the new pressure methods. Over the years the Committee grew and so did the membership. Wheelchairs and seating became part of the remit in the latter half of the eighties, encouraged by Ellis's defining of a wheelchair as an assistive device, just as an orthosis is. The story of the Group's transformation from SIGOP to CIGOPW during the 1990s is told in the next chapter.

Special interest and local support groups concerned with research started in the early 1980s. For example, in May 1981, BJOT reported a research special interest annual meeting attended by more than 50 people,[133] and a year later J. Stowe reported the establishment of a special research interest group in Yorkshire designed to encourage research and the exchange of ideas and assistance.[134]

Another early starter was the special interest group in mental health which was formed in 1981, the initial meeting being attended by 22 occupational therapists. The

Group compiled a chart illustrating the types of treatment they used. The list recorded treatment according to usage from the most to the least used: encouraging use of normal social activities and assessment; home management and social skills training; day centres; relaxation training; counselling, advising other disciplines or working in or with other agencies; family work; physical fitness; creative therapy (projective techniques); crisis intervention and group homes and hostels; and self-help groups.[135]

The group especially interested in hand therapy claims a longer history, but was formally established in 1984.

# British Association of Hand Therapists (BAHT)
## By Annette Leveridge[136]

In order to trace the history of the British Association of Hand Therapists (BAHT) over the last two decades, it is necessary to note the development of hand therapy in Great Britain from as early as 1916. Nathalie Barr (née Smythe), a pioneer of hand therapy, presented the opening paper Development of the Hand Therapist at the first Conference of BAHT at Warwick in July 1986. She spoke of the roles of physiotherapists and occupational therapists that emerged through the work of groups of surgeons developing expertise in hand surgery during the wars that occurred in England and Europe in 1914-18 and again in 1939-45, but added:

> ...there is little evidence that much attention was focused in relation to specialised hand therapy in the United Kingdom until well into the Second World War. The frightful injuries suffered by airmen in particular resulted in the establishment by the Royal Air Force in Surrey of one of the first specific rehabilitation centres at Chessington.[137]

Nathalie Barr and Mary S. Jones from Farnham Park are recognised particularly by the Association as pioneers of BAHT.

In the 1950s and 1960s, hand units started to emerge throughout the British Isles, and occupational therapists and physiotherapists became recognised as integral members of the hand team. From the 1960s and 1970s, and into the 1980s, there was a remarkable advance in knowledge and interest by therapists throughout the world. Farnham Park had become a leader in programming teaching seminars and study days, along with other established hand centres such as the one at Derby Royal Infirmary. SIGOP, too, was programming workshops and seminars.

On 4 February, 1984, BAHT was established at the London Hospital, Whitechapel, under the chairmanship of Margaret Ellis. It followed a meeting of occupational therapists and physiotherapists with special interest in the rehabilitation of the hand and upper limb. The 1st Annual General Meeting of BAHT held later that year attracted 100 people. At the time there were 114 members—56 OTs, 55 PTs and 3 commercial members. Congratulations were received from the British Society for Surgery of the Hand, and from the American Society of Hand Therapists established in the previous decade. In 1989 a working party on postgraduate education for hand therapists was formed. A course structure was envisaged within which it would be possible for therapists to progress from one level to another and perhaps accumulate credits or modules which could eventually lead to a higher qualification. Three levels of validated courses were defined.

BAHT offers several awards. Barr donated money to the Association in 1985, followed by a further donation, to initiate an Annual Award for full BAHT members. Another Award given by the Association in Barr's honour has been made on three occasions to hand therapists who have made special contributions to the development and recognition of the Association throughout the world. Recipients of the award have been Maureen Salter, Annette Leveridge and Victoria Frampton. A Training and Travel Award became available in 1989 to help therapists with travelling expenses and course fees, not only in the UK but also to centres of excellence throughout the world. BAHT has benefited from generous bequests more recently and consequently has changed its charity status to that of a limited company. Members are now given the opportunity to apply for various awards and bursaries to forward their careers. Opportunities for travel, exchange visits to other countries, research and further study are available to members. Postgraduate Education is developing fast. Following the setting up of the working party in 1989, a BAHT Education Subcommittee was established, setting guidelines and standards for organisation of Level I, II and III Courses and Accredited Prior Learning leading to certification.[138,139] The first validated BAHT Basic Hand Course was run in April 1991 at Bristol Royal Infirmary.

The Group continues to widen its horizons and raise standards. The early 1990s brought hand therapists together internationally with the formation of International Federation of Societies for Hand Therapy (IFSHT) and the European Federation of Societies for Hand Therapy (EFSHT). British hand therapists were in the forefront at their inauguration and on their Executive Councils.

Another special interest group was formed in 1987 by a small group of occupational therapists dedicated to rheumatology. Known as OTSIGiR, originally the group was formed as a branch of the British Health Professionals in Rheumatology (BHPR) with links to the European and International Leagues Against Rheumatism. Meetings were held during BHPR conferences and study days until the first independent study day was held on 5 December, 1987, to discuss The Management of Osteoarthritis. The group was involved in the initial discussions regarding the affiliation of Special Interest Groups to COT, and its story continues in the next chapter.[140]

The final group to be discussed here is one concerned with occupational therapy paediatric practice

# The National Association of Paediatric Occupational Therapists

## By Felicity McElderry

The role of occupational therapy has been recognised increasingly as paediatric services have expanded, but demand continues to far outstrip resources. Clinicians have largely led developments and one of the current challenges is the need to undertake efficacy research that relates directly to clinical practice and service provision.

During the 1960s and 1970s, paediatric occupational therapists met in regional groups and through a London-based organisation called Paediatric Interest People (PIP). This was made up largely of occupational therapists, but included speech and language therapists and physiotherapists. By 1989, the growing number of paediatric occupational therapists and the need to develop a more permanent professional organisation resulted, at the first Annual Conference in Preston, in a resolution to form the National Association of Paediatric Occupational Therapists (NAPOT). Its continuance and growth in the 1990s feature in Chapter 11.

Common to all those special groups is the need to based practice on a sound and well researched base, and so, as would be expected, the 1980s saw a greater acceptance of research as the foundation of practice and professional development.

# Research: becoming accepted

## By Irene Ilott

In the 1970s medical practitioners had expressed an urgent need for occupational therapists to redress the knowledge gap through research.[141,142] By the beginning of the 1980s, the Research and Degree Committee of COT were continuing their encouragement of research activity in plans for the future. These included organising study days, encouraging the formation of research interest groups, offering advice, preparing guidelines on research and research funding, and developing a Register.[143] A listing of research projects being undertaken had been published in BJOT for a few years following the call from Margaret Ellis mentioned in the previous chapter.[144] In 1980 the entry contained the titles of 28 projects.[145] In 1982, the first special research issue of the Journal, 34 projects were reported.[146] From that time the number declined gradually; the following year 18 projects were reported,[147] and in 1984 only 14.[148] In the annual reports for 1983–4 the decreasing number of reports was noted, and COT urged members once more to send details of their research. 1988 saw the publication of a report entitled Research Register in which the authors thanked members for sending information about 220 projects. They suggested the contents would be used to identify priorities and facilitate information exchange, as well as for the College to respond to consultation exercises.[149] During the late 1980s research began to appear in the Annual Conference and

Exhibition, first as sessions and then integrated as an expectation in the criteria used by the scientific panel for selecting abstracts. In the spirit of the decade, Ellis' 1987 Casson Memorial Lecture proposed as one of five conclusions that research is essential to maximise efficiency.[150]

The professional body also promoted the establishment of local research support groups and special interest groups. This started in the early 1980s with a report of a 1981 research special interest annual meeting attended by more than 50 people.[151] A year later a special research interest group was established in Yorkshire to encourage research and the exchange of ideas and assistance.[152] BJOT continued to publicise details of funding opportunities to undertake research training. In 1980 there was an advertisement for Chest Heart and Stroke Association Research Scholarships for members of the remedial professions, which included salary, university fees and expenses for advanced study.[153] Five years later there was an advertisement for four Research Training Fellowships in physiotherapy and occupational therapy offered by the DHSS and Scottish Home and Health Department.[154]

As well, BJOT featured articles about research methods, the process of research and how to disseminate findings. For example, there was advice by Rosemary Barnitt on how to approach a research advisor,[155] and an article by H.G. Clancy outlined the structure and function of literature reviews.[156] In 1983 a literature review workshop was held with students at the Northampton School of Occupational Therapy based around the topic of pressure sores. [157] Four years later, the literature review was promoted as a research method in it own right, and one that it was possible for all occupational therapists to attempt at least once. A review about the asymmetrical tonic neck reflex was used as an example.[158] 1988 saw a description of qualitative research methods and the start of the debate and polarity between quantitative and qualitative methodologies.[159]

Despite all such endeavours there remained a need to advocate acceptance of career researchers. In 1988, a member of the Research and Development Committee wrote 'there are too few occupational therapists involved in research and unfortunately, unlike many other professions, research is not considered to be an integral part of our career development.'[160] This deficiency was also noted in a letter published a year later in which it was suggested that a 'radical change in strategy is required to maintain our professional standing in the wake of the NHS reforms' along with 'clearer recognition (by the COT) of the specialist skills that research occupational therapists can offer their profession.'[161] That letter was answered by the Chair of Research and Development Committee who suggested that although, as in other disciplines, only a minority of about 2–7% would be researchers, a research unit 'with emphasis on national concerns and initiatives would be beneficial.'[162] The need to present the results of research in plain English was advocated by a member of the COT Research and Development Committee in 1989 who noted that 'research is frequently viewed as an elitist activity' and that the 'more jargonised and technical a professional language becomes, the greater the divide between the researcher and the researched.'[163] As well as specialist researchers the COT recognised the need for all occupational therapists to consider research as integral to their practice, to be informed consumers of research. In a BJOT editorial C. Ravetz suggests that:

*...new therapists should be encouraged to continue research activity and undertake projects of suitable size to fit workload thus allowing research to become part of a normal working pattern and not slip into the realms of esoteric possibility that someone else may make into reality.*[164]

Most research of the decade continued to be of an applied nature, such as Mayers' into a model for community occupational therapy practice for clients with long-term disability/handicap which was 'understandable to clients, their carers, society in general, other health professions, and that focuses on the ordinary but crucial aspects of everyday living.'[165] Other examples included: a pilot study to investigate ways of increasing participation by mentally handicapped patients in an occupational therapy department within existing staff resources;[166] ten single subject studies: of the engagement level in hospitalised demented patients using time sampling;[167] a questionnaire survey focusing on patients' views of occupational therapy in a therapeutic milieu (which revealed that two-thirds of patients considered occupational therapy to be helpful);[168] a follow-up study, funded by Mersey Regional Health Authority, about motor problems among 53 low birth weight children in mainstream education;[169] and a double blind randomised control trial in which activities of daily living assessments were used to measure the effectiveness of vitamin D supplements in elderly long stay patients. (Three occupational therapists were amongst the 10 authors with a senior lecturer statistics, a biochemist, 5 medical consultants, and 1 professor.[170]) A striking example of research findings improving services was provided by Alicia Mendez, in a seminar entitled Collaboration in Health Care at the London Hospital in October 1983. She described a multi-professional and multi-centre trial that evaluated a myoelectric prosthesis for younger children that resulted in DHSS provision of the device. The Chairman, Mr Heinz Wolff, suggested that 'members of the remedial professions are now emerging as equals in medical research teams' and he hoped the seminar would demonstrate this new equality.[171]

A couple of studies investigated new products. One was research undertaken as part of the MSc. at Southampton into staff perceptions of the value of computers. Most of the 51 subjects taking part considered computers to be valuable for patient care and to have a beneficial effect.[172] The other research used a single case methodology to evaluate an automatic calendar as an aid to assist recall of day and date.[173] Twenty-two research articles in the BJOT between 1983–85 related to reports of the development of standardised assessments. These included the Rivermead Activities of Daily Living Assessment,[174] and the Rivermead Perceptual Assessment.[175] On a similar but slightly different tack, another article critiqued diagnostic and assessment measures used in identifying bulimia. It contained different authors' interpretation and measures, including surveys, sampling, interviews and questionnaires.[176]

A letter to *BJOT* suggested that basic as well as applied research was required. J. Wilson wrote 'we should concentrate our research efforts on developing our understanding of what normal activities have to offer and the relationship between activities and the health of the individual' instead of altering and adapting activities to create specialised treatments whilst overlooking their 'innate value.'[177] In the same spirit another study applied the recommendation of *The Way Ahead* Working Party to focus upon occupation as the identifying feature of occupational therapy interventions. Published in 1982, this was an exploratory study of therapeutic play with psychologically disturbed children that involved analysing the current use of activities in different diagnostic categories.[178]

In the 1985 Casson Memorial Lecture, D.L. McLellan articulated a vision of inculcating research into the training from day one, describing how the capacity for research grows in an environment of friendship and informal interchange between teachers who are involved in it and students and later on colleagues.[179] Educators had already reported introducing occupational therapy students to the research process. For example, in October 1980, M.L. Malcolm described a project for second and third years students at the Salford School of Occupational Therapy. This was intended to enable the students to acquire research skill, contribute new knowledge to the profession, develop a critical approach and the ability to express the findings concisely and unambiguously in a 2000 word project, with suitable ones being submitted to the Journal.[180] The first textbook about research, written by occupational therapists based in the UK, was *Research Guidelines: A Handbook for Therapists* by Partridge and Barnitt.[181]

In BJOT, the publication of a first authors guide in January 1983 marked a new era. The guide described two categories of articles. These were scientific, structured fully referenced articles, comparable in value and format to those in any learned profession's publications, and descriptive articles based on personal experience. A change in the composition and authorship patterns from descriptive to referenced articles was supported by the introduction of a peer review process. Between 1975 and 1984 articles increased in size, number, and use of references. The majority (63%) were by single authors, the most popular topics being physical occupational therapy, psychiatry, equipment/aids, and teaching subjects.[182] From the early 1980s the Editorial Board sought to secure the Journal's inclusion in Index Medicus.[183]

Occupational therapy researchers also published in other journals. In a letter to BJOT Clephane Hume, Chair of the Editorial Board, described occupational therapists' contribution to other journals as an 'excellent way of furthering knowledge.' She pointed to examples such as *Community Care, Health Service Journal, Age and Ageing, International Medicine and Mental Handicap*.[184] The BJOT had, over the years published many reprints from medical journals written by medical experts, but in 1987 it was time for one by two occupational therapists, AJ Turton and CM Fraser, which had been published previously in *International Rehabilitation Medicine*.[185] British occupational therapists also contributed papers about research to conferences primarily for other than occupational therapists, or in other places. J. Stowe, for example, gave a paper about equipment at the European Congress of Rheumatology in Moscow, which was attended primarily by medical practitioners.[186] Margaret Smith delivered a keynote address on research at the 15th Federal Conference of the Australian Association in February 1989.[187]

In a final cautionary note, L. Jones, Chair of the Research and Development Committee of COT made the link between cost effectiveness and professional survival in an editorial in April 1988. She noted that:

> *...occupational therapy has a difficult and uneasy place in the world of research. As a practice based profession, we are reluctant to engage in research activities at the cost of patient care or education of our students—recently the profession has been asked to justify its role, treatments and methods, both to its paymasters and to other professional groups. Scientific evidence and numbers are being demanded if we are to survive as a profession, it will be necessary to internalise research and evaluative practice. It is important that we accept the challenge and continue to develop an atmosphere where research and evaluative work thrive and form an acceptable and credible part of our role.[188]*

**In summary,** the 1980s was a time of social upheaval and change of a fundamental nature. That was reflected in the ongoing questioning of direction manifest by two major inquiries, by industrial action taken by the professional body, by major changes in education, and greater acceptance of the need for research. The development of interest groups told of increasing specialisation, noted as a sign along the road of most professions. Some of the patterns of change to which Hester Monteath alluded in a keynote paper presented at the Federal Conference of the Australian Association of Occupational Therapists in 1980 conclude the chapter. She said:

> *A glance at proceedings of some local, national, federal, and international conferences of recent years demonstrates that occupational therapists are involved in highly specialised areas of work and individuals are undoubtedly respected and valued for their skill and competence. But I find it difficult to extract from many excellent and erudite papers what these individuals have in common and what it is that is exclusive to occupational therapy...It is right and proper that we are concerned with all aspects of human existence within a changing society...*

There are...five necessary tasks to be tackled:

*...stocktaking...look at what we are doing*
*...restate our own raison d'etre and describe the boundaries of our professional competence*
*...be articulate in our communication with others, and our limitation in this is our undoubted uncertainty about our professional identity*
*...evaluation of every technique we apply*
*...research remains the keynote to our credibility.[189]*

[1]Jones M. Thatcher's Kingdom: A View of Britain in the Eighties. Sydney: William Collins Pty Ltd., 1984: cover.
[2]Jones M. Thatcher's Kingdom: A View of Britain in the Eighties...: cover.
[3]Cited in: British Association of Occupational Therapists. The Way Ahead: Report on the Working Party. London. 1981.
[4]Draper P. Director of the Unit for the Study of Health Policy at Guy's Medical School. Unemployment can seriously damage your health. Guardian, 1981; November.
[5]Thatcher M. House of Commons, 1983. Cited in: Jones. Thatcher's Kingdom...: 35.
[6]Plea to Prime Minister. BAOT News No. 11. September 1980: 1.
[7]Jones. Thatcher's Kingdom...: 169–71.
[8]Cleary Y. Announcements: BAOT Marches for the NHS British Journal of Occupational

Therapy 1988; 51(4).

[9]Gripper J. Correspondence. British Journal of Occupational Therapy 1988; 51(3): 101.

[10]Kirby H, Langton T, Emck S, Daykin T, Horne A, Wood Y, Kay S, Greenwood C, Gardener G, Leslie J, Moon J, Lochery G, Slorence J, Burford A. Concerns Regarding the NHS. British Journal of Occupational Therapy 1988; 51(6): 210.

[11]Reported in OT News. December 1987.

[12]Ellis M. Concerns Regarding the NHS. British Journal of Occupational Therapy 1988; 51(6): 210.

[13]DHSS. The Next Steps. London: HMSO, 1984; 2, Cited in: DHSS. Working for Patients. London: HMSO, 1989.

[14]Correia S. General Management in the NHS. British Journal of Occupational Therapy 1989; 52(3): 79.

[15]Warren B. From McColl to the DSA and Beyond. British Journal of Occupational Therapy 1988; 51(3): 75.

[16]Etherington K. The Disabled Persons Act 1986: The Need for Counselling. British Journal of Occupational Therapy 1990; 53(10): 430–1.

[17]Promoting Better Health: the Government's Programme for Improving Primary Health Care. CMND 249. London: HMS0, 1987.

[18]Evans E. Promoting Better Health: The Government's Programme for Improving Primary Health Care. British Journal of Occupational Therapy 1988; 51(2): 66.

[19]Royal Commission on the NHS. A Service to Patients: Conclusions and Recommendations of the Royal Commission's Report. London: HMSO (22.78), 1979.

[20]Office of Population and Census and Surveys. Population Trends. London: HMSO, 1981.

[21]Central Statistical Office. Social Trends 11. London: HMSO, 1981.

[22]DHSS. Report of a Study on the Respective Roles of General, Acute and Geriatric Sectors in Care of the Elderly Hospital Patient. London: HMSO, 1981.

[23]DHSS. Care in Action: A handbook of Policies and Priorities for the Health and Personal Social Services in England. London: HMSO, 1981.

[24]British Association of Occupational Therapists. The Way Ahead: Report on the Working Party. London. 1981; 42.

[25]BAOT. The Way Ahead...; 41.

[26]Central Statistical Office. Social Trends 11...

[27]Department of Education and Science and Scottish Education Department. Higher Education into the 1990s. A Discussion Document. London: HMSO. 1978.

[28]BAOT. The Way Ahead...

[29]Grove E. Working Together. British Journal of Occupational Therapy 1988; 51(5): 150–6.

[30]Grove E. Figure 5: Working together with the Occupational Therapy Officer. British Journal of Occupational Therapy 1988; 51(5): 156.

[31]BAOT News. 1, November 1979.

[32]BAOT and College News. 2(1): 1981.

[33]Grove E. Working Together...

[34]COT. A Special Meeting: Research and Occupational Therapy. The King's Fund Centre, London, 15 February 1982.

[35]BAOT. The Way Ahead...; 5.

[36]BAOT. The Way Ahead...; 8

[37]BAOT. The Way Ahead...; 9–10.

[38]British Journal of Occupational Therapy. The College meets the DHSS on OT Manpower. 1981; 44(4): 113.

[39]BAOT. The Way Ahead...; 13.

[40]COT. Recommended Minimum Standards for Occupational Therapy Staff Patient Ratios. February 1980

[41]Green S. 'Occupation': When Do We have it Right? British Journal of Occupational Therapy 1989; 52(8): 291.

[42]SCC. Reflections on the Congress. British Journal of Occupational Therapy 1985; 48(8): 225.

[43]Hopson S, Hume C, Kelly G, Barnett U. The second European Congress of occupational therapy: A Report. British Journal of Occupational Therapy 1985; 48(9): 269–74.

[44]SCC. Reflections on the Congress...

[45]Warren, B. Chairman of Council 1986–87' 2000 .

[46]HRH, The Princess Royal. Foreword. Occupational Therapy. An emerging profession in health care. Report of a Commission of Inquiry 1989. London: Duckworth, 1990; 7.

[47]BAOT Annual Report, 1980.

[48]Jay P, Mendez A, Monteath HG. The Diamond Jubilee of the Professional Association, 1932–1992: An Historical Review. British Journal of Occupational Therapy 1991; 55 (7): 252–6.

[49]Carnduff A, Richards S. Official Opening of the New Headquarters and the Disability Information and Study Centre. British Journal of Occupational Therapy 1989; 52(11): 429–32.

[50]Carnduff & Richards. Official opening of the new headquarters...

[51]Carnduff & Richards. Official opening of the new headquarters...

[52]Blom-Cooper L. Occupational Therapy. An emerging profession in health care. Report of a Commission of Inquiry 1989. London: Duckworth, 1990; 9–10.

[53]Blom-Cooper. Occupational Therapy...; 14.

[54]Blom-Cooper. Occupational Therapy...; 15.

[55]Blom-Cooper. Occupational Therapy...; 44, 56.

[56]Blom-Cooper. Occupational Therapy...; 16–18.

[57]Blom-Cooper. Occupational Therapy...; 21, 34–6.

[58]Blom-Cooper. Occupational Therapy...; 89.

[59]Blom-Cooper. Occupational Therapy...; 85–9.

[60]Announcements. Publication of Independent Commission Report: and Carnduff A. Discussions of recommendations by BAOT Members. British Journal of Occupational Therapy 1989; 52(10): 400–401.

[61]Craik C. Informed written comment provided to AAW. 2001.

[62]BAOT. The Way Ahead.

[63]Grove E. Figure 2: Working together. British Journal of Occupational Therapy 1988; 51(5): 153.

[64]Blom-Cooper. Occupational Therapy...; 69.

[65]BAOT and College News. Vol. 2. No. 2. September 1981.

[66]Whitley Council accepted that art and music therapists with approved post-graduate training should have their own grading structure independent of occupational therapy.

[67]BAOT. The Way Ahead...; 20.

[68]Blom-Cooper. Occupational Therapy...; 67–8.

[69]Blom-Cooper. Occupational Therapy...; 72–5.

[70]Jay P. Occupational Therapy Helpers and Assistants in Health and Social Services. London: Disabled Living Foundation. 1991: 6.

[71]Jay P. Occupational Therapy Helpers and Assistants in Health and Social Services. London: Disabled Living Foundation. 1991

[72]BAOT. The Way Ahead...; 11

[73]College of Occupational Therapists. Helpers/Technical Staff-in-service Handbook .1979.

[74]Blom-Cooper. Occupational Therapy...; 65

[75]BAOT. The Way Ahead...; and Blom-Cooper. Occupational Therapy...

[76]Blom-Cooper. Occupational Therapy...; 72–5.

[77]DHSS and Paterson CF. Cited in: Grove E. Working together. British Journal of Occupational Therapy 1988; 51(5): 151.

[78]Stewart AM. Study of Occupational Therapy Teaching Resources in the United Kingdom. London: CPSM 1979.

[79]Blom-Cooper. Occupational Therapy...; 18.

[80]Fraser-Holland N. Casson Memorial Lecture: Moving Targets and 20:20 Vision. British Journal of Occupational Therapy 1990; 53(8): 326-327

[81]College of Occupational Therapists. Diploma Course 1981: Training in Occupational Therapy. London: COT, 1981.

[82]College of Occupational Therapists. Diploma Course 1981: Training in Occupational Therapy. London: COT, 1981.

[83]Fraser-Holland N. Casson Memorial Lecture: Moving Targets and 20:20 Vision. British Journal of Occupational Therapy 1990; 53(8): 326–7.

[84]Blom-Cooper. Occupational Therapy...; 65.

[85]British Association of Occupational Therapy. 'The Way Ahead' Report of the Working Party, London, 1981: 32.

[86]Research and Degree Committee. A Review of the Needs for Degrees for Occupational Therapists: A Statement from Council. London: College of Occupational Therapists, September, 1981.

[87]BAOT. The Way Ahead.

[88]Research and Degree Committee. A Review of the Needs for Degrees for Occupational Therapists: A Statement from Council. London: College of Occupational Therapy, September, 1981.

[89]Fraser-Holland N. Casson Memorial Lecture: Moving Targets and 20:20 Vision. British Journal of Occupational Therapy 1990; 53(8): 323–8.

[90]Ellis M. Personal recollection to AAW, 2001.

[91]Jarvis P. Professional Education. London: Croom Helm, 1983.

[92]King, JD. "Competence to Practise". British Journal of Occupational Therapy, Vol. 43. No. 6, June 1980

[93]Council for Professions Supplementary to Medicine. PSM Education and Training— The Next Decade. London: Council for Professions Supplementary to Medicine, November, 1979.

[94]Keilhofner G. A Model of Human Occupation: Theory and Application. Baltimore: Williams and Wilkins, 1985.

[95]Reed KL. Models of practice in occupational therapy. Baltimore: Williams & Wilkins, 1984

[96]Green M. Planning for Change in Education. British Journal of Occupational Therapy 1988; 51(3): 78–80.

[97]Goodlad S, Pippard B, Bligh D. The curriculum of higher education. In: Bligh D, ed. Professionalism and flexibility in learning. Guildford: Society for Research into Higher Education, 1982: 76, 81.

[98]British Journal of Occupational Therapy 1983; 46(12): 373.

[99]British Journal of Occupational Therapy 1985; 48(9): 286.

[100]British Journal of Occupational Therapy 1988; 51(2): 89.

[101]Barnitt R. Post-Registration, Education in the UK: Staying Alive Practically and Intellectually. Cited in: Hopson S, Hume C, Kelly G, Barnett U. The second European Congress of occupational therapy: A Report. British Journal of Occupational Therapy 1985; 48(9): 270.

[102]Hopson S, Hume C, Kelly G, Barnett U. The second European Congress of occupational therapy: A Report. British Journal of Occupational Therapy 1985; 48(9): 270.

[103]Atkinson L. Casson Memorial Lecture: Unique To Occupational Therapy. British Journal of Occupational Therapy 1980; 43 (7): 221–4.

[104]DHSS. Care in Action: A Handbook of Policies and Priorities for the Health and Personal Social Services in England. London: HMSO, 1981.

[105]DHSS (SR7) Annual Census of NHS, Non Medical Manpower. London: DHSS, 1986.

[106]Edwards JD. Occupational Therapy Role and Education. MSc. thesis, University of Manchester. 1980.

[107]BAOT. The Way Ahead...; 43.

[108]Turner A, ed. The Practice of Occupational Therapy: An Introduction to the Treatment of Physical Dysfunction. Edinburgh: Churchill Livingstone, 1981.

[109]Hopson S, Hume C, Kelly G, Barnett U. The second European Congress of occupational therapy: A Report. British Journal of Occupational Therapy 1985; 48(9): 269–74.

[110]Hopson S, Hume C, Kelly G, Barnett U. The second European Congress of occupational therapy: A Report. British Journal of Occupational Therapy 1985; 48(9): 269–74.

[111]Penso DE. Occupational Therapy for Children with Disabilities. London: Croom Helm, 1987.

[112]Gwilym Roberts was Group Head Education and Practice at COT.

[113]Meikle F. In: Gray JA. The Edinburgh City Hospital. East Linton: Tuckwell Press.1999; 364–66.

[114]Williams D, Harrison J, Newell C, Holt J. Crafts: A Criminal Offence? British Journal of Occupational Therapy 1987; 50(1): 12–15.

[115]Riley PM. The OT's role with the younger disabled child. British Journal of Occupational Therapy 1980.

[116]Bray J, Wright S. The Use of Technology in the Care of the Elderly and Disabled. Tools for Living. Opportunities for the Application of Recent Technical Advances. 1980. Chapter 14, 108–12.

[117]Bumphrey EE, ed. Occupational Therapy in the Community. Cambridge: Woodhead-Faulkner, 1987; x.

[118]Bumphrey EE. Occupational Therapy within the Primary Health Care Team. British Journal of Occupational Therapy 1989; 52(7): 252-255.

[119]Smith S. How Occupational Therapy Staff Spend their Work Time. British Journal of Occupational Therapy 1989; 52(3): 82, 85, 87.

[120]Ford L. Maintaining mental health. In: Bumphrey...Occupational Therapy in the Community...; 194.

[121]Phipps S. Working in a Community Mental Health Team. British Journal of Occupational Therapy 1989; 52(2): 69.

[122]Collis M, Ekdawi MY. Psychiatric rehabilitation: needs of a health district. Interim Report. Coulsdon, Surrey: Netherne Hospital Rehabilitation Service, 1981.

[123]Wing JK, Bennett DH, Denham J. The industrial rehabilitation of long-stay schizophrenic patients. Medical Research Council memo no. 42. London: HMSO, 1964.

[124]Acharya S, Ekdawi MY, Gallagher L, Glaister B. Day Hospital rehabilitation: a six year

study. Social Psychiatry 1982; 117: 1–5.

[125]Gilman S. Alternatives to Open Employment in the Community. British Journal of Occupational Therapy 1987; 50(5): 158–9.

[126]Wansbrough N, Cooper P. Open Employment After Mental Illness. London: Tavistock, 1980.

[127]Wing JK, Morris B, eds. Handbook of Psychiatric Rehabilitation Practice. London: Oxford University Press, 1981.

[128]Bennett DH. The value of work in psychiatric rehabilitation. Social Psychiatry 1970; 5: 224.

[129]Wing JK, Brown GW. Institutionalism and Schizophrenia. Cambridge: Cambridge University Press, 1970.

[130]Miles A. Long-stay schizophrenia patients in hospital workshops: a comparative study of an industrial unit and an occupational therapy department. British Journal of Psychiatry 1971; 119: 611.

[131]BAOT. The Way Ahead...; 79.

[132]Sue Kennedy is Newsletter Editor and Membership Secretary to CIGOPW.

[133]British Journal of Occupational Therapy 1981; 44(5): 145–6.

[134]Stowe J. British Journal of Occupational Therapy 1982; 45(3): 99–100.

[135]Ford L. Maintaining mental health. In: Bumphrey... Occupational Therapy in the Community...; 198.

[136]Annette Leveridge is Hon. Secretary, British Association of Hand Therapists, Education Sub-Committee, Secretary General of the International FS Hand Therapists (IFSHT) and Past Historian, IFSHT.

[137]Barr N. Development of the Hand Therapist. Opening paper: British Association of Hand Therapists' 1st conference. Warwick. British Association of Hand Therapists Newsletter 5, 1986.

[138]Leveridge A. A History of the BAHT. Part 1. The British Journal of Hand Therapy 1997; 2(7); and A History of the BAHT Part II. The British Journal of Hand Therapy 1997; 3(1).

[139]Leveridge A. BAHT: Its Formation and Development. British Association of Hand Therapists Handbook. London: BAHT, 1998.

[140]Information provided by OTSIGiR.

[141]Tooley Dr. Round the Regions: AGM of North East Metropolitan regional group. British Journal of Occupational Therapy 1971; 34(5): 32.

[142]The Royal College of Physicians of Edinburgh. Reprint from booklet: Co-operation between medical and other health professions. British Journal of Occupational Therapy 1977; 40(7): 154–5.

[143]COT. The Research and Degree Committee Annual Report for 1979/80. 1980; 235.

[144]British Journal of Occupational Therapy 1976; 39(7): 178.

[145]British Journal of Occupational Therapy 1980; 43(2): 39.

[146]British Journal of Occupational Therapy 1982; 45(2): 57.

[147]British Journal of Occupational Therapy 1983; 46(7): 203.

[148]British Journal of Occupational Therapy 1984; 47(7): 218.

[149]Brown J, Jones L. Research Register. British Journal of Occupational Therapy 1988: 51(9): 325.

[150]Ellis M. The 1987 Casson Memorial Lecture. Quality: who cares? British Journal of Occupational Therapy 1987; 50(6): 195-200.

[151]Report of a research special interest annual meeting. British Journal of Occupational Therapy 1981; 44(5): 145–6.

[152]Stowe J. Report of a special research interest group. British Journal of Occupational

Therapy 1982; 45(3): 99–100.

[153]Chest Heart and Stroke Association Research Scholarships. British Journal of Occupational Therapy 1980; 43(1): 35.

[154]Research training fellowships in physiotherapy and occupational therapy. British Journal of Occupational Therapy 1985; 48(11): 111.

[155]Barnitt R. On giving research advice. British Journal of Occupational Therapy 1980; 43(9): 285–7.

[156]Clancy HG. The literature review: its structure and function. British Journal of Occupational Therapy 1980; 43(6): 206–8.

[157]Gillott H, et al. Current thinking on pressure sores; results of a literature review workshop held at Northampton School of Occupational Therapy. British Journal of Occupational Therapy 1983; 46(2): 41–4.

[158]Kelly G. Keeping up with the journals: the strange case of the disappearing asymmetrical tonic neck reflex. British Journal of Occupational Therapy 1987; 50(9): 298–9.

[159]Robertson L. Qualitative research methods in occupational therapy. British Journal of Occupational Therapy 1988; 51(10): 344–6.

[160]Nouri F. Assessment. British Journal of Occupational Therapy 1988; 51(8): 268.

[161]Mountain G. Correspondence. British Journal of Occupational Therapy 1989; (10): (page unkown)

[162]Jones L. Correspondence. British Journal of Occupational Therapy 1989; (10): (page unkown)

[163]Cowley J. Research and Development Committee: COT the language we use: facilitative or obstructive? British Journal of Occupational Therapy 1989; 52(3) 98.

[164]Ravetz C. Editorial: The rights and responsibilities of qualification. BJOT 1987; 50(8): 255.

[165]Mayers CA. British Journal of Occupational Therapy 1989; (6): 244.

[166]Bush A, Williams J, Morris S. An activity period for the mentally handicapped. British Journal of Occupational Therapy 1980; 43(8): 297–300.

[167]Conroy MC, Fincham F, Agard-Evans C. Can they do anything? 10 single subject studies of the engagement level of hospitalised demented patients. British Journal of Occupational Therapy 1988; 51(4,): 129–32.

[168]Stockwell R, Powell A, Bhat A, Evans C. Patients' views of occupational therapy in a therapeutic milieu. British Journal of Occupational Therapy 1987; 50(12): 406–10.

[169]Roberts BL, Marlow N, Cooke RWI. Motor problems among children of very low birthweight. British Journal of Occupational Therapy 1989; 52(3): 97–9.

[170]Corless D, et al. Using activities of daily living assessments to measure the effectiveness of vitamin D supplements in elderly long-stay patients. British Journal of Occupational Therapy 1987; 50(2): 60–62.

[171]Seminar report: Collaboration in health care working report on collaborative research. British Journal of Occupational Therapy 1984; 47(1): 84–5.

[172]Rugg S. A preliminary study of occupational therapy staff concerning the use of computers in the profession. British Journal of Occupational Therapy 1986; 49(3): 71–5.

[173]Lincoln NB, Edmans JA, Walker MF, Noble T, Addison L. The provision of an automatic calendar on a stroke ward. British Journal of Occupational Therapy 1988; 51(6): 195–6.

[174]Whiting S, Lincoln N. An ADL assessment for stroke patients. British Journal of Occupational Therapy 1980; 43(2): 44–6.

[175]Bhavnani G, Cockburn J, Whiting S, Lincoln N. The reliability of the Rivermead Perceptual Assessment. British Journal of Occupational Therapy 1983; 46 (1): 17–19.

[176]Martin JE. Research methodology used in identifying bulimia. British Journal of Occupational Therapy 1989; 52(5): 175–80.

[177]Wilson J. Correspondence. British Journal of Occupational Therapy 1988; (1): 25.

[178]Jeffery LIH. Occupational therapy in child and adolescent psychiatry the future—applying the deliberations of The Way Ahead Working Party to a particular clinical field. British Journal of Occupational Therapy 1982; 45(10): 330–4.

[179]McLellan DL. Casson Memorial Lecture. British Journal of Occupational Therapy 1985; 48(8): 228-232.

[180]Malcolm ML. Training in research at Salford school of Occupational Therapy. British Journal of Occupational Therapy 1980; 43(10): 361–2.

[181]Partridge C, Barnitt R. Research Guidelines—A Handbook for Therapists 1986.

[182]Trevan-Hawke JA. British Journal of Occupational Therapy: composition and authorship patterns 1975-1984. British Journal of Occupational Therapy 1986; 49(9): 301–4.

[183]Hume C, Smith M. BJOT readership survey: result. British Journal of Occupational Therapy 1984; 47(2): 35.

[184]Hume C. Letter. British Journal of Occupational Therapy 1986; 49(8): 270.

[185]Turton AJ, Fraser CM. A test battery to measure the recovery of voluntary movement control following stroke. British Journal of Occupational Therapy 1987; 51(1): 11–14.

[186]Stowe J. Xth European Congress of Rheumatology, Moscow. British Journal of Occupational Therapy 1984; 47(4 ): 123.

[187]Smith ME. Conference report: focus on Australia. British Journal of Occupational Therapy 1989; 52(2): 59–60.

[188]Jones L. Editorial. British Journal of Occupational Therapy 1988; 51(4): 111.

[189]Monteath HG. Focus on Psychiatry—The challenge of change. Keynote paper: Proceedings Federal Conference of the Australian Association of Occupational Therapists. Tasmania, 1980: 19–20.

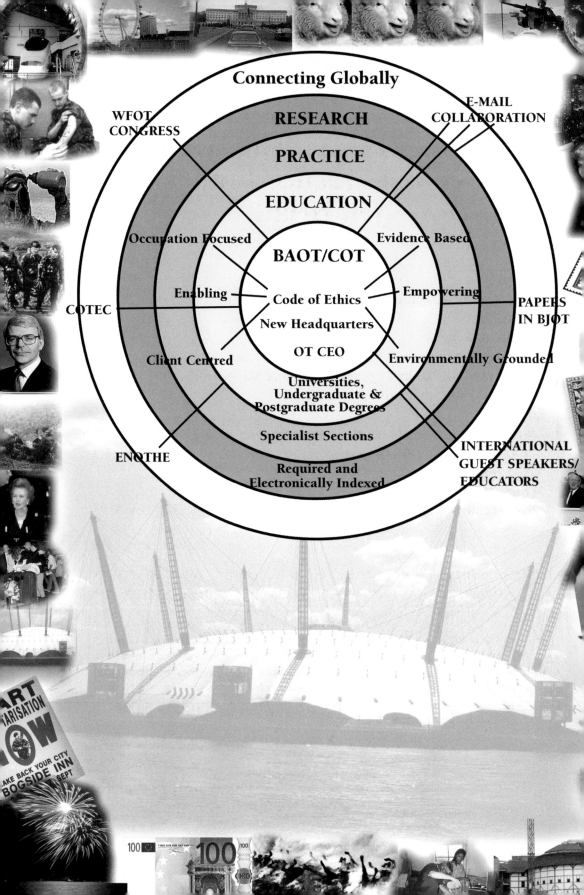

Connecting Globally

RESEARCH

PRACTICE

EDUCATION

BAOT/COT

Code of Ethics
New Headquarters
OT CEO

WFOT CONGRESS

E-MAIL COLLABORATION

Occupation Focused

Evidence Based

Enabling

Empowering

COTEC

PAPERS IN BJOT

Client Centred

Environmentally Grounded

Universities, Undergraduate & Postgraduate Degrees

Specialist Sections

ENOTHE

Required and Electronically Indexed

INTERNATIONAL GUEST SPEAKERS/ EDUCATORS

# Chapter 11

# Enabling Occupation and Client Centred Practice Towards Self Health

This penultimate chapter tells the story of happenings in occupational therapy during the last decade of the twentieth century. Across the globe anticipation grew as the new millennium approached, with suggestions and plans for new beginnings in almost every sphere of activity. It was no less so in occupational therapy, and how the professional Association and its members in the UK positioned themselves for an exciting and effective twenty-first century provides the substance of the chapter. Degrees and postgraduate opportunities were available at last. Alongside these a more holistic understanding of personal rights and responsibilities with regard to health and social justice; and a rebirth of ideas about the importance of occupation in all people's lives, gave added zest to forward planning.

# Context of the times: connecting globally

In Britain, the burgeoning of multiculturalism continued rapidly, as travel and relocation across Europe increased with the advent of the European Union. As well, global travel became an accepted part of business and leisure, with air services competing or co-operating to grab a lucrative and expanding market. Multiculturalism escalated too as people sought refugee status from far-flung corners of the globe. All impacted on local scenes, and as customs and styles of living changed, multiculturalism was variously bemoaned or tolerated, condemned or welcomed and celebrated, and multicultural policies become imperative.

Compounding any issues arising from multiculturalism, were changes within the employment market, with people often having to accept short-term work contracts rather than full time permanent jobs. Many were 'out of work' for short or long periods of time, and more than a few had to think about or make career changes more often than had previously been the case. Issues of social and community health assumed greater significance. Local authorities became increasingly involved in supporting different types of communities, by allocating resources and supporting initiatives established by small local groups, as well as by providing the services required of them by Health and Social Services Legislation. Occupational therapists were engaged in programmes addressing more than the traditional ways of life of earlier British custom, and in facilitating the development of self-help programmes for people with disabilities and socio-economic handicap. By the end of the century the value of what they had to offer was being recognised afresh at Government level when Lord Hunt, Minister of Health, launched *Meeting the Challenge: A Strategy for the Allied Health Professions* in November, 2000. That document set out the contribution of the Allied Health Professions to patient care, and highlighted their potential role to lead innovative approaches towards achieving the targets of the most recent NHS plans. The strategy acknowledged that the role of the Professions Allied to Medicine (PAMS) had been undervalued or neglected. It made a commitment to changing that, with the proposal to establish over 6,500 more therapists and other health professionals by 2004, to educating more, and to establishing new therapist consultant posts.[1]

A particular feature of this decade was the accelerating pace of information exchange. Rapid progress in the area of electronic information technology resulted in both new and old data being readily available in expanding spheres of interest, accessed from a computer terminal. That enabled people singly or collectively to become aware of, respond to, challenge, or influence ideas and theories as soon as they were published. The impact was global: communication could occur instantly between people in neighbouring rooms, around the country, or in distant locations worldwide. As a result, issues of importance in one country, such as the death of Princess Diana, Nelson Mandela's release from prison, warfare in the Middle East and General Schwarzkopf leading Desert Storm troops, the re-unification of Germany after 43 years, or floods in Bangladesh, became immediate concerns as unrestricted film and personal experiences were relayed across the world almost as they happened.

The same technologies facilitated global exchanges between people who shared similar interests and missions. Particular concerns of this decade, such as the fragile ecology, preservation of endangered species, the continuing prevalence of HIV/AIDS, and the growing numbers of asylum seekers, engaged diverse groups around the world. There was an increased emphasis on accountability of governments and social institutions. People were beginning to understand they had the right to determine their own future and, for example, in the health field, to participate in decisions about treatment options and approaches. In spite of, or because of, such understanding, many altruistic people held concerns about the social and health injustices experienced by huge numbers of people around the world. At times, the resources of diverse groups combined to address or compensate for such injustices as co-operation between many, but not all, countries and cultures led to greater levels of tolerance and understanding. Political differences and protecting separate identities became less important in some places, whilst in others fundamentalism gained ground to protect identity, religious, and cultural practices.

Within occupational therapy electronic communication enabled the strengthening of collaboration between Associations in Europe and other parts of the world. A case in point was the Committee of Occupational Therapists for the European Communities (COTEC) which flourished following its establishment in the previous decade after the success of the second European Congress held in London.[2] The membership rose throughout the 1990s to 21 national associations, with a number of others having observer status at meetings. A website advises of meetings held in different European countries twice a year to plan and co-ordinate the ongoing work.[3] The aim of the organisation is to enable national associations of occupational therapists in European countries to develop, harmonise, and improve standards of professional practice and education, as well as to advance the theory of occupational therapy throughout Europe. Financed entirely by member associations, COTEC not only supports the development of new associations, education and services, it has produced a European Code of Ethics, maintains collaborative links with European organisations, WFOT, and the World Health Organisation (WHO) amongst others; and supports a European Occupational Therapy Congress every four years. In 1994, COTEC delegates met at the WFOT Congress held in London. Jennifer Creek reported that delegates experienced a sense that occupational therapy is an expanding and dynamic profession with speakers emphasizing the value of its European and international nature.[4] At the Congress in Paris *ERGO 2000* held at the end of the century, Maeve Groom, from Derbyshire, UK, was elected as President.

**Figure 2.11.1:  COTEC delegates at a meeting held in Vienna in 1999. Maeve Groom is second from the left.** *(Courtesy of COTEC)*

As it is an organisation established during the last decades of the twentieth century, it is useful to consider how COTEC has defined itself in terms of goals and philosophical stance and to reflect on the constancies and differences found between these and those used in the early periods of the profession's establishment. Although the definition of occupational therapy it holds has changed little from earlier ones, the goal and philosophy reflects contemporary thought:

> *The goal of Occupational Therapy is to promote peoples' health and well being by enabling meaningful occupation. Occupational Therapists believe that health can be influenced by occupation.*
>
> *In partnership with the individual, the occupational therapist assesses the physical, psychological and social functions, identifies areas of dysfunction and involves the individual in a structured program of activities. The overall aim is to help each individual to achieve maximum independence and quality of life. The activities selected will relate to the individual's personal, social, cultural and economic needs and will reflect the environmental factors that govern his/her lifestyle.*
>
> *The philosophy of the profession is based on problem solving and on the use of a diversity of techniques. The emphases on the individual's ability to function adequately within his/her own environment requires that the occupational therapist is sensitive to social, technological and demographic influences and changes.*[5]

Notable differences are the emphasis on health and well-being as distinct from illness, the involvement of individual recipients of occupational therapy in problem solving, and the nature of lifestyle outcomes rather than 'cure,' along with recognition of the potential impact and importance of contextual circumstances.

Also facilitated by information technology is another organisation set up in 1995 by COTEC. This is the Educational Network for Occupational Therapists in Higher Education (ENOTHE) which links occupational therapy education programmes in Europe, assisting in the gathering and exchange of information about education issues. The Network works to set European standards according to WFOT guidelines and provides assistance to institutions seeking to start occupational therapy education programmes. The secretariat under the charge of Beryl Steeden was hosted at the British Association throughout most of the 1990s.

In other examples of global connections, Judy Briggs, the BAOT WFOT delegate from Nottinghamshire, UK, became one of four programme co-ordinators as part of the new management structure of WFOT, introduced at its 2000 Council meeting in Sapporo in Japan. A WFOT/BAOT joint initiative in the Gulf Region included a joint exhibition stand at *Rehab 2000* in Dubai, where a group for occupational therapists in the Middle East (OTMEG) was formed.[6]

# The Association

During this decade, as in previous ones, the BAOT experienced change and growth. The Code of Ethics was reviewed and altered to reflect end-of-the-century values, not once, but several times; negotiations and changes of Trade Union affiliation occurred; another move to a new headquarters became necessary; another WFOT Congress was hosted; and for the first time an occupational therapist was appointed as the Chief Executive of the professional organisation.

## Code of Ethics

The Code of Ethics was first reviewed during the decade in 1990. It was explained that the purpose of the Code was:

> ...to promote voluntary standards of professional behaviour. It has no status as a formal requirement for any certification award, made solely by the COT or in association with any other certification body.

> ...It is for guidance only and should not be seen as a definitive statement on professional conduct or behaviour.

> ...It is without prejudice and bestows no rights on any person for its indiscriminate use for purposes other than those stated above. It replaces any previous code in circulation. [7]

A couple of years after the review a series of articles *Ethics in Practice*[8] were published in BJOT in order to:

> ...familiarise members with the way in which the Code can and should be used to support them in everyday practice at all professional levels. By using actual problems and situations that have been brought to the Committee's attention in the past, each article will clarify and expand on one principle, showing how detailed reference to the 'Principle' and accompanying 'Notes' can suggest an appropriate course of action or resolution to the dilemma.[9]

Further reviews of the Code occurred in 1995 and in 2000. Mid-decade the Code provided a set of principles that recognised the COT's strong commitment to 'client-centred practice.'[10] It prescribed the response of occupational therapists towards clients as one that respected their individual needs, choices and circumstances.[11]

> Occupational therapists should at all times recognise and respect the autonomy of clients receiving their services, acknowledging their role in an episode of care, the need for client choice and the benefits of working in partnership. The occupational therapist is expected to act as an advocate for the client in relation to upholding the autonomy of the individual. Individual therapists have a responsibility to promote the dignity, privacy and safety of all clients with whom they come into contact.[12]

In the same tone the 2000 version recommends that 'services should be client centred and needs led'[13] because:

> Each client is unique and, therefore, brings an individual perspective to the occupational therapy process. Normally, clients have a right to make choices and decisions about their own health and independence, and such choices should be respected even when in conflict with professional opinion.[14]

Such statements became part of the messages published in some form or other by COT for consumer or service provider advice. A good example is provided by a leaflet Not Just

Quality of Care, Quality of Life about occupational therapy in residential and nursing homes. In this the philosophical beliefs of the therapists were described:

> We believe that occupations (activities) describe who you are and how you feel about yourself. If you are unable to do the things you want, or need to do, to live and enjoy your life, your general well-being may be affected. Occupation is important for everyone's life.[15]

This resurgence of commitment to occupation as a necessary component of health can be linked to the growth of models of practice such as Keilhofner's Model of Human Occupation[16], and the development of a new international discipline known as Occupational Science.

## Headquarters

It was a decade of anniversaries. In 1999 a Silver Jubilee celebration of the formation of the BAOT, following the profession's Diamond Jubilee in 1992 which had commemorated the formation of the first Association of Occupational Therapists in Britain sixty years earlier in Scotland.[17] To mark the latter anniversary, BJOT published a landmark historical review of SAOT, AOT, and BAOT/COT during the previous sixty years, compiled by Peggy Jay, Alicia Mendez, and Hester Monteath. In terms of the early 1990s, although regretting changes in the NHS which led to 'the erosion of some of our most senior managerial posts at District and Area levels,' they recognised beneficial changes that had taken place in the staffing of headquarters, noting that by 1992 key posts were:

> ...the Secretary/Chief Executive, Head of Professional Affairs/Deputy Secretary, Head of Industrial Relations and Head of Business Affairs. The very new post of Head of Professional Affairs/Deputy Secretary is held by an occupational therapist, as is the post of Disability Information and Study Centre Manager which was created last year. This is in line with policy adopted by other long-established professional associations.[18]

The number of positions and the range of duties of senior staff at headquarters changed as the decade progressed, so that at its finish the Association was serviced by three groups of staff to deliver the objectives of three Boards: Education and Practice, Membership and External Affairs, and Research and Development. The groups were managed by Group Heads, who were all occupational therapists, whilst a fourth Board concerned with Resource Management was in the direct charge of the Chief Executive. The latter is responsible for the day-to-day running of Headquarters, working with the Group Heads and together forming the Senior Management Team (SMT). There was also an Executive Management Group (EMG) which implements policies approved by Council and cannot make policy decisions without reference to it. There is also a Secretariat. Officers concerned with Clinical Audits and Effectiveness; a COT Advisory Service; Pre and Post Registration; Professional Affairs; Regional Support; Specialist Sections; Support Workers; and Students were in place. Other people employed at Headquarters are involved in a wide variety of areas, including administration, finance, membership, catering, communications and the library. By the late 1990s there were six co-opted members of Council:

- the Department of Health Occupational Therapy Officer
- the Occupational Therapy Advisor to the Scottish Executive
- the BAOT COTEC delegate
- the BAOT WFOT delegate

- a representative from the BAOT/UNISON (Trade Union) Occupational Therapy Panel
- a representative nominated by the CPSM Occupational Therapists' Board.

**Figure 2.11.2: College of Occupational Therapists Organisational Chart 2000**

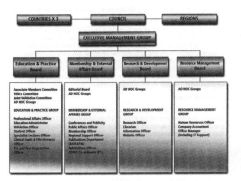

The three management groups at Headquarters, which deal with the day-to-day concerns of members, and the growth, development and promotion of the profession, are extremely active. In the year 1999–2000, the External Affairs team dealt with over 5000 enquiries from the media, issued over 200 media statements, handled nearly 3000 requests for publicity materials, provided courses, conferences, and seminars for some 2000 delegates, published 80 peer reviewed articles in BJOT, and generated £1,337,190 in advertising revenue. The Education and Practice team made 108 visits to occupational therapy training departments, gave 194 presentations on education, training and practice, held 28 workshops on clinical governance, and dealt with over 3000 enquiries about professional practice and other issues. The Research and Development team was directly involved in 16 partnership projects, produced 5 new publications, dealt with over 7000 enquiries, responded to 13 consultation documents, and presented at 14 seminars, courses, and workshops.[19]

In 1999, the Scottish Parliament, and Assemblies in Wales and Northern Ireland, assumed devolved responsibility for health and social services.[20] This led to BAOT Country Boards being established further to the activity of the Devolution Working Group. These new structures were put in place and members elected to sit on them. The Boards are mandated to liaise with their respective national assemblies on behalf of BAOT/COT. Receiving an annual budget to assist them, and remaining an integral part of and supported by officers employed by the Association, they were formed to take forward local issues in their countries, such as in education and workforce planning. They all represent occupational therapy to statutory, voluntary and private sectors; influence the planning and delivery of the integrated health and social care services; and maintain effective communication links between the members and Headquarters. The Scottish Board works with a devolved Scottish Parliament, and the Welsh and Irish Boards provide information to their respective Assemblies. An elected member from each of the three Boards has a seat on the Association's Executive Management Group as well as a seat at Council.

**Figure 2.11.3:  Gwilym Roberts, Group Head, Education and Practice and Mary Gilbert, Cardiff School, uphold the Welsh flag**

Also in 1999, Council of COT, to facilitate the achievement of 'healthy outcomes through occupation,' produced a new Vision Statement: 'Members First.' To benefit all users of occupational therapy it aimed to provide the 'highest standard of expert, professional opinion and advice informed by research, scholarship, innovation and the promotion of excellence in practice'; 'timely, responsive, specialist support for all members'; and the establishment of an accountable, responsive, learning professional organisation, managed with integrity, probity and sound financial stewardship.[21] In October 2000 Sheelagh Richards, who had been Occupational Therapy Officer at the Department of Health, and a former COT Chairman of Council, was appointed the new Chief Executive. The first woman as well as the first occupational therapist to take the role, in line with the vision statement and the client centred approach of the Code of Ethics, she proposed at the time of her appointment that the profession needed to 'develop new frameworks, which start with users of our service.'[22] In the Annual Report 1999–2000 she talked about partnerships:

*'Partnership' is now at the top of the Government agenda, but once again, it has been a strong theme in the College's Activities. Those partnerships span statutory agencies, international networks and organisations that represent the profession's service users. It is particularly pleasing to see a greatly enhanced level of joint working with other health and social care professionals—on research, clinical effectiveness and audit, education and training activities, and on the development of the proposed new regulatory framework. It is through such collaboration that we break down age-old barriers which inhibit best practice and through which we better understand and value the role of other colleagues.[23]*

**Figure 2.11.4:  Sheelagh Richards: The first occupational therapist Chief Executive of BAOT/COT**

Richards took up office in the purpose-designed headquarters, situated in Borough High Street close by the former one at Marshalsea Road. The new facility was opened in 1998 by HRH, the Princess Royal.[24] Four floors of the building house a library, and spacious meeting and conference facilities available for use by members in addition to the offices and workstations of staff and executive. By chance it connects in a small way with a site of historic interest to occupational therapists, in that from some of its windows Red Cross Hall, Cottages and Gardens, where Elizabeth Casson worked for Octavia Hill early in the century, are clearly visible.

**Figure 2.11.5:  The opening of the Borough High Street headquarters**

Casson would have been pleased at the developments of the profession she was so instrumental in establishing in the UK. The rapid need for more extensive Headquarters buildings certainly highlights the growth of its members. By the 1999–2000 annual report, these numbered 22 130.

**Table 2.11.1:  Number of members per category and percentage increases from 1997-2000**

| Categories | 1997/98 | 1998/99 | %increase | 1998/99 | 1999/2000 | %increase |
|---|---|---|---|---|---|---|
| Professional members | 13755 | 15,072 | 9.5 | 15,072 | 16,102 | 6.8 |
| Associate members | 1473 | 1,285 | -12.76 | 1,285 | 1,267 | -1.4 |
| Overseas members | 375 | 403 | 7.4 | 403 | 432 | 7.1 |
| Retired members | 90 | 130 | 44.4 | 130 | 166 | 27.6 |
| Students | 4419 | 3,992 | -9.6 | 3,992 | 4,131 | 3.5 |
| Others | | 32 | | 32 | 32 | |
| Total | 20112 | 20914 | 3.9% | 20914 | 22130 | 5.8% |

Note that the students figures above are not a true reflection of the actual end of year figures as some students obtain professional memberships before the end of the membership year in October.

Over the years a number of organisations had supported the work of the profession. It is timely to note two that were still important at the end of the century. One was the Occupational Therapists Board of the Council for Professions Supplementary to Medicine (CPSM). This had a statutory function quite different from the protective, and welfare roles of COT or BAOT to promote member interests. The Occupational Therapists Board, from the time of the 1960 PSM Act, had scrutinised and approved training establishments, courses and qualifications, standards of behaviour and practice, and had published an annual register of state registered practitioners. Elected representatives of the profession who regulated in the interest of the public, consisted of nine registered occupational therapists including two from Scotland, one from Wales, and one, without voting rights, from Northern Ireland. In addition there were five medical practitioners, a person from industry or technical education, a teaching member of a University, and one other. A Board Member was co-opted onto the COT Council to aid collaboration between the Board and the Professional Body and observer status to the Board given to the College. As the 1990s drew to a close, plans for new legislation and a Health Professions Council to replace the CPSM were in place.

There was also the Federation of Professional Organisations (FPO) of the Professional and Technical 'A' (PTA) Whitley Council, which had been formed in May 1981. The FPO was 'listed' by the Trades Union Certification Officer, and BAOT was a very active member as one of the eight constituent organisations.[25] It ceased to function in the mid 90s as the industrial relations climate for the allied health professions started to change.

To meet the demands of membership to be represented at local and national levels of bargaining, the Industrial Relations section at BAOT headquarters had, by 1992, grown from a single officer some 13 years earlier to four officers based in London, a further three who were field-based, and administrative support.[26] The following year, a decision was taken that the principal trade union functions should best be carried out in conjunction with a national union, in the light of the fragmentation of the NHS into Trusts and the threat to local pay bargaining. Following a ballot of the membership, an agreement was signed with UNISON, the largest union in the UK, for provision of trade union services to BAOT members. By 2000, all UNISON regions had occupational therapist contact officers, and most had regional stewards. These met at a successful seminar Partnerships—BAOT/UNISON and Health and Social Services held at Coventry in November 1999 where they were joined by a significant number of local government and health based stewards.[27]

## Information, publishing, archiving, and advertising

The Disability, Information and Study Centre (DISC) at the Marshalsea Road headquarters was established in the summer of 1991 to provide information from a centralised resource about occupational therapy and related fields.[28] The products generated by DISC began to appear in the professional journal. For example, in January 1995 information resources and a study day about work practice were promoted.[29] The first Register of Current Research, containing subject index, abstract and researcher contact details was published in 1995, and in 1996 a PhD network was established to share information and advice among those undertaking a research degree. Further to the move to expanded facilities in the Borough High Street premises it became the College of Occupational Therapists Library.

An enquiry service is open every working week day afternoon. It is designed to assist professional development in either practice or research, and to that end literature searches and current research listings are available. During 1999–2000 there were 1331 visitors to the library, 941 enquiries, 1651 literature searches conducted, 258 theses loaned, and 7466 photocopies dispatched. In line with this the College website has expanded from 20 pages to more than 200. The aim is to use the site as an interactive communication tool for members and external audiences, and to support COT becoming a knowledge community and cyber society.[30]

The BAOT/COT continued to provide two major publications each month—the *British Journal of Occupational Therapy* and *Occupational Therapy News.*

The *British Journal of Occupational Therapy* remains the 'public face' of occupational therapy in the UK. In addition to articles of practice and research interest the monthly publication, edited by Upma Barnett, publishes items of general interest such as lists of Council Members and Regional Officers, Committee Reports, news about WFOT, Letters to the Editor, Book and Equipment Reviews, and Announcements. Since 1978, when the BAOT became a trades union, only clinical and professional matters can appear within its pages. This is because, as the official publication of the COT, to retain the registered charity status formerly enjoyed by AOT anything affecting salaries or conditions of service must be excluded.

Greg Kelly made a review of letters published over sixty years, and found that issues of contemporary interest had been evident in very early correspondence, such as the standardised tests referred to in 1939 by Miss English, the founding sub-editor, and the call for research and scientific method by Joyce Hombersley in 1944. Those topics were two of the themes Kelly extrapolated from his review. Others were concerned with: spirituality and religion; other therapies; a change of title; and issues of gender.[31]

One of the roles of *BJOT* has been to encourage directions taken by the professional body, although it is limited to some extent according to the types of paper submitted. From time to time it has run special themed editions, such as in the 1999–2000 year when it offered an edition concentrating on older people and falls, one on sexuality and gender, and another on occupational science. *BJOT* is now research based. As well as the results of particular studies, over the years, it has featured papers about research methods, how to disseminate findings and the process of research as well. During the 1990s, such papers have ranged from the role of a Research Ethics Committee,[32] to a series titled *Symposium on Writing for Publication*, which included how to write a research article.[33] Articles have described the process of research, such as Jenkins' personal reflection of research as 'a cathartic exercise.'[34] The problems of conducting a multi-centre rehabilitation trial were discussed,[35] and philosophical approaches underpinning research methods have been explored. Kelly, for example, described the hermeneutic approach.[36] In such ways BJOT continued to build up the evidence base for the profession. However, in a review of the literature in BJOT from 1989–1996, Gail Mountain found that the majority of papers were descriptive in nature:

> Of the papers with a research orientation, the most reported area of interest was physical disability. However much of this research was small scale and there was a notable absence of funded projects. Nevertheless, the number of papers describing research activity increased markedly during the latter years, as did the application of evidence-based material.[37]

As well as the Journal, *Occupational Therapy News*, with its different brief of being the key member news tool of the Association, has also provided a forum for discussion among members at all levels. It is less formal and more political than its fellow publication. Using the final issue for 2000 as a sample, in that edition can be found: news of someone struck off the Occupational Therapists Register, and comment relating to that from the Occupational Therapists Board of the CPSM; news of the launch of the Government strategy for PAMS; a report of occupational therapists being 'overstretched' in local authorities; the scrutiny of the occupational therapy service of the North Lakeland Trust by the Commission for Health Improvement; a report of a national conference which considered the Audit Commission's survey of community equipment services; an article about the BAOT personal accident policy; another about celebrating diversity in the NHS; a short paper on race equality; an HIV/Aids feature; others about the Cochrane Collaboration (an international organisation that aims to help people make informed decisions about health care through systematic reviews), and virtual conferencing; and 14 pages of classified advertisements.[38]

Other special publications for the whole membership produced and managed from headquarters have included various pamphlets promoting the profession or providing careers advice; handbooks for occupational therapy helpers and technical staff; directories of private practitioners and other specialist sections of COT; Annual Reports; and Occupational Therapists' Reference Books and Membership Handbooks. Five Occupational Therapists' Reference Books were produced between 1983 and 1992. In the Forward to one of the earliest editions, Julia Robbins, Chairman of Council, described their purpose as 'for the use of practising Occupational Therapists who have seen the need for an authoritative, concise and up-to-date publication containing most of the facts and information which they need to have at hand daily in their work.'[39] Over the years a wealth of COT promotional leaflets, posters, and goods for a wide range of audiences explained occupational therapy. That culminated in 1998 when a series of leaflets, posters, and newspaper adverts, published as the first national advertising campaign *Able to Make You Able*, was unveiled.

**Figure 2.11.6:** *Able to Make You Able* **campaign**

A copy of most of these publications is now housed in the archival section of the Wellcome Institute for the History of Medicine in London. The BAOT/COT established the Archive there in 1997 because:

> ...*The Institute will ensure that the collection is put in safe storage, catalogued and made available for academic study under secure conditions. Work started on 13 August, 1997 when the material held at headquarters was collected and transported to the Wellcome Institute for cataloguing by the archivist. It will eventually be housed in the Contemporary Medical Archives Centre of the Wellcome Institute at 183 Euston Rd, London NW1 2BP, where it will join that of the Chartered Society of Physiotherapy and other similar bodies.*[40]

## National and international conferences

In the 1990s the College held its annual conferences at various sites throughout the country as had become the current trend, and in 1998 Belfast was the chosen venue giving occupational therapists from Northern Ireland the opportunity to host the event for the first time. Its theme was *Occupation for Health*, which not only was a sign of the changing interests of the times, but also provided the title and theme for this history. Illustrative of the journey from self-health to prescription and back to self-health was a paper by Dr Frances Reynolds, a psychologist from Brunel University, which received much acclaim. Almost a blast from the past, and a possible portent of the future, her paper *Alleviating stress through creative activity: a qualitative study of needlework practitioners* told how 36 of the 40 participants used embroidery to manage their depression or anxiety. Gaynor Sadlo, in her account of the paper, argued that 'a relatively simple research design, well conducted, can yield important information to add to our understanding of occupation.' She added, 'Although needlework was the craft in this study, similar results might be found for any creative activity. It seemed to me that these subjects became their own occupational therapists, in the real sense.'[41] Sheelagh Richards gave an outstanding Casson Memorial Lecture, which she titled *Occupation for Health—and Wealth?* In this she provided an insightful view of Government, linking national initiatives with those of occupational therapy and exhorting the profession to a more active political future, a theme that other Casson lecturers have argued is important.[42]

In April 1994, BAOT welcomed the 11th World Federation of Occupational Therapists Congress to London. The theme was 'Developing Opportunities' and Margaret Ellis was the convener. The opening ceremony took place at The Royal Albert Hall, with people from over fifty countries attending. Keynote speakers were Michelle Hahn from Brazil, Chris Henrikson from Sweden, and Jenny Wilson from Uganda; and a further 1200 presentations of some form or other were accepted on a wide range of topics. Keen to involve the maximum number of people, in part, to help them acquire financial support to attend, the scientific committee led by Naomi Fraser-Holland, offered varied lengths of time for presentations, some as short as 4 minutes in Discussion Sessions.[43]

The wide range of topics included some traditional interests—such as mental handicap where the use of holistic practice, music workshops, Keilhofner's *Model of Human Occupation*, sheltered and supported employment, and computer training were reported as being found effective.[44] Many papers addressed issues relating to children, such as adventure play, communication, developmental assessment of pre-schoolers, and a feedback system for attention deficit hyperactivity. One given by Elizabeth Harris, a second year student from the London School, was awarded the best paper relating to children. She described her own interactions in the life of children in a Romanian institution, prior to and following her becoming an occupational therapy student, and the effectiveness of the application of what she was learning.[45] Community Care was also a popular topic, with overcoming physical, cultural and social barriers one of its themes. Community-based rehabilitation was another. The involvement of communities, families and people with disabilities in decision making, planning and evaluation of rehabilitation was addressed by several speakers as they described work with local people trained for a short time by professionals visiting developing or disadvantaged countries. Many speakers were in tune with theme of person centred practice, which was described as one of the highlights of the Congress.[46]

In a three hour seminar on building bridges between people who use and people who provide services, Sheelagh Richards reflected, sadly, on the pervasive nature of passive and patronising stereotypes which portray 'the disabled' within society. Campaigning for change and seeking to foster collaborative partnerships between users and providers she reminded delegates of the United Nations rules concerning equalisation of opportunities. Nick Stone, in his recording of the forum, argued that services should be provided in a way that was neither judgmental nor prescriptive whether the people occupational therapists worked alongside were disabled by ill-health, poverty, ethnicity, sexuality or other factors. In similar vein, in his summing up of the Congress at the closing ceremony,[47] The Rt Hon. Nicholas Scott, Minister for Disabled People, talked about the need felt by disabled people not to be the recipients of special favours, but rather to have barriers removed. Occupational therapy was important in that, he said, and in changing the attitudes of society as a whole because disabled people had 'pools of ability still untapped.'[48]

The Congress was preceded by the WFOT 21st Council Meeting, the largest held to that date, in Edinburgh. There were 63 delegates representing 40 countries. The outgoing president, Maria Schwartz, planted a tree outside the Astley Ainslie Hospital to commemorate the meeting and the 40th anniversary of the first WFOT Congress in

Edinburgh. She exhorted delegates to:

> ...*speak up at all levels and articulate our contribution but we also have to convince by results....To meet the increasing challenges we are well advised to strengthen our transnational network, exchanging expertise across geographical and cultural borders.*[49]

Barbara Tyldesley, from the UK was elected as the new WFOT president.

Tyldesley, at the 1999 COT Annual Conference, held at the University of Liverpool provided a wonderful, but very different, Casson Memorial Lecture. She told the story of Liverpool's great occupational therapy pioneer, Constance Owens. It is a great story, told in brief in Appendix B of this history, and illustrates how one person can create, change and shape the world we live in:

> *The present location of her [Constance Owens'] 'original school' within the Medical Faculty of the University of Liverpool would have been the fulfillment of her dreams and academic aspirations for the profession.*[50]

At the final conference of the decade held at Keele University, Kay East, Chairman of Council, echoed Maria Schwartz's words when she called for British occupational therapists to be a 'powerful voice with Government.' As a starter, she urged members to lobby their Council members to speak up, as only about one-third of them did so at meetings. Council Members, in response, suggested that Council was too large and unwieldy, had a huge agenda which prevents discussion, and that it was 'a rubber stamping body.' They experienced difficulties in getting comment or even interest from members in their regions.[51] Earlier in the year, as a member of the Government Modernisation Action team, East had explained that this was the 'chance to shape the future of the NHS and of our profession, and we have to make the most of it.' She asked members to make their views known as part of the Department of Health campaign to receive public comment by letters, leaflets, public meetings and e-mail.[52]

# Education

Teamwork and interdisciplinary study were becoming integral in professional education at all levels. They were being explored and implemented in undergraduate courses, and at professional association level. For example, a Health Care Professions Education Forum had been launched in 1989 to identify issues of multi-professional concern, for collaboration in projects of common benefit, and to co-ordinate efforts in tackling current educational issues and development. The Forum's Constitution was published in Autumn 1991, with committee posts being rotated among representatives from the wide range of health care professions which made up the Forum. Membership included: the British Dietetic Association, the British Orthoptic Society, the British Psychological Society, the Chartered Society of Physiotherapy, the College of Radiographers, the College of Speech Therapists, the English National Board for Nursing, Midwifery and Health Visiting, the Institute of Medical Laboratory Sciences, and the Society of Chiropodists, as well as the College of Occupational Therapists.

The 1991 Annual Conference, held at the University of East Anglia, had 'Education and Advancement into 2000' as its theme. This was appropriate, for by this time degrees for pre-registration education were becoming a reality for all occupational therapists after decades of commitment, hard work and much lobbying. Postgraduate opportunities were also expanding. But the change was not welcomed by everyone. There were those who thought occupational therapists would be over qualified for the jobs they did,[53] and that degrees would lead to the ultimate demise of the profession.[54] Rosemary Barnitt in the Casson Memorial Lecture given at the 1991 Conference dared to present those negative ideas for inspection. Following the conference, Sandra Benson, Chairman of the Education and Research Board of COT, picked up another concern caused by the introduction of degrees. That was the anxieties felt by a large number of the profession who regarded their qualification as of lesser status. Benson reminded everyone that the Blom-Cooper Commission had found the Diploma equivalent to an ordinary degree, and also pointed to the availability of post registration opportunities such as those that allowed part-time credit accumulation.[55] The subject was revisited some years later, when a survey of occupational therapists in education, practice and management found it remained a matter of concern.[56]

Barnitt had started by reminding her audience of Casson's link with education and, 'clearly a lady of tactics and politics', of her tenacity in the face of apparently hopeless odds.[57] Following in the founder's tenacious footsteps, Barnitt went on to talk about politics and education.

> It is now five years since I advised our first student who had been elected to the National Union of Students how to man a picket line...It is now four years since the student body asked me why our professional body, and in particular the Journal, was not running articles and leaders on political issues as were evident in the medical and nursing journals. In other words why weren't we fighting systems which led to inequity for students, patients, and social services and NHS staff.
>
> ...We are no longer in a position to avoid political activity and to leave it to our Union representatives and Council members to deal with those issues on their own.[58]

With regard to that student's query, however, it should be noted that the rules of the Charity Commission preclude COT (a registered charity) from political activity, and this applies to *BJOT*, which is produced by the College. The restriction, however, does not apply to *OT News* (a BAOT product).

In turning to discuss what would happen when occupational therapists with degrees entered the workforce, where management was drawn increasingly from non-health professional personnel, Barnitt recommended making them aware:

> ...that therapists with degrees are not being educated to sit in ivory towers doing research and keeping clear of patients who want to go to the lavatory. Our degree students will be able to initiate, process and evaluate their service delivery. If dressing, making cups of tea and toast, and carrying out home visits are still the bedrock of professional practice, these are the therapists the degree programmes will produce. However I would also expect them to challenge this existing practice and make recommendations about who should deliver these skills to the patient.[59]

Perhaps Barnitt's paper was one factor provoking a more proactive political stance. For example, in *OT News*, May 2000, Darren Ayres, a second year student at Canterbury Christ Church University College, wrote about how 'we shouted at the Government'! He explained that was not literally, but 'by a petition drop in which 38 000 members of the public committed their support in the hope of obtaining more money for occupational therapy.' He described how he had learned well, in his course, that the promotion of occupational therapy is as important as 'assessment, planning, intervention and reflection,' and how he, with five more from his school, had donned uniform to join with others who made the drop at 10 Downing Street.[60] This initiative was part of a national petition drive organised by the COT External Affairs team to raise awareness of workforce and resource shortages. A letter writing campaign, urging members to write to their Members of Parliament or Assemblies was launched at the same time.[61] Although successful, in view of East's comments noted above and which were made a few months later, there remained much to be done. On the question of workforce shortages, Christine Craik made a plea not to regard those who moved to another area of employment as a loss. Instead, she said, occupational therapists should be encouraged to seek positions where they could exert an influence in positive ways, creating policy and participating in decision making in other spheres of endeavour based on the philosophies, principles and values of occupational therapy which they took with them.[62]

By the end of the decade twenty-one universities and colleges offered occupational therapy degree programmes over three years. These were at Aberdeen, Canterbury, Cardiff, Coventry, Derby, Edinburgh, Exeter, Glasgow, Lancaster, Liverpool, London (Brunel University), Middlesborough, Newcastle, Northampton, Norwich, Oxford, Salford, Sheffield, Southampton, York, and Ulster. In addition, in Eastbourne and London Hospital Medical College, two year accelerated courses for graduates of other disciplines were offered, and four year part time in-service courses for mature students employed in health or social services were available in Bristol, Crawley, Essex, London (Southbank University), and York. All WFOT-approved courses, they are jointly monitored and validated by COT and the CPSM, although the degree is awarded by the particular institution of higher education which the student attends. Students can be funded privately, but most have financial help from bursaries provided by Regional Health or Local Education Authorities. Global connections are possible at student level with opportunities for links and exchanges within Europe and, farther afield, in Australia, Hong Kong, and the USA. The stories of the courses are told in Appendix A.

**Figure 2.11.7:  Map indicating qualifying courses in Occupational Therapy**

In June 2000, pre-registration students were accepted as student members of BAOT. Before that they had not been included in the Articles of Association and had no recognition within it. Instead, all had been registered with the COT, which provided educational support and professional indemnity insurance cover. Ritchard Ledgerd, COT Student Officer, explained that 'the move demonstrates the organisation's commitment to supporting students, and recognises their contribution as stakeholders in the profession's future.'[63]

**Figure 2.11.8:   Pictured at COT Conference in Keele are students from York and Bristol with COT President Baroness Dean and COT Student Officer Ritchard Ledgerd**

A most timely event in the Diamond Jubilee year was the award to Averil Stewart of the first chair of occupational therapy in the UK. Head of the Department of Occupational Therapy at Queen Margaret College in Edinburgh, Professor Stewart's award recognised her professional leadership over many years.[64] In her Inaugural Professorial Lecture, 'Empowerment and Enablement: Occupational Therapy 2001' Stewart concluded:

> ...we have come a long way as a profession over the past 60 years: from working within institutions, where discipline, control, and work ethics had considerable influence, to now giving opportunities for personal development and choice with emphasis on community living.
>
> Changes have never been more rapid than over the past decade. Government policies, hospital trusts, privatisation, and community care provide many challenges...
>
> Health care professionals and many others are being exhorted by the Government to empower their clients and enable them to choose and live their own lifestyles....I hope, however, that I have demonstrated that occupational therapists have long held such attitudes and that we are truly enabling people to achieve their aspirations.[65]

Prior to receiving that honour, in the 1992 Casson Memorial Lecture Stewart had recognised the newer directions the profession was taking towards self-health, by initiatives aimed at illness prevention and health promotion. Applying the principles of occupational therapy to all people, not only those with medically diagnosed disability, she explained how:

> we have moved from close partnerships with individual patients to more global partnerships, collaborating with teams in the promotion of health. In promoting healthy

*living, therapists should apply to themselves some of the values and coping strategies which they present to their clients.*[66]

By the end of the century, there were three professors of occupational therapy in the UK, as Pamela Eakin in Northern Ireland, and Surya Shah in England were appointed to personal chairs.

In 1994, at the WFOT Congress, there were many sessions about education, and presentations from UK participants expressed wide-ranging interests. In one about course development, Gaynor Sadlo described a problem-based learning approach used at the London School and presented the results of an international survey that supported its use. Problem-based learning was fast becoming a favoured teaching approach in many occupational therapy schools. In another session about opportunities to learn, Martin Boey considered what was needed in the move away from the medical model towards occupational science. He suggested a shift in paradigms within education so that holism, client-centredness and problem solving became the underpinning elements. Margaret Robinson, from the University of Northumbria, spoke about how a Personal Competencies Model had been adopted for that University's pre-registration occupational therapy course. The model had the advantage of providing a lifelong record of personal development. Rona Howard from University College, Salford, argued for creative, reflective thinking, problem solving, adaptiveness and 'vision in a changing world' in preference to 'competence', and a student from Queen Margaret College, Caroline Symons, highlighted positive experiences, good role models, enthusiasm, prompt feedback, and learning contracts. Naomi Fraser-Holland challenged the student educator relationship suggesting that partnership and self directed learning would promote increased skills and responsibility and, with some similarity, Sue Beecraft described the use of interview, participant observation, and small group discussion without formal structure to facilitate reflective practice. Both the Fraser-Holland and Beecraft papers related to accelerated graduate entry course students. Barbara Tyldesley discussed a national survey on the relevance of studying anatomy and found that 95% of the sample agreed it was essential. In a totally different vein, Greg Kelly talked about the relevance of Zen ideas to complement Western Science. He argued that asking the right questions was as important as problem setting in clinical reasoning. The use of inter-professional educators was the focus of Anne Loch's paper, and was also the topic addressed by T. N. Evans and Lisa Scobbie—although they considered it within post-graduate education. With undergraduates, Elizabeth Cracknell described a lighthearted 'How to Study' workshop for new students at the Northampton School at the start of their programme, as helpful in addressing any illiteracy problems. With regard to fieldwork, Daphne Piegrome compared UK and USA evaluation tools and questioned the reliability and validity of differing models used by the different schools across Britain, whilst Helena Culshaw described a 'needs of the service' approach using a clinical audit model. Catherine F. Paterson considered methods of student selection having that found time pressures made the traditional use of interviewing difficult, and Irene Ilott spoke about investigating student failure in order to ensure the quality of graduating occupational therapists.[67,68, 69, 70]

# Practice: occupational and client centred

Not only were conceptual statements being made about education issues, they were also made in relation to practice. It is enlightening to consider examples as a background for understanding the changing nature of practice. A COT position statement, for example, about core skills and concepts for practice in the mid-1990s put forward the values and beliefs on which practice was based. They differed greatly from those of the early formative years of the profession in the UK, when such statements were tied to medical prescription. The following extract demonstrates re-adoption of something similar to the probably unspoken occupation for self-health values of early humans as discussed in Volume 1 of this history—plus, of course, the addition of occupational therapist's intervention:

*Occupational therapists seek the active involvement of people, empowering them to be participants and partners in improving their life skills. This enables them to influence their own environment and to maintain and enhance their own health and opportunities.*

*The partnership involves the understanding and creative use of the environment and resources; the person's abilities, skills and aspirations; and the occupational therapist's broadly based knowledge and experience.* [71]

**Figure 2.11.9:** **The essential role of occupational therapy in cost effective primary care**[72]

The unique core skills of occupational therapy were listed as:

*The use of purposeful activity and meaningful occupation as therapeutic tools in the promotion of health and well-being.*

*The ability to enable people to explore, achieve and maintain balance in the daily living tasks and roles of personal and domestic care, leisure and productivity.*

*The ability to assess the effect of, and then to manipulate, physical and psychosocial environments to maximise function and social integration.*

*The ability to analyse, select and apply occupations as specific therapeutic media to treat people who are experiencing dysfunction in daily living tasks, interactions and occupational roles.*[73]

The word 'occupation' was beginning to replace 'activity,' which had taken pride of place since the 1960s. Irene Ilott went so far as to title an article *Let's Have a Moratorium on Activities (the Word, not the Deed)*. She did this to promote pride in the word which features in the profession's name. Occupation, she wrote, suffered from misuse, embarrassment and intermittent proposals to change that name. The time was right, she argued, with the increasing interest in and understanding of humans as occupational beings, and illustrated the argument with quotes from Helene Polatajko's Muriel Driver Lecture for the Canadian Association[74] that 'occupational therapy enables a powerful need—occupation' and that 'occupational therapy is enabling living.'[75] Others, too, debated this issue; Janet Golledge, for example, in 1998, suggested that both the terms *occupation and purposeful activity* should be used. *Activity*, used by itself, was thought to be different and not favoured.[76]

In mid-decade Christine Craik described some of the other issues that occupational therapists had to take into account in practice, apart from planning, implementing and evaluating treatment:

> *Now we have become accustomed to considering more than just our own judgement: we take into account contracts, current target groups and catchment areas and debate about which profession should be involved in treatment. Now there are other people— consumers, managers, purchasers and other members of the multidisciplinary team— affecting the direction and priorities of occupational therapy…How confident are we that those who influence our practice fully understand the complexities of occupational therapy, with its emphasis on working with clients to achieve their goals, the use of activity as the focus of intervention, the adoption of an holistic framework and the measurement of quality of life as an outcome?[77]*

Such lack of understanding, she believed could restrict and inhibit the evolution of new aspects of work.

There are other pressures, too, which prevent occupational therapists from being able to enable and empower clients towards health though the occupations they need and want to engage in. Sharon Green described it vividly in a BJOT editorial *Dealing with Paradoxes*. First she talked about how the use of the word 'end-users' in relation to the role of patients and clients in research made her feel uncomfortable, as the image did not match a client-centred practice ideal. Next she described how students were disappointed at the little use of occupation in the therapeutic processes they shared in final fieldwork placements. It was replaced with 'assessing, home visiting and arranging equipment' along with 'ever-increasing paperwork, electronic mail items and planning meetings', which, ironically, were meant to aid rather than prevent them from engaging in quality treatment. Green sympathised with them:

> *…as on a particularly quiet day in a nursing home a staff nurse responded to my question on the value of an activity programme for elderly mentally ill people with 'Well, of course it is valuable; it is activity that gives life its meaning, isn't it?…but there just isn't the time; the work has to be done first.'[78]*

In part as a result of such scenarios, despite commitment to a revisited and strengthening philosophical and theoretical base, Rosemary Hagedorn, in the 1995 Casson Memorial Lecture, urged occupational therapists to become more visible, cautioning that:

> *…there is still a gap between our professional perceptions of the scope and potential of our interventions, and the distorted image that others perceive.…To be visible, one must be sure of being seen; it is a matter of confidence, of pride, of making positive statements about ourselves.[79]*

Arguing that the four core components of occupational therapy are the person, the occupation, the therapist and the environment, she identified occupation as the unique element forming the focus and vehicle for therapy. She went on to describe various kinds of models to help explain the richness and diversity of practice, and as a base for personal paradigms. These, she said, depended on education based on a new version of the 'three Rs'—reasoning, reflection and research.

## Evidence-based practice

The word 'occupation,' which had made a comeback in the previous decade, was being used increasingly. As well as it becoming a catchword, the need for practice to be evidence based, also became recognised as a central issue. It was addressed by Pamela Eakin, in the 1997 Casson Memorial Lecture, who concluded that 'evidence based practice is an issue, indeed a duty, for all occupational therapists.'

> *The challenge for the profession is to shift the balance, now and in the future, towards the integration of research and practice into a seamless whole for the benefit of those who use our services and for the development of the profession.*[80]

The concept of evidence-based practice was picked up in a special issue of BJOT published in November 1997[81]. Other special issues highlighting the interdependence of clinical audit[82] and clinical governance[83] followed. Taylor's *Evidence-Based Practice for Occupational Therapists* published in 2000, described how, over the last three decades, management of health care had developed from principles of efficiency ('doing things cheaply') and quality ('doing things better'). That did not always result in the 'best' intervention being used. Management was, in those cases, in conflict with the health and social care practitioner's philosophy, particularly if it was not possible to argue that the 'best' intervention was based on anything other than common sense. This suggested the need for practice being underpinned by sound evidence.[84]

The term 'evidence-based practice' is easy to confuse with 'research' and 'audit' because of the many similarities between them. All are systematic processes for finding evidence or information to improve interventions. However, research aims to generate new knowledge, whilst audit and evidence-based practice aim to review and improve interventions, the first of these using existing practice, and the second existing knowledge as the focus of the review process. Table 2.11.2 is how Taylor summarises the crucial differences.

**Table 2.11.2: Comparison of research, audit and evidence-based practice**[85]

| Research | Audit | Evidence-based practice |
|---|---|---|
| Systematic investigation to increase the sum of knowledge | Systematic approach to improvements and mechanisms to bring them about | Systematic review of evidence to identify possible guide to clinical interventions |
| Aims to identify the most effective form of treatment | Aims to compare actual performance against agreed standards of practice | Aims to use evidence to underpin clinical decision making, intervention and outcome |
| Results extend to the general population | Results apply only to the population examined | Results apply to a particular problem |
| May be a one-off study | The process is ongoing and continuous | Philosophy for decision making |
| Data collection is complex, new data being collected | Data collection is via records and follow-up of patients | Data is drawn from existing research |

As part of the debate that followed the session held on evidence-based practice at the 1997 Annual Conference, the subject of randomised controlled trials (RCTs) became quite a hot topic. Many saw this form of research as being foisted on them by the medical establishment and as an inappropriate tool to assess the effectiveness of occupational therapy interventions. Andrew Clegg and Katrina Bannigan sought to present a more balance view in an 'Opinion' paper published in *BJOT*. They concluded that, 'RCTs are the most appropriate method for assessing different therapeutic, diagnostic and preventive interventions, where some doubt exists as to their relative effectiveness, safety, acceptability or cost effectiveness.' However, despite that, they added 'RCTs should not be used to the exclusion of other methodological designs' as other tools may be more appropriate to provide evidence of effectiveness of some kinds of practice.[86]

As part of the initiatives towards evidence-based practice, in July 2000 COT launched a Clinical Audit Network Database to enable therapists to make contact with others when carrying out an audit.[87] This contains a national collection of audits carried out by occupational therapists in various practice settings. It is linked to the Clinical Improvements Database on the website of the National Institute for Clinical Excellence.[88,89]

## Community based practice

Whilst calls for evidence-based practice were coming to the fore, work for many was based in the community with occupational therapists employed in health and social care, across the four countries. The Minister of State for Health at the start of the decade stated that community care was aimed at providing 'the services and support which will enable people affected by ageing or disability to live as independently as possible.'[90] The introduction of the NHS and Community Care Act of 1990 was widely recognised as introducing the most fundamental change in the organisation of services since the NHS was established, as it decreed a market oriented health and social care system. Markets were to replace bureaucracy and incentives were to replace administrative control in order to meet patient demands more effectively, efficiently and economically. Hospitals could opt out of health authority control and become self-governing trusts, which became known as NHS trusts. Those under health authority management were to be known as Directly Managed Trusts (DMUs). Trusts had authority to own and dispose of assets, could borrow money within agreed limits for capital works, and could determine staff pay and conditions. Health authorities and fund-holding general practices were known as purchasers, and trusts or the independent sector became known as providers. Purchasers and providers were linked with contracts. Between 1991 and 1994, 95% of hospitals and community services came to hold trust status. A major concern of many occupational therapists was that the altruistic, caring motives of public service could be lost in business contracts and work for pay motives. The multiple needs of clients could not always be 'neatly costed, packaged and sold,' and the changes 'may lead to a therapy no longer focused on occupation as a central theme.'[91]

Rosemary Bowden, in 1991, explained her view of the changes:
> ...the policy of community care has been explicit now for nearly a decade. last year saw it enshrined in legislation. But the move to community care is much more than simply providing the same services to people in a different environment. It is about a change in

*culture and a fundamental change in the power base of service delivery. It is about developing a needs-led provision rather than service-driven. It is about negotiating with users and carers what it is that meets their agenda rather than the prescription of service following an assessment. It requires considerable skills in assessment, in negotiating, in networking and in imaginative problem solving.* [92]

She reassured readers that the profession had nothing to fear from a community oriented policy, as its roots were planted firmly in practical problem solving, and it was not subject to the status and mysticism of the medical model. COT efforts to forge closer links with user groups were applauded and Bowden recommended that therapists listen to the language used as well as clients' views in order to be user focused.

The concept of a mixed market of service providers with no framework for consistency or comparison followed different interpretations and time lines in different venues and did, indeed, challenge the concept of community occupational therapy services as they had been. Putting forward this view, Sheelagh Richards concluded, similarly to Bowden, that community occupational therapists needed to take a proactive stance putting the interests of purchasers and clients ahead of those of the profession and, as well, adopting the language of the marketplace to illustrate value for money. [93]

COT, in an interim statement on the implementation of the reforms, noted that approximately 2000 occupational therapist were employed by LASS departments and, after social workers, were the second largest group of qualified staff employed. The College provided advice to directors of occupational therapy services to get involved in planning the reforms; to occupational therapists that they could become care managers particularly of those clients who were severely or multiply disabled; that they combine assessment and service provision when possible; and that they should work to retain the distinctive nature of the profession. COT was 'particularly concerned about the legal implications of occupational therapists having to undertake work, and make judgements, in areas of practice in which they are neither trained nor competent.' Their view held that, 'Authorities' objectives should be to use the core skills of all occupational therapists...for the full benefit of service users with physical disabilities, learning difficulties or mental health problems.' [94] COT ran a seminar on care management in 1992 when pilot schemes with some positive promise in Gloucester, Wiltshire and Kent were explored. However, overall, a variable rate of implementation was evident, waiting lists remained an issue of concern, and the role of the care manager was not clearly defined at that date. [95]

In fact, there were almost as many types of care/case management as there were multidisciplinary teams. These included 'case co-ordination' between workers and needs; 'budget-holding case management' in which the manager controlled the purse strings as well as co-ordinating services; 'independent case management' in which the manager was, essentially an advocate; and 'client-funded case management' in which, after assessment, the client or carer organised and paid for services from an allocated budget. All had advantages and disadvantages. [96]

Community care resulted in a steep rise in demand for occupational therapy services, and waiting lists continued to grow. Occupational therapists were seen as having vital roles in housing adaptation, assisting people to adapt to disability, and ensuring effective discharge from hospital. By 1995 senior officers in health and social services called for 'urgent action to increase the recruitment and education of occupational therapists working in social services departments.'[97]

In a 1997 report of a qualitative study that considered how 15 occupational therapists from trusts and non-trusts experienced the changes, Lloyd-Smith found a central role was played by professional leaders who protected against 'service fragmentation and loss of professional direction.' He concluded:

> ...staff adopted a pragmatic position towards trust status, attempting to make trust status work to their own and their patients' advantage....The change of management status did create tensions and anxieties for staff, but it appeared that these were rarely discussed openly. The reported experience...revealed the importance they attached to measures of outcome in order to demonstrate the clinical effectiveness of occupational therapy both to support continued input and for the future development of services.[98]

Community occupational therapy was also provided as part of the NHS. In terms of adults with physical disability a survey reported in 1996 that the numbers of therapists varied between venues, and that the majority of occupational therapists provided functional assessment and advisory services regarding specific therapy and the provision of aids and equipment. More detail is provided in the adjacent figure.[99]

**Figure 2.11.10: Occupational therapy intervention offered in NHS Community Services**

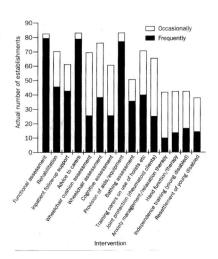

In terms of mental health a national survey into the structure and working practices of Community Mental Health Teams (CMHTs) launched in 1995 found a lack of continuity between hospitals and community services. 'Widespread dissatisfaction at the lack of a clear sense of leadership or common purpose within CMHTs' had led to 'burnout or emotional exhaustion.' This was not attributed to the challenging behaviours of clients, despite the fact that 89% of CMHTs offered services to people with severe and long term mental health problems. In fact that was seen as the major source of job satisfaction.[100] The move to the community, although welcomed initially, had raised questions about whether occupational therapy had lost its direction. To consider the issues more closely, and to provide a future strategy for research, education and practice in the mental health field, COT established a 'Mental Health Project' and published a special issue of BJOT in 1998.[101]

As part of community care and along side it was primary care practice, for which various delivery models emerged as more integrated services were put together through community care and primary care trusts. A COT brochure *Who Makes Doctors Better?* focused on the essential role of occupational therapy in cost effective primary care. It outlined how practitioners could support GPs. The brochure went on to detail areas of assessment, treatment, education and care delivered by occupational therapists to maintain health, prevent disease, provide rehabilitation and cost effective ways of achieving *Health of the Nation* targets. It mentioned specifically coronary heart disease and stroke rehabilitation, mental illness, accidents, HIV/Aids and sexual health, cancer, independence for the elderly, safe discharge from hospitals and rehabilitation centres, and learning disabilities. The types of service encompassed ADL, equipment and environmental adaptation, splinting and pressure garments for hand injuries and burn patients, work rehabilitation, and social skills and anxiety management.

**Figure 2.11.11: COT brochure of the mid 1990s. *(Who Makes Doctors Better)***

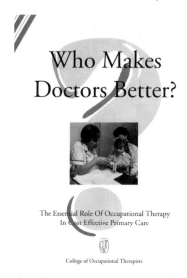

## Specialisation

During the decade eleven Specialist Sections of the COT were developed as a national resource for members, and a Specialist Sections Officer was employed to maintain and develop their links with the College. Advice, publications, newsletters, annual conferences, and study days linked undergraduate and postgraduate education. A look at the growing number of Specialist Sections provides an overview of practice in the 1990s, as well as telling how each developed and became part of the COT structure. In some places aspects of 1990s literature relevant to the area of practice is also included.

# CIGOPW (formerly SIGOP)
## By Sue Kennedy

In 1995 the Special Interest Group in Othotics and Prosthetics changed its name to the Clinical Interest Group in Orthotics, Prosthetics and Wheelchairs (CIGOPW). This was prompted by the COT wanting to regulate the Special Interest Groups. Because of too few members and lack of a regional structure the group became an Associate Specialist Section. However after a big campaign by committee and individual members, Specialist Section status was achieved in 1996, with the certificate being presented at the COT Conference dinner in Leeds. Specialist Section status has continued to be reconfirmed and membership by the end of the decade approached 300. The group celebrated its 21st year of serving the profession in 1998 with a two-day conference in the historic setting of Worcester College, Oxford.[102]

---

In the 2000 COT membership handbook CIGOPW interests were clarified as promoting awareness, knowledge and skills in the areas of Orthotics, Prosthetics, Wheelchairs and Special Seating. It is particularly concerned with continuing education at postgraduate level. CIGOPW involvement in orthotics, to meet the functional needs of clients, is in the manufacture of temporary orthoses in low temperature thermoplastics, as well as soft splints in neoprene and lycra. In the area of prosthetics members are involved in assessment for upper or lower limb prostheses aimed at enabling functional ability, and in subsequent rehabilitation. In the area of wheelchairs and special seating, members may work in dedicated wheelchair centres or, at the other end of the spectrum, in a surgical wards assessing basic chairs and seating for amputees for example.[103]

## Occupational Therapy for Elderly People (OCTEP)[104]

It was in the late 1970s that a group of London-based occupational therapists had set up the first special interest group to be established known as the Care of the Elderly Special Interest Group (CESIG). Although other regional groups also formed, the London group became recognised as the national one. However, its size and activity level fluctuated over the years.

The group was re-launched in January 1994 and grew rapidly, being one of the first to receive Specialist Section status as Occupational Therapy for Elderly People (OCTEP). When Council voted to admit representatives of specialist sections, OCTEP took its seat. As a Specialist Section of the COT it has a regional support network, sharing and disseminating advice and information to members and the College about work in the field of care of the elderly. At least two National Study Days are organised which prove very popular and have recently covered diverse topics from 'Outreach Services' to 'Leisure Activities.' Well-established regional groups also arrange their own study days. Membership includes occupational therapists, support workers and students and overseas members.

OCTEP recognises and embraces the changes that are occurring in care of the elderly. In the late 1990s the first clinical forum in Dementia Care was established with its own database and website to bring together therapists working in specific fields. In such a diverse field of practice, a need to focus on specific areas was recognised. Three further clinical forums on general medicine, functional psychiatry, and day hospital practice were set up. Another recent innovation is the awarding of grants towards study and research projects being undertaken by members to encourage innovative work by therapists working with older people.

# National Association of Paediatric Occupational Therapists (NAPOT)
## By Felicity McElderry

The story of the genesis of NAPOT, which was formed in 1989, was told in Chapter 10. The organisation, which is the largest Specialist Section in COT, provides support to over 1200 occupational therapists throughout the United Kingdom and in twenty-three countries overseas who work with children and young people. NAPOT aims to promote the most effective policies and services to meet children's needs; and to develop high standards of practice in all areas of paediatric occupational therapy, including those with mental health needs, physical, or learning disabilities. It emphasises a holistic, child-centred view with approaches that take as much account of psychological as of physical needs. It has retained the original PIP enthusiasm for working with other paediatric therapists who are welcomed as associate members, and with professional bodies and other organisations involved in developing children's services and which include parent support groups. NAPOT provides a range of services to members which include: a journal;[105] an Annual Conference; a comprehensive network of regional groups; local and national networking and training, including an information databank; and a professional advisory service.

With the current healthcare agenda changing rapidly, NAPOT seeks to identify major trends in order to support members in meeting children's needs. Following devolution, this now has to take account of policy variations across the United Kingdom. NAPOT is consulted through the College on many Government initiatives relating to children's services. The emphasis on more integrated care is providing a springboard for paediatric occupational therapists to launch innovative ways of working. One long-term trend has been the increasing inclusion in mainstream school of children with special educational needs. Occupational therapy services have matched this inclusion, providing therapists to work directly with the child and in a consultative role with the school team. Publication of the NAPOT *Guidelines for Good Practice* has added to resources available to paediatric occupational therapists. Raising awareness of the role of occupational therapy with all children, but especially in mental health, is important in the climate of developing primary care.[106]

# National Association of Occupational Therapists in Rheumatology (NAROT)[107]

The Special Interest Group in Rheumatology (OTSIGiR) had been formed in 1987 by a small group of occupational therapists as a branch of the British Health Professionals in Rheumatology (BHPR). That organisation had links to the European and International Leagues Against Rheumatism. Meetings were held during BHPR conferences and study days until December 1987 when the first independent study day was held. This focused on 'The Management of Osteoarthritis.' In 1994 the group changed its name to NAROT

Involved in the initial discussions with COT about affiliation of special interest groups, NAROT, with over 100 BAOT members, became a Specialist Section in 1995. It accepted a seat on Council in 1997 along with all other Specialist Sections. By 2000 membership exceeded 250. Members have access to bi-annual journal publications, the *Journal of Rheumatology Occupational Therapy*, annual conferences and general meetings, a website, resource collection, regional meetings and communication links with fellow specialists. At present NAROT is writing standards of practice for occupational therapists working in rheumatology.

# National Association of Occupational Therapists in Neurology (NANOT)[108]

The inaugural meeting of the group known as the 'Occupational Therapy Special Interest Group in Neurology (OTSIGN)' had been held at the National Hospital for Neurology and Neurosurgery in London in 1982. From that time, regular meetings in the capital had promoted clinical awareness and a chance to network with colleagues. In 1984 the group contributed a chapter to an Occupational Therapy Reference book about 'perception.' A member survey, the following year, highlighted postgraduate education as an issue and the London group agreed to co-ordinate a nationwide network to address this for members nationally. In 1986 the first newsletter was produced, the original logo was designed, and a representative attended the first meeting of special interest groups at COT. The next year saw the first regional groups being set up in Bristol and Wessex; others were established later. The first national conference was held in 1989. Member surveys showed that stroke was the most commonly encountered condition treated by its members, and the most common area of work was neurorehabilitation.

By the early 1990s a more formalised structure was developed within the regional and national framework, leading to a national committee and financial structure. Closer links were developed with COT and in 1994, OTSIGN was granted Specialist Section status, and established clinical forums in stroke and brain injury. A new logo was introduced, and in 1996 the name was changed to the National Association of Occupational Therapists in Neurology (NANOT). About that time, links with charities were developed, and, in conjunction with the Parkinson's Disease Association, a resource pack was developed for occupational therapists working with people with the disease.

After 1997 when Specialist Sections were granted the right to vote on COT council, NANOT contributed to the COT student handbook, a membership pack was produced, and national practice standards and clinical guidelines were developed. By 2000 membership had risen to over 600, a social services representative was voted onto the national committee to meet their needs, and the 'stroke forum' produced a book on Occupational Therapy and Stroke.

## HIV/AIDS, Oncology, Palliative Care and Education (HOPE)[109]

Palliative care was first recognised as a medical specialty within the UK in 1987. The impact of this recognition was tremendous within hospice and specialist palliative care units the number of which expanded rapidly with care provided by a multi-professional team. In the early 1990s a group of occupational therapists working in the Oxford and Gloucestershire region met to discuss issues relating to their new emerging caseload of patients with cancer. Their motivation and interest led them to seek a wider network throughout the country as the contribution of occupational therapy for this patient group was at a very formative stage. A Special Interest Group in Oncology and Palliative Care was formed and its informal committee facilitated *ad hoc* study days.

In 1992 the original committee resigned and a more formal regionalised structure was implemented. Links were established with COT, and formal recognition of the occupational therapy contribution to palliative care occurred. A representative of the new committee was given a seat on the Professional Committee (now Clinical Issues Committee) of the National Council for Hospice and Specialist Palliative Care Services (NCHSPCS). Additionally, a representative was given one on the education board of 'Help the Hospices.' These are still held today and both organisations are very supportive of the role and contribution of occupational therapy and of HOPE as an organisation. Around that time, talks took place with the occupational therapists' HIV & AIDS group who were meeting in London on a bi-monthly basis. The rapid growth in numbers of clients and dedicated government monies had resulted in many occupational therapists being employed in inner cities to work solely with them. Outside the inner cities, clients received care through hospice and palliative care units. SIGOP felt they could work with the HIV & AIDS group on many common issues. Talks took place for a number of years during which monies, specifically for treatment of HIV & AIDS clients, dried up. Coupled with that, as advances in medication caused the trajectory of the disease to change considerably, clients were seen within palliative care services and specialised rehabilitation units. In 1995 the partnership and umbrella organisation HOPE was formed. Membership includes overseas occupational therapists working in New Zealand, Australia, Sweden, Hong Kong and Ireland.

When the group's status changed to a COT Specialised Section, HOPE expanded its aims not only to support members with up to date information and a networking structure, but also to facilitate sound education initiatives to maximise continued professional development. Three study days are held annually throughout the UK, particularly to support the majority who work in sole positions, and a national conference was held in York. This 2-day event was a tremendous success, and gave the members more opportunity to share and discuss practice related issues. HOPE publishes a member newsletter three times a year and has produced documents such as *Guidelines for Clinical Practice* (1997) and *Guidelines for Measuring Occupational Therapy Outcomes in HIV Aids, Oncology and Palliative*

*Care* (2000). It works closely with NCHSPS in the production of all their publications, and played a key role in the production of *Rehabilitation—Fulfilling Lives*. Individual members have produced a book about occupational therapy in oncology and palliative care, contributed chapters to another on palliative day-care, and are writing a chapter about occupational therapy for a definitive Oxford text on palliative care. Despite HOPE's hard work in promoting the role of occupational therapy, they are not part of teams in all of the 240 Specialist Palliative Care Units.

Within this specialty, as in many others, intervention is based on a holistic client-centred approach, which is flexible and is constantly being reassessed according to the needs of the client and their carers. Occupational therapy may include a range of interventions such as:

- The use of functional activities for the treatment of physical, psychological and emotional difficulties.
- Retraining in personal and domestic activities of daily living.
- Retraining of cognitive and perceptual dysfunction.
- Splinting to prevent deformities and control pain.
- Home assessment and / or referral to Social Services for provision of equipment to enable optimum independence.
- Relaxation training and stress management.
- Lifestyle management, energy conservation, time management.
- Support and education to carers.
- Facilitating psychological adjustment to loss of function.
- Facilitating a therapeutic programme of activities within palliative day care.

## The Association of Occupational Therapists in Mental Health (AOTMH)

The Association of Occupational Therapists in Mental Health (AOTMH) promotes and develops the many facets of the profession in that field, emphasising holistic approaches to clients with mental health problems. As a body AOTMH represents the opinion of occupational therapists in mental health by providing comments on current issues across the range of fields of practice: forensic, community, hospital-based, substance misuse, homelessness, and mental health aspects of physical disability. To enable that, it has members from each of those fields on its Committee. It provides support and encouragement to therapists working within mental health practice acting as a national network for exchange and dissemination of information amongst members. As well, AOTMH promotes public awareness of the role of occupational therapists in mental health, and provides opportunities for specialist training.

As noted in earlier chapters mental health practice had evolved in quite major fits and starts over the last decades in response to the changing needs of society and to treatment fashions. By the 1990s occupational therapists were working in primary care, out-patient services, community teams, and day hospitals, as well as with in-patients in hospitals. The latter number was decreasing as hospitals were shut down and patients moved into the community under the rationale of 'normalisation.' Community mental health teams often had to support clients struggling to cope with their own health whilst trying to carry on family, social and work roles. The emphasis and contributions of occupational therapy as environments had changed according to mental health policy and practice had not been subjected to systematic review over the years, and the idea that practice remained centred on craftwork, recreational, and social pursuits was no longer accurate across the field. For example many occupational therapists had specialist skills in psychotherapy, dramatherapy, family therapy, and counselling.[110]

It was noted in the last chapter that counselling skills had become a topic of growing interest amongst occupational therapists in the 1980s. The interest continued into the 1990s although COT had made no position statement on counselling and some therapists, like Hagedorn,[111] held concerns about whether occupational therapists should be involved in it to a great extent. Creek argued that 'talking is only a legitimate tool for occupational therapists if it is used to support activity.'[112] In 1997, in a paper published in *BJOT* challenging that view, the authors suggesting that 'therapeutic dialogue is intrinsically valuable and, therefore, assertions that it should always be linked to activity appear somewhat unrealistic in today's context.'[113] They thought it time to acknowledge the importance of counselling skills in occupational therapy. Indeed, they described it as vital, because in surveys of the time it was rated by mental health service users as one of the two most beneficial therapies, and headed a list in *The Health of the Nation* information booklets as an 'effective' treatment method for mental health problems. That same source had indicated that some 91.5 million working days were lost through mental illness in 1991.[114] Two levels of counselling were suggested in the BJOT paper: first there was building a therapeutic relationship in day-to-day work by engaging with clients and understanding their issues and concerns; and secondly, there was counselling as a therapeutic strategy to promote change, personal growth and decision making. The authors suggested that definitions of counselling which included facilitating choice, reducing confusion, collaboration between helper and client, and helping people to use their own resources, appeared to be in line with occupational therapy values and had evolved alongside the recognition of the rights and potential of individuals. They further argued that 'for many people, taking part in activity or occupation is not perceived as a problem, whereas taking time out for themselves may well be so, alongside balancing conflicting demands. Occupation can be used as a defence or a distraction to avoid addressing serious personal difficulties.' They went on to suggest that activity without counselling 'does not help clients to understand what is happening or how to move forward and does nothing to enhance the professional credibility of the occupational therapist.'[115] Those conflicting views about the basic substance of professional intervention remain central in the professional debate.

Forensic services was one of the newer areas of practice within mental health. It had its own special interest group, OTWISE, which aimed to support occupational therapists working in forensic psychiatry and secure environments. At the WFOT Congress, Mary Crawford, the Director of Rehabilitation at Broadmoor Hospital, explained the services there and how occupational therapy fitted into the total picture, not least how they coped with therapy versus security roles. Mike Fowler from the Fromeside Clinic in Bristol provided a historical perspective explaining how forensic psychiatry and occupation used as therapy started back in 1800. He saw future challenges as a need to increase awareness generally, that the specialty is covered sufficiently in undergraduate education, and that opportunities to move into new and developing areas were taken when they arose.[116]

## Occupational Therapy in Work Practice and Productivity (OTWPP)

Another Specialist Section had grown from the profession's long time interest in work practice and productivity for people with any kind of impairment. Occupational Therapy in Work Practice and Productivity (OTWPP), which started as an interest group in 1995, not only provides a professional network for support and development of occupational therapists working in that field, but also aims to increase awareness and raise the profile of the contribution of occupational therapy in work related issues. It does that within employment in the statutory, private and voluntary sectors. OTWPP also provides specialist professional representation to and on behalf of COT for policy and/or consultation purposes on: development of work skills; work hardening and rehabilitation; work skills and productivity as a means of self discovery and change; and litigation, health and safety, and 'occupational health'. It plays a mediator role acting to advise and negotiate with employers on behalf of individual clients and to advise them about compliance with the Disability Discrimination Act. Membership is open to any occupational therapist, occupational therapist support workers, and students, as well as to others through commercial and associate membership.[117]

The establishment of OTWPP was one indication that rehabilitation aimed at 'return to work' was once more assuming importance in the 1990s. As was obvious in the 1950s and 1960s, in particular, it had earlier been a central concern of practice. Over the ensuing years of high unemployment and changing values, return to work programmes had disappeared from centre stage, but an interest in and commitment to it had been maintained. Joanne Pratt, in a special issue of BJOT relating to the topic, discussed work practice as one aspect of occupational therapists' long time valuing of engagement in productive activity as a therapeutic medium and a goal in itself. The process of enhancing clients' work performance could be educational, social, vocational or rehabilitative extending the notion of 'work rehabilitation,' which had derived from biomedical concepts. Pratt used an informal survey of media reports to consider some factors with the potential to influence future practice, such as:

> ...the demise of jobs for life, the delayering and downsizing of many corporations, short-term contracts, the impact of new technology on the workplace and reported increases in occupational stress. Added to this, many therapists continue to deal with some of the most profound changes in the delivery of health and social care that the UK has seen in 40 years.[118]

The special issue provided a snapshot of UK practice related to work performance in 1997. The topics on the theme were diverse covering: 'the role of work with clients recovering from mental health problems; teleworking as an example of the changing nature of work patterns in our society; the statistical concepts that underpin objective assessment of work performance; and the legislative context of practice.'[119] Despite it being a small area of practice in Britain, during that the same year a workshop on 'Work practice and productivity' afforded an international perspective as presenters from Australia, Denmark, USA as well as the UK joined in discussion. This identified common parallels and themes in issues such as 'industrial legislation, community-based care, cost, effectiveness, efficacy, the changing nature of work and skill levels of the work force.'[120]

The special issue was appreciated and applauded. A letter to the Editor read:

*We are writing to express our appreciation of the June 1997 edition of BJOT. The theme of work practice is timely, and the interesting variety of papers covered a wide spectrum on this subject. The concept of a themed issue is useful, since it places a significant number of articles in the same location, something students in particular find helpful! The only thing we felt was missing in the issue was an overview of the legislation, particularly the Disability Discrimination Act, and the possible implications for occupational therapists. Perhaps this could be included in a future issue of the journal to round off this important subject.*[121]

A second letter expressed some similar thoughts:

*I am writing with reference to the June special issue of BJOT on work practice. As a whole I found the edition interesting and the idea of having themed issues is attractive. My concern about them, however, is that often one has to wait months (or in this case years) to read and hear opinions, news, research and new ideas regarding a particular issue. I am particularly disturbed that the theme of work and employment appears to attract so little attention, publicity and interest within the BJOT and the occupational therapy profession in general.*

*While many of the views expressed in the issue advocate the importance of, occupation (of course they do, we are occupational therapists after all), it would appear that there is a rather negative attitude regarding the appropriateness and possibility of paid employment within the realms of rehabilitation.*

*I feel strongly that employment (and by this I mean real paid jobs in the local community) is one of the most meaningful occupations that any individual can choose to undertake. Yet, all too often, we see real employment replaced by 'industrial therapy', 'training' or 'coaching' when a real job would be far more purposeful.*

*Few human activities are regarded with such universal approval as work. In most societies, some form of work is, in itself, a prerequisite for life's essentials. Constructive employment is a fundamental adult human experience. Not only is it a means of participating in families and social organisations, but work also assumes a role and an identity and channels energy into activities, which are generally seen as desirable for the community at large as well as for the individual.*[122]

## Occupational Therapists for People with Learning Disabilities (OTPLD)

The National Association of Occupational Therapists for People with Learning Disabilities (OTPLD) is diverse. Client needs differ so occupational therapist members working in this specialty do so in a variety of settings to address issues such as 'challenging behaviour,' 'profound learning and multiple disability,' or 'parents with learning disability.' The occupations, models of practice and approaches employed by therapists vary to meet the individual needs.

OTPLD supports and promotes occupational therapy to achieve high standards of practice that is evidenced-based. It produces regular newsletters, holds study days and conferences, offers regional networking to facilitate frequent and local meetings, and provides a database.

## Occupational Therapists in Private Practice (OTiPP)[123]

Unlike other Specialist Sections, OTiPP represents a method of service delivery rather than a clinical specialty or a particular type of work. As such its development has followed a different path. In 1988 a letter was published in BJOT inviting members who were interested in or already practising outside statutory services to attend a seminar. Following this a two-day conference was held in Harrogate in November 1989. An Association was formed to act as an independent self-help support group, a constitution was drafted and a committee was formed. At the AGM in November 1990 consideration was given to becoming a Special Interest Group (SIG). It was felt that this would not meet the needs of the members and OTiPP continued as an Association until November 1993. At this time an affiliation document had been negotiated by Council enabling groups to become Specialist Sections affiliated to COT and it was agreed that OTiPP should apply for Associate Affiliation. OTiPP was fully accredited as a Specialist Section in 1994.

The prime objective of OTiPP has always been to provide support, advice and encouragement both for new members and for those who have been working independently for many years. Members represent a very wide range of areas of work and depth of involvement. A large number work independently full-time; some run their own companies with teams of OTs and other staff. Another group divide their time equally between independent work and statutory employment, and a further group work principally within statutory services only undertaking a small amount of independent work.

The range of work undertaken by OTiPP members reflects the fact that opportunities for OTs within the independent sector have increased considerably during the past few years and continue to do so. Changes in the structure and management of the NHS and social services have encouraged individuals to become more business orientated and to market themselves and their services to other agencies in areas such as training, domiciliary assessments, and work with housing associations and residential care establishments. Occupational therapists are now recognised as making a valuable contribution in many areas outside statutory bodies, in addition to their long-standing role within charitable and voluntary organisations. They are now well established within the field of personal injury litigation where they work closely with the legal profession in preparing reports for court, and in assisting claimants to obtain the services that they require.

Increasingly, insurance companies have recognised occupational therapists' value in relation to assessing qualification for claims for long term and permanent health care and the associated organisation of care packages and rehabilitation programmes. Within business, large companies are now employing occupational therapists to advise on work practices and to manage graded work programmes. Some of these opportunities have arisen as a result of the Disability Discrimination Act (1995) which, because of requirements concerning access to public buildings, has given further scope for occupational therapists' skills.

The membership of OTiPP has grown steadily and now numbers about 270. Typically, a proportion of OTiPP members join speculatively when they are considering developing their professional role outside statutory services but then do not pursue this path. Others may be a member of OTiPP for a few years whilst they become established, and then do not renew their membership. The majority, however, retain their membership, gain support from their fellow members, keep up to date with relevant issues through a quarterly Newsletter and benefit from networking opportunities available through regional meetings and annual conferences. A National Conference has become an annual event and study days are also held.

Private practice is not suited to newly qualified therapists or to people returning to work after a significant break, as a good grounding in current trends and practices in the statutory sector or established voluntary and private fields is essential to maintain high professional standards. Most practitioners have worked for several years and are usually at senior level. Many start on a part-time basis in existing establishments, others find a gap in the market and offer a specialist service using their home as a base. OTiPP has a code of business standards for its members. It works closely with the COT on many issues, and the latter recommend that all occupational therapists who practice privately should join OTiPP. Jointly they publish a *Directory of Private Practitioners*.

## College of Occupational Therapists Specialist Section in Housing (COTSSIH)

The College of Occupational Therapists Specialist Section in Housing (COTSSIH) was established to promote and share the interests, skills and experience of occupational therapists working in the field of housing. Members are employed in a variety of areas, including social services, housing departments, housing associations, housing improvement agencies, private work, disability housing services and health trusts and authorities. They work with clients of all ages and range of disabilities. COTSSIH has broad ranging aims similar to other Specialist Sections. It acts as a resource for information and good practice, and to support and promote education opportunities in the field. As well it liaises with service users, professional bodies and providers of housing to achieve good functional design and adaptations in both new and old property; campaigns for improved policies and better standards in housing; encourages research and development in the field; and serves as a resource to the COT on housing and community matters.

In 1992 several items in BJOT discussed the housing issue. In an editorial Dr R.S. Ramaiah, a Director of Public Health Medicine in Middlesborough, pointed to the Government's Green Paper *The Health of the Nation*. This recognised an association between health and housing thus provoking wider debate on the issue. Based on earlier roles, he explained, public health physicians would have an advisory role on medical priority for rehousing. However there was a growing feeling, he said, that the assessments should be undertaken by occupational therapists employed by local authorities. He recommended that the issue warranted discussion at local and national level.[124] In the next issue, a letter to the editor in response to Ramaiah's editorial, told how occupational therapists were already involved in the rehousing scheme in Ashfield, Nottinghamshire. Assessments were carried out by all social services occupational therapists alongside their normal duties.[125]

In the same edition, a paper addressed 'housing and occupational therapists' as a developing field. It was based on a report by the London Borough's Occupational Therapists' Housing Group. The report used case histories to highlight a range of housing difficulties experienced by disabled people, and the role occupational therapists can play in the provision of suitable housing for them. It was based on the premise that without suitable housing people with disabilities will be hampered and frustrated in a range of occupational needs such as personal independence, employment and socio-cultural pursuits. It recommended that occupational therapists work with local authority housing/development sections, housing associations, architects, disabled users and voluntary groups. The group saw occupational therapists' input as analysis of mobility, access and function. The latter included the 'function to enjoy a lifestyle as free from impediments to independence as the user, carer and occupational therapist can devise. This will include self-care, care of dependents, and domestic, culinary and extramural aspects of daily living.' The provision of housing for disabled people was the subject of considerable discussion between service users, voluntary organisations, property designers and builders in Europe and the UK at the time.[126]

Special Interest Groups as distinct from Specialist Sections are not accredited by COT. However, close working relations are maintained with some of the groups such as: the National Occupational Therapy Pain Association; the Special Interest Group in Orthopaedics; the Cardiac Rehabilitation Occupational Therapy Special Interest Group; the Association of Occupational Therapists in Computer Technology; the British Association of Hand Therapists; Gardening & Horticulture for Training, Therapy and Health; British Association of Bobath Trained Therapists; the Occupational Therapy in Accident and Emergency Special Interest Group; the Burns Therapy Interest Group; and the National Forensic Head OTs' Forum.[127]

In all those particular areas of interest there was a growing requirement for research. Indeed the requirement was manifest across the profession, and Irene Ilott picks up that story in the final section of the chapter.

# A requirement for research
## By Irene Ilott

The 1990 BAOT Code of Ethics and Professional Conduct featured research in paragraph 17. The principle stated: 'occupational therapists shall promote: an understanding of and research into occupational therapy,' with a note added to the effect that:

> *...occupational therapists have a responsibility to contribute to the continuing development of the profession by critical evaluation and research. Any research undertaken has additional ethical implications which occupational therapists must respect.*[128]

That paragraph is indicative of one of the principal objectives of the College: the promotion of the knowledge base—the science—of occupational therapy. The founders stated this primary objective in the AOT Articles of Association. They were reaffirmed in the mission statement that was approved by Council in August 1999. This states:

> *...the College of Occupational Therapists aims to provide a clear identity for all its members through the provision of the highest standard of expert, professional opinion and advice informed by research, scholarship, innovation and the promotion of excellence in practice.*[129]

Additionally, the most recent version of the Code of Ethics and Professional Conduct states that 'occupational therapists have a duty to ensure that wherever possible their professional practice is evidence based and consistent with established research findings.' As well, there is a requirement for all occupational therapy personnel to be informed 'consumers' of research.[130] Christine Craik, who was reviewing her term of office as Chairman of the Council in June 1994, expanded the concept: 'all occupational therapists have a responsibility to be discerning consumers of research and to be able to incorporate the results of research in their field of interest into their everyday practice.'[131]

To be an informed consumer of research is dependent upon several factors, not least of which is access to knowledge in real or virtual libraries. Some of the first articles about using medical libraries had appeared in *BJOT* in the 1980s.[132,133] In the 1990s Roberts gave an overview of *Index Medicus and Medline* and indexing methods,[134,135] whilst Barber provided a detailed introduction to indexes and abstracts. It was noted that occupational therapists 'tended to rely on their own professional journal publication rather than researching the literature in depth via existing indexes,' and recommended that a central information resource be provided in the Disability and Information Study Centre at COT's new headquarters.[136] Local research networks were encouraged.[137] In 1994, a report described how to set up a local support group for networking purposes based upon a multidisciplinary group in Southampton. A one-year evaluation, completed by ten people indicated that the benefits were networking and support, sharing information and ideas, discussion of problems, increased knowledge and personal development.[138]

The main ways in which research and development (R&D) has been promoted are through publications (particularly in the peer reviewed BJOT which is the principal medium for disseminating the process and outcome of occupational therapy research in the UK), and by providing training, courses and conferences. The more strategic approach, which had emerged during the 1980s, was built upon by an increasing awareness of national research policy and funding,[139] establishing collaborative alliances with the Joint Therapies Research Group and the Research Forum for Allied Health Professions, and by endorsing R&D strategies for the profession.[140]

Many early initiatives undertaken by the professional body to increase the research capacity of members have already been noted. For example, small grants and awards had been available to enable occupational therapists to undertake post-qualification degree courses that contained a research element. As time passed the opportunities increased, and although relatively modest, such awards have led to success with other sources of funding. Funding sources have featured in a regular 'Research and Development' (R&D) page published in *Occupational Therapy News* since November 1997.

In the 1990s R&D strategies highlighted the interdependence of capacity, productivity and quality services.[141] They also reflected the vision expressed in Stewart's inaugural professorial lecture in which she said that 'research is not just an add-on but must be an integral part of how we serve our patients.'[142] Constance Owen, the first occupational therapist to be awarded a PhD, had lived that vision and encouraged others to follow it. She did not resign from her part-time position in the Medical Research Unit on Ageing at the University of Liverpool until 1993 when she was in her 80s.[143]

Reports of members gaining higher research degrees featured in BJOT from the early 1990s. For example, there were four between October 1992 and February 1993. Thesis titles illustrate the diversity of occupational therapy research. These were *Continuing Education: Study of the Professional Development of Occupational Therapists* by Jill Ashton, who was awarded a PhD from the University of Exeter; *Factors Contributing to Work-related Stress in Occupational Therapy: Implications for Personal, Managerial and Organisational Sources of Change* by Grace Sweeney, who was awarded an MPhil from the University of Exeter; *Clinical Reasoning in Community Occupational Therapy: Processes and Patterns* by Heli Munroe, who was awarded a PhD from Heriot-Watt University of Edinburgh; and *Very Low Birth Weight Children in Primary School* for which Lynne Roberts was awarded a PhD from the University of Liverpool. In April 1994, it was announced that the first doctorate in occupational therapy from the University of Ulster had been awarded to Pamela Eakin for a DPhil thesis entitled *Disability and Community Care: the Development of an Instrument to Assess Need and Measure Outcome.*[144]

Because research resources are too scarce to squander on repetitious projects, the Research Register was reconstituted. The COT accepted an offer from the British Library for it to be published quarterly in the *Occupational Therapy Index* heralding the future use of electronic databases. By the end of the decade technological advances transformed the register of projects. It was replaced by the *Thesis Collection: the National Collection of Unpublished Occupational Therapy Research* which is constantly updated on the College website.[145] The thesis collection had started in 1979 with donated theses submitted for the Fellowship by examination. By 1999 there were over 300 items in the national collection. Most were masters dissertations, with 29 doctoral dissertations and 30 work-based, evaluative studies. There are 718 subjects in the subject index reflecting the rich diversity of titles, topics and methods. It is growing collection with theses donated for reference and loan. A Register of Therapy Researchers, a collaborative project with the Chartered Society of Physiotherapy, and the Royal College of Speech and Language Therapists and COT, was funded by the National Health Service Executive.[146]

During the 1990s themes that reflect changing emphases within occupational therapy debuted in research and research dialogue. The study of human occupations, for example, prompted Fossey to propose some research questions relating to effective occupational function, occupations and health and occupational analysis, and to suggest that qualitative methods were needed to understand people's subjective experience of participation in occupation.[147] The need for research to be emancipatory for consumers and carers was highlighted in an editorial by Payling when she was coming to the end of her term as chair of the R&D Committee. She reported that she was:

> ...overwhelmed by the distance still required to be travelled to ensure that occupational therapy research is investigating topics of interest to the users of our services and in a way that is acceptable to them; users achieve the status of active participants in research rather than observed subjects in samples; research that is emancipatory of our users and will enable occupational therapists to work as agents of change in partnerships with people with disabilities of all kinds, to challenge society to break down the barriers to full and equal integration of everyone in our communities.[148]

During the 1990s clinical studies continued investigating topics such as: satisfaction of adults using upper limb prostheses,[149] occupational and dietetic therapy with female psychiatric patients,[150] the role of occupational therapy and physiotherapy for female patients with proximal femoral fractures,[151] the value of functional assessment of older people with dementia,[152] and developmental history of children with motor/learning difficulties.[153] A review of the literature published between 1989 and 1996 revealed that most papers were related to clinical work and descriptive in that they illustrated, rather than evaluated, current practice.[154] Notwithstanding that finding, during 1996 there was a heated exchange on the letters page of BJOT between readers who considered the research published irrelevant, incomprehensible and conducted by an academic elite divorced from the reality of practice; and those who did not.

Additionally, new technologies and educational approaches were evaluated, such as the use of teleconferencing with students on clinical placement,[155] and problem based learning.[156] Qualitative methods were used to understand differences in clinical reasoning between students and experienced therapists,[157] and Pinnington and Bagshaw highlighted the importance of ethical screening for student research projects. They also summarised the development of diploma and degree projects over the past 10 years and the need to expand clinical reasoning.[158] Electronic databases available via the Internet became an easy way to share research in progress and outcomes both locally and internationally. The Cochrane Collaboration is a prime example being promoted by COT as a valuable resource for evidence based practice.[159,160] Two examples of systematic reviews with occupational therapy authors are Rehabilitation by Drummond and colleagues,[161] and Life Skills Programmes for Chronic Mental Illness by Nicol, Robertson and Connaughton.[162]

A landmark *Research In Practice* conference was held in October 1993, chaired by Professor Heinz Wolff, and Rick Telford, the Chairman of the Research and Development Committee, who inaugurated an annual research forum for the presentation of papers. The Patron, HRH the Princess Royal, who attended, congratulated the College on fostering the new research attitude within the profession by setting up annual research grant awards and by establishing the Disability Information Study Centre. She stressed that the research should be relevant to the profession rather than to please other professional groups.[163]

The need for the professional body to adopt a more strategic approach to research increased during the 1990s particularly in response to the evidence-based movement. Policy makers, commissioners/purchasers of occupational therapy, members of the multidisciplinary team and patients began to demand evidence about clinical and cost effectiveness. In 1995, Helena Culshaw concluded an editorial with the challenge 'we need our practice to be evidence based to compete and our outcomes to be measurable and/or desirable. If not, who will buy it?'[164] As well as an imperative for evidence of the benefits, outcomes and value for money of specific interventions, there was also the expectation that practitioners would use the best available research evidence to inform their clinical reasoning and decision making. An emerging strategic awareness was manifest in a variety of ways. These included identifying priorities for occupational therapy research, references to policy documents and national sources of funding, and developing collaborative alliances with other professional bodies and research organisations.

Barnitt highlighted the need for the profession to link research priorities with the new Department of Health national and regional strategies if funding was to be secured. She advised that 'as a profession, it is time we decided what the function of research should be within our professional context—so how do we select key areas for research priorities—unless your topic has relevance to your employer or the national research strategy, it will become more difficult to get funding.'[165] A set of priority topics was stated in an invitation to apply for the Research Awards administered by the R&D Committee. Set for 1991–95 they were intended to keep occupational therapy at the forefront of developments, and would be reviewed annually. The topics were client centred and multidisciplinary assessment, and ways in which occupational therapy assessment is unique; case management with young people, school leavers and elderly people; collaboration between agencies with the occupational therapy contribution in the statutory, voluntary and independent sectors, particularly in the fields of psychiatry, mental health and elderly people; occupational therapy practice including educational, clinical and management projects which could change practice. The results of a live research project conducted to identify the research priorities in mental health undertaken at the AOTMH annual conference were published in March, 2000.[166] The top three priority areas were related to understanding activity/occupation, group work, and occupational performance skills. A nation wide consultation exercise, held between October 1997 and July 1998 at 25 workshops, involved 766 people most of whom were occupational therapy practitioners working in NHS Trusts. There was a remarkable consensus that the priority for research was evaluating the effectiveness of specific interventions, either as stand-alone interventions or as part of a multi-professional, inter-agency package of care; understanding the relationship between occupation, health and well being, and the impact of occupational deprivation on the health of individuals, groups and communities; and the way services are delivered and organised. These are being used to formulate research priorities for the COT Strategic Vision and Action Plan.

Establishing strategic alliances has taken a pivotal role throughout the history of the profession. Working in partnership with service users and carers, other members of the multi-professional team, and congruent organisations, has been a constant theme. For example, a letter from J. Stowe, head research occupational therapist at the Rheumatology and Rehabilitation Research Unit in Leeds, encouraged members to become involved with the group.[167] Arguably the most important strategic alliances during the last decade have been with other professional bodies, firstly through the Joint Therapies Research Group and, later, the Research Forum for Allied Health Professions. The alliance between the professional bodies emerged in response to the Department of Health Report of the Taskforce on the Strategy for Research in Nursing, Midwifery and Health Visiting in 1993.[168] Between then and 2000 there were regular meetings of the Joint Therapies Research Group. The membership comprised officers and members from the three therapy professions. The Group conducted high level lobbying, organised conferences and produced joint responses to policy initiatives such as the Research Assessment Exercise, and obtained Department of Health funding for the 1997 and 1999 versions of the Register of Therapy Researchers—a database of expertise. In 2000 it was agreed to expand the membership to the 12 professions regulated under the CPSM, and the inaugural meeting was held in November 2000 at COT headquarters.

Demands for a response to earlier requests for the professional body to commit substantial investment in supporting research were made at an R&D Committee research networking day in 1991. As well, radical changes in strategy were called for to maintain professional standing in the wake of the NHS reforms.[169] Priorities for action included establishing a central research co-ordinator post to promote research, provide advice and to update indexes and databases; and enhancing the profile of research throughout the profession and within the professional body. In 1997 the first Research and Development Strategy was published in the special, evidence-based practice issue of the Journal.[170] The Strategy addressed three levels, for occupational therapists as research consumers, participants in research and as proactive researchers. The establishment of the Research and Development Board and Group in 1997 to lead and deliver on the Strategy was seen as heralding 'the start of a new era.'[171]

During 2000 the Research and Development Board reviewed the 1997 Strategy and prepared a new Strategic Vision and Action Plan for endorsement by the Council of the COT. The intention was to create a whole system, integrated approach to R&D to achieve coherence between clinical governance, statutory regulation, education, knowledge management and life long learning.

**In summary** this penultimate chapter has told of events and ideas that featured in occupational therapy during the last decade of the twentieth century. The Professional Association moved into a new and extensive purpose designed building, with library and meeting facilities, and electronic links with colleagues around the world. A global fraternity started fifty years earlier had grown, and new international organisations and affiliations had developed to meet expanding needs, aided by the technological revolution. Education of occupational therapists came of age with basic degrees for all and opportunities for higher qualifications for those who sought them. Research became a requirement, and the appointment of the first professors of occupational therapy enhanced its academic standing. Alongside those achievements were the more holistic understanding of people's rights and responsibilities, and the rebirth of ideas about the importance of occupation linked with concepts of enabling and empowering people within their own communities. They infiltrated, education, research and practice, which more and more sought evidence to support what it attempted to achieve. Practice was wide ranging, and embraced specialties that were a close fit with earlier paradigms of care, and those that followed newer directions. The importance of the socio-political environment in the changes was paramount. The BAOT and COT appear well positioned to move forward into the new millennium, but there is no doubt that occupation for health will follow different paths from those of the twentieth century.

The final chapter will consider the journey of occupation for health from prescription to self-health that was traced in this volume, and compare it with the earlier journey from self-health to prescription. It will pick out and reflect on themes and ideas that surfaced as contexts changed and make tentative suggestions for the next phase of the journey.

---

[1]BAOT. PAMS strategy launched. Occupational Therapy News. December 2000, 8/12: 4.

[2]In May 2001 the name became Council of Occupational Therapists for the European Countries to cover inclusion of countries not members of the European Union but which, as part of Europe, share the same aims.

[3]www.cotec-europe.org

[4]Creek J. Occupational therapy in Europe -COTEC. British Journal of Occupational Therapy 1995; 57(5): 188.

[5]www.cotec-europe.org

[6]Becoming part of a global family: International report. Shaping the future 2000 and beyond: Annual Report 1999–2000. London: BAOT/COT, 2000: 15.

[7] Code of professional conduct. British Journal of Occupational Therapy 1990; 53(4): 143–8.

[8] Warren B. Ethics in practice. British Journal of Occupational Therapy 1993; 56(5): 163; Confidentiality. British Journal of Occupational Therapy 1993; 56(6): 206; Cruelty. British Journal of Occupational Therapy 1993; 56(8): 292; Personal relationships. British Journal of Occupational Therapy 1994; 57(1): 14; Respecting consumer rights. British Journal of Occupational Therapy 1994; 57(40): 130; Maintenance of service to consumers; British Journal of Occupational Therapy 1994; 57(9): 353.

[9] Warren. Ethics in practice....

[10] Ethics Committee: Code of Ethics and Professional Conduct for Occupational Therapists. College of Occupational Therapists, July 1995: 3.

[11]Ethics Committee: Code of Ethics and Professional Conduct for Occupational Therapists....: 4.

[12]Ethics Committee: Code of Ethics and Professional Conduct for Occupational Therapists....: 4.

[13]Ethics Committee: Code of Ethics and Professional Conduct for Occupational Therapists....: 5.

[14]Ethics Committee: Code of Ethics and Professional Conduct for Occupational Therapists....: 2.

[15]COT. Not Just Quality of Care, Quality of Life. Leaflet.

[16]Keilhofner G. A Model of Human Occupation. Baltimore: Williams and Wilkins. 1995.

[17] COT. Occupational Therapists Reference Book 1992. London: Parke Sutton Publishing Ltd. 1992.

[18]Jay P, Mendez A, Monteath HG. The Diamond Jubilee of the Professional Association, 1932–1992: An Historical Review. British Journal of Occupational Therapy 1991; 55 (7): 252–6.

[19]BAOT/COT. Shaping the future 2000 and beyond: Annual Report 1999–2000....: 4–9.

[20]BAOT/COT. Shaping the future 2000 and beyond: Annual Report 1999–2000....: 12.

[21]COT. Members First: Membership Handbook 2000. London: COT, 2000: 1.

[22]New Chief Executive for COT. Occupational Therapy News. October 2000, 8/10: 1.

[23]Richards S. Chief Executives Report. Shaping the future 2000 and beyond: Annual Report 1999–2000:...: 3.

[24]Occupational Therapist's Reference Book 1992....

[25]Occupational Therapist's Reference Book 1992...

[26]Jay, Mendez & Monteath. The Diamond Jubilee of the Professional Association, 1932–1992...

[27]Campaigning for Better Pay and Conditions. Shaping the future 2000 and beyond: Annual Report 1999–2000....: 18.

[28]Croft S. Disability and Information Study Centre. British Journal of Occupational Therapy 1991; 55 (8): 314–5.

[29]MacDonald G. Current Awareness Bulletin: Occupational therapy in work practice. British Journal of Occupational Therapy 1995; 58(1): 13.

[30]BAOT/COT. Shaping the future 2000 and beyond: Annual Report 1999–2000....: 5, 9.

[31]Kelly G. Letters to the Editor: The Last 60 Years. British Journal of Occupational Therapy 1997; 60(10): 436–40.

[32]King J. Role of the research ethics committee. British Journal of Occupational Therapy 1990; 53(4): 148.

[33]Drummond A. Writing a research article. British Journal of Occupational Therapy 1994; 57(8): 303–5.

[34]Jenkins M. The doctoral route. British Journal of Occupational Therapy 1994; 57(9): 349–350.

[35]Drummond AER, Parker CJ. Multi centre trials. British Journal of Occupational Therapy 2000; 63(10): 476–80.

[36]Kelly G. Understanding occupational therapy: a hermeneutic approach. British Journal of Occupational Therapy 1996; 59(5): 237–42.

[37]Mountain G. A review of the literature in the British Journal of Occupational Therapy from 1989-1996. British Journal of Occupational Therapy 1997; 60(10): 430–5.

[38]BAOT. Occupational Therapy News. December 2000, 8/12.

[39]Robbins J. Occupational Therapists' Reference Book 19834. Norwich: Parke Sutton Publishing in Association with the British Association of Occupational Therapists, 1984: Foreword.

[40]The British Association/College of Occupational Therapists archives. British Journal of Occupational Therapy. 1997; 60(8): 364.

[41]Sadlo G. Leisure occupations. COT 22nd Annual Conference, 24–26 June 1998, Ulster: Paper Presentations. Occupation for Health. British Journal of Occupational Therapy. 1998; 61(9): 426.

[42]Richards S. The Casson Memorial Lecture: Occupation for Health—and Wealth? British Journal of Occupational Therapy 1998; 61(7): 294-300

[43]Ellis M. WFOT 11th World Congress. British Journal of Occupational Therapy 1994; 57(1): 19.

[44]WFOT 11th International Congress, London: Scientific Programme. British Journal of Occupational Therapy 1994; 57(5): 188.

[45]WFOT 11th International Congress, London: Scientific Programme. British Journal of Occupational Therapy 1994; 57(7): 266–74.

[46]WFOT 11th International Congress, London: Scientific Programme. British Journal of Occupational Therapy 1994; 57(6): 228–36.

[47]WFOT 11th International Congress, London: Scientific Programme. British Journal of Occupational Therapy 1994; 57(7): 270.

[48]WFOT 11th International Congress, London: Scientific Programme. British Journal of Occupational Therapy 1994; 57(5): 193.

[49]Schwartz M. In Hume  C. WFOT 21st Council Meeting, 10–15 April 1994, Edinburgh. British Journal of Occupational Therapy 1994; 57(5): 194.

[50]Tyldesley B. The Casson Memorial Lecture 1999: Alice Constance Owens —Reflections upon a remarkable lady and a pioneer of occupational therapy in England. British Journal of Occupational Therapy 1999; 62(8): 359–66.

[51]Walker C. Annual Conference: Kay East—We have to be a powerful voice with Government. Occupational Therapy News. September 2000, 8/9: 4.

[52]East K. In The NHS: a chance to have your say. Occupational Therapy News. June 2000, 8/6: 1.

[53]O'Brien T. Cited in Challenge and Opportunity—occupational therapy and community care. British Journal of Occupational Therapy. 1990; 53(12): 515.

[54]Caines E. Therapy Weekly 1990; 13 December: 1.

[55]Benson S. Educational Change: Threat or Challenge? British Journal of Occupational Therapy. 1991; 54(5): 161.

[56]Gape N, Hewin P. A Matter of Degree: Has Occupational Therapy Graduated as a Profession? British Journal of Occupational Therapy. 1995; 58(2): 50–54.

[57]Collins B. The Story of Dorset House School of Occupational Therapy. Oxford: Dorset House, 1987.

[58]Barnitt RE. The Casson Memorial Lecture: Through a Glass Darkly. British Journal of Occupational Therapy. 1991; 54(6): 208–15.

[59]Barnitt RE. The Casson Memorial Lecture …

[60]Ayres D. Petition Drop (part 2): You know you make me want to shout. Occupational Therapy News, May 2000, 13.

[61]BAOT/COT. Shaping the future 2000 and beyond: Annual Report 1999–2000….: 4.

[62]Craik C. Once an occupational therapist... British Journal of Occupational Therapy. 1991; 54(10): 369.

[63]Student News: Students become members of the British Association of Occupational Therapists. Occupational Therapy News, September 2000, 8/9: 15.

[64]Jay, Mendez & Monteath. The Diamond Jubilee of the Professional Association, 1932–1992…: 256.

[65]Stewart AM. Empowerment and Enablement: Occupational Therapy 2001. British

Journal of Occupational Therapy. 1994; 57(7): 248-254.

[66]Stewart AM. The Casson Memorial Lecture 1992: Always a Little Further. British Journal of Occupational Therapy. 1992; 55(8): 296-302.

[67]Kelly G. Education: Course Development. WFOT 11th International Congress, London: Scientific Programme. British Journal of Occupational Therapy 1994; 57(5): 192.

[68]Woodward M. Student session: undergraduate teaching and its challenges. WFOT 11th International Congress, London: Scientific Programme. British Journal of Occupational Therapy 1994; 57(7): 268.

[69]Woodward M. Education: Developments and Progression. WFOT 11th International Congress, London: Scientific Programme. British Journal of Occupational Therapy 1994; 57(7): 267–9.

[70]WFOT 11th International Congress, London: Scientific Programme. British Journal of Occupational Therapy 1994; 57(6): 234–6.

[71]COT. Core Skills and Conceptual Framework for Practice–A Position Statement. 1994.

[72]COT Who Makes Doctors Better? 1995: 3.

[73]COT. Core Skills and Conceptual Framework for Practice...

[74]Polatajko H. Naming and framing occupational therapy: A lecture dedicated to the life of Nancy B. Who??Canadian Journal of Occupational Therapy 1992; 59(4): 189–99.

75Ilott I. Let's Have a Moratorium on Activities (the Word, not the Deed). British Journal of Occupational Therapy 1995; 58(7): 297–8.

[76]Golledge J. Distinguishing between occupation, purposeful activity and activity, part 1: Review and explanation. British Journal of Occupational Therapy 1998; 61(3): 100–104.

[77]Craik C. Stakeholders in the future of occupational therapy. British Journal of Occupational Therapy 1995; 58(12): 517.

[78]Green S. Dealing with Paradoxes. British Journal of Occupational Therapy 1996; 59(2): 49.

[79]Hagedorn R. The Casson Memorial Lecture 1995: An Emergent Profession—A Personal Perspective. British Journal of Occupational Therapy 1995; 58(8): 324–31.

[80]Eakin P. The Casson Memorial Lecture 1997: Shifting the Balance—Evidence-based Practice. British Journal of Occupational Therapy 1997; 60(7): 290–4.

[81]British Journal of Occupational Therapy 1997; 60(11).

[82]British Journal of Occupational Therapy 1999; 62(6).

[83]British Journal of Occupational Therapy 2000; 63(11).

[84]Taylor MC. Evidence-Based Practice for Occupational Therapists, Blackwell Science Ltd, 2000; 3.

[85]Taylor MC. Evidence-Based Practice for Occupational Therapists, Blackwell Science Ltd, 2000; Introduction: 3.

[86]Clegg A, Bannigan K. Shifting the Balance of Opinion: RCTs in Occupational therapy. British Journal of Occupational Therapy 1997; 60(11): 510–12.

[87]Contact staff on clinical.audit@cot.co.uk

[88]www.nice.org.uk

[89]Audit Database Launched. Occupational Therapy News. July 2000, 8/7: 1.

[90]COT. Who Makes Doctors Better? 1995.

[91]Lloyd-Smith W. Misplaced Trust? Occupational Therapy and NHS Trusts. British Journal of Occupational Therapy 1994; 57(2): 40–44.

[92]Bowden R. Power to the User. British Journal of Occupational Therapy 1991; 54(8): 281.

[93]Richards S. Community occupational therapy: Past dreams and new visions. British Journal of Occupational Therapy 1992; 55(7): 257–9.

[94]COT Interim Statement on the Implementation of Community Care Reforms and the Use of Occupational Therapy Resources. British Journal of Occupational Therapy 1992; 55(2): 80.

[95]Care Management. British Journal of Occupational Therapy 1992; 55(5): 206–207.

[96]Ovretveit J. Concepts of case management. British Journal of Occupational Therapy 1992; 55(6): 225–8.

[97]Announcements: Occupational Therapists a 'missing link' in vital community care services. British Journal of Occupational Therapy 1995; 58(3): 134.

[98]Lloyd-Smith W. Moving to Trust Status: The experiences of Staff of Occupational Therapy Departments. British Journal of Occupational Therapy 1997; 60(7): 309–14.

[99]Sessions D. A Survey of NHS Community Occupational Therapy Services for Adult Physical Disability. British Journal of Occupational Therapy 1996; 59(3): 119–24.

[100]Community mental health services: New Survey. British Journal of Occupational Therapy 1995; 58(2): 89.

[101]Craik C. Pioneers for the next century. British Journal of Occupational Therapy 1998; 61(5): 185.

[102]Kennedy S. Newsletter Editor and Membership Secretary

[103]COT. Membership Handbook. 2000.

[104]Contributed by OCTEP group.

[105]NAPOT Journal (ISSN 1465-8305)

[106]Felicity McElderry is NAPOT Professional Adviser. (12.2.01)

[107]Contributed by NAROT group. 2000.

[108]Contributed by NANOT group.

[109]Contributed by HOPE group.

[110]Job T, Broom W, Habermeh lF. Coming Out! Time to Acknowledge the Importance of Counselling Skills in Occupational Therapy. British Journal of Occupational Therapy 1997; 60(8): 357–8.

[111]Hagedorn R. Occupational Therapy: Perspectives and Processes. Edinburgh: Churchill Livingstone, 1995.

[112]Creek J, ed. Occupational Therapy and Mental Health. 2nd ed. Edinburgh: Churchill Livingstone, 1997: 83.

[113]Job, Broom, & Habermeh. Coming Out!…

[114]Department of Health. The Health of the Nation information booklets. London: HMSO, 1994.

[115]Job, Broom, & Habermeh. Coming Out!…

[116]Flood B. Psychiatry: Developments in Forensic Services. British Journal of Occupational Therapy 1994; 57(7): 269.

[117]Occupational Therapy in Work Practice and Productivity. British Journal of Occupational Therapy 1997; 60(6): 285.

[118]Pratt J. Work Practice: Moving Ahead. British Journal of Occupational Therapy 1997; 60(6): 237.

[119]Pratt. Work Practice: Moving Ahead.…

[120]Pratt J. Work Practice and Productivity. British Journal of Occupational Therapy 1997; 60(8): 375.

[121]Howard L, Stewart S. Letter to the Editor: Work practice. British Journal of Occupational Therapy 1997; 60(9): 423.

[122]Caulfield J. Work practice: the Clubhouse model. British Journal of Occupational Therapy 1997; 60(9): 423.

[123]Contributed by OTiPP group

[124]Ramaiah RS. Occupational therapy and medical priority rehousing. British Journal of

Occupational Therapy 1992; 55(2): 41.

[125]Weaver J. Letters to the Editor: Medical Priority rehousing. British Journal of Occupational Therapy 1992; 55(3): 116.

[126]Ross R. Housing and Occupational Therapists. British Journal of Occupational Therapy 1992; 55(3): 123–4.

[127] COT. Membership Handbook. 2000: 70.

[128]BAOT. Code of Professional Conduct. British Journal of Occupational Therapy 1990; 53(4): 143–8.

[129]COT. Members first. Membership Handbook 2000. London: COT. 2000: 1.

[130]College of Occupational Therapists. Code of Ethics and Professional Conduct for Occupational Therapists. London: COT, 2000: 13.

[131]Craik C. Opinion: What could occupational therapists not achieve? British Journal of Occupational Therapy 1994; 57(6): 217–8.

[132]Valentine P. Using the medical library. British Journal of Occupational Therapy 1982; 45(1): 25–7.

[133]Howard PA. How to borrow a book, or obtain copies of journal articles, if you are an OT working in the NHS. British Journal of Occupational Therapy 1982; 45(1): 27–8.

[134]Roberts D. Index Medicus and Medline for occupational therapists. Part 1 An overview of coverage and searching methods. British Journal of Occupational Therapy 1990; 53(8): 317–20.

[135]Roberts D. Index Medicus and Medline for occupational therapists: Part 2 An introduction to indexing methods for searchers. British Journal of Occupational Therapy 1990; 53(9): 376–8.

[136]Barber G. Searching the occupational therapy journal literature. British Journal of Occupational Therapy 1990; 53(7): 275–9.

[137]Ballinger C, Curtin M. Research network. British Journal of Occupational Therapy 1993, 56(1): 39.

[138]Ballinger C, Pomeroy V, Melville H. Networking between therapists interested in research: how to set up a support group. British Journal of Occupational Therapy 1994; 57(5): 185-187.

[139]Barnitt RE. Editorial: Watching your back. British Journal of Occupational Therapy 1992; 55(10): dd.

[140]Eakin P, Ballinger C, Nicol M, Walker M, Alsop A, Ilott I. College of Occupational Therapists: Research and Development Strategy. British Journal of Occupational Therapy 1997; 60(11): 484-486.

[141] Eakin et al. College of Occupational Therapists: Research and Development Strategy....

[142]Stewart A. Empowerment and enablement: occupational therapy 2001. British Journal of Occupational Therapy 1994; 57(7): 248–54.

[143]Alice Constance Owens 1906–1976 Remembered by her friends. British Journal of Occupational Therapy 1977; 40, (1): 7–9.

[144]Announcement. British Journal of Occupational Therapy 1994; 57(4): 156.

[145]Carr.Thesis Collection: the National Collection of Unpublished Occupational Therapy Research. London: COT, 1999.

[146]Register of Therapy Researchers, Version 2, CD-ROM. April 1999.

[147]Fossey E. The study of human occupations: implications for research in occupational therapy. British Journal of Occupational Therapy1992; 55(4):148–52.

[148]Payling J. Editorial: Research for disabled people. British Journal of Occupational Therapy 1993; 56(10): 359.

[149]Fraser C. A survey of users of upper limb prostheses. British Journal of Occupational

Therapy 1993; 56(5): 166-7.

[150]Merriman SH, Kench K. Occupational therapy and dietetic therapy with a group of female psychiatric patients: an evaluation of outcome. British Journal of Occupational Therapy 1993; 56(12): 437–40.

[151]Burns A, Park K. Proximal femoral fractures in the female patient: a controlled trial. The role of the occupational therapy and physiotherapy. British Journal of Occupational Therapy 1992; 55(10): 397–400.

[152]Tullis A, Nicol M. A systematic review of the evidence for the value of functional assessment of older people with dementia. British Journal of Occupational Therapy 1999; 62(12): 554–63.

[153]Stephenson E, McKay C, Chesson R. An investigative study of early developmental factors in children with motor/learning difficulties. British Journal of Occupational Therapy1990; 53(1): 4–6.

[154]Mountain GA. A review of the literature in the British Journal of Occupational Therapy 1989–1996. British Journal of Occupational Therapy 1997; 60(10): 430–35.

[155]Clark C, Homer S, Paul B. The use of teleconferencing with occupational therapy students. British Journal of Occupational Therapy 1990; 53(5): 187–9.

[156]Sadlo G, Piper DW, Agnew P. Problem based learning in the development of an occupational therapy curriculum. Part 1: the process of problem based learning. British Journal of Occupational Therapy 1994; 57(2): 49–54.

[157]McKay EA, Ryan S. Clinical reasoning through story telling: examining a student's case study on a fieldwork placement. British Journal of Occupational Therapy 1995; 58(6): 234–8.

[158]Pinnington L, Bagshaw A. The requirement for ethical reasoning in occupational therapy education. British Journal of Occupational Therapy 1992; 55(11): 419–22.

[159]Miller E, Willis M. The Cochrane Collaboration and occupational therapy: emerging partnership. British Journal of Occupational Therapy 2000; 63(6): 288–90.

[160]Hooper D. Cochrane Collaboration and occupational therapy: emerging partnerships. Occupational Therapy News 8(12); 2000: 20–21.

[161]Drummond A, Lincoln N, House A, Enderby P, Majid M, Dewey M. The Stroke Collaborative Review Group: Rehabilitation. Stroke Research Unit, Nottingham City Hospital NHS Trust, Department of Liaison Psychiatry, Leeds General Infirmary, Community Science Centre, Northern General Hospital, Trent Institute for Health Services Research, 1996.

[162]Nicol MM, Robertson L, Connaughton JA. Life skills programmes for chronic mental illness 1998. (Cochrane Review) In: The Cochrane Library, 2, 2001. Oxford: Update Software.

[163]Research In Practice. British Journal of Occupational Therapy 1993; 56(1): 421.

[164] Culshaw HMS. Editorial: Evidence-based practice for sale? British Journal of Occupational Therapy 1995; 58(6): 233.

[165]Barnitt RE. Editorial: Watching your back. British Journal of Occupational Therapy 1992; 55(10): dd.

[166]Fowler, Davis S, Bannigan D. Priorities in mental health research: the results of a live research project. British Journal of Occupational Therapy 2000; 63(3): 98–104.

[167]Stowe J. Letter to the Editor. British Journal of Occupational Therapy 1992; 55(10): 401.

[168]British Journal of Occupational Therapy 1993; 56(12): 465.

[169]Curtin M. Research and Development Committee research networking day. British Journal of Occupational Therapy 1991; 54(9): 358.

[170]Eakin, Ballinger, et al. COT: Research and Development Strategy...1997....

[171]Eakin, Ballinger, et al. COT: Research and Development Strategy...1997...: 486.

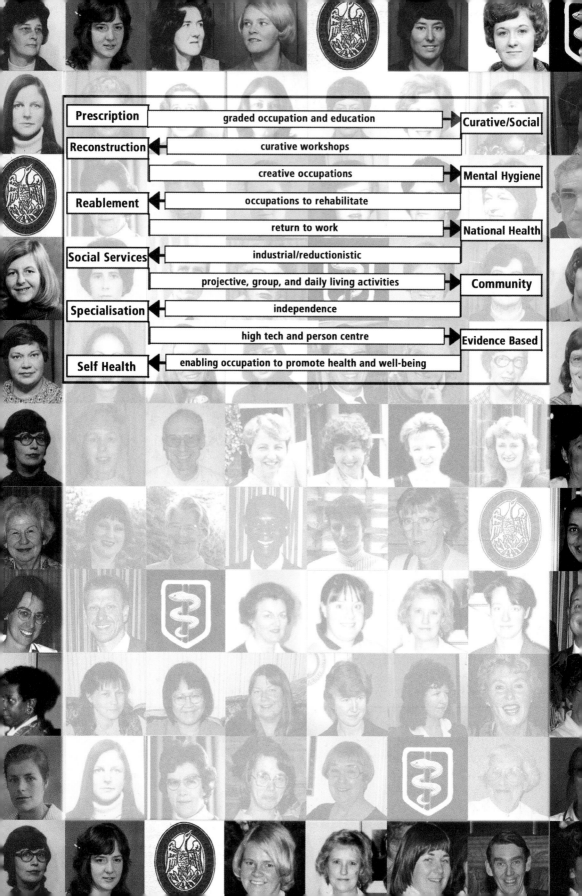

| Prescription | graded occupation and education | Curative/Social |
|---|---|---|
| Reconstruction | curative workshops | |
| | creative occupations | Mental Hygiene |
| Reablement | occupations to rehabilitate | |
| | return to work | National Health |
| Social Services | industrial/reductionistic | |
| | projective, group, and daily living activities | Community |
| Specialisation | independence | |
| | high tech and person centre | Evidence Based |
| Self Health | enabling occupation to promote health and well-being | |

# Chapter 12

# Serpent and Phoenix: Self Health and Revitalisation

## Contents

This chapter, which recalls the revitalisation myths of serpent and phoenix in the title, is concerned with analysing the past and projecting into the future of occupational therapy. The last decades of the twentieth century saw the revitalisation of basic concepts concerned with occupation, with the need for practice to be evidence based, and for it to be centred on clients' own needs as they perceive them. All suggest a focus towards the concept of self health through what people do on a daily basis. Providing evidence of the sorts of occupational regimes and constructs which appear to be health giving through developing a scientific base, and following this up with practice that enables and empowers people to work towards their own goals, potential and self health, seems to bring full circle, the long journey from pre-history to the present.

In this volume of the history of occupation for health the evolving saga of occupational therapy in the United Kingdom during the twentieth century has unfolded. Added to the tales in the first volume of occupational regimes for health prior to the twentieth century, it is possible to get an overview of the total picture of how instrumental what people 'do' is to their health from a holistic point of view. Combined, the two volumes have also provided the stories of who has used occupation therapeutically to help others throughout time. Considered together, the stories told, provide an understanding of how socio-cultural-political contexts affect what professions such as occupational therapy do (or do not do) in day-to-day practice. It seems that changing technologies, spiritual beliefs, political will and philosophical mores affect the provision of health care practices as much as the current understandings of biological effects and advances in medical techniques.

The sub-title of this volume *a journey from prescription to self health* was not chosen at the outset of the project, but emerged as the data unfolded. The first volume saw the very gradual build up of Western professionalism as society became more ordered and subject to greater control. This occurred as populations increased and occupations became more complex and less grounded in ways of life where nature imposed its own controls. The second volume picked up the story just as medical prescription was becoming accepted as commonplace across much of the population. The power of the medical profession increased as understanding of the human body and technical ways to fix problems improved. It was at the start of such developments that occupational therapy, as a profession in the United Kingdom, came into existence. From the beginning its use was circumscribed by medical prescription. For much of the twentieth century that remained the case, although almost as soon as care in the community became widespread the question of prescription for occupational therapy became problematic as other than medical personnel became referring agents. Gradually, the importance of people assuming greater control over the state of their own health came more to the fore. This was manifest within occupational therapy with the development of interest and practice based on enabling occupation which was deemed important by the people it sought to assist, by concepts of striving towards client driven or centred intervention, and by developing philosophies and research aimed at understanding the relationship between occupation and health. As part of that, in recent years the suggestion of occupation for health—occupational therapy—having a different and self-regulated purpose apart from medical prescription for illness, has been discussed openly provoking debate about important conceptual issues. That raises thoughts about where the occupation for health journey might lead to in the 21st century. In the discussion within this chapter prescription, conceptual issues about the notion of occupation for health in its own right, and future possibilities for occupational therapy will be addressed.

It can be hoped that, whatever the route forward brings, an understanding of occupational therapy's long history, before and after the profession emerged, will inform decision making. To that end, an overview of the ports of call made in the twentieth century journey is undertaken with reference to earlier paradigms of occupation for health, and in Figure 2.12.1 both ancient and recent aspects of the long track from pre-history are illustrated.

**Figure 2.12.1:** Ancient and recent aspects of occupational therapy's long track from pre-history to the end of the twentieth century

| PERIOD | SOCIAL FOCUS | HEALTH FOCUS | OCCUPATIONAL FOCUS |
|---|---|---|---|
| Prehistory | Survival | Natural Health Regimes | Self Health |
| Classical | Conquest | Humoral Gymnasia /Prevention | Strength & Beauty of Body & Mind |
| Medieval | Life after Death | Humoral-Spiritual | Monastic Creeds -Labour/Prayer |
| Renaissance/ Reformation | Rebirth of Individualism | Humoral-Social | Individual /Economic |
| Enlightenment | Growth of Science | Humoral-Prevention Morally Curative | Action & Rest Individual |
| Industrial | Capitalism | Occupational & Public Health | Industriousness Economic |
| **TWENTIETH CENTURY** | | | |
| 1900-1913 | Suffrage Social Justice | Remedial & Social | Education Work |
| 1914-1918 | War- Patriotism | Reconstructive | Curative Workshops |
| 1920-1938 | Economic Depression | Utilitarian Mental Hygiene | Creative |
| 1939-1945 | War | Rehabilitation | Reablement |
| 1946-1965 | Post War Boom | National Health | Return to Work |
| 1966-1986 | Recession | Social Services | Independence Reductionistic |
| 1987-2000 | Technological & Multicultural | High Tech., Community & Health Promoting | Enabling Person Centred Evidence Based Self Health |

# An overview of the twentieth century journey

Against the background of nineteenth century charitable notions of the better educated, and their valuing of industriousness, the poor, disadvantaged or disabled became subject to initiatives aimed at improving their lot in life. Examples abound, and those identified as associated with occupation for health include the social activist and public health reformer drives to improve working and domestic conditions, to ensure green environments for play and recreation, to provide impetus for making everyday objects things of beauty, and to establish education and work institutions for those unable to take advantage of what was on offer without special consideration of their needs. Such initiatives, led by people like Robert Owen, John Ruskin, William Morris, Thomas Southwood Smith and Octavia Hill, contained the seeds of social justice and occupational therapy which flourished in the twentieth century, and which were sprouting at its dawning.

As the century opened, social justice issues, particularly concerned with women's rights and those of crippled children, had surfaced as important. The successful fight for women's suffrage, and the necessity of increased opportunities for education for both women and crippled children resulted in women being able and more than ready to engage in careers in the health professions. Their focus, in the first place, was on the educational needs of crippled children. Disabled herself, and having some concept of the ill effects of occupational deprivation, Agnes Hunt was a prime example of such pioneers. Her work established a tradition of other than medical care being required in cases requiring hospitalisation over a long period. In her case, it was based on meeting the education and play needs of children in institutions providing orthopaedic services. This broke new ground and opened up possibilities for more wide ranging ideas about the occupational requirements of people hospitalised for a long term. Agnes Hunt's initiatives were probably instrumental in orthopaedics  being one of the first areas of occupational therapy intervention within the field of physical health.

In some cases women needed to go so far as to establish new professions, because some aspects of care had not been addressed sufficiently to that date—as Elizabeth Casson had found when working first with Octavia Hill's tenants, and then with psychiatric patients. Particularly because medicine had been a province of men, some of the health needs of women and children had been overlooked. In the past they had often been the province of women within their domestic environments, and so were an aspect of their occupational roles which also included doctoring, nursing and rehabilitating. In occupational therapy, the idea that people's occupational roles could be health giving and curative was expanded into medical environments. The earlier history showed that occupation for health had sometimes, but not consistently, been addressed by previous providers of health and social care. Before and after the advent of monastic care, for example, the fate of the homeless, the sick and the needy had been subject to the skills and beliefs of their families and communities. Monasteries had established hospitals, hospices and lay institutional care for the needy. These had disappeared with the reformation when the State took over the Church. Community based workhouses replaced monastic care and, later, mad houses and asylums became places for those with mental illness, in all of which occupation was used as the principal means of intervention.

Families had also had to care for the 'consumptive.' Tuberculosis, at the turn of the century, was the other diagnosis that ensured occupational as well as medical intervention for many. Pioneered by Sir Robert Philip, graded occupations were used as treatment from the last decade of the nineteenth century, and programmes were expanded early in the next. Holding that a correct balance of activity and rest were central issues in health, his curative view of occupational treatment was administered according to specific dosage, a prescription carried forward and adhered to in many occupational therapy departments of a later date. Philip was to become a member of the Board of Governors of the Astley Ainslie Occupational Therapy Department and Training School. Tuberculosis programmes were another of the earliest 'physical' treatments that engaged occupational therapists, and were major employers for decades, until the advent of modern drugs that changed the picture dramatically. Treatment varied between large-scale developments of whole villages where patients lived and worked, to more traditional sanatoria. Dr Jane Walker, of the Nayland Sanatorium, was an early leading exponent of occupational therapy, and became a vice president of the AOT when it was formed in the 1930s.

World War I provided another stepping stone in the recognition of the part occupation could play alongside or as part of curative medicine, particularly in the field of orthopaedics. Sir Robert Jones, assisted by Manuel, ex-King of Portugal, established curative workshops for injured servicemen throughout the length and breadth of the country. Remarkably similar, in many respects, to later rehabilitation centres, these established a tradition of splints and appliances being made in the workshops—a precursor of the things to come during and following World War II. Whilst war and conquest, and its social consequences had led to the establishment of gymnasia in the classical world to develop and maintain strength and beauty of body and mind, the rationale for the curative workshops of World War I was much more pragmatic. It sought to return injured servicemen to the fight as quickly as possible, and so, unlike the gymnasia, when the war ended the perceived purpose ended too, and the workshops were closed. During the war acknowledgement of the needs of people with disability was not a government priority, although industrial scientists (work study experts—ergonomists) had, like occupational therapists did later, made remarkable contributions to establishing routines, training and equipment to assist injured people to overcome dependence.

The War had also provided the impetus for approximately 116 proto-occupational therapists known as 'civilian aides' recruited in the USA to serve abroad. In the main, they worked with victims of shell shock, in make-shift quarters, with make-shift equipment. Some of the establishments in which they received preliminary training continued after the conflict ended, but others, like the curative workshops, folded at the cessation of hostilities. Despite that disappointment, World War I saw the establishment of the first formal Society of Occupational Therapists in the USA. Although not recognised as one of the six founders of occupational therapy, the work of Adolf Meyer, a psychiatrist, was instrumental in its development. His interest in occupation used for remedial purposes within mental hygiene was supported and carried forward in the UK by David Henderson and others who had worked with Meyer in America. Those psychiatrists recognised the worth of moral and industrial treatment, which had been the mainstay of programmes in asylums throughout the nineteenth century, and which had flourished because of the inspirational work of people such as Philippe Pinel in Paris, William and Samuel Tuke in York, William Ellis at Wakefield and Hanwell, and W.A.F. Browne in Scotland.

Henderson, a Scot, played a major role in promoting the profession in the UK, and Scotland saw appointment in 1925 of Margaret Barr Fulton—the first trained occupational therapist in Britain. She was later to become the founding President of WFOT. In the 1920s Elizabeth Casson heard Henderson speak of occupational therapy, and this quickened her already substantial interest in the subject, leading eventually to the establishment of Dorset House, the first British School of Occupational Therapy. At a time of economic depression, it is remarkable that four schools were instigated during the 1930s. As well as Dorset House, there was one at the Maudsley Hospital, another based in Tottenham Court Road which metamorphosed into the London School and later the programme based at Brunel University. A fourth school at the Astlie Ainsley Institution in Edinburgh was to provide, eventually, the first occupational therapy degree programme on the mainland, as part of Edinburgh's Queen Margaret College. The establishment of the schools reflected considerable government interest in improving treatment within mental institutions at that time. Occupational treatment or therapy became a 'hot' topic, featured in prestigious medical journals and government memoranda. Such interest stimulated two British associations of occupational therapists, SAOT and AOT, to be established and constituted during the 1930s. Members and officials represented a mix of occupational therapists. Some were trained but many others were pioneers who had been occupation treatment practitioners before training was available. And there were more than a few interested others. Those were largely members of the medical profession with a particular interest in the use of occupation as treatment. They must have been 'heady' days!

Occupational therapy at that time found craft work to be the medium of choice. It had been recognised as useful in the treatment of patients with mental disorders in the nineteenth century and carried over into the twentieth. Readers will recall from Chapter 5 how Dr R. Eager, in one of the earliest texts, discussed the notion of diversion as an overtaking of negative or sick behaviours. That idea, which has emerged many times throughout the history, still begs answers to questions about whether it is possible to divert unhealthy thoughts by occupation, and whether that in itself is therapeutic as many claimed it to be. Eager said of the results of those creative remedies that, 'the Mental Hospital which practises Occupational Therapy creates a spirit of hopefulness and happiness which is absent in one which does not do so.'[1] Considering the link between happiness, health and well-being which many latter day researchers, including myself, have found, revisiting rather than trying to forget, or actively rejecting, creativity would be a more positive way forward. We need to know more, rather than less about all the aspects of occupation that have been used with success.

Then along came World War II. This was a time of enormous growth and consolidation, and one of substantial pride, in the profession. Its members felt needed and respected, and that what they had to offer was of 'essential national importance.'

Indeed, two occupational therapists, Dorothy Bramwell and Margaret Lewthwaite, had their work in the Middle East recognised by the award—Member of the British Empire (MBE). At home, training opportunities mushroomed with the government and armed forces providing much of the impetus to increase the numbers of workers in the field. In a time like none other, before or since, occupational therapists, as has proved to be the case more often than not, worked with tremendous energy and initiative despite almost non-existent facilities, equipment or material. One example that typifies the flair many displayed was the programme to provide materials to prisoners of war overseas; it was led by Miss English who recognised and acted on the need to overcome what can be devastating consequences of occupational deprivation. Readers may recall how Miss English explained in *The Times* that, '...physical and mental deterioration, caused from monotony and lack of occupation, is one of the greatest problems for prisoners of war...'[2] An international comradeship between occupational therapists was also manifest, and a particular relationship grew from earlier contact between Scottish and Canadian occupational therapists when the latter established occupational therapy services in Scotland, as well as some of strategic note south of the border. During this war, unlike the previous one, the provision of rehabilitative facilities was recognised as having industrial and economic significance, and so became an accepted and ongoing part of the British health structure. It is fascinating, indeed, to speculate on the twists and turns of the fate of occupational therapy because of occupation's many roles within human life, and how each were valued (or not) at particular periods.

As the two World Wars came and went, the pace of social change increased. Central Government became more and more concerned with the health as well as the wealth of its people. As was noted in Volume 1, that had started with the Elizabethan Poor Law Act of 1601 when Parliament had recognised that the care of poor, infirm and homeless rested with it. Under the central control of the Privy Council, the Act laid this duty upon each parish to be administered by local justices of the peace, and resourced by the raising of a local community tax—the poor rate. For well over 100 years, whilst a strong Privy Council and a settled agricultural life provided a stable context, the system worked well. Occupation was central for reasons of self-respect, economy, and health—action and rest still being deemed central to their preservation, as they had been in the *Regimen Sanitatis* of classical and medieval medicine. Local authorities were required to provide work when it was not otherwise available and to buy raw materials for that purpose. It was not until 1948, that the National Assistance Act finally replaced the old Elizabethan Poor Law amid cheers in the House of Commons. Perhaps Members forgot that the original conception of the old Poor Law was to help those in need within their own local environments, a concept to be revisited in community care initiatives of later in the century.[3]

The idea that health and social services should rank with justice and defence as a benefit provided by the state had gained ground during the early part of the century, but did not eventuate until after World War II. The foundations were laid by the 1908 Old Age Pensions Acts, the founding of Employment exchanges in 1910, and the National Insurance Act of 1911. Between the two wars local authorities had assumed more responsibility for the care of the blind, crippled and chronic unfit, and by 1939 two-thirds of the hospital beds in the country were administered by them. However, it was the establishment of the Emergency Medical Service during World War II that pre-empted modern national health and social services, along with the Beveridge and Tomlinson Reports in 1942 and the Disabled Persons (Employment) Act of 1944. After the war, as has been seen, a whole series of Acts were passed re-organising health and social services, with the jewel in the crown being the establishment of the National Health Service in 1948. This was designed 'to secure improvement in the physical and mental health of the people of England and Wales and the prevention, diagnosis, and treatment of illness, and for that purpose to provide or secure the effective provisions of services.'

A 'return to work' ethos characterised the decade following the war. There was paid employment in abundance as the country sought to re-establish patterns of life in peacetime. These were to be remarkably different from what had gone before, not least for occupational therapists. For a start there were many more therapists available, and people in government and the health services were much more aware of what they had to offer as they had become part of the health care establishment. No longer to be seen mainly in psychiatric hospitals working to improve patients' mental health through largely creative and social means, most were at the forefront of the medical rehabilitation workforce in assisting people with physical disorders to return to work. Practice was focused on occupations for remedial as well as for social purposes, and the term reablement was coined. This came to include domestic and personal activities of daily life, for which a mainly female profession at that time appeared to be well suited. Occupational therapists were not, as a rule, employed in industrial rehabilitation centres. In hindsight this appears to be illogical. While gender issues may have had some part in that decision, the main reason appears to have been an attempt to prevent the medicalisation of socio-economic retraining immediately prior to recipients' re-entry into the workforce. This was not appreciated by medical rehabilitation experts, who believed that their establishments were well able to take patients from injury to work most effectively and economically. Occupational therapists, at that time, were closely aligned with medicine and medical rehabilitation specialists, and so were seen by industrial rehabilitation experts as inappropriate providers of industrial rehabilitation.

From the late 1930s both curative and preventive aspects of medicine had improved significantly as pharmacological developments made it possible to prevent or treat infectious diseases, and to control mental disorders to a much greater extent, while new technologies enabled progressive diagnosis and surgery.[4] Over time the length of stay of patients in hospitals was reduced; more returned home straight from acute care, and those requiring lengthier rehabilitation were those with long term or permanent disability, and the elderly. Rehabilitation began to be focused more and more on assisting people with personal and domestic activities of daily living to become and remain independent. This coincided with an economic downturn, and as return to work became uncertain this reinforced the direction of practice towards ADL. It was reinforced further with the implementation of the Chronically Sick and Disabled Persons Act of 1970. Until that Act there had been relatively little legislation for the benefit of disabled people.

That Act, and the later one of 1986, led to an essentially needs based service provided by local authorities according to their reading of requirements, but with the level of provision and criteria of need not specified. Alf Morris, who had presented the Private Members Bill from which preceded the 1970 Act, propounded a philosophy which sat well with occupational therapy ideology at that time, and remains relevant to end of the century direction towards enabling self health and well-being:

> If we could bequeath one precious gift to posterity, I would choose a society in which there is genuine compassion for the very sick and the disabled, where understanding is unostentatious and sincere, where, if years cannot be added to the lives of the chronically sick, at least life can be added to their years; where the mobility of disabled people is restricted only by the bounds of technical progress and discovery; where the handicapped have a fundamental right to participate in industry and society according to their ability; where socially preventable disease is unknown and where no man has cause to be ill at ease because of his disability.[5]

As rehabilitation toward return to work tended to decline in the physical rehabilitation field, industrial rehabilitation tended to increase in mental health. Difficulties began to surface between nursing and occupational therapy in some places as both claimed it as an area of practice. In part, that overlap of interests appears to have mirrored the blurring of roles which was beginning to occur, encouraged by an economic incentive to cut down the number of specialist services. That incentive had some merit in that common and agreed outcomes of therapy between treatment team members appear common sense. Other new directions in psychiatry, such as the use of group therapy and the setting up of therapeutic communities, also adopted a multi-professional approach.

The 1970s saw the start of a recurring pattern, every 3–5 years, of reorganisation, restructuring, reform, or review of the NHS. Whilst better use of scarce resources prompted such initiatives, their regularity caused upheavals in practice, increased record keeping and, as well, highlighted a need for more occupational therapists. Recruitment became a major issue as it had been in World War II.[6] In the 1977 Jubilee Issue of BJOT, 'Agag' recognised that the role of hospitals had begun to decline for a combination of economic and social reasons. The tradition of ongoing care being given in hospitals was challenged, replaced by the notion of community care as the way forward.[7] Community care could more effectively address social health needs, as well as many of a physical and psychological nature. Cosin had raised the idea of social medicine as early as the 1950s. With reference to special geriatric units, he said of social medicine, that the aim was to combine 'preventive medicine, medical treatment, and physical, psychological and social rehabilitation.'[8] Whilst community care did eventuate in large measure, true social health care still remains a tantalising vision as what is provided in its stead are, in the main, social services for those who are diagnosed according to medical criteria. Pertinent to many of today's problems, and to the future directions of occupational therapy, is recognition that there are many people with occupational dysfunction who would benefit from occupational therapy intervention, but who have not reached a point at which symptoms are recognisable as medical problems. To intervene early, and enable healthier occupational regimes, is a health-promoting, illness-preventing occupational approach of the future.

Occupational therapists gradually became associated in the public domain as 'providers of equipment for the disabled' and the image of 'special craft teachers in hospitals' receded somewhat. The growth of paediatric services, and many areas of specialisation from toy libraries to housing, orthoses to driving, and sensory-motor to medico legal assessments, to name but a few, give the lie to those stereotypes. Yet with a much wider role and many areas of specialisation it is difficult to understand why by the end of the 1980s the Blom-Cooper Commission of Inquiry was still able to legitimately describe occupational therapy as a 'submerged profession.' Indeed, before the Commission felt able to carry out its inquiry, it felt it necessary to establish just what professional work was done by those called occupational therapists. They saw its difference to many of the other allied health professions, in that it:

> *...did not develop primarily to enable medicine to exploit new technologies: it developed when it became possible to save the lives of those who would in earlier times have died. With this increased ability there was a growing awareness that the job of restoring individuals to health and maximising their functional capacity was not completed by the physician, the surgeon or even the bed-side nurse exercising their various skills. Many hospitalised patients who had survived invasive surgical or medical procedures were nevertheless listless and pessimistic about the future pattern of their lives. They often lacked the motivation even to leave the hospital, where at least they were sheltered from the realities of a possibly hostile world. In the world outside hospital they needed to be given sympathy, advice and practical assistance if they were to regain the skills required for them to function adequately in paid employment or domestic tasks—in short to establish as much personal autonomy and independence as possible. The health service needed to develop a rehabilitation thrust as an integral part of its therapeutic purpose. Slowly it dawned on the few, dotted throughout the services, who were being employed to proffer such support to patients, that a new approach was required. These few were acutely aware that they themselves, by professional training, had to acquire a systematic body of knowledge and skills. It could not be given satisfactorily by amateur, self-taught well-wishers.*[9]

Chapter 10 listed several factors that the Blom-Cooper Commission recognised as contributing to occupational therapy's problems of identity. These included the dominant position held by medicine and social work, which required occupational therapists either to court those professions for patronage or to form alliances with other professions to erect common platforms. Both of these options have been utilised to largely good effect by the COT. Such efforts did, however, take time and resources which could, instead, have been available to take the profession forward in directions aimed at its own autonomous future. Additionally, dependence on doctors and social workers for access to clients resulted in the work of occupational therapists often being attributed to some other agency, so that false stereotypes of their function were maintained. This was aggravated by the pronounced female composition of the profession, which continued to influence pecuniary rewards and status derived from their work.[10]

Throughout all the changes a dynamic but often frustrated and sometimes criticised British Association and its antecedents threaded a path through a veritable minefield of sociopolitical legislation. It appears that they did so with courage and determination and, mostly, with surprising success—if success is measured by the profession's growth from a handful of enthusiasts in the early 1930s to over 20 000 occupational therapist members by the end of the century. A chart depicting its major national and international milestones is shown as Figure 2.12.2. Success is also the case if it is measured by the degree of change and development the profession has negotiated successfully, and its adaptability to altered health needs as technology and contexts evolved. To a large extent that journey has been recorded in the professional journals. Jenny King looked back to the first issue of *Occupational Therapy* in 1938 and the editorial of Miss Ross and Miss English where they explained their basic editorial knowledge as 'a complete and utter blank,' and compared it with the BJOT of the 1990s. King described how the modern version, with a professional editor and her editorial team, tried to draw information from the full range of settings in which practitioners worked, commissioning in areas from which papers were not forthcoming; how it tried to assist those finding difficulty with the newer type of research articles by providing guidelines on writing for publication, editorial assistance and study days; and how, different from many other totally research-oriented occupational therapy journals, it provided for different types of presentation such as short reports and opinion pieces as well as research articles.[11]

**Figure 2.12.2: National and international highlights in the journey**

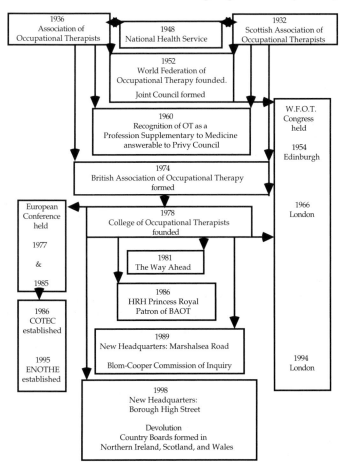

The health and social care environment changed markedly over the last two decades of the century as projects concerned with skill mix, re-profiling and the introduction of commercial values to health services, for example, typified the flavour of the times. This resulted in altered roles for occupational therapists and occupational therapy helpers, which led to many being involved mainly in assessment, supervision and discharge planning rather than in the hands on treatment of earlier times. Some changes, like GPs becoming purchasers when the concept of 'fund-holding' was introduced, have once more increased medical control over occupational therapy services. Yet despite the changes having fundamental significance, occupational therapists have tended to leave socio-political debate to the Professional Association, raising very little voice about concerns. As health and social care policy affect the way occupational therapists work on a daily basis, it is becoming imperative that occupational therapists and educators give more attention to the formation and implementation of health-related government policy.[12]

Just as occupational therapists seemed hesitant to take on a more political role, so too did they hesitate to embrace research, despite it being called for from an early date by some of their respected medical advisors. Fortunately, that corner seems to have been turned, especially since the idea of evidence based practice has found fertile ground. That coincided with the long battle to base pre-registration education in universities, with subsequent access to post-graduate opportunities. Significantly, many members of the profession began to embrace qualitative methodologies to capture individual experiences and relationships in a more holistic way, and alongside that, took to the idea of clinical reasoning as the heart of practice.[13]

As the world at large went 'high tech' in the last decade so too did the COT, at least in some spheres. That enabled contact with fellow occupational therapists throughout the world, and global visions for the future of occupational therapy began to emerge. First there was a revisiting of the almost forgotten notion of occupation as an agent for health as the foundation of practice. Then came the push for client-centred practice and an enabling rather than a prescriptive attitude to therapeutic initiatives. Both suggest a proactive rather than a reactive approach, and a return to the age-old values of promoting self health as the way forward. Auldeen Alsop in the mid-1990s maintained:

> *Enabling clients to manage change in their lives is part of our core business. The competent performance of each individual in his or her personal environment is within the profession's domain of concern. Being aware of, and managing, the influences of the sociopolitical and economic context in which we work must also be of concern if the profession is to survive. Whilst changes in the wider environment may challenge the homeostasis of the profession, the transitions we make are often reassuringly stabilised by the roots of the profession which are grounded in the past.*

> *These roots embrace a history and a philosophy which are uniquely different from those of other professions...*

> *...It is the understanding of both the historical and the contemporary significance of activity, occupation and employment in people's lives that leads us to approach clients' problems in a unique, professional way.*[14]

That brief overview of the occupational therapy journey from prescription to self health provides food for thought and reflection to guide the way forward. However, there are some issues emerging from the material that need to be addressed, albeit briefly. There are, needless to say, issues of defining and overviewing concepts of occupational therapy and occupation for health for the 21st century, which have proved to be so difficult to do throughout the profession's twentieth century history. Part of that process needs to be concerned with the relationship between occupation and health, how it articulates with medical views, and how it will fit into health care in the coming years. First, though, some discussion about the largely female composition of occupational therapy is needed. It was women being able to engage in careers other than those of a menial nature or home duties that proved to be essential in the establishment of the profession—which was, in the first instance, supplementary to medicine.

# The work of women and the patronage of medical men

Historically, the work of women in the public arena has been less well recorded than that of men. That, in itself, supports the many male dominance theories that abound. The question of male dominance has attracted many authors of different disciplines to describe or research the issues that surround it in the workplace This is not the forum for detailed debate on the issue, but it is appropriate to question why most occupational therapists are women, and what impact that has had on its historical development; the way forward can then be considered with some of those thoughts in mind. The question is of relevance to both men and women in the profession as the past and current preponderance of women has given it a particular cast and way of working, and influenced how it is perceived by fellow professions, the public, and employing and governing bodies.

Although men were instrumental in the beginning of the profession, as both instigators and organisers, it has been quite clear that, in the main, women have found the work described as occupational therapy more to their liking than have men. Men have been more evident in the field as technical instructors, in socio-economic health arenas, as well as in medical rehabilitation. In curative workshops and establishments for people with tuberculosis, for example, it was often technical instructors with particular trade skills who were employed. Such gender division could be an artefact of how the profession was allowed to grow by both medical patronage and socio-political initiatives. Readers may recall Dr David Henderson's very early supposition, for example, that occupational therapy would be, essentially, 'women's work' which called for a good education, intelligence and refinement.[15] Occupational therapy itself and the vocational paths of occupational instructors (not called occupational therapy) were controlled externally to the extent of what aspect of occupation for health either could work in. Some of the decisions about what was inclusive or exclusive to occupational therapy were undoubtedly driven by issues about medical patronage from inside medicine's ranks, and by powerful groups outside medicine to control it's sphere of influence. As, latterly, occupational therapists begin to understand occupation for health as their domain of concern in its entirety, the extent of socio-political manoeuvres and medical control or patronage issues become clearer. Some can be seen as counter-productive in terms of ultimate benefits to the public in terms of health through occupation. Even if a variety of interested professions remain involved in the future, some overriding philosophies need to be articulated and decisions need to be taken to make sense of the whole, and to guide health initiatives for all people towards understanding the relationship between it and occupation.

Another early contributing factor to male/female ratios was that the first British School, Dorset House, was a female establishment. Based at a residential clinic run by Dr Elizabeth Casson for women psychiatric patients, the first students and teachers were women. That may have established a precedent. Only a few schools accepted male students for decades to come. Although, in the present, the numbers of male occupational therapists are increasing, there remains a preponderance of women. It has been suggested that the work itself taps into the same capacities evident in the caring roles previously undertaken by women in the domestic sphere, in a way similar to nursing and teaching infants. Certainly, in the earliest days of the twentieth century it was, largely, nurses and teachers who provided occupational instruction in orthopaedic and mental hospitals. Accepting their role as supplementary to medicine, the fledgling female occupational therapists assumed an aura of amazing confidence as they promoted and established services in places where none had existed before. It was only gradually, and in more recent years when feminist ideas have been to the fore, that questions about the drawbacks, as well as the advantages of the feminine nature of occupational therapy have been discussed more openly.

Despite some evidence of negative reactions when the word 'feminism' is used, as Hamlin and colleagues found when surveying American occupational therapists,[16] some articles discussing the issues have appeared in the profession's journals. In BJOT, for example, Jackie Taylor reflected on the female dominance of occupational therapy 'in a world primarily managed, controlled and informed by men.'[17] In agreement with other writers in the field, she suggested that creative work and helping the sick to perform activities of daily life has its roots in women's work. A difference of moral viewpoint between women and men, she thought, could be a reason for some of the difficulties in the development of occupational therapy. She found useful the notions put by Gilligan that moral reasoning for males centres on rights, principles and fairness, whilst for women it is based on an ethic of care which has three levels. Those range from care of self, through care of others, to a morality of non-violence in which attempts are made to resolve issues in ways that cause least hurt.[18] Although not exclusive to women, an ethic of care in occupational therapy enables therapists to empower clients to voice their needs. However, Taylor suggests that 'disempowerment is not experienced solely by those receiving care. Occupations that are predominantly female suffer low status and disempowerment also.'[19] That has been the case in occupational therapy under the patronage, guiding hand and control of medicine. The concerns of the Blom-Cooper Commission of Inquiry about the controlling hand of medicine in occupational therapy come to mind immediately, and there are many other examples sprinkled throughout this text. Taylor suggests that examination of feminist thought may facilitate questioning of occupational therapy's links with medicine and with objective science, and help to affirm its original base in activity and its relationship with health and well-being.[20] Another view, put by Greg Kelly, confirms that there are some particular strengths to be gained by recognising and integrating the feminine principle into the profession. He, however, suggests that 'in the balanced viewpoint...any system based upon the feminine principle or the masculine principle alone will not be sufficient; they must merge and actualise in the practice of occupational therapy.'[21]

That seems reasonable, in the light of this history, which has been testament to the many ways in which occupational therapy has allied itself with medicine and with male patronage since the earliest days. It can even be suggested that the profession would not have evolved at all had it not been for the interest and involvement of physicians and surgeons. Let us consider that thought briefly. Certainly, before the twentieth century, there were many, apart from those in the medical field who promoted occupation for health purposes. Some of their stories are chronicled in the first volume of this history. But their contribution, if not of a medical nature, is seldom called to mind when occupational therapists discuss their background or describe the basis of their therapy to others. In the twentieth century it was indeed doctors of medicine who promoted and established occupational therapy in the United Kingdom. Experts in tuberculosis like Philip, McDougall, and Walker, orthopaedic surgeons such as Jones and Girdlestone, medical superintendents like Cunningham, and psychiatrists such as Henderson, Casson, and Tennent could truly be described as occupational therapists in their own right, so great was their contribution. They were visionary in attempting to meet the holistic health needs of their patients, but, it is true, they saw it as essential that the occupation in occupational therapy was medically prescribed and had to be seen to be so. The therapists, at that time, appear happy for it to have been that way. Perhaps that was to do with their gratitude for a way out of the domestic roles they would otherwise have been confined too, and their acceptance of male dominance in the world of paid employment and medicine. Indeed, the Association of Occupational Therapists' first 'official' definition of an occupational therapist was:

> ...any person who is appointed as responsible for the treatment of patients by occupation and who is qualified by training and experience to administer the prescription of a Physician or Surgeon in the treatment of any patient by occupation.[22]

Casson's definition of an occupational therapist was equally prescriptive. It described:

> ...one who has gone through a specific and strenuous professional training such as has a masseuse, a dispenser, or a nurse, and who is ready to be given a doctor's prescription and carry out that treatment with all the skill it requires.[23]

Occupational therapists for many decades were totally committed to the idea of medical prescription. It gave acceptance, purpose, and status to their chosen occupation. It provided a place for them in the complex scheme of health care, and a rationale for the sorts of subjects they chose to found their practice upon. Medical prescription was a source of pride. So much was that the case that medical staff not only allotted patients to 'suitable classes' but some actually prescribed the occupations which should be used. In the 1933 *Memorandum on Occupation Therapy for Mental Patients* issued by the Board of Control, it was the Medical Superintendent himself who was seen as the appropriate person to organise occupational therapy aimed at 'promoting recovery, of creating new habits, and of preventing deterioration.' That was in addition to a doctor being the person to direct and keep in touch with the patient's work, prescribe treatment, and supervise its application.[24] As Dr Eager explained a little later in the 1930s 'the prescribing of suitable occupations for patients is as important as the prescribing of drugs.' Indeed, if the former was done well, drugs might not be needed at all.[25] Similarly, Dr John Iveson Russell during the same period proclaimed 'therapeutic occupations must be conducted under medical supervision, and in some cases specifically prescribed,' and that the doctor's 'instructions regarding a new patient may be called the prescription.'[26] However, he added that 'the main secret of success lies in the method and the manner in which the occupation is presented' for to prescribe precisely what 'a patient shall do and to tell him when he dislikes it that "the doctor knows best" is nothing better than charlatanism.' As well as making the case records available, he used the formulary shown in Figure 2.12.3 as the record of prescription to make sure the occupational officer had all the required information.[27]

**Figure 2.12.3: Formulary used at the North Riding of Yorkshire Mental Hospital 1938** [28]

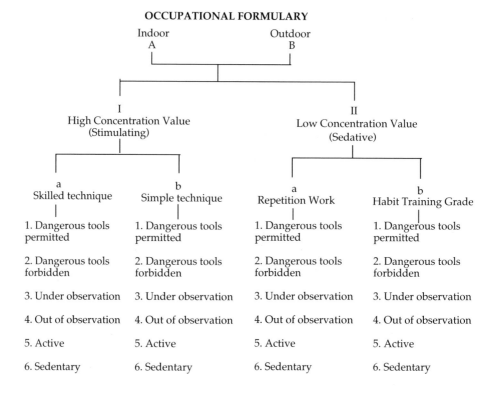

Dr H. Ashley Cooper, at the 1941 annual general meeting of AOT, reflected on the difficulty of prescribing occupational therapy for patients with mental illness. He said, 'it is as if a doctor had to prescribe drugs whose action and dosage he did not know, to be dispensed by a chemist ignorant of measuring devices.' Whilst the results may be excellent it could not be claimed as 'a masterpiece of scientific therapy.' He suggested as imperatives the collection of data about cases as a basis for controlled experiments to test findings, and to test new techniques against control groups.[29] As such research did not start in earnest for many years, and were seldom controlled trials, it is hardly a surprise that ultimately there was a drop in the standard of prescriptions, and even in a readiness to prescribe. Another reason for that might be that, like Adolf Meyer, many potential prescribers felt that occupational therapy 'must provide opportunities rather than prescriptions.'[30]

The issue of prescription was a two-way process of the giving and the welcoming of medical patronage. This took many years to resolve, and indeed, it remains a somewhat murky issue to ascertain where both occupational therapists and medical personnel stand on this issue. There has certainly been much debate over the years, particularly when many occupational therapists started to be employed outside the health field within local authorities. A more recent factor has been a more mature appreciation of the depth and potential of occupation as a health-promoting agent in its own right and with sometimes a different purpose from reductionist medical views of treatment. The debate is in urgent need of being re-opened so that a way forward becomes clear for the profession, as an autonomous health discipline with something valuable to offer within acute medical care, social, and population health spheres.

In hindsight, though, alliance with medicine was a strategic move by the many women and few men who worked as occupational therapists in those early days, and by those who guided the profession forward as officers in the fledgling associations. Medicine had entrées into many spheres of influence not open to a young and largely female profession, and the benefit of doctors helping to carry forward the message of how occupation could assist those who were ill was deemed, and proved to be, invaluable.

Such assistance was still being sought in the 1960s. Readers will recall *Occupational Therapy, Present and Future,* the report of a committee chaired by Dr Francis Bach, which advanced a changing role for occupational therapists but reinforced the need for their interventions to be under medical direction. To define the parameters of the scope and function of occupational therapy, for example, numerous medical organisations were called on to express their opinion including: the Association of Industrial Medical Officers; the British Association of Physical Medicine; the British Orthopaedic Association; the Medical Society for the Care of the Elderly; the Royal College of Physicians; the Royal College of Surgeons; and the Society of Medical Officers of Health.

One of the problems has been that, like prescription, the patronage did not continue to the same extent as in the early days. Medical interest turned to other matters as contexts and technology altered procedures and outcomes, and their practice became more reductionist and technical. For a while occupational therapy followed suit, until it became obvious that the new paradigms of care did not fit the basically holistic nature of occupation for health philosophies. The decline of medicine as a close and influential ally added to an apparent loss of direction for occupational therapists, which was evident from the 1960s. While some exceptional medical personnel with particular visions such as Dott, Wyn-Parry, Nicholls, or Aitken continued to work alongside occupational therapists as patrons, advisors, and colleagues, those were the exception rather than the rule. Patronage was sought amongst others with different kinds of expertise. Presidents of BAOT were selected from the ranks of those who might have influence in government, for example, and chief executives were appointed from people with business and organisation skills. Whilst it is possible to question the potential dilemmas created by seeking such patronage from a feminist point of view, or from that of an autonomous profession, the pragmatics of such action for a relatively small organisation, which in the main was made up of women, are apparent in this history. On the whole, patronage was chosen wisely and well, and association with others with a voice eased difficult times. What is very significant in the light of those earlier choices is the present appointment of a female patron, HRH, The Princess Royal, a female President, Baroness Dean of Thornton-le Fylde, and a female occupational therapist as Chief Executive of the British Association and College of Occupational Therapists.

It has been mentioned how the fundamental change in the relationship between doctors and occupational therapists appeared to create a feeling of vulnerability. It also triggered the search for ways for the profession as a whole to regain respect for what it had to offer. An initial reaction was to attempt to change the image. This was done by occupational therapists reducing many aspects of 'creativity' deemed important in earlier times, and by side-lining 'diversion' as unscientific. They also even put aside, for some thirty years, the word 'occupation.' Despite that, probably, unconscious act they were unable to agree on a better descriptor for the profession's nomenclature, despite many suggestions that they should do so.

That leads to the next part of this overview, which considers changing definitions of occupational therapy, and the development of concepts about occupation and how it relates to health.

# Defining occupational therapy

In one of the earliest definitions of occupation therapy in the UK, from the 1933 *Memorandum on Occupation Therapy for Mental Patients*, are some important issues worthy of note for the future. They are: the absence of social health, and many would add spiritual health; the separation but inclusion of occupation and recreation; and the health maintenance role of occupational therapy acknowledged in the phrase 'creating new habits,' as well as both remedial and preventive roles. It read that occupational therapy was:

> *...the treatment, under medical direction, of physical or mental disorders by the application of occupation and recreation with the object of promoting recovery, of creating new habits, and of preventing deterioration.*[31]

Also in the 1930s, Iveson Russell described it as a:

> *...deliberately planned means of attaching a patient's interests to material objects and their common relationships, in a manner that will persistently emphasise his own value and importance, and so prevent the troubled mind from seeking refuge in morbid introspection in which it can find but a nightmare of unworthiness and despair.*[32]

That very deep definition suggests that some thought could be given to the very old but rejected notion of diversion, which has raised its head, again and again, throughout the first and second volumes of the history. Other of Iveson Russell's words resonate with modern ideas about individual values and the relationship between objects and occupation.

Those early definitions were soon to be narrowed, much simplified and jargonised as the profession got underway. Even Casson, who set up her clinic somewhat in the style of more recent therapeutic communities with holistic aims and occupational therapy encased within broadly based, holistic occupation programmes, defined it narrowly. Her definition, 'any activity, mental or physical, prescribed and guided for the definite purposes of contributing to, and hastening recovery from disease or injury,' remained unquestioned for decades.[33] As, until fairly recent times, did many who followed her she differentiated clearly between the benefits of occupation and occupation 'prescribed to help to cure the particular disability,' which in her mind set the boundary to occupational therapy.[34] Such differentiation, which acknowledges a medical but not a holistic health-giving value to occupation, was fairly representative of Casson's time, just as a spiritual view of health was representative of the middle ages. What is interesting, in the case of Casson, is that, despite her words, in deed she acted upon a much broader concept of occupation for health as her story showed. Also, despite narrow definitions of the time, John Cunningham's acceptance of school work as a form of occupational therapy at Astlie Ainsley Institution, in the formative years, likewise demonstrates a broader understanding of the extent of occupation for health.

By the 1950s, O'Sullivan was arguing that the patient, 'who looks forward with obvious interest to the perusal of his daily newspaper, is as active a recipient of occupational therapy as the patient who passes from the rand to the wale in the completion of a basket.'[35] That view appears consistent with the description of occupational therapy which readers may recall from an article in *The Lancet* as 'primarily a psychological treatment, whether it is practised upon physical or psychiatric cases.' It was explained that its 'therapeutic value essentially depends upon the transference of the patient's focus of attention from a subjective to an objective centre,' and that, 'in all cases, the patient's interest must be diverted from preoccupation with his disability and inadequacy to purposeful activity and achievement.' It was claimed that the success of occupational therapy would be limited if body and mind failed to be regarded as an organic whole in relationship with the environment.[36] Those descriptors also allude to issues of latter day occupational therapists' interest in enabling potential according to individual capacities and strengths. Not a new thought, that picks up, for example, on Alfred Adler's postulate about 'the importance of achieving self-realization through the use of abilities, interests and skills, and adaptation to the environment.'[37]

Adolf Meyer, too, had defined occupational therapy in relation to the environment when he argued that where the treatment took place needed to be homelike, and that staff and patients alike should share in the occupations.[38] According to David Henderson, Meyer believed that 'the wholesome pluralism of practical life' should not be surrendered to medical ideology, maintaining use of the 'broad concepts of instincts, habits, interests and specific experiences and capacities.'[39] Similarly, Nesta Clarke, a British occupational therapist, stated publicly in 1938 that occupational therapy involved 'the patient's whole day, so that work, leisure, recreation, eating and sleeping formed a balanced whole, varied and directed in accordance with his individual needs.'[40]

By the time of the 1960s report *Occupational therapy, Present and Future* it was being recognised that expansion and adaptation of occupational therapy because of advances in medical, social and economic environments meant a reappraisal. The report describes the major aim of the profession, which might be considered a definition, as forwarding the recovery of patients from mental or physical illness through training aimed at use of returning function or residual abilities to gain maximum social, and vocational adjustments. Practice would foster a sense of well-being, independence, initiative, responsibility, judgement and resettlement according to the demands of home and job, and provide advice on equipment, home alterations, avocational interests and social contacts.[41] Those interesting social and positive health ideas were seldom articulated clearly in formal definitions about occupational therapy although they clearly annunciated the spirit of the profession at the time. In the following decade when Elizabeth Grove reported on a definition put together by a small international group in Paris during the WFOT Council meeting, elements traditionally found within formal definitions of the profession remained. But added to them were new terms that referred to social or developmental problems, and fulfilling people's needs for optimum function in social environments.[42]

Social and environmental issues were picked up once more in the recent goals and philosophies of COTEC reported in the previous chapter. So too was the concept of promoting 'peoples' health and well-being by enabling meaningful occupation,' because 'occupational therapists believe that health can be influenced by occupation.' Other contemporary ideas are alluded to by the use of the words—'partnership,' 'personal, social, cultural and economic needs,' 'lifestyle,' 'problem solving,' and sensitivity to 'social, technological and demographic influences and changes.'[43]

Interestingly, definitions have not appeared recently in annual reports of BAOT/COT. Perhaps to publish a definition each decade would be useful, both as a fundamental reminder of what the profession is about, and as an exercise in mapping growth and change, reviewing new or lost directions, and for guiding future plans.

As the definition has changed so too has the understanding of occupation. As people returned to the tradition of occupational therapy with its roots in 'doing' in recent years, they brought with them skills in analysis picked up along the profession's journey. Instead of looking simply at the positive effects on an individual's health, apparent when patients became engaged in an occupation which provided meaning and interest for them, therapists were able to consider a whole range of inferences and possibilities of the media. They realised and began to research factors such as the effects of occupational deprivation or imbalance; or the notion of community occupations as well as individual ones; or the dimensions which were brought to bear when thinking about how to 'enable' or how to measure individual differences in need according to cultural mores, to name but a few. So to help future therapists a review of ideas about occupation pertinent to twentieth century occupational therapy are added to those found in the long journey from pre-history to the end of the nineteenth century.

## Conceptual issues about occupation for health

In the first volume of this history it was found that throughout time occupation had been a primary mechanism for health, the basis of economic life, and been prescribed for specific purposes, socially, legally and medically. Those three factors, which are very much entwined, continued in the twentieth century.

## Occupation as a primary mechanism for health

The fundamental truth that occupation is the inbuilt mechanism that enables humans, and other animals, to obtain the requirements for living, for survival, and for health, forms the essence of occupational therapists' claim that people's occupations influence physical, mental, social and spiritual health. However, occupation has been so fundamental to all aspects of people's lives that, even since the advent of occupational therapy, how it contributes to the well working of individuals as a whole is easily overlooked. As a consequence, in the future, it seems probable that to survive healthily people will need to adapt, adapt to, or reverse the effects of physiological, psychological, social, spiritual, and environmental occupational deprivation that humans have set in motion. In that vein, Rene Dubos in the *Mirage of Health* wrote that:

> *...the more civilization increases in complexity and the more it compels its members to become specialized, the more it is necessary to maintain a certain number of human activities in a primitive, unorganized state. In a wise society leisure and holidays—instead of becoming stereotyped as they presently are—should play a role similar to that of national parks and wildlife reservations, where plants and animals retain some chance to practice the mechanisms which have permitted evolutionary adaptation. Fortunately for his biological and social future, man has in reserve a large store of unspecialized tissue cells in his body and many unexploited potentialities in his brain that still permit him to evolve adaptively and achieve fitness to many unexpected situations. But fitness will never be a static condition with which he can be satisfied. All living things and their environments change endlessly and no permanent equilibrium between them can ever be reached. Man has added still further complexities to the biological situation by urges and strivings that have nothing to do with species survival. As long as he continues to reach further into the*

*unknown and to create for himself situations governed by parabiological values, problems of adaptation will endlessly arise.*[44]

The concept of people using occupation to maintain their own health in a natural and largely unconscious way can be recognised as the cornerstone of occupational therapy. It was, and is, through physical effort and rest, mental planning and creativity, social organisation and spiritual fulfillment that people maintain or enhance self-health. Questioning the relationship between occupation and health was an early manifestation of writers in the field. Iveson Russell, in the 1930s, was concerned with occupation as a problem 'of human nature...Undoubtedly idleness has an evil influence, and worthy occupation a beneficial influence, on the human mind'[45]. Readers may also recall how Eager, at about the same time, posed different and apparently simple but very important questions about how to define occupation. He recognised that 'one person's work may be another person's recreation' and the perennial problems which result when occupation is not viewed as a whole but divided into work, labour, recreation and amusement as discrete entities.[46] Such reflection on the potential extent and value of occupation as an agent of health is epitomised in a section of a letter from Miss Castle which was quoted in Chapter 8: '...to struggle to do is to continue to live...occupation does more than divert, it nourishes and sustains.'[47]

There has been a gradual return to an appreciation of each person's right and responsibility to maintain and enhance their own health and well-being. In part that has been driven by initiatives of the World Health Organisation and by countries responding to its concern to aim health initiatives at health promotion and preventive programmes. It makes economic sense, even in affluent countries where the costs of sophisticated medicine are hard to contain. Such appreciation and direction makes it imperative for occupational therapists to increase their concern with the health and well-being potential of occupation and to become pro-active in medico-socio-political debate about 'Health of the Nation' issues. The COT has certainly made moves in that direction, but they require the support of visible programmes and public dialogue from members.

## Occupation as the basis of economic life

Occupation became understood, more and more, in economic terms as manufacturing and materialism became dominant. Additionally, because health had come to be associated with medicine, preventive and health giving occupational regimes had been forgotten, particularly as many occupations were superseded by machines to make life easier. However, economic factors are not unimportant in themselves in terms of health, for any event which touches a person modifies, even if only slightly, the balance between 'his or her organs and functions.'[48] There is certainly a difference in the health status of affluent as opposed to poor groups of people, between the employed and the unemployed, for example, and those able to engage in a range of occupations which hold meaning for them rather than a restricted range. Although most would immediately assume that the poorer person will automatically experience the poorer health, it is not necessarily always the case. Iveson Russell, in the 1930s, contemplated that although it might be said that:

> *...the retired old man and the unemployed young man suffer not from lack of work but*
> *from lack of wages. It is not so...both suffer from the painful feeling of being*
> *ineffective...In each case the ideal self is frustrated and idleness depresses them as much as*
> *it does those who experience privation.*[49]

Russell may well have seen the results of such occupational deprivation during the
1914–18 War, and afterwards during the economic depression. The economic factor was
particularly significant in both World Wars, in the depression that followed the first, and
in the period of reconstruction that followed the second. The latter was manifest in a
'return to work' ethos and a concurrent medical interest in work-based rehabilitation
where many occupational therapy programmes played a central role.

Occupational therapists by the very nature of their therapy are bound up in both the
economics of health care and of normal life. That should be a source of strength for the
profession. Mary Jones explained in the early 1950s that in most communities, 'living a
normal life' is integral to the economic structure of the state. Part of the day is spent in
occupations that are 'directed towards obtaining necessities and something extra to
provide amenities, while the rest of the waking hours are spent in enjoying those
amenities.' She went on:

> *At the moment in England, we are in the middle of an experiment in the development*
> *of the responsibility of society to the individual. Perhaps insufficient emphasis is being laid*
> *on the equally necessary responsibility of the individual to society. When the habits of life*
> *are grossly interrupted by ill health, this sense of responsibility is easily shed. The*
> *reablement team has been set up to expedite, or to make possible, the return of the patient*
> *to normal life. If success is to be other than passing, the patient must himself be enlisted*
> *as a full-time member of the team—the reablement team.*[50]

Her reablement approach anticipated the enablement approach of the 1990s, and the
need for all people to take responsibility once more for their own health. This does not
mean that occupational therapists would work themselves out of employment, but that
they have an increased role in enabling all people to recognise the relationship between
what they do and their health. That will mean making and taking different roles towards
the whole population as well as maintaining their current ones.

Taking a different perspective of economic issues, it is often the shortage of resources
that dictates changes in health policy as well as perceived new directions of growth in the
material wealth of a nation. Authorities are often accused of overlooking the perceived
needs of a minority, and that has long been the case. Even in spite of the manpower
shortage of World War I, Amar, like occupational therapists at present, had to have
economy firmly in mind as he helped to 'reconstruct' injured servicemen. Readers may
recall that he suggested the use of beech wood to make wooden toys because it required
'little in the matter of outlay.'[51] In similar vein, early occupational therapists held sales of
work and charged patients for the cost of articles they made to recoup ongoing material
expenses. Such 'housekeeping' requirements maintained occupational therapists in a
subordinate role, and helped to develop a culture of making do, of putting up with less

that ideal circumstances in order to be compliant and quietly effective, as women were expected to be in the domestic situation. Maintaining small-scale economies in many ways prevented occupational therapists from looking at the bigger economic picture.

If the bigger economic picture were to be taken seriously by occupational therapists, the profession could be well positioned astride the health/economics interface. The focus of professional ideology, and much of its history points that way. Between acceptance and implementation of that position lies consultation, research, education, development of practice directions, and public exposure to the concepts and facts of the interface.

## Occupation prescribed for social, legal and medical purposes

As civilizations became more sophisticated, social leaders and legal authorities devised rules about what people should or could do in particular circumstances. These are in reality a form of prescription for community and social health and well-being. As community health affects individual health, and vice versa, these become an issue for occupational therapists to consider and, in cases of concern at the very least, to act upon.

In the first volume of this history a pertinent example was provided by the establishment of Bridewell, one of only five Royal hospitals in London after the closure of monastic institutions. Bridewell came about as the result of public action aimed towards alleviating social and community problems caused by occupational depravation and occupational deprivation. Occupation was prescribed as the therapy to overcome the effects of the socio-economic ills that inmates had suffered from in the community. In more recent times occupational programmes run in jails, for street kids, for substance abusers and suchlike, and programmes aimed to assist refugees to re-establish viable economic and health giving occupations in impoverished, war-torn, or famine situations are examples of a similar nature. Some, but not many, occupational therapists get involved in programmes like those as they did, for example, after World War II in Germany.

Prescriptions of 'what to do' at times when individuals were ill had been part of the advice given out by health experts of many persuasions throughout time. Shamans, priests, 'mouthpieces' for the 'gods,' philosophers, monks, wise-women, physicians, nurses and anyone who cared to assume the mantle of doctor of medicine, all prescribed in some way what people needed to do to be healthy or to overcome illness. The *Regimen Sanitatis* originating in Classical times, and a central health doctrine in Europe from the 11th to the 19th century was a major source of curative and preventive prescriptions, occupation as exercise, action, or motion and rest being one of the six rules which were all enmeshed with one another when interpreted. They gave way in the twentieth century to medical prescriptions, often pharmaceutical in nature, which were very much the province of registered medical practitioners. For half a century at least, medical prescriptions held a status as at no other time in history. Occupational therapy was part of that dominant medical prescription pattern.

# Future possibilities for occupational therapy

When thinking of the future, it is as important to identify those attributes have been seen to rest with occupational therapists, as it is to uncover their weaknesses. Readers may find and enumerate many in the text, but some, such as a pioneer attitude, an intense determination to meet the needs of patients or clients, and a commitment to team work, are worthy of a brief mention here because they are important in the future.

An ongoing 'pioneer attitude' has occurred, in part, because of the profession's difference from other allied health disciplines. Practitioners, educators and researchers have had to battle continually for a hearing, for facilities, for resources, for positions, and for respect. Status and respect are not automatic on qualification as an occupational therapist, as often appears to be the case for those qualifying in more established careers like law or medicine, or more obviously medically-related ones like nursing, physiotherapy, or medical imaging. Whilst the battling has resulted in the loss of some personnel, it has also resulted in strength, adaptability, resilience and openness to new ideas as characteristics of the discipline. It is evident in the creativity and inventiveness of practitioners. K.G. Garrold of Nottingham Handicaft Company, for example, recognised that 'as a generalisation…virtually every piece of equipment emanates from designs originated by occupational therapists.'[52] Not only noticeable in practitioners, educators too maintained a pioneer spirit:

> The schools of the sixties and seventies owed much to the enthusiasm and foresight of their principals who encouraged their staff to explore the variety of teaching methods being developed in higher education on a national and international basis. Peer teaching, small-group instruction and problem-based learning became the currency of occupational therapy educators. The aim was to provide the best possible conditions for learning. This pursuit of excellence moulded our teachers into facilitators. As a consequence, occupational therapy benefited from the best of educational advances while the rest of higher education was still thinking about the 'new methods.'[53]

This has continued in the university schools of the 1990s, as well as in wide ranging areas of practice, and so it is likely to persist as an occupational therapist's trait as students absorb attitudes as well as philosophies and competences from their teachers in both lecture rooms and practice venues.

With regard to occupational therapists' determination to meet the needs of their clients, the inaugural Presidential Address to the AOT in 1950 of Lord Webb-Johnson is interesting to note. It could be suspected he was talking to the converted when he said:

> …Occupational therapy is a calling, and unless you feel the urge to serve your fellow-men, then you have chosen your work wrongly.

*...Remember you have very often to carry the patient: you have to give him something of yourself. Remember that phrase 'full knowledge, exquisite judgement and skill in the highest to be put forth not at any self-chosen moment but daily at the need of others.'*[54]

Another strength referred to often in the stories told and issues discussed in the professional journals, has been the notion of working with others as part of a team. Occupational therapists have, indeed, expressed pride in being team players. That ability has grown from initiatives taken in the early roles of lone therapists in large psychiatric hospitals and later as group therapists and members of therapeutic communities. It also grew from being part of the rehabilitation effort of World War II and after. To help patients return to employment required the forming of a co-operative working relationship with others such as disablement resettlement officers, and staff within industry as well as others working within allied health services on a daily basis. Occupational therapists could relate to messages of people like James Sommerville when he said:

*A specialist in rehabilitation is not a specialist at all. He considers himself a member of a team of workers, both lay and medical, directed towards the patient as a whole.*[55]

One of the ways teamwork has manifest is in the commitment to international colleagues, which has developed from the seeds sown in the first decades of the twentieth century between colleagues in the USA, Canada and the United Kingdom. In the very early days help was forthcoming from the direction of the New World, especially during times of war. Since then, occupational therapists from the UK have been very much part of initiatives to assist other countries to get established. Alicia Mendez, who took a major role in the internationalisation of occupational therapy, recalled the important part played in that process by therapists in Britain. Not only did Britain host the first International Congress which launched WFOT in 1952, but throughout its existence it has consistently been a major source of people willing to take on leadership roles within the organisation. There have, for example, been three British Presidents of the World Federation, Peg Fulton, Alicia Mendez, and Barbara Tyldesley.[56]

Directions for the future will certainly call upon the continuance of occupational therapists' long held pioneer spirit; commitment to enabling both traditional clients and the population at large to experience well-being and health through daily occupations; and through teamwork at local and global levels. The change to enabling populations to understand better and act upon the developing appreciation of occupation's relationship to health and well-being is a major challenge to the way forward.

## Enabling population health and well-being through occupation

Many of the early patrons of occupational therapy, as well as even earlier exponents of occupation for health, recognised that what people did was either health giving or contributed to illness. From Greek physicians such as Hippocrates and Celsus, through a range of different contexts and points of view typified by Ramazzini, Pare, Mercurialis, Burton, Cheyne, Pinel, Brown, Smiles and Southwood-Smith, different occupations have been suggested as important to maintain health, or to avoid because of unhealthy consequences. Following the advice provided by the World Health Organisation in documents such as the *Ottawa Charter for Health Promotion*[57] all health professionals need to be turning their attention to population health as well as providing the best possible interventions for those who are unwell. Henderson, who was so instrumental in the foundation of occupational therapy in Britain, recognised and advocated such directions for occupational therapists. That was partly because he understood 'there can be no division of body and mind...the one reacts on the other.' Occupation, he argued, 'will lead to the preservation of health but will also prevent illness. Life and work are indivisible just as mind and body are.'[58] James Sommerville, another Scot of great influence within occupational therapy some years later, pointed to prevention as the first leg of intervention followed by 'diagnosis, treatment and rehabilitation.'[59] Yet another, Cairns Aitken in the 1976 Casson Memorial Lecture, explained:

> *Over the centuries there has been ample evidence proving the effects of social circumstances on the pattern of disease...Many of the principal disorders in our society are known to be influenced by our behaviour (occupation), such as in relation to drug addiction (tobacco, alcohol and barbiturates), violence (accident and aggression), and habit (diet and exercise.)*[60]

Views such as his point in the future to the type of research necessary to demonstrate not only the positive impact of occupation on health, but also the negative effects that poorly chosen occupational factors may have. They can impact to the point of disease, disability and death, and to community disorders of monumental scale. It seems timely to harness the strong voices of past authorities to light a proactive way forward for practice. This is also required to enable our traditional client group to experience health and well-being through their occupations. Dr Muir Gray's words, reported in Chapter 9, are recalled. He said that occupational therapists must become 'revolutionaries, changing society to prevent handicap being caused for people with disabilities who are often unable to effect change themselves.'[61] That brings to mind a question posed at about the same time, with a few additions that relate to current directions:

> *Are we as a profession, or as individuals, prepared to do anything about social injustice* (especially occupational injustice) *towards our clients,* (and populations in general) *and if so, how?*[62]

**In this summative chapter** the history of occupational regimes for health has been woven together so that readers may consider directions for the future. The changing nature of philosophies and practice assists recognition of the part played by contexts, beliefs, socio-cultural mores, and technologies, as well as advances in knowledge. In Volume I, because of the fundamental nature of occupation across the broad spectrum of the everyday lives of all people, whatever their socio-cultural and environmental context, it was complex to appreciate the scope of the practice of 'occupation for health.' For very different reasons it has been equally complex to piece together the twentieth century story of occupational therapy in the United Kingdom. Indeed, despite the size of this volume, it feels as if only the surface has been scratched. Many more histories of particular events, people, environments, approaches, specialties and professional issues are called for. It is hoped that this volume, as well as the first, will encourage a greater range of questions, research and initiatives to facilitate growth and direction based on in-depth and investigative practices. Hopefully, however, what has been provided is an appreciation of the extensive roots of occupational therapy as it journeys on into the twenty-first century. As Alsop put it: 'These roots embrace a history and a philosophy which are uniquely different from those of other professions.'[63]

[1]Eager R. Aids to Mental Health: The Benefits of Occupation, Recreation and Amusement. Exeter: W.V.Cole, 1936; 6.

[2]English AM. Training War Prisoners. The Times 1943; August.

[3]Randle APH. Rehabilitation and Society. Occupational Therapy 1974; 37(1): 15–17.

[4]Blom-Cooper L. Occupational Therapy. An Emerging Profession in Health Care. Report of Commission of Inquiry 1989. London: Duckworth, 1990; 12.

[5]Etherington K. The Disabled Persons Act 1986: The Need for Counselling. British Journal of Occupational Therapy 1990; 53(10): 430–1.

[6]Fraser-Holland EN. The Casson Memorial Lecture: Moving Targets and 20:20 Vision. British Journal of Occupational Therapy 1990; 53(8): 323–8.

[7]'Toward a wider view' by Agag. British Journal of Occupational Therapy 1977; 40 (9): 218.

[8]Cosin LZ. The place of the day hospital in the geriatric unit. Occupational Therapy 1956; 1: 13–22. (Reprinted in Occupational Therapy by kind permission of the Author and International Journal of Social Psychiatry.)

[9]Blom-Cooper L. Occupational Therapy...; 13.

[10]Blom-Cooper L. Occupational Therapy...; 18–19.

[11]King J. Change and challenge. British Journal of Occupational Therapy 1997; 60(10): 429.

[12]Cameron A, Masterton A. The changing policy context of occupational therapy. British Journal of Occupational Therapy 1998; 61(12): 556–60.

[13]Ryan S. Thinking, reasoning and reflecting. British Journal of Occupational Therapy 1996; 59(5): 195.

[14]Alsop A. The origins of our species: A brief history of our time. British Journal of Occupational Therapy 1996; 59(4): 155.

[15]From our own Correspondents. Scotland: Occupational therapy in early mental disorder. The Lancet March 22, 1924; ccvi: 621.

[16]Hamlyn RB, Loukas KM, Froehlich J, MacRae N. Feminism: an inclusive perspective. American Journal of Occupational Therapy 1992; 46(11): 967–70.

[17]Taylor J. A different voice in occupational therapy. British Journal of Occupational Therapy 1995; 58(4):170–73.

[18]Gilligan C. In a Different Voice. London: Harvard University Press, 1982.

[19]Hugman R. Power in Caring Professions. London: Macmillan, 1983.

[20]Taylor J. A different voice in occupational therapy....

[21]Kelly G. Feminist or feminine? The feminine principle in occupational therapy. British Journal of Occupational Therapy 1996; 59(1): 2–6.

[22]MacDonald EM. The history of the Association of Occupational Therapists: Chapter 2, 1936–39. Occupational Therapy 1957; 20(4): 14–16.

[23]Casson E. Occupational Therapy. (Reprinted from a report of conference on 'Welfare of cripples and invalid children' held at the Drapers' Hall, London, on November 7th and 8th, 1935.) Occupational Therapy 1955; 18 (3): 98–100.

[24]Board of Control. Memorandum on Occupation Therapy for Mental Patients. His Majesty's Stationery Office, London, 1933; 2.

[25]Eager R. Aids to Mental Health: The Benefits of Occupation, Recreation and Amusement. Exeter: W. V. Cole, 1936; 6.

[26]Russell JI. The Occupational Treatment of Mental Illness. London: Bailliere, Tindall & Cox, 1938; 31–2.

[27]Russell. The Occupational Treatment of Mental Illness...; 31–2.

[28]Russell. The Occupational Treatment of Mental Illness...; 34.

[29]Astley Cooper H. Some reflections on occupational therapy. Occupational Therapy 1941; Spring: 9–12.

[30]Meyer A. The philosophy of occupational therapy. (Read at Fifth Annual Meeting of the National Society for the Promotion of Occupational Therapy). Archives of Occupational Therapy, 1922, 1(1): 1–10.

[31]Board of Control. Memorandum on Occupation Therapy for Mental Patients. His Majesty's Stationery Office, London, 1933; 2.

[32]Russell. The Occupational Treatment of Mental Illness...; 8.

[33]Casson E. Occupational Therapy. (Reprinted from a report of conference on 'Welfare of cripples and invalid children' held at the Drapers' Hall, London, on November 7th and 8th, 1935.) Occupational Therapy 1955; 18 (3): 98–100.

[34]Casson. Occupational Therapy...

[35]O'Sullivan ENM. Textbook of Occupational therapy: With Chief Reference to Psychological Medicine. London: H.K. Lewis, 1955; 4.

[36]The Association of Occupational Therapists. Reprinted from The Lancet 1951; (further details of date not given): 1.

[37]Macdonald EM. World-wide conquests of disabilities: The history, development and present functions of the remedial services. London: Bailliere Tindall, 1981: 106.

[38]Meyer A. 1895. Cited by Gelder M. Adolf Meyer and his influence on British psychiatry. Chapter in: Berrios GE, Freeman H., ed. 150 Years of British Psychiatry, 1841–1991. London: Gaskell, 1991; 422.

[39]Henderson DK. Introduction. In: Winters EE, Ed. The collected papers of Adolf Meyer, Volume II: Psychiatry. Baltimore: The Johns Hopkins Press, 1951, p. xiii.

[40]Clarke NIR. Work as a stimulant: Value of Occupational Therapy. Birkenhead News 1938; 27th August. Also reported in Birkenhead Advertiser 1938; 27th August.

[41]Dunkin EN. Summary of the Report—Occupational therapy, Present and Future—to the Council of the Association of Occupational Therapists from the Advisory Board of the Sub-Committee. Occupational Therapy 1966; 29(8): 6–13.

[42]Grove E. Occupational Therapy in the United Kingdom. Ist European Congress, Edinburgh, May, 1977.

[43]www.cotec-europe.org

[44]Dubos R. Mirage of Health: Utopias, Progress and Biological Change. New York: Harper and Row, 1959; 60–61.

[45]Russell. The Occupational Treatment of Mental Illness…; 2.

[46]Eager. Aids to Mental Health…; 13.

[47]Castle P. Correspondence. Occupational Therapy 1961; 24(10): 17.

[48]Dubos. Mirage of Health…; 122.

[49]Russell. The Occupational Treatment of Mental Illness…; 2.

[50]Jones MS. Uses of Occupational Therapy in Physical Medicine. Reprinted from The Lancet, London: August, 18, 1951; 308.

[51]Amar J. The physiology of industrial organisation and the re-employment of the disabled. Translated by Bernard Miall, edited with notes and an introduction by

Professor AF Stanley Kent. London: The Library Press, 1918; 343.

[52]Garrold KG. Letter. Occupational Therapy 1972; 36(11): 874.

[53]Fraser-Holland EN. The Casson Memorial Lecture: Moving Targets and 20:20 Vision. British Journal of Occupational Therapy 1990; 53(8): 323–8.

[54]Webb-Johnson, Rt Hon. Lord. Presidential Address. Occupational Therapy 1950; 13(3): 50–7.

[55]Sommerville J. Medical Rehabilitation. Scottish Journal of Occupational Therapy 1954; March: 30–43.

[56]Mendez A. Personal communication. 2001.

[57]World Health Organisation, Health and Welfare, Canada, Canadian Public Health Association. Ottawa Charter for Health Promotion. Ottawa, Canada: 1986.

58Henderson DK. Life and work. Scottish Journal of Occupational Therapy, 1957 (30) 7–10.

[59]Sommerville. Medical Rehabilitation…

[60]Aitken C. The Casson Memorial Lecture: Rehabilitation: Facts and fantasies about occupational therapy British Journal of Occupational Therapy 1976; 39 (7): 172–3.

[61]Muir Gray JA. You must be revolutionaries. British Journal of Occupational Therapy 1975; 38(6): 126.

[62]IM. Conferences: What should O.T.s do about social injustice? British Journal of Occupational Therapy 1975; 38(6): 137.

[63]Alsop A. The origins of our species: A brief history of our time. British Journal of Occupational Therapy 1996; 59(4): 155.

# Appendices

# Appendix A
## Stories of Educational Establishments

Brief stories of the schools are provided. They are important in their own right, and were central to the reminiscences of participants in the history focus groups conducted around Britain. Individuals frequently told stories of their own history as occupational therapists remembering, very clearly, incidents relating to the educational institutions they attended as students. Schools were approached to provide their own stories for inclusion in the history. Some, but not all complied, and some, but not all, cited authors. The style of the stories as well as what is told, therefore, differs from school to school and, unfortunately, most have had to be been shortened considerably.

### 1930  Dorset House: Oxford  (The story continues)

material provided by the School
During the war Dorset House moved from Bristol to Bromsgrove in the Midlands and was for a time the only school of occupational therapy in the country. At the request of the Ministry of Health, the School agreed to organise wartime training courses to ensure a rapid and reasonably adequate supply of workers. Many candidates, such as nurses, physiotherapists and craft teachers, were selected and given courses to extend their previous qualifications. At the end of the war Mary Macdonald, the principal, moved the School to spacious hutted premises in the grounds of the Churchill Hospital, Oxford, which offered excellent facilities for training with the University and several hospitals in the area helping with lectures, clinics and hospital practice. In 1948, a non-profit making, limited company was formed to take the School over. Elizabeth Casson, the Schools founder, remained the Medical Director, and in the following year she created a Trust in which the School was the primary beneficiary.

In 1964, the year Macdonald was awarded an MBE for her contribution in the field of rehabilitation, the School moved from the huts at the Churchill Hospital to Headington. In 1971, which saw the retirement of Macdonald, the Casson Trust offered AOT money to support what was to be known as The Casson Memorial Lecture to be given at the Association's AGM. Macdonald's successor was Betty Collins who had been vice-principal for 17 years. Dorset House gave up its independent status to integrate, in 1992, with Oxford Polytechnic which in 1994 became Oxford Brookes University, and three years later, within it, part of the School of Health Care. Multi-professional modules are part of the curriculum shared with nursing, midwifery and physiotherapy students.

### 1932- c 1939 The Maudsley Hospital: London

The story of this school is told in chapter 5.

### 1935 The London School (The story continues)

by Christine Craik
The Occupational Therapy Centre and Training School was moved in 1937 to Great Ormond Street, having outgrown it's Tottenham Court Road premises. It closed

in 1940 following the outbreak of war because of conditions in London, which Muriel Tarrant and Angela Rivett described as 'the Blitz', 'chaos in Government Departments', and uncertainty about the place of occupational therapists in the E.M.S. It remained closed for a couple of years, although contacts were kept and work was carried on until it was re-opened in 1942 in Hampstead. At that time it offered a two and a half year training with specialisation in either physical or mental illnesses. For the first two years students paid a fee of seventy guineas per annum, then the cost differed according to the speciality chosen in the last six months. Because of the war emergency, shortened courses were offered to students who held diplomas in nursing, massage, or craft teaching.

Later in the 1940s the School moved to Merton Rise, and then extended into premises at St Johns Wood Park. 1945 was the first year the dual qualification was offered and the training was extended to three years. Two scholarships, by open competition, were offered which were advertised in *The Times and Daily Telegraph*. Students gained access to the course via an entrance examination held six times a year which cost a guinea, in addition to a general Certificate of Education, and a personal interview. The examination consisted of 'an intelligence test, a general knowledge paper, essay, and craft and dexterity test.' During the 1950s the School had an arrangement to send students, newly qualified as therapists, who wished to avail of the opportunity, to Boston and to Basel for a three month placement.

In 1976, the first interprofessional studies teaching started, with students attending Anatomy and Physiology lectures at the Polytechnic of Central London. Additionally, the School became a pioneer of problem based learning approaches in occupational therapy education. As the School was privately owned by Miss Tarrant and Miss Rivett, and the lease on its properties were about to terminate in a few years urgent measures were called for. No forward plans had been made, and as it was one of the largest occupational therapy schools in the UK a serious loss of manpower was feared as it came under threat of closure. In 1980, after extensive negotiations, the School joined the West London Institute of Higher Education in Isleworth, West London. Eventually that was to become Brunel University College and later in 1998 a part of Brunel University by which time there were over 120 students enrolling. In 1996 a Masters degree in Occupational Therapy was designed and the first cohort started, graduating in 1999.

### 1937  Astley Ainsley Instsitution: Edinburgh (The story continues)

by Averil Stewart

Wartime circumstances led to the course started at the Astley Ainslie Institution in Edinburgh in 1937 being halted temporarily after the first diplomas were awarded in 1939. Studies were resumed in 1941. War casualties put pressure on beds and the value of occupational therapy was realised. The shortage of therapists, even with the support of eight graduate therapists from Toronto, was such that the number of places on the full-time, two and a half year course was augmented by a six-month course for assistant occupational therapists. Teachers and nurses were also given 'top up' courses to help swell the number of therapists. The first training school in Scotland, it was unique in that its existence depended on an Act of Parliament. Previously the will of the hospital's benefactor, David Ainslie, did not allow for the education of staff. Hence in 1946, the Astley Ainslie Order Confirmation Act extended the training school to admit students to the Occupational Therapy Training Centre of the hospital, to arrange courses of study and training, and to issue diplomas.

From the 1940s to the 1960s the course continued with growing student numbers and international links, particularly with Scandinavian students seeking places. These links led to requests for expert advice during the establishment of schools in Belgium and later in Portugal and Finland. The course was extended to three full calendar years and intakes to around 36 each year. Funding came from the Scottish Office and students became active in student politics, with membership of the Scottish Union of Students being approved in 1963. In 1966 Mary Cunningham succeeded her cousin, Dorothy Bramwell, as head of school until her retirement in 1982. It was during her period of leadership that the hospital-based school transfered into the higher education sector as part of Queen Margaret College in 1979. This paved the way for validation of the first degree course in the UK. The School was also to house the first British professor of occupational therapy when Averil Stewart was appointed to a personal chair in the last decade of the century.

The 80s and 90s were a time of enormous change. For example: undergraduate intake numbers increased to 70, and students had the option of honours degree programmes; a conversion course for diplomates; an MScOT; a fast-track, graduate entry Postgraduate Diploma, and PhD studies. The first

doctorate was gained by Maggie Nicol in 1994. Links were established with schools abroad and accreditation sought through the American Association of Occupational Therapists. Occupational Therapy is managed alongside Art Therapy within the Faculty of Social Science and Health in the renamed Queen Margaret University College.

### 1941 St Andrews: Northampton

St Andrew's Hospital for the treatment of all forms of nervous and mental disorders had been opened in 1838 to provide private treatment at a reasonable cost. Occupational and recreational activities had always been prominent but a dearth of capable occupational therapists led to the School being formed to help to overcome the problem. Dr Thomas Tennent, who had pioneered occupational therapy teaching at the Maudsley, had moved to St Andrews in 1938 as Medical Superintendent and was a powerful force in establishing the School and its programme. He, like Henderson, had spent time at the Phipps' Psychiatric Clinic where Meyer had pioneered occupational therapy in the USA.

Official recognition for the School was obtained in 1941 when three students were already undergoing instruction. By 1943, seven students were engaged in a two-year course with Mabel Thompson. Joyce Hombersley became the Director of Training a year later. The aim of St Andrews School was to offer a complete training to students at a fee within their means. The Committee of Management considered that by subsidising such a course they were indirectly offering benefits to patients within the hospital and elsewhere. Until the building of an occupational therapy and recreational block, the school was housed in a series of rooms separated from the hospital by bomb damage and standing in its own garden. Lectures took place in the well-equipped lecture room in the nurses' home and were given by the Medical Staff of the hospital and by visiting lecturers. The majority of craftwork was done at the Northampton School of Arts and Crafts a couple of miles from the hospital and bicycles were the usual form of transport.

The School differed from others in that all students, rather than those who chose too, took the Psychological Diploma at the end of the second year's training. The physical diploma, which was taken at the end of the third year, followed attendance at Creaton Sanatorium for experience with patients suffering from tuberculosis, and Manfield Orthopaedic Hospital, where they also had lectures. The appointment of a Representative of the Central Council of Physical Recreation to the staff of the Hospital made it possible for all students to receive a two-year course of physical and recreational activities. Students took the patients under their supervision for physical training classes and organised parties for them throughout the winter months. Hostel accomodation was provided for first year students. By 1948, the fees were 30 guineas per annum, and at least six scholarships of £80 each were granted by the hospital to second year students. The hospital also granted a Fellowship for an exchange of postgraduate students with those attending training schools in the USA.

By 1980, there was an intake of 45 students each year, and a building programme to meet the increasing needs was set in train. Staff from Nene College, Northampton, provided the lectures in anatomy, physiology, psychology and sociology. The College was later to become the Nene Centre for Healthcare Education and St Andrews Occupational Therapy School became a part of that higher education facility as degree programmes were implemented in the 1990s.

### 1942-1949  The Retreat: York

The Occupational Therapy School at the Retreat in York was unique, in that it was the only occupational therapy course recognised by the Association which was combined with one for nursing and which together lasted four years. The director of the school was Percy T. Oliver who had been vice chairman of the Association in 1938. Students sat both the General Nursing Council Examination in mental nursing, and the Occupational Therapy Association Examinations. The Preliminary Occupational Therapy Papers were taken at the end of the second year of study. The fourth year of training was devoted entirely to occupational therapy, and it was during that time that a period of three months was spent on a 'physical' placement, such as in an orthopaedic hospital or a tuberculosis sanatorium. At the end of the fourth year the students took the Final Examinations of the Association. Students were paid a first year nurse's salary during the first three years of training, and no salary, but free board and lodging, during the fourth year.

In 1949, the Association's Annual Report noted the cessation of the School. This was due to the small numbers of students who underwent training there. In the Retreat's Annual Report for 1949 Arthur Poole, the Physician Superintendent, recorded:

*In May 1949 the Occupational Therapy Association notified us of their new regulation viz: 'No Training School could continue to be recognised unless it had 12 students in training and an annual intake of 12 so that at the end of three years the number shall not be less than 25.' And as the Committee felt it would not be right for us to allocate so much space and time to this one section of the hospital auxiliary training we reluctantly decided to close down the training school.*

### 1945  St Loyes: Exeter

by Catherine Mounter & Graeme Barber

The Occupational Therapy School in Exeter was founded by Dame Georgiana Buller, under the auspices of St Loye's Training Centre for Cripples which had been established in 1937. The first intake of students commenced training in 1944. Nancy Ross, a founder member of AOT, of the first Council, and the first editor of the profession's Journal, was appointed Principal and she remained in the post until her retirement in 1955. At the start she was the only full-time member of staff. During her tenure the student intake increased from seven to over sixty. Initially, the School was housed in the bomb-damaged premises of 'Newstead' in Matford Avenue. Shortly after it was established, 'Larkby', a large house opposite, was also acquired enabling the rapidly expanding School to increase both its intake and its activities. In December 1953, when larger premises were needed the School moved to its current site of Millbrook House, the original home of St Loye's Training Centre for Cripples.

Connie Henson took over as principal when Ross retired. She had qualified in 1942 from the Training School in Tottenham Court Road, was very active in AOT committee work and, like her predecessor, edited the Journal. She dealt successfully with a range of administrative problems, always ensuring that the professional education offered to her students kept pace with national and international developments. She frequently led such developments, introducing innovative and challenging methods and encouraging her staff to capitalise on the individual talents of her students at every opportunity. Under her guidance, the School became financially viable, was noted for high academic and professional standards, had a greatly increased student intake, and is thought to have been the first School to admit male students. Henson initiated important improvements to the facilities available for students such as a common room and extra classroom. When she retired in 1974, after 20 years at St Loye's, her contribution had been recognised with the award of an MBE in 1970, and an Honorary MA from the University of Exeter in 1976. Katherine Ingamells, who had been a tutor at the School since 1964, took over as Principal in 1975 remaining in the post until 1984 during which time the Casson building, which housed an assessment and rehabilitation flat and teaching rooms was opened by Sir Hugh Casson in honour of his aunt, Dr Elizabeth Casson.

Whilst Dr Rita Goble was Principal from 1984 until 1994 many developments in the fields of pre-registration, continuing and postgraduate education, research and professional practice took place at the School. Bachelors, BPhil and MSc Degrees in Occupational Therapy were introduced in the 1990s, the course became available via distance learning methods, and the School further expanded its buildings and facilities. In 1986 the first Independent Living Centre in the South West had been opened at the School which was understood to be the only teaching facility offering this service outside the NHS. St

Loye's initiated and hosted a series of Standing Conferences, which enabled occupational therapists and other health care professionals to debate a variety of pertinent issues. Guest presenters included distinguished occupational therapists from the United States of America, Canada and Australia.

Increases to the student intake and modifications to the occupational therapy course necessitated further expansion to the premises and in 1991 a new building with an impressive lecture theatre, computer room and other teaching facilities was opened. The School continued to develop and expand its courses and facilities after Barbara Paul became Principal in 1994. The Advanced Course in Occupational Therapy, for example, offered stand alone modules from 1998 onwards, including the first ever credit-rated electronically delivered course on evidence-based practice. The School is now affiliated to the University of Exeter.

### 1947 The Liverpool School
material provided by the School

Six young women working with Constance Owens at the Deva EMS Hospital at Upton during the war were officially designated as students but, at the end of the war, no authority was interested in taking on the responsibility for continuing their training. Owens determined to do so herself, and with that in mind purchased two houses in Huyton, one to live in, and another which became the Liverpool School of Occupational Therapy. With herself as Principal, and one other member of staff, the School opened early in 1947 with two intakes a year. Owens believed that hospital practice must run parallel to lectures, so students spent part of the week in school and part in local hospitals. For quite a number of years she,

herself, employed qualified occupational therapists, many from her own School, and seconded them to the hospitals. The last hospital took over the employment of their own occupational therapists in 1974! She also employed her past students to assist with teaching. Cecile Dorward, who at 35 had taken up occupational therapy at the suggestion of her friend Owens, stayed on to tutor anatomy. She demonstrated synovial cartilage on the remains of her weekend roast. Conditions were indeed, different from today.

When Owens started to study for a Doctorate she retired as Principal, and Joy Rook took on the role of Director of Training in 1961. The following year the School was made into a Limited Company with a Board of Governors, of which Owens was a member. The School became known as 'The College of Occupational Therapy (Liverpool) Ltd.' In 1963 another house was acquired for teaching and for additional sleeping accommodation. By 1970, the total number of students had risen to 135, but as the College was still independent, receiving no funding from either the Departments of Education or of Health, in order to extend the facilities Phyllis Howie, the principal at the time, launched an appeal to raise money to build a hall large enough for lectures, exams, practical and social activities. It was furnished with tables and chairs obtained from the collection of 'Green Shield' stamps! When Department of Health Bursaries were made available to all Occupational Therapy schools the further expansion of physical facilities became possible. During the 90s the first students to qualify with a degree graduated and the school made the transition over two years into the University of Liverpool. It became part of the School of Health Sciences in the Faculty of Medicine.

## 1948 The Derby School
### by Margaret Foster

A draft scheme for the establishment of a School of Occupational Therapy in Derby was prepared in 1947 by Dr R.G. Cooke, a physician, Dr E.U.H. Pentreath, a psychiatrist, and Mr F.W. Houndsell, who was Principal of the School of Art for the County Borough of Derby. The School started in 1948, and was officially opened by Dr Balme, the Chief Medical Officer of the Rehabilitation and Resettlement Department of the Ministry of Health. Iris Fitchett was appointed Principal of the School, which was the first to be run under the auspices of the National Health Service through the Sheffield Regional Hospital Board. The School began in Ward 10 of the Derbyshire Royal Infirmary, transferred to Hartington St two years later, and in 1954 moved to Highfields. A house close by, the Cedars, was acquired soon after for student accommodation. As numbers increased, residential accommodation for students was also provided at the Women's Hospital Nurses Home. Students recall curfews, green and grey uniforms at lectures as well as on hospital practice, long gowns at the bi-annual balls, and the production of lavish entertainments on the Cedar's lawns at the annual graduation ceremonies. The annual intake increased from an initial nine students to 30 by 1967.

During Mary Burdon's tenure as Principal the School expanded to an intake of over 60 students per year, the School library was extended and plans were drawn up for building extensions on the Cedars site to accommodate teaching facilities. In the 1970s open days were introduced to promote the School. Compulsory wearing of uniforms while in School was also abandoned during this period. In 1976 the School saw the development of the first accelerated programme to enable students with a first degree to gain the Diploma in Occupational Therapy with two years of study. Vivien Wallace who took over as Principal in 1978 negotiated the School through many changes in its organisation and management, including the transition from the Southern Derbyshire Health Authority to Derbyshire College of Higher Education in 1990. In 1991 new teaching and library facilities in what was to be known as the Fitchett Building was opened by HRH the Princess Royal, and the School was fully transferred onto the Cedars site. The BSc(Hons) in Occupational Therapy was validated and commenced in the same year with 90 full time students. In 1992 Derbyshire College of Higher Education, of which the School was now a part, became the University of Derby. In a restructuring of the Institute, the BSc(Hons) Occupational Therapy programme became part of the Division of Allied Health within the School of Health and Community Studies. Students also had the opportunity to study in European partner institutions. In 1998 an integrated accelerated two year pathway for graduates commenced.

Through negotiation with employers in Health and Social Services, Irene Ilott, In-Service Programme Leader between 1990 and 1994 developed an in-service four year part time programme for support workers in occupational therapy, with students' funding sponsored by their employers. Without adequate sponsorship the programme ceased after one cohort. An integrated four and a half year part time route for support workers to study the same programme was validated and commenced in 1994. This maintained an annual intake of twelve students, and was extended to include applicants not employed in a support worker capacity.

### 1949 Botley's Park
by a group of Botley's Park trained occupational therapists

Botley's Park Hospital for the care of mentally handicapped people (later 'learning disabled' and now 'with special needs') at Chertsey in Surrey catered for all ages and was built on the villa system in large rural grounds. Dr Paddle, the Physician Superintendent wanted a school attached to his hospital because he realised the need for more occupational therapists with expertise in the treatment of people with special needs. He took a keen interest in the Occupational Therapy Training School which opened in 1949, and unlike most of the other schools the academic year started in January. Barbara Bushell, the Head of the Occupational Therapy Department and of the Hospital Children's School was appointed as the first Principal remaining in charge until her retirement in 1974. The Vice Principal, who was full time in the school, was Olive Edmondson. It was the only school that gave all students a course of lectures and three months practical experience on the problems and treatment of people with special needs. Initially there was an intake of six students, this was increased to ten and by 1967 to 15. The small size of the school was a great strength, allowing teaching to be on a more informal basis and when necessary for students to be given additional help and extra tutorials.

For some years the management of Botley's Park Hospital had been concerned about the future of the school and latterly there was no Physician Superintendent to champion the cause. Many discussions had taken place about increasing the fees, upgrading the accommodation and providing more equipment. After Barbara Bushell's retirement, existing staff continued to run the school while unsuccessful attempts were made to find a new Principal. Connie Henson, the recently retired Principal of the St Loyes School, was invited to carry out a viability study and compiled a detailed report on the situation. She concluded that the school could be made viable, that examination results were excellent despite the staffing problem, and with increased fees and upgrading of buildings the school's future would be secure. Paula Juffs, a tutor from St Loyes, was appointed Principal in March 1976. Despite this, a decision was made that the school should be closed by the end of 1976. Alicia Mendez, the Chairman of the Occupational Therapy Board of the CPSM and Sidney Lock, the Chairman of Council of BAOT held discussions with the Botley's Park authorities to that end. The main consideration was that no student should be disadvantaged by this action. Paula Juffs supervised the students until the end of the year when those still in training moved to St Loyes to complete their course in Exeter.

### 1962 The Glasgow School

Doris Sym was the prime mover in the establishment of the Glasgow School. Sym had been a schoolteacher in South Africa and Edinburgh before taking up occupational therapy at the Astley Ainslie Hospital Training Centre. She foresaw that many occupational therapists would be required in the future, so in a very determined manner set about convincing the Greater Glasgow Health Board of the need to establish a school in the west of Scotland. After much hard work, and support from the Scottish Association, whose Chairman at the time was Jean Waterston, the school opened in a large Victorian mansion in Sherbrooke Avenue on Glasgow's south side.

The Glasgow School had an original intake, in 1962, of 15 students which number increased over the next 18 years to 42. The Scottish Association became the examining body when the school opened, its first diplomas being awarded in 1965. It had close associations with Glasgow University, the University of Strathclyde, Langsdale College of Further Education and Jordan Hill College of Education, in addition to resources within the Health Service. Its foundation stimulated growth in the clinical field in the west of Scotland, and a close association between School and practitioners was encouraged, the School being seen as a resource centre for them.

When Sym retired as Principal in 1975, first Betty Hudson, and later Ann Carnduff, took her place. The School became part of the Glasgow Caledonian University, and ran a modular degree course within a semester system which had three main thrusts: a human occupation perspective, research, and the development of critical awareness of the dynamics of the employment environment. In 1997 Sym was awarded an Honorary Fellowship of Glasgow Caledonian University. Resplendent in her blue gown, Ann Carnduff reported, she gave a characteristically feisty speech.

### 1963 The York School

The second York School of Occupational Therapy started in the autumn of 1963 with Miss M.W. Stamper as Principal, and Freda Sampson as Vice-Principal, the latter having, for many years, been the Head Occupational Therapist at the London Hospital. The School was first established at the Military Hospital, but the closure of that institution in 1977 required the finding of a new venue. The School was re-sited at the College of Ripon and York St John following a 1974 amalgamation of two earlier institutions, which created a new

College of Advanced Education. Between then and 1980 enrolment increased from 24 to over 40 students each year. By that time there were eight members of the occupational therapy teaching staff. They were responsible for both academic and practical subjects such as orthotics, home economics, and creative skills. Other practical subjects were learned with students from other courses thus providing them with the exposure to different vocational orientations as well as with expert tuition. Some academic subjects being taught by lecturers from other departments supplemented that experience.

The degree programme which developed in the 1990s was modular in design, and took an occupational performance approach towards behaviour and well-being. Student learning was assisted by approaches such as self directed learning and guided choice. By then the institution had become the University College of Ripon and St. John, and was an autonomous part of the University of Leeds.

### 1964 The Cardiff School
by Martin Booy

Occupational therapy education in Wales began in September 1964 with the opening of the Welsh School of Occupational Therapy, based at the Cardiff Royal Infirmary. The building was in a terrace of three-storey Victorian houses adjacent to the hospital, together with the Cardiff School of Physiotherapy and the Welsh School of Orthoptics. These premises, formerly staff residences were far from ideal, but were seen as a temporary arrangement as a new University Hospital was planned. John Bement, the hospital's Head Occupational Therapist at the time, became the first Vice-Principal under the leadership of Desmond Connor. Within the first intake of 19 were two male students, an unusual phenomenon in occupational therapy at the time, just as it was unusual for the Principal and Vice-Principal of an occupational therapy School to be male. The first students qualified for the Association of Occupational Therapists Diploma in 1967 under the national examination system, which continued into the 1980s.

In 1973 all the health professional training schools formerly at Cardiff Royal Infirmary transferred to the University Hospital site. Schools of Nursing, Occupational Therapy, Orthoptics, Physiotherapy, Radiography, and a new School of Remedial Gymnastics were accommodated in a new, purpose-built teaching block known as the Combined Training Institute (CTI). By this time the School was accepting 25–30 students per year. This building has remained the home of occupational therapy education in Wales until the present day, although there have been many organisational and philosophical changes over time.

An important milestone occurred in 1986 when the first students were admitted onto the School's 'Diploma 81' Course, and also in that year two members of staff, Anne Green and Jo Hobman left to set up the All-Wales in-service training scheme for occupational therapists. In its 35-year history the school has had four Principals, Desmond Connor (1964–68), Joyce Johns (1968–79), Norma Fraser (1979–89), and Martin Booy (1989–present), and has trained nearly 1000 occupational therapists.

### 1967 The Salford School of Occupational Therapy

The Salford School of Occupational Therapy in the North West of England was established in 1967. In 1971 it became part of the Science Department of Salford College of Technology, along with courses in physiotherapy, radiography and chiropody. Teaching of theoretical subjects such as physiology and psychology was shared with students of the other courses, and in some cases was provided by consultants from local hospitals. The School also benefited from facilities and staff available from other departments in the College in the teaching of practical subjects. For example, teachers of trade apprentices taught students woodwork, metalwork, bricklaying, painting and decorating in the building department. Most clinical practice was undertaken for the whole of the second and third year, apart from a fortnight's intensive theoretical work during the summer. Their placements were widely dispersed throughout the country.

By 1980 the School had an annual intake of 30 students, which included a mix of school leavers and mature students. Its situation had some disadvantages, which were recognised by School staff. It was scenically unattractive, had limited opportunities for work or play, and good accommodation was hard to find. Apparently, though:

> ...everybody seems to be happy. The assets of the School include a relaxed atmosphere and positive staff student relationships. Students describe the staff as being accessible, approachable and occasionally, formidable. Staff describe students as being highly individual, enjoyable, critical and – occasionally – absent.

In the 1990s the school became part of the University of Salford, in the Faculty of Health Care and Social Work Studies. Its degree with modular design, emphasised problem oriented learning, active enquiry and resource investigation.

## 1973 The Ulster School: Jordanstown

Serious efforts to open an occupational therapy school in Northern Ireland (NI) started in the late 1950s. As a first step, throughout the '60s a small number of local occupational therapists approached all the major hospitals to urge them to establish departments. Their persistence had paid off by 1970, with the opening of the occupational therapy department at the Royal Victoria Hospital. By then, there were 48 occupational therapists in NI. Forty-two worked for the NI Hospitals Authority, one for NI Council for Orthopaedic Development, and five in Welfare (the equivalent of Social Services). Based on this, the local occupational therapists were able to assure the AOT that, 'There could be places for 34 students in a variety of hospital situations.' In the initial planning two advisers, Mary Macdonald from Oxford and Doris Sym from Glasgow, were invited to NI to advise on the establishment of the school. They visited in 1971 during a period of great social and political unrest to carry out the groundwork for the course approval. On one occasion, as Macdonald was speaking, a bomb exploded in the distance and she did not appear to bat an eyelid!

The Ulster Polytechnic in Belfast, was approved for the school's location, and in September 1973 the Occupational Therapy Training School opened. Joy Rook, previously at the Dublin School, become its Principal Lecturer. Helen Baird, who was a member of a number of COT education committees joined the School as Director of Occupational Therapy in 1976, where she was to remain for 18 years. The first intake of 20 students was chosen from 100 applications much to the delight of the organising committee. In the following 21 years the course 'produced' 467 occupational therapists. The majority of students were from NI, plus a small number from the Republic of Ireland, one or two from England and Scotland, and a small number of students from beyond the British Isles. Faciliteies included a rehabilitation flat, a remedial workshop shared with physiotherapy, and the use of a simulated social skills training centre.

Three main themes occurred repeatedly in the activities of the course over the years. They were: progress towards a degree level training; numbers on the course; and resources, mainly accommodation. The first record of a possible degree level training course appeared in the Senior Course Tutor's Diary of 1975, where Joy Rook noted a special meeting to discuss degree proposals—possibly a degree in Rehabilitation Studies with physiotherapists. However, it was to be ten years before a degree course was approved for occupational therapists. Many factors prevented it, such as a change of Government policy and a ban on any degree proposals going through. Other factors helped, such as the development of the Diploma '81 award by the COT, and the merger of the Polytechnic with the New University of Ulster. It was the first in the UK to have a course approved at honours degree level when it began in 1986, and the second to appoint a professor of occupational therapy, Dr Pamela Eakin.

## 1976 The Newcastle School

A School in the North East of England had been anticipated for some years. In 1972, for example, Council of COT had sent material about the possibility to the deputy governor of the Royal Newcastle Infirmary, and to BAOT members in the Newcastle Region. But it was not until four years later, in September 1976, that the Newcastle Occupational Therapy Course started at Newcastle Polytechnic. Situated in the School of Health Studies which was part of the Faculty of Community Social Studies, students on the course had access to all the educational and recreational facilities of a Polytechnic with a student population of 9000. By the end of the decade, the intake was 25 students each year. Students at all levels of training had the opportunity to participate in all decision-making relating to the Course and the School, and there were student members on both relevant committees and on the School Board. Throughout the Course, peer teaching was a central aspect. In both the academic setting and the clinical field students were encouraged to learn from, and to teach, each other at a formal and an informal level.

The overall running of the Course was the responsibility of the Course Committee made up of all tutors, student representatives, and representatives from the clinical field, the medical profession, and the physiotherapy course. It was chaired by the Course Leader. Particular features were the open structure of the Course designed to allow students to develop skills they already had and to learn new ones, and in particular to develop social skills and interpersonal relationships. In the 1990s it became part of the Faculty of Health, Social Work and Education in the University of Northumbria at Newcastle, and, as part of its honours degree offered opportunities for shared units with physiotherapy. It also offers an MS, and an Advanced Diploma in Fieldwork Education.

### 1978  West Midlands School: Wolverhampton & Coventry

Occupational therapy education was established in the West Midlands in 1978,

with the opening of the Wolverhampton School of Occupational Therapy. The school, based at New Cross Hospital, was self-funding and emerged as a direct response to an identified shortfall of occupational therapists in the West Midlands region. It was to serve a population of five million people throughout the five counties of the region. Mary Keer was appointed to the post of Principal in January 1978, to begin the preparatory work for the School. The first intake of 24 students commenced with 3.5 whole time equivalent (wte) teachers. The official opening ceremony was held on 12 March 1979, with Mr Tredrea, Chairman of Wolverhampton Area Health Authority and the Rt Hon Lord Byers, President of the COT presiding.

The School worked closely with other schools in the Combined Education Centre although clinical skills were often taught in single profession groups with the instruction tailored accordingly. Multidisciplinary instruction was considered a sensible use of scarce resources, as it could develop 'student awareness of respective roles'. Occupational therapy and physiotherapy students shared anatomy and physiology lectures, some clinical skills such as splint-making and mobility, and a member of staff from the school provided a series of psychology and psychiatry lectures for physiotherapy students. Students learnt some of their practical skills from specialist instructors at the Adult Education Centre in Wolverhampton.

In 1986, following a review of education for occupational therapists within the West Midlands, additional training places were deemed necessary. The proposed increase, to double the number was not viable within New Cross

provided by the School

Hospital and plans were made to relocate the School in an Institute of Higher Education. In 1987 regional universities and polytechnics were invited to tender for the provision of occupational therapy education. The then Coventry Polytechnic was successful in its bid and in the summer of 1988 the students and staff of the Wolverhampton School, transferred to become part of its Faculty of Social Biological and Health Sciences. In October 1988, 56 students commenced the course. HRH, The Princess Royal, officially opened the West Midlands School of Occupational Therapy on 11 May 1989.

The BSc (Hons) Occupational Therapy, validated in 1990, provided new opportunities for students. The modular structure, flexible in design, enabled students some degree of choice in studies during the final year. Further developments in student choice and opportunities for shared learning with other health and social care students were realised in 1995 as the degree programme was reviewed. Throughout the 1990s student numbers continued to increase to meet the demands of practice, with an annual intake of 125 full time and a maximum of 15 part-time in-service route students entering the course in 1999. Additionally the school offers a range of courses to meet practitioners continuing professional development needs, including courses in therapeutic horticulture, fieldwork education and an MSc Occupational Therapy.

## 1977 The Grampian School: Aberdeen
by Catherine F. Paterson

The Department of Occupational Therapy of the Robert Gordon University, School of Health Studies, started with 12 students in January 1977. Initially called the Grampian School of Occupational Therapy, the most northern school in the UK and the third in Scotland, it was the outcome of vigorous campaigning by the SAOT. In March 1973, the Scottish Home and Health Department responded to a staffing crisis and authorised the North-Eastern Regional Hospital Board to establish a school. The Board duly allocated the well appointed third floor of the Victoria Pavilion of Woolmanhill Hospital, the original Aberdeen Royal Infirmary, with every intention of providing purpose built premises for paramedical education within ten years. The School was formally opened in March 1977 by Professor Cairns Aitken. The first intake of students to qualify were privileged to be presented with their diplomas by Miss Margaret (Peg) Barr Fulton, MBE, who took a very special interest in the school since she had worked nearby.

The original target intake was 15 students with an establishment for five lecturers. This favourable student to staff ratio was not maintained. The intake was increased to 22 in 1980 and some money earmarked for teaching staff salaries was used to employ a part-time librarian and develop a library service. Whilst that quite unusual decision in occupational therapy schools at the time was beneficial, it was also unfortunate in failing to maintain the high student/staff ratios. The Grampian School was established with teacher-based, externally moderated examinations, which paved the way for further educational reforms in the 1980s. As early as 1982, talks began with COT, the Scottish Office and the Scottish schools, to discuss the profession's aspiration for degree-level entry to the profession. Progress was slow, the Government being reluctant to encourage a development, which would lead to demands for higher salaries. In the meantime, the Grampian School prepared for validation in relation to Diploma '81 which was approved in 1984.

Aberdeen sought approval for its diploma course from the Council for National Academic Awards through the Robert Gordon Institute of Technology (RGIT), which was granted in April 1989. The school was finally transferred to RGIT on 1 April 1990, with the other NHS schools of physiotherapy and radiography, providing further opportunities for close co-operation. Another year on and at last, not only was the course validated for the award of a BSc degree but retrospective approval was given for two years, so that the first students were capped in July 1992, by which time RGIT had become The Robert Gordon University (RGU). Further course developments led to a four year honours degree in 1994.

The push towards degrees necessitated intensive staff development. Staff had initially pursued qualifications in teaching at the certificate level, but from 1982, lecturers were progressively allowed on the diploma, masters and doctorate programmes. Helena Munro was awarded a PhD in Education in 1992. The move to RGU resulted in an increase in the annual intake to 36 by the end of the decade but with little increase in staffing. However, over the years, the school has benefited from a succession of valued lecturers, including Jennifer Creek and Christine Craik. The RGU Department of Occupational Therapy now looks forward to the new Faculty of Health and Social Studies, which is due for completion in the summer of 2002. This transfer will mark the end of an era, since it coincides with the retirement of its founding principal Catherine F. Paterson after 26 years.

## 1979 The Essex School: Colchester
by Lynne Askham

The school began in 1979 as the brainchild of Mavis Wallis, who had the idea of training Occupational Therapy Assistants through a four year, part time, in-service course with the intention of meeting local staff shortages. The scheme would also satisfy the desire of local assistants who wished to qualify, but who were tied to the area by family, and partners' work. In 1978, following three years' research, scepticism from the BAOT, and some assistance from the North Thames Regional Health Authority, Wallis had submitted a report to the CPSM and the BAOT. Approval for one intake of students was granted. The course was planned to be accomplished in four years using day release, tutorials, residential sessions, and extra study days; much rested on the students' willingness to undertake a great deal of private study. This pattern, excluding residential periods, became the national model for part time education in Occupational Therapy.

A partnership was formed with Colchester Institute and the first group of 18 students enrolled there in September 1979. All five Districts within the local Health Authority sponsored students to the 'Essex Scheme'. Wallis and Mary Collins, a sociology lecturer at Colchester Institute, shared the course management. Tutorials were held in the students' workplaces and Summer School took place at St Loye's School in Exeter where Katherine Ingamells and her staff greeted this new challenge with enthusiasm. Early clinical placements provided very mixed experiences for students as few occupational therapists in the area had been involved with students in the past. However, the organisation of local meetings, courses and study days for clinical supervisors, along with the secondment of their assistants to future courses, gave the supervisors some 'ownership' of the course. This team approach was to remain a unique feature of the school.

There were some difficulties in the early years. The second intake, planned for 1981 was given approval only at the last minute, resulting in the hasty recruitment of students who were ill-prepared. Consequently, the drop out rate was high, leading to further scepticism on the part of the professional bodies. However, a sudden increase in occupational therapy positions and widespread interest from assistants across the region, highlighted the need to continue with the scheme. Agreement was finally given to continue, with the proviso that extra tutors were employed. From then on the school employed a range of occupational therapists and maintained input from a variety of subject tutors at Colchester Institute. The School came of age with the production of a badge, the official title 'Essex School of Occupational Therapy' and a place of its own at the Area Health Authority in Witham.[1]

In 1986 Wallis started an Accelerated two year Diploma for graduates which was the first of its kind. In 1996 this became the first accelerated course to become a degree programme and followed validation of the Essex School's four year part-time BSc (Hons) Occupational Therapy in 1995. The School merged with Colchester Institute in 1994, and is now part of the Centre for Health and Therapy Studies, with degrees awarded by the Anglia Polytechnic University.

## 1986: The All Wales In-Service Training Scheme for Occupational Therapists: Hensol

by Ann Geen & Deb Hearle

The All Wales Part Time Occupational Therapy Programme was established in 1986 by Mid Glamorgan Health Authority, to address a profound short-fall of qualified occupational therapists in Wales. Despite the confirmed success of the in-service training model, pioneered in Essex (1979), there was doubt and resistance about an all Wales equivalent. Many people, including members of the Welsh Office, envisaged insurmountable problems which drove a few initial enthusiasts to prove the sceptics wrong.

Following a feasibility study commissioned by Mid Glamorgan Health Authority and led by Sue Jenkins and Christine Court, The All Wales In-Service Training Scheme for Occupational Therapists was established. Initially planned for only two cohorts, it was designed to tap the valuable potential of experienced Occupational Therapy Helpers and Technicians in Wales and enable them to qualify as occupational therapists. Funding was provided by all health authorities in Wales with additional fees levied on those local authorities seconding students.

The scheme was launched with two full time staff, Ann Geen and Jo Hobman who shared the District Occupational Therapists's office in Glanrhyd Hospital, Bridgend. The scheme's headquarters soon progressed to a bathroom, complete with Victorian bath! Dodging milk floats and sheep, the first twenty-four students set off, some at five o'clock in the morning, to converge on Bridgend College of Technology where the teaching took place. Ann and Jo were assisted by Gail Williams, and Dr Angela Feltham, part-time occupational therapy and medical sciences tutors respectively.

In 1989, a second cohort and third full time member of staff, Deb Hearle, joined what was soon to become The All Wales School of Occupational Therapy; the offices moved to an old pharmacy department in Pen-y-Fai Hospital. Soon after, in 1992, the school was offered purposely-adapted premises within Hensol Castle and became an outreach course of the University of Glamorgan, it's first link with Higher Education.

In 1994, The All Wales School sought academic affiliation with the University of Wales to integrate more closely with other courses for Professions Allied to Medicine. This also helped to continue preparations for the Degree which was finally validated in 1995. Commitment continued to the in-service model, however, to take account of the changes within service provision, admission was extended to those in the voluntary and private sectors with relevant experience. The course hence became known as 'part-time' as opposed to 'in-service' to encompass this wider demand.

In 1998, The All Wales School integrated with the University of Wales, College of Medicine, to form part of the Department of OT Education and joined colleagues from what was previously known as The Welsh School. This marked the end of or education as part of the Health Service in Wales.

Although only established for two cohorts, the success of this mode of education together with the commitment of the team, has led to four Diploma intakes followed by ongoing BSc (Hons) intakes. By 2002, the programme had three full and six part time staff and had produced over one hundred new therapists, the majority of whom have remained in Wales forming a stable, high quality workforce with a unique understanding of the needs of Wales.

### 1987 Bristol Polytechnic
provided by the School

Bristol is proud to be the home of the first occupational therapy school in the UK founded by Dr Elizabeth Casson in 1930. In 1987, at Bristol Polytechnic, a new in-service, part-time occupational therapy programme welcomed its first cohort of 21 students. The programme, based in the South West of England, was only the second of its kind in the UK, the first having been established in the early 1980s in Crawley in Surrey. The philosophy of 'in-service education' or 'learning on the job' is common in many workplaces and is based on the belief of maintenance of standards and retaining staff, through work-based education. In this collaboration, the staff were occupational therapy support workers who were given the opportunity to study part-time for a professional occupational therapy qualification at a higher education establishment, in conjunction with fieldwork placements as students and employment as support workers. Four years later, the programme delivered 17 diplomates into their first posts as state registered occupational therapists.

This in-service programme was established in response to a specific and acute regional shortage of occupational therapists. In the early 1980s, Bristol and the area immediately surrounding had three health authorities providing hospital based services and one large local government authority providing domiciliary services. In the hospital based services, out of a possible 148 qualified occupational therapy positions, 32 were vacant and had been so for more than a year. In-service students were recruited every two years attending the Polytechnic for one and a half days (now two days) a week for four years. The host institution is the University of the West of England which resulted from a merger of several higher education establishments with the Bristol Polytechnic in 1996. Students now graduate with a Bachelor of Science honours degree in occupational therapy. The annual intake has increased to 36 students.

### 1987 The Canterbury School

provided by the School

The occupational therapy programme at Christ Church College, Canterbury was developed in the mid 1980s and validated in 1987. The first cohort of just over 20 students began their education and training in September of that year. The programme was at that time a three year diploma with an additional fourth year to convert this to an ordinary Bachelor of Science degree. The fourth year was to be self funded. Prior to the first cohort completing their training, the programme was awarded ordinary degree status. This was the first programme in England to be awarded degree status. Thus the first cohort of students graduated with a BSc degree awarded by the University of Kent at Canterbury, to which the College was affiliated. Since the inception of the programme, eligible students have been bursaried from Regional Health Authorities, originally South East and North East Thames.

During the first two years of the programme teaching accommodation was found within the College campus. Towards the end of the 1988/89 academic year, the programme moved into purpose built accommodation. This was substantially funded by South East Thames Regional Health Authority. This modern home for the School was officially opened by HRH, The Princess Royal in November 1991. From the first intake in 1987 the student numbers progressively increased, the programme intake is currently 80 students per year, the majority of whom are bursaried. In addition, there are places available for European Union students and those who are self funded.

In 1992 the programme was re-validated as an honors degree and re-validated again in 1997 where substantial changes were made in all three years to both the academic and fieldwork aspects. There was an increased expectation that students should take responsibility and actively participate in their learning. This, to ensure that as graduates they would be reflective practitioners committed to life-long learning. Another significant change was the inclusion of fieldwork assessments in the degree classification to give an accurate reflection of the educational achievements of the new graduate practitioners. During the academic year 1998/99, the College was awarded University College status from the Privy Council. Thus, all graduates will be awarded degrees from Canterbury Christ Church University College.

### 1987 The Harrow In-service Diploma Course

A four-year in-service diploma programme for OT assistants was validated in 1987 and delivered at the Harrow campus of the Polytechnic of Central London which is now the University of Westminster. It closed in 1996.

### 1987 The Crawley School: Surrey
by Zielfa B. Maslin

An in-service Diploma Course in Occupational Therapy was set up in 1987 following a joint initiative by a consortium of three West Sussex health authorities (Chichester, Mid-Downs and Worthing), West Sussex Social Services and Crawley College. The first Course Director was Rosemary Hagedorn. The diploma course produced three cohorts of state registered occupational therapists: 1988-92; 1990-94; 1992-96. This course is primarily aimed at enabling occupational therapy support workers in health and social services to qualify as state registered occupational therapists whilst working. For the students, it is a route to qualification that suits their work, personal and family commitments.

Zielfa B. Maslin assumed the course directorship in January 1993, and the Course now offering two courses: a four-year part-time BSc (Honours) Occupational Therapy programme in partnership with the University of Brighton; and a one-year Certificate for Occupational Therapy Support Workers (Social Services). In 1994, the course was validated to a four-year part-time BSc (Hons) in Occupational Therapy with a degree awarded by the University of Brighton with whom the course continues to develop partnership schemes. In 1997, approval for an annual intake was granted by the Joint Validating Committee of the College of Occupational Therapists and the Council of Professions Supplementary to Medicine. The first cohort of BSc (Hons) graduates qualified in 1998. Alumni from the course are actively practising occupational therapists in Jersey, Berkshire, Essex, Kent, Sussex, Surrey, Hertfordshire, London and Hampshire.

A Certificate for Occupational Therapy Support Workers (Social Services) was developed in partnership with Essex Social Services. The course is an innovative mix of formal teaching in college; distance learning by guided study packs; telephone tutorials; and exercises done with supervisors in the workplace. As far as is known, this is the first distance learning course for occupational therapy support workers. Students need only attend college for ten days over a period of one year. This course started in 1997 and Beverley Meeson was its first course leader.

### 1989 St. Bartholomew's and Royal London School
by Lynn Summerfield-Mann

Located in the East End, one of the most vibrant parts of London with diverse communities and rich history is the St. Bartholomew's and Royal London School. The planning and development of the School began in the 1980s between the District Occupational Therapist for Tower Hamlets and Chairman of COT, Margaret Ellis, the Dean of the London Hospital Medical College, Professor Roy Duckworth, Head Therapists from within the North East Thames Region and Dr Naomi Fraser-Holland.

The original course which was approved in 1989 was designed to deliver a student-centred and accelerated curriculum with core curriculum modules and problem based modules. The core curriculum modules presented the principles of professional theory and practice, basic and applied sciences in a combination of lectures, seminars and tutorials. The problem based modules required students to work in small groups investigating individuals needs and difficulties due to bio-psycho-social dysfunction. The first year of the course emphasised professional studies and there was an early fieldwork placement to promote appreciation of service delivery. The principle of self-assessment applied throughout the course which covered 25 months including fieldwork. The first intake came from ten different disciplines, with most having degrees in psychology. Student numbers continued to rise and the course is now validated to take in 62 students per intake. There are 8 staff, all with either Master's degrees or PhDs.

In 1995 a merger took place between London Hospital Medical College, St Bartholomews Medical School and Queen Mary and Westfield College, University of London. As a result, in 1998, the School of Occupational Therapy became an academic department within the Division of Community Science, St Bartholomew's and the Royal London School of Medicine and Dentistry alongside departments such as General Practice and Primary Care, and Care of the Elderly. The School's Research and Development strategy and staff development takes account of responsibilities for the local community in terms of health improvement. In 1999 it became a member of the first Interprofessional Training Ward in the UK. This brought together students of medicine, physiotherapy, nursing and occupational therapy from three universities to deliver services within the Musculo-Skeletal Directorate of the Trust. Another initiative involved students in a pilot project led by Dr Linda Lovelock which addressed elder abuse in East London. A Masters course is part of future planning.

### 1989 Southbank: London
by Catherine Usher & Anna Forte

The teaching at South Bank was based on the belief that selected occupational therapy support workers have the capacity to undertake academic study and reach a level of competence that satisfies the requirements for state registration as an occupational therapist. The original Diploma course was exclusively designed to meet the needs of individuals who were unable to access a full-time occupational therapy programme, those with non-traditional entry qualifications or those who particularly wished to integrate their studies with employment. With Maggie Cummings as its first Course Director, the occupational therapy programme had its first intake of students in October 1989 and since then successfully attracted students from diverse cultural and personal backgrounds, with ages ranging between 21 and 56, the current average age of the students being 35. South Bank has a central London location, which allows students from a wide geographical area to gain access to the course.

In 1992 South Bank Polytechnic was granted University status, and the programme became part of the School of Education and Health Studies in the Faculty of Science, Technology, Health and Society, which more recently became the Faculty of Health. South Bank University now has over 700 academic staff and 20,000 students. Under the Directorship of Auldeen Alsop, the South Bank programme became the first four-year, part-time BSc (Hons) in Occupational Therapy in the country, with its first intake of degree students in September 1993, graduating in 1997. More recently, in late 1998, the Occupational Therapy course moved its teaching rooms into new, purpose built accommodation in one of the main university buildings. The current Occupational Therapy programme has a validated annual intake of up to 30 students, and is delivered by nine full and part time staff and visiting lecturers, with service user involvement on a regular basis. The course has a community emphasis and recognises the need to prepare practitioners who are fit for practice in a multicultural society, paying particular attention to new trends in health and social care and their potential impact on occupational therapy service provision.

### 1990 The Sheffield School

An occupational therapy programme was validated and commenced at the Sheffield Hallam University in 1990. The programme is part of the School of Health and Community Studies, and some subjects are shared with other disciplines. It offers an honours degree programme of three years full time and, since 1997, a four year part-time route has also been available. There are between 25-32 places open to both school leavers and mature students and opportunities are available for worldwide placements and for linking with European Schools.

### 1991 The Norwich School

An honours degree programme at the University of East Anglia in Norwich commenced in 1991. This was jointly validated with a similar programme in physiotherapy with which it shares some aspects of the curriculum. Such sharing is based on the philosophy, similar to other schools with joint teaching, of enhancing future interdisciplinary work. The programme comprised three years full time study and offered 34 places to applicants with requisite academic ability and following an individual interview. It took an interesting and innovative direction, reflecting research based practice, and

maximum opportunity is given to students to provide choice and flexibility to their programmes. Designed to encourage students to acquire skills through practice, and knowledge through teaching others, it requires them to participate in active enquiry. To that end, a research project in the third year allows students to focus on a particular area of interest and specialist professional knowledge whilst developing skills of enquiry.

### 1992 St Martin's College: Lancaster

provided by the School

The Department of Occupational Therapy Studies was initiated at St Martin's College (SMC) Lancaster in 1992. Its development followed successful tendering to provide occupational therapy education as a result of the changes in provision when funds were devolved from National to Regional level. SMC successfully contracted with the then North West Regional Health Authority and the Northern Regional Health Authority to provide pre-registration occupational therapy education to degree level to serve the manpower needs of Northern Lancashire and Cumbria. The resultant honours degree is an award from Lancaster University. The initial course was started through close liaison with the district occupational therapists from the catchment area and the College. Funding from occupational therapy services was allocated to support the development. This close liaison between practising therapists and the Department has been a valued and valuable hallmark of the development. The initial pre-registration degree course was devised by a steering group comprising clinicians, college staff and fieldwork colleagues who had always been involved in teaching and scrutiny of the course.

The first intake of 24 students began in 1993 sharing accommodation with the Lancaster School of Radiography at Lancaster Moor Hospital. During that year an architect designed facility was built on the main Lancaster College Campus overlooking Morecambe Bay and the Lakeland Hills. The two departments moved into this facility in 1994. The Department of Occupational Therapy Studies, in line with the SMC Mission Statement, has always had close links with the surrounding community. It was the first occupational therapy education establishment to run clinics within its physical environment which offer unique educational opportunities to students as well as service to the community. These included clinics for people with head injury, activities of daily living, dysphasia and a Carer's Support Group. Other student work involved community projects within Lancaster, for example, working with local families and their children with disabilities; local schools regarding Disability Awareness within the National Curriculum and constructing equipment and programmes for local institutions and services. A manageable continuous professional development programme has been developed towards Masters level courses.

---

### 1993 The Southampton School

                             provided by the School Southampton University School of Occupational Therapy and Physiotherapy was founded in 1993 by the then Wessex Regional Health Authority whose members felt that there was a need for such a school to implement staffing strategies in Hampshire, Dorset and the Isle of Wight. The authority was also committed to interdisciplinary working and commissioned a joint educational programme between Occupational Therapy and Physiotherapy. Southampton already had a School of Medicine and a School of Nursing and in 1994 a new Faculty was founded in the University titled the Faculty of Medicine, Health and Biological Sciences. The founder members of the new School were Dr Rosemary Barnitt, an occupational therapist, and Paul Standing, a physiotherapist. Both commenced work on 1st April 1992. and spent the first year recruiting staff, designing course documentation for validation and planning building and teaching facilities, helped by the University of East Anglia who had carried out a similar development two years previously and were generous with support and advice. An additional bonus was the local availability of the Rehabilitation Masters course which meant that there were very suitable local clinicians and researchers available to staff the new School. Sadly, Paul Standing died in 1993 and Fleur Kitsell was appointed as Head of Physiotherapy. The School was represented at a Senior Level in the University by a Dean who could be elected from any of the constituent Schools, the Heads of which have equal voting rights.

The first intake of 30 Physiotherapy and 30 Occupational Therapy students commenced in September 1993 with eight full time equivalent academic staff and three support staff. The course design was such that approximately 60% of Year One was shared, 40% of Year Two, and between 20% and 40% of Year Three depending on Options selected. All clinical/fieldwork hours were profession specific. The year groups were named after the Greek Alphabet so the first intake was Alpha followed by Beta and so on. Commissions to educate therapists increased and by the 1998 intake there were 67 physiotherapy and 68 occupational therapy students. A part time option commenced for the occupational therapists in 1995 with a further intake in 1996 and 1998. The School moved premises three times between 1992 and 1995 when it arrived at a purpose built building on the University site, designed by Sir Norman Foster. The first two intakes of students appeared to accept moving as part of their educational programme and soon found all the University facilities.

By 1999 staffing of the School had risen to 52, plus seven in the School's Health Research Unit, plus PhD/MPhil students. The Research Unit proved very successful and steadily pulled in grants and students. In August 1999, the School was taking on board the School of Podiatry from New College in Southampton and the Rehabilitation Research Unit from the School of Medicine. There are plans to offer a flexible programme of Masters Studies. A graduate school and a cross faculty Masters programme are also in the planning stage.

---

### 1994 University of Teesside: Middlesborough

by Claire Brewis

Occupational therapy education commenced at the University of Teesside in Autumn, 1994. This followed a campaign by local occupational therapy managers over some time, and funding being devolved to the region for occupational therapy training. Based within the University's School of Human Studies, 28 students enrolled in the first cohort. The Course was led by Jennifer Creek, with Angela Birleson and Claire Brewis, previously local clinicians, as lecturers. From the outset, a particular feature of the Teesside Course was an evenly mixed student cohort of school-leavers and mature entrants. A terraced house in King Edward's Square was allocated to the Course and converted to provide activities of daily living facilities for teaching purposes. The majority of the teaching took place in the main University buildings.

With the second cohort of 30 students Eric Charlton, another local clinician, joined the teaching team, and a number of part-time lecturers also contributed to the teaching. Local trusts assisted with funding of special posts. South Tees Mental Health and Community NHS Trust funded a post of research occupational therapist, and a lecturer practitioner post was established with South Tees Acute NHS Trust. The Course moved into the newly established School of Health in 1996, which comprised of physiotherapy, medical imaging, social work, nursing and midwifery as well as occupational therapy. The summer of 1997 saw the first graduates from Teesside. There was particular delight in two first class honours awards being conferred on local mature students accepted for the course with non-traditional qualifications. They were Sandra Crowther and Margaret Perkins. In that year Surya Shah, from Australia, joined the team and in the following year was made the first professor of occupational therapy in England.

The following year, 1998, saw another three first class awards to local mature students, Doreen Yeoh, Marion Wotherspoon and Alison Bullock. In that year Jennifer Creek stepped down as Course Leader, and Claire Brewis and Angela Birleson took over until Mala Vacara was appointed as Subject Group Leader the next year. In 1998 and 1999 diplomates from Singapore joined the Course for the final semester of Year 3 to convert their diplomas in occupational therapy to degrees. Similarly, a local clinician converted her occupational therapy diploma to a degree. A bigger and better activities of daily living suite was provided in 1999 as the students had outgrown the one in King Edward's Square. Funding was granted for an assessment test library for teaching purposes and for the use of local clinicians. A new programme of study was approved by the Joint Validation Committee to commence the following autumn.

---

**1994 The Eastbourne School: Brighton**
provided by the School

This two-year full time accelerated programme in occupational therapy for graduates was jointly validated in May 1994 by the University of Brighton, the College of Occupational Therapists and the Council for Professions Supplementary to Medicine. In recognition of the advanced entry and the level of study of management principles applied to occupational therapy services, the award was originally validated as a Postgraduate Diploma in Occupational Therapy (one of three in the United Kingdom). After the first intake of 25 students, thereafter 30-33 students annually have been admitted to the Course. The programme was promoted by South Thames Regional Health Authority, as commissioners of occupational therapy education, to meet local needs, in consultation with the University of Brighton. Sited on the Eastbourne campus as part of the Faculty of Health, it now stands within the newly formed School of Healthcare Professions along with Physiotherapy and Podiatry. The two-year schedule was initially designed to complement existing occupational therapy courses within the region, which include traditional three-year full time and four-year part-time education programmes, both of which led

to BSc Honours degrees in Occupational Therapy. The initial contract with South Thames was from 1994, for a five-year period. In 1997, the year when other Healthcare courses in the South East of England were required to re-contract, this course was exempted, it being agreed that the contract period would be permitted to roll forward to synchronise with the next general tendering period, in 2002. The School maintains close collaboration with the new Sussex Educational Consortium, and discussions about satisfying future needs are in progress.

All students admitted to the occupational therapy programme have a first degree in a relevant subject with classification of 2.2 or above, and have experience of health or social care work environments. Those selected undertake an accelerated course of 45 weeks per year for two calendar years. An extended academic year allows for the same amount of weeks to be devoted to the study of occupational therapy as any other validated occupational therapy programme. However, educational strategies have been incorporated which take advantage of students' previous university experience and which encourage students to reflect on their learning both clinically and academically, to expedite theory/practice integration. A modified version of Barrows and Tamblyn 1980 validated innovative educational strategy, problem based learning (PBL) was adopted to foster the highest quality of learning for these graduate students.

---

[1] Askham L. Senior Tutor. The Essex School of Occupational Therapy. Unpublished report. June 1999.

# Appendix B

## Stories of Fellows of the College of Occupational Therapists

### 1972 Nathalie Barr, MBE

Nathalie Barr (nee Smythe) was born in 1910. She spent four years working as a VAD in the Navy during the Second World War before undertaking one of the special wartime occupational therapy training courses at Dorset House in 1945, upgrading to full qualification in 1947. She worked with orthopaedic surgeon Guy Pulvertaft at Grimsby Royal Infirmary and later in Derby where she helped to establish Etwall Rehabilitation Centre. She also worked with Norman Capener, an Exeter surgeon who, like Pulvertaft had a special interest in hands. Nathalie's interest in hand therapy was nurtured. The opportunity to develop that further occurred in 1954 when she moved to the Medical Rehabilitation Unit, Royal Air Force, Chessington, and worked with hand surgeon Kit Wynn Parry. She experimented with and developed innovative and original techniques in mobilisation and the use of dynamic, lively wrist and hand splints using the workshops at Chessington to produce metal hinges and springs for them. Details of her innovative work appears in the first edition of Wyn Parry's *Rehabilitation of the Hand*, published in 1958, of which she was a co-author. The book established her reputation nationally and internationally in the field of hand therapy and rehabilitation, and Nathalie was awarded an MBE. In 1955 she became a co-opted member of AOT Council and between 1957 and 1959 was its Chairman. She also served on Joint Council and various other AOT committees. In 1960, after her marriage, she was invited to assist in developing rehabilitation services in Hong Kong. Her contribution there is well remembered. On her return to the UK in 1965 she became a tutor at the Welsh School of Occupational Therapy. As well as being one of the first Honorary Fellows of the AOT she was also an Honorary Fellow of the American Association of Occupational Therapists. In 1972 she was re-elected to the Council of AOT as a National member for three years. In 1975, her book *The Hand: Principles and Techniques of Simple Splint Making in Rehabilitation* was published. It was re-issued in 1988, modified and updated. She became an active founder member of the British Association of Hand Therapists in 1984, funding a training and travel award that is competed for annually by therapists. As well she endowed a lectureship. A Nathalie Barr lectureship was already established in the USA for the American Society of Hand Therapists. In addition she endowed the Pulvertaft Fellowship for hand surgeons to undertake higher surgical training at an approved centre in either the UK or France, and gave a generous bequest to COT.

---

### 1972 Mary S. Jones

Mary S. Jones (affectionately known as either Mrs Jones or Molly), trained as a physiotherapist at St. Thomas' Hospital. She married, travelled, and lived in various parts of the world, until at the outbreak of World War II, encouraged by orthopaedic surgeon, Mr Rowley Bristow, she completed a shortened war-time occupational therapy course at Dorset House. In 1940 she started an occupational therapy department at the Rowley Bristow

Hospital, Pyrford, Surrey mainly for patients with nerve lesions, TB spines and TB hips. During this period she pioneered hand splints and devised special equipment to enable patients on long-term bed rest to engage in productive work for the war effort. She took an active role in the developing AOT, as part of or chairing many of its committees. In 1946 Molly began planning for the occupational therapy programme at Farnham Park, one of the first civilian rehabilitation centres. Between 1947 and her retirement in 1961, she built up a department that became world famous and attracted a constant stream of visitors. Molly devised graded programmes of occupational therapy and designed remedial equipment, splints and prostheses for the specific treatment of lower and upper limb injuries. Many of her designs were, later, commercially produced. Her methods of treatment were published in *The Lancet, the British Journal of Physical Medicine*, in Macdonald's *Occupational Therapy in Rehabilitation*, and in her 1960 book, *An Approach to Occupational Therapy*. That was based on a research approach to daily practice. Molly was an inspiring teacher, taking a very active role as a clinical supervisor for students of Dorset House, Derby, Exeter, London and Northampton. She held a profound belief in the value of occupational therapy for physical rehabilitation, which she chose to call reablement, and did a great deal to establish its reputation as an important branch of treatment.

---

### 1972 Grizel MacCaul, MBE

Grizel MacCaul was born in Canada in 1908. Aged seven when her mother died she went to live with an aunt in Scotland. She first trained to teach physical education at Bedford College. Later she trained as an occupational therapist at Dorset House, qualifying in 1940. From then until 1946 Grizel remained on the staff of Dorset House and worked in rehabilitation for war casualties. Next she became Occupational Therapist in Charge at The London Hospital, and then, in 1949, Head Occupational Therapist at King's College Hospital department where she worked with Dr Frank Cooksey. Her department at King's College became internationally recognised and attracted visitors from all over the world. There, Grizel created an ADL unit, which included one of the first rehabilitation kitchens, then, the first Functional Assessment Unit, jointly staffed by an occupational therapist and a physiotherapist. She was the first to employ a research occupational therapist to do a study of problems for disabled housewives in their kitchens. Over the years, Grizel served on both national and international professional committees. She was one of the signatories of the original Memorandum and Articles of the AOT and Chairman of Council from 1947-1948, and again in 1955. She was a Governor of the Liverpool School and Westminster Hospital, and was awarded an MBE in 1957. Grizel was an inspiring teacher, commanding respect from her students and staff by her wide breadth of knowledge, her quickness of mind and her ability to stimulate everyone to give of their best. People were also enthused by her personal charisma, sense of fun, kindness and concern for others. She was an examiner, was involved in syllabus revision, initiated and taught the first clinical supervisors' course, and collaborated with Macdonald on *Occupational Therapy in Rehabilitation*. Grizel was one of the great pioneers in establishing the role of occupational therapy in the treatment of physical disability and made a major contribution to changing occupational therapy from a predominantly craft-based exercise regime to one that largely concentrated on enabling people to overcome the practical problems of daily life.

### 1972 E. Mary Macdonald, MBE

Mary Macdonald, 'Mac', as she was universally known, was born in South America where she spent her childhood until her family returned to England. As the only girl, it was assumed she would be a companion for her parents, but instead she became a craft teacher at a school in Wales. In the early 1930s she met Elizabeth Casson and accepted her invitation to become a student at Dorset House. Afterwards, with the help of a Pilgrim Trust grant she spent a year in the USA before returning to Bristol to become Principal of Dorset House. She remained its Principal for 33 years, retiring in 1971. She was awarded a BLitt by the University of Oxford for a research thesis, *Worldwide Conquests of Disabilities*, a comprehensive survey of remedial services around the world, which she conducted in her retirement years. Mac was instrumental in the start of the AOT and became its first Secretary at an inaugural meeting in 1936. She served on Council, many of its various committees, and represented the AOT on many occassions, such as on the Cope Committee which led to the setting up of the CPSM. Additionally, she acted as adviser in the setting up of rehabilitation projects overseas, for example, establishing a training school and clinical facilities in Argentina. Mac collaborated with Nora Haworth, a physician, in writing an early English textbook on occupational therapy and later edited several editions of *Occupational Therapy in Rehabilitation*. In 1964, she received the MBE for her contribution in the field of rehabilitation, and was awarded an Honorary Fellowship of WFOT.

### 1972 Dr Constance Owens, MBE

Alice Constance Tebbit, Conn to her family and friends, was born in 1906. As a student at Birmingham University, she chose to work for an Honours Degree in English and a Diploma in Education. At an early stage of her studies a friend suffered a mental illness and was admitted to hospital. The restrictive and harsh life of a patient in a mental hospital in the 1920s shocked and distressed her and led to a change of career interests. She was unsure of how to progress until she met Elizabeth Casson, who infected Conn with her enthusiasm to improve psychiatric treatment and to start occupational therapy. A lifelong friendship developed from this meeting. Conn attended the Philadelphia School of Occupational Therapy in the USA, graduating in 1930 and on returning to Bristol became the principal of Dorset House. Three years later she established an occupational therapy department at the County Mental Hospital at Upton by Chester, but because she married in 1934, was obliged to leave her job. In 1941 she was asked to the hospital to develop occupational therapy in the new EMS Hospital for War Casualties. There, she started training 6 students. At the end of the war, since no authority was interested in continuing their training, Conn established, and became Principal, of the Liverpool School of Occupational Therapy early in 1947. In 1951 she chaired the meeting in Stockholm where the idea of WFOT was initiated, and in the following year organised its first meeting at the Liverpool School. She was made an Honorary Fellow of WFOT in 1964. By that time she had been awarded the MBE, and gained an MA at

Liverpool University. In 1962 she became the first British occupational therapist to gain a PhD for her work on '*Imagery*' and took up a part-time research post at the University. She had served the AOT on many committees, and as Chairman of Council between 1936 and 1942, and again in 1966.

### 1972 Angela Rivett

Angela Rivett was a quiet and gracious person, who, like many of the early occupational therapists, brought a wealth of experience from other fields. Having gained her Art Teacher's Diploma, she taught in schools in Yorkshire and North London coming to appreciate the therapeutic potential of creative activities in mental illness. Trained as an occupational therapist at the Maudsley Hospital, she returned there after working in several private hospitals, and eventually became the Head Occupational Therapist. In the 1930s, Angela, with her friend Muriel Tarrant, established the Occupational Therapy Centre and Training School in Tottenham Court Road, London, which became known as the London School of Occupational Therapy, and is now part of Brunel University. In 1944, she became a signatory to the Memorandum of the AOT and held a seat on the first Council of the newly formed professional body. For many years she took a committed role in the affairs of the Association as a member of the Council and on numerous committees. She was involved, in an advisory capacity, with the establishment of occupational therapy training schools in Denmark and elsewhere.

### 1972 E. Muriel Tarrant

In the early 1930s, Muriel Tarrant in collaboration with her friend Angela Rivett, opened a treatment centre in Tottenham Court Road, London. Students who held appropriate qualifications were accepted for a 'month course in occupational therapy' and so began her long career as a co-principal at the Occupational Therapy Centre and Training School. She enthused her students, especially in the field of physical medicine. She established what is reputed to have been the first 'physical' occupational therapy department in London at the Royal Free Hospital. Her forthright manner instilled respect and enabled her to win the support of many eminent doctors in spite of misgivings about this new profession. Her great concern for the personal well-being of her students assisted many through problematic times. Muriel served on the Council of the AOT on several occasions and on its various committees. In 1951 she organised the first National Conference. She represented occupational therapists on the Joint Negotiating Committee and subsequently on the newly formed Whitley Council. Muriel's personality, knowledge and expertise in industrial relations matters enabled her to develop good rapport with other paramedicals as well as union officials and management.

### 1974 E. Margaret Hollins

Prior to the Second World War, E. Margaret Hollins, known as Betty, studied Fine Art at the Slade, specialising in painting and sculpture. She brought a real appreciation of the value of creative activities to the field of rehabilitation. During the war she served in the Land Army in Kent, ploughing and tending livestock directly under the flight path of the German bombers. Then in 1945, Betty entered Dorset House, joining the last wartime course run by the Government, specifically designed for mature students.

In 1951 she became Head Occupational Therapist successively at the Queen Elizabeth Hospital, Birmingham, the Wolverhampton Royal, and the Royal Surrey County Hospital, Guildford, before starting her long term commitment to the Nuffield Hospital in Oxford, where she remained until her retirement in 1978. During her time at Nuffield, Betty became wellknown worldwide for her work in physical rehabilitation. She was involved in the planning and setting up of the Disabled Living Research Unit at the Mary Marlborough Lodge and its development and growth to a national centre. She initiated the publication *Equipment for the Disabled*, contributed to many books and journals, and presented papers at conferences worldwide. During 1956-57 she joined a team of physiotherapists, who were sent to Argentina by the British Government, to help in a polio epidemic. In 1962 she assisted with a course at Chicago University Medical Centre on children's prosthetics and, in 1972, she presented a series of lectures in Czechoslovakia at the invitation of the British Council for Rehabilitation. Betty served on AOT Council and various committees and chaired her regional group.

---

### 1974 M. Alicia Mendez, OBE

During the Second World War, Alicia Mendez completed a wartime short course at Dorset House, upgrading to full qualification in occupational therapy in 1946. In 1948 she developed occupational therapy services at Queen Mary's Hospital, Roehampton, initiating and continuing specialised work in the field of prosthetics. By 1961, her area of responsibility had extended to include all occupational therapy services in the Westminster Hospital Teaching Group. From 1968 she developed clinical teaching and post-graduate courses in conjunction with physiotherapy and other disciplines, and initiated married women's refresher courses. From 1958, from time to time, Alicia served on the AOT Council and some of its subcommittees, and was Chairman from 1959-1961. From 1962-1968 she was a delegate to Whitley Council and secretary of Committee 'C' of the P.T.A. Council. She was an elected member of the Occupational Therapy State Registration Board from its inception in 1962, serving as its chairman from November 1965, being also the nominated representative to the Council. In 1969, she was a member of the Remedial Professions Tunbridge Committee. From 1963-1972 she was a United Kingdom delegate to the World Federation Council and attended meetings in Israel, London, Sweden, Switzerland and Norway. Alicia was first Vice-President of WFOT from 1968 until 1972 when she was elected President. In the New Year Honours List of 1975 she was awarded an OBE and in the same year she was awarded an Honorary Fellowship of the International Society of Prosthetics and Orthotics. Alicia was the first occupational therapist to have the honour of giving the Casson Memorial Lecture in 1987. Her title was *Processes of Change: Some Speculations for the Future*. She published *A Chronicle of the World Federation of Occupational Therapists. The First Thirty Years: 1952–1982* in 1986.

---

### 1974 Barbara Stow, MBE

Barbara Stow became interested in occupational therapy after working as a VAD during the early part of the Second World War. She trained at the Liverpool School, qualifying in 1944. After three months at Belmont Hospital in Surrey she became head of the department at St. Thomas' Hospital in London. There she established and developed a department that was renowned for good practice and was used widely for student clinical training. After visiting the USA in 1947 for three months, she returned to St. Thomas' and set up one of the earliest rehabilitation kitchens and ADL units in the country. Barbara left St. Thomas' Hospital in 1963 to become Director of the Disabled Living Activities Group, set up by Lady Hamilton under the auspices of the Central Council for the Disabled. In 1970, she was appointed the first Director of the renamed Disabled Living Foundation. That innovation brought together, in one place, a wide variety of equipment for disabled people, which could be tried out by them and for other Disabled Living Centres in the UK and overseas. The Information service she set up within the Foundation was the first of its kind in the country. She retired at the end of 1977 but continued to act as a Trustee until 1983. Her contribution to AOT was as Chairman of the Council from 1949-1951, again in 1954, and from 1962-1963. She was awarded an MBE in 1969 for her contribution to rehabilitation. In 1966, Barbara was the convenor of the Fourth WFOT Congress in London. She served as a member of the Executive Committee of the Royal Association for Disability and Rehabilitation from its inception until 1982, and for many years, was a Governor and member of the Executive and Management Committees of the Queen Elizabeth Foundation for Disabled people.

### 1977 Betty Collins

Towards the end of the Second World War, Betty Collins trained at Dorset House. She practised in both physical and psychiatric hospitals before becoming Assistant Director at the School of Occupational Therapy in Melbourne,

Australia, in 1951. She returned to Dorset House as Vice-Principal and Tutor in 1954 where she remained, becoming Principal in 1971. She wrote *The Story of Dorset House School of Occupational Therapy 1936-1986*, which was privately published by the Governors of the School. In 1959 she carried out a national survey of occupational therapists in psychiatric hospitals. During her career Betty served for a total of 12 years as a member of the AOT Council and at different times she held the positions of Chairman of the Joint Council, of the Board of Studies, and of the Education Committee, the latter for six years, was a Vice Chairman of Council, and was Chairman of Council from 1979 to 1980. From 1964 to 1966 she was Chairman of the Programme Planning Committee for the WFOT Congress, which was held in London in 1966. Betty was elected as a delegate to WFOT two years later, and became one of two WFOT Vice-Presidents. From 1970 to 74 she was Chairman of WFOT Education Board, and it was under her leadership that the minimum standards for student education were revised and updated. In her capacity as delegate, Betty attended meetings in Sweden, Switzerland, Norway, Canada and France. She was made a Fellow of WFOT in 1982.

### 1977 Elizabeth Grove

Elizabeth Grove, known affectionately as Liz, trained at the London School of Occupational Therapy from 1945 to 1948. Subsequently, she held posts as Deputy Head Occupational Therapist at Holloway Sanatorium and later at the West Middlesex Hospital. A particular interest in the clinical training of students led to her being appointed an Examiner in 'Occupational Therapy Applied to Physical Disabilities', on many occasions.

In 1958 she designed an adjustable raised lavatory seat and an adjustable bath seat which were subsequently marketed by Homecraft and other firms. Illustrative of her wide ranging interests, in 1969 Liz was the author of the chapter on 'Head Injuries' in Macdonald's *Occupational Therapy in Rehabilitation* and, in 1973, she contributed to the book *Comprehensive Care of Psychiatric Patients*. At the 1970 and 1974 WFOT Congress she presented papers on the *Assessment of Neurological Disabilities* and *The Delivery of Occupational Therapy Services*, respectively. She has participated in various research programmes, including supervising and organising research into the treatment of brain-damaged patients and an investigation into the need for occupational therapy for psychiatric patients in community settings. On two occasions, Liz was a member of Council, and from 1971 to 1972 she was its' Chairman. From 1972, for some years, she served as a member of the Occupational Therapists' Board of the CPSM. In 1973 she was elected alternate delegate representing the UK at WFOT. Also, in that year she was appointed a member of the working party set up by the Secretary of State to review the Remedial Professions (McMillan Report). She was appointed as the first Occupational Therapy Officer to the Department of Health and Social Security. Initially this was in addition to her post as District Occupational Therapist of the Wandsworth and East Merton District, and Head Occupational Therapist of the St. George's Hospital Group. Later it became full time and she was joined by another occupational therapist. Liz remained in this prestigious post until her retirement. In 1988, she gave the Casson Memorial Lecture, entitled *Working Together*. Currently she works voluntarily having established a very successful rehabilitation service for clients with long term disability

close to her London home.

### 1977 Jean Waterston, MBE

Jean (Waterston) Blades, qualified at the Astley Ainslie Occupational Therapy Training Centre in 1942. From 1944 to 1951 as Head Occupational Therapist she established a department at Princess Margaret Rose Hospital in Edinburgh. During the following nine years she worked at the Astley Ainslie Hospital and taught 'Occupational Therapy Applied to Orthopaedics and Resettlement' at the Training Centre. In 1960, she was awarded the Teacher's Diploma (SAOT), and from 1960 to 1978 she held the appointment of Head Occupational Therapist at the Simon Square Centre, in charge of the Community and Work Centre Occupational Therapy Services for Edinburgh. Jean was a member of the committee which met in Stockholm in 1951 prior to the formation of WFOT. She presented papers at the WFOT Congress in Copenhagen in 1958 and at the post WFOT Study Course in New York in 1962. In 1968 she represented WFOT on a working party at Killarney, Eire, with the International Society for the Rehabilitation of the Disabled to plan rehabilitation aids for under-developed countries. From 1960 she served on various committees with the Scottish Council on Disability and acted as Assistant Honorary Secretary to the Edinburgh Committee for the Co-ordination of Services for the Disabled. Between 1960 and 1962 she was Chairman of the SAOT, at the time when the Glasgow School was being planned. She was also President of the Joint Council of Occupational Therapists, and a member of the 1977 BAOT Congress Committee. In 1976, Jean was awarded the MBE in the New Year's Honours List.

## 1978 Margaret E. Smith

Margaret Smith first graduated from the Royal Academy of Music in London and then went on to gain her Diploma in Education at Jordanhill College in Glasgow. The next four years were spent teaching music in the West of Scotland. Margaret trained at the Occupational Therapy Training Centre of the Astley Ainsley Institution. She was invited to work at Crichton Royal Psychiatric Hospital in Dumfries after being a student there, and this was followed by an invitation to join a team at the Department of Psychological Medicine at the University of Glasgow to plan and open the first day hospital. Another invitation to set up a similar day hospital at Cornell University led to a year spent in the USA before returning to Scotland and marriage. After raising her family, Margaret moved into the field of research which was to become her major interest and contribution to the profession. Her study of the problems of mentally handicapped school leavers was responsible for legislation which allowed such young people to stay at school until the age of 19. She became the first occupational therapist to be employed in full-time research by a Scottish University when she was appointed Research Fellow in the Department of Community Medicine in Edinburgh. Her research covered areas such as the effectiveness of stroke units, projects for hand surgeons in training, and the outcome of severe injury with particular emphasis on legal compensation. In 1978 Margaret was awarded a Fellowship by Examination with honours. Her thesis was entitled *Familiar Daily Living Activities as a Measure of Neurological Deficit after Stroke.* She became widely sought after as a speaker at conferences, not only in her own profession, nationally and internationally,

but by other organisations such as the Royal College of Physicians and Surgeons. Throughout her career, Margaret served on many committees and she was one of four who organised the Second European Congress in London in 1985. In addition, she was a founder member and on the Council of the Society for Research in Rehabilitation.

## 1979 Averil Stewart

Averil Stewart gained her Diploma in Occupational Therapy in Edinburgh in 1964. She spent the next 18 years working as an occupational therapist, interspersed with teaching and research, and became manager of Worthing District Service, in charge of a team of over 40 staff. Averil became interested in the development of courses for support workers. After gaining her teaching diploma in 1972, she taught for two years at the Glasgow School and contributed to the occupational therapy helpers courses in Sussex. As Secretary of the Scottish Association in the late 1960s she was involved in negotiations which led to the formation of the BAOT in 1974. She has since served as a member of Council and on various committees and working parties. She was also Chairman of the Occupational Therapists Board of CPSM for some years, and was its first Education Development Officer. Her thesis for Fellowship by Examination of the COT was entitled *The Study of Occupational Therapy Teaching Resources.* She returned to Scotland and to Queen Margaret College in 1983 as a senior lecturer, and quickly became involved in the development of mainland Britain's first BSc degree in occupational therapy. This was validated in 1986 just before Averil was promoted to Head of Department. The Department of Occupational Therapy at Queen Margaret College expanded and diversified under her leadership. Research activity also increased with the appointment of specialist researchers and a growth in research funding obtained by the department. In 1992, she was invited to give the Casson Memorial Lecture. She titled it *Always a Little Further*. Averil was promoted to a personal chair in 1992, becoming the first professor of occupational therapy in the country.

---

### 1979 Diana M. Whysall

Diana Wallis (nee Whysall) qualified in 1971 from the Derby School of Occupational Therapy and, unusually for those times, was a mature student. Key moments in her career include: 1975-79 - working with people with epilepsy and mental health problems at the Maudsley Hospital; 1983-85 - completing attachments with the Health Advisory Service; 1986-89 - assisting in the development of the innovative two-year postgraduate occupational therapy course at the London Hospital Medical College. Diana was awarded a Fellowship by Examination in 1979 for a thesis entitled: *Socialisation in People with Epilepsy and an associated Psychological Disorder*.

---

### 1980 Sidney J. Lock

Sidney Lock worked in commerce before training as a general nurse during the Second World War, and working, for a time, at the Epileptic Colony at Lingfield. This led him to occupational therapy and the London School where he qualified in 1948. His first job was at the Kent & Sussex Hospital at Tunbridge Wells. Whilst there he started three decades of voluntary service to the profession. In the early 1950s Sidney began campaigning for enlargement of Council, realised that a fast developing profession needed greater

representation, and that every member should be able to nominate and vote for a local representative. He sat on Council of AOT, and was it's Chairman in 1976. He was Chairman of the Editorial Board, and Honorary Editor of *Occupational Therapy*, the journal of AOT. He was a Regional Group Officer for several terms and a delegate on PTA Whitley Council for some 11 years. He took his delegate responsibilities seriously, working countless hours to ensure occupational therapists were properly and fairly represented as testified by the records of meetings which were used at the time of the Halsbury and other inquiries. Besides that he was committed to excellence in his clinical work where he devised special remedial equipment like the FEPS, and wrote booklets about adapted equipment for worldwide sales. He was also an Examiner, and a tutor at St. Loye's College. After his retirement, Sidney was persuaded to take on the Chairmanship of the Salaries and Industrial Relations Committee, involvement with the Publicity Committee, and his former employers utilised his expertise in wheelchair clinics.

---

### 1980 Joan E. Martin

Joan Martin trained at the Northampton School, qualifying in 1972. She first worked at King's College Hospital and then at Atkinson Morley Hospital. There, whilst working with Professor Crisp, in the psychiatric department, she became interested in anorexia nervosa and she did a considerable amount of work to develop treatment programmes. In 1975 she undertook the basic clinical supervisors course and in 1976 her intermediate clinical supervisors course. In 1979 she qualified as a teacher, gaining both the CNAA Certificate in Education and the COT's teaching diploma. In 1981 she was awarded a Fellowship by Examination of the COT for her thesis entitled *The Art of Treating Anorexia Nervosa: The Condition, the Different Treatment Models and the Role of Occupational Therapy*. She returned home to Northern Ireland and began her teaching career at the University of Ulster. In 1986 she was awarded an MA from Warwick University for her thesis *Bulimia Nervosa an exploration of its social origins*. She continued her scholastic journey gaining a DPhil. through published works from the University of Ulster, and is thought to be the first occupational therapist in the UK to do so.

---

### 1980 Doris Sym, MBE

Doris Sym was a school teacher in South Africa and in Edinburgh before studying occupational therapy at the Occupational Therapy Training Centre at the Astley Ainslie in 1946. She gained her Scottish Teachers' Diploma in 1952, and worked as Head Occupational Therapist at Bangour Hospital before returning to the Astley Ainslie to teach. Recognising a need for more occupational therapists, and a shortage of training opportunities in Scotland, she crusaded for the establishment of a school of occupational therapy in Glasgow. Eventually the Greater Glasgow Health Board came to the party in 1962 and Doris became its Principal. Apart from running the Glasgow School, she helped to set up study programmes of neuroanatomy for occupational therapy students, and helped to run the first WFOT Congress in Edinburgh in 1952. She was Chairman of the SAOT in 1963, before the merger with AOT, President of the Joint Council, Vice Chairman of the Occupational Therapists Board of the CPSM, and Chairman of the

Fellowship Committee. She was also a member of several education committees. Doris was an Honorary Life Member of BAOT and an Honorary Member of the Finnish Association, having spent three months in Helsinki as Adviser. She was awarded an MBE for her work in occupational therapy. After her retirement in 1975, she maintained her interest in the Glasgow School, pleased by its transition into the university sector and the development of its degree courses. In 1997 she was awarded an Honorary Fellowship of Glasgow Caledonian University.

---

### 1981 Lily Jeffrey

Lily Jeffrey qualified at the Derby School in 1955 working at Dingleton Hospital, Melrose, before moving in 1967 to the Fleming Memorial Hospital, Newcastle-upon-Tyne where she specialised in Child Psychiatry. She then became Head Occupational Therapist at the Nuffield Psychology and Psychiatry Unit of the University of Newcastle, which was based at the Fleming Memorial Hospital. In 1992 Lily Jeffrey gained a Fellowship by Examination for her thesis titled *Exploration of the use of therapeutic play in the rehabilitation of psychologically disturbed children*.

---

### 1982 Lalage Dawson Jones

Lalage Dawson Jones trained as an occupational therapist at Dorset House between 1946-1949 and on graduating went to work with Beryl Johnson, the first occupational therapist at Bexley Hospital. She took over as Head in 1951 and remained in that post till retiring in November 1979. In the later years Lalage was designated District Occupational Therapist for the Bexley Health District by which time there were over 40 occupational therapists at the Hospital. She took a keen interest in clinical training, and during the late 1950s and 1960s was an Examiner in 'Applied Psychiatric Occupational Therapy and Departmental Management'. Lalage became especially interested in the need to treat psychiatric patients in the community. Between 1960-1969 she ran an out-patient Social Club in Greenwich, mainly single-handed, and was one of three Bexley staff members to set up and support Group Homes. She was a member of the South East Thames Regional Health Authority Psychiatric Specialist Sub Committee from 1961-1979. Lalage was a member of the BAOT Helpers Training Committee and started training courses for Helpers in 1974. A founder and Executive Committee member for three years of the National Association of Industrial Therapy Mangers, she also served on various committees in the Boroughs of Lewisham, Greenwich and Bexley mainly associated with Mental Health and Health Care Planning. In the 1950s and 1960s Lalage served on the AOT Council and was its representative on the National Association for Mental Health Committee. She attended WFOT Congresses in Scotland, Denmark, London and Zurich.

### 1983 Phyllis M. Howie

Phyllis Howie trained as a Froebel teacher during World War II, teaching for ten years before undertaking occupational therapy. In 1956 when she qualified from Dorset House School, she won the Student of the Year award. After working, first, at the Royal Surrey County Hospital, Guildford, Phyllis moved to King's College Hospital to work with Grizel MacCaul in 1958. There she was employed with Margaret Stewart, a physiotherapist, in establishing a Functional Assessment Unit. They produced a joint report on their pioneer work in 1961. Phyllis went back to Dorset House to teach, gaining her teacher's diploma in 1964. She then returned to King's College, sponsored by the Central Council for the Disabled, to carry out a pilot study of the problems of the disabled housewife in her kitchen which was published in 1967. In that year she went back to teaching, this time at the Liverpool College of Occupational Therapy where she became Principal the following year, and stayed until her retirement in 1983. Phyllis served on many Committees, Boards and working parties, including Council and its Executive. She made a particular contribution to education. She sat on the Board of Studies, the Validating Board for Diploma '81 and was also involved on committees concerned with clinical training, clinical supervisor training, teacher training, examining both students and teachers, and several revisions of the syllabus.

### 1984 Susan Woodward

Susan Woodward gained a degree in English and Philosophy and worked for two years in Tanzania as a VSO English teacher, prior to training as an occupational therapist in Edinburgh. She qualified in 1981. She was awarded a Fellowship by Examination for her thesis entitled: *An assessment of the value of horticultural therapy at Hillside Market Garden.*

### 1985 Margaret Ellis

Margaret Ellis, known as Maggie, trained at the London School of Occupational Therapy, qualifying in 1961. Her first appointment was at St. Olave's Hospital where she became Head Occupational Therapist and then she worked at the Old Manor Hospital, Salisbury, Wiltshire. She was appointed

Group Head Occupational Therapist at the London Hospital and, in 1974, the District Therapist for Tower Hamlets District Health Authority. Maggie developed a wide range of interests in both psychiatric and physical medicine, and a special interest in orthotics. In 1981 she was awarded Fellowship of the International Society for Prosthetics and Orthotics and was Chairman of the National Committee. She was co-opted in 1982 as a member of the Committee on Hand Assessment of the British Society for Surgery of the Hand. She contributed to a chapter on Hand Orthotics in *The Practice of Hand Surgery* edited by Lamb and Kuczynski, and was instrumental in the formation of the British Association of Hand Therapists, of which she was Chairman for some time. She was central in the establishment of the School of Occupational Therapy at St. Bartholomew's and the Royal London Hospital. Maggie served on international, national and community committees, as well as COT Council, many COT Committees and Boards and was Chairman of Council between 1987 and 1989 commissioning the Blom-Cooper Commission of Inquiry. As Chairman of the Education Board and of the Research and Degree Committee she worked tirelessly for the acceptance and development of degree status. She also encouraged the growth of research in the profession organising numerous research courses and study days. In 1994, Maggie was invited to give the Casson Memorial Lecture, which she titled *Quality: Who Cares?* She was Convenor of the 1994 WFOT Congress in London.

### 1985 Peggy Jay

After service as an air radio mechanic in the Fleet Air Arm between 1950-54, Peggy Jay trained at the London School of Occupational Therapy between 1954 and 1957. She went as a post registration student to Switzerland to work at Burgerspital in Basel. In 1958, she took a post with Molly Jones at Farnham Park Rehabilitation Centre, becoming Head Occupational Therapist in 1960 when Molly retired. There, Peggy was responsible for a number of workshops which provided daily treatments for an average of 80 patients with a wide range of physical disabilities. She supervised the clinical practice of students from four training schools. Peggy remained at Farnham Park until 1967, when she began a freelance research and writing career in the interests of disabled people. She wrote widely and two of her books – *Coping with Disablement* and *Help Yourselves* became recognised textbooks. In 1977 she published an extensive revision of Mary S. Jones' book *An Approach to Occupational Therapy*. In 1974 she initiated courses on assessment techniques, including psychological testing for occupational therapists with the approval of the British Psychological Society. Subsequently these courses, which continued to the end of the century, became known as 'Objective and Standardised Assessment for Occupational Therapists' with courses for therapists with specialised interest in paediatrics, neurology, and adult mental health. Peggy was a member of the Council of AOT, and was its last Chairman. In 1974 she became the first Chairman of BAOT, serving in that capacity until 1976. Peggy also convened the second European Occupational Therapy Congress in London. An articulate spokesperson for the profession and for the causes of disabled persons, she was also a member of the British Council for the Rehabilitation of the Disabled (which became the Royal Association for Disability and Rehabilitation), the Disabled Living Foundation, and a founder member and Council member of the Society for Research in Rehabilitation.

## 1985 Hester Monteath, MBE

Hester Monteath trained at the Occupational Therapy Training Centre in Edinburgh between 1948 and 1950. Following her graduation she worked in general medical, surgical and psychiatric areas at Edenhall Hospital, Midlothian, Bangour General Hospital, West Lothian and Bangour Village Hospital before becoming Head Occupational Therapist at the Royal Edinburgh Hospital, a psychiatric teaching institution. Her particular interests included the development of new techniques of treatment in psychiatry and clinical team involvement, the contribution of professional staff in management structures, and also the clinical training of students. Hester was a Vice Chairman of SAOT Council, and served on various of its committees including its Board of Studies. She held similar positions with BAOT after amalgamation, in which she played an influential role. She held a particular interest in pre and post registration education issues, including Fellowship by Examination. She was an alternate member of the Occupational Therapists Board of the CPSM. She chaired the committee which organised the First European Congress held in Edinburgh in 1977. As an alternate delegate to WFOT, she gave unstintingly of her expertise to help other professional associations, devoting time and effort to representing the profession on numerous national and local working parties and planning groups. In 1989, Hester was invited to give the Casson Memorial Lecture but, sadly, was unable to do so due to ill-health.

## 1986 Lyndia Jones

Lyndia Jones graduated as an occupational therapist in 1980 from Mohawk College, Hamilton, Ontario. She was appointed to Riverdale Hospital Toronto, where she worked with people with cardiac and neurological conditions, and those needing chronic care. In 1981, she travelled to England and began work in oncology at the Royal Marsden Hospital in London. Two years later she moved to the National Hospital for Nervous Diseases. Whilst employed there, she fulfilled a research contract to develop a standardised and reliable measure of disability. She was involved with the development of a post-registration course for neurology, and was Secretary of the Special Interest Group in Neurology. Lyndia was awarded a Fellowship by Examination in 1986, for her thesis entitled *Evaluation of the Jebsen test: reliability, validity and usefulness as a measure of hand function in neurological patients.*

## 1987 Julia Robbins

Julia Robbins was trained at Dorset House. She began her professional career working in child psychiatry in Birmingham and at the Maudsley Hospital. After this she travelled to West Pakistan where she stayed for four years. While there, Julia set up a unit for mentally handicapped children and young adults. On her return to England, she became a tutor at Dorset House, there gaining her teaching diploma. She returned to the field to Knowle Hospital, in Farnham, and subsequently became the District Occupational Therapist for the Southampton Health Authority. Whilst in Southampton, she initiated a three year staff development programme. Her interest and involvement in mental handicap services continued and in 1985 she became the first occupational therapist to move into the post of a General Manager for Tatchbury Mount Hospital. Julia gave papers on a wide variety of subjects, most of which are on management skills, and on services for handicapped people. In Wessex, she served on a number of Regional Group Committees, became a Regional Council Member to COT and was elected Chairman of Council between 1981-1983. She energetically visited members throughout the country, dispensing encouragement. As Chairman, Julia attended the WFOT congress in Hamburg and following her Chairmanship, in 1984, undertook an extensive lecture tour of Australia and New Zealand. She then joined the growing number of freelance occupational therapists, undertaking work, for example, towards the establishment of the School at Southampton University, and as a consultant to the Centre for Mental Health Services Deveopment.

### 1987 Mary Loggie

Mary Loggie qualified as an occupational therapist at the Astley Ainslie Training Centre in Edinburgh and worked in Edinburgh hospitals until 1966. She returned to the Astley Ainslie as an educator, and became Head of Department, remaining in that position until she retired from Queen Margaret College in 1986. Between 1950 and 1974, she held various offices in the SAOT, including the Chairmanship between 1955 and 1956. She was a member of many committees including the Scottish Board of Studies, the CPSM, and the Education and Research Board of COT. During her career she was a member of the Organising Committee of the First International Congress of WFOT in 1954 and later became the alternate UK delegate on WFOT Council. The culmination of Mary's long and exceptional career was the establishment of a degree course in occupational therapy at Queen Margaret College. Her leadership, diplomacy and wisdom, led the way forward into university education for occupational therapists in the 1990s.

### 1991 Dr E. Naomi Fraser-Holland

Naomi Fraser-Holland achieved a unique combination of multi-professional education and training as a nurse, physiotherapist, and psychologist, as well as an occupational therapist holding a COT teaching diploma. She began her occupational therapy career in Canada in 1953. Early in her career she taught at McGill University where there was a joint physiotherapy and occupational therapy course. In the UK, in 1962, Naomi joined the staff of St. Loye's School in Exeter as a senior tutor. Her contribution to St. Loye's in that capacity was to last until 1985 when she became a research fellow at the University of Exeter and Course Coordinator of the Multidisciplinary MSc in Health Care, in the Department of General Practice. By that time Naomi held a PhD in Psychology (Human Learning) which she was awarded in 1971. From 1978, Naomi gave a long and continuous service to COT committees. She encouraged and enabled post-graduate study and research as a tutor on the Continuing Education Course for Professions Complementary to Medicine. She was professional adviser, examiner and validator for many courses from the 1980s and through the 1990s. In 1988 she became Course Director/Senior Lecturer at the School of Occupational Therapy at the London Hospital Medical College and London University. She was chosen to give the 1990 Casson Memorial Lecture which she called *Moving Targets and 20:20 Vision*.

## 1998 Dr Rosemary Barnitt

Rosemary Barnitt graduated from St. Andrews School of Occupational Therapy in 1964. Between 1966 and 1969 she worked at the Children's Hospital in Adelaide, South Australia, setting up a new programme which included play therapy, and community services to Aboriginal people in the Northern Territory. Back in the UK she worked, first, at the Queen Elizabeth Hospital, Hackney, before becoming interested in research. On a new track she took a post as a research fellow for the Industrial Training Unit in Cambridge, then the DHSS, and then the Department of Employment. In 1975 she gained a BSc in Psychology and, in 1977, an MSc in Occupational Psychology. In 1981 she returned to clinical work at St. Bartholomew's and Hackney Hospitals before turning to education two years later. Rosemary accepted the appointment as Principal of the Liverpool College of Occupational Therapy. There she stayed until 1992 when she took on the challenge to create and lead a new School of Occupational Therapy and Physiotherapy at the University of Southampton, where she was also made Reader in Occupational Therapy. Regarded as one of the pioneers in the field of research, she is an active member of the multi professional Society for Research and Rehabilitation. Her interests in education and in research were central in her 1991 Casson Memorial Lecture, *Through a Glass, Darkly*.

---

## 1998 Rosemary Hagedorn

Rosemary Hagedorn trained at the London School qualifying in 1965. She began working at St. Mary's Hospital, Paddington, becoming Head Occupational Therapist there in 1968, but since then has lived and worked in Sussex for much of her career. She became Head Occupational

Therapist at Southlands Hospital, Shoreham, which opened in 1975. That post was followed by District Occupational Therapy positions in Chichester and Worthing at which time she became very interested in horticulture. In 1987 she gained a Diploma in Teaching and Course Development from the University of London, and seven years later an MSc from the University of Exeter. Rosemary was appointed as Director of the four year In-Service Course at the Crawley College. She is, perhaps, best known for two major publications. After writing a student guide on 'Models of Practice' she extended it as the basis of a text *Foundations for Practice in Occupational Therapy*, published in 1972. In 1995, her second book, *Occupational Therapy Perspectives and Processes*, was published. Her Casson Memorial Lecture in the same year reflected the concepts she elucidated in her texts. It was called An *Emergent Profession - A Personal Perspective*.

---

## 1998 Sheelagh E. Richards

Sheelagh Richards qualified from the Edinburgh School in 1970, and started her career as an occupational therapist in Kilbride, Scotland, in the first integrated social work department in the UK. That was followed by an appointment as first full time occupational therapist in the County of Argyll, a job which involved developing services for people in remote communities. In 1973 she established the first training centre in Campbletown for adults with learning disabilities. This was followed by positions in social services and health in Cambridgeshire and Bedfordshire until the early 1990s when she entered the political arena as Occupational Therapy Officer at the Department of Health. In this role she resolutely represented and promoted the profession across two different political parties in government, and gave support in high places and on a personal basis to colleagues throughout the UK. Sheelagh was elected to Council in 1978 and was Chairman from 1989-1991. In 1998, at the first annual conference held in Northern Ireland, Sheelagh discussed insights she had gained in the political sphere, along with perspectives for the way forward as the Casson Memorial Lecturer in a paper titled *Occupation for Health - and Wealth?* In December 2000 she was appointed Chief Executive of the BAOT/COT, as the first occupational therapist and the first woman to take on this role.

### 1998 Barbara Tyldesley

Barbara Tyldesley trained at Dorset House, qualifying in 1956. She worked at Birch Hill Hospital, Rochdale, for three months before going to Malaysia where she worked with children at Sungei Bulch Leper Settlement near Kuala Lumpur. On her return to the UK, she developed clinical independence as a single handed occupational therapist at Bolton District Hospital. In 1968 she joined the staff of the Liverpool School later becoming Vice-Principal. She obtained a COT Teaching Diploma in 1970, and an MEd from the University of Liverpool in 1994. Specialising in anatomy and physiology, Barbara was a co-author of Muscles, Nerves and Movement. In contrast to that interest, Barbara also taught horticultural therapy following a particular and long term interest. A proponent of peer group teaching, her education expertise made her in demand as an external examiner for schools around the country. Barbara served on both Manchester and Merseyside Regional Group Committees, and at national level, the CPSM, and the COT Council where she was a member and Chairman of various of its committees. In 1981 she became 2nd Alternate Delegate to

WFOT which led to her becoming Chairman of its Education Committee, and her eventual election to President of WFOT from 1994 to 1998. In 1999, Barbara was invited to give the Casson Memorial Lecture. Her topic was the story of the founder of the School where she herself provided warm and committed leadership for many years. She titled it *Alice Constance Owens - Reflections upon a Remarkable Lady and a Pioneer of Occupational Therapy in England.*

### 1999 Upma Barnett

An Honorary Fellowship for exceptional support to the College and the profession was presented to Upma Barnett, who has edited the *British Journal of Occupational Therapy* since 1983. The profession has been promoted worldwide through this high quality publication.

### 1999  Janet Brown

An Honorary Fellowship for exceptional support to the College was presented to Janet Brown for her loyalty, commitment and dedication to BAOT/COT and the membership. Janet had been with the organisation since 1982, firstly with the Education Department and latterly as Secretary to Council.

### 1999 Professor Nadina Lincoln

An Honorary Fellowship of the College was awarded to Professor Nadina Lincoln for being a strong proponent of the profession encouraging occupational therapists in research and practice. She has held positions as clinical psychologist at Rivermead Rehabilitation Centre, Oxford, and Nottingham City Hospital, and at the time of the award held a personal chair in the Department of Psychology of Nottingham University.

### 2000 Ann Turner

After qualifying as an occupational therapist, Ann Turner worked in Oswestry, Leicester and Derby, before spending a couple of years in the British Voluntary Programme in Honduras. She was Head Occupational Therapist at Battle Hospital, Reading, between 1973 and 1975, before moving into the area of education. She worked first at St. Loye's in Exeter, and then at St. Andrews, now the University College Northampton, where she became Divisional Leader of Occupational Therapy in 1996. Ann made a major contribution to the profession through her Editorship of *Occupational Therapy and Physical Dysfunction* which at the turn of the century was close to its fifth edition. Ann was influential, at a national level as a member of COT Council, and a member of its Education and Practice Board. At an international level, she supported development of occupational therapy in Latvia and Argentina. Ann made a particular contribution by assisting many occupational therapists to define and expand their understanding of the theory base of the profession, and affirming beliefs in occupation as essential to well-being and as a medium for treatment.

### 2000 Professor M. Anne Chamberlain

An Honorary Fellowship of the College was awarded to Professor M. Anne Chamberlain in recognition of her strong advocacy for occupational therapy. Over the previous 25 years, Anne consistently involved occupational therapists in research and encouraged development and evaluation of innovative practice. As well, she demonstrated the effectiveness of rehabilitation and the unique contribution of occupational therapy leading to the development of the National Demonstration Centre for Rehabilitation.

She upheld the importance and value of occupational therapy in the national arena through membership of several national decision-making bodies, such as the Disabled Living Centres Council.

### 2000 Catherine F. Paterson

Catherine F. Paterson trained at the Occupational Therapy Training Centre in Edinburgh between 1960 and 1963. She worked as a practitioner in the fields of mental health, spinal injuries, and care of the elderly. She was a key figure in SAOT serving as Chairman during 1971 and 1972. She was awarded a Winston Churchill Memorial Trust Fellowship in 1972 to study clinical and educational aspects of occupational therapy in Australia for three months. Between 1974 and 1976 she worked as a full time fellow for the King's Fund studying the needs of the remedial professions. She was also a founder member of the Society for Research in Rehabilitation in Scotland which is an interdisciplinary forum. Catherine made a significant impact on the education of undergraduates with the establishment of the Grampian School of Occupational Therapy, now part of the Robert Gordon University. She was its founder in 1976 and the Schools only Director to the present. She is the author of over 40 publications, papers and chapters on occupational therapy, covering a range of subjects some based on surveys and particular educational studies. Many are about specific aspects of the history of occupational therapy. Indeed, Catherine could be described as a historian of occupational therapy. Currently, she is completing her PhD, documenting the history of the profession in Scotland from 1900-60 within its international context. It is fitting that she should be the last subject of this history as her assistance has been of great value.

# Appendix C

## Chairmen of the Associations of Occupational Therapists

| year | SAOT | year | BAOT | year | AOT |
|------|------|------|------|------|-----|
| 1932 | Miss M Menzies | | | | |
| 1933 | Miss S Thomson | | | | |
| 1934 | Miss J Miller | | | | |
| 1935 | Miss N Kennedy | | | | |
| 1936 -1937 | Miss A George | | | 1936-1942 | Mrs G Owens |
| 1938 | Miss G Longsmead | | | | |
| 1939 -1945 | no meetings (war years) | | | 1943-1945 | Miss I F Hilton |
| 1946 -1948 | Miss B Fulton | | | 1946 | N I R Clarke |
| | | | | 1947-1948 | Miss G MacCaul |
| 1949-1950 | Miss R E Begg | | | 1949-1951 | Miss B Stow |
| 1951-1952 | Miss I D Bramwell | | | 1952 | Miss E Osborn |
| 1953-1954 | Miss J Meader | | | 1953 | Miss G Thornley |
| | | | | 1954 | Miss B Stow |
| 1955-1956 | Miss M E C Loggie | | | 1955 | Miss G MacCaul |
| 1957-1958 | Miss C L Henderson | | | 1956 | Mr G Albon |
| 1959-1960 | Miss J Waterson | | | 1957-1958 | Miss N Smythe |
| 1961-1962 | Miss R E Begg | | | 1959-1960 | Miss M A Mendez |
| 1963 | Miss D Sym | | | 1961 | Miss E Sampson |
| 1964 | Mrs M Crowther | | | 1962-1963 | Miss Stow |
| 1965-1966 | Miss E A Proctor | | | 1964-1965 | Miss W G Hewstone |
| 1967 | Miss E McRae | | | 1966 | Dr G Owens |
| 1968 | Miss E A Proctor | | | 1967-1968 | Miss R Higgins |
| 1969 | Miss C Henderson | | | 1969 | Mr A J Paice |
| 1970 -1971 | Miss CF Paterson | | | 1970-1971 | Mrs E Grove |
| 1972 | Mrs M McDonald | | | 1972 | Mrs M Davies |
| 1973 | Miss P McLean | | | 1973 | Miss P Jay |
| | | 1974 - 1975 | Miss P Jay | | |
| | | 1976 | Mr S J Lock | | |
| | | 1977 - 1978 | Mrs E E Bumphrey | | |
| | | 1979 - 1980 | Miss B E G Collins | | |
| | | 1981 - 1983 | Mrs J M Robbins | | |
| | | 1984 - 1985 | Mrs L M Mackenzie | | |
| | | 1986 | Mrs B E Warren | | |
| | | 1987 - 1989 | Mrs M Ellis | | |
| | | 1990 - 1991 | Mrs S E Richards | | |
| | | 1992 - 1993 | Mrs C Craik | | |
| | | 1994 - 1995 | Ms J Clayton | | |
| | | 1996 - 1998 | Mrs C J Minto | | |
| | | 1999 - 2000 | Ms K East | | |

# Appendix D

## Casson Memorial Lecturers

The Casson Memorial Lecture was established in 1971 with money presented by the Casson Trust, in memory of Dr Elizabeth Casson, founder of the first school of occupational therapy in the United Kingdom in 1930. She died in 1954 aged 73 years.

| YEAR | LECTURER | TITLE |
|------|----------|-------|
| 1973 | George Godber | Inaugural lecture:  Interpersonal Relationships in the Health Service |
| 1974 | Hugh Casson | Envirotecture (not published) |
| 1975 | Hugh Glanville | From Pioneer Occupational Therapy School to Chair of Rehabilitation:  A Review of Progress |
| 1976 | Professor Cairns Aitken | Rehabilitation:  Facts and Fantasies about Occupational Therapy |
| 1977 | Geoffrey Shaw | -not published |
| 1978 | Alicia Mendez | Processes of Change:  Some Speculations for the Future |
| 1979 | Professor V Wright | Patients Matter |
| 1980 | Leigh Atkinson | Unique To Occupational Therapy |
| 1981 | Elizabeth Fanshawe | The Importance of Rehabilitation to Disabled People |
| 1982 | Judith Farrell | - untitled |
| 1983 | Joan Bicknell | Mentally Handicapped People: Their Rights and Responsibilities |
| 1984 | Professor H Woolf | - not published |
| 1985 | Professor D L McLellan | Training for a Rehabilitation Team |
| 1986 | J H Walker | Out into the Community |
| 1987 | Margaret Ellis | Quality:  Who Cares? |
| 1988 | Elizabeth Grove | Working Together |
| 1989 | Hester Monteath | No lecture given due to ill-health |
| 1990 | Naomi Fraser-Holland | Moving Targets and 20:20 Vision |
| 1991 | Rosemary Barnitt | Through a Glass, Darkly |
| 1992 | Averil Stewart | Always a Little Further |
| 1993 | Stephanie Correia | Traditions and Transitions - Issues for the Future |
| 1994 | | (WFOT Congress) (No lecture given) |
| 1995 | Rosemary Hagedorn | An Emergent Profession - A Personal Perspective |
| 1996 | J Elizabeth Yates | Equalising Opportunities |
| 1997 | Professor Pamela Eakin | Shifting the Balance Towards Evidence-Based Practice |
| 1998 | Sheelagh Richards | Occupation for Health - and Wealth? |
| 1999 | Barbara Tyldesley | Alice Constance Owens - Reflections upon a Remarkable Lady and a Pioneer of Occupational Therapy in England |
| 2000 | Dr Christine Mayers | Reflect on the Past to shape the Future |

# Legends of Frontispieces

## Volume Frontispieces

The main frontispiece of each volume is based on the wonderful sepia frontispiece of Robert Burton's Anatomy of Melancholy which is pictured in chapter 5 of the first volume. The collage for this volume illustrates different aspects of occupational therapy in different periods of the twentieth century. They are linked with the current British Association badge, and the early badges of English and Scottish Associations. The classical gods represent Asclepius, the God of medicine, and Hygiea, the goddess of health. The photographs are from the archives of Dorset House (Oxford Brooks University), the Royal Star and Garter Homes, Richmond, and the British Association of Occupational Therapists.

The chapter frontispieces provide a conceptual map of the content within the chapter. They are encased in material illustrative of the times. That material is from photographs and art work of the period from the Archives of the British Red Cross, the Middlesex Hospital, the Imperial War Museum, the Octavia Hill Birthplace Museum, Hulton Getty, the British Association of Occupational Therapists, and other sources for which copyright was unable to be traced.

# Index